Payroll Accounting 2017

Payroll Accounting 2017

Third Edition

**Jeanette M. Landin,
Ed.D., M.B.A.**
Landmark College

**Paulette Schirmer,
D.B.A., M.B.A.**
University of Phoenix

Mc
Graw
Hill
Education

PAYROLL ACCOUNTING 2017

Published by McGraw-Hill Education, 2 Penn Plaza, New York, NY 10121. Copyright © 2017 by McGraw-Hill Education. All rights reserved. Printed in the United States of America. Previous editions © 2016 and 2015. No part of this publication may be reproduced or distributed in any form or by any means, or stored in a database or retrieval system, without the prior written consent of McGraw-Hill Education, including, but not limited to, in any network or other electronic storage or transmission, or broadcast for distance learning.

Some ancillaries, including electronic and print components, may not be available to customers outside the United States.

This book is printed on acid-free paper.

1 2 3 4 5 6 7 8 9 RMN 21 20 19 18 17 16

ISBN 978-1-259-57218-0
MHID 1-259-57218-8
ISSN 2373-2644

Chief Product Officer, SVP Products & Markets: *G. Scott Virkler*
Vice President, General Manager, Products & Markets: *Marty Lange*
Managing Director: *Tim Vertovec*
Marketing Director: *Natalie King*
Brand Manager: *Steven Schuetz*
Director, Product Development: *Rose Koos*
Director of Digital Content: *Peggy Hussey*
Associate Director of Digital Content: *Kevin Moran*
Lead Product Developer: *Kris Tibbetts*
Product Developer: *Randall Edwards*
Marketing Manager: *Michelle Williams*
Market Development Manager: *Erin Chomat*
Digital Product Analyst: *Xin Lin*
Director, Content Design & Delivery: *Linda Avenarius*
Program Manager: *Daryl Horrocks*
Content Project Managers: *Dana M. Pauley / Brian Nacik*
Buyer: *Jennifer Pickel*
Design: *Egzon Shaqiri*
Content Licensing Specialists: *Ann Marie Jannette / Lori Slattery*
Cover Image: *Ralf Hiemsich*
Compositor: *SPi Global*
Printer: *R. R. Donnelley*

The Internet addresses listed in the text were accurate at the time of publication. The inclusion of a website does not indicate an endorsement by the authors or McGraw-Hill Education, and McGraw-Hill Education does not guarantee the accuracy of the information presented at these sites.

About the Authors

Jeanette Landin

Landmark College

Jeanette Landin is an assistant professor of business and accounting at Landmark College in Putney, Vermont, where she teaches undergraduate accounting and business courses to an at-risk student population. She is the faculty advisor for the college's Phi Beta Lambda chapter. Professor Landin is also a certified advanced facilitator with the University of Phoenix, where she teaches online undergraduate courses and workshops, and adjunct faculty with John F. Kennedy University, where she teaches upper-division and graduate-level accounting courses. Dr. Landin earned her B.A. degree from the University of California at Irvine before receiving her M.B.A. and Ed.D. from the University of Phoenix, where she conducted research into college success strategies for at-risk students. She has earned master's certificates in accounting and in autism spectrum disorders.

Jeanette is an active member of the Institute for Management Accountants (IMA), Teachers of Accounting Curriculum at Two-Year Colleges (TACTYC), and Vermont Women in Higher Education (VWHE), and she previously served as an active member of the California Business Educators Association and the Western Business Educators Association. Dr. Landin currently serves on the IMA's Committee for Academic Relations and as a peer reviewer for the American Accounting Association. She is a peer reviewer for the *Transnational Journal of Business* and a member of the Business Editorial Board with the Multimedia Educational Resource for Learning and Online Teaching (MERLOT).

Paulette Schirmer

University of Phoenix

Paulette Schirmer is an accountant with the Division of Finance for the State of Alaska and a certified advanced facilitator for the University of Phoenix, where she teaches accounting courses at the bachelor's and master's levels. Dr. Schirmer also works with the University of Alaska Southeast as an online instructor for its payroll accounting course. She received her BS in accounting from Metropolitan State College of Denver (now Metropolitan State University of Denver), her MBA from Regis University, and her DBA from University of Phoenix, where she conducted research on globalization strategies for small businesses.

Dr. Schirmer is active in the preparation of Alaska's Comprehensive Annual Financial Reports and that state's annual Compensation and Travel Report, as well as training state employees on the state's financial and reporting systems.

Dedications

The authors dedicate this book to the following individuals:

For Chris, Kierstan, and Meaghan, who are the center of my universe.

—Jeanette Landin

For Royce and Elizabeth, who kept me grounded and reminded me to have fun.

—Paulette Schirmer

A Note from the Authors

Businesses employ people, and part of employing people is compensating them for their labors. Labor costs often represent the largest company expenditure as well as the most complex one. According to a 2016 article published by the Institute of Management Accountants (IMA), attention to the connection between accounting and human resources is a critical element in successful business strategy. We believe that payroll is one facet of this intersection and is also the connection between financial and managerial accounting. Payroll accounting is detailed, deadline driven, and of utmost importance for the successful functioning of a business. The changing, detailed nature of payroll accounting involves legal challenges, economic changes, technological advances, and—above all—governmental obligations. We are passionate about college education. Our aim in *Payroll Accounting 2017* is to provide instructors with a payroll accounting text that allows them to teach students how to navigate this highly specialized and extremely necessary aspect of accounting.

We continue to rely on the guidance of our colleagues, instructor feedback from the first and second editions, and the information gained from our peers. Additions to the third edition reflect industry and student needs, and we continue to follow these trends to inform future updates. Based on the feedback we have received, we have compiled a table of topics presented on payroll certification exams and have used that as a guide to the information presented in this edition.

Our approach to payroll accounting is different from other existing texts because we have chosen to include both the financial and the managerial accounting pieces so that students can understand both the techniques involved and the importance of their work in the broader scope of business. We present content that is concise, thorough, and easy to follow. We are excited to produce this work through McGraw-Hill because of the top-quality teaching and learning resources that the company makes available. Teaching traditional payroll accounting and Internet-based financial accounting via McGraw-Hill's Connect platform for several years has been a wonderful experience for both our students and ourselves.

Our text features many interesting real-world connections throughout. We've drawn examples from many different disciplines to help make payroll accounting come alive for teachers and students alike. Two discussions are unique: (1) the content in Chapter 5 that explores labor planning (Learning Objectives 5-5 and 5-6) and (2) the discussion in Chapter 6 about the function of labor costs in business and employee benefit reports as strategic tools (Learning Objective 6-7). We believe that this information contributes to a comprehensive understanding of payroll accounting in the 21st century and that it will make accounting students more valuable to the organizations they work for in their careers.

Many payroll frauds and scandals occur in the real world. Payroll fraud continues to be a major source of loss for companies, and it is surprising to find how commonly it happens. We've included examples of the frauds that employees have perpetrated in recent years. One notable case that highlighted the scope of payroll fraud involved a $700 million scheme that resulted in hundreds of jobs lost and for which the perpetrators remain at large. Students are interested in these stories, which enliven and enrich class discussion. We've also included a section in each chapter about ethics and internal controls to teach students how to prevent payroll fraud and to identify potential data breaches. We believe that this information about internal controls will become increasingly important as sensitive personnel information becomes more readily accessible with the inclusion of cloud-based payroll systems.

Payroll accounting and the associated fields of economics and finance are continually evolving. As a result, the payroll industry contains an ever-changing array of rules and regulations, and the "Trends to Watch" box in each chapter will highlight the trends known at the time of publication. On the legal front, we are watching the ripple effects of the Supreme Court's affirmation of the Affordable Care Act, which has affected employee benefits and tax reporting. Another issue of interest is the change to the exempt minimum wage and the challenge it presents to businesses. Other trends we are watching include issues of cybersecurity that challenge the notion of secure electronic payroll deposits and cause internal control guidelines and new regulations to respond to the changing needs of the economy. In the "Internet Activities" sections at the end of each chapter, we provide Internet links for students who want to explore payroll topics in more depth.

In addition, we provide both a continuing problem, which is located at the end of each chapter, and a full-quarter additional continuing problem, located in Appendix A. Technological integration of the continuing problem and Appendix A within Connect provides a good tool for student learning. Smartbook, LearnSmart, and walkthrough examples of tax forms are used to reinforce the questions and key terminology. A shortened version of Appendix A is another option for instructors who want a comprehensive problem with fewer payroll periods.

From our perspective, payroll accounting is complex enough to warrant specific attention in the curriculum. *Payroll Accounting 2017* is designed to fit the needs of terms as short as 3 weeks and as long as 15 weeks. The instructor may choose to assign the exercise sets found at the end of each chapter, the continuing payroll project in each chapter, or the continuing problem. The Continuing Payroll Project in Appendix A of which instructors may assign either one month (December) or the entire fourth quarter of payroll accounting complete with year-end tax forms. We designed the content to give instructors curricular flexibility by offering many options for formative and summative assessments.

We are proud of what we have accomplished with this text and strongly believe that we have taken payroll accounting education to a higher level of rigor. The content of *Payroll Accounting 2017* has grown in depth and detail yet is readily understandable by students who may have little or no prior accounting information. We have included materials to show the integration of payroll in other aspects of both managerial and financial accounting as well as business operations. Within Appendix E, we have provided materials that allow readers to learn about payroll within the context of their own state's legal framework and links to each state's revenue department to facilitate specific learning. We hope that you enjoy reading and learning from this text as much as we enjoyed writing it.

Jeanette Landin
Paulette Schirmer

Changes to the Third Edition

Based on feedback from our reviewers and users, we have included additional content in this third edition of *Payroll Accounting*. We appreciate all the feedback and user recommendations we have received because they have helped us create a stronger, more complete text. The changes we have made have added clarity, updated information, and given additional opportunities for students to demonstrate their understanding of the concepts presented. We have created end-of-chapter exercises to complement end-of-chapter problems to offer variety in academic rigor for each chapter. We have also included tables that correlate different payroll certification exams with the content in this text.

The following are specific changes to each chapter.

Chapter 1

In Chapter 1, we updated payroll-related legislation to reflect as many changes as possible prior to publication. We included specific information about Affordable Care Act reporting, both paper-based and online. We updated the information about worker classifications, including specific IRS guidance about exempt and nonexempt classifications. We incorporated information about mandatory sick leave legislation.

Chapter 2

In Chapter 2, we included highlights of guidance about exempt employee duties tests. We shared updates about the change to the exempt minimum wage. We discussed proposed paycard legislation that would both facilitate employee access to compensation and guard employees against fraud.

Chapter 3

Chapter 3 opens with updated minimum wage and tipped minimum wage information. We included the payroll register as a tool for computing gross pay in different pay situations and to prepare students for its use in later chapters. We shared examples to depict different gross pay situations to facilitate student computations and understanding of gross pay concepts.

Chapter 4

We extended the presentation of pre-tax deductions and explained qualified Section 125 cafeteria plans in detail in Chapter 4. We included several examples of pay computations with different combinations of pre-tax and post-tax deductions. We incorporated specific guidance about Section 125 and 401(k) effects on tax computations, and we compared federal income tax deductions computed using percentage and wage-bracket methods. We presented an explanation of potential fraud when employers use paper checks as a pay method.

Chapter 5

In Chapter 5, we updated employer payroll tax information and all tax forms with the current year's editions. We shared examples of tax computations in different situations to facilitate student understanding of employer tax obligations. In addition, we included a section about workers' compensation insurance and added end-of-chapter problems on the topic.

Chapter 6

Chapter 6 begins with a reintegration of the payroll register to facilitate connections between it and payroll-related accounting entries. We included explicit guidance about the connection between payroll computations and accounting transactions. We updated the transactions to reflect current-year tax rates and updated all accounting reports to match the presentation students will see in the end-of-chapter exercises.

Appendix A: Continuing Payroll Project

In Appendix A, we have significantly revised the setup from customer reviews and feedback. We removed the requirement to complete paper paychecks as part of the project. We placed more emphasis on completion of the payroll register and the transfer of data to both employees' earnings records and accounting entries. We included Forms W-2 and W-3 to the year-end reporting.

Appendix C: Federal Income Tax Tables

We updated both the percentage and the wage-bracket methods of determining federal income tax withholding to reflect the most current tax rates available.

Appendix D: State Income Tax Tables

We updated the tax rates for each state in Appendix D.

Appendix F: Payroll Certification Information

We correlated the learning objectives in this text with the topics included on payroll certification examinations offered by the National Association of Certified Professional Bookkeepers (NACPB), the American Institute of Professional Bookkeepers (AIPB), and the American Payroll Association (APA). We also included the certification exam requirements and contact information for each certification organization.

Text Features

Chapter Opener

Each chapter opens by focusing on a payroll accounting topic related to a real-world company to set the stage for the topic of the chapter.

Chapter One

Payroll Practices and System Fundamentals

Payroll systems are an integral part of job planning and strategic human resource management, cost management for products and services, and benefits analysis for a company. A company's payroll system has historically connected human resources and accounting departments. In contemporary businesses, payroll has taken on a strategic role in terms of company direction and future plans. A well-designed payroll system can serve the company; for this reason, an understanding of payroll foundations is imperative. In this chapter, we will explore the need for a payroll system, legal requirements, ethical guidelines, best practices, and variations in payroll practices among different-sized companies.

LEARNING OBJECTIVES

After studying Chapter 1, you should be able to:

LO 1-1 Explain the Purpose of Studying Payroll Accounting

LO 1-2 Discuss the Legal Framework for Payroll Accounting

Stop & Check

The Stop & Check feature allows students to review their understanding of the content just read. It also enables instructors to conduct formative assessments at multiple points throughout each chapter, testing the students' understanding informally as well as offering opportunities to expand on the material.

Which Law?

Stop & Check

1. Requires employers to verify the employee's legal right to work in the United States?	a.	COBRA
2. Protects the rights of disabled workers?	b.	ERISA
3. Governs the management of retirement plans?	c.	Civil Rights Act of 1991
4. Protects discrimination of workers older than age 40?	d.	PRWOR
5. Creates safe work environments for employees?	e.	SOX
6. Mandates equal pay for equal work?	f.	ADEA
7. Extends medical benefits for terminated employees?	g.	HIPAA
8. Ensures that child support obligations will be paid?	h.	ADA
9. Protects workers and families with preexisting medical conditions?	i.	OSHA
10. Enforces payment of monetary damages because of discrimination?	j.	Equal Pay Act of 1963
11. Requires internal controls on payroll practices of pub-		

Trends to Watch

Each chapter contains a feature box that connects payroll-related recent events with industry trends that shape the future of the profession. These trends offer instructors more opportunities to expand upon chapter topics, fostering discussion and application.

Trends to Watch

LEGAL ENVIRONMENT

To say that the legal environment of payroll is continually evolving is an understatement. During the early part of the 2010s, we have witnessed the following legal challenges:

- IRS revenue rulings about FICA refunds resulting from employee overpayment of taxes.
- Increasing numbers of states legislating paycard use to protect employee rights and improve access to wages.
- Enhanced enforcement of the Equal Pay Act by the EEOC to protect the rights of women and minorities.
- Repeal of the Defense of Marriage Act, which changed the definition of married couples to include same-sex unions.

Some trends to watch include the following:

- Debate about the proposed Mobile Workforce Income Tax Simplification Act, which creates a 30-day safe harbor for employees who travel across state lines as a normal part of their employment.
- Increasing numbers of private employers and localities raising the minimum wage significantly to close the gap between the minimum wage and the living wage.
- Increasing scrutiny about state-level changes and clarification of the Equal Pay Act.
- Continued legislation and action to increase the federal minimum wage for both exempt and

End-of-Chapter Assessments

Students can demonstrate their understanding through assessments designed to complement the chapter's learning objectives. Each chapter has review questions, exercises, and problems, with the exercises and problems having two sets each chapter (Set A and Set B). Each type of assessment is designed to measure student learning as follows:

- Questions for review are designed to check for students' remembrance of concepts.
- Exercises check for understanding and application of chapter concepts.
- Problems allow students to apply and analyze payroll accounting principles,

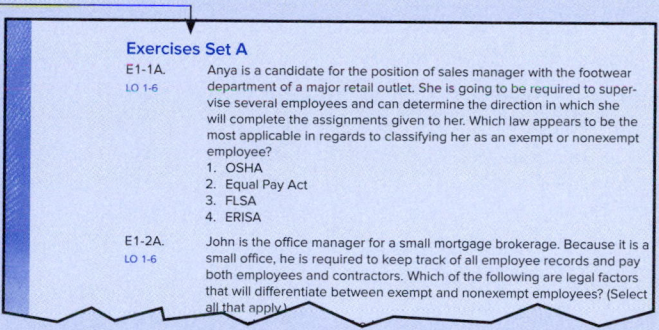

Exercises Set A

E1-1A.
LO 1-6
Anya is a candidate for the position of sales manager with the footwear department of a major retail outlet. She is going to be required to supervise several employees and can determine the direction in which she will complete the assignments given to her. Which law appears to be the most applicable in regards to classifying her as an exempt or nonexempt employee?
1. OSHA
2. Equal Pay Act
3. FLSA
4. ERISA

E1-2A.
LO 1-6
John is the office manager for a small mortgage brokerage. Because it is a small office, he is required to keep track of all employee records and pay both employees and contractors. Which of the following are legal factors that will differentiate between exempt and nonexempt employees? (Select all that apply)

Critical Thinking Exercises

Critical Thinking

CT1-1. You have been hired as a consultant for a company facing an IRS audit of its accounting records. During your review, you notice anomalies in the payroll system involving overpayments of labor and payments to terminated employees. What should you do?

CT1-2. Lee Chen is the accountant for a local nonprofit organization. He has been tasked with managing the costs of the payroll so that staffing levels may remain the same even if funding levels change. He considers outsourcing the payroll to a payroll processing company. What are some factors that Lee should consider in his decision? Why are these factors important?

Want to challenge your students further? The Critical Thinking exercises require students to consider complex real-world situations that build confidence and turn learning into mastery. These exercises offer possibilities for team presentations or class debate.

In the Real World: Scenarios for Discussion

Each chapter contains a discussion scenario that is drawn from real-world events. These scenarios encourage the expansion of chapter content and allow students to apply their learning to real situations.

In the Real World: Scenario for Discussion

The Brinker Restaurant Group, owners of restaurant franchises such as Chili's Grill &Bar and Maggiano's Little Italy, was sued by its employees for not providing adequate meal and rest breaks for employees. According to the California Labor Code §512 and Wage Order no. 5, employees must be provided with rest periods—specifically, a 30-minute meal break— every five hours that they work. After 10 hours of consecutive work, the employee must be given a second meal break. The California Supreme Court ruled that the rest breaks had to be offered, but the employer did not have to ensure that the employee actually rested.

Internet Activities

The Internet Activities at the end of each chapter offer students the chance to use their web navigation skills to expand on their learning. These exercises attract tech-savvy learners, allowing them to form their own understanding of payroll concepts on their own terms.

Continuing Problem: Prevosti Farms and Sugarhouse

Continuing Payroll Project: Prevosti Farms and Sugarhouse

Toni Prevosti is opening a new business, Prevosti Farms and Sugarhouse, which is a small company that will harvest, refine, and sell maple syrup products. In subsequent chapters, students will have the opportunity to establish payroll records and complete payroll information for Prevosti Farms and Sugarhouse.

Toni has decided that she needs to hire employees for the business to grow. Complete the application for Prevosti Farms and Sugarhouse's Employer Identification Number (Form SS-4) with the following information:

Prevosti Farms and Sugarhouse is located at 820 Westminster Road, Bridgewater, Vermont, 05520 (which is also Ms. Prevosti's home address), phone number 802-555-3456. Bridgewater is in Windsor County. Toni has decided that Prevosti Farms and Sugarhouse, the responsible party for a sole proprietorship, will pay its employees on a biweekly basis. Toni's Social Security number is 055-22-0443. The beginning date of the business is February 1, 2016. Prevosti Farms and Sugarhouse will use

© API/Alamy, RF

Starting with Chapter 1, each chapter has an integrated, continuing problem—about fictional company Prevosti Farms and Sugarhouse—that matches the chapter content and affords students a macro-level understanding of how each piece of payroll fits together.

Continuing Payroll Project

The Continuing Payroll Project (Appendix A) allows students to track a quarter's worth of payroll transactions for a company. This Continuing Payroll Project offers instructors increased flexibility in teaching and assessment by offering a simulation equivalent to a full quarter of a fictitious company's payroll activities, including payroll transactions, pay processing, and tax form completion. The Continuing Payroll Project may be presented in different lengths—as short as one month or in its three-month entirety—to meet curricular needs.

Appendix A

Continuing Payroll Project: Wayland Custom Woodworking

Wayland Custom Woodworking is a firm that manufactures custom cabinets and woodwork for business and residential customers. Students will have the opportunity to establish payroll records and to complete a month of payroll information for Wayland.

Wayland Custom Woodworking is located at 1716 Nichol Street, Logan, Utah, 84321, phone number 435-555-9877. The owner is Mark Wayland. Wayland's EIN is 91-7444533, and the Utah Employer Account Number is 999-9290-1. Wayland has determined it will pay their employees on a semimonthly basis. Federal income tax should be computed using the *percentage* method.

Connect Accounting for *Payroll Accounting 2017*

- SmartBook® is the market-leading adaptive study resource that is proven to strengthen memory recall, increase retention, and boost grades. SmartBook, which is powered by LearnSmart, is the first and only adaptive reading experience designed to change the way students read and learn. It creates a personalized reading experience by highlighting the most impactful concepts a student needs to learn at that moment in time. As a student engages with SmartBook, the reading experience continuously adapts by highlighting content based on what the student has mastered or is ready to learn. This ensures that the focus is on the content he or she needs to learn, while simultaneously promoting long-term retention of material. Both student and Instructors can use SmartBook's real-time reports to quickly identify the concepts that require more attention from individual students—or the entire class. The end result? Students are more engaged with course content, can better prioritize their time, and come to class ready to participate.

- End-of-Chapter Content is a robust offering of review and question material designed to aid and assess the student's retention of chapter content. The End-of-Chapter content is composed of both static and algorithmic exercises, problems, critical thinking exercises, and continuing payroll projects, which are designed to challenge students using McGraw-Hill Education's state-of-the-art online homework technology. Guided example videos are also provided with select end-of-chapter problems, which help walk students through complex payroll processes. Instructors can also assign test bank questions to students in both static and algorithmic versions.

- The Continuing Payroll Project from Appendix A is available on Connect in an auto-graded format. Students will apply skills, such as preparing tax forms and payroll registers, to complete the payroll process for a company from start to finish. Instructors can choose from the full 3-month version or the shorter 1-month version for their Connect assignment.

- Templated payroll and tax forms are integrated into Connect and are assignable. Students can complete the forms in these problems to gain a better understanding of how payroll forms are prepared in today's digital world.

- Test Bank - The Test Bank for each chapter has been updated for the 3rd edition to stay current with new and revised chapter material, with all questions available for assignment through Connect. Instructors can also create tests and quizzes from the Test Bank through our TestGen platform.

Exercise 3-8A

Telemarketers receive $15 commission on all new customers they sign up for phone service through Birch Phones. Each telemarketer works 40 hours. The company ran a competition this week to see who could sign up the most new people and the winner would get a bonus of $50. Because these employees are paid solely on commission, the employer must ensure that they earn the federal minimum wage for 40 hours each week. Compute the gross pay for each of the following outbound sales representatives.

Employee	Number of New Customers Signed	Total Commission		Difference Between Commission and Minimum Pay		Total Gross Pay	
Kenny	22	$	330			$	330
Charles	18	$	270	$	20	$	290
Laurie	29	$	435			$	485
Phyllis	16	$	240	$	50	$	290

Adam is a part-time employee who earned $570.00 during the most recent pay period. He is married with two withholding allowances. Prior to this pay period, his year-to-date pay is $7,548.82. How much should be withheld from Adam's gross pay for Social Security tax?

- ○ $46.09
- ○ $35.34
- ○ $43.69
- ○ $32.73

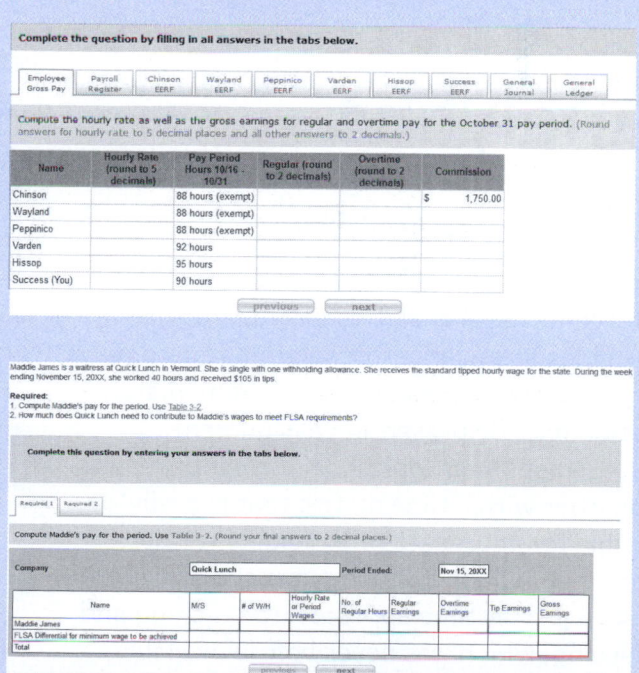

McGraw-Hill Connect®
Learn Without Limits

Connect is a teaching and learning platform that is proven to deliver better results for students and instructors.

Connect empowers students by continually adapting to deliver precisely what they need, when they need it, and how they need it, so your class time is more engaging and effective.

73% of instructors who use Connect require it; instructor satisfaction increases by 28% when Connect is required.

Connect's Impact on Retention Rates, Pass Rates, and Average Exam Scores

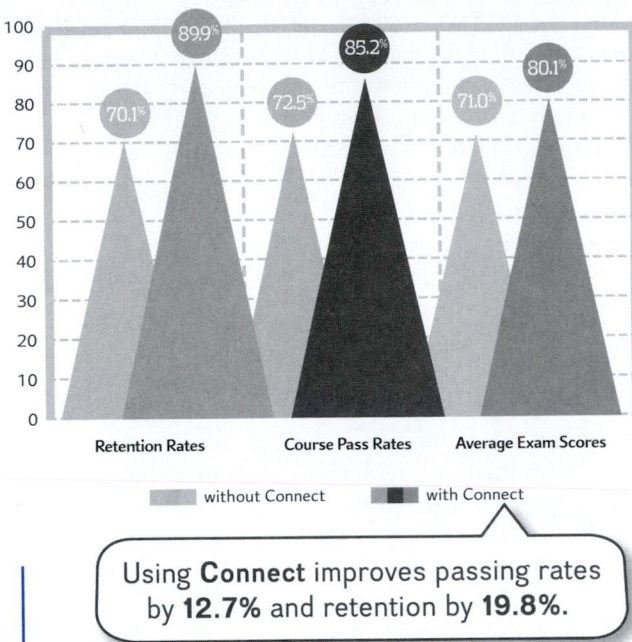

Using **Connect** improves passing rates by **12.7%** and retention by **19.8%**.

Analytics

Connect Insight®

Connect Insight is Connect's new one-of-a-kind visual analytics dashboard that provides at-a-glance information regarding student performance, which is immediately actionable. By presenting assignment, assessment, and topical performance results together with a time metric that is easily visible for aggregate or individual results, Connect Insight gives the user the ability to take a just-in-time approach to teaching and learning, which was never before available. Connect Insight presents data that helps instructors improve class performance in a way that is efficient and effective.

Impact on Final Course Grade Distribution

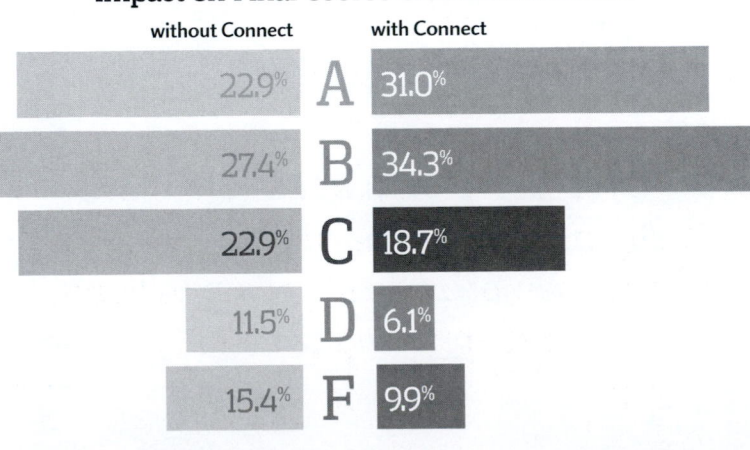

Adaptive

©Getty Images/iStockphoto

THE **ADAPTIVE** **READING EXPERIENCE** DESIGNED TO TRANSFORM THE WAY STUDENTS READ

> More students earn **A's** and **B's** when they use McGraw-Hill Education **Adaptive** products.

SmartBook®

Proven to help students improve grades and study more efficiently, SmartBook contains the same content within the print book, but actively tailors that content to the needs of the individual. SmartBook's adaptive technology provides precise, personalized instruction on what the student should do next, guiding the student to master and remember key concepts, targeting gaps in knowledge and offering customized feedback, and driving the student toward comprehension and retention of the subject matter. Available on smartphones and tablets, SmartBook puts learning at the student's fingertips—anywhere, anytime.

> Over **5.7 billion questions** have been answered, making McGraw-Hill Education products more intelligent, reliable, and precise.

www.mheducation.com

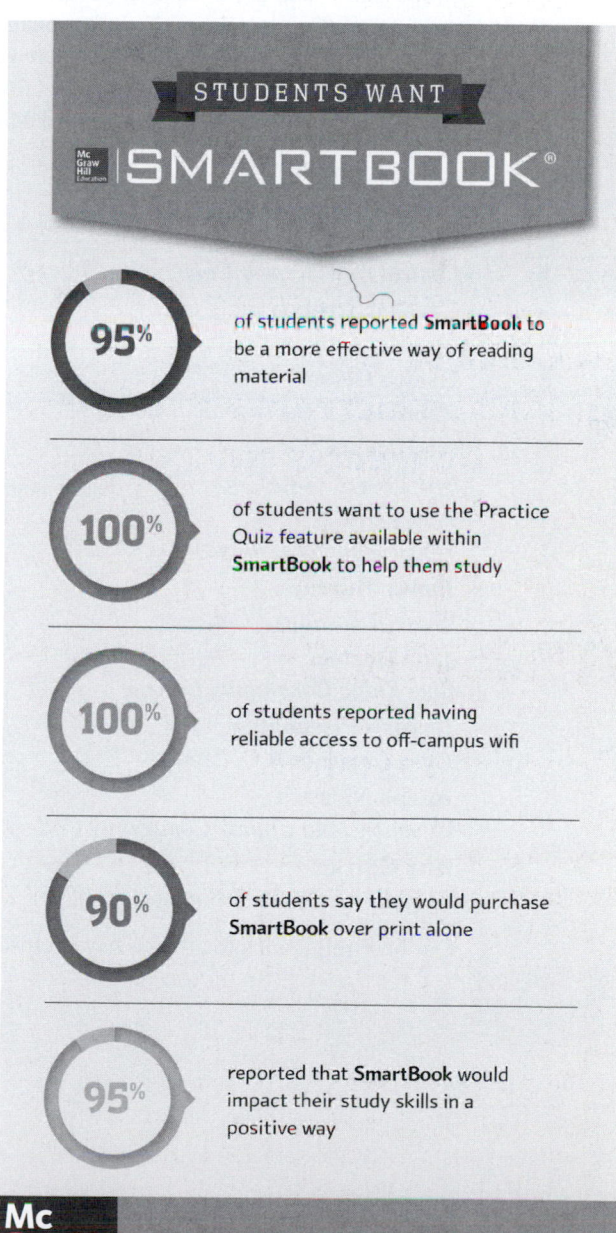

STUDENTS WANT

Mc Graw Hill Education **SMARTBOOK**®

95% of students reported SmartBook to be a more effective way of reading material

100% of students want to use the Practice Quiz feature available within **SmartBook** to help them study

100% of students reported having reliable access to off-campus wifi

90% of students say they would purchase **SmartBook** over print alone

95% reported that **SmartBook** would impact their study skills in a positive way

Mc Graw Hill Education

*Findings based on a 2015 focus group survey at Pellissippi State Community College administered by McGraw-Hill Education

Acknowledgments

This third edition of *Payroll Accounting* would not have been possible without the patience, guidance, and encouragement of Steve Schuetz, brand manager; the diligence and commitment of Randall Edwards, product developer; the support and leadership of Dana Pauley and Brian Nacik, content project managers; the incredible form templates designed by Kitty O'Donnell; and the amazing artwork of Egzon Shaqiri, designer. We further want to thank Michelle Williams, marketing manager; Melissa Homer and Lorraine Buczek, content licensing specialists; Peggy Hussey, director of digital content; Kevin Moran, associate director of digital content; Xin Lin, digital product analyst; and the compositing team at SPi Global. Special thanks go to Anna Hoppmann, digital asset librarian, and to Connie Schleisman and the technical support team for facilitating our online access and asset location needs. Thanks go to our project development team who handled every formatting request with professionalism.

Countless other colleagues have offered their feedback, insights, and inspiration during various stages of this project. We want to extend sincere thanks to the reviewers and TACTYC session attendees who helped us shape the third edition:

Annette Frank
Mott Community College

Carol Rogers
Central New Mexico Community College

Carolyn Strauch
Crowder College

Danica Olson
MIlwaukee Area Technical College

Ira Hickam
Kaskaskia College

Ivan Lowe
York Technical College

James Murray
Western Technical College

Jana Hosmer
Blue Ridge Community College

Jerrilyn Eisenhauer
Tulsa Community College

Joseph Nicassio
Westmoreland County Community College

Kim Gatzke
Delgado Community College

Kirk Lynch
Sand Hills Community College

Larry Ardner
Stark State College

Lina Fedynyshyn
Emily Griffith Technical College

M. Jeff Quinlan
Madison College

Marilyn Ciolino
Delgado Community College

Mellissa Youngman
National Institute for the Deaf

Merrily Hoffman
San Jacinto College

Molly McFadden-May
Tulsa Community College

Rick Street
Spokane Community College

Susan Davis
Green River College

Susan L. Pallas-Duncan
Southeast Community College

Our heartfelt thanks to all who have helped make this project a reality.

Jeanette Landin

Paulette Schirmer

Brief Contents

Contents

Chapter 3
Gross Pay Computation   94

Chapter 4
Employee Net Pay and Pay Methods   138

Chapter 5
Employer Payroll Taxes and Labor Planning   188

Chapter 6
The Payroll Register, Employees' Earning Records, and Accounting System Entries   258

Payroll Practices and System Fundamentals

Payroll systems are an integral part of job planning and strategic human resource management, cost management for products and services, and benefits analysis for a company. A company's payroll system has historically connected human resources and accounting departments. In contemporary businesses, payroll has taken on a strategic role in terms of company direction and future plans. A well-designed payroll system can serve the company; for this reason, an understanding of payroll foundations is imperative. In this chapter, we will explore the need for a payroll system, legal requirements, ethical guidelines, best practices, and variations in payroll practices among different-sized companies.

LEARNING OBJECTIVES

After studying Chapter 1, you should be able to:

LO 1-1   Explain the Purpose of Studying Payroll Accounting

LO 1-2   Discuss the Legal Framework for Payroll Accounting

LO 1-3   Discuss the Ethical Guidelines for Payroll Accounting

LO 1-4   Identify Contemporary Payroll Practices

LO 1-5   Compare Payroll Processing Options for Different Businesses

LO 1-6   Differentiate Between Exempt and Nonexempt Workers

© McGraw-Hill Education/John Flournoy, photographer

Payroll Challenges for the World's Largest Employer

Walmart, based in Bentonville, Arkansas, is the largest American private employer. In early 2016, Wal-Mart Stores, Inc., (d.b.a. Wal-Mart) employed 2.2 million workers, making it the largest private employer in the world. More than 1.4 million of Wal-Mart Stores' employees work in the United States. As of February 2016, Wal-Mart Stores announced that it would increase the minimum starting wage to $10.00 per hour for more than 1.2 million employees due to long-standing pressure from labor organizations, and it would increase the average wage for full-time workers to $13.38 per hour. This wage increase represents an additional $2.7 billion in personnel costs to the company. In addition to these pay increases, Walmart instituted a new paid-time-off policy that replaced a former requirement to wait one day before receiving sick time. Walmart's philosophy behind these changes was that these investments in their employees would lead to strategic long-term effects. (Sources: *Reuters, Employer Benefits News, 24/7 Wall Street, Corporate.Walmart.com*)

The need for organized payroll practices grows in proportion to the business size. Companies have many options for their payroll management, depending on the firm's structure and size. In Chapter 1, we will explore the basics of payroll systems, including legal and ethical issues involved with employee pay.

LO 1-1 Explain the Purpose of Studying Payroll Accounting

Unlike many other types of accounting, payroll affects most (if not all) members of an organization. Payroll errors can lead to serious internal and external problems. Internal errors may cause a company to pay excessive wages for unneeded overtime, forego profits, or employ the wrong number of workers during seasonal or other workflow changes. Managers use internal reports about labor usage, staffing levels, and employee compensation trends to ensure operational effectiveness. Organizational decision makers use these reports to control labor costs, hire additional employees to meet surge demands, and manage the cost of goods sold. Payroll errors can result in governmental fines, taxes, or legal charges related to the violation of labor laws. Employers provide external reports to the Internal Revenue Service (IRS), state government tax departments, and many more agencies, depending upon the nature of the company.

> The New York County District Attorney indicted Sky Materials Corporation as of March 1, 2016, for underreporting $3 million in payroll during 2015 to avoid paying workers' compensation insurance premiums. After investigation, court records revealed a history of payroll understatement that resulted in more than $1 million of unpaid insurance premiums. (Sources: *ManhattanDA.org, New York Post*)

According to the United States Bureau of Labor Statistics, in 2016, employment in accounting jobs is expected to increase 11% through 2024. Salaries average $36,430 for accounting clerks who have completed some college work and $65,940 for accountants with bachelor's degrees. (Source: www.bls.gov/ooh)

The legislative framework governing employers' payroll systems is complex. These laws reflect societal evolution over time. Note how some of these laws have been challenged or changed since their inception.

The Equal Pay Act of 1963 mandated that males and females be paid equally for equal work. Any employees who feel that they have been paid unequally based upon gender have legal options to rectify the situation.

- First, they should gather documentation regarding the differential and determine if other employees in question are willing to substantiate the difference.
- Second, they should speak with their supervisor to question the pay differential.
- Should the supervisor be unwilling to discuss or adjust, an attorney may become a necessary third step.

This Act was modified by the **Lilly Ledbetter Fair Pay Act of 2009,** which removed the 180-day statute of limitations on claims of unequal treatment.

> In 1979, Lilly Ledbetter, an employee of Goodyear Tire and Rubber Company, started at the same rate of pay as males in the same position. Over time, she was declined raises by management, which based its decisions on negative reviews that Ms. Ledbetter later claimed were discriminatory. Under the provisions of the 1963 Equal Pay Act, the claimant had 180 days to file a complaint. Although the U.S. Supreme Court agreed with her discrimination claims, it ruled in favor of Goodyear because of the lack of timeliness of Ms. Ledbetter's filing. This ruling ultimately led to the Lilly Ledbetter Fair Pay Act of 2009. (Source: www.govtrack.us)

The Civil Rights Act of 1964 prohibited discrimination based on race, creed, color, gender, and national origin. Since 1964, this Act has been extended by Executive Order 11478 to protect people with AIDS, pregnant workers, people with different sexual orientations,

© Shutterstock/www.BillionPhotos.com

and people with disabilities. As of June 2015, the United States Supreme Court ruled in *Obergefell v. Hodges* that same-sex marriage was legal and could not be banned in any state. This extension of the Civil Rights Act of 1964 represented another step toward the legal protection of worker dignity. (Source: www.eeoc.gov, U.S. Supreme Court No. 14-556)

The Age Discrimination in Employment Act of 1967 (ADEA) prevents mandatory retirement of older employees (older than age 40) and prohibits age-based discrimination in hiring.

The Occupational Safety and Health Act of 1970 (OSHA) defined and enforced healthy and safe working environments for employees.

Several landmark cases followed ADEA enactment. Some of the most notable cases involved commercial airline pilots who were discriminated against based on their age, not their ability to pilot an airliner. In the case of *Trans World Airlines v. Thurston* (1985), the defendant disputed the FAA's mandatory retirement age for pilots, claiming that older pilots should be given the same rights as disabled pilots, which involved reassigning these individuals as flight engineers. The U.S. Supreme Court upheld Thurston's claim but denied the double damages that Thurston sought. (Source: legal-dictionary.thefreedictionary.com)

Employee safety programs and personal protective equipment represent an additional cost to the employer, but fines for noncompliance and payments made following workplace injuries are often far more costly.

© Martin Barraud/Caia Image/Glow Images, RF

The Employee Retirement Income Security Act of 1974 (ERISA) regulates the management of retirement and pension plans. ERISA has been extended by the Consolidated Omnibus Budget Reformation Act of 1986. During the recession of 2007–2009, the value of some employee retirement funds decreased, causing employees to postpone retirement. The Internal Revenue Service imposes limitations on retirement plan contributions, and those limits have shifted to reflect the need for employees to recoup losses sustained during the recession. Since that time, employee retirement benefits have shifted from being a financial burden to becoming an employee hiring and retention strategy, and retirement researchers are contemplating proposing a mandatory retirement savings law. (Source: *Employee Benefit News*)

In *CIGNA v. Amara* (2011), the U.S. Supreme Court ruled on communications issued by retirement plan administrators. CIGNA was found in violation of ERISA because of its misleading and incomplete communications to plan participants that resulted in misunderstandings about the benefit level due to the participant. The Court ruled that the benefit level accrued under the plan needed to be commensurate with the benefits received upon the participant's retirement. (Source: www.nixonpeabody.com)

The Consolidated Omnibus Budget Reconciliation Act of 1985 (COBRA) extended medical benefits for terminated employees at the employee's expense. The federal government, in response to the high unemployment rates at the start of 2010, briefly subsidized COBRA insurance. The temporary reduction in COBRA remains available, but only for employees who were terminated between September 1, 2008, and March 31, 2010. The repeal of the Defense of Marriage Act (DOMA) in 2013 forced employers to offer COBRA coverage to same-sex spouses. (Sources: U.S. Department of Labor, SHRM)

The Immigration Reform and Control Act of 1986 (IRCA) requires employers to verify that employees are legally able to work in the United States. Form I-9 is the most common payroll-related application of this law. Immigration and citizenship laws require the collection of information within an I-9, and retention is three years from date of hire or one year from date of termination (whichever is longer).

Several pieces of Federal legislation have been proposed to limit immigration, target immigration in targeted industries, and address the issue of refugee employment. According to National Conference of State Legislators, there is a 2016 limit restricting the number of refugees allowable to 85,000; the number of allowable refugees is expected to climb to 100,000 in 2017. As the laws increase allowable number of refugee employees, the complexity of payroll regarding how each group of refugees is treated for tax purposes may become a hot topic of debate. (Source: www .congress.gov; http://www.ncsl.org/bookstore/state-legislatures-magazine/statestats-february-2016.aspx)

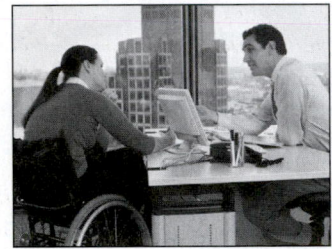

The Americans with Disabilities Act of 1990 (ADA) extended the provisions of the Civil Rights Act of 1964 by ensuring that people with disabilities have the same opportunities as those without mental or physical impairment. This law applies to employers with 15 or more employees on the payroll, including full-time and part-time workers. In 2011, changes to the definition of disability expanded the ADA provisions to allow individuals broader protection under the Act.

© Image Source/PunchStock, RF

The Civil Rights Act of 1991 granted employees who have been discriminated against the chance to be paid monetary damages through legal proceedings. This Act applies to American employers and American-controlled employers with internationally based operations.

In the case of *Pollard v. DuPont* (2000), Sharon Pollard sued DuPont for her managers' knowledge of a hostile work environment created by sexual harassment. Under Section VII of the Civil Rights Act of 1964, Ms. Pollard would not have received compensation for her complaint. However, the 1991 revision of the Civil Rights Act allowed her to receive $300,000 in compensation for damages. (Source: www .oyez.org)

The Family and Medical Leave Act of 1993 (FMLA) granted employees the right to take medical leave under reasonable circumstances without fear of job loss. The employee may have to take unpaid leave, but medical benefits must continue under FMLA provisions. Upon return from family leave, the employer must provide an equivalent position with equivalent pay, benefits, and terms of employment. The employer has many responsibilities under the FMLA that involve employee notification of benefits and processes while on leave. The repeal of DOMA provoked the need to clarify the term "family member." Following the U.S. Supreme Court decision in *Obergefell v. Hodges (2015),* the U.S. Department of Labor updated the definition of spouse to include same-sex marriages, regardless of where they live. (Source: U.S. Department of Labor)

In the case of *Young v. Wackenhut,* the plaintiff was on unpaid leave according to FMLA provisions. Ms. Young had completed all forms provided by Wackenhut, her employer; however, Wackenhut neglected to issue a specific, individual notice about requirements involved with her return to work. The New Jersey District Court ruled in favor of Ms. Young because Wackenhut did not satisfy all stipulated notification requirements of FMLA. (Source: www.lexology.com)

© Blend Images/Alamy, RF

The Uniformed Services Employment and Reemployment Rights Act of 1994 (USERRA) governs the rights of military service members in terms of length of military service, return to work, and accommodations for injured veterans. USERRA was amended as to service members' rights in 2005. In 2011, USERRA was further amended by the Veterans Opportunity to Work, which allowed USERRA to recognize claims of a hostile work environment resulting from an individual's military status.

The U.S. Department of Labor investigates many cases involving service members' rights. A notable case involved an Army reservist, Colonel Scott Harrison, who served multiple tours in the Middle East, during which he received many rank promotions for his military work. His civilian employer denied him promotions, stating that his military service detracted from his work performance. USERRA states that service members must receive the same promotions and compensation that they would have received if they had not been absent for military purposes. Colonel Harrison received a promotion plus $96,000 in lost wages because of USERRA. (Source: U.S. Department of Labor)

The Personal Responsibility and Work Opportunity Reconciliation Act of 1996 (PRWOR) mandated that employers file a new hire reporting form within 20 days after an employee initially commences work. This Act protects children and needy families by enforcing child support obligations. The child support provisions of PRWOR were strengthened by the passage of the **Personal Responsibility, Work and Family Promotion Act of 2002.**

The Health Insurance Portability and Accountability Act of 1996 (HIPAA) protects workers and their families who have preexisting medical conditions from discrimination based on those conditions. The Ebola outbreak in 2014 led to additional guidance about HIPAA rights and notifications to interested parties, including employers, during emergency situations,

In *Equal Employment Opportunity Commission v. Boston Market* (2004), the plaintiff claimed that Boston Market, an employer, sought access to employees' private psychological and medical records. Although the Supreme Court ultimately found that state law was more stringent than HIPAA legislation, Boston Market was found in violation of patient privacy law by seeking communication with medical professionals without prior specific authorization. (Source: www.americanbar.org)

The Sarbanes–Oxley Act of 2002 (SOX) provided criminal penalties for violations of ERISA. SOX provides protections for whistleblowers and mandates the rotation of auditors among publicly owned companies. An addition consideration for public companies of SOX regarding payroll is that the internal controls of a payroll system must be reported under the guidelines set out in Section 404. Costs of SOX compliance have sparked discussion about the Act's effectiveness, especially following the 2008 financial crisis.

> An employee of Countrywide Mortgage, a Bank of America subsidiary, alerted OSHA officials to fraud in the company's financial records. This employee led internal investigations that revealed significant fraud in monetary transactions, as well as a history of retaliation against other whistleblowers. In 2011, the U.S. Department of Labor found Bank of America to be in violation of the Sarbanes–Oxley Act's whistleblower provision and awarded $930,000 to the employee. (Source: www.osha.gov)

The American Recovery and Reinvestment Act of 2009 (ARRA) provided tax credits for employers and employees through the Making Work Pay provisions. Changes in withholding allowances reduced the amount of taxes collected from workers, and unemployed individuals received between $400 and $800 on their tax return based upon specific qualifications within the Act. Although ARRA's provisions have expired, parts of it were reinstated through the *American Taxpayer Relief Act of 2012 (ATRA)*. Many of the ATRA provisions were extended through 2015 by the extension of the Work Opportunity Tax Credit.

The Defense of Marriage Act of 1996 (DOMA) restricted payroll-related taxes and benefits to include only traditionally married couples, denying married status to people in same-sex unions. The U.S. Supreme Court overturned DOMA in its ruling in *U.S. v. Windsor* on September 6, 2013; the Internal Revenue Service subsequently mandated that all married same-sex couples must be treated as married for all tax purposes. The repeal of DOMA had a ripple effect throughout all phases of payroll because of the need to amend business and personal tax return filings back to 2011, owing to the three-year amendment rule. The effects of DOMA's repeal have had a ripple effect on employee rights, highlighting the need for additional legislative clarification.

> In *U.S. v. Windsor,* Ms. Windsor and her wife were recognized as a married couple by the State of New York, and her compensation was taxed accordingly. However, the IRS sued Windsor for unpaid taxes because her same-sex marriage violated DOMA. The U.S. Supreme Court found that DOMA violated Windsor's Fifth Amendment right to liberty and overturned DOMA. The IRS subsequently dropped its lawsuit. (Source: www.supremecourt.gov)

As times change, new legislation will be enacted, and existing laws are sometimes repealed and amended. An example of evolving legislation includes new state laws about paid sick time for all employees, such as those enacted in Massachusetts, Oregon, and Vermont.

The payroll accountant's job is one of consistent and continual learning and research to ensure that the company is complying with all current regulations and reporting requirements. Many states, but not all, have additional payroll tax laws.

(See www.americanpayroll.org/weblink/statelocal-wider/ for more information.)

LO 1-2 Discuss the Legal Framework for Payroll Accounting

Why did businesses start withholding taxes from people's paychecks? Federal income tax withholding was temporarily instituted in 1861 as a way to recover from the high costs of the Civil War; this tax was repealed in 1872. Throughout the 19th century, cities were growing in the wake of the Industrial Revolution, as factories and companies increased

© Pixtal/age Fotostock, RF

Which Law?

Stop & Check

1. Requires employers to verify the employee's legal right to work in the United States? K
2. Protects the rights of disabled workers? H
3. Governs the management of retirement plans? B
4. Protects discrimination of workers older than age 40? F
5. Creates safe work environments for employees? I
6. Mandates equal pay for equal work? J
7. Extends medical benefits for terminated employees? A
8. Ensures that child support obligations will be paid? D
9. Protects workers and families with preexisting medical conditions? G
10. Enforces payment of monetary damages because of discrimination? C
11. Requires internal controls on payroll practices of public companies E

a. COBRA
b. ERISA
c. Civil Rights Act of 1991
d. PRWOR
e. SOX
f. ADEA
g. HIPAA
h. ADA
i. OSHA
j. Equal Pay Act of 1963
k. IRCA

automation and institutionalized mass production. People were moving from rural to urban areas in unprecedented numbers, and the need for infrastructure and civil services grew. Roads needed to be built, law enforcement personnel needed to be increased, and outbreaks of disease prompted a need for sanitation systems. Therefore, the U.S. Congress formalized the permanent continuation of the federal income tax instituted during the Civil War as a means to fund the infrastructure improvements of the booming cities. After many failed attempts to reinstate a federal income tax, Congress passed the **Sixteenth Amendment to the U.S. Constitution**, in 1909, which was ratified by states in 1913. This version incorporated a tiered income tax, including exemptions and deductions to limit the tax imposed on wages earned; it was the harbinger of many employment-related laws (see Figure 1-1).

During the Great Depression of the 1930s, the stock market collapsed, financial institutions went bankrupt, and companies released workers or ceased business operations. The

FIGURE 1-1
Timeline of Payroll Legislation

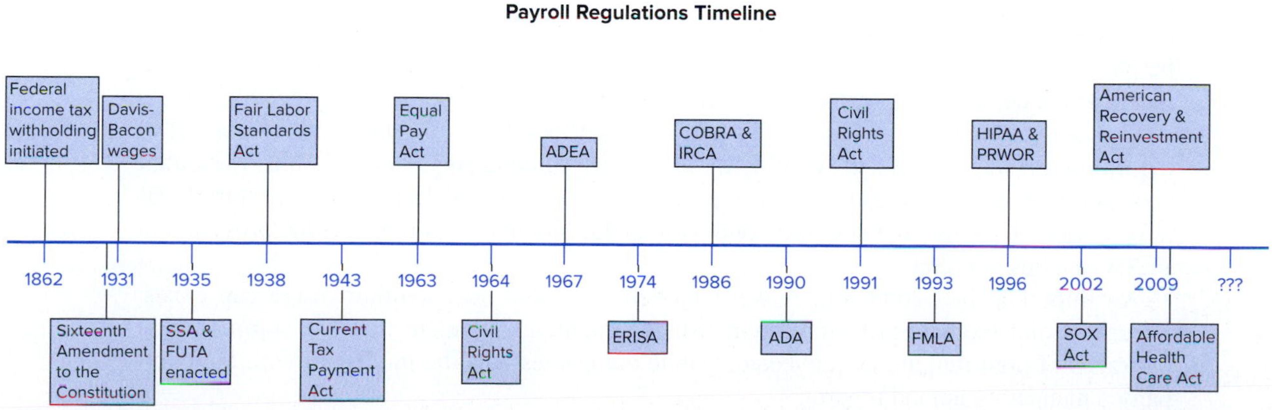

Payroll Regulations Timeline

government needed money to fund programs that would stimulate economic recovery. Additionally, the need for a social welfare system emerged as the number of displaced workers increased. The 1930s became a decade of landmark employment legislation that defined the legal environment for employers and employees, most of which remains enforced in 2017.

In 1931, Congress passed the ***Davis-Bacon Act***, creating a standard of wages for governmental contracts totaling more than $2,000. The increased standard wages created under the Davis-Bacon Act brought additional revenue to small businesses and the communities where the contact workers lived, bought groceries, and purchased other services or goods. The Davis-Bacon Act comprised more than 60 different federal statutes, providing a prevailing wage and wage classification strategy to guide employers and contractors.

In 1935, the ***Social Security Act* (SSA)**, also known as the ***Federal Insurance Contributions Act* (FICA)**, established a contribution-driven fund that would help the average U.S. worker achieve a level of financial stability when he or she became too old or infirm to work. A contribution-driven fund's employees and employers pay a percentage of gross earnings into the Social Security fund. Originally, the fund was designed to be earmarked for a specific individual upon retirement, but the fund currently provides assistance for families who experience diminished wages and working situations because of infirmity of the worker or a family member. Social Security is synonymous with **Old-Age, Survivors, and Disability Insurance (OASDI)**. ***Medicare tax***, a government-mandated health insurance program for individuals older than 62 years of age, was also included in the SSA legislation.

The ***Walsh-Healey Public Contracts Act*** of 1936 affected governmental contractors providing goods or services exceeding $10,000. The Act required companies to pay workers a minimum wage for all hours worked under 40 per week and time and a half (regular pay times 1.5) per hour for any hours over 40 per week. The Walsh-Healey Public Contracts Act also prohibited the employment of individuals younger than 16 years of age. Compliance with this act is enforced through the Employment Standards Administration Wage and Hour Division of the Department of Labor. These standards also apply to workers within the District of Columbia.

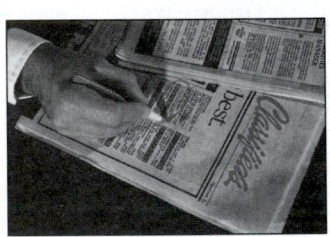

© Royalty-Free/Corbis, RF

As another part of its social welfare legislation, the U.S. Congress passed the ***Federal Unemployment Tax Act* (FUTA)** as a way to help displaced workers, individuals from the workforce who find themselves unemployed and meet certain state or federal qualifications. FUTA and its state counterpart, **SUTA**, are based upon the wages earned by the employees. Unlike Social Security taxes, only employers pay FUTA. Some states require both employers and employees to contribute to SUTA. For example, Alaskan employees contribute up to an annual amount of $198.50 (2016 figure) to SUTA, which is collected at a rate of 0.50% of wages; employers contribute up to 2.6% of employee wages until they reach $38,700 in annual gross earnings. Should an employee have more than one employer, the employee is allowed to request a return for the amounts over the annual earnings maximum in the following year.

The enactment of the ***Fair Labor Standards Act* (FLSA)** of 1938 required better record-keeping and worker protection. This Act regulates the minimum wage, a topic with which most workers are familiar, stated as the lowest an individual under certain classifications can be paid. Less commonly known, minimum wage applies only to workers at businesses that meet certain conditions. For example, small businesses that conduct no interstate commerce, such as a restaurant that serves only locally obtained food from one state, are not subject to the minimum wage provisions of FLSA. Additionally, tipped employees, such as restaurant servers, are exempt from minimum wage standards under FLSA. In the contemporary business world, a business that does not conduct interstate commerce is rare, but the provision in FLSA remains in effect.

An important fact about FLSA wage guidelines is that no maximum wage cap exists. Securities and Exchanges Commission (SEC) regulations stipulate that the compensation packages of high-ranking employees of public companies must be published with the company's mandatory annual report.

The minimum wage may differ from a "living wage," which is an amount needed to meet basic subsistence needs. Certain localities have enacted living wage ordinances to rise in relation to the Consumer Price Index. Some of these cities include (but are not limited to):

- San Leandro, California
- Pine Bluff, Arkansas
- Asheville, North Carolina
- Pittsburgh, Pennsylvania
- Albuquerque, New Mexico

(Source: Employment Policies Institute)

One of the major provisions of FLSA is the classification of employees for overtime pay purposes. The U.S. Department of Labor is clarifying and narrowing the guidelines for workers who are exempt from the FLSA overtime regulations. New guidelines for employee classifications are scheduled to became effective in July 2016, which may involve FLSA re-classifications for certain employees. The 2016 re-classifications include revised guidelines regarding overtime pay for administrative, executive, and professional employees. (Source: DOL, SHRM)

FLSA guidelines define maximum hours, minimum age, pay rates, and mandatory break times. This part of the FLSA is an outgrowth of the industrial environment of the early 20th century, when no such guidelines existed. Horror stories about working conditions and children working 12- to 14-hour days abounded during the 1930s. The FLSA created the classifications of exempt and nonexempt workers. Exempt workers are salaried workers who are not subject to certain wage and overtime provisions of FLSA. Overtime is the payment of wages at one-and-a-half times the normal rate for qualifying hours. Nonexempt workers are subject to wage and overtime provisions.

Additionally, under FLSA, pay periods are not regulated, nor is the amount of paid time off given to employees. Those two items are at the discretion of the employer. Paid time off has become a topic of discussion since 2010, and companies such as McDonald's have begun offering it to nonexempt employees in 2015 as a regular part of employee benefit packages in response to pressure from labor leaders. Certain states, including Massachusetts,

© David Schaffer/age fotostock

Oregon, Connecticut, California, and Vermont, instituted paid sick leave for employees (Sources: *Bloomberg,* Seyfarth Shaw LLP)

A third class of workers, independent contractors, is not subject to the pay provisions of the FLSA. ***Independent contractors*** are typically treated as vendors of a business. Independent contractors are not employees of the business and are not reflected on payroll records. In July 2015, the Department of Labor ruled that improper classification of workers diminished workers' legal protections under the FLSA and declared that the following items must be considered when classifying a worker as an employee or an independent contractor:

1. The extent to which a worker is an integral element of the employer's business.
2. Whether the worker's managerial skills affect his or her opportunity for profit or loss.
3. Relative investments in facilities and equipment by ***both*** the employee and the employer.
4. The extent to which the worker exercises independent business judgment.
5. The permanent nature of the working relationship between the employer and employee.
6. The type and extent of the control that the employer has over the employee.

To obtain the remittance of employers' withholding taxes, the federal government needed a way to standardize the collection of taxes from employers. Before the ***Current Tax Payment Act (CTPA)*** of 1943, no formalized guidelines for remittance of taxes existed. During the time before the CTPA, the remittance of taxes from employers was inconsistent and unreliable as a funding source for governmental projects. The CTPA was passed during World War II as a means of guaranteeing a source of funds to support the country's involvement in the war. The CTPA created the requirement for the submission of estimated taxes on wages earned during the year of earning instead of after the end of the year as previously required.

© aabejon/Getty Images, RF

Another employer obligation is *worker's compensation*, commonly known as *worker's comp*. Unlike other payroll-specific laws, state laws govern worker's compensation laws. Worker's compensation is an insurance policy carried by employers to provide wage continuation and to pay for medical services for workers injured in the course of doing business. The amounts assigned to the policy vary by type of work being performed and associated risks for various professions. For example, heavy equipment operators would have a higher worker's comp rate than office workers because their exposure to injury is deemed higher by the insurance industry. Worker's compensation plans are subject to annual audits and are based upon payroll wages, less exempt employees (typically working owners). Employers must report all wages earned by the employee; however, only one-third of overtime hours are reported to the worker's compensation auditor. Each state has different requirements for coverage and eligibility. Because worker's compensation is an insurance program, it is not considered a tax, but it is a state-mandated employer payroll expense. The nature and extent of the worker's compensation insurance varies per state. (Source: NFIB)

The *Affordable Care Act of 2010* was one of the most significant changes in payroll accounting in recent years. Although the primary focus of the Act was to ensure health care coverage for all Americans, employers have several reporting responsibilities related to the Act. One of the responsibilities included in Section 1003 is the disclosure and justification for rates of plans and any increases in premiums. Another reporting requirement is the number of full-time equivalent (FTE) employees, the cost of insurance coverage provided to employees, and the elimination of a waiting period for health insurance coverage. The legislation of the Affordable Care Act is 974 pages containing many provisions and contingencies, including a requirement for continuing premium review. (Source: HHS)

According to the Internal Revenue Service, employers must report whether they provide Minimum Essential Coverage that is part of their company-sponsored benefits including any group health plans, COBRA plans, or preexisting insurance coverage. Health insurance coverage is reported on IRS Form 1095 A, B, or C as follows:

- Form 1095-A is for individuals who have purchased insurance from the Healthcare Marketplace, not through an employer. This form is issued by the Marketplace.

- Form 1095-B is for individuals covered under minimum essential coverage, such as governmental and some qualified employer-sponsored plans. This form is issued by insurers and self-insured employers.

- Form 1095-C is for large employer health insurance where the employer is responsible for the shared responsibility provision of the Act. This form is issued by employers who offer coverage but are not self-insured.

The employer must file IRS form 1095-B or 1095-C and furnish a copy to the insured if the insured received medical insurance benefits for as few as one day of one month during a calendar year. (Source: IRS)

LO 1-3   Discuss the Ethical Guidelines for Payroll Accounting

Professional *ethics* is critical in any accounting context, and especially so in payroll accounting. The payroll accountant is entrusted to handle money belonging to the firm and owed to the government and employees. After the Enron accounting scandal and the passage of

Which Payroll Law?

1. Established requirements for employer recordkeeping? D
2. Provided government assistance for workers who are too old or infirm to work? A
3. Established protection for displaced workers? F
4. Required employers to file taxes collected in a timely manner? C
5. Set aside funds for health insurance? G
6. Regulated wages for employees whose employer engaged in governmental contracts? H
7. Is governed on a state-to-state basis and protects employees injured during the course of work activities? B
8. Is responsible for reporting requirements of minimum essential coverage for full-time equivalent employees? E

a. Social Security Act
b. Worker's compensation
c. Current Tax Payment Act
d. Fair Labor Standards Act
e. Affordable Care Act
f. Federal Unemployment Tax Act
g. Medicare
h. Davis-Bacon Act

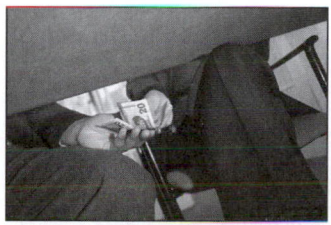

© Thinkstock Images/Getty Images, RF

the *Sarbanes–Oxley Act of 2002*, ethics became a focus of the accounting profession as a whole. The American Institute of Certified Public Accountants (AICPA) defined a code of ethics that is commonly applied in the accounting profession. The basic guidelines of the AICPA Code of Ethics include the following tenets:

- Responsibility
- The Public Interest
- Integrity
- Objectivity and Independence
- Due Care

> Ethisphere maintains an annual list of the most ethical companies in the world. In 2016, the list included many companies based in the United States, such as Cisco, Hasbro, USAA, and several others. Although the companies on the list are in a variety of industries, certain ethical principles are common to all: integrity, social responsibility, care for all stakeholders, and honesty and transparency in all business dealings. (Source: Ethisphere)

Responsibility

An accountant is responsible for maintaining confidences and exercising moral judgment in all actions. A payroll accountant deals with sensitive personnel information that must remain confidential. Social Security numbers, employee legal obligations, and an employer's tax liabilities are a few examples of information that a payroll accountant must protect.

> In 2009, DuPont sued a former employee who stole approximately 600 files by loading them onto a portable flash drive before leaving the company. These files contained confidential company information, and 550 of the 600 files were found on the former employee's home computer. The employee was sentenced to an 18-month prison term. (Source: Law360)

The Public Interest

Accountants must uphold the ***public interest*** by maintaining confidentiality and exhibiting professionalism in their practice. In terms of payroll accounting, the term *public interest* includes the needs of the firm, its employees, and associated governmental entities. A payroll accountant must complete all tasks and adhere to deadlines, despite any personal issues. Personal honesty and transparency of transactions are the core of acting in the public interest.

> 99.7% of all U.S. businesses are classified as small businesses. These small businesses experience periods of financial distress, and sums needed to meet payroll obligations occasionally are unavailable. During times of financial distress, it is vital that the payroll accountant communicate with employees to build trust. It is equally important that the payroll accountant communicate with management to develop crisis plans. In this way, the payroll accountant upholds the public interest. (Source: Financial Executives International)

Integrity

In the workplace, integrity is the most important asset a professional can possess. ***Integrity*** involves doing the right thing despite any external pressure, personal temptations, or conflicts of interest. The main question when weighing the integrity of a decision is, Am I doing what is right and just for everyone concerned? Any course of action that lacks integrity potentially restricts the rights of interested parties and compromises the best interests of the company.

> Payroll fraud can happen anywhere that pressures, opportunities, and rationalizations exist. In *Perrenod v. U.S.* (2013), the CEO of a company was held liable for the remittance of payroll taxes that the CFO (who had been fired) had embezzled. The CFO had issued the tax remittance checks to himself, which became apparent only when the IRS sent the company a notice of a tax default. The CEO, Perrenod, sued the United States, claiming that he had no knowledge of the liability and should be absolved of the late penalties. The Supreme Court ruled that Perrenod was liable for all penalties because, as CEO, he was responsible for all actions of the company's personnel. (Source: *Forbes*)

Objectivity and Independence

Accountants must take care to be free of any pressures that would compromise the integrity of their work. These pressures can come from business or personal relationships that may affect a payroll accountant's judgment concerning the best interests of all concerned in a given situation. ***Objectivity*** in accounting means that the accountant considers only facts relevant to the task at hand, independent of all other pressures.

Social obligations may compromise a payroll accountant's objectivity. The AICPA Code of Ethics section 17 specifically addresses social club membership as a factor in the loss of an accountant's independence or objectivity. Such club membership could create a social debt that may cause an accountant to commit payroll fraud. (Source: AICPA)

Due Care

Due care revolves around an accountant's competence and assumes that the accounting professional is equally competent as other people in a similar role. According to the AICPA, an accountant must remain current with accounting practices and legal developments to comply with due care requirements. Payroll laws and tax guidelines change regularly. As a payroll accountant, it is extremely important to remain aware of annual changes that the IRS and other accounting bodies publish through participation in professional accounting organizations, subscriptions to accounting industry publications, and participation in discussions at accounting conferences.

Staying current with payroll changes is an ongoing task. Some of the sources for this information include:

- IRS (www.irs.gov)
- AICPA (www.aicpa.org)
- Financial Accounting Standards Board (FASB) (www.fasb.org)
- American Payroll Association (www.apa.org)
- U.S. Department of Labor (www.dol.gov)
- Compliance Tools for HR Professionals (www.hr.blr.com)

What's Ethical?

1. Giles is the payroll accountant for his company. His boss informs him that the company is considering switching payroll systems and asks for his input. What are some ethical concerns involved in changing accounting software?

2. Liza, the payroll manager, is in a sorority. At a social event, she discovers that one of her sorority sisters works for the same company. Her sorority sister asks Liza for confidential information about one of the employees in her department, claiming that the sorority oath requires Liza's compliance. What should Liza do?

LO 1-4 Identify Contemporary Payroll Practices

Contemporary accounting practices reflect the effects of technology and electronic communications on business. Payroll practices have adapted to include modern tools that facilitate data transmission, and new challenges have emerged. Some examples include:

- Direct deposit regulations for employee pay and tax remittances
- Electronic filing requirements

© Anatolii Babii/Alamy, RF

- New timekeeping methods
- The availability of paycards as a method of wage and salary disbursement
- Government contract influences on payroll
- International employees
- Simultaneous in-house and outsourced payroll personnel
- Integration of payroll into other company functions

Payroll is no longer a stand-alone department. Integrated software packages such as QuickBooks and Sage 50 allow business owners to view data across departments and synthesize the information to make large-scale decisions. Contemporary payroll systems serve as a tool for strategic planning, performance measurement, and customer/vendor relations. Payroll accountants are a key element in the decision-making process and must remain educated about legal and compliance issues.

The payroll accountant plays a vital role in a company's structure, no matter how large or small. Payroll and other employee benefits often represent the largest category of a company's expenses. McDonald's Corporation reported more than $4.4 billion in payroll expense alone during fiscal year 2015. The McDonald's Corporation operates more than 35,000 restaurants in 118 countries and has more than 1.7 million employees worldwide.

OPERATING COSTS AND EXPENSES (in millions)			
Company-Operated Restaurant Expenses	2015	2014	2013
Food & Paper	5,552.2	6,129.7	6,361.3
Payroll & Employee Benefits	4,400.0	4,756.0	4,824.1
Occupancy & Other Operating Expenses	4,024.7	4,402.6	4,393.2
Franchised Restaurants-Occupancy Expenses	1,646.9	1,697.3	1,624.4
Selling, General & Administrative Expenses	2,434.3	2,487.9	2,385.6
Total Operating Costs	18,267.5	19,492.1	19,341.4
Net Income	4,529.3	4,757.8	5,585.9

Source: McDonald's Financial Highlights, 2016

Payroll Preparation Options

Several options exist for payroll preparation. The most frequently used method for contemporary payroll preparation is electronic accounting programs. Other options available are manual calculation of payroll using spreadsheets and charts prepared by the Internal Revenue Service, and payroll preparation by outsourcing the process to a third party such as ADP, Paychex®, and myPay Solutions.

Regardless of the payroll preparation method, it is important for the payroll accountant to understand how the process should work. In the event of hardware failure, legislative actions, or tax changes, the accountant must ensure accurate payroll preparation. Companies can lose credibility as the result of flawed payroll, as well as be subject to substantial fines, IRS audits, and civil litigation. Cases in which companies have paid fines for improper payroll practices abound.

> Innovative Payroll, Inc., was accused in 2016 of defrauding customers, including the city of Trenton, New Jersey, of more than $5.6 million. The defendant in the case diverted clients' payroll tax amounts to his personal accounts, which led to the clients receiving IRS penalties for unpaid payroll taxes. (Source: *Courier-Post*)

Some companies have seriously shortchanged employees' paychecks, paying fines in addition to the standard payroll expenditures. Other tales of employee overpayment in the public sector highlight problems in payroll systems, such as computer glitches that have delayed payment of the company's wages. The volume of legislation and stories of problems involving payroll administration point to the need for a well-established payroll system. Despite the legislation concerning payroll practices, no legislation specifies the format and precise delivery of a payroll system.

The information contained in the personnel records is highly sensitive and must be protected against intrusion from unnecessary parties. The ***Privacy Act of 1974*** guaranteed the safeguarding of information contained in private personnel records and mandates information safekeeping as well as due process rights to individuals. Consider the implications of the legal requirements of information safekeeping:

- Personnel records contain information about an individual's marital status, children, other dependents, and legal residence—sensitive information that must be protected under the Privacy Act of 1974.
- Payroll records generally have information about the hourly rate and salary information for each employee. Access to these records is protected by provisions of the **Equal Employment Opportunity Commission (EEOC)** and could provoke or inhibit discrimination lawsuits.

© Rob Daly/age fotostock, RF

- The information contained in payroll records influences the accuracy and integrity of a company's accounting records. The recording of payroll expenses and liabilities affect the profitability of a company, which influences investor and customer relations.
- Companies engaging in business with the federal government must comply with the Davis-Bacon Act (for federal contracts) and potentially the ***Copeland Anti-Kickback Act of 1934*** (for construction projects, protecting taxpayers from unethical pay practices).
- The number of hours worked by an employee must comply with the provisions of the Fair Labor Standards Act (1935).
- Deductions for payroll, especially for retirement plans, must be documented and verified in accordance with the Sarbanes–Oxley Act of 2002.

Employers are required to file tax deposits for employee withholding, Social Security, Medicare, FUTA, and SUTA taxes according to an identified timeline depending upon the size of the company's payroll. Taxes may be remitted via telephone, Internet, mail, or the company's payroll software program. Additional reports are required from the employer on either a quarterly or an annual basis. A company has many responsibilities within its payroll system:

- Tax withholding must be done consistently, reflecting the requirements of federal, state, and local authorities.
- Employers must match amounts withheld from employee paychecks for certain payroll taxes.
- Withholding of deductions that the employee voluntarily elects, such as health care, insurance, and investments, must be correctly recorded and reported.
- Timely and accurate payment must be made to the employee, government agencies, and companies for which the employee has designated the voluntary deductions.
- Tax and other liabilities must be reported to governmental agencies in accordance with established deadlines.

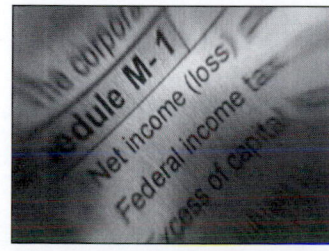

© Don Carstens/Brand X Pictures, RF

An accurate payroll system allows managers to focus on the firm's business, not payroll administration. As such, a well-designed system benefits the employees and governmental agencies, and thus the firm. The timely forwarding of any monies withheld from employees, either by governmental regulation or voluntary election, is critical to a firm's success. If the establishment and implementation of a payroll system sounds complex, it is!

Besides administrating employee pay, a well-designed and accurately maintained payroll system is necessary during inevitable governmental audits. An audit is a process by which a third-party organization, either a public accounting firm or a government agency, inspects the accounting records of a firm for accuracy, integrity, and compliance with federal rules and regulations. During a payroll audit, the auditor inspects the company's records of employee pay, tax remittance, and voluntary deduction maintenance. The thought of audits instills fear into the hearts of even the most seasoned accounting professionals. Their salvation, however, is to establish and maintain an accurate payroll system.

Consider the growth of some companies:

Tom's of Maine started in 1968 as a local organic personal care product company and is now a nationally recognized leader in environmental stewardship and sustainability. (Source: www.tomsofmaine.com)

© McGraw-Hill Education/John Flournoy, photographer

© Japser White/Image Source, RF

Ben and Jerry's, which started as a $5 correspondence course in ice-cream making and a $12,000 investment in 1978, has become an icon of premium ice cream and environmental causes. (Source: www.benjerry.com)

McDonald's Corporation was started in 1955 by the McDonald brothers when they sold their hamburger business to Ray Kroc. The brand is now an international icon for fast food, serving approximately 68 million customers each day. (Sources: www.mcdonalds.com, *The Fiscal Times*)

All these companies share similar beginnings: one location, a few employees, and a relatively simple payroll. As each company has grown, so has the payroll complexity, including multiple departments and facilities in many states and countries. At the heart of each company is a well-run business model and a sound payroll system that has evolved with it.

Tracking and monitoring employee hours, locations, and applicable governmental requirements within various nations requires a knowledgeable payroll staff, willing to remain current with accounting trends and international regulations. Sophisticated payroll systems enable companies to create, populate, and file a multitude of documents using current software and Internet technology.

Privacy Protection

A company must make every reasonable effort to protect personnel information contained in payroll records. This is a critical part of any payroll accountant's job. Several privacy acts exist to protect the information contained in payroll and personnel records. Some of the privacy acts include (but are certainly not limited to):

- U.S. Department of Labor OCFO-1, which pertains to the privacy of information in payroll files.
- U.S. Department of Health and Human Services Privacy Act 09-40-0006, which pertains to eligibility of public employees for pay, entitlements, raises, and benefits.
- Common Law Privacy Act, which pertains to freedom from misuse or abuse of one's private affairs.
- Privacy Act of 1974, pertaining to the use of information about private citizens.
- Computer Fraud and Abuse Act (CFAA) of 1986, which addresses cybercrime, an issue that has grown in importance in recent years.

The General Accounting Office of the federal government has been working to revise guidelines about records privacy and release of information as the Internet and e-business evolve. The Cyber Privacy Fortification Act of 2015 (H.R. 104) was proposed as an amendment to the CFAA that mandated notification to the U.S. Secret Service or FBI in the event of data breaches of records containing highly sensitive information. As proposed, H.R. 104 reinforces employer responsibility for the privacy of personnel records.

Online privacy is a growing concern, and it affects the security of payroll data. In October 2013, the Internal Revenue Service used the first seven letters of employee last names and truncated Social Security numbers to verify employee information. IRS Publication 1075, published in 2015, delineated specific encryption requirements governing remote access, data transfers, cloud-based services, and mobile devices. (Sources: IRS, *Thomson Reuters*)

The common element among these laws is the protection of sensitive employee information such as addresses, dependents, compensation amounts, and payroll deductions. The payroll accountant is also responsible for discretion in discussing pay rates, bonuses, or other compensation-related topics with employee and management. Sensitive topics should never be discussed with anyone other than the employee or appropriate managers. All employment-related items may be viewed during an audit of payroll records, and auditors must treat the information with absolute confidentiality.

One way that the federal government keeps track of employers is with Employer Identification Numbers (EINs). The EIN allows the IRS to know which companies may have employees, therefore generating employment tax revenue for the government and creating tax liabilities for employers. Form SS-4 (see Figure 1-2) is used to report the personal Social Security number, type of business, and existence of any prior EINs for a business owner. The EIN is required for all tax deposits, tax returns, and informational returns. It will appear on the company's Form W-2s, 940s, 941s, any state tax forms, and the annual tax return for the company. Form SS-4 may be completed either on paper or through an online request portal processed by the IRS that contains the same information as the paper form. (Source: IRS)

Confidential Records

You are the payroll clerk of a company. A group of students approaches you to work on a class project and asks to see confidential personnel and payroll records. What would you do? What are the laws regarding the situation?

LO 1-5 Compare Payroll Processing Options for Different Businesses

Companies have several options for payroll processing. The option a company chooses depends on the size of the business, the complexity of the business in terms of geographic placement and business model, the capital available for payroll processing, and the availability of trained personnel.

During the middle of the 20th century, measuring worker time was managed largely through punch clocks and handwritten time sheets. Contemporary time-collection devices serve as more than simple time clocks. Although the old-fashioned punch clocks still exist, companies have integrated different time collection systems as part of their office security and computer access procedures. Time clocks are used as part of a security system to log when people enter a building for work, which can yield analysis of simple on-site versus working-hour time. Many companies now use biometric devices such as fingerprint readers to collect time for their hourly employees. Systems such as Kronos offer biometric badges and time-collection devices that connect with office telephones.

© D. Hurst/Alamy Images, RF

FIGURE 1-2

Example of Form SS-4

Form **SS-4**	**Application for Employer Identification Number**	OMB No. 1545-0003

Form **SS-4** (Rev. January 2010) Department of the Treasury Internal Revenue Service	**Application for Employer Identification Number** (For use by employers, corporations, partnerships, trusts, estates, churches, government agencies, Indian tribal entities, certain individuals, and others.) See separate instructions for each line. Keep a copy for your records.	OMB No. 1545-0003 EIN 12-5555555

1 Legal name of entity (or individual) for whom the EIN is being requested BD2 Enterprises		

2 Trade name of business (if different from name on line 1) IC Snow Resort	**3** Executor, administrator, trustee, "care of" name	

4a Mailing address (room, apt., suite no. and street, or P.O. box) 1234 Main Street	**5a** Street address (if different) (Do not enter a P.O. box.)
4b City, state, and ZIP code (if foreign, see instructions) Granite, NH 03942	**5b** City, state, and ZIP code (if foreign, see instructions)

6 County and state where principal business is located
 Winchester NH

7a Name of responsible party Kris King	**7b** SSN, ITIN, or EIN 111-22-3333

8a Is this application for a limited liability company (LLC) (or a foreign equivalent)? .... ☐ Yes ☐ No	**8b** If 8a is "Yes," enter the number of LLC members ....

8c If 8a is "Yes," was the LLC organized in the United States?   Yes   No

9a **Type of entity** (check only one box). **Caution.** If 8a is "Yes," see the instructions for the correct box to check.

Sole proprietor (SSN) 111 22 3333	Estate (SSN of decedent) _____
Partnership	Plan administrator (TIN) _____
Corporation (enter form number to be filed) _____	Trust (TIN of grantor) _____
Personal service corporation	National Guard State/local government
Church or church-controlled organization	Farmers' cooperative Federal government/military
Other nonprofit organization (specify) _____	REMIC Indian tribal governments/enterprises
Other (specify)	Group Exemption Number (GEN) if any _____

9b If a corporation, name the state or foreign country (if applicable) where incorporated	State	Foreign country

10 **Reason for applying** (check only one box)

Started new business (specify type) Ski Resort	Banking purpose (specify purpose) _____
	Changed type of organization (specify new type) _____
	Purchased going business
Hired employees (Check the box and see line 13.)	Created a trust (specify type) _____
Compliance with IRS withholding regulations	Created a pension plan (specify type) _____
Other (specify)	

11 Date business started or acquired (month, day, year). See instructions. 09/01/2015	**12** Closing month of accounting year December
13 Highest number of employees expected in the next 12 months (enter -0- if none). If no employees expected, skip line 14.	**14** If you expect your employment tax liability to be $1,000 or less in a full calendar year **and** want to file Form 944 annually instead of Forms 941 quarterly, check here. (Your employment tax liability generally will be $1,000 or less if you expect to pay $4,000 or less in total wages.) If you do not check this box, you must file Form 941 for every quarter.

Agricultural	Household	Other
		25

15 First date wages or annuities were paid (month, day, year). **Note.** If applicant is a withholding agent, enter date income will first be paid to nonresident alien (month, day, year)   09/15/2015

16 Check **one** box that best describes the principal activity of your business.

		Health care & social assistance	Wholesale-agent/broker
Construction Rental & leasing	Transportation & warehousing	Accommodation & food service	Wholesale-other Retail
Real estate Manufacturing	Finance & insurance	Other (specify) Recreation	

17 Indicate principal line of merchandise sold, specific construction work done, products produced, or services provided.
 Downhill and cross-country skiing

18 Has the applicant entity shown on line 1 ever applied for and received an EIN?   Yes   No
 If "Yes," write previous EIN here

Third Party Designee	Complete this section **only** if you want to authorize the named individual to receive the entity's EIN and answer questions about the completion of this form.	
	Designee's name	Designee's telephone number (include area code) ( )
	Address and ZIP code	Designee's fax number (include area code) ( )

Under penalties of perjury, I declare that I have examined this application, and to the best of my knowledge and belief, it is true, correct, and complete.

Name and title (type or print clearly) Kris M. King, Owner	Applicant's telephone number (include area code) (603) 555-4411
	Applicant's fax number (include area code)

Source: Internal Revenue Service.

Using computer access as another type of collection device serves a similar function and can offer the additional functionality of specific task tracking and precise timekeeping. With the growth of mobile connectivity, companies now have a large number of smartphone apps to track employee attendance and productivity. These practices relating to time collection impact and are integrated with payroll.

The basic elements of a payroll system are similar for all companies, but this is a case when size does matter. However, it is not only the size of the company but also the complexity of the laws that affect payroll procedures. Let's look at the differences between large and small company payrolls and then explore certified payroll issues.

Large Businesses

Large companies present intricate problems for payroll accountants. Companies such as Apple, Google, and Microsoft have multiple divisions, many of which exist in different geographical locations. General Electric has different companies that operate as separate entities within GE's framework. Payroll procedures reflect the intricacy of the company's structure and may take many forms.

One of the major challenges in larger organizations is the existence of multiple departments in which an individual employee may work on any given day. Some companies can have shared employees, who will have allocable time to more than one department; for example, one employee may work for both the marketing and the production departments. When this occurs, the payroll accountant will have to record the time worked for each department, and pay rates may differ based on the tasks that the employee performs for each department.

A common payroll procedure with large companies involves employee portals on company websites. On the company's payroll website, employees may enter vacation time, overtime, and other issues that need to be entered into the payroll system. Through the same website, employees may change withholding allowances and voluntary deductions and maintain certain other aspects of their employee files. Such web-based portals contain highly sensitive information, and security of the information is an obvious concern for the companies who use them. Multiple identity checks and security measures are in place to ensure privacy of employee data, such as SSL (secure sockets layer) encryption, *VPN* (virtual private network), and CAPTCHA programs that are designed to differentiate between humans and other computer programs.

> Providing employees with Internet-based access to their personnel files is a challenging issue. Federal laws do not grant employees the right to access their personnel files, and companies must be aware of state laws before providing access. Questions of assigning access to other parties (such as union representatives), access to file artifacts, and the right of the employee to challenge items contained in their file are issues that a firm should address when creating a web portal through which employees may access payroll records. In addition, issues of cybersecurity must be addressed. (Source: SHRM)

To overcome some of the issues with payroll processing, large companies may rely heavily on payroll service vendors to assist with payroll preparation and human resources integration. Providers such as myPay Solutions work with the security needs of the company to offer websites that are secure and integrate multiple personnel functions seamlessly. Some larger firms will work with software engineers to develop independent systems specifically meeting unique company needs.

Large companies face other issues related to accurate timekeeping, such as the volume of employee records. Companies with computerized time-measurement systems may link employees' computer logins, telephone logins, or building access with the payroll system. Companies working with radio frequency time cards and electronic payroll monitoring can properly allocate employee time to specific machines or production lines. With the computer software and services currently available, large companies have many options to maintain the accuracy and integrity of their payroll systems.

© Comstock Images/Jupiter Images, RF

Small Businesses

One apparent difference between large and small businesses is the volume and handling of payroll records. A small number of employees generally leads to fewer payroll-related transactions. Manual payroll systems may be maintained in very small businesses, including the use of handwritten time cards. Outsourcing of payroll activities may not be as prominent. With a small company, the amount of time to complete payroll-related tasks may be less than in a large company. For a small company, the task can be performed without disrupting the revenue-producing tasks of the business.

Small companies have the option of processing payroll in-house with a minimum of difficulty. However, small companies may lack specifically trained payroll personnel, which may place the responsibility for employee pay and benefits on other personnel and may increase the risk of pay or tax inaccuracies. The human resource director, office manager, and payroll professional may frequently be the same person. Using payroll software and a properly designed payroll system, the task of payroll for a small company is generally manageable by minimal company staff. Small companies may choose to explore outsourcing as the company grows. Outsourcing payroll may be a viable option if the task becomes unwieldy or legal obligations become unmanageable.

> Small companies have an option to use hosting services as a way to access low-cost, cloud-based services and the security of on-site accounting software. Hosted payroll accounting software can change in scale without the need for additional software licensing or hardware. (Source: *Accounting Today*)

Depending on the size of the company, number of employees, and complexity of the payroll process, the company may choose to purchase a computer-based accounting system, it may continue to prepare worksheets and manual payroll checks, or it can decide to outsource the payroll preparation and associated tasks. Whichever decisions the company makes as it grows, the importance of understanding the mechanics of the payroll process is paramount. Following is an overview of the various computer-based systems available.

> According to *Accounting Today,* common payroll mistakes made by small firms include:
>
> - Misclassifying employees as independent contractors
> - Omitting the value of gift cards awarded to employees as part of their taxable income
> - Failure to make timely payroll tax deposits
> - Improper treatment of expense reimbursements made to employees
> - Incorrect treatment of taxable fringe benefits

Large vs. Small

Stop & Check

What are some of the payroll processing methods available for large companies?

How does payroll processing differ between large and small companies?

Computer-Based Systems

Various accounting software packages exist to facilitate payroll-related accounting tasks, including QuickBooks, Sage50, and Microsoft Dynamics GP. According to the American

Payroll Association, computerized payroll systems eliminate approximately 80% of payroll processing time and errors. Computerized accounting systems foster the integration of payroll data with other company financial functions, which allows decision makers to develop a comprehensive understanding of the operational needs of the company. Although payroll professionals must verify employee data and update the software at regular intervals, computerized systems reduce the burdens of manual pay calculations, pay disbursement, and report compilation from the payroll accountant. (Source: *Inc.*)

When used properly, small companies may benefit from a computerized payroll system. Although concerns about confidentiality of personnel records exist, electronic access to records may streamline certain tasks like employee information updates and overtime reporting. Additionally, as year-end approaches, companies can deliver the employees' W-2 (see Figure 1-3) tax forms electronically, ensuring employees rapid access to their tax documents.

A trend in payroll processing involves the issuance of electronic paycards, much like preloaded credit cards, as opposed to paper checks. Paycards offer the employees the flexibility of not having to wait for their paycheck to be deposited at a bank. Companies that offer direct deposit as a pay option must offer paycards as an option to employees who do not have bank accounts. However, a paycard can be lost or stolen, and with it, the employee's paycheck, too. Additionally, employers may be charged fees for loading a paycard. When companies consider paycards as an option, it is important to communicate to employees an understanding that there may be costs assessed by the card issuer.

Internet-Based Systems

Internet-based accounting software is an option for a company that does not have the need for or the resources to purchase a computer-based accounting system. Computer-based accounting systems such as QuickBooks, Oracle, and Sage50 offer both desktop and Internet-based services for businesses. In addition, companies such as Zero, Intacct, and Wave have developed Internet-only accounting packages that are accessible for a monthly fee. Advantages of using Internet-based services include the ease of access for accounting personnel and managers and automatic software updates. A potential disadvantage of relying on Internet-based software for a company's accounting is information security issues.

FIGURE 1-3

Form W-2 Wage and Tax Statement

22222 | Void ☐ | a Employee's social security number: 444-44-4444 | For Official Use Only ► OMB No. 1545-0008

b Employer identification number (EIN): 12-1234567	1 Wages, tips, other compensation: 21689.20	2 Federal income tax withheld: 2488.46
c Employer's name, address, and ZIP code: SOME COMPANY NAME, 1111 SOME ADDRESS DRIVE, SOMECITY, OK 00000	3 Social security wages: 22360.00	4 Social security tax withheld: 1386.32
	5 Medicare wages and tips: 22360.00	6 Medicare tax withheld: 324.22
	7 Social security tips	8 Allocated tips
d Control number	9	10 Dependent care benefits
e Employee's first name and initial / Last name / Suff.	11 Nonqualified plans	12a See instructions for box 12
CONNIE BARNES, P.O. BOX 11211, OKLAHOMA CITY, OK 73127	13 Statutory employee ☐ Retirement plan ☒ Third-party sick pay ☐	12b
	14 Other	12c
f Employee's address and ZIP code		12d D 670.80

15 State	Employer's state ID number	16 State wages, tips, etc.	17 State income tax	18 Local wages, tips, etc.	19 Local income tax	20 Locality name
OK	12-1234567	21689.20	936.00			

Form **W-2** Wage and Tax Statement **2016** Department of the Treasury—Internal Revenue Service

Source: Internal Revenue Service.

Accounting Today conducted case studies with firms that had used Internet-based accounting software and highlighted the following:

Positive Aspects	Challenges
Timely identification of financial issues because of the ease of access to company records	Users cannot usually customize certain information layouts to suit specific company needs
Low price for software access and "real time" knowledge of business information	Not suitable for highly complex businesses such as large manufacturing operations
Increased opportunity for collaboration in the business planning and monitoring process	Employee resistance to learning about new software and company accounting process
Continual software updates for changes in tax rates or other related practices	More options available than company personnel knew how to use

(Source: *Accounting Today*)

Manual Systems

With manual payroll systems, the payroll employee relies on deduction percentages that come presented in publications from the Internal Revenue Service. ***Publication 15*** (also known as Circular E) is the manual payroll accountant's best friend, along with periodic updates and supplemental publications. (Source: www.irs.gov)

The largest challenges the manual payroll preparer faces are time constraints and updated tax tables. Companies can determine the length of time between the end of the payroll period and the employee payments with some degree of latitude. However, employees who do not receive accurate and timely pay for their labor are likely to become disenchanted with the organization.

Manual payroll accountants may use spreadsheet programs, such as Excel, in which the accountant can create lookup formulas or other connecting formulas to facilitate the accurate completion of the payroll process. Spreadsheets with formulas or macros should be used only if the accountant understands the formulas and can verify the linkage prior to finalizing payroll to ensure that calculations are correct.

According to the IRS, approximately one-third of all small businesses make payroll errors. The average annual IRS penalty is $845 per small business. (Source: BASIC)

Outsourced Payroll Systems

Outsourced payroll processing has become rather popular as a way to ensure compliance with the changing legal structure and withholding requirements. When a company chooses to use an outsourcing firm for the completion of the payroll processes, there are several considerations: records retention, confidentiality, compliance, timeliness, and thoroughness. Managers should review the cost/benefits of outsourcing a firm's payroll processes prior to making the commitment.

External payroll providers offer flexibility and advanced data analysis that might be challenging for smaller internal departments. During a survey of more than 2,000 accounting professionals, an overwhelming margin stated that they would prefer to outsource payroll functions because of the time involved in the process. External payroll management providers such as ADP and Paychex® assist company owners and managers with strategic planning and related human resources issues. However, outsourcing is not a wise decision for all companies. For a small company, outsourcing may not be cost effective. For large or international

© Barry Gregg/Royalty-Free/CORBIS, RF

companies, outsourcing may be the only option to manage the payroll complexity. (Source: *Accounting Today*)

A recent trend in payroll accounting involves cloud-based computing, meaning that the data is housed on a server external to the firm and accessible via an Internet connection. Companies such as ADP and Volt offer cloud-based payroll and human resource functions for businesses. These services reduce costs by allowing a company to avoid hardware and software costs associated with payroll. However, some issues have arisen with payroll vendor stability and information security. Before turning to a cloud-based service, a company needs to determine its needs to ensure that it makes the appropriate choice. (Source: www.payrolllab.com)

Certified Payroll

Companies who do business with the federal government under the Davis-Bacon Act are required to file a report (see Figure 1-4 for Form WH-347) delineating the payroll paid as part of the government contract with each payroll. *Certified payroll* is a way that the federal government keeps track of the money spent as part of government contracts. Davis-Bacon wages and the state versions of those regulations require special handling and knowledge. Certified payroll facilitates governmental internal accountability and verifies that Davis-Bacon requirements are met.

FIGURE 1-4
Form WH-347 Certified Payroll

U.S. Department of Labor — Wage and Hour Division	PAYROLL (For Contractor's Optional Use; See Instructions at www.dol.gov/whd/forms/wh347instr.htm)	**≡WHD** U.S. Wage and Hour Division

Persons are not required to respond to the collection of information unless it displays a currently valid OMB control number.

Rev. Dec. 2008

NAME OF CONTRACTOR ☐ OR SUBCONTRACTOR ☐	ADDRESS	OMB No.: 1235-0008 Expires: 02/28/2018

PAYROLL NO.	FOR WEEK ENDING	PROJECT AND LOCATION	PROJECT OR CONTRACT NO.

(1) NAME AND INDIVIDUAL IDENTIFYING NUMBER (e.g., LAST FOUR DIGITS OF SOCIAL SECURITY NUMBER) OF WORKER	(2) NO. OF WITHHOLDING EXEMPTIONS	(3) WORK CLASSIFICATION	OT OR ST	(4) DAY AND DATE / HOURS WORKED EACH DAY	(5) TOTAL HOURS	(6) RATE OF PAY	(7) GROSS AMOUNT EARNED	(8) DEDUCTIONS — FICA	WITH-HOLDING TAX		OTHER	TOTAL DEDUCTIONS	(9) NET WAGES PAID FOR WEEK
			o										
			s										
			o										
			s										
			o										

Source: U.S. Department of Labor

What is the Difference?

In a few words, compare the following:

a.   Manual payroll systems

b.   Computerized payroll systems

c.   Outsourced payroll systems

d.   Certified payroll

© Ariel Skelley/Blend Images LLC, RF

LO 1-6   Differentiate Between Exempt and Nonexempt Workers

Company employees may be classified as either exempt or nonexempt workers. The distinction between the two terms is how the wage and hour provisions of FLSA apply to the worker. Exempt workers are not subject to the FLSA wage and hour provisions; wage and hour laws usually apply to nonexempt workers. Many different types of employees are classified as exempt from FLSA provisions, including certain computer profession-als and outside salespersons. Companies will typically classify highly skilled workers such as accountants, general managers, human resource managers, and upper management as exempt, salaried employees. Because job titles alone are not a basis for classification of employees as exempt from FLSA provisions, the U.S. Department of Labor has issued guidelines for the most common types of employees. Note that for workers to be classified as exempt, they must meet *all* elements in the following tests to achieve exempt status.

- Executive Exemption
  - Salary compensation must be no less than $913 per week.
  - Managing the firm must be a primary duty of the employee.
  - The employee must supervise and otherwise direct the work of at least two other full-time employees (or an equivalent).
  - The employee must have the authority to hire and fire other employees.
- Administrative Exemption
  - Salary compensation must be no less than $913 per week.
  - The primary duty must include the performance of office or other nonmanual labor that relates directly to the management of the firm's operations.
  - The employee must exercise independent judgment in the performance of normal duties.
- Professional Exemption
  - Learned Professional
    - Salary compensation must be no less than $913 per week.
    - This employee must perform work that is characterized by advanced learning or that is primarily academic in nature and requires consistent discretion and judgment.
    - The employee's advanced knowledge must be in a field that involves science or learning.
    - The employee must have acquired that knowledge through specialized intellectual education.
  - Creative Professional
    - Salary compensation must be no less than $913 per week.
    - This employee's primary work duty must involve invention, imagination, or originality that requires judgment and discretion. (Source: DOL)

> 2016 marked the first time in several years that the minimum salary for exempt work-ers was addressed legislatively. The previous minimum salary of $455 per week rep-resented an average wage of $11.38 per hour. This weekly amount was raised to place the minimum salary for exempt workers at $47,476 annually. The increase to the weekly minimum salary represented an increase in labor costs; the full effects of this change to employers are unknown as yet. This increase in the salary threshold for exempt employers is designed to be increased every three years. (Source: SHRM)

When workers are employed under a salary basis, they are paid to perform a specific job regardless of the number of hours worked to accomplish that job. A recent Gallup Work and Education poll (see Figure 1-5) reflected that more than half of the salaried workers surveyed

© Photodisc/Getty Images, RF

worked in excess of 40 hours per week; however, it should be noted the law currently provides that if salaried employees show up or are called by their employer for even an hour, the company may be required to pay them for the full eight-hour day.

A primary difference is that nonexempt salaried individuals receive overtime pay for any hours exceeding 8 per day and 40 per week. We will discuss overtime calculations in depth later in the text. The difference between salaried and hourly workers in reference to overtime calculation is that salaried workers will receive their normal shift hours of pay, even when not working the full shift, and do not receive overtime when they work more than 40 hours per week.

Hourly (nonexempt) employees receive a predetermined amount per hour of work performed (or fraction thereof). Hourly employees must receive overtime pay for hours worked in excess of 8 per day and 40 per week. Some employers may make an election that permits four 10-hour shifts; should the election be made, the employee would be subject to overtime rates only after the 10 hours per day and 40 hours have been performed.

Certain individuals who work for a company but are not employees of the company are classified as **independent contractors**. These individuals may work for a firm, but the firm can control only the content and deliverables of the individual's work. The firm does not control the manner in which the work is done or provide the tools that the individual uses to complete the work. An independent contractor is not considered an employee of the firm and is not subject to payroll-related laws; however, it is important to understand what differentiates an independent contractor from an employee to avoid the financial consequences resulting from misclassification. These penalties may include back pay, fines, and legal fees.

FIGURE 1-5
Gallup Work and Education Poll Results

Average Hours Worked by Full-Time U.S. Workers, Aged 18+

Self-reported hours typically worked each week, based on pay structure

	Paid a salary	Paid hourly
	%	%
60+ hours	25	9
50 to 59 hours	25	17
41 to 49 hours	9	12
40 hours	37	56
Less than 40 hours	3	8
Weekly average	49 hours	44 hours

Based on Gallup's 2014 Work and Education poll, conducted Aug. 7–10, 2014

GALLUP

LEGAL ENVIRONMENT

To say that the legal environment of payroll is continually evolving is an understatement. During the early part of the 2010s, we have witnessed the following legal challenges:

- IRS revenue rulings about FICA refunds resulting from employee overpayment of taxes.
- Increasing numbers of states legislating paycard use to protect employee rights and improve access to wages.
- Enhanced enforcement of the Equal Pay Act by the EEOC to protect the rights of women and minorities.
- Repeal of the Defense of Marriage Act, which changed the definition of married couples to include same-sex unions.

Some trends to watch include the following:

- Debate about the proposed Mobile Workforce Income Tax Simplification Act, which creates a 30-day safe harbor for employees who travel across state lines as a normal part of their employment.
- Increasing numbers of private employers and localities raising the minimum wage significantly to close the gap between the minimum wage and the living wage.
- Increasing scrutiny about state-level changes and clarification of the Equal Pay Act.
- Continued legislation and action to increase the federal minimum wage for both exempt and nonexempt employees.

Exempt vs. Nonexempt

1. What is the difference between exempt and nonexempt workers?
2. What is the difference between an employee and an independent contractor?

Summary of Payroll Practices and System Fundamentals

Accounting practices have existed for centuries, and a need continually exists for employers to compensate employees for the work they have performed. Once the United States began taxing personal income, payroll processing became increasingly complex. During the 20th century, payroll practices evolved to include provisions for withholding taxes from employees, remitting payroll taxes to government agencies, maintaining accurate and confidential records, and incorporating civil rights–related legislation. Payroll accounting is a field that, due to its changing nature, requires precision and attention to minute details. Additionally, because of the nature of their work, payroll accountants must adhere to ethical guidelines including due care, objectivity, independence, integrity, and the public interest.

The establishment of a payroll system involves careful, deliberate planning. The framework used for the payroll system must have ample room for company growth, structure to ensure system stability, and trained payroll personnel to ensure that company and government deadlines are met. Using the best practices outlined in this chapter may help a company implement a robust payroll system, whether the system is maintained by company personnel, outsourced, completed manually, or accomplished through the use of specifically designed software. Robust payroll system design may reduce or prevent problems with employees and governmental entities.

Key Points

- Legislation that has affected employees' working conditions has mandated many aspects of the workplace, including civil rights, retirement and health benefits, and reinvestment in American workers.
- Payroll-specific legislation has influenced working hours and employee wages.
- Employer and employee taxes have been enacted, and the remittance of tax obligations has been mandated.
- Payroll accountants must adhere to ethical guidelines because of the nature of the work performed.
- Payroll practices have evolved to include the electronic transmission of employee pay and tax obligations.
- Security of employee information is an ongoing concern for companies, especially with electronic transmission of sensitive data.
- Payroll may be processed at a central corporate site or through an outsourced payroll processing company.
- Many companies use payroll accounting software such as QuickBooks and Sage 50, and cloud computing has become a new option for businesses.
- Employees are classified as either exempt or nonexempt from the FLSA provisions, based on the scope of their work and the job classification.

Vocabulary

ACA	ERISA	OSHA
ADA	Ethics	Privacy Act of 1974
ARRA	FICA	PRWOR
ATRA	FLSA	Public interest
Certified payroll	FMLA	SOX
COBRA	FUTA	SUTA
Copeland Anti-Kickback Act	HIPAA	USERRA
Current Tax Payment Act	Independent contractor	VPN
Davis-Bacon Act	Integrity	Walsh-Healey Public
DOMA	IRCA	Contracts Act
Due care	Medicare tax	Worker's compensation
EEOC	Objectivity	

Review Questions

1. What is the purpose of a payroll system?

2. What are some differences between large- and small-company payroll practices?

3. What is certified payroll? Which companies must use it?

4. Why might it be a good idea to let employees manage their pay records? What are some of the pitfalls?

5. What are some ways that a payroll system may protect a company in the event of a visit from a government auditor?

6. What is payroll outsourcing? When might a company consider outsourcing its payroll?

7. Give three examples of federal laws that are essential to ensure legal, fair hiring practices.

8. What are the major types of payroll processing methods?

9. What are two laws governing the taxes that employers must withhold from employees?

10. What are two of the main provisions of FLSA?

11. Why was the Social Security Act of 1935 important? What did it provide?

12. What are the advantages of a computerized payroll system over a manual system?

13. Which Act created the term "Full-Time Equivalents"? What are these employee types used for?

Exercises Set A

E1-1A.

LO 1-6

Anya is a candidate for the position of sales manager with the footwear department of a major retail outlet. She is going to be required to supervise several employees and can determine the direction in which she will complete the assignments given to her. Which law appears to be the most applicable in regards to classifying her as an exempt or nonexempt employee?

1. OSHA
2. Equal Pay Act
3. FLSA
4. ERISA

E1-2A.

LO 1-6

John is the office manager for a small mortgage brokerage. Because it is a small office, he is required to keep track of all employee records and pay both employees and contractors. Which of the following are legal factors that will differentiate between exempt and nonexempt employees? (Select all that apply.)

1. Number of hours worked
2. Type of work performed
3. Location where the work is performed
4. Amount of supervisor-given direction

E1-3A.

LO 1-1, 1-2

Consolidated Construction obtained a job working for a nearby international airport, a project contracted with the federal government for $500,000, welding the support structures for the new extension of the terminal. What laws govern the wages Consolidated Construction pays to its welders for this project? (Select all that may apply.)

1. Davis-Bacon Act
2. Sarbanes–Oxley Act
3. Walsh-Healey Act
4. FLSA

E1-4A.

LO 1-1, 1-2

Roxie works as the payroll clerk for an agricultural firm that hires many temporary and immigrant workers on an hourly basis. What law governs the hiring or documenting of these workers?

1. ADEA
2. FLSA
3. IRCA
4. USERRA

E1-5A.

LO 1-1, 1-2

Kim-Ly is a member of the hiring board for her company. As the board reviews candidates for a position, one of the other board members wants to exclude Eric, a man in his 50s, because his age might pose an insurance risk for the company. What law protects Eric against this practice?

1. FLSA
2. ADEA
3. ADA
4. Civil Rights Act of 1991

E1-6A.
LO 1-1, 1-2

Ovenet Inc. is a company that provides health insurance to its employees. The company is self-insured. Which of the following forms should the company provide its employees to comply with the Affordable Care Act?
1. 1095-A
2. 1095-B
3. 1095-C

E1-7A.
LO 1-3

Ashlee is the new payroll accountant for a company. While she was exercising at the gym, she encountered Madison, the president of the company. Madison explained that he was under pressure to report certain levels of profit and asked her to meet with him about payroll expenses. What ethical guidelines should Ashlee consider before agreeing to meet (Select all that apply)?
1. Due Care
2. Objectivity and Independence
3. Public Interest
4. Integrity

E1-8A.
LO 1-4, LO 1-5

Kevin owns a new golf pro shop. As a small business owner, he has several options for payroll processing. What factors should he consider when deciding on payroll processing? (Select all that apply.)
1. The number and types of employees of the business
2. The physical size of the office facility
3. The amount of money he has to spend on payroll processing
4. The computer technology used by the business

Match the following terms with their definitions:

E1-9A.	Manual payroll	a.	A preloaded credit card used to pay employees
E1-10A.	Time card	b.	The process of gathering information about hours worked for one or more employees
E1-11A.	Paycard	c.	A web-based application wherein employees can modify certain payroll-related information
E1-12A.	Employee Internet portal	d.	Governs accounting for firms with federal government contracts in excess of $2,000
E1-13A.	Certified payroll	e.	A record of the time worked during a period for an individual employee
E1-14A.	Outsourced payroll	f.	Examples of companies used for outsourcing payroll processing
E1-15A.	Auditor	g.	A way for governmental agencies to track the payroll associated with a government contract
E1-16A.	ADP and Paychex®	h.	Payroll administration using a paper payroll register
E1-17A.	Time collection	i.	The use of an external company to track time and benefits and pay employees
E1-18A.	Davis-Bacon Act	j.	A person or group who examines a company's accounting records for accuracy

Problems Set A

P1-1A.
LO 1-2, 1-6

Kristina is the accounting manager for a small, local firm that has full- and part-time staff. What must Kristina consider when classifying employees as exempt or nonexempt?

P1-2A.
LO 1-4, 1-5

Jeff is an accountant for his firm, a medium-sized company with 125 employees. The firm has traditionally maintained the administration of its payroll. His co-worker, the only other accountant in the firm, retires.

Because of budget concerns, the firm chooses not to refill the position. What options does Jeff have regarding administration of the payroll?

P1-3A.
LO 1-1, 1-2

Juan is the office manager and payroll clerk for his company, which is composed of 12 employees. An employee, Joe, stops by Juan's office and wants to view his payroll record. What privacy regulations must Juan consider before granting his co-worker access?

P1-4A.
LO 1-3

A group of employees, who read on a website that income tax collection is illegal, approach Tarik, the controller for a large company. They request that he stop withholding income taxes from their pay unless he can explain what laws govern income tax collection. What should Tarik tell them?

P1-5A.
LO 1-1, 1-2

Sheri is a warehouse worker for a small grocery market. As she was moving some merchandise, the loading dock door unexpectedly fell and injured her. How does OSHA apply to Sheri for this type of injury?

P1-6A.
LO 1-4

Ben is a new payroll accountant at his company. In his review of previous manual payroll records, he noted several errors that required the issuance of additional checks to employees for unpaid payroll amounts. What are his options to avoid similar problems in the future?

P1-7A.
LO 1-3

Charli and Sarah are friends who work for the same company. Charli manages a manufacturing department and Sarah supervises the payroll clerks. Which ethical guidelines or rules would these friends need to remember when discussing work?

P1-8A.
LO 1-1, 1-2

At Denniston Industries, employees have the option of choosing employer-sponsored health insurance at no additional cost or receiving additional pay so that they may purchase medical insurance elsewhere. What responsibilities does the employer have according to COBRA upon termination of an employee who opts to receive the additional pay to purchase medical insurance?

P1-9A.
LO 1-6

RaeLeene is a new manager at Resterra Inc. She is reviewing the FLSA classification of each employee, and approaches you for clarification about differences between exempt and nonexempt employees. What are three differences between exempt and nonexempt employees?

P1-10A.
LO 1-4

Mahala is a new employee in the payroll department for Winhook Industries. She has had several employees approach her with questions but is unsure how privacy regulations could affect her response. What advice would you give her about privacy laws and payroll?

Exercises Set B

E1-1B.
LO 1-6

Hunter is a candidate for the position of marketing clerk with the promotions department of a film production company, earning $10.25 per hour. He will work occasional overtime in his new position and will not have managerial or supervisory duties as a regular part of his job description. Why should Hunter be classified as a nonexempt employee? (Select all that apply.)
1. His annual wages are lower than the minimum exempt salary.
2. He has no supervisory or managerial duties.
3. He has the term "clerk" in his job title.
4. He will work occasional overtime.

E1-2B.
LO 1-1, 1-2

Bernie manages a ski resort that has year-round and seasonal employees. Assuming that the ski resort engages in interstate commerce, which are FLSA requirement(s) that Bernie should consider?
1. Hourly wages paid to employees
2. Safety of the working conditions

3. Number of hours worked per week
4. Employee age and weekly work schedule

E1-3B.

LO 1-1, 1-2

Carl is a military veteran who requires many absences for medical reasons. His boss has demanded that he reduce the number of sick days unless he provides his medical history. Which law(s) protect Carl? (Select all that apply.)
1. ADA
2. FLSA
3. USERRA
4. HIPAA

E1-4B.

LO 1-1, 1-2

Valerie is a production worker at a large automobile manufacturing plant. After working there for 10 years, she discovers through conversations with a colleague with the same title and similar seniority that her wage is 20% lower than his wage. She feels that she has been a victim of discrimination. Which law(s) govern her situation?
1. FLSA
2. Civil Rights Act of 1964
3. ADEA
4. Equal Pay Act

E1-5B.

LO 1-4, 1-5

Skylar is the new bookkeeper for a small company and was hired to replace a long-time employee who retired. Upon starting the position, Skylar notices that the prior bookkeeper used a purely manual system. The company owner has said that Skylar may update the payroll system. What options are available?

E1-6B.

LO 1-6

Jeffrey is the accounting manager for a company that provides computer-consulting services. The computer-consulting company has a staff that includes five full-time employees and eight on-call workers who independently determine the number of hours and their work location. The on-call consultants claim that they should be classified as employees. What criteria should Jeffrey use to determine the workers' employment status? (Select all that apply.)
1. The extent to which the on-call workers control their hours and working locations
2. The number of hours worked by the on-call workers
3. The number and types of job-specific tools that the employer provides
4. How the workers are compensated for their work, by the job or by hours

E1-7B.

LO 1-3

Paola is the payroll accountant for an import-export firm. Her most recent experience with accounting educational courses was when she was in college, which was eight years ago. What body recommends the ethical guidelines of public interest, integrity, objectivity and independence, and due care?
1. IRS
2. AICPA
3. EEOC
4. USERRA

E1-8B.

LO 1-5

Harris is the payroll accountant for a company that engages in work on federal contracts. He wants to ensure that the company is compliant with the provisions of the Davis-Bacon Act. What is the name for the process used to monitor payroll compliance in this situation?
1. Contracted Payroll
2. Davis-Bacon Verification
3. Certified Payroll
4. Outsourced Payroll

Match the following items with their definitions:

E1-9B.	USERRA	a.	A provision of the Sarbanes–Oxley Act
E1-10B.	*U.S. v. Windsor*	b.	Instituted a tiered income tax on workers
E1-11B.	Mandatory auditor rotation	c.	Prohibited employment of individuals younger than 16 years of age
E1-12B.	HIPAA	d.	Strengthened the child support provisions of PRWOR
E1-13B.	Lilly Ledbetter Fair Pay Act	e.	Legislation that governs the treatment of military service personnel
E1-14B.	Sixteenth Amendment	f.	A worker who is not subject to a company's direction or its payroll laws
E1-15B.	Walsh-Healey Public Contracts Act	g.	Repealed the 180-day statute of limitations on equal pay complaints
E1-16B.	Independent contractor	h.	Mandates completion of form I-9
E1-17B.	Personal Responsibility, Work and Family Promotion Act of 2002	i.	The case responsible for the U.S. Supreme Court's repeal of DOMA
E1-18B.	IRCA	j.	Protects the confidentiality of employee medical records

Problems Set B

P1-1B.
LO 1-4, 1-5
Roxie is the payroll administrator for a small company. Because of economic conditions, her boss has assigned her the additional duties of office management, and Roxie is considering outsourcing her payroll duties. What are the pros and cons of outsourcing the company's payroll?

P1-2B.
LO 1-1, 1-2
Jim is the payroll clerk for a company in a state where same-sex marriage recently became legal. One of the company's employees informs Jim that he has been in a same-sex marriage since January 2011. What actions does Jim need to take regarding prior-year taxes?

P1-3B.
LO 1-3
Rosita is STB Incorporated's payroll accountant. During a casual conversation with coworkers, she learns that another co-worker is deliberately overstating the number of hours worked during each pay period because of a personal economic situation. Which ethical guidelines pertain to this situation? What should Rosita do with this knowledge?

P1-4B.
LO 1-6
Michaela is a payroll accountant for Top Table Industries. She is asked to explain the differences between exempt and nonexempt employees. What job elements should she highlight as the difference between exempt and nonexempt employees?

P1-5B.
LO 1-1, 1-2, 1-3,
During a review of payroll records, LaTieya notices that a female employee in Department A is receiving a significantly lower salary than similarly skilled male employees in the same department. What actions should LaTieya take in this situation?

P1-6B.
LO 1-3
Nic is an accountant for a large, multinational firm. During payroll processing, he notices that the new state payroll tax updates have not been installed in the firm's software. What ethical guidelines govern his behavior in this situation?

P1-7B.
LO 1-2
Hector is an employee of a contractor that provides governmental construction services in Washington, D.C. The current contract is for $250,000. Hector is 22 and is paid $9.50 per hour. How does the Walsh-Healey Public Contracts Act affect Hector?

P1-8B.
LO 1-4
Sean works as a payroll clerk at Drink Pocket Inc. He shares an office with three other co-workers and must examine documents containing personal information as a regular part of his duties. Based on the provisions of the Privacy Act of 1974, what responsibilities does Sean have regarding the payroll records he handles?

P1-9B.
LO 1-5
Jaelle is a senior payroll administrator for Jericho Home Design. The company has 15 employees and annual revenues of $50 million. She has been using and maintaining manual payroll records for the last 20 years of her career, and the president of Jericho Home Design wants to explore options for computerized payroll processing. Which payroll option is the most suitable for both Jaelle and Jericho Home Design? Why?

P1-10B.
LO 1-2
You are the payroll accountant for your company and have been asked for information about employees and independent contractors. What are three key differences between employees and independent contractors?

Critical Thinking

CT1-1. You have been hired as a consultant for a company facing an IRS audit of its accounting records. During your review, you notice anomalies in the payroll system involving overpayments of labor and payments to terminated employees. What should you do?

CT1-2. Lee Chen is the accountant for a local nonprofit organization. He has been tasked with managing the costs of the payroll so that staffing levels may remain the same even if funding levels change. He considers outsourcing the payroll to a payroll processing company. What are some factors that Lee should consider in his decision? Why are these factors important?

In the Real World: Scenario for Discussion

The Brinker Restaurant Group, owners of restaurant franchises such as Chili's Grill &Bar and Maggiano's Little Italy, was sued by its employees for not providing adequate meal and rest breaks for employees. According to the California Labor Code §512 and Wage Order no. 5, employees must be provided with rest periods—specifically, a 30-minute meal break—every five hours that they work. After 10 hours of consecutive work, the employee must be given a second meal break. The California Supreme Court ruled that the rest breaks had to be offered, but the employer did not have to ensure that the employee actually rested.

Food for thought:
1. Should employers ensure that employees on breaks not perform any work? Why or why not?

2. What laws pertain to employee rest breaks? How would they apply in this situation?

3. How might an employer ensure that employees actually rest during a break?

Internet Activities

1-1. Using the website www.jstor.org, search for articles about payroll-related laws or relevant employment legislation. Once you find an article, summarize the article, and explain how the legislation influenced contemporary payroll practices.

1-2. Visit the website of the American Payroll Association at www.americanpayroll.org. On the right side of the Home page, you will find articles about recent developments in payroll practices and legislation. Choose an article and create a presentation to your class about how its content affects payroll practice.

1-3. Want to know more about the specifics of some of the concepts in this chapter? Check out these websites:

www.dol.gov/whd/

www.taxhistory.com/1943.html

www.workerscompensationinsurance.com

www.Kronos.com

www.adp.com

www.paychex.com

www.businessmanagementdaily.com/19717/organizing-personnel-files-4-faqs

© API/Alamy, RF

Continuing Payroll Project: Prevosti Farms and Sugarhouse

Toni Prevosti is opening a new business, Prevosti Farms and Sugarhouse, which is a small company that will harvest, refine, and sell maple syrup products. In subsequent chapters, students will have the opportunity to establish payroll records and complete payroll information for Prevosti Farms and Sugarhouse.

Toni has decided that she needs to hire employees for the business to grow. Complete the application for Prevosti Farms and Sugarhouse's Employer Identification Number (Form SS-4) with the following information:

Prevosti Farms and Sugarhouse is located at 820 Westminster Road, Bridgewater, Vermont, 05520 (which is also Ms. Prevosti's home address), phone number 802-555-3456. Bridgewater is in Windsor County. Toni has decided that Prevosti Farms and Sugarhouse, the responsible party for a sole proprietorship, will pay its employees on a biweekly basis. Toni's Social Security number is 055-22-0443. The beginning date of the business is February 1, 2016. Prevosti Farms and Sugarhouse will use a calendar year as its accounting year. Toni anticipates that she will need to hire six employees initially for the business, three of whom will be agricultural and three who will be office workers. The first date of wage disbursement will be February 15, 2016. Toni has not had a prior EIN.

Answers to Stop & Check Exercises

Which Law?
1. E
2. H
3. B
4. F
5. I
6. J
7. A
8. D
9. G
10. C

Which Payroll Law?
1. D
2. A
3. F
4. C
5. G
6. E
7. B

Form **SS-4** (Rev. January 2010) Department of the Treasury Internal Revenue Service	**Application for Employer Identification Number** (For use by employers, corporations, partnerships, trusts, estates, churches, government agencies, Indian tribal entities, certain individuals, and others.) ▶ See separate instructions for each line. ▶ Keep a copy for your records.	OMB No. 1545-0003 EIN

Type or print clearly.

1	Legal name of entity (or individual) for whom the EIN is being requested

2	Trade name of business (if different from name on line 1)	3	Executor, administrator, trustee, "care of" name

4a	Mailing address (room, apt., suite no. and street, or P.O. box)	5a	Street address (if different) (Do not enter a P.O. box.)
4b	City, state, and ZIP code (if foreign, see instructions)	5b	City, state, and ZIP code (if foreign, see instructions)

6	County and state where principal business is located

7a	Name of responsible party	7b	SSN, ITIN, or EIN

8a	Is this application for a limited liability company (LLC) (or a foreign equivalent)? . . . . ☐ **Yes** ☐ **No**	8b	If 8a is "Yes," enter the number of LLC members . . . . . ▶

8c	If 8a is "Yes," was the LLC organized in the United States? . . . . ☐ **Yes** ☐ **No**

9a   **Type of entity** (check only one box). **Caution.** If 8a is "Yes," see the instructions for the correct box to check.

☐ Sole proprietor (SSN) _____ | ☐ Estate (SSN of decedent) _____
☐ Partnership | ☐ Plan administrator (TIN) _____
☐ Corporation (enter form number to be filed) ▶ _____ | ☐ Trust (TIN of grantor) _____
☐ Personal service corporation | ☐ National Guard   ☐ State/local government
☐ Church or church-controlled organization | ☐ Farmers' cooperative   ☐ Federal government/military
☐ Other nonprofit organization (specify) ▶ _____ | ☐ REMIC   ☐ Indian tribal governments/enterprises
☐ Other (specify) ▶ | Group Exemption Number (GEN) if any ▶

9b	If a corporation, name the state or foreign country (if applicable) where incorporated	State	Foreign country

10   **Reason for applying** (check only one box)

☐ Started new business (specify type) ▶ _____ | ☐ Banking purpose (specify purpose) ▶ _____
 | ☐ Changed type of organization (specify new type) ▶ _____
☐ Hired employees (Check the box and see line 13.) | ☐ Purchased going business
☐ Compliance with IRS withholding regulations | ☐ Created a trust (specify type) ▶ _____
☐ Other (specify) ▶ | ☐ Created a pension plan (specify type) ▶ _____

11	Date business started or acquired (month, day, year). See instructions.	12	Closing month of accounting year
13	Highest number of employees expected in the next 12 months (enter -0- if none). If no employees expected, skip line 14.	14	If you expect your employment tax liability to be $1,000 or less in a full calendar year **and** want to file Form 944 annually instead of Forms 941 quarterly, check here. (Your employment tax liability generally will be $1,000 or less if you expect to pay $4,000 or less in total wages.) If you do not check this box, you must file Form 941 for every quarter. ☐

Agricultural	Household	Other

15	First date wages or annuities were paid (month, day, year). **Note.** If applicant is a withholding agent, enter date income will first be paid to nonresident alien (month, day, year) . . . . ▶

16   Check **one** box that best describes the principal activity of your business.

☐ Construction ☐ Rental & leasing ☐ Transportation & warehousing ☐ Health care & social assistance ☐ Wholesale-agent/broker
☐ Real estate ☐ Manufacturing ☐ Finance & insurance ☐ Accommodation & food service ☐ Wholesale-other ☐ Retail
 ☐ Other (specify)

17	Indicate principal line of merchandise sold, specific construction work done, products produced, or services provided.

18	Has the applicant entity shown on line 1 ever applied for and received an EIN? ☐ **Yes** ☐ **No** If "Yes," write previous EIN here ▶

Third Party Designee	Complete this section **only** if you want to authorize the named individual to receive the entity's EIN and answer questions about the completion of this form.	
	Designee's name	Designee's telephone number (include area code) ( )
	Address and ZIP code	Designee's fax number (include area code) ( )

Under penalties of perjury, I declare that I have examined this application, and to the best of my knowledge and belief, it is true, correct, and complete.

Name and title (type or print clearly) ▶	Applicant's telephone number (include area code) ( )
Signature ▶ Date ▶	Applicant's fax number (include area code) ( )

For Privacy Act and Paperwork Reduction Act Notice, see separate instructions.   Cat. No. 16055N   Form **SS-4** (Rev. 1-2010)

Source: Internal Revenue Service.

What's Ethical?

1. Answers will vary. Some concerns include data privacy and integrity in the software switchover, tax and employee pay integrity on the new software, and employee pay methods.

2. Answers will vary. Liza could choose to ignore her sorority sister's request, claiming professional responsibility. She could also discontinue active participation in the sorority. In any case, Liza must not consent to her sorority sister's request for confidential information.

Confidential Records

As a payroll clerk, your task is to protect the privacy and confidentiality of the information you maintain for the company. If a student group—or any personnel aside from the company's payroll employees and officers—wishes to review confidential records, you should deny their request. If needed, you should refer the group to your department's manager to discuss the matter in more depth. The laws that apply to this situation are the Privacy Act of 1974, the Freedom of Information Act, and potentially HIPAA.

Large vs. Small

Large companies have computer-based accounting packages such as QuickBooks, Sage 50, and Microsoft Dynamics GP available. Additionally, they may consider outsourcing their payroll functions to companies such as ADP and Paychex®, which provide companies with comprehensive payroll services and tax reporting.

For small companies, the cost of outsourcing the payroll function needs to be considered. On one hand, a small company may not have personnel who are proficient with payroll regulations and tax reporting requirements, which leaves a company vulnerable to legal actions and stringent fines. However, engaging a payroll service company may be cost prohibitive. The decision to outsource the payroll for a small company should take into account the number of personnel, locations, and types of operations in which the company engages.

What Is the Difference?

a. Manual payroll systems involve the use of paper and pencil recordkeeping or a spreadsheet program, such as Microsoft Excel. This is most appropriate for very small firms.

b. Computerized payroll systems can be used by any company, regardless of size. Examples of computerized systems include QuickBooks, Sage 50, and Microsoft Dynamics GP. These computer packages range in price, depending on the company size and operational scope.

c. Outsourced payroll involves the engagement of a third party to manage a company's payroll data, issue employee compensation, and prepare tax forms.

d. Certified payroll pertains to companies with employees who work on federal government contracts. Certified payroll ensures that a company reports payroll expenditures of contractually allocated money.

Exempt vs. Nonexempt

1. Exempt workers are exempt from the overtime provisions of FLSA. Exempt workers tend to be employees in a company's managerial or other leadership functions, in which they may need to work more than 40 hours per week to complete their tasks. Exempt workers usually receive a fixed salary per period that is not based on the number of hours worked. Nonexempt workers tend to be compensated on an hourly basis and often do not have managerial or leadership responsibilities. It should be

noted that some nonexempt workers do have managerial or leadership responsibilities and may receive a fixed salary; however, these particular employees are covered by the overtime provisions of FLSA.

2. An employee is defined as a person who works solely for one company. Most or all work-related materials are provided by the company. Employee payroll taxes are paid by the company, and the employee may be eligible for fringe benefits. In contrast, an independent contractor may have more than one company as a client. Independent contractors provide their own tools and materials, pay their own income taxes, and generally establish their working hours. An employee of a company is considered to be part of the payroll expense, whereas an independent contractor is a vendor of the company who submits invoices for payment.

Chapter Two

Payroll System Procedures

Payroll procedures have a dual focus: (1) governmental rules and (2) the company's needs. The company must abide by the applicable governmental and industrial regulations or face potential fines, sanctions, or closure. To comply with regulations, a company must make several decisions: pay frequency, pay types (e.g., direct deposit, paycards, or paper checks), employee benefits, and handling of pay advances. The payroll accountant must prepare for the integration of new hires, transfer of employees among departments, and terminations that occur during the normal course of business. Employee benefits and government-required payroll deductions complicate the pay process.

Accountants handle documents that have varying levels of confidentiality. Some items include receipts for expenses, invoices from vendors, and other business-related documents that are not confidential. The employees' documents that payroll accountants handle are usually private and often contain highly sensitive personal information. Different regulations regarding the length of retention and storage procedures apply to payroll documents. An important note about financial or personnel documentation is this: Any documents connected with fraudulent activity have no time limit for retention purposes. In the event of suspected fraud, investigators may request relevant fraud-related documents at any time.

LEARNING OBJECTIVES

After studying Chapter 2, you should be able to:

LO 2-1   Identify Important Payroll Procedures and Pay Cycles

LO 2-2   Prepare Required Employee Documentation

LO 2-3   Explain Pay Records and Employee File Maintenance

LO 2-4   Describe Internal Controls and Record Retention for a Payroll System

LO 2-5   Discuss Employee Termination and Document Destruction Procedures

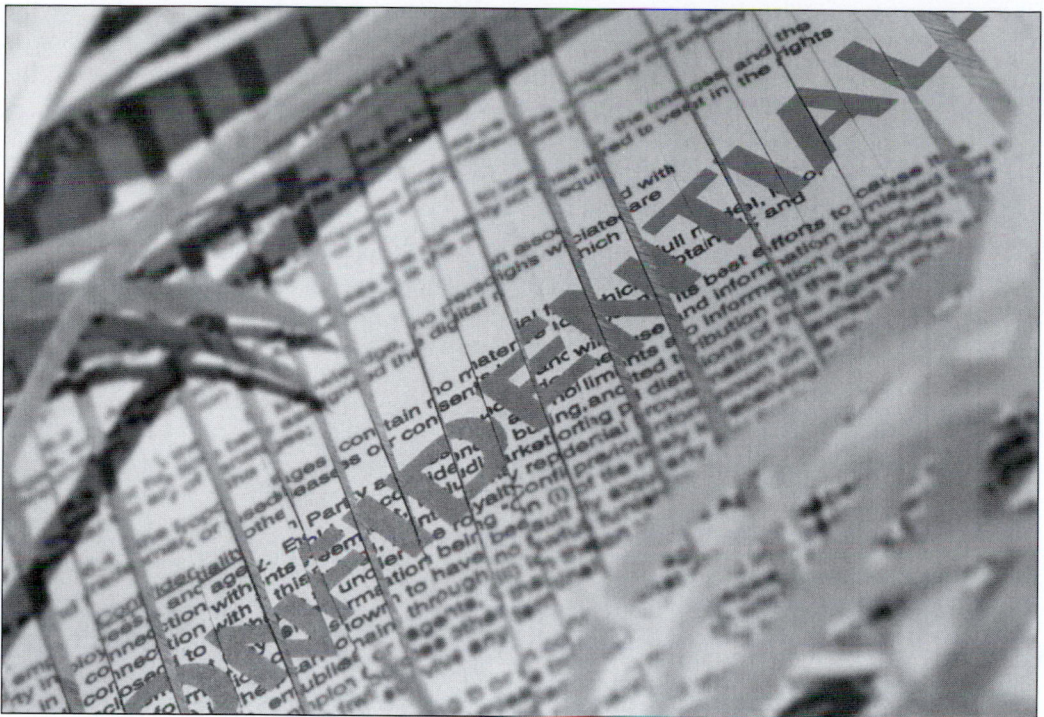

© Steve Cole/Getty Images, RF

Document Destruction and Arthur Andersen's Downfall

In the late 1990s, Enron was one of the biggest names in the energy business. The company leveraged contracts and used "mark-to-market" accounting to adjust energy contracts to fair market values and reported a pretax profit of $1.41 billion in 2000. However, irregularities in the firm's accounting practices led to a congressional investigation into financial documents. During its probe, Congress found that Enron's auditing firm, Arthur Andersen, had destroyed many documents that would have contained information relevant to the investigation. Missing data included revenue transfers and payroll records. Although the U.S. Supreme Court ultimately overturned Arthur Andersen's conviction for obstruction of justice during the Enron investigation, the American Bar Association has delineated guidelines for document retention, including relevance, industry, compliance standards, and litigation needs. Congressional legislation regarding documentation is contained in 18 U.S.C. §1512(c) and 18 U.S.C. §1519. (Sources: American Bar Association, *Journal of Accountancy,* Greenberg Traurig LLP)

Personnel and payroll files are closely related. In Chapter 2, we will explore payroll system procedures, including information about file security, legally required documents, and internal controls.

LO 2-1   Identify Important Payroll Procedures and Pay Cycles

© Sam Edwards/age fotostock, RF

The documentation required for paying employees starts before the first employee is hired. The EIN, obtained online from the IRS, is the first step in employer documentation, closely followed by the employee information files. Under FLSA, certain information is required in every employee file. According to the U.S. Department of Labor, the list of required information to be maintained in the employee file includes:

1. Employee's full name as used for Social Security purposes, and the employee's identifying symbol or number, if such is used in place of the employee's name on any time, work, or payroll records.
2. Address, including zip code.
3. Birth date, if younger than 19.
4. Sex and occupation.
5. Time and day of week when employee's workweek begins.
6. Hours worked each day and total hours worked each workweek.
7. Basis on which employee's wages are paid.
8. Regular hourly pay rate.
9. Total daily or weekly straight-time earnings.
10. Total overtime earnings for the workweek.
11. All additions to or deductions from the employee's wages.
12. Total wages paid each **pay period**.
13. Date of payment and the pay period covered by the payment.

Payroll documentation regulations protect employees by ensuring that they receive accurate paychecks. These regulations also keep employers in compliance with tax regulations and provide an audit trail for government bodies. **New hire reporting** requirements ensure that employees pay legal obligations such as child support and garnishments. Figure 2-1 shows an Employee Information Form, which contains elements of the information from the employee file. Note that the employee file is maintained by the firm's human resources department, and the employee information form shown in Figure 2-1 is maintained by the payroll department, so some FLSA elements may not appear on the form.

FIGURE 2-1
Sample Employee Information Form

EMPLOYEE EARNINGS RECORD

NAME   **Jonathan A. Doe**   Hire Date   **1/1/2015**

ADDRESS   **100 Main Street**   Date of Birth   **4/16/1983**

CITY/STATE/ZIP
Anytown, MD 21220   Position   **Sales**   PT/(FT)

TELEPHONE   **202-555-4009**   No. of exemptions   **4**   (M)/S

SOCIAL SECURITY

NUMBER   **987-65-4321**   Pay Rate   **$15.00**   (Hr)/Wk/Mo

Period Ended	Hrs. Worked	Reg Pay	OT Pay	Gross Pay	Social Sec. Tax	Medicare	Fed Inc. Tax	State Inc. Tax	401(k)	Taxable income	Total Deduc	Net pay	YTD
1/7/15	40	600.00	0.00	600.00	37.20	8.70	14.00	12.00	25.00		96.90	503.10	600.00

The EEOC's protection of employee rights, especially when it leads to a lawsuit, involves the firm's personnel documentation. Accurate and correctly maintained payroll records are especially important because they reflect the firm's treatment of its employees.

When a company develops or reviews its payroll system, the payroll accountant faces a multifaceted task. The employer must answer several questions:

- How will the company handle new hires?
- What will the procedure be when an employee transfers from one department to another?
- What is the procedure to follow upon employee termination?
- What processes should the company establish to ensure government compliance?
- How will employee time and attendance be tracked?

Pay Cycles

Let's start with a basic question: How often should the company pay its employees? Regardless of which accounting system the company is using, the determination of pay cycle, or pay periods, is the first thing a new company needs to establish. Some options for payroll cycles include the following:

Daily payroll is typically paid at the end of the day or by the end of the next business day. This method of payroll processing is typical in day labor situations; however, it should be noted that day labor could be treated as independent contractor work and thus not be subject to payroll, payroll taxes, or a W-2. Daily payroll could potentially have 365 or 366 pay periods.

Weekly payroll is typically used in a Monday through Friday workweek. The employees receive their paychecks the following Friday. Several types of companies use a weekly payroll system, including grocery stores, construction, and professional offices. This pay frequency may lead to 52 pay periods per year.

Biweekly payroll is typically processed based on a two-week period, and employees receive their paychecks approximately a week after the end of the pay period. Pay dates may be any weekday. This pay frequency generally has 26 pay periods per year. On rare occasions there may be 27 pay periods in a biweekly payroll; however, this is rare, and typical calculations will use 26.

Semimonthly payroll is paid twice a month. Examples of semimonthly payroll pay dates include (1) the 1st and 15th of the month and (2) the 15th and last day of the month. This is not the same as biweekly payroll, and taxation and hours paid are different. Employees receive 24 pay disbursements per year when using a semimonthly payroll system.

Monthly payroll is less frequently used than other methods. Some companies process payroll once per month and may allow a semimonthly draw to the employees. When employees

Stop & Check

What's in the File?

1. Which of the following artifacts must be included in the employee file?

   a. Full name and address.
   b. Occupation.
   c. Mother's maiden name.
   d. Pay rate.
   e. Date of payment.
   f. Spouse's name.

Match the pay frequencies:

2. Monthly
3. Semimonthly
4. Biweekly
5. Weekly

Number of pay periods:

a. 26
b. 12
c. 52
d. 24

are allowed to draw their wages at mid-month, the employer may or may not take payroll taxes out of the draw. If the mid-month draw does not have payroll taxes withheld, the month-end payroll will need to recover all taxes and withholdings for the month from the employee.

LO 2-2 Prepare Required Employee Documentation

Employees versus Independent Contractors

People who work for a company may be classified as either employees or independent contractors depending on the nature of the work and the withholding of payroll-related taxes from the worker's compensation. According to the IRS, millions of workers have been misclassified, which has led to employers not depositing the full amount of taxes due and employees missing out on benefits. IRS form SS-8 (available at www.irs.gov) is a way that employers may receive official guidance about worker classification.

© Monty Rakusen/cultura/Corbis, RF

Employees

The determination of a worker as an employee has two primary criteria according to labor laws. The first is *work direction,* which means that the employer substantially directs the worker's performance. The employer provides the primary tools that an employee uses; for example, the employee may be given the use of a desk, computer, company car, or other items needed to complete the assigned work. The other criterion is *material contribution,* which means that the work that the employee completes must involve substantial effort. An employer withholds payroll taxes from an employee's compensation, provides company-specific benefits, and includes the worker on governmental reports.

Independent Contractors

Classification of a worker as an independent contractor (IC) means that the employer does not direct the worker's specific actions and does not provide the tools needed to complete the work. For example, if a worker performed accounting services for a company but used a privately owned computer and printer, as well as determined the number and timing of the hours worked for the company, the worker could be classified as an independent contractor. An independent contractor may or may not perform work that constitutes material contribution for the employer. The treatment of independent contractors is important because cases in which independent contractors have been reclassified as employees have occurred and do contribute to fraud and potential tax avoidance by employers.

©Marc Romanelli/Blend Images LLC, RF

In two notable cases, *United States v. Silk* (1947) and *Bartels v. Birmingham* (1947), both of the employers reclassified ICs as employees for tax purposes, resulting in violations and fines under IRS section 530, which prevents such reclassification when an IC is clearly working in a nonemployee capacity. According to the U.S. Department of Labor (DOL), investigations into employee misclassification usually involve examination of two years of employee records. When intentional misclassification is suspected, the DOL will examine more years of employee records. (Source: American Payroll Association)

Payment records for ICs, although maintained separately from payroll records, are an instance in which payroll accountants must be aware of employee classification and record-keeping requirements to avoid fraudulent activity. Independent contractors are responsible for their own payroll taxes. They are paid through a company's accounts payable, not payroll. This subject has become increasingly important in the past decade as many employers have sought to reduce liabilities through the incorrect classification of IC workers.

The IRS has three tests to clarify if a worker is an employee or an independent contractor:

1. **Behavioral Control:** To what extent does the employer have the right to control and direct the worker's actions?

2. **Financial Control:** This guideline pertains to the worker's unreimbursed expenses, investment in job-related tools, availability of worker's services to other entities outside the company, and how the worker is paid.

3. **Relationship of the Parties:** This includes details related to any work-related contracts between the employer and the worker, benefits offered, permanency of the relationship, and relationship between the worker's services and the firm's normal business operations. (Source: IRS)

Further clarification about determining employment status may be located in IRS Form 1779. Upon request, the firm may request official guidance from the IRS by submitting form SS-8. Penalties are assessed to employers who deliberately misclassify employees in an effort to cut payroll costs; in addition to the penalties, the employers may have to provide unpaid wages to misclassified employees. In fiscal year 2015, the U.S. Wage and Hour Division mandated more than $74 million in back wages to employees who were misclassified as independent contractors. (Source: DOL)

Reporting New Employees

Reporting newly hired employees is considered important by governmental bodies. Why is this so?

- First, reporting employees creates a registry to monitor people who owe child support.
- Second, it helps immigration agencies track immigrants to ensure that they are still legally able to work in the United States.
- Third, for certain professions such as teaching, the new hire reporting system can be used to communicate issues such as ethical violations for which the professional has been censured by governmental or accrediting bodies.
- Finally, the new hire reporting system assists with the administration of COBRA medical benefits.

All newly hired employees must have certain specific documentation. For legal purposes, the minimum amount of documentation allowed is the *W-4* (see Figure 2-2) and *I-9* forms (see Figure 2-3). The W-4 is a publication of the Internal Revenue Service. The main purpose behind the W-4 is to help the employer determine the correct amount of federal income taxes to withhold from the employee's payroll. The I-9 form is published by the Department of Homeland Security, which stipulates that all new hires be reported within 20 days of their start date. Registration of employees by using the I-9 form minimizes negative implications associated with monitoring legally authorized workers in the United States and tracking people with legal obligations such as child support and other garnishments.

> As of the 2010 U.S. census, the estimated amount of child support transferred between custodial and noncustodial parents for children younger than the age of 21 in the United States exceeded $41.7 billion. Source: U.S. Census Bureau

Please refer to the following information for the Form W-4 shown in Figure 2-2 and the I-9 shown in Figure 2-3. The final page of the I-9 form contains the employee-provided documents needed to verify identity and eligibility to work in the United States. Employees must provide either one item from List A *or* one item from both List B *and* List C.

Jonathan A. Doe was born on 5/17/1981 and lives at 123 Main Street, Anytown, Kansas 54932. He is single. His Social Security number is 987-65-4321. His employer is Homestead Retreat at 9010 Old Manhattan Highway, Olathe, Kansas 59384. His email address is jonathandoe@anymail.com, and his phone number is (620)552-2299. When he filled out his new hire paperwork on January 2, 2015, Jessica Stolpp in Human Resources for Homestead Retreat verified his identity with both his Social Security card and his driver's license (G93847562), which expires on his birthday in 2017.

FIGURE 2-2

Form W-4 Employee Withholding Allowance Certificate

Form W-4 (2016)

Purpose. Complete Form W-4 so that your employer can withhold the correct federal income tax from your pay. Consider completing a new Form W-4 each year and when your personal or financial situation changes.

Exemption from withholding. If you are exempt, complete **only** lines 1, 2, 3, 4, and 7 and sign the form to validate it. Your exemption for 2016 expires February 15, 2017. See Pub. 505, Tax Withholding and Estimated Tax.

Note: If another person can claim you as a dependent on his or her tax return, you cannot claim exemption from withholding if your income exceeds $1,050 and includes more than $350 of unearned income (for example, interest and dividends).

Exceptions. An employee may be able to claim exemption from withholding even if the employee is a dependent, if the employee:

• Is age 65 or older,

• Is blind, or

• Will claim adjustments to income; tax credits; or itemized deductions, on his or her tax return.

The exceptions do not apply to supplemental wages greater than $1,000,000.

Basic instructions. If you are not exempt, complete the **Personal Allowances Worksheet** below. The worksheets on page 2 further adjust your withholding allowances based on itemized deductions, certain credits, adjustments to income, or two-earners/multiple jobs situations.

Complete all worksheets that apply. However, you may claim fewer (or zero) allowances. For regular wages, withholding must be based on allowances you claimed and may not be a flat amount or percentage of wages.

Head of household. Generally, you can claim head of household filing status on your tax return only if you are unmarried and pay more than 50% of the costs of keeping up a home for yourself and your dependent(s) or other qualifying individuals. See Pub. 501, Exemptions, Standard Deduction, and Filing Information, for information.

Tax credits. You can take projected tax credits into account in figuring your allowable number of withholding allowances. Credits for child or dependent care expenses and the child tax credit may be claimed using the **Personal Allowances Worksheet** below. See Pub. 505 for information on converting your other credits into withholding allowances.

Nonwage income. If you have a large amount of nonwage income, such as interest or dividends, consider making estimated tax payments using Form 1040-ES, Estimated Tax for Individuals. Otherwise, you may owe additional tax. If you have pension or annuity income, see Pub. 505 to find out if you should adjust your withholding on Form W-4 or W-4P.

Two earners or multiple jobs. If you have a working spouse or more than one job, figure the total number of allowances you are entitled to claim on all jobs using worksheets from only one Form W-4. Your withholding usually will be most accurate when all allowances are claimed on the Form W-4 for the highest paying job and zero allowances are claimed on the others. See Pub. 505 for details.

Nonresident alien. If you are a nonresident alien, see Notice 1392, Supplemental Form W-4 Instructions for Nonresident Aliens, before completing this form.

Check your withholding. After your Form W-4 takes effect, use Pub. 505 to see how the amount you are having withheld compares to your projected total tax for 2016. See Pub. 505, especially if your earnings exceed $130,000 (Single) or $180,000 (Married).

Future developments. Information about any future developments affecting Form W-4 (such as legislation enacted after we release it) will be posted at *www.irs.gov/w4.*

Personal Allowances Worksheet (Keep for your records.)

A	Enter "1" for **yourself** if no one else can claim you as a dependent	**A** 1
B	Enter "1" if: { • You are single and have only one job; or • You are married, have only one job, and your spouse does not work; or • Your wages from a second job or your spouse's wages (or the total of both) are $1,500 or less. } . . .	**B** 1
C	Enter "1" for your **spouse**. But, you may choose to enter "-0-" if you are married and have either a working spouse or more than one job. (Entering "-0-" may help you avoid having too little tax withheld.)	**C** _____
D	Enter number of **dependents** (other than your spouse or yourself) you will claim on your tax return	**D** _____
E	Enter "1" if you will file as **head of household** on your tax return (see conditions under **Head of household** above) . .	**E** _____
F	Enter "1" if you have at least $2,000 of **child or dependent care expenses** for which you plan to claim a credit . . .	**F** _____
	(**Note:** Do **not** include child support payments. See Pub. 503, Child and Dependent Care Expenses, for details.)	
G	**Child Tax Credit** (including additional child tax credit). See Pub. 972, Child Tax Credit, for more information.	
	• If your total income will be less than $70,000 ($100,000 if married), enter "2" for each eligible child; then **less** "1" if you have two to four eligible children or **less** "2" if you have five or more eligible children.	
	• If your total income will be between $70,000 and $84,000 ($100,000 and $119,000 if married), enter "1" for each eligible child . .	**G** _____
H	Add lines A through G and enter total here. (**Note:** This may be different from the number of exemptions you claim on your tax return.) ▶ **H**	**H** 2

For accuracy, complete all worksheets that apply.	• If you plan to **itemize** or **claim adjustments to income** and want to reduce your withholding, see the **Deductions and Adjustments Worksheet** on page 2. • If you are **single and have more than one job** or are **married and you and your spouse both work** and the combined earnings from all jobs exceed $50,000 ($20,000 if married), see the **Two-Earners/Multiple Jobs Worksheet** on page 2 to avoid having too little tax withheld. • If **neither** of the above situations applies, **stop here** and enter the number from line H on line 5 of Form W-4 below.

-------------------- ▶ Separate here and give Form W-4 to your employer. Keep the top part for your records. --------------------

Form **W-4** Department of the Treasury Internal Revenue Service	**Employee's Withholding Allowance Certificate** ▶ Whether you are entitled to claim a certain number of allowances or exemption from withholding is subject to review by the IRS. Your employer may be required to send a copy of this form to the IRS.	OMB No. 1545-0074 20**16**

1 Your first name and middle initial	Last name	**2** Your social security number
Jonathan A.	Doe	987-65-4321

Home address (number and street or rural route)	**3** ☑ Single ☐ Married ☐ Married, but withhold at higher Single rate.
123 Main Street	Note: If married, but legally separated, or spouse is a nonresident alien, check the "Single" box.
City or town, state, and ZIP code	**4** If your last name differs from that shown on your social security card,
Anytown, KS 54932	check here. You must call 1-800-772-1213 for a replacement card. ▶ ☐

5	Total number of allowances you are claiming (from line **H** above **or** from the applicable worksheet on page 2)	**5** 2
6	Additional amount, if any, you want withheld from each paycheck	**6** $ _____
7	I claim exemption from withholding for 2016, and I certify that I meet **both** of the following conditions for exemption.	
	• Last year I had a right to a refund of **all** federal income tax withheld because I had **no** tax liability, **and**	
	• This year I expect a refund of **all** federal income tax withheld because I expect to have **no** tax liability.	
	If you meet both conditions, write "Exempt" here . . . . ▶	**7**

Under penalties of perjury, I declare that I have examined this certificate and, to the best of my knowledge and belief, it is true, correct, and complete.

Employee's signature
(This form is not valid unless you sign it.) ▶ *Jonathan A. Doe*   **Date** ▶ 1/2/2016

8 Employer's name and address (Employer: Complete lines 8 and 10 only if sending to the IRS.)	**9** Office code (optional)	**10** Employer identification number (EIN)

For Privacy Act and Paperwork Reduction Act Notice, see page 2.   Cat. No. 10220Q   Form **W-4** (2016)

Source: Internal Revenue Service.

FIGURE 2-3
I-9 Employment Eligibility Verification Form

Employment Eligibility Verification

Department of Homeland Security
U.S. Citizenship and Immigration Services

USCIS
Form I-9
OMB No. 1615-0047
Expires 03/31/2016

▶**START HERE.** Read instructions carefully before completing this form. The instructions must be available during completion of this form.
ANTI-DISCRIMINATION NOTICE: It is illegal to discriminate against work-authorized individuals. Employers **CANNOT** specify which document(s) they will accept from an employee. The refusal to hire an individual because the documentation presented has a future expiration date may also constitute illegal discrimination.

Section 1. Employee Information and Attestation *(Employees must complete and sign Section 1 of Form I-9 no later than the **first day of employment**, but not before accepting a job offer.)*

Last Name *(Family Name)*	First Name *(Given Name)*	Middle Initial	Other Names Used *(if any)*
Doe	Jonathan	A	

Address *(Street Number and Name)*	Apt. Number	City or Town	State	Zip Code
123 Main Street		Anytown	KS	54932

Date of Birth *(mm/dd/yyyy)*	U.S. Social Security Number	E-mail Address	Telephone Number
05/17/1981	9 8 7 - 6 5 - 4 3 2 1	jonathandoe@anymail . com	(620) 552-2299

I am aware that federal law provides for imprisonment and/or fines for false statements or use of false documents in connection with the completion of this form.

I attest, under penalty of perjury, that I am (check one of the following):

[X] A citizen of the United States

[ ] A noncitizen national of the United States *(See instructions)*

[ ] A lawful permanent resident (Alien Registration Number/USCIS Number): _____

[ ] An alien authorized to work until (expiration date, if applicable, mm/dd/yyyy) _____ . Some aliens may write "N/A" in this field.
(See instructions)

For aliens authorized to work, provide your Alien Registration Number/USCIS Number **OR** *Form I-94 Admission Number:*

1. Alien Registration Number/USCIS Number:_____

OR

2. Form I-94 Admission Number: _____

If you obtained your admission number from CBP in connection with your arrival in the United States, include the following:

Foreign Passport Number: _____

Country of Issuance: _____

Some aliens may write "N/A" on the Foreign Passport Number and Country of Issuance fields. *(See instructions)*

3-D Barcode
Do Not Write in This Space

Signature of Employee:	Date *(mm/dd/yyyy)*: 01/02/2015

Preparer and/or Translator Certification *(To be completed and signed if Section 1 is prepared by a person other than the employee.)*

I attest, under penalty of perjury, that I have assisted in the completion of this form and that to the best of my knowledge the information is true and correct.

Signature of Preparer or Translator:	Date *(mm/dd/yyyy)*:

Last Name *(Family Name)*	First Name *(Given Name)*

Address *(Street Number and Name)*	City or Town	State	Zip Code

🛑 *Employer Completes Next Page* 🛑

Source: United States Citizenship and Immigration Services

Section 2. Employer or Authorized Representative Review and Verification

(Employers or their authorized representative must complete and sign Section 2 within 3 business days of the employee's first day of employment. You must physically examine one document from List A OR examine a combination of one document from List B and one document from List C as listed on the "Lists of Acceptable Documents" on the next page of this form. For each document you review, record the following information: document title, issuing authority, document number, and expiration date, if any.)

Employee Last Name, First Name and Middle Initial from Section 1: Doe, Jonathan A,

List A	OR	List B	AND	List C
Identity and Employment Authorization		**Identity**		**Employment Authorization**

List A	List B	List C
Document Title:	Document Title: Driver's License	Document Title: Social Security Card
Issuing Authority:	Issuing Authority: State of Kansas	Issuing Authority: Social Security Administration
Document Number:	Document Number: G93847562	Document Number: 987-65-4321
Expiration Date *(if any)(mm/dd/yyyy)*:	Expiration Date *(if any)(mm/dd/yyyy)*: 05/17/2017	Expiration Date *(if any)(mm/dd/yyyy)*:
Document Title:		
Issuing Authority:		
Document Number:		
Expiration Date *(if any)(mm/dd/yyyy)*:		
Document Title:		
Issuing Authority:		**3-D Barcode** **Do Not Write in This Space**
Document Number:		
Expiration Date *(if any)(mm/dd/yyyy)*:		

Certification

I attest, under penalty of perjury, that (1) I have examined the document(s) presented by the above-named employee, (2) the above-listed document(s) appear to be genuine and to relate to the employee named, and (3) to the best of my knowledge the employee is authorized to work in the United States.

The employee's first day of employment *(mm/dd/yyyy)*: 01/01/2015 _____ *(**See instructions for exemptions**.)*

Signature of Employer or Authorized Representative	Date *(mm/dd/yyyy)* 01/02/2015	Title of Employer or Authorized Representative Human Resources
Last Name *(Family Name)* Stolpp	First Name *(Given Name)* Jessica	Employer's Business or Organization Name Homestead Retreat

Employer's Business or Organization Address *(Street Number and Name)* 9010 Old Manhattan Highway	City or Town Olathe	State KS	Zip Code 59384

Section 3. Reverification and Rehires *(To be completed and signed by employer or authorized representative.)*

A. New Name *(if applicable)* Last Name *(Family Name)* First Name *(Given Name)*	Middle Initial	**B.** Date of Rehire *(if applicable) (mm/dd/yyyy)*:

C. If employee's previous grant of employment authorization has expired, provide the information for the document from List A or List C the employee presented that establishes current employment authorization in the space provided below.

Document Title:	Document Number:	Expiration Date *(if any)(mm/dd/yyyy)*:

I attest, under penalty of perjury, that to the best of my knowledge, this employee is authorized to work in the United States, and if the employee presented document(s), the document(s) I have examined appear to be genuine and to relate to the individual.

Signature of Employer or Authorized Representative:	Date *(mm/dd/yyyy)*:	Print Name of Employer or Authorized Representative:

LISTS OF ACCEPTABLE DOCUMENTS
All documents must be UNEXPIRED

Employees may present one selection from List A
or a combination of one selection from List B and one selection from List C.

LIST A Documents that Establish Both Identity and Employment Authorization OR	LIST B Documents that Establish Identity AND	LIST C Documents that Establish Employment Authorization
1. U.S. Passport or U.S. Passport Card	1. Driver's license or ID card issued by a State or outlying possession of the United States provided it contains a photograph or information such as name, date of birth, gender, height, eye color, and address	1. A Social Security Account Number card, unless the card includes one of the following restrictions: (1) NOT VALID FOR EMPLOYMENT (2) VALID FOR WORK ONLY WITH INS AUTHORIZATION (3) VALID FOR WORK ONLY WITH DHS AUTHORIZATION
2. Permanent Resident Card or Alien Registration Receipt Card (Form I-551)		
3. Foreign passport that contains a temporary I-551 stamp or temporary I-551 printed notation on a machine-readable immigrant visa	2. ID card issued by federal, state or local government agencies or entities, provided it contains a photograph or information such as name, date of birth, gender, height, eye color, and address	2. Certification of Birth Abroad issued by the Department of State (Form FS-545)
4. Employment Authorization Document that contains a photograph (Form I-766)	3. School ID card with a photograph	3. Certification of Report of Birth issued by the Department of State (Form DS-1350)
5. For a nonimmigrant alien authorized to work for a specific employer because of his or her status: a. Foreign passport; and b. Form I-94 or Form I-94A that has the following: (1) The same name as the passport; and (2) An endorsement of the alien's nonimmigrant status as long as that period of endorsement has not yet expired and the proposed employment is not in conflict with any restrictions or limitations identified on the form.	4. Voter's registration card	4. Original or certified copy of birth certificate issued by a State, county, municipal authority, or territory of the United States bearing an official seal
	5. U.S. Military card or draft record	
	6. Military dependent's ID card	5. Native American tribal document
	7. U.S. Coast Guard Merchant Mariner Card	6. U.S. Citizen ID Card (Form I-197)
	8. Native American tribal document	7. Identification Card for Use of Resident Citizen in the United States (Form I-179)
	9. Driver's license issued by a Canadian government authority	
6. Passport from the Federated States of Micronesia (FSM) or the Republic of the Marshall Islands (RMI) with Form I-94 or Form I-94A indicating nonimmigrant admission under the Compact of Free Association Between the United States and the FSM or RMI	**For persons under age 18 who are unable to present a document listed above:** 10. School record or report card 11. Clinic, doctor, or hospital record 12. Day-care or nursery school record	8. Employment authorization document issued by the Department of Homeland Security

Illustrations of many of these documents appear in Part 8 of the Handbook for Employers (M-274).

Refer to Section 2 of the instructions, titled "Employer or Authorized Representative Review and Verification," for more information about acceptable receipts.

The payroll accountant should retain a copy of the Employment Eligibility Verification Form (I-9) and a current Employee Withholding Allowance Certificate (W-4) in every employee's permanent file. The employer should request a new W-4 from employees annually in January to ensure that all addresses, life situations, and other information remain current. Because of the timing constraints on the release of annual tax documents such as the W-2 and W-3, employers should verify employees' W-4 information as close to January 1 as possible each year.

> The U.S. Congress is considering the Legal Workforce Act (H.R. 1147), which would mandate electronic verification of an employee's eligibility to work in the United States. If H.R. 1147 is signed into law, the paper I-9 form would be repealed in favor of the electronic verification system, which would improve communication among agencies such as the Department of Homeland Security and the Social Security Administration and reduce fraud. The paper I-9 form expired in March 2016, but employers are required to use it until the U.S. Citizenship and Immigration Services (USCIS) completes the conversion to a smart form, which will be done online. (Source: SHRM)

Hiring Packet Contents

© Ariel Skelley/Getty Images, RF

The **hiring packet** maintained by many companies may be as basic as a simple W-4 and I-9 form or may be incredibly complex if foreign workers and multiple types of voluntary deductions are involved. Common items in a hiring packet are the federal forms mentioned earlier, state and local withholding allowance forms, elections for voluntary deductions, insurance paperwork, and the offer letter that specifies the pay rate and start date. Not all companies have the same items in the hiring packet, and no legislative guidelines exist. The firm's management, after reviewing the needs of the company and the legal requirements for the position, determines the hiring packet contents. Many companies also are including diversity self-declaration papers to ensure compliance with equal opportunity legislation, requirements under federal contracts, and other special requirements.

Notification of New Hires to State Offices

The Immigration Reform and Control Act mandates that employers notify state offices within 20 days of an employee's start date. State forms for fulfilling this requirement vary, and the reporting of new hires is a complex task with high potential for errors for companies with employees in multiple states.

The Office of Management and Budget (OMB) has designed a form (see Figure 2-4) for multistate employers to register and designate one state as the primary place to which they will send new hire reports. They can designate on the form the other states in which they have employees. The use of the multistate registry helps employers ensure they remain in compliance with the law. The penalty for noncompliance is strictly enforced and ranges from $25 per unreported employee to $500 for intentional nonreporting.

Foreign Workers

Employers who hire non–U.S. citizens face additional challenges. The employer must verify that the employee is legally allowed to work in the United States. Generally, the I-9 form serves this purpose, but there may be occasions when the prospective employee does not have an appropriate government-issued visa for working in the United States. If no visa exists, the employer may file a petition with the U.S. Citizenship and Immigration Services office to gain permission for the foreign employee to work in the United States. Some exceptions exist to the rules for the visa. The fees for permanent workers not in the protected classes can range

OMB Control No: 0970-0166
Expiration Date: 05-31-2016

MULTISTATE EMPLOYER NOTIFICATION FORM FOR NEW HIRE REPORTING

Employers who have employees working in two or more states may use this form to register to submit their new hire reports to one state or make changes to a previous registration. Multistate employers may also visit https://ocsp.acf.hhs.gov/OCSE/ to register or make changes electronically.

Federal law (42 USC 653A(b)(1)(A)) requires employers to supply the following information about newly hired employees to the State Directory of New Hires in the state where the employee works:

- Employee's name, address, Social Security number, and the date of hire (the date services for remuneration were first performed by the employee)

- Employer's name, address, and Federal Employer Identification Number (FEIN)

  If you are an employer with employees working in two or more states AND you will transmit the required information or reports magnetically or electronically, you may use this form to designate one state where any employee works to transmit ALL new hire reports to the State Directory of New Hires.

Source: United States Department of Health and Human Services.

from $0 to $1,435, depending on the petitioner and the worker concerned. For information about the Permanent Worker Visa Preference Categories, please visit the U.S. Citizenship and Immigration Services website (www.uscis.gov).

> The U.S. Senate has proposed the H-1B and L-1B Visa Reform Act of 2015, which limits the number of foreign workers and the length of time they are allowed to work in the United States. The purpose of this proposed legislation was to prevent abuse among employers who hire a disproportionately high number of foreign workers as compared to U.S. citizens. (Source: U.S. Congress)

© Getty Images/Blend Images/Ariel Skelley

Statutory Employees

Some personnel who would normally be classified as independent contractors must be treated as employees for tax purposes. The IRS classifies ***statutory employees*** as personnel who meet any of the following guidelines:

- A driver who distributes beverages (other than milk) or meat, vegetable, fruit, or bakery products or who picks up and delivers laundry or dry cleaning, if the driver is a single company's agent or is paid on commission.

- A full-time life insurance sales agent whose principal business activity is selling life insurance or annuity contracts, or both, primarily for one life insurance company.

- An individual who works at home on materials or goods that a company supplies and that must be returned to that company or a designated agent in accordance with furnished specifications for the work to be done.

- A full-time traveling or city salesperson who works on a single company's behalf and turns in orders from wholesalers, retailers, contractors, or operators of hotels, restaurants, or other similar establishments. The goods sold must be merchandise for resale or supplies for use in the buyer's business operation. The work performed for that single company must be the salesperson's principal business activity.

Recall that the primary differences between an employee and an independent contractor are that the independent contractor sets his or her own hours and provides the tools necessary to complete the task. Statutory employees are a hybrid of employee and independent contractor. To ensure proper and timely remittance of employment taxes, the IRS has mandated that the employer withhold FICA taxes from statutory employees in the same manner as other company personnel; however, federal income taxes are not withheld from statutory employees' pay. (Source: IRS Publication 15-A)

U.S. Workers in Foreign Subsidiaries

Many companies have foreign subsidiaries and divisions that employ U.S. expatriate workers. The *Foreign Account Tax Compliance Act (FATCA)* of 2010 requires employers to report to the IRS the wages of employees who are permanent U.S. citizens working in foreign locations in order to facilitate appropriate taxation of such workers. Under the IRS Foreign Earned Income Exclusion, expatriate workers must file Form 673 with their employer to exclude the first $101,300 of annual wages (2016 figure) from U.S. taxation but must pay income tax on income in excess of that amount.

Entering New Employees into the Database

The method of entering a new employee into the payroll system depends upon the system in place. A manual system would require minimal work, adding the employee to the federal, state, and local lists for taxes withheld as well as adding the new hire to the list of employees to pay. Manual systems should have a checklist of all employees to ensure that no one is missed in the process.

Who Are You?

1. Go to the website for the U.S. Citizenship and Immigration Services, located at www.uscis.gov, and type I-9 into the search box on the website. Click on the link for the PDF version of the I-9 form to obtain a digital copy. What are two different ways that you would be able to prove your eligibility for work in the United States?

2. Go to the IRS website, located at www.irs.gov, and type W-4 into the search box on the website. Click on the link for the PDF version of the W-4 to obtain a digital copy. Before you start, ask yourself how many exemptions you think you should claim. Complete the Personal Allowances Worksheet. How did the number of allowable exemptions compare with your estimate? Explain.

3. What are three examples of statutory employees?

FIGURE 2-5
Employee Database Information Sample

Personal Information

Salary

Vacation

Tax Details

Benefits & Deductions

Employee Files

Direct Deposit

Employee History

$14.59/hour

Salary History

Amount	Effective on
$14.59/hour	04/04/2016
$13.75/hour	01/01/2015

© McGraw-Hill Education/John
Flournoy, **photographer**

Setting up a new employee in an automated system involves many more steps. The payroll employee enters in the pertinent data (see Figure 2-5). Employee number, name, address, Social Security number, wage, pay frequency, withholding information from W-4, department, and contact information are typically included. The payroll employee must designate a worker's compensation classification, state of employment, and local jurisdiction (when local taxes are applicable). Depending on state requirements, additional location codes, job classification codes, and identifying characteristics may also be required.

LO 2-3   Explain Pay Records and Employee File Maintenance

© Corbis, RF

One of the most important parts of any payroll system is the maintenance of employee pay records. The maintenance of accurate and detailed records that reflect the pay period, pay date, pay rate, and deductions is critical not only because it is a legal requirement, but also for positive employee relations. Pay records may be manual, computerized through programs such as Sage 50 or QuickBooks, or maintained by external companies whose sole function is employee payroll implementation. Employers retain physical copies of employees' time records, pay advice, and any other documentation processed with the paycheck. Some other types of documentation include:

- Request for a day off.
- Reports of tardiness or absenteeism.
- Detailed records of work completed during that day's shift.

Technological advances allow employers to scan and save this information digitally, such as using an Adobe Acrobat file, within the payroll accounting system. The availability of digital copies facilitates managerial, auditor, or authorized executives' review, approval, or commentary on the documentation attached to payroll documents. Digital copies also permit transparency of records between the employer and employee, reducing miscommunication and payroll discrepancies.

Pay Records

Employee wages involve far more than simple hourly rates or periodic salary payments. Employees can be subject to the Fair Labor Standards Act, and many provisions of that law affect employee pay. In this section, we will look at how different pay periods and methods influence the payment of employee wages.

The first payroll decision a company should make is the company's pay frequency (daily, weekly, biweekly, semimonthly, monthly). Choice of pay frequency affects the applicable amounts for employee income tax withholding. Separate schedules for federal income taxes are provided in *IRS Publication 15* (available at www.irs.gov), which is released in November for the following year (i.e., 2017 tax information is released November 2016). Once the pay frequency has been determined, the payroll accountant can establish the payment schedule for federal and state payroll liabilities. Employers must submit government tax liabilities in a timely manner. Depending upon the level of payroll, more frequent tax deposits may be required.

Pay Rate

Pay rate is the amount per hour per pay period the company determines the employee should be compensated. The determination of pay rate depends upon many employee variables: experience, education, certifications, governmental regulations (i.e., minimum wage, Davis-Bacon, etc.), hours worked, or a combination of all of the above. Employers may also pay specific rates for jobs performed. For example, employees working in a manufacturing environment may be subject to a different pay scale when cross-trained and working in a sales capacity. Minimum wage rates vary per state, and different parts of the same state may have different minimum wages.

> The idea of paying a living wage continues to be a prominent issue. Companies such as Walmart, Target, and McDonald's have all established minimum employee wages that are significantly higher than the federal minimum wage. Other smaller-scale employers such as Gravity Payments, a merchant services firm, have significantly increased the wages paid to all employees.

Classifying employee wages as salary versus hourly is a basic determination, linked to the type of work performed and the position within the company. ***Salaried exempt employees*** are not subject to overtime, are paid to do a specific job, and fulfill the FLSA requirement of self-direction; however, not all salaried employees are classified as exempt. Certain jobs such as nurses, police officers, and upper-level administrators may earn a fixed salary but are classified as ***nonexempt*** because of the nature of management direction in their function. Nonexempt workers do not generally supervise other employees and generally work under the direction of a supervisor.

> ### EXAMPLE: PAY PERIOD COMPUTATION, BIWEEKLY EMPLOYEE
> Juan is a manager for a textiles firm. He earns $52,000 per year, is classified as an exempt employee, and is paid biweekly. He normally works 40 hours per week.
>
> During June, the following occurred:
>
> Pay period ending June 15: Juan worked 85 hours.
>
> Pay period ending June 29: Juan worked 78 hours
>
> Salary for the June 15 pay period = $52,000/26 periods per year = $2,000
>
> Salary for the June 29 pay period = $52,000/26 periods per year = $2,000
>
> Juan's salary for each pay period would be the fixed amount no matter how many hours he worked because he is classified as an exempt employee.

> The concept of a fluctuating workweek for salaried nonexempt employees has been a source of confusion for employers. Some salaried nonexempt employees work in industries that require them to be available at different times based on company needs. If an employee is nonexempt and salaried but has hours that are changeable due to the nature of their job, then they must receive overtime during periods when they work more than 40 hours in a given week. (Source: *Inside Counsel*)

Hourly employees are protected by the FLSA and eligible for overtime pay. When overtime pay is applied, hourly employees may earn more than their salaried counterparts. Overtime rules and rates are determined by FLSA; however, some states may have additional requirements for overtime pay. Overtime is calculated at one-and-a-half times the employee's hourly rate. For FLSA, overtime applies only to hours worked exceeding 40 in a week (with some exceptions). Some states may also require that employees receive overtime pay for any hours worked exceeding 8 per day in addition to the 40 hours per week, making it possible for an hourly employee to earn overtime pay without reaching the 40 hours in the week. In this textbook, all nonexempt employees receive overtime pay for hours worked in excess of 40 hours per week.

© Vladimir Godnik/Beyond Fotomedia
GmbH/Alamy, RF

Commissions and piece rate compensation offer employees incentives for specific jobs. **_Commissions_** are a percentage of sales or services performed by an individual. An example of a commission would be a sales representative receiving 1% of all sales he or she initiates. **_Piece rate_** connect employee compensation with the production of a good or service. Piece rate compensation was widely used in the United States prior to industrialization and automated manufacturing. For example, when a shoe was being made, the person preparing the sole would receive a set rate per item.

> The California state legislature passed Assembly Bill 1513, which established guidelines about productive time and rest time for piece rate employees. This Bill also established a specified time period for employers to pay employees back pay because of the legal change. (Source: California Department of Industrial Relations)

Compensation structures can become complex if the employee is compensated using multiple pay types. A sales representative may receive a salary and commissions while working on the sales floor but receive hourly and piece rate if filling in on the manufacturing floor. Proper classification of the various aspects of the employee's workday becomes exceptionally important for the correct processing of the payroll.

Entering Hours

When it is time to prepare the payroll, an automated system will provide the payroll employee with a simple form to complete, typically including wage type and number of hours worked. In complex organizations, an additional classification of job location may be required if the employee works in multiple departments or locations. The automated systems will complete the mathematics to obtain gross pay, and most automated systems will calculate overtime and shift differentials (i.e., higher pay for working during times not considered "normal business hours").

> Many web-based applications exist to track employee attendance and calculate pay. TimeStation, FishBowl, and TimeDock use Quick-Read (QR) codes, employee PINs, and GPS location tagging to verify employee work. These apps may be useful tools for companies with employees at remote locations. Apps such as Weekly Hours allow employees to calculate their hours worked and to email the time sheet to a supervisor. Other apps, such as iTookOff Paid Leave Tracker, allow employees to manage their paid time off through a synchronized app.

Calculations of Weekly Regular Time and Overtime

Even with the use of automated systems, the payroll accountant must determine the breakdown of each employee's regular and overtime hours. Recall the discussion regarding the FLSA standard of 40 hours in a week. This is where the calculation of overtime becomes important.

The employee's hours are added up, the total for the pay period is computed to determine if the employee worked more than 40 hours total for any given week, and overtime is separated from regular hours worked for wage calculations. If the employee did not work more than 40 hours, the total regular hours are noted on the time card. If the employee did work more than 40 hours, hours worked will be divided between the 40 hours and the overtime pay computation.

EXAMPLE: NONEXEMPT PAY CALCULATION

Monique works as a maintenance worker at a busy hospital. She earns $52,000 annually, is paid weekly, and is classified as nonexempt. Her standard work week is 40 hours.

During April, the following occurred:

Pay period ending April 22: Monique worked 50 hours.

Because Monique is classified as a nonexempt employee, she would receive her weekly pay *plus* overtime at the rate of 1.5 times her hourly wage. To determine her hourly wage, divide her annual pay by the total hours worked during the year:

Hourly wage = $52,000/(52 weeks × 40 hours per week)

Hourly wage = $25

Overtime rate = $25 × 1.5 = $37.50 per hour

Total pay for the week = Regular pay + overtime pay

= ($25 × 40 hours) + ($37.50 × 10 hours) = $1,000 + $375

Total pay for the April 22 pay period = $1,375

Monique is classified as a nonexempt worker, so she is eligible to receive overtime for any hours worked in excess of 40 per week.

Depending upon company policy, the existence of paid holidays or sick days may alter payroll calculations. However, holiday hours, sick time taken, and vacation days are not usually included in the worked hours to determine overtime.

According to the FLSA, employers are not required to pay for employee sick time; however, many states have either passed legislation or have pending bills that would mandate employer-paid sick time. As of 2016, the following locations have mandatory paid sick time:

Connecticut	California	Massachusetts
Oregon	Washington, D.C.	Vermont

Washington County, Maryland

Employees subject to Davis-Bacon or Walsh-Healey provisions were granted paid sick leave as of September 2015. (Source: A Better Balance)

Worker Facts

1. Which classification of workers is subject to the wage and hour provisions of the Fair Labor Standards Act?

2. What is the difference between exempt and nonexempt employees in overtime pay requirements?

3. What is the difference between commission and piece rate pay as far as the basis for the compensation?

LO 2-4 Describe Internal Controls and Record Retention for a Payroll System

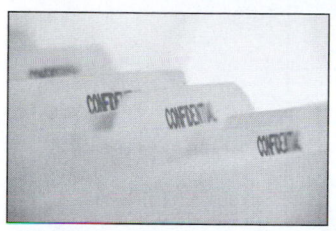

© Tetra Images/Corbis, RF

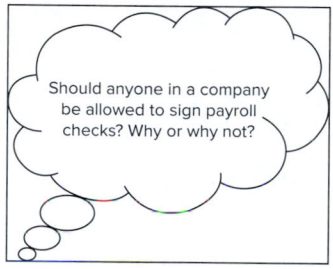

Should anyone in a company be allowed to sign payroll checks? Why or why not?

Internal controls are critical to ensure the integrity of a payroll system. Confidentiality of payroll information is one of the most important controls in establishing a payroll system. Pay records such as time records are considered confidential documents, and personnel who handle or maintain such records must ensure the privacy of the information they contain. Small firms may be able to maintain the confidentiality of handwritten time sheets; however, multifacility companies may need to use more secure time-collection methods to ensure information privacy.

Strategic planning of the payroll system prior to its inception can prevent data errors and losses related to inadequate *internal controls*. Most importantly, the payroll system design should be reviewed at regular intervals to determine its effectiveness and appropriateness for the company size and to correct errors before they become magnified.

A company with many departments and many employees will generally have a more complex *review process* than a small company will. In an organization that has one office and a dozen or fewer employees, certain steps of the verification process may be omitted and fewer people are required to conduct it. Conversely, a large organization with several departments and many employees could have several levels of verification in the *payroll review* process. Even outsourced payroll requires levels of the review process. The payroll executed by an external company is only as accurate as the data provided. For instance, a company could have a payroll review process such as the one shown in Figure 2-6.

An extremely important issue within internal controls is the determination of authorized signers. A common (and good!) practice in a company is to have at least one designated signatory for payroll checks. Often, these signers are different people than those involved in the review process. In many companies, more than one person signs the payroll checks as another level of review of the accuracy. Remember that the most important part of payroll is *accuracy*. The extra time it takes to review and obtain the necessary signatures is time well spent, as long as it prevents costly errors.

Documentation of the payroll process is vital. As should be clear by now, execution of payroll is not merely writing checks to employees. Proper documentation of payroll entails a well-delineated procedure and properly trained personnel. Table 2-1 contains examples of different documentation controls, the activities involved in each, and the personnel who may be required.

FIGURE 2-6
Payroll Review Process: Steps to Ensure Accurate Payroll

| Employee completes time card | Manager verifies the employee's time card | Payroll clerk computes the period wages for the employee | Payroll supervisor verifies the payroll clerk's math | Employee's check is presented with payroll register for verification and signatures |

TABLE 2-1
Documentation Controls

Procedure	Example of Internal Control Activities	Could Be Performed by
Review and approval of time data from time cards or other time collection devices	Complete the time collection procedure Review of time collection for accuracy and approval	Employee's Supervisor
Overtime approval	Approve the amount and type of overtime to be paid	Employee's Supervisor
Approval for leave of absence or other unpaid time off	Obtain all prior approvals for unpaid time away due to FMLA or other reasons	Employee's Supervisor
Timely entering of payroll data	Enter the payroll data into the payroll system in a timely manner, and check for data integrity and accuracy	Payroll clerk
Payroll system security	Make sure that only designated employees or payroll vendors have access to payroll data	Payroll supervisor
Approval of the payroll prior to issuance	Obtain the approval from signatory prior to issuing checks	Authorized signer(s)
Maintenance of paid time off (i.e., vacation, sick, etc.)	Ensure that employees receive the exact amount agreed upon	Payroll clerk; employee; supervisor; other designee
Access to payroll data	Ensure that payroll data is confidential and secure	Payroll supervisor
Separation of duties	Make sure that different people verify data, enter data, verify checks	Payroll supervisor
Training of payroll staff	Ensure that payroll department employees and other department supervisors are aware of and follow company payroll policies	Payroll supervisor

Review of Time Collected

The time reported manually on time cards or electronically through other methods must be verified for accuracy prior to the completion of any payroll. Simple issues in employee underpayment (which can cause federal penalties) or overpayment (which can erode the company's available cash) can occur even with sophisticated systems. Time collection and employee payment errors can lead to reduced employee morale, lawsuits, and fines.

Overtime Approval

Hourly employees are subject to federal overtime provisions, commonly known as time-and-a-half, but may include other pay bases such as double-time, and so forth. The Fair Labor Standards Act (FLSA) guarantees nonexempt employees' rights to appropriate pay for the hours worked; however, employees can misreport the overtime they work, costing the company money in the process. Therefore, a good practice is to obtain supervisor approval on all employee-reported overtime.

Computerized systems can also affect the reported overtime. The data is only as accurate as the person who entered it. One of the authors worked at a company that once paid her for 75 hours of overtime in one pay period—when she should have had only 7.5! This kind of error can cause chaos for both the employee, who must return the money, and the employer, who should not have paid it in the first place. Once again, improper pay can erode the morale of the employees. Overpayment on hours can create a myriad of other overpayments; federal withholding taxes, Medicare, Social Security taxes, and pension or 401(k) contributions that are driven by gross wages are just a few examples.

A payroll specialist in Florida was HIV-positive and was afraid to reveal his illness to employers. Instead, he just took the money from his employer to pay for expensive medications. Despite a strong internal controls system, the employee found ways to

(continued)

circumvent the safeguards. He would memorize his co-workers' usernames and passwords to create "ghost" employees. These ghosts' pay would go to the payroll specialist's bank account. To cover his trail, he would falsify the payroll summaries he submitted for approval. The payroll specialist was found guilty of embezzling $112,000 before his termination. (Source: *Journal of Accountancy*)

Approval for Leave of Absence or Other Unpaid Time Off

The employee's supervisor is one level of oversight to ensure that the payroll data reaches the payroll department accurately and in a timely fashion. Supervisors work closely with their employees and should approve overtime and paid time off. Supervisors review individual timesheets for accuracy prior to delivery to the payroll department. Control of time away from work is the responsibility of the employee's supervisor, at the very minimum. The department supervisor should approve the time off. This approval needs to be tracked and maintained by the payroll department to ensure integrity in the payroll records. A suggested best practice is to keep requests for time away attached to the payroll stub for the affected pay period. The use of leave forms provides companies with a paper trail used to clarify perceived discrepancies in pay.

Web-based services facilitate requests, approvals, and tracking for paid time off. Apps such as Zenefits allow managers to adjust paid time off, approve and track employee requests, synchronize calendars, and download reports detailing employee time away from work. (Source: www.zenefits.com)

File Security

According to many different pieces of federal and state legislation, all files pertaining to payroll, whether paper or electronic, must be kept secure from tampering. Another reason for *file security*, or restriction of personnel file access, is the firm's governmental payroll obligations. The tax information contained in the payroll records is required to prepare timely and accurate payment of payroll taxes, a factor that is nearly as important as paying the employees. Examples of methods to secure payroll records include multiple passwords for system access, locking of file cabinets with controlled key disbursement, and encryption programs.

Because payroll data contains highly personal and private information, security of the information is important. To maintain file security, access to payroll records is restricted to a relatively small number of people. Paper-based payroll data is stored in a secure location; similarly, electronic payroll data is securely backed up and encrypted. Many federal and state laws, including the Privacy Act of 1974, protect payroll information.

Paycard use for payroll disbursement was estimated to be nearly $57 billion in 2015, so data privacy and fund protection are a high priority for companies and legislators. Preventing breaches of payroll record security is a high priority and an evolving issue. The Electronic Fund Transfer Act of 1978, created to prevent problems with newly created ATM cards, has been expanded to address fraud and theft issues with *paycards*, a pre-loaded credit card that allows an employee to access funds without needing a bank account.

In *Jessie Chavez v. PVH Corporation (2013)*, the defendant had to pay $1.85 million to Chavez because of fees deducted from the plaintiff's payroll card, which meant that the full amount of the wages was reduced; additionally, the plaintiff had not agreed to paycard use in advance. The Consumer Financial Protection Bureau (CFPB) proposed legislation in 2014 that would include specific language on paycards, informing employees of their right to request another form of pay disbursement. Additionally, the CFPB is seeking legislation that would mandate the provision of paycard fee disclosures and additional terms and conditions of paycard use. As of spring 2016, this proposed legislation was still awaiting final ruling (Sources: American Payroll Association, Lexology, CFPB Monitor)

Alternating Duties and Cross-Training

The cross-training of payroll professionals can act as a safeguard of payroll information. One of the goals of the Sarbanes–Oxley Act of 2002 was to protect the integrity of accounting data by legislating document retention requirements and the rotation of duties by auditors. The same principle applies to payroll system workers. Cross-training and alternating the duties of the people in the payroll process may avoid or minimize errors and potential issues stemming from corruption. Furthermore, cross-training and rotation of duties foster professional development and proficiency with multiple tasks. This rotation of payroll duties refers only to personnel within the payroll department, not opening the payroll processing to non-accounting departments.

Who Does Which Job?

Imagine that you have been approached to assist a business owner who is concerned about the security of his or her company's payroll. In a team of three or four people, decide how you would distribute payroll responsibilities to implement excellent internal control procedures. How did you divide the responsibilities? Explain.

Best Practices Involved in Employee File Maintenance

Maintenance of employee files is as important as the protection of employee information. IRS Regulation 26 CFR 1.6001 clearly states that the method of *file maintenance* is the responsibility of the employer. The Internal Revenue Code recommends record labeling, creation of backup copies, and secure record storage. An important note is that despite the choice of record maintenance, the employer retains all liability for auditor access to the information upon demand. Items such as time and work records, including time cards and electronic work records, must be maintained to be available for auditors because these items are vital components of a payroll system audit.

---

26 CFR 1.6001–1 Records.

(a) *In general.* Except as provided in paragraph (b) of this section, any person subject to tax under subtitle A of the Code (including a qualified State individual income tax which is treated pursuant to section 6361(a) as if it were imposed by chapter 1 of subtitle A), or any person required to file a return of information with respect to income, shall keep such permanent books of account or records, including inventories, as are sufficient to establish the amount of gross income, deductions, credits, or other matters required to be shown by such person in any return of such tax or information. (Source: www.gpo.gov)

Payroll record maintenance is important for employees at all levels of the organization. IRS Revenue Procedure 98-25, 1998-1 CB 689, was enacted in 1998 to govern the maintenance procedures and duration of recordkeeping for companies with employees. Some provisions of the law include payroll transaction details such as time worked, pay dates, employee status, record reconciliation, and correlation of IRS reports and employee records. With regard to executive-level pay, the company must keep records of how the executive's pay was derived, including benchmarks from similar companies, payout period, and scheduled increases. All pay disbursed must be justified according to the amount and type of work performed, regardless of employee level or classification. A company's payroll and legal department should work closely to determine and implement a maintenance and record destruction program that complies with IRS requirements but avoids the inaccessibility of data that occurs with information overload.

© Danil Melekhin/E-plus/Getty Images, RF

Electronic Records

Many companies have moved to electronic, scanned copies of payroll records that allow immediate access to employee files from a password-protected format. In remote locations, payroll accountants can send the managers and employees Adobe files requiring a password to access pay records. Several data encryption programs are currently on the market allowing payroll managers to select the best fit for their individual company. All hard copies (i.e., paper versions) of payroll information must be in a locked file cabinet with limited access.

Computers have become a necessary part of business and offer significant benefits to the accounting department. Most accounting software for the preparation of payroll includes password requirements that the company can control, limiting access to electronic information about employees, pay, and personal information. Many regulatory agencies have addressed the issue of record security and safeguarding procedures; for example, the Food and Drug Administration enacted 21 CFR Part 11 that delineates electronic record security and safeguarding procedures.

Payroll accounting, according to the definition by the Internal Revenue Code, is a closed system because only certain employees are granted access to the information contained in the electronic records. All aspects of information security are the employer's responsibility, including access to, creation of, and maintenance of electronic personnel and pay records. Record identifiers would log who had accessed an electronic file, when, and from what location. Record logging provides an additional measure of security and protection against unauthorized access (also called "hacking") as well as tracking whether unauthorized changes occur on records.

> Ransomware is code placed into a computer system by hackers, aimed at obtaining a monetary fee to release access to a company's computerized information. The city of Plainfield, New Jersey, encountered ransomware that was downloaded onto the city's computer system during a city-related Internet search. According to the FBI, more than $24 million has been lost to hackers using ransomware. (Source: *The Washington Post*)

Like other payroll records, electronic records, especially those accessible over the Internet, must be safeguarded to prevent fraudulent activity and data corruption. Employers can provide access to information via a company's intranet (inside the organization) or via the Internet using encryption programs, passwords, and secured website locations. It is important to note that once a company has allowed Internet access to its payroll files, the company is opening itself up to additional risks from hacking or wrongful use of the payroll information. It is the payroll accountant's responsibility to report any suspicious activity to company managers or the information security department of the company.

Payroll as a Non-Solo Effort

One best practice is to have more than one person involved in the generation and maintenance of payroll records. Many errors can occur when the total payroll responsibility rests with one person. Errors that occur may be the result of a complex hacking effort or a simple failure to remove the system access from a former employee.

- Nonexistent or "ghost" employees could be created and paid via the payroll system. The person committing the fraud could circumvent the payroll system and divert the funds to himself or an accomplice.
- Terminated employees could continue to be paid via the payroll system, or the funds could be subverted to someone else perpetrating the fraud.
- Sales commission plans, employee bonus plans, incentive programs, and other arrangements intended to induce particular behaviors are subject to the employee's and management's manipulation.
- The payroll checks distributed to employees could be stolen individually or en masse prior to their distribution. In addition, check fraud could be perpetrated using actual checks or just the account information.
- The company's payroll system or payroll service provider could suffer a breach of the security protocols protecting the computer systems, which could allow any combination of fraud or theft to be perpetrated. (Source: *Houston Chronicle*)

Other instances of payroll fraud could have been avoided with a ***separation of duties***, which involves the division of related tasks to prevent fraud.

- A payroll worker, disgruntled with his job, stole almost $300,000 from different companies by transferring the organizations' money into different bank accounts that he owned.
- A former bookkeeper forged $80,000 in payroll checks before the company owner discovered the discrepancy.
- In the Los Angeles Unified School District, internal inspectors found that the pay system was issuing paychecks to deceased employees.
- In a recent audit of Department of Transportation records in Florida, the auditors found that the paper files supporting the payroll system had been discarded to make room in the office. The audit revealed overpayments to employees caused by an incorrect calculation and a lack of payroll verifications. Of the employees who were overpaid, only one returned the money.

Internal controls promote improved accuracy when more than one person is involved in payroll preparation and disbursement. A division of record maintenance, employee verification, and the spread of pay disbursement responsibilities among different employees, depending upon the size of the company, would prevent many of the preceding problems. This not only protects the employer from complaints and potential legal issues stemming from payroll anomalies, but also provides a level of protection and verification to employees. Auditors look for well-defined internal controls within organizations to ensure legal compliance and file integrity.

Document Retention Requirements

According to the IRS Regulation 26 CFR 1.6001, records pertaining to any financial transaction must remain available for ***payroll audit***, the inspection by regulating bodies, at all times. The purpose of the tax code is to maintain records for legal purposes in the event of the suspicion of fraudulent activity. IRS Regulation 26 CFR 1.6001 pertains to both manual and computerized records, including payroll records prepared by third-party sources. Both manual and electronic documents must be maintained in such a way that they maintain accessibility for the duration similar to tax record retention.

When a company institutes a retention schedule, the requirements of legislation and the IRS must be considered. The retention period does not begin until the disbursement of pay occurs or the employee terminates employment, whichever occurs last. Remember: In the event of fraudulent activity, retention requirements no longer apply, and all company records can be requested by the courts.

Companies must abide by both state and federal law regarding document retention. Employee payroll records, consisting of all forms and payroll compensation statements, must be retained for a period of seven years following *termination* or separation. Although no regulations exist for the retention and archiving of internal payroll documents (e.g., a *payroll register*), a general guideline is that the internal documents should be stored with the other payroll accounting records and destroyed in accordance with accounting record guidelines.

In 2012, the U.S. Supreme Court issued specific guidelines to the IRS about the statute of limitations for audits. In *U.S. v. Home Concrete Supply, LLC,* the Court directed the following guidelines about records audits:

- Three years to assess a taxpayer's deficiency.
- Six years if the taxpayer's gross assets were understated by more than 25%.
- Unlimited time if intent to commit fraud exists. (Source: www.supremecourt.gov)

The agencies that have the right to audit payroll records include:

- The Internal Revenue Service (IRS).
- Federal and State Departments of Labor.
- Department of Homeland Security.
- Other state and local agencies.
- Labor unions.

The following is a chart that explains federal record retention requirements, including relevant laws and types of documents. (Source: SHRM)

Payroll Records (time sheets, electronic records, etc.)	• 3-year retention period • An additional 5-year post-termination retention is recommended due to Lilly Ledbetter Act • Includes employee data, any pay records and all compensation, financial and nonfinancial
Employee Federal, State, and Local Tax Records	• 4 years from date the tax is due or paid • Includes all W-4s, state and local tax withholding forms, requests for additional tax withholding, and tax remittances
Form I-9 and Accompanying Employment Eligibility Documents	• 3 years after hire OR • 1 year after termination, whichever is longer
Employee Benefits and Contributions	• 6 years • All retirement plan contributions, plan changes, records pertaining to any other employee voluntary deductions
Health Plan Documentation	• No written guidelines, but a minimum of 6 years is recommended • All written notices about changes in health coverage, especially for health coverage after termination of employment

Even if your company outsources payroll activities, it is still accountable for all records and the information transmitted to the payroll service companies. The third-party payroll service provider attends only to the processing of company payroll but is not responsible for payroll tax payments. Tax remittance remains the liability of the company. Instances in which companies have diverted payroll tax liabilities for personal purposes have resulted in sizable fines and sanctions for companies.

Internal Controls and Audits

Stop & Check

1. Which of these is *not* a payroll internal control procedure?

   a. Overtime approval.

   b. Removal of payroll oversight.

   c. Cross-training.

   d. File security.

2. Which of these records should be retained in the event of a payroll audit?

   a. Employee medical records.

   b. Employee reviews.

   c. Employee time and work records.

   d. Employee nonpayroll correspondence.

LO 2-5 Discuss Employee Termination and Document Destruction Procedures

When employees are terminated, either voluntarily or involuntarily, the employer has payroll issues unique to the situation. The common element to each termination is the paperwork needed. When an employer terminates a worker's employment involuntarily, the burden of proof for the termination is on the employer, should the case ever require legal scrutiny.

In *Graziadio v. Culinary Institute of America* (2016), the plaintiff was terminated involuntarily after taking two consecutive three-week leaves to care for her children because the Culinary Institute of America claimed that Graziadio had not filed the required paperwork for leave under the FMLA. At first, the court ruled in favor of the Culinary Institute of America because the proper paperwork was not on file. However, further investigation found that the human resources director of the Culinary Institute of America, who refused to allow Graziadio to return to work, had not responded to Graziadio's numerous email requests for FMLA paperwork to justify her absence and to return to work. (Source: JD Supra Business Advisor)

©John Lund/Drew Kelly/Blend Images LLC, RF

Employee Termination

There are two different methods of separation of an employee from the company: termination and ***resignation***. When an employee leaves a company, the payroll accountant must complete several steps with regard to the employee's and the firm's records. The employee's final paycheck will be a culmination of hours worked, and possibly, depending on the company policies, vacation earned and not taken, and sick time earned and not taken. Depending on the company's policies, if the employee's compensation is commission based, there should be an agreement between management and the employee regarding sales and timing of the final paycheck to ensure payment of all earned commissions.

Final hours are calculated the same as for any normal pay period. The employee's daily hours are calculated to determine regular and overtime, and the week is added together to reach weekly hours and weekly overtime. If the employee earned any vacation or sick time, then those hours also need to be paid out on the final paycheck. Vacation and sick time are not included in the worked hours for the determination of overtime. No legislation exists that requires severance packages upon termination.

In terms of payroll accounting, the major difference between the termination and the resignation of an employee is the timing of the delivery of the final pay disbursement. When an employee quits, any compensation due will be processed and disbursed on the company's next scheduled pay date. However, when the employee is terminated, the company may be mandated to issue the final paycheck immediately or within a short time frame to comply with state labor laws. There is no federal regulation for the immediate issuance of the employee's final pay, although the Department of Labor explicitly mandates back pay owed to former employees. Table 2-2 contains information about states' employee termination pay guidelines.

TABLE 2-2
States' Termination Pay Guidelines

State	Guideline	State	Guideline
AL	No termination pay guidelines	MO	On the day of discharge or within seven days if employee requests pay to be mailed
AK	Within three business days	MT	Next regular payday or 15 days from termination, whichever is soonest
AZ	Within seven working days or the end of the next pay period, whichever is sooner	NE	Next pay or within two weeks, whichever is soonest
AR	Within seven days of discharge	NV	Immediately upon discharge
CA	At time of discharge	NH	Within 72 hours
CO	Immediately upon discharge	NJ	By the next regular payday
CT	No later than the next business day	NM	Within five days when wages are definite; otherwise within 10 days if wages are indefinite
DE	Next regularly scheduled payday	NY	Next regular payday
DC	No later than the day following discharge	NC	Next regular payday
FL	Next pay period	OH	Next regular payday
GA	No termination pay guidelines	OK	Next regular payday for the pay period
HI	At time of discharge unless conditions render pay impossible; next business day in that case	OR	First business day after discharge or termination
ID	Within 10 days, excluding weekends and holidays	PA	Next regular payday
IL	No later than the next payday, but immediately if possible	RI	Next regular payday
IN	Next regular payday	SC	Within 48 hours
IA	Next regular payday for the pay period	SD	Next regular payday or whenever the terminated employee returns all of the employer's property
KS	No later than the next regular payday	TN	Next regular payday or 21 days, whichever comes later
KY	Next regular payday or 14 days, whichever is sooner	TX	No later than six days after discharge
LA	Next regular payday or 15 days, whichever is sooner	UT	Within 24 hours

(continued)

TABLE 2-2   *(concluded)*

State	Guideline	State	Guideline
ME	Within a reasonable time after demand, either the next day or within two weeks	VT	Last regular payday or the following Friday if no regular payday exists
MD	Next regular payday	VA	On or before the next regular pay date
MA	Next regular payday or the following Saturday if no regular payday is scheduled	WA	Next regular payday
MI	Immediately upon severance after due diligence	WV	72 hours after demand or when wages become due under employment contract
MN	Within 24 hours of termination	WI	Next regular payday or monthly, whichever is sooner
MS	Next regular pay date	WY	Within five working days of termination date

(Source: www.bizfilings.com)

Document Destruction

Although many state and federal laws delineate the time requirement for document retention, there are also several methods for regulated ***document destruction*** of sensitive payroll data. How must these confidential documents be destroyed? It is not as simple as throwing old payroll documents in the trash. Preferred destruction methods of confidential payroll documents include incineration, confidential shredding services, or pulping of the paper records. Electronic records must be purged from the server. Although specific destruction procedures and regulations vary among states and localities, the basic guidelines of confidential destruction after the required retention period are common to most areas. From small-scale record destruction using in-office paper shredders to large-scale operations such as ProShred, Iron Mountain, and many other companies, destruction of confidential business documents is a serious concern because of the federal privacy laws governing payroll documents.

Destroy and Terminate

1. How should paper payroll records be destroyed? How about electronic records?

2. Charlie, a resident of Hawaii, is terminated without cause from his job on October 12. When must he receive his final pay? Is the employer required to pay him a severance package? Explain.

Trends to Watch

PAYROLL PROCEDURES

As we move further into the digital age, payroll procedures are changing to meet employer needs, technological availability, and employee accessibility. Some procedures that have changed during the early 2010s include the following:

- Affordable Care Act employer reporting requirements clarified.
- An increase in the use of Internet-based employee files, which requires increasingly sophisticated security software and company protocols.

- Increased "job swapping" that requires employees to be cross-trained and employers to consider compensation needs of different positions.
- An increase in the "virtual marketplace," in which employers and employees will telecommute or otherwise perform work from geographically dispersed locations.

Some trends to watch include the following:

- Deeper scrutiny of data security efforts aimed at preventing data breaches involving employee information.
- Specific guidelines regarding the classification of exempt and nonexempt employees, including a revised exempt employee minimum salary.
- Increased documenting of job leveling to improve equal pay efforts.
- Increased federal intervention in worker's compensation claims in response to states' reduction of worker's compensation award amounts.

Summary of Payroll System Procedures

The establishment of a payroll system involves careful planning and deliberation. The framework used for the payroll system needs to have enough room for company growth and enough structure to make sure that company and governmental deadlines are met. Using some of the best practices outlined in this chapter can help a company implement a robust payroll system, whether the system is maintained by company personnel or outsourced, completed manually or electronically with the use of specifically designed software. Adequate payroll system design can save a company from problems with employees and with governmental entities.

Although pay processes and methods vary among companies, the framework of internal review and the necessity for accuracy remain the fundamental aspects of any payroll system. Documentation of an employee's eligibility to work in the United States as well as compensation method, rates, tax liabilities, and voluntary withholdings are critical elements of employee files that the payroll accountant must maintain. The process of entering items into a payroll system varies depending on the type of work done and the compensation rates, for which the payroll accountant must have documentation. Depending on the company's preferences, anything from manual records to computerized records to external payroll vendors may be used to track the payroll. At employee termination, final pay must be issued, but the timing of that final pay depends on state legislation.

Payroll recordkeeping and maintenance are complex issues and subject to several federal and state regulations. Employee personal information must be safeguarded at all times, and information privacy is paramount. Now that many companies are resorting to electronic pay records, information safeguarding is especially important, and encryption efforts are multidimensional, involving the accounting, legal, and information systems departments of an organization. Destruction of payroll-related documents after the required retention period is a serious concern, and an entire industry focuses on document retention and destruction.

Key Points

- Communication protocol varies among companies and departments within companies.
- Ethical payroll practices require protection of information and dissemination only to the employee or specifically relevant supervisory staff.
- Control of the payroll system involves regular system design review and delineation of specific tasks.
- Payroll, whether completed internally or by an **outsourced vendor** (a payroll service external to the company), is only as accurate as the information provided.

- Pay periods are at the discretion of the company. The IRS has developed *tax tables* (withholding amounts) for each pay interval that are contained in **Publication 15**, an annual IRS guide to payroll.
- File security is of utmost importance, especially when files are stored electronically and accessed via an Internet portal.
- Documentation for payroll exceptions such as time away from work should be maintained separately from regular work time documentation.
- Calculations of pay can involve many variables and require review of each employee prior to pay issuance.
- Final pay needs to reflect all earned compensation, paid time off, and deductions up to the date of termination.
- The timing of final pay disbursement when an employee is terminated depends on state law.

Vocabulary

Biweekly payroll	Internal control	Resignation
Commission	Monthly payroll	Review process
Daily payroll	New hire reporting	Semimonthly payroll
Document destruction	Nonexempt	Separation of duties
Exempt	Outsourced vendor	Statutory employee
File maintenance	Pay period	Tax table
File security	Paycards	Termination
Foreign Account Tax	Payroll audit	W-4
Compliance Act	Payroll review	Weekly payroll
Hiring packet	Piece rate	
I-9	Publication 15	

Review Questions

1. What constitutes internal controls for a payroll department?

2. Why should more than one person prepare/verify payroll processing?

3. What documents should be included in all new-hire packets?

4. Why are new hires required to be reported to the state's employment department?

5. For the state in which you live, when must a terminated employee be paid his or her final paycheck?

6. What are the five main payroll frequencies?

7. What are some of the best practices in establishing a payroll system?

8. What are the important considerations in setting up a payroll system?

9. What are the different tasks involved in payroll accounting?

10. When does a payroll record retention period begin?

11. What agencies or organizations can audit a company's payroll records?

12. How long must employers keep terminated employee records?

13. Are independent contractors included in company payroll? Why or why not?

14. What is the difference between termination and resignation?

15. What is the difference among daily, weekly, biweekly, semimonthly, and monthly pay periods?

Exercises Set A

E2-1A.
LO 2-1, 2-3

Amanda, a nonexempt employee at Old Tyme Soda Distributing, works a standard 8:00–5:00 schedule with an hour for lunch each day. Amanda received overtime pay for hours in excess of 40 per week. During the week, she worked the following schedule:

Monday 8:00–11:00, 12:00–4:30
Tuesday 8:00–11:00, 12:00–5:15
Wednesday 8:00–11:00, 12:00–5:00
Thursday 8:30–5:00 (no lunch)
Friday 8:00–6:00 (no lunch)

How many hours of overtime did Amanda work this week?
1. 0 hours
2. 1.5 hours
3. 2 hours
4. 2.25 hours

E2-2A.
LO 2-1

Carlie receives her pay twice per month. Which of the following choices describes her pay frequency?
a. Biweekly
b. Semimonthly
c. Weekly
d. Monthly

E2-3A.
LO 2-2

Roberto is a new employee for McGee's Windows. Which federal forms must he complete as part of the hiring process?
1. W-4
2. W-2
3. SS-8
4. I-9

E2-4A.
LO 2-4, 2-5

Angela, a resident of Texas, ended her employment on December 8, 2016. The next pay date for the company is December 20. By what date should she receive her final pay?
1. December 8
2. December 14
3. December 20
4. December 31

E2-5A.
LO 2-4

Corey is a new nonexempt sales clerk for Cohen Real Estate. He completes his time card for the pay period. To ensure proper internal control, what is the next step in the payroll review process?
1. Submit the time card to the payroll clerk.
2. Have a friend check his math for accuracy.
3. Submit the time card to his manager for review.
4. Enter the time card data directly into the payroll system.

E2-6A.
LO 2-5

Jacob needs additional filing space at the end of the year in the company's offsite, secured storage. He sees several boxes of payroll records marked for the current year's destruction. What methods can Jacob use to dispose of the payroll records? (Select all that apply.)
1. Contact an offsite record destruction service.
2. Place the boxes containing the records in the company trash disposal.
3. Shred the records, and then dispose of the shredded paper.
4. Incinerate the payroll records marked for destruction.

E2-7A.
LO 2-1

Rachael is verifying the accuracy and amount of information contained in the employee records for her company. Which of the following items should be present in the employee information? (Select all that apply)

1. Job title
2. Social Security number
3. Birth date (if under 19)
4. Previous addresses

E2-8A.
LO 2-2

Camber is the payroll clerk for Multisound Speakers. A colleague who is classified as an independent contractor requests to be classified as an employee. What factors should Camber consider? (Select all that apply.)
1. Relationship of the parties.
2. Behavioral control.
3. Method of compensation.
4. Financial control.

E2-9A.
LO 2-2

What are the forms of identification that establish *identity* for the I-9? (Select all that apply.)
1. Driver's license.
2. Native American tribal document.
3. Voter registration card.
4. Social Security account card.

E2-10A.
LO 2-2

What are the forms of identification that establish **employment authorization** for the I-9? (Select all that apply.)
1. U.S. Citizen I.D. Card.
2. U.S. Passport.
3. School record.
4. Certified copy of the birth certificate.

Problems Set A

P2-1A.
LO 2-1

Jason is a salaried employee earning $75,000 per year. What is Jason's period pay for each of the following pay frequencies?
1. Biweekly
2. Semimonthly
3. Weekly
4. Monthly

P2-2A.
LO 2-2, 2-3

Jonathan is in the payroll accounting department of Moran Industries. An independent contractor of the company requests that Social Security and Medicare taxes be withheld from future compensation. What advice should Jonathan offer?

P2-3A.
LO 2-4

You are the new payroll supervisor for your company. Which payroll documentation control procedures are now your responsibility?

P2-4A.
LO 2-2

Naia is a new employee in the payroll department of Redtap Inc. After working at the company for one week, she asks you why it is so important to submit new hire documentation. What guidance will you offer her?

P2-5A.
LO 2-3, 2-4

You are the payroll accounting clerk for your company, which has 50 employees. The controller has asked for assistance in determining which accounting software package is best suited to the company's payroll needs. What factors should you consider in your decision?

P2-6A.
LO 2-2

Sue is a citizen of the Northern Pomo Indian Nation. In completing her I-9, she provides an official Northern Pomo Indian Nation birth certificate to establish identification and employment eligibility. Is this sufficient documentation? Why or why not?

P2-7A.
LO 2-3

The controller has requested your assistance to price various accounting software programs available for document retention, payroll preparation, and financial reporting. What requirements should you ensure are present in the computer program?

P2-8A.
LO 2-5

Large Laptops, a California corporation, has internal corporate requirements that stipulate a three-year payroll document retention period. They enter into a contract with an international company that mandates a six-year payroll document retention requirement. How should Large Laptops balance these requirements?

P2-9A.
LO 2-2

Manju is a full-time life insurance agent with a small insurance company. The company has classified her as an employee, and she feels that she should be classified as an independent contractor because she receives no company benefits and sets her own office hours. Should she be reclassified as an independent contractor? Why or why not?

P2-10A.
LO 2-2

Genevieve is an employee of Lux Lights, a company with headquarters in Providence, Rhode Island. She lives and works in Tillicoultry, Scotland, and earns an annual salary of $85,300. The company has been withholding U.S. federal income taxes from her pay, but Genevieve believes that she should be exempt because she is an expatriate. What course of action should Genevieve take?

P2-11A.
LO 2-2, 2-3

Complete the W-4 for employment at Bernie's Bar and Grill

Kierstan Amber Winter-Casey
542 Sole Point Road
Sitka, Alaska 99835
SSN: 988-65-3124
Single, head of household
Two dependents

She is eligible for the child tax credit because of her two allowances and an annual salary of $36,000. She is not claiming an additional amount to be withheld, nor is she claiming exemption from withholding. She has $1,500 annually in child care expenses.

P2-12A.
LO 2-2, 2-3

Complete the I-9 for employment at Excelsior College. Be sure to complete the "preparer" section.

Meaghan Ariel Lambert
Maiden name: Smith
Social Security number: 123-45-6789
Date of Birth: 7-1-1984
552 Coddington Road
Rio Nido, California 95555
U.S. Citizen

Meaghan presented her passport for her employer to review.

Passport number 5397816, issued by the United States State Department, expires 10/31/2018

Form W-4 (2016)

Purpose. Complete Form W-4 so that your employer can withhold the correct federal income tax from your pay. Consider completing a new Form W-4 each year and when your personal or financial situation changes.

Exemption from withholding. If you are exempt, complete **only** lines 1, 2, 3, 4, and 7 and sign the form to validate it. Your exemption for 2016 expires February 15, 2017. See Pub. 505, Tax Withholding and Estimated Tax.

Note: If another person can claim you as a dependent on his or her tax return, you cannot claim exemption from withholding if your income exceeds $1,050 and includes more than $350 of unearned income (for example, interest and dividends).

Exceptions. An employee may be able to claim exemption from withholding even if the employee is a dependent, if the employee:

• Is age 65 or older,

• Is blind, or

• Will claim adjustments to income; tax credits; or itemized deductions, on his or her tax return.

The exceptions do not apply to supplemental wages greater than $1,000,000.

Basic instructions. If you are not exempt, complete the **Personal Allowances Worksheet** below. The worksheets on page 2 further adjust your withholding allowances based on itemized deductions, certain credits, adjustments to income, or two-earners/multiple jobs situations.

Complete all worksheets that apply. However, you may claim fewer (or zero) allowances. For regular wages, withholding must be based on allowances you claimed and may not be a flat amount or percentage of wages.

Head of household. Generally, you can claim head of household filing status on your tax return only if you are unmarried and pay more than 50% of the costs of keeping up a home for yourself and your dependent(s) or other qualifying individuals. See Pub. 501, Exemptions, Standard Deduction, and Filing Information, for information.

Tax credits. You can take projected tax credits into account in figuring your allowable number of withholding allowances. Credits for child or dependent care expenses and the child tax credit may be claimed using the **Personal Allowances Worksheet** below. See Pub. 505 for information on converting your other credits into withholding allowances.

Nonwage income. If you have a large amount of nonwage income, such as interest or dividends, consider making estimated tax payments using Form 1040-ES, Estimated Tax for Individuals. Otherwise, you may owe additional tax. If you have pension or annuity income, see Pub. 505 to find out if you should adjust your withholding on Form W-4 or W-4P.

Two earners or multiple jobs. If you have a working spouse or more than one job, figure the total number of allowances you are entitled to claim on all jobs using worksheets from only one Form W-4. Your withholding usually will be most accurate when all allowances are claimed on the Form W-4 for the highest paying job and zero allowances are claimed on the others. See Pub. 505 for details.

Nonresident alien. If you are a nonresident alien, see Notice 1392, Supplemental Form W-4 Instructions for Nonresident Aliens, before completing this form.

Check your withholding. After your Form W-4 takes effect, use Pub. 505 to see how the amount you are having withheld compares to your projected total tax for 2016. See Pub. 505, especially if your earnings exceed $130,000 (Single) or $180,000 (Married).

Future developments. Information about any future developments affecting Form W-4 (such as legislation enacted after we release it) will be posted at *www.irs.gov/w4*.

Personal Allowances Worksheet (Keep for your records.)

A	Enter "1" for **yourself** if no one else can claim you as a dependent	**A** _____
B	Enter "1" if: { • You are single and have only one job; or • You are married, have only one job, and your spouse does not work; or • Your wages from a second job or your spouse's wages (or the total of both) are $1,500 or less. } . . .	**B** _____
C	Enter "1" for your **spouse.** But, you may choose to enter "-0-" if you are married and have either a working spouse or more than one job. (Entering "-0-" may help you avoid having too little tax withheld.)	**C** _____
D	Enter number of **dependents** (other than your spouse or yourself) you will claim on your tax return	**D** _____
E	Enter "1" if you will file as **head of household** on your tax return (see conditions under **Head of household** above) . .	**E** _____
F	Enter "1" if you have at least $2,000 of **child or dependent care expenses** for which you plan to claim a credit . . .	**F** _____
	(**Note:** Do **not** include child support payments. See Pub. 503, Child and Dependent Care Expenses, for details.)	
G	**Child Tax Credit** (including additional child tax credit). See Pub. 972, Child Tax Credit, for more information. • If your total income will be less than $70,000 ($100,000 if married), enter "2" for each eligible child; then **less** "1" if you have two to four eligible children or **less** "2" if you have five or more eligible children. • If your total income will be between $70,000 and $84,000 ($100,000 and $119,000 if married), enter "1" for each eligible child . .	**G** _____
H	Add lines A through G and enter total here. (**Note:** This may be different from the number of exemptions you claim on your tax return.) ▶	**H** _____

For accuracy, complete all worksheets that apply.	• If you plan to **itemize** or **claim adjustments to income** and want to reduce your withholding, see the **Deductions and Adjustments Worksheet** on page 2. • If you are **single and have more than one job** or are **married and you and your spouse both work** and the combined earnings from all jobs exceed $50,000 ($20,000 if married), see the **Two-Earners/Multiple Jobs Worksheet** on page 2 to avoid having too little tax withheld. • If **neither** of the above situations applies, **stop here** and enter the number from line H on line 5 of Form W-4 below.	

-------------------- **Separate here and give Form W-4 to your employer. Keep the top part for your records.** --------------------

W-4
Form
Department of the Treasury
Internal Revenue Service

Employee's Withholding Allowance Certificate

▶ **Whether you are entitled to claim a certain number of allowances or exemption from withholding is subject to review by the IRS. Your employer may be required to send a copy of this form to the IRS.**

OMB No. 1545-0074

2016

1 Your first name and middle initial	Last name	2 Your social security number
Home address (number and street or rural route)	3 ☐ Single ☐ Married ☐ Married, but withhold at higher Single rate.	
	Note: If married, but legally separated, or spouse is a nonresident alien, check the "Single" box.	
City or town, state, and ZIP code	4 If your last name differs from that shown on your social security card, check here. You must call 1-800-772-1213 for a replacement card. ▶ ☐	

5	Total number of allowances you are claiming (from line **H** above **or** from the applicable worksheet on page 2)	**5**	
6	Additional amount, if any, you want withheld from each paycheck	**6**	$
7	I claim exemption from withholding for 2016, and I certify that I meet **both** of the following conditions for exemption. • Last year I had a right to a refund of **all** federal income tax withheld because I had **no** tax liability, **and** • This year I expect a refund of **all** federal income tax withheld because I expect to have **no** tax liability. If you meet both conditions, write "Exempt" here . . . . ▶	**7**	

Under penalties of perjury, I declare that I have examined this certificate and, to the best of my knowledge and belief, it is true, correct, and complete.

Employee's signature
(This form is not valid unless you sign it.) ▶ _____   **Date** ▶ _____

8	Employer's name and address (Employer: Complete lines 8 and 10 only if sending to the IRS.)	9 Office code (optional)	10 Employer identification number (EIN)

For Privacy Act and Paperwork Reduction Act Notice, see page 2.   Cat. No. 10220Q   Form **W-4** (2016)

Employment Eligibility Verification

Department of Homeland Security
U.S. Citizenship and Immigration Services

USCIS
Form I-9
OMB No. 1615-0047
Expires 03/31/2016

▶**START HERE.** **Read instructions carefully before completing this form. The instructions must be available during completion of this form.**
ANTI-DISCRIMINATION NOTICE: It is illegal to discriminate against work-authorized individuals. Employers **CANNOT** specify which document(s) they will accept from an employee. The refusal to hire an individual because the documentation presented has a future expiration date may also constitute illegal discrimination.

Section 1. Employee Information and Attestation *(Employees must complete and sign Section 1 of Form I-9 no later than the **first day of employment**, but not before accepting a job offer.)*

Last Name *(Family Name)*	First Name *(Given Name)*	Middle Initial	Other Names Used *(if any)*

Address *(Street Number and Name)*	Apt. Number	City or Town	State	Zip Code

Date of Birth *(mm/dd/yyyy)*	U.S. Social Security Number	E-mail Address	Telephone Number
	☐☐☐-☐☐-☐☐☐☐		

I am aware that federal law provides for imprisonment and/or fines for false statements or use of false documents in connection with the completion of this form.

I attest, under penalty of perjury, that I am (check one of the following):

☐ A citizen of the United States

☐ A noncitizen national of the United States *(See instructions)*

☐ A lawful permanent resident (Alien Registration Number/USCIS Number): _____

☐ An alien authorized to work until (expiration date, if applicable, mm/dd/yyyy) _____ . Some aliens may write "N/A" in this field.
(See instructions)

For aliens authorized to work, provide your Alien Registration Number/USCIS Number **OR** *Form I-94 Admission Number:*

1. Alien Registration Number/USCIS Number:_____

OR

| 3-D Barcode |
| **Do Not Write in This Space** |

2. Form I-94 Admission Number: _____

If you obtained your admission number from CBP in connection with your arrival in the United States, include the following:

Foreign Passport Number: _____

Country of Issuance: _____

Some aliens may write "N/A" on the Foreign Passport Number and Country of Issuance fields. *(See instructions)*

Signature of Employee:	Date *(mm/dd/yyyy)*:

Preparer and/or Translator Certification *(To be completed and signed if Section 1 is prepared by a person other than the employee.)*

I attest, under penalty of perjury, that I have assisted in the completion of this form and that to the best of my knowledge the information is true and correct.

Signature of Preparer or Translator:	Date *(mm/dd/yyyy)*:

Last Name *(Family Name)*	First Name *(Given Name)*

Address *(Street Number and Name)*	City or Town	State	Zip Code

🛑 *Employer Completes Next Page* 🛑

Section 2. Employer or Authorized Representative Review and Verification

(Employers or their authorized representative must complete and sign Section 2 within 3 business days of the employee's first day of employment. You must physically examine one document from List A OR examine a combination of one document from List B and one document from List C as listed on the "Lists of Acceptable Documents" on the next page of this form. For each document you review, record the following information: document title, issuing authority, document number, and expiration date, if any.)

Employee Last Name, First Name and Middle Initial from Section 1:

List A Identity and Employment Authorization	OR	List B Identity	AND	List C Employment Authorization

List A	List B	List C
Document Title:	Document Title:	Document Title:
Issuing Authority:	Issuing Authority:	Issuing Authority:
Document Number:	Document Number:	Document Number:
Expiration Date *(if any)(mm/dd/yyyy)*:	Expiration Date *(if any)(mm/dd/yyyy)*:	Expiration Date *(if any)(mm/dd/yyyy)*:
Document Title:		
Issuing Authority:		
Document Number:		
Expiration Date *(if any)(mm/dd/yyyy)*:		
Document Title:		**3-D Barcode** **Do Not Write in This Space**
Issuing Authority:		
Document Number:		
Expiration Date *(if any)(mm/dd/yyyy)*:		

Certification

I attest, under penalty of perjury, that (1) I have examined the document(s) presented by the above-named employee, (2) the above-listed document(s) appear to be genuine and to relate to the employee named, and (3) to the best of my knowledge the employee is authorized to work in the United States.

The employee's first day of employment *(mm/dd/yyyy)*: _____ (*See instructions for exemptions.*)

Signature of Employer or Authorized Representative	Date *(mm/dd/yyyy)*	Title of Employer or Authorized Representative	
Last Name *(Family Name)*	First Name *(Given Name)*	Employer's Business or Organization Name	
Employer's Business or Organization Address *(Street Number and Name)*	City or Town	State	Zip Code

Section 3. Reverification and Rehires *(To be completed and signed by employer or authorized representative.)*

A. New Name *(if applicable)* Last Name *(Family Name)* First Name *(Given Name)*	Middle Initial	**B.** Date of Rehire *(if applicable) (mm/dd/yyyy)*:

C. If employee's previous grant of employment authorization has expired, provide the information for the document from List A or List C the employee presented that establishes current employment authorization in the space provided below.		
Document Title:	Document Number:	Expiration Date *(if any)(mm/dd/yyyy)*:

I attest, under penalty of perjury, that to the best of my knowledge, this employee is authorized to work in the United States, and if the employee presented document(s), the document(s) I have examined appear to be genuine and to relate to the individual.

Signature of Employer or Authorized Representative:	Date *(mm/dd/yyyy)*:	Print Name of Employer or Authorized Representative:

LISTS OF ACCEPTABLE DOCUMENTS
All documents must be UNEXPIRED

Employees may present one selection from List A
or a combination of one selection from List B and one selection from List C.

LIST A		LIST B		LIST C
Documents that Establish Both Identity and Employment Authorization	OR	**Documents that Establish Identity**	AND	**Documents that Establish Employment Authorization**

LIST A	LIST B	LIST C
1. U.S. Passport or U.S. Passport Card	1. Driver's license or ID card issued by a State or outlying possession of the United States provided it contains a photograph or information such as name, date of birth, gender, height, eye color, and address	1. A Social Security Account Number card, unless the card includes one of the following restrictions: (1) NOT VALID FOR EMPLOYMENT (2) VALID FOR WORK ONLY WITH INS AUTHORIZATION (3) VALID FOR WORK ONLY WITH DHS AUTHORIZATION
2. Permanent Resident Card or Alien Registration Receipt Card (Form I-551)		
3. Foreign passport that contains a temporary I-551 stamp or temporary I-551 printed notation on a machine-readable immigrant visa	2. ID card issued by federal, state or local government agencies or entities, provided it contains a photograph or information such as name, date of birth, gender, height, eye color, and address	2. Certification of Birth Abroad issued by the Department of State (Form FS-545)
4. Employment Authorization Document that contains a photograph (Form I-766)	3. School ID card with a photograph	3. Certification of Report of Birth issued by the Department of State (Form DS-1350)
5. For a nonimmigrant alien authorized to work for a specific employer because of his or her status: a. Foreign passport; and b. Form I-94 or Form I-94A that has the following: (1) The same name as the passport; and (2) An endorsement of the alien's nonimmigrant status as long as that period of endorsement has not yet expired and the proposed employment is not in conflict with any restrictions or limitations identified on the form.	4. Voter's registration card	4. Original or certified copy of birth certificate issued by a State, county, municipal authority, or territory of the United States bearing an official seal
	5. U.S. Military card or draft record	
	6. Military dependent's ID card	
	7. U.S. Coast Guard Merchant Mariner Card	5. Native American tribal document
	8. Native American tribal document	6. U.S. Citizen ID Card (Form I-197)
	9. Driver's license issued by a Canadian government authority	7. Identification Card for Use of Resident Citizen in the United States (Form I-179)
6. Passport from the Federated States of Micronesia (FSM) or the Republic of the Marshall Islands (RMI) with Form I-94 or Form I-94A indicating nonimmigrant admission under the Compact of Free Association Between the United States and the FSM or RMI	**For persons under age 18 who are unable to present a document listed above:** 10. School record or report card 11. Clinic, doctor, or hospital record 12. Day-care or nursery school record	8. Employment authorization document issued by the Department of Homeland Security

Illustrations of many of these documents appear in Part 8 of the Handbook for Employers (M-274).

Refer to Section 2 of the instructions, titled "Employer or Authorized Representative Review and Verification," for more information about acceptable receipts.

Exercises Set B

E2-1B.

LO 2-1, 2-3

Connie, a nonexempt employee of Westside Motel, works a standard 6:00–3:00 p.m. schedule with an hour for lunch. Connie works in a state requiring overtime for hours exceeding 8 per day and for those exceeding 40 in a week. During the week, she worked the following schedule:

Monday 6:00–10:30, 11:15–3:00
Tuesday 6:15–10:45, 11:45–3:15
Wednesday 5:45–10:00, 11:00–3:30
Thursday 7:00–12:00, 1:00–3:00
Friday 6:00–3:00 (no lunch)

Based on a 40-hour workweek, how much overtime has Connie worked during the period?
1. 2 hours
2. 0.5 hour
3. 1 hour
4. 1.5 hours

E2-2B.

LO 2-1

Paolo is a salaried employee earning $84,000 per year who receives pay every two weeks. Which of the following best describes the pay frequency?
a. Biweekly
b. Semimonthly
c. Weekly
d. Monthly

E2-3B.

LO 2-3, 2-5

On October 31, 2016, Terri quit her job after four years with Aspen Tree Service in Colorado. Aspen Tree Service pays employees weekly on Fridays. Upon quitting, Terri had 38.5 hours of vacation accrued that she had not used, and she had worked 45 hours, 5 hours of which was subject to overtime. When must she receive her final paycheck?
1. On the next pay date.
2. Within seven days.
3. Immediately upon discharge.
4. Whenever she demands it.

E2-4B.

LO 2-4, 2-5

Brad terminated his employment with Whiz Records on December 15, 2016. When is the earliest that Whiz Records may destroy his payroll records?
1. December 15, 2017
2. December 15, 2018
3. December 15, 2019
4. December 15, 2020

E2-5B.

LO 2-4

Zachary is a new payroll clerk at RC Imports, a company with 250 employees. He has completed entering all time card data for the pay period. What should Zachary's next step in the payroll review process be?
1. Ask employees to verify that the time Zachary entered is accurate.
2. Generate pay checks and prepare them for signature.
3. Ask his supervisor to verify the accuracy of the payroll data.
4. Have another payroll clerk verify the data accuracy.

E2-6B.

LO 2-4

Martin needs additional filing space at the end of the year in the company's office and chooses to use offsite, secured storage. Upon arriving at the storage facility, he discovers that the unit is nearly full and sees several boxes marked for destruction at the end of the next calendar year. What are Martin's options regarding the destruction of the payroll records marked for destruction? (Select all that apply.)
1. He should take the oldest year's boxes to the closest recycling facility.
2. He should make arrangements to pulp or burn the payroll records marked for destruction.

3. He should arrange to have a document destruction service pick up the boxes marked for destruction.
4. He should bring a shredding machine to the storage facility and prepare to shred the records marked for destruction.

E2-7B.

LO 2-1

Monika is conducting a review of the payroll files for each employee. Which of the following items must be present in the file? (Select all that apply.)
1. Basis upon which compensation is paid.
2. Overtime pay earned during each pay period.
3. Hours worked during each pay period.
4. Break times taken each day.

E2-8B.

LO 2-2

Kevin is preparing to compute employee pay and needs to determine the amount of employee federal income taxes to be withheld. Which of the following should he consult?
1. USCIS I-9
2. IRS Publication 15
3. DHS Schedule F
4. SSA Schedule 8

E2-9B.

LO 2-2

Embry is a new employee of the Peak House restaurant. Which of the following will provide proof of *identity* for the completion of the I-9? (Select all that apply.)
1. U.S. Passport.
2. U.S. Military Identification Card.
3. U.S. Citizen Identification Card.
4. Oklahoma driver's license.

E2-10B.

LO 2-2

Stephanie is completing the I-9 for her new employment at Pass Time Driving School. Which of the following provides proof of her employment authorization? (Select all that apply.)
1. Social Security Card.
2. Certificate of birth abroad, issued by the U.S. Department of State.
3. Idaho driver's license.
4. U.S. Passport.

Problems Set B

P2-1B.

LO 2-2

Sandy is an independent contractor for your company, where you are the payroll accountant. She feels that she should receive employee benefits because of the number of hours that she dedicates to the company. What guidance could you offer Sandy?

P2-2B.

LO 2-5

Frank was terminated for cause from Pineland Industries in Georgia, on August 21, 2016. As of the date of his termination, he had accrued 22 hours of regular time. Employees at Pineland are paid semimonthly on the 15th and last day of the month. Frank would like to know when he will be paid for the accrued hours. What will you tell him?

P2-3B.

LO 2-2

Quinn is a member of the Menominee Indian Nation and is a new employee at Raven Enterprises. During the process of completing his I-9, he claims that the only way to prove his identity is the Menominee Indian Nation official birth certificate. Is this document sufficient to prove identity for the purposes of the I-9? Why or why not?

P2-4B.

LO 2-2

Carol is a new employee of Eartheon Batteries. She is curious about the purpose of the requirements for new hire documentation to be forwarded to government agencies. What should you tell her?

P2-5B.

LO 2-1

Levon wants to start his own company. As a seasoned payroll professional, he approaches you for guidance about the differences between weekly, biweekly, and semimonthly pay periods. What would you tell him?

P2-6B.
LO 2-4

Helena is a new payroll clerk for Hope Sinks and Drains. She is curious about the purpose of the different steps in the payroll review process and asks you, her supervisor, for guidance. What would you tell her?

P2-7B.
LO 2-3

Pierre started as a payroll accountant at a company with 70 employees. He soon notices that the former payroll accountant had been processing payroll manually, and suggests that the company immediately switch to cloud-based payroll. Although the company is switching to an electronic payroll processing system, what types of paper documentation must be maintained in employee records?

P2-8B.
LO 2-4

Jiana, a payroll clerk, has received a promotion and is now the payroll supervisor for her company. What document control items could now become her responsibility?

P2-9B.
LO 2-2

You are in the payroll department of Yinkeng Imports, a multistate company. The company has historically been filing employee information with each state. What alternative exists for multistate employers?

P2-10B.
LO 2-1

Christianne is the payroll supervisor for PSN Freight. Her company is preparing to merge with another distribution company that has a different pay cycle. The president of the company wants to know the difference between biweekly and semimonthly pay cycles as far as pay dates and pay amounts. What should Christianne tell him?

P2-11B.
LO 2-2, 2-2

Complete the W-4 for employment at Dark Forest Ranch:

Madeline Emma Jenkins
203 County Road 4
Douglas, Wyoming 82036
SSN: 545-02-1987
Married filing jointly
Three dependents. She has no child care expenses but is able to claim the child tax credit and does not wish to withhold additional amounts.
She has a second job as a waitress at the Douglas Café, where she earns $12,000/year.

P2-12B.
LO 2-2, 2-3

Complete the I-9 for employment with the Tennessee Department of Corrections. Be sure to complete the "preparer" section.

Martin Allan Davis
Social Security number: 987-65-4312
Date of Birth: 5-29-1975
5923 Bunker Hill Road
Clarksville, Tennessee 38205
U.S. Citizen
Martin presented his driver's license and Social Security card for his employer to review.
Tennessee Driver's License #U30290688, Expires 5/29/2018

Critical Thinking

2-1. When BirMax was looking to implement a payroll accounting system, the manufacturing firm had several options. With only 40 employees, the manual preparation of payroll through spreadsheets and handwritten time cards was a comfortable option for the firm. Another option is to convince the senior management of BirMax to implement a software program for payroll processing. What are the key points to consider? If the company has more than one department, how can this transition be accomplished?

2-2. You have been hired as a consultant for a company facing an IRS audit of its accounting records. During your review, you notice anomalies in the payroll system involving overpayments of labor and payments to terminated employees. What would you do?

Form W-4 (2016)

Purpose. Complete Form W-4 so that your employer can withhold the correct federal income tax from your pay. Consider completing a new Form W-4 each year and when your personal or financial situation changes.

Exemption from withholding. If you are exempt, complete **only** lines 1, 2, 3, 4, and 7 and sign the form to validate it. Your exemption for 2016 expires February 15, 2017. See Pub. 505, Tax Withholding and Estimated Tax.

Note: If another person can claim you as a dependent on his or her tax return, you cannot claim exemption from withholding if your income exceeds $1,050 and includes more than $350 of unearned income (for example, interest and dividends).

Exceptions. An employee may be able to claim exemption from withholding even if the employee is a dependent, if the employee:

• Is age 65 or older,

• Is blind, or

• Will claim adjustments to income; tax credits; or itemized deductions, on his or her tax return.

The exceptions do not apply to supplemental wages greater than $1,000,000.

Basic instructions. If you are not exempt, complete the **Personal Allowances Worksheet** below. The worksheets on page 2 further adjust your withholding allowances based on itemized deductions, certain credits, adjustments to income, or two-earners/multiple jobs situations.

Complete all worksheets that apply. However, you may claim fewer (or zero) allowances. For regular wages, withholding must be based on allowances you claimed and may not be a flat amount or percentage of wages.

Head of household. Generally, you can claim head of household filing status on your tax return only if you are unmarried and pay more than 50% of the costs of keeping up a home for yourself and your dependent(s) or other qualifying individuals. See Pub. 501, Exemptions, Standard Deduction, and Filing Information, for information.

Tax credits. You can take projected tax credits into account in figuring your allowable number of withholding allowances. Credits for child or dependent care expenses and the child tax credit may be claimed using the **Personal Allowances Worksheet** below. See Pub. 505 for information on converting your other credits into withholding allowances.

Nonwage income. If you have a large amount of nonwage income, such as interest or dividends, consider making estimated tax payments using Form 1040-ES, Estimated Tax for Individuals. Otherwise, you may owe additional tax. If you have pension or annuity income, see Pub. 505 to find out if you should adjust your withholding on Form W-4 or W-4P.

Two earners or multiple jobs. If you have a working spouse or more than one job, figure the total number of allowances you are entitled to claim on all jobs using worksheets from only one Form W-4. Your withholding usually will be most accurate when all allowances are claimed on the Form W-4 for the highest paying job and zero allowances are claimed on the others. See Pub. 505 for details.

Nonresident alien. If you are a nonresident alien, see Notice 1392, Supplemental Form W-4 Instructions for Nonresident Aliens, before completing this form.

Check your withholding. After your Form W-4 takes effect, use Pub. 505 to see how the amount you are having withheld compares to your projected total tax for 2016. See Pub. 505, especially if your earnings exceed $130,000 (Single) or $180,000 (Married).

Future developments. Information about any future developments affecting Form W-4 (such as legislation enacted after we release it) will be posted at *www.irs.gov/w4*.

Personal Allowances Worksheet (Keep for your records.)

A	Enter "1" for **yourself** if no one else can claim you as a dependent	**A** _____
B	Enter "1" if: { • You are single and have only one job; or • You are married, have only one job, and your spouse does not work; or • Your wages from a second job or your spouse's wages (or the total of both) are $1,500 or less. } . . .	**B** _____
C	Enter "1" for your **spouse.** But, you may choose to enter "-0-" if you are married and have either a working spouse or more than one job. (Entering "-0-" may help you avoid having too little tax withheld.)	**C** _____
D	Enter number of **dependents** (other than your spouse or yourself) you will claim on your tax return	**D** _____
E	Enter "1" if you will file as **head of household** on your tax return (see conditions under **Head of household** above) . .	**E** _____
F	Enter "1" if you have at least $2,000 of **child or dependent care expenses** for which you plan to claim a credit . . .	**F** _____
	(**Note:** Do **not** include child support payments. See Pub. 503, Child and Dependent Care Expenses, for details.)	
G	**Child Tax Credit** (including additional child tax credit). See Pub. 972, Child Tax Credit, for more information.	
	• If your total income will be less than $70,000 ($100,000 if married), enter "2" for each eligible child; then **less** "1" if you have two to four eligible children or **less** "2" if you have five or more eligible children.	
	• If your total income will be between $70,000 and $84,000 ($100,000 and $119,000 if married), enter "1" for each eligible child . .	**G** _____
H	Add lines A through G and enter total here. (**Note:** This may be different from the number of exemptions you claim on your tax return.) ▶	**H** _____

For accuracy, complete all worksheets that apply.	{ • If you plan to **itemize** or **claim adjustments to income** and want to reduce your withholding, see the **Deductions and Adjustments Worksheet** on page 2. • If you are **single and have more than one job** or are **married and you and your spouse both work** and the combined earnings from all jobs exceed $50,000 ($20,000 if married), see the **Two-Earners/Multiple Jobs Worksheet** on page 2 to avoid having too little tax withheld. • If **neither** of the above situations applies, **stop here** and enter the number from line H on line 5 of Form W-4 below. }

--------- Separate here and give Form W-4 to your employer. Keep the top part for your records. ---------

---

Form W-4
Department of the Treasury
Internal Revenue Service

Employee's Withholding Allowance Certificate

▶ Whether you are entitled to claim a certain number of allowances or exemption from withholding is subject to review by the IRS. Your employer may be required to send a copy of this form to the IRS.

OMB No. 1545-0074

2016

1 Your first name and middle initial	Last name	2 Your social security number

Home address (number and street or rural route)	3 ☐ Single ☐ Married ☐ Married, but withhold at higher Single rate.
City or town, state, and ZIP code	**Note:** If married, but legally separated, or spouse is a nonresident alien, check the "Single" box. 4 If your last name differs from that shown on your social security card, check here. You must call 1-800-772-1213 for a replacement card. ▶ ☐

5	Total number of allowances you are claiming (from line **H** above **or** from the applicable worksheet on page 2)	**5** _____
6	Additional amount, if any, you want withheld from each paycheck	**6** $ _____
7	I claim exemption from withholding for 2016, and I certify that I meet **both** of the following conditions for exemption.	
	• Last year I had a right to a refund of **all** federal income tax withheld because I had **no** tax liability, **and**	
	• This year I expect a refund of **all** federal income tax withheld because I expect to have **no** tax liability.	
	If you meet both conditions, write "Exempt" here . . . . ▶	**7**

Under penalties of perjury, I declare that I have examined this certificate and, to the best of my knowledge and belief, it is true, correct, and complete.

Employee's signature
(This form is not valid unless you sign it.) ▶ _____ Date ▶ _____

8 Employer's name and address (Employer: Complete lines 8 and 10 only if sending to the IRS.)	9 Office code (optional)	10 Employer identification number (EIN)

For Privacy Act and Paperwork Reduction Act Notice, see page 2.   Cat. No. 10220Q   Form **W-4** (2016)

Employment Eligibility Verification

Department of Homeland Security
U.S. Citizenship and Immigration Services

USCIS
Form I-9
OMB No. 1615-0047
Expires 03/31/2016

▶**START HERE.** Read instructions carefully before completing this form. The instructions must be available during completion of this form.
ANTI-DISCRIMINATION NOTICE: It is illegal to discriminate against work-authorized individuals. Employers **CANNOT** specify which document(s) they will accept from an employee. The refusal to hire an individual because the documentation presented has a future expiration date may also constitute illegal discrimination.

Section 1. Employee Information and Attestation *(Employees must complete and sign Section 1 of Form I-9 no later than the **first day of employment**, but not before accepting a job offer.)*

Last Name (*Family Name*)	First Name (*Given Name*)	Middle Initial	Other Names Used (*if any*)

Address (*Street Number and Name*)	Apt. Number	City or Town	State	Zip Code

Date of Birth (*mm/dd/yyyy*)	U.S. Social Security Number	E-mail Address	Telephone Number
	☐☐☐-☐☐-☐☐☐☐		

I am aware that federal law provides for imprisonment and/or fines for false statements or use of false documents in connection with the completion of this form.

I attest, under penalty of perjury, that I am (check one of the following):

☐ A citizen of the United States

☐ A noncitizen national of the United States *(See instructions)*

☐ A lawful permanent resident (Alien Registration Number/USCIS Number): _____

☐ An alien authorized to work until (expiration date, if applicable, mm/dd/yyyy) _____ . Some aliens may write "N/A" in this field. *(See instructions)*

For aliens authorized to work, provide your Alien Registration Number/USCIS Number **OR** Form I-94 Admission Number:

1. Alien Registration Number/USCIS Number: _____

OR

2. Form I-94 Admission Number: _____

If you obtained your admission number from CBP in connection with your arrival in the United States, include the following:

Foreign Passport Number: _____

Country of Issuance: _____

Some aliens may write "N/A" on the Foreign Passport Number and Country of Issuance fields. *(See instructions)*

3-D Barcode
Do Not Write in This Space

Signature of Employee:	Date (*mm/dd/yyyy*):

Preparer and/or Translator Certification *(To be completed and signed if Section 1 is prepared by a person other than the employee.)*

I attest, under penalty of perjury, that I have assisted in the completion of this form and that to the best of my knowledge the information is true and correct.

Signature of Preparer or Translator:	Date (*mm/dd/yyyy*):

Last Name (*Family Name*)	First Name (*Given Name*)		

Address (*Street Number and Name*)	City or Town	State	Zip Code

🛑 *Employer Completes Next Page* 🛑

LISTS OF ACCEPTABLE DOCUMENTS
All documents must be UNEXPIRED

Employees may present one selection from List A
or a combination of one selection from List B and one selection from List C.

LIST A		LIST B		LIST C
Documents that Establish Both Identity and Employment Authorization	OR	Documents that Establish Identity	AND	Documents that Establish Employment Authorization

LIST A	LIST B	LIST C
1. U.S. Passport or U.S. Passport Card	1. Driver's license or ID card issued by a State or outlying possession of the United States provided it contains a photograph or information such as name, date of birth, gender, height, eye color, and address	1. A Social Security Account Number card, unless the card includes one of the following restrictions: (1) NOT VALID FOR EMPLOYMENT (2) VALID FOR WORK ONLY WITH INS AUTHORIZATION (3) VALID FOR WORK ONLY WITH DHS AUTHORIZATION
2. Permanent Resident Card or Alien Registration Receipt Card (Form I-551)		
3. Foreign passport that contains a temporary I-551 stamp or temporary I-551 printed notation on a machine-readable immigrant visa	2. ID card issued by federal, state or local government agencies or entities, provided it contains a photograph or information such as name, date of birth, gender, height, eye color, and address	
4. Employment Authorization Document that contains a photograph (Form I-766)		2. Certification of Birth Abroad issued by the Department of State (Form FS-545)
5. For a nonimmigrant alien authorized to work for a specific employer because of his or her status: a. Foreign passport; and b. Form I-94 or Form I-94A that has the following: (1) The same name as the passport; and (2) An endorsement of the alien's nonimmigrant status as long as that period of endorsement has not yet expired and the proposed employment is not in conflict with any restrictions or limitations identified on the form.	3. School ID card with a photograph 4. Voter's registration card 5. U.S. Military card or draft record 6. Military dependent's ID card 7. U.S. Coast Guard Merchant Mariner Card 8. Native American tribal document 9. Driver's license issued by a Canadian government authority	3. Certification of Report of Birth issued by the Department of State (Form DS-1350)
		4. Original or certified copy of birth certificate issued by a State, county, municipal authority, or territory of the United States bearing an official seal
		5. Native American tribal document
		6. U.S. Citizen ID Card (Form I-197)
	For persons under age 18 who are unable to present a document listed above:	7. Identification Card for Use of Resident Citizen in the United States (Form I-179)
6. Passport from the Federated States of Micronesia (FSM) or the Republic of the Marshall Islands (RMI) with Form I-94 or Form I-94A indicating nonimmigrant admission under the Compact of Free Association Between the United States and the FSM or RMI	10. School record or report card 11. Clinic, doctor, or hospital record 12. Day-care or nursery school record	8. Employment authorization document issued by the Department of Homeland Security

Illustrations of many of these documents appear in Part 8 of the Handbook for Employers (M-274).

Refer to Section 2 of the instructions, titled "Employer or Authorized Representative Review and Verification," for more information about acceptable receipts.

In the Real World: Scenario for Discussion

The Lilly Ledbetter Fair Pay Act of 2009 centered on a case in which Ms. Ledbetter discovered documents that revealed discrimination against her that resulted in unequal pay practices. The company argued that the documents were confidential and scheduled for destruction and that Ms. Ledbetter should not have had access to the information. What are the issues in this case in terms of document privacy and retention? How could the situation have been prevented in the first place?

Internet Activities

2-1. Using a search engine such as Google, Yahoo, or Bing, search the Internet for the term "new hire packet contents." Compile a list of the different new hire packet items that you find in at least three companies. What are some unique items that you found on the companies' lists?

2-2. Go to www.irs.gov and search for IRS e-file security. List the facts that the IRS cites about why e-filing is secure. What about these practices makes the customer's information secure? How could the IRS improve e-filing security?

2-3. Want to know more about some of the concepts discussed in this chapter? Check out:

www.uscis.gov

www.irs.gov/businesses

www.archives.gov/federal-register/cfr/subject-title-26.html

www.proshred.com

www.ironmountain.com

Continuing Payroll Project: Prevosti Farms and Sugarhouse

Prevosti Farms and Sugarhouse pays its employees according to their job classification. The following employees make up Sugarhouse's staff:

Employee Number	Name and Address	Payroll information
A-Mille	Thomas Millen 1022 Forest School Rd Woodstock, VT 05001 802-478-5055 SSN: 031-11-3456 401(k) deduction: 3%	Hire Date: 2-1-2016 DOB: 12-16-1982 Position: Production Manager PT/FT: FT, nonexempt No. of Exemptions: 4 M/S: M Pay Rate: $35,000/year
A-Towle	Avery Towle 4011 Route 100 Plymouth, VT 05102 802-967-5873 SSN: 089-74-0974 401(k) deduction: 5%	Hire Date: 2-1-2016 DOB: 7-14-1991 Position: Production Worker PT/FT: FT, nonexempt No. of Exemptions: 1 M/S: S Pay Rate: $12.00/hour
A-Long	Charlie Long 242 Benedict Road S. Woodstock, VT 05002 802-429-3846 SSN: 056-23-4593 401(k) deduction: 2%	Hire Date: 2-1-2016 DOB: 3-16-1987 Position: Production Worker PT/FT: FT, nonexempt No. of Exemptions: 2 M/S: M Pay Rate: $12.50/hour

Employee Number	Name and Address	Payroll information
B-Shang	Mary Shangraw 1901 Main Street #2 Bridgewater, VT 05520 802-575-5423 SSN: 075-28-8945 401(k) deduction: 3%	Hire Date: 2-1-2016 DOB: 8-20-1994 Position: Administrative Assistant PT/FT: PT, nonexempt No. of Exemptions: 1 M/S: S Pay Rate: $10.50/hour
B-Lewis	Kristen Lewis 840 Daily Hollow Road Bridgewater, VT 05523 802-390-5572 SSN: 076-39-5673 401(k) deduction: 4%	Hire Date: 2-1-2016 DOB: 4-6-1950 Position: Office Manager PT/FT: FT, exempt No. of Exemptions: 3 M/S: M Pay Rate: $32,000/year
B-Schwa	Joel Schwartz 55 Maple Farm Way Woodstock, VT 05534 802-463-9985 SSN: 021-34-9876 401(k) deduction: 5%	Hire Date: 2-1-2016 DOB: 5-23-1985 Position: Sales PT/FT: FT, exempt No. of Exemptions: 2 M/S: M Pay Rate: $24,000/year base plus 3% commission per case sold
B-Prevo	Toni Prevosti 10520 Cox Hill Road Bridgewater, VT 05521 802-673-2636 SSN: 055-22-0443 401(k) deduction: 6%	Hire Date: 2-1-2016 DOB: 9-18-1967 Position: Owner/President PT/FT: FT, exempt No. of Exemptions: 5 M/S: M Pay Rate: $45,000/year

The departments are as follows:

Department A: Agricultural Workers

Department B: Office Workers

1. You have been hired to start on February 1, 2016, as the new accounting clerk. Your employee number is B-XXXXX, where "B" denotes that you are an office worker and "XXXXX" is the first five letters of your last name. If your last name is fewer than five letters, use the first few letters of your first name to complete the employee number. Your Social Security number is 555-55-5555, and you are full-time, nonexempt, and paid at a rate of $34,000 per year. You have elected to contribute 2% of your gross pay to your 401(k). Complete the W-4 and the I-9 to start your own employee file. You are single with only one job (claiming two exemptions). You live at 1644 Smitten Road, Woodstock, VT 05001. Your phone number is (555) 555-5555. Your date of birth is 01/01/1991. You are a citizen of the United States and provide a Vermont driver's license #88110009 expiring 1/1/2018 in addition to your Social Security card for verification of your identity.

2. Complete the employee information form for each employee. Enter the pay rate earnings for each employee.

Form W-4 (2016)

Purpose. Complete Form W-4 so that your employer can withhold the correct federal income tax from your pay. Consider completing a new Form W-4 each year and when your personal or financial situation changes.

Exemption from withholding. If you are exempt, complete **only** lines 1, 2, 3, 4, and 7 and sign the form to validate it. Your exemption for 2016 expires February 15, 2017. See Pub. 505, Tax Withholding and Estimated Tax.

Note: If another person can claim you as a dependent on his or her tax return, you cannot claim exemption from withholding if your income exceeds $1,050 and includes more than $350 of unearned income (for example, interest and dividends).

Exceptions. An employee may be able to claim exemption from withholding even if the employee is a dependent, if the employee:

• Is age 65 or older,

• Is blind, or

• Will claim adjustments to income; tax credits; or itemized deductions, on his or her tax return.

The exceptions do not apply to supplemental wages greater than $1,000,000.

Basic instructions. If you are not exempt, complete the **Personal Allowances Worksheet** below. The worksheets on page 2 further adjust your withholding allowances based on itemized deductions, certain credits, adjustments to income, or two-earners/multiple jobs situations.

Complete all worksheets that apply. However, you may claim fewer (or zero) allowances. For regular wages, withholding must be based on allowances you claimed and may not be a flat amount or percentage of wages.

Head of household. Generally, you can claim head of household filing status on your tax return only if you are unmarried and pay more than 50% of the costs of keeping up a home for yourself and your dependent(s) or other qualifying individuals. See Pub. 501, Exemptions, Standard Deduction, and Filing Information, for information.

Tax credits. You can take projected tax credits into account in figuring your allowable number of withholding allowances. Credits for child or dependent care expenses and the child tax credit may be claimed using the **Personal Allowances Worksheet** below. See Pub. 505 for information on converting your other credits into withholding allowances.

Nonwage income. If you have a large amount of nonwage income, such as interest or dividends, consider making estimated tax payments using Form 1040-ES, Estimated Tax for Individuals. Otherwise, you may owe additional tax. If you have pension or annuity income, see Pub. 505 to find out if you should adjust your withholding on Form W-4 or W-4P.

Two earners or multiple jobs. If you have a working spouse or more than one job, figure the total number of allowances you are entitled to claim on all jobs using worksheets from only one Form W-4. Your withholding usually will be most accurate when all allowances are claimed on the Form W-4 for the highest paying job and zero allowances are claimed on the others. See Pub. 505 for details.

Nonresident alien. If you are a nonresident alien, see Notice 1392, Supplemental Form W-4 Instructions for Nonresident Aliens, before completing this form.

Check your withholding. After your Form W-4 takes effect, use Pub. 505 to see how the amount you are having withheld compares to your projected total tax for 2016. See Pub. 505, especially if your earnings exceed $130,000 (Single) or $180,000 (Married).

Future developments. Information about any future developments affecting Form W-4 (such as legislation enacted after we release it) will be posted at *www.irs.gov/w4*.

Personal Allowances Worksheet (Keep for your records.)

A	Enter "1" for **yourself** if no one else can claim you as a dependent	**A** _____
B	Enter "1" if: { • You are single and have only one job; or • You are married, have only one job, and your spouse does not work; or • Your wages from a second job or your spouse's wages (or the total of both) are $1,500 or less. } . . .	**B** _____
C	Enter "1" for your **spouse.** But, you may choose to enter "-0-" if you are married and have either a working spouse or more than one job. (Entering "-0-" may help you avoid having too little tax withheld.)	**C** _____
D	Enter number of **dependents** (other than your spouse or yourself) you will claim on your tax return	**D** _____
E	Enter "1" if you will file as **head of household** on your tax return (see conditions under **Head of household** above) . .	**E** _____
F	Enter "1" if you have at least $2,000 of **child or dependent care expenses** for which you plan to claim a credit . . .	**F** _____
	(**Note:** Do **not** include child support payments. See Pub. 503, Child and Dependent Care Expenses, for details.)	
G	**Child Tax Credit** (including additional child tax credit). See Pub. 972, Child Tax Credit, for more information. • If your total income will be less than $70,000 ($100,000 if married), enter "2" for each eligible child; then **less** "1" if you have two to four eligible children or **less** "2" if you have five or more eligible children. • If your total income will be between $70,000 and $84,000 ($100,000 and $119,000 if married), enter "1" for each eligible child . .	**G** _____
H	Add lines A through G and enter total here. (**Note:** This may be different from the number of exemptions you claim on your tax return.) ▶ **H**	_____

For accuracy, **complete all worksheets that apply.**	• If you plan to **itemize** or **claim adjustments to income** and want to reduce your withholding, see the **Deductions and Adjustments Worksheet** on page 2. • If you are **single and have more than one job** or are **married and you and your spouse both work** and the combined earnings from all jobs exceed $50,000 ($20,000 if married), see the **Two-Earners/Multiple Jobs Worksheet** on page 2 to avoid having too little tax withheld. • If **neither** of the above situations applies, **stop here** and enter the number from line H on line 5 of Form W-4 below.

--------------------------------- **Separate here and give Form W-4 to your employer. Keep the top part for your records.** ---------------------------------

---

Form W-4

Department of the Treasury
Internal Revenue Service

Employee's Withholding Allowance Certificate

▶ **Whether you are entitled to claim a certain number of allowances or exemption from withholding is subject to review by the IRS. Your employer may be required to send a copy of this form to the IRS.**

OMB No. 1545-0074

2016

1	Your first name and middle initial	Last name		2	Your social security number
	Home address (number and street or rural route)		3 ☐ Single ☐ Married ☐ Married, but withhold at higher Single rate. **Note:** If married, but legally separated, or spouse is a nonresident alien, check the "Single" box.		
	City or town, state, and ZIP code		4 If your last name differs from that shown on your social security card, check here. You must call 1-800-772-1213 for a replacement card. ▶ ☐		

5	Total number of allowances you are claiming (from line **H** above **or** from the applicable worksheet on page 2)	**5**	
6	Additional amount, if any, you want withheld from each paycheck	**6**	$
7	I claim exemption from withholding for 2016, and I certify that I meet **both** of the following conditions for exemption. • Last year I had a right to a refund of **all** federal income tax withheld because I had **no** tax liability, **and** • This year I expect a refund of **all** federal income tax withheld because I expect to have **no** tax liability. If you meet both conditions, write "Exempt" here . . . . ▶	**7**	

Under penalties of perjury, I declare that I have examined this certificate and, to the best of my knowledge and belief, it is true, correct, and complete.

Employee's signature
(This form is not valid unless you sign it.) ▶

Date ▶

8	Employer's name and address (Employer: Complete lines 8 and 10 only if sending to the IRS.)	9 Office code (optional)	10 Employer identification number (EIN)

For Privacy Act and Paperwork Reduction Act Notice, see page 2.

Cat. No. 10220Q

Form **W-4** (2016)

Employment Eligibility Verification

Department of Homeland Security
U.S. Citizenship and Immigration Services

USCIS
Form I-9
OMB No. 1615-0047
Expires 03/31/2016

▶**START HERE.** Read instructions carefully before completing this form. The instructions must be available during completion of this form.
ANTI-DISCRIMINATION NOTICE: It is illegal to discriminate against work-authorized individuals. Employers **CANNOT** specify which document(s) they will accept from an employee. The refusal to hire an individual because the documentation presented has a future expiration date may also constitute illegal discrimination.

Section 1. Employee Information and Attestation *(Employees must complete and sign Section 1 of Form I-9 no later than the* **first day of employment,** *but not before accepting a job offer.)*

Last Name *(Family Name)*	First Name *(Given Name)*	Middle Initial	Other Names Used *(if any)*

Address *(Street Number and Name)*	Apt. Number	City or Town	State	Zip Code

Date of Birth *(mm/dd/yyyy)*	U.S. Social Security Number	E-mail Address	Telephone Number
	☐☐☐-☐☐-☐☐☐☐		

I am aware that federal law provides for imprisonment and/or fines for false statements or use of false documents in connection with the completion of this form.

I attest, under penalty of perjury, that I am (check one of the following):

☐ A citizen of the United States

☐ A noncitizen national of the United States *(See instructions)*

☐ A lawful permanent resident (Alien Registration Number/USCIS Number): _____

☐ An alien authorized to work until (expiration date, if applicable, mm/dd/yyyy) _____ . Some aliens may write "N/A" in this field. *(See instructions)*

For aliens authorized to work, provide your Alien Registration Number/USCIS Number **OR** Form I-94 Admission Number:

1. Alien Registration Number/USCIS Number: _____

OR

2. Form I-94 Admission Number: _____

If you obtained your admission number from CBP in connection with your arrival in the United States, include the following:

Foreign Passport Number: _____

Country of Issuance: _____

Some aliens may write "N/A" on the Foreign Passport Number and Country of Issuance fields. *(See instructions)*

3-D Barcode
Do Not Write in This Space

Signature of Employee:	Date *(mm/dd/yyyy)*:

Preparer and/or Translator Certification *(To be completed and signed if Section 1 is prepared by a person other than the employee.)*

I attest, under penalty of perjury, that I have assisted in the completion of this form and that to the best of my knowledge the information is true and correct.

Signature of Preparer or Translator:	Date *(mm/dd/yyyy)*:

Last Name *(Family Name)*	First Name *(Given Name)*		

Address *(Street Number and Name)*	City or Town	State	Zip Code

STOP   *Employer Completes Next Page*   **STOP**

Section 2. Employer or Authorized Representative Review and Verification

(Employers or their authorized representative must complete and sign Section 2 within 3 business days of the employee's first day of employment. You must physically examine one document from List A OR examine a combination of one document from List B and one document from List C as listed on the "Lists of Acceptable Documents" on the next page of this form. For each document you review, record the following information: document title, issuing authority, document number, and expiration date, if any.)

Employee Last Name, First Name and Middle Initial from Section 1:

List A Identity and Employment Authorization	OR	List B Identity	AND	List C Employment Authorization
Document Title:		Document Title:		Document Title:
Issuing Authority:		Issuing Authority:		Issuing Authority:
Document Number:		Document Number:		Document Number:
Expiration Date *(if any)(mm/dd/yyyy)*:		Expiration Date *(if any)(mm/dd/yyyy)*:		Expiration Date *(if any)(mm/dd/yyyy)*:
Document Title:				
Issuing Authority:				
Document Number:				
Expiration Date *(if any)(mm/dd/yyyy)*:				
Document Title:				**3-D Barcode Do Not Write in This Space**
Issuing Authority:				
Document Number:				
Expiration Date *(if any)(mm/dd/yyyy)*:				

Certification

I attest, under penalty of perjury, that (1) I have examined the document(s) presented by the above-named employee, (2) the above-listed document(s) appear to be genuine and to relate to the employee named, and (3) to the best of my knowledge the employee is authorized to work in the United States.

The employee's first day of employment *(mm/dd/yyyy)*: _____ *(See instructions for exemptions.)*

Signature of Employer or Authorized Representative	Date *(mm/dd/yyyy)*	Title of Employer or Authorized Representative		
Last Name *(Family Name)*	First Name *(Given Name)*	Employer's Business or Organization Name		
Employer's Business or Organization Address *(Street Number and Name)*	City or Town		State	Zip Code

Section 3. Reverification and Rehires *(To be completed and signed by employer or authorized representative.)*

A. New Name *(if applicable)* Last Name *(Family Name)* First Name *(Given Name)*		Middle Initial	B. Date of Rehire *(if applicable) (mm/dd/yyyy)*:

C. If employee's previous grant of employment authorization has expired, provide the information for the document from List A or List C the employee presented that establishes current employment authorization in the space provided below.

Document Title:	Document Number:	Expiration Date *(if any)(mm/dd/yyyy)*:

I attest, under penalty of perjury, that to the best of my knowledge, this employee is authorized to work in the United States, and if the employee presented document(s), the document(s) I have examined appear to be genuine and to relate to the individual.

Signature of Employer or Authorized Representative:	Date *(mm/dd/yyyy)*:	Print Name of Employer or Authorized Representative:

LISTS OF ACCEPTABLE DOCUMENTS
All documents must be UNEXPIRED

Employees may present one selection from List A
or a combination of one selection from List B and one selection from List C.

LIST A **Documents that Establish Both Identity and Employment Authorization**	LIST B **Documents that Establish Identity**	LIST C **Documents that Establish Employment Authorization**
OR		AND
1. U.S. Passport or U.S. Passport Card	1. Driver's license or ID card issued by a State or outlying possession of the United States provided it contains a photograph or information such as name, date of birth, gender, height, eye color, and address	1. A Social Security Account Number card, unless the card includes one of the following restrictions: (1) NOT VALID FOR EMPLOYMENT (2) VALID FOR WORK ONLY WITH INS AUTHORIZATION (3) VALID FOR WORK ONLY WITH DHS AUTHORIZATION
2. Permanent Resident Card or Alien Registration Receipt Card (Form I-551)		
3. Foreign passport that contains a temporary I-551 stamp or temporary I-551 printed notation on a machine-readable immigrant visa	2. ID card issued by federal, state or local government agencies or entities, provided it contains a photograph or information such as name, date of birth, gender, height, eye color, and address	
4. Employment Authorization Document that contains a photograph (Form I-766)		2. Certification of Birth Abroad issued by the Department of State (Form FS-545)
	3. School ID card with a photograph	3. Certification of Report of Birth issued by the Department of State (Form DS-1350)
5. For a nonimmigrant alien authorized to work for a specific employer because of his or her status: a. Foreign passport; and b. Form I-94 or Form I-94A that has the following: (1) The same name as the passport; and (2) An endorsement of the alien's nonimmigrant status as long as that period of endorsement has not yet expired and the proposed employment is not in conflict with any restrictions or limitations identified on the form.	4. Voter's registration card	
	5. U.S. Military card or draft record	4. Original or certified copy of birth certificate issued by a State, county, municipal authority, or territory of the United States bearing an official seal
	6. Military dependent's ID card	
	7. U.S. Coast Guard Merchant Mariner Card	
	8. Native American tribal document	5. Native American tribal document
	9. Driver's license issued by a Canadian government authority	6. U.S. Citizen ID Card (Form I-197)
	For persons under age 18 who are unable to present a document listed above:	7. Identification Card for Use of Resident Citizen in the United States (Form I-179)
6. Passport from the Federated States of Micronesia (FSM) or the Republic of the Marshall Islands (RMI) with Form I-94 or Form I-94A indicating nonimmigrant admission under the Compact of Free Association Between the United States and the FSM or RMI	10. School record or report card	8. Employment authorization document issued by the Department of Homeland Security
	11. Clinic, doctor, or hospital record	
	12. Day-care or nursery school record	

Illustrations of many of these documents appear in Part 8 of the Handbook for Employers (M-274).

Refer to Section 2 of the instructions, titled "Employer or Authorized Representative Review and Verification," for more information about acceptable receipts.

EMPLOYEE EARNINGS RECORD

NAME		Hire Date	
ADDRESS		Date of Birth	
CITY/STATE/ZIP		Position	PT/FT
TELEPHONE		No. of exemptions	M/S
SOCIAL SECURITY NUMBER		Pay Rate	Hr/Wk/Mo

Period Ended	Hrs. Worked	Reg Pay	OT Pay	Gross Pay	Social Sec. Tax	Medicare	Fed Inc. Tax	State Inc. Tax	SDI	401(k)	Other	Total Deductions	Net pay	YTD

EMPLOYEE EARNINGS RECORD

NAME	Thomas Millen	Hire Date	
ADDRESS		Date of Birth	
CITY/STATE/ZIP		Position	PT/FT
TELEPHONE		No. of exemptions	M/S
SOCIAL SECURITY NUMBER		Pay Rate	Hr/Wk/Mo

Period Ended	Hrs. Worked	Reg Pay	OT Pay	Gross Pay	Social Sec. Tax	Medicare	Fed Inc. Tax	State Inc. Tax	SDI	401(k)	Other	Total Deductions	Net pay	YTD

EMPLOYEE EARNINGS RECORD

NAME	Avery Towle	Hire Date	
ADDRESS		Date of Birth	
CITY / STATE / ZIP		Position	PT/FT
TELEPHONE		No. of exemptions	M/S
SOCIAL SECURITY NUMBER		Pay Rate	Hr/Wk/Mo

Period Ended	Hrs. Worked	Reg Pay	OT Pay	Gross Pay	Social Sec. Tax	Medicare	Fed Inc. Tax	State Inc. Tax	SDI	401(k)	Other	Total Deductions	Net pay	YTD

EMPLOYEE EARNINGS RECORD

NAME	Charlie Long	Hire Date	
ADDRESS		Date of Birth	
CITY / STATE / ZIP		Position	PT/FT
TELEPHONE		No. of exemptions	M/S
SOCIAL SECURITY NUMBER		Pay Rate	Hr/Wk/Mo

Period Ended	Hrs. Worked	Reg Pay	OT Pay	Gross Pay	Social Sec. Tax	Medicare	Fed Inc. Tax	State Inc. Tax	SDI	401(k)	Other	Total Deductions	Net pay	YTD

EMPLOYEE EARNINGS RECORD

NAME	Mary Shangraw	Hire Date	
ADDRESS		Date of Birth	
CITY/STATE/ZIP		Position	PT/FT
TELEPHONE		No. of exemptions	M/S
SOCIAL SECURITY NUMBER		Pay Rate	Hr/Wk/Mo

Period Ended	Hrs. Worked	Reg Pay	OT Pay	Gross Pay	Social Sec. Tax	Medicare	Fed Inc. Tax	State Inc. Tax	SDI	401(k)	Other	Total Deductions	Net pay	YTD

EMPLOYEE EARNINGS RECORD

NAME	Kristen Lewis	Hire Date	
ADDRESS		Date of Birth	
CITY/STATE/ZIP		Position	PT/FT
TELEPHONE		No. of exemptions	M/S
SOCIAL SECURITY NUMBER		Pay Rate	Hr/Wk/Mo

Period Ended	Hrs. Worked	Reg Pay	OT Pay	Gross Pay	Social Sec. Tax	Medicare	Fed Inc. Tax	State Inc. Tax	SDI	401(k)	Other	Total Deductions	Net pay	YTD

EMPLOYEE EARNINGS RECORD

NAME   Joel Schwartz   Hire Date

ADDRESS   Date of Birth

CITY/STATE/ZIP   Position   PT/FT

TELEPHONE   No. of exemptions   M/S

SOCIAL SECURITY NUMBER   Pay Rate   Hr/Wk/Mo

Period Ended	Hrs. Worked	Reg Pay	OT Pay	Gross Pay	Social Sec. Tax	Medicare	Fed Inc. Tax	State Inc. Tax	SDI	401(k)	Other	Total Deductions	Net pay	YTD

EMPLOYEE EARNINGS RECORD

NAME   Toni Prevosti   Hire Date

ADDRESS   Date of Birth

CITY/STATE/ZIP   Position   PT/FT

TELEPHONE   No. of exemptions   M/S

SOCIAL SECURITY NUMBER   Pay Rate   Hr/Wk/Mo

Period Ended	Hrs. Worked	Reg Pay	OT Pay	Gross Pay	Social Sec. Tax	Medicare	Fed Inc. Tax	State Inc. Tax	SDI	401(k)	Other	Total Deductions	Net pay	YTD

Answers to Stop & Check Exercises

What's in the File?

1. a, b, d, e
2. b
3. d
4. a
5. c

Who Are You?

1. Student answers will vary. One possible way to prove both identity and employment is a current U.S. passport. Alternatively, a current state-issued driver's license and a Social Security card will work for the purposes of the I-9.
2. Student answers will vary. Many students may underestimate their estimated exemptions.

Worker Facts

1. Nonexempt.
2. Exempt workers receive a fixed amount of money and generally direct the actions of other employees; nonexempt workers are eligible for overtime and generally have their work directed by a manager.
3. Commission workers are typically tied to sales completed by the individual; piece-rate pay is determined by the number of pieces the employee completes during a shift or period.

Who Does Which Job?

Student answers will vary. The answer should reflect a clear separation of duties, cross-training, rotation of tasks, and security protocols.

Internal Controls and Audits

1. b
2. c

Destroy and Terminate

1. Paper payroll records should be shredded or burned. Computer records should be purged from the server and all other storage devices.
2. Charlie should receive his final pay on October 12, and no later than October 13. His employer is not required to provide him with a severance package, although he may be eligible for his accrued vacation pay.

Chapter Three

Gross Pay Computation

Two important terms in payroll accounting are gross pay and net pay. **Gross pay** is the amount of wages earned before deducting amounts for taxes or other deductions. **Net pay** is the amount of money the employee actually receives in a paycheck, after all taxes and other deductions have been subtracted. In this chapter, we will focus on computing gross pay.

The calculation of an employee's gross pay is the first step for payroll processing. Employee pay may be calculated in different ways. **Hourly** employees are paid for each hour, or fraction thereof, that they work in a given day. Salaried employees are broken into two classifications, based on FLSA classification: **exempt** and **nonexempt**. Salaried exempt employees receive pay based on the job they perform, regardless of the number of hours it takes. Salaried nonexempt employees may receive both **salary** and **overtime**. Another class of employees work on a **commission** basis, which means that some or all of their wages are based on sales revenue. Commission-based employees receive wages only when they complete sales or perform duties, outlined in their employment contract, that qualify them for a commission. A final classification is **piece-rate** employees. Typically found in manufacturing environments, employees are paid based upon the number of pieces completed during a work shift. Production reports are required and authorized by a supervisor as accurate, and the compensation per piece is calculated based in part on the labor dedicated to a specific job.

LEARNING OBJECTIVES

After studying Chapter 3, you should be able to:

LO 3-1   Analyze Minimum Wage Pay for Nonexempt Workers

LO 3-2   Compute Gross Pay for Different Pay Bases

LO 3-3   Calculate Pay Based on Hours and Fractions of Hours

LO 3-4   Create a Payroll Register

LO 3-5   Apply Combination Pay Methods

LO 3-6   Explain Special Pay Situations

© Ryan McVay/Getty Images, RF

The Minimum Wage Controversy: What Constitutes a Living Wage?

The idea of establishing a minimum wage for workers began in New Zealand in 1896. In the United States, minimum wage laws existed in various states but were not federally mandated until the passing of the Fair Labor Standards Act of 1938, which set the minimum wage at 40 cents per hour. The minimum wage has been raised over time, but many parties, including labor unions, contend that the current federal minimum wage of $7.25 is too low for workers to support their families. Opponents of the minimum wage laws maintain that legislation of a mandatory minimum wage leads to overpayment of workers for the level of service they provide a company.

In 2015, more than 1.25 million wage-based workers earned the federal minimum wage. As of 2016, 17 states either have increased or will increase their minimum wages. Additionally, several cities and companies have adopted a significantly higher minimum wage. (Source: U.S. Department of Labor, *Opposing Viewpoints in Context*)

Employee pay is the focus of Chapter 3. We will examine different bases for gross pay computations and how these compensation bases differ.

LO 3-1 Analyze Minimum Wage Pay for Nonexempt Workers

Two primary classifications of employees exist: exempt and nonexempt. These classifications refer to the provisions of the Fair Labor Standards Act (FLSA). The FLSA provisions protect nonexempt employees, including clerical, factory, and other nonmanagerial employees. Nonexempt employees are operative workers whose workdays may vary in duration, whose tasks do not meet the U.S. Department of Labor guidelines for exempt employees, and who do not generally have supervisory or managerial duties. Exempt employees include employees who meet U.S. Department of Labor guidelines for exempt classification, which includes job titles such as Department Supervisor or Warehouse Manager.

© Creatas/Getty Images

For hourly workers, FLSA contains wage provisions that stipulate the *minimum wage* an employer may pay an employee. However, the law exempts some employers from the minimum-wage requirements. According to the U.S. Department of Labor, the following conditions exempt an employer from paying the federal minimum wage:

- Firms that do not engage in interstate commerce as part of their business production.
- Firms with less than $500,000 of annual business volume.

Certain firms are covered by the FLSA provisions, regardless of their participation in interstate commerce or annual business volume. These businesses include hospitals, schools for mentally or physically disabled or gifted children, preschools, schools of any level, and governmental agencies. Under FLSA section 3(y), law enforcement and fire protection employees may have specified work periods ranging from 7 to 28 days, during which employees would be paid for overtime only after a predefined number of working hours.

FLSA was modified in 1974 to include explicit provisions about domestic workers. Since 1974, minimum-wage provisions cover domestic service workers, such as nannies and chauffeurs, who earn more than $1,700 in wages annually. Note that the 1974 modification specifically excluded occasional babysitters and employees who provide domestic companion services for the elderly. In 2015, the U.S. Congress further amended FLSA to include caregivers and other direct care employees who provide in-home companionship services.

Minimum Wage

An important consideration with the minimum wage provision of the FLSA is the existence of separate tiers of minimum wage. Wages for *tipped employees* are lower than those of nontipped employees. Federal wage and hour laws as of 2016 stipulate a federal minimum wage of $7.25 and a minimum hourly wage of $2.13 for tipped employees. States may enact additional minimum wage laws to address the specific economic needs of their population. This minimizes the legislative need to continually revisit the minimum wage. For example, the District of Columbia declared its minimum wage to be $10.50. Many other states have minimum wage rates that are higher than the federal minimum wage.

As of 2016, there were 10 states (AZ, CO, FL, MO, MT, NJ, NV, OH, OR, and WA) that had tied their minimum wage to the consumer price index. A map depicting minimum wage changes for 2016 is shown in Figure 3-1, and the details of specific minimum wage rates are shown in Table 3-1. Some examples involving different minimum wages follow. Note that a few states have a minimum wage that is less than the FLSA minimum wage. These lower minimum wages may be paid by employers who are not subject to FLSA provisions because they do not conduct interstate commerce.

FIGURE 3-1
Minimum Wage Hourly Rates for 2016

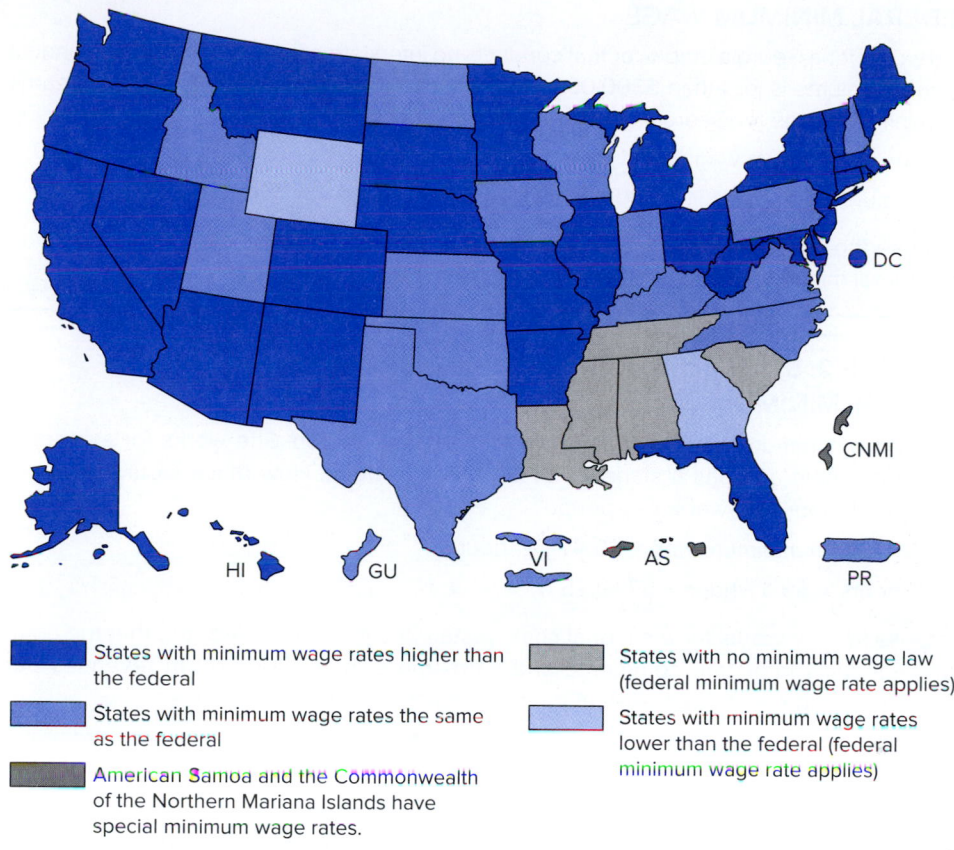

States with minimum wage rates higher than the federal

States with minimum wage rates the same as the federal

American Samoa and the Commonwealth of the Northern Mariana Islands have special minimum wage rates.

States with no minimum wage law (federal minimum wage rate applies)

States with minimum wage rates lower than the federal (federal minimum wage rate applies)

Source: U.S. Department of Labor, 2016

TABLE 3-1
Minimum Wage Hourly Rates by State

AK	$9.75	**IA**	$7.25	**MS**	None**	**PA**	$7.25
AL	None**	**ID**	$7.25	**MT**	$8.05*	**RI**	$9.60
AR	$8.00	**IL**	$8.25	**NC**	$7.25	**SC**	None**
AZ	$8.05	**IN**	$7.25	**ND**	$7.25	**SD**	$8.55
CA	$10.00*	**KS**	$7.25	**NE**	$9.00	**TN**	None**
CO	$8.31	**KY**	$7.25	**NH**	$7.25	**TX**	$7.25
CT	$9.60	**LA**	None**	**NJ**	$8.38	**UT**	$7.25
DC	$10.50	**MA**	$10.00	**NM**	$7.50	**VA**	$7.25
DE	$8.25	**MD**	$8.75	**NV**	$8.25*	**VT**	$9.60
FL	$8.05	**ME**	$7.50	**NY**	$9.00*	**WA**	$9.47*
GA	$5.15	**MI**	$8.50	**OH**	$8.10*	**WI**	$7.25
HI	$8.50	**MN**	$9.50*	**OK**	$7.25*	**OR**	$9.25
		MO	$7.65	**OR**	$9.25	**WY**	$5.15

*Variances exist depending on metropolitan area, business size, or employee benefits availability. Be sure to check with the state revenue department for specific metropolitan areas and businesses.
**In states with no minimum wage mandate, the federal minimum wage prevails.
Source: U.S. Department of Labor, 2016

EXAMPLE 1: STATE MINIMUM WAGE LOWER THAN FEDERAL MINIMUM WAGE

Don works for a Georgia employer that conducts no interstate commerce and whose annual business volume is less than $300,000. He is a janitor in a manufacturing plant and earns the minimum wage for Georgia. How much would he earn for a 40-hours pay period?

Georgia minimum wage: $5.15 per hour

40 hours × $5.15/hour = $206

Because the employer does not meet the requirements that would force it to pay Don the federal minimum wage, it may pay the state's minimum wage.

EXAMPLE 2: STATE MINIMUM WAGE HIGHER THAN FEDERAL MINIMUM WAGE

Wendy is a minimum wage worker in the state of Washington. She works for a national restaurant chain and has a standard 37.5 hour workweek. How much would she earn during a 75-hour, two-week pay period?

Washington minimum wage: $9.47 per hour

75 hours × $9.47/hour = $710.25

Because Wendy works for a national chain restaurant, it is safe to assume that the company conducts interstate commerce and earns more than $500,000 in revenues per year. She would be compensated at the state minimum wage in any case.

Tipped Employees

Workers in professions such as waiters, waitresses, bartenders, food service workers, and some hotel service personnel may receive an hourly wage less than the minimum wage rates listed in Table 3-1. The rationale for the decreased minimum wage is that these employees have the opportunity to earn tips from patrons of the establishments as a regular part of their employment. The federal minimum wage for tipped employees is $2.13 per hour; however, many states have different regulations about how much the employee must earn in tips to meet federal wage and hour laws.

The difference between the tipped employee minimum wage and the federal minimum wage is known as the *tip credit*. Federal wage and hour laws mandate that the tip credit is $5.12 per hour. Note that the tip credit is the difference between the minimum wage and the tipped employee minimum wage ($7.25 − $2.13 = $5.12). Some states such as Alaska, California, and Montana do not allow tip credit; instead, all workers receive minimum wage. Table 3-2 contains the details about tip credit for each state.

EXAMPLE: TIPPED EMPLOYEE IN OKLAHOMA, MINIMUM WAGE MET

Abigail is a tipped employee in Stillwater, Oklahoma. During a 40-hour workweek and pay period, she earned $220 in tips.

Hourly tipped minimum wage: $2.13 per hour

$2.13 per hour × 40 hours = $85.20 in wages

Tips earned: $220

Total wages and tips earned during the pay period:

$220 + $85.20 = $305.20

The federal and state minimum wage are $7.25 per hour. The minimum wage for a 40-hour workweek:

$7.25 per hours × 40 hours = $290

Therefore, Abigail has earned more than the federal and state minimum wage. The employer does not need to contribute to Abigail's pay during the pay period.

TABLE 3-2

Table of 2016 Minimum Hourly Wages for Tipped Employees by State

Jurisdiction	Basic Combined Cash and Tip Minimum Wage Rate	Maximum Tip Credit Against Minimum Wage	Minimum Cash Wage	Definition of Tipped Employee by Minimum Tips Received (monthly unless otherwise specified)
Federal: Fair Labor Standards Act (FLSA)	$7.25	$5.12	$2.13	More than $30
State Law Does Not Allow Tip Credit				
Note: The minimum rate is the same for tipped and nontipped employees				
Alaska			$9.75	
California			$10.00	
Minnesota:				No tip credit allowed
Large employer Annual receipts > $625,000 per year			$9.00	
Small employer Annual receipts < $625,000 per year			$7.25	
Montana:				
Business with gross annual sales exceeding $110,000			$8.05	
Business with gross annual sales of $110,000 or less			$4.00	
Nevada			$8.25	With no health insurance benefits provided by employer and received by employee
			$7.25	With health insurance benefits provided by employer and received by employee
Oregon			$9.25	
Washington			$9.47	
State Law Allows Tip Credit				
Arizona	$8.00	$3.00	$5.05	Not specified
Arkansas	$8.00	$5.37	$2.63	More than $20
Colorado	$8.31	$3.02	$5.29	More than $30
Connecticut:	$9.60			At least $10 weekly for full-time employees or $2.00 daily for part-time in hotels and restaurants. Not specified for other industries.
Hotel, restaurant		34.8% ($3.37)	$5.78	
Bartenders who customarily receive tips		18.5% ($1.69)	$7.46	
Delaware	$8.25	$6.02	$2.23	More than $30
District of Columbia	$10.50	$7.73	$2.77	Not specified
Florida	$8.05	$3.02	$5.03	
Hawaii	$8.50	$0.75	$7.75	More than $20
Idaho	$7.25	$3.90	$3.35	More than $30
Illinois	$8.25	40% ($3.30)	$4.95	$20

(continued)

Jurisdiction	Basic Combined Cash and Tip Minimum Wage Rate	Maximum Tip Credit Against Minimum Wage	Minimum Cash Wage	Definition of Tipped Employee by Minimum Tips Received (monthly unless otherwise specified)
Indiana	$7.25	$5.12	$2.13	Not specified
Iowa	$7.25	$2.90	$4.35	More than $30
Kansas	$7.25	$5.12	$2.13	More than $20
Kentucky	$7.25	$5.12	$2.13	More than $30
Maine	$7.50	50% ($3.75)	$3.75	More than $30
Maryland	$8.25	$4.62	$3.63	More than $30
Massachusetts	$10.00	$6.65	$3.35	More than $20
Michigan	$8.50	$5.27	$3.23	Not specified
Missouri	$7.65	50% ($3.825)	$3.825	Not specified
Nebraska	$8.00	$5.87	$2.13	Not specified
New Hampshire	$7.25	55% ($3.9875)	45% ($3.2625)	More than $30
New Jersey	$8.38	$6.25	$2.13	Not specified
New Mexico	$7.50	$5.37	$2.13	More than $30
New York:	$9.00			Not specified
Food service workers		$1.50	$7.50	
Service employees		$1.50	$7.50	
Service employees in resort hotels if tips average at least $5.05 per hour		$1.50	$7.50	
North Carolina	$7.25	$5.12	$2.13	More than $20
North Dakota	$7.25	33% ($2.39)	$4.86	More than $30
Ohio: *The increased minimum wage will apply to employees of businesses with annual gross receipts of greater than $297,000 per year.*	$8.10	$4.05	$4.05	More than $30
Oklahoma	$7.25	$5.12	$2.13	Not specified
Pennsylvania	$7.25	$4.42	$2.83	More than $30
Rhode Island	$9.60	$6.21	$3.39	Not specified
South Carolina	$7.25	$5.12	$2.13	Not specified
South Dakota	$8.50	50% ($4.25)	$4.25	More than $35
Texas	$7.25	$5.12	$2.13	More than $20
Utah	$7.25	$5.12	$2.13	More than $30
Vermont: *Employees in hotels, motels, tourist places, and restaurants who customarily and regularly receive tips for direct and personal customer service*	$9.60	50% ($4.80)	$4.80	More than $120
Virginia	$7.25	$5.12	$2.13	Not specified
West Virginia	$8.75	70% ($6.13)	$2.62	Not specified
Wisconsin	$7.25	$4.92	$2.33	Not specified
Wyoming	$5.15	$3.02	$2.13	More than $30

Source: U.S. Department of Labor, 2016

EXAMPLE: TIPPED EMPLOYEE IN RHODE ISLAND, MINIMUM WAGE *NOT* MET

Grayson is a tipped waiter in Warwick, Rhode Island. During a 40-hour work and pay period, he earned $75 in tips.

Hourly tipped minimum wage: $3.39 per hour

$3.39 per hour × 40 hours = $135.60 in wages

Tips earned: $75

Total wages and tips earned during the pay period:

$135.60 + 75 = $210.60

The state minimum wage for Rhode Island is $9.60 per hour. During a 40-hour work-week and pay period, the minimum pay for an employee is:

$9.60 per hours × 40 hours = $384.00

Because Grayson has not earned the minimum wage, the employer must pay the difference between the earned wages and tips and the minimum wage:

$384.00 − $210.60 = $173.40 to be added to Grayson's pay by the employer

The employer must pay the additional $173.40 to Grayson to bring his pay to the minimum wage.

Pay Your Employees Correctly

Stop & Check

1. Heather works as a clerk receiving minimum wage for a pharmaceutical company in North Carolina that pays its employees on a biweekly basis. She is classified as nonexempt, and her standard workweek is 40 hours. During a two-week period, she worked 88 hours and received $638.00. Was Heather's pay correct? Explain.

2. Tony works as a publisher's representative receiving minimum wage in New York. He works 39.5 hours during a one-week period. How much should he receive?

3. Mary is an intern for a popular radio station, which is a large employer in Minnesota. She receives minimum wage and works 32 hours per week. How much should she receive for two weeks of work?

4. Tony is a tipped minimum wage worker for a Minnesota company with $615,000 in annual revenues. He worked 75 hours during a biweekly pay period, in which he earned $1,000 in tips. What is his gross pay (excluding tips)?

© PhotosIndia.com/Glow Images

LO 3-2 Compute Gross Pay for Different Pay Bases

Salaried Workers

Employees in highly technical, qualification-driven positions within a company are generally classified as exempt from FLSA regulations. Accountants, engineers, lawyers, managers, and supervisors are included in this classification. Section 13(a)(1) of the FLSA defines the eligible exempt employees in the following job descriptions: executives, administrative personnel, professionals, and outside sales representatives. Section 13(a)(17) of the FLSA also allows specific computer-related employees to be included in the classification of salaried workers. The FLSA provides a minimum wage for salaried workers of not less than $913 per week effective 12/1/2016.

> Companies often use a technique called "job leveling" to determine salaries for exempt employees. This technique uses job descriptions to define common types of responsibilities in an effort to generate pay grades. This practice has led to staffing imbalances, multiple titles for similar jobs, and issues with employee morale. Solutions to the job-leveling issue include a comparison of each employee's duties and a holistic view of the actual size of the job. Once these variables are measured, the job is compared to similar roles in the industry to determine appropriate compensation. (Source: SHRM)

The division of salaried workers into exempt and nonexempt statuses has historically correlated with company policy more than legal requirements. However, in 2015 the U.S. Department of Labor began to investigate employee classifications to ensure compliance with FLSA stipulations. Remember that overtime pay is the payment of wages at one-and-a-half times the employee's normal wage rate.

For nonexempt salaried workers, the employment contract entered into between the employee and the employer determines at what level of hourly work they would receive overtime pay. Many salaried nonexempt worker contracts, when specified, are for 45 hours per week. If the contract stipulates that 45 hours per week is the standard workweek for a salaried, nonexempt employee, then the employee is still subject to FLSA overtime rules for hours worked past 40. However, if the worker's contract stipulated that the employee is only eligible for overtime after working 45 hours, then only the hours worked in excess of 45 per week would be eligible for overtime pay.

EXAMPLE: SALARIED, NONEXEMPT EMPLOYEE

A salaried, nonexempt employee earns $1,000 per week and has a standard 45-hour workweek.

   Hourly compensation: $1,000/45 hours = $22.22 per hour

   Overtime rate = $22.22 × 1.5 = $33.33 per hour

Because this employee is classified as nonexempt according to FLSA guidelines, the employee is subject to overtime compensation, and the hourly rate is needed to compute overtime pay.

   For the same salaried, nonexempt employee, if the contract between employee and employer stated that all hours *exceeding* 45 were considered for overtime, then the individual would need to work 45.25 hours or more in the week to qualify for overtime.

   However, *if* the contract stated that only 40 hours were required before overtime rates applied, then the 5 hours would be paid at overtime rates.

Note: A salaried *exempt* worker would be paid $1,000 per week regardless of the number of hours worked.

Employers may not prorate a salaried worker's pay when the number of hours worked is fewer than the contractual hour requirement. An exception to this would be time away from work in accordance with the employer's sick or vacation policy. The company would allow employees to take paid time off under either of these programs to supplement their missed wages. Companies may also offer salaried employees the option of leave without pay for missed days; however, contractual hours covered under leave without pay must be documented and signed by both a manager and the employee.

Salary Translation to Hourly Rates

The calculation of gross pay for salaried employees depends on the firm's choice of pay periods. An employee's gross pay is determined by dividing the annual pay by the number of pay periods in a year. For instance, if a firm paid employees on a monthly basis, then the salary calculation would be $\frac{1}{12}$ of the yearly amount. It is occasionally necessary to determine the hourly rate for salaried employees. To get the hourly rate, you would use the following equation:

$$\text{Hourly rate} = \frac{\text{Annual amount}}{\text{Total hours worked per year}}$$

To arrive at the total number of hours worked per year, multiply the number of weeks in a year (52) by the number of hours worked in a standard workweek without overtime.

$$\text{Hourly rate} = \frac{\text{Annual salary}}{\text{Number of hours in a standard workweek} \times 52 \text{ weeks/year}}$$

Because the calculation of overtime, holiday, or vacation time for salaried workers could be based upon the hourly rate of the individual, knowing how to calculate that amount will enable accurate pay.

EXAMPLE:

Jackie earns a salary of $60,000 per year for ABD Industries. ABD Industries pays its employees on a monthly basis.

Gross pay = $60,000 per year/12 months = $5,000 per month.

If she were a ***nonexempt*** employee, it would become necessary to calculate her hourly rate. When calculating the hourly rate, using the correct number of hours in a regular workweek is critical in determining the overtime pay rate. Note how the following examples computing the hourly rate using different regular workweeks.

Number of hours in the regular workweek	$\dfrac{\text{Annual salary}}{\text{\# of hours} \times 52 \text{ weeks}}$	Hourly rate
40	$\dfrac{60{,}000}{(40 \times 52)}$	$28.85
37.5	$\dfrac{60{,}000}{(37.5 \times 52)}$	$30.77
35	$\dfrac{60{,}000}{(35 \times 52)}$	$32.97

What happens if the salaried employee decides to take unpaid leave during a pay period? That amount must be deducted from the gross pay amount. In the case of unpaid leave, the amount of time taken and the number of regular hours in the pay period are the major factors.

EXAMPLE:

Jackie wants to take two extra days off around a holiday but has no paid time off remaining for the year. The company pays Jackie on a biweekly basis, and there are 80 hours in a pay period. At 8 hours per day, she will be taking 16 hours of unpaid leave (8 hours × 2 days).

(continued)

(concluded)

Using the previous example for Jackie's work with ABD Industries with her regular working hours as 40 hours per week, her normal salary is:

80 hours × $28.85/hour = $2,308 per pay period.

To calculate her pay, including the unpaid leave, we need the proportion of her paycheck that will be unpaid. We calculate the proportion of the total paycheck she will be taking as unpaid leave.

Unpaid portion: 16 hours

Normal hours per pay period: 80

Unpaid portion = 16/80 = 0.20

That means she will receive 100 − 0.20 = 0.80 (or 80%) of her normal gross pay.

Gross pay per period with 16 hours unpaid time:

$2,308 × 0.80 = $1,846.40

Note: Using a rounded hourly rate (as shown in this example) to compute period pay will differ from results using nonrounded hourly rates.

In many instances, nonexempt employees are paid on a salary basis to avoid paperwork such as *time cards* or pay sheets if they consistently work a fixed number of hours per week. According to 29 CFR 778.113(a), the employer and employee must agree on the standard number of hours to be worked each week for which the employee shall receive fixed pay. If the employee is classified as a nonexempt worker, however, the FLSA requires that these salaried workers are eligible for overtime. For a nonexempt salaried worker, the hourly rate is necessary to compute pay beyond the agreed-upon weekly hours per 29 CFR 778.113(a).

If the employee works less than the agreed-upon number of hours during the week, some states have provisions by which the employee's salary may be reduced. In this case, the hourly rate is again necessary to make sure the gross pay is correctly calculated.

Salaried Workers and Minimum Wage Comparisons

In the case of a salaried nonexempt worker for whom FLSA provisions apply, the fixed weekly salary must adhere to minimum wage guidelines. The minimum wage applies to salaried nonexempt employees whose wages do not exceed $913 per week. The U.S. Department of Labor has established this salary level as one of the tests for exemption from FLSA provisions.

EXAMPLE: SALARIED NONEXEMPT EMPLOYEE PAY

Sally is a receptionist for KTC Incorporated, located in California. She is salaried and works 40 hours per week, but she is nonexempt because her job classification is nonmanagerial.

If she were paid $275 per week

Hourly wage = $275/40 hours per week = $6.88/hour.

This amount is below the federal minimum wage test for exempt employees. Sally would need to be paid a minimum of *$290* per week for her work to meet FLSA minimum wage requirements because of her weekly 40-hour work agreement with her employer. To meet this requirement, the employer must contribute additional money to meet the minimum-wage requirement.

Hourly Workers

Hourly workers are paid for any hour or fraction of an hour they work. These employees may be either skilled or unskilled. Hourly employees must receive overtime for hours worked in excess of 40 per week, according to FLSA. Overtime is the same for hourly workers as it is for the salaried nonexempt workers. Hourly workers may be paid for each minute worked, and the computation of those minutes depends upon company policy. Companies may offer different work shifts and workday lengths, such as four 10-hour shifts or five 8-hour shifts, to reach the 40 hours needed. State regulations may require the company with the 10-hour shifts to file an election to pay no overtime for the two additional hours per day. The reason stated should not be overtime avoidance, but a deemed economic benefit for the longer schedules. For example, set-up time in a manufacturing environment can eliminate anywhere from half an hour to an hour of productive time. By working the longer schedules, manufacturing efficiency can be improved.

> The city of Pocatello, Idaho, needed to install a new water system for parts of the metropolitan area. Departmental executives determined that the project required approximately 4,000 man-hours to complete the work. To complete the work in an eight-week period, the city elected to have employees work 10-hour shifts. The use of 10-hour shifts was determined to optimize energy costs and optimize efficiency. (Source: *Idaho State Journal*)

© Liam Bailey/Image Source, RF

An employee working for an hourly wage may work in more than one job classification. When this occurs, the employee's pay per classification may vary. For example, a manufacturing employee may work on the sales counter where the pay differential provides an additional $1.50 per hour. When situations like this occur, the payroll accountant must be informed of hours performed for each of the job classifications to provide accurate pay, classification, and reporting. Methods used to communicate this include notes on the time card, schedules provided to the payroll clerk, or job duty notification forms.

EXAMPLE: HOURLY PAY WITH DIFFERENT RATES

Merrill is an hourly worker for a fast-food establishment and earns $7.25 per hour. He occasionally is the crew chief, during which he receives a $2.00/hour differential. During a 40-hour workweek, he worked 16 hours as a crew chief and 24 hours as a regular employee. His pay would be calculated as follows:

Regular pay: 24 hours × $7.25/hour = $174.00

Crew chief pay: $7.25/hour + $2.00/hour differential = $9.25/hour

16 hours × $9.25/hour = $148.00

Gross pay = $174.00 + $148.00 = $322.00

Commission Work

Commissions are compensation based on a set percentage of the sales revenue for a product or service that the company provides. Commission-based compensation is appropriate in the following types of situations:

- Retail sales personnel
- Automotive sales personnel
- Media databases or monitoring that pertains to media relations
- Marketing sales agents

> ## EXAMPLE: COMMISSION WORKER PAY
>
> An ice machine company may have sales representatives earning 5% commission on all sales made. If sales representative A sells $100,000 worth of ice machines during July, the commission due is computed as follows:
>
> Sales Price × Commission Rate = $100,000 × 5% = $5,000
>
> **Note:** Commissions may be contingent upon the company's return/warranty policy.
>
> If sales representative A had returns of $7,500 during August, the commission for that month could be reduced:
>
> Returns × Commission Rate = deduction from commissions $7,500 returns × 5% commission rate = $375 deducted from commissions during August.

An important classification of a sales representative's job is the difference between inside and outside sales. An inside sales representative is one who conducts business via telephone, email, or other electronic means and does not travel to customer sites. An outside sales representative meets with customers either at the customer's facility or another agreed-upon location. Some inside sales representatives are covered under the FLSA and must receive at least minimum wage for their labors. Outside sales representatives are excluded from minimum wage requirements under FLSA. In a 2010 circuit court decision, the judge ruled that inside sales representatives are nonexempt from FLSA wage and hour provisions, whereas outside sales and retail sales representatives are exempt.

> ## EXAMPLE: INSIDE SALES REPRESENTATIVE, LESS THAN MINIMUM WAGE
>
> Sally works as an inside sales representative in the company store and receives 5% commission for all sales she makes during her shift. During the week, she made 15 sales via telephone with a total dollar value of $1,500.
>
> Commissions = Dollar value of sales × Commission rate
>
> Commissions = $1,500 × 5% = $75
>
> Based upon a 40-hour workweek, she would have constructively earned **$1.88** per hour; thus, the employer would be responsible for meeting the minimum wage requirements under FLSA. The employer would have to adjust Sally's compensation to meet the minimum wage requirements.

> ## EXAMPLE: OUTSIDE SALES REPRESENTATIVE, LESS THAN MINIMUM WAGE
>
> Samantha works as an outside sales representative for the same company. She made sales this week of $2,000 and has an agreed commission percentage of 10% of her total sales revenue. Commission = 2,000 × 10% = $200 $200 per week/ 40 hours = $5.00 hour. Because she is an outside sales representative, she is exempt from minimum wage regulations under FLSA.

Gross Pay for Commission-Based Employees

In situations where the employee is principally engaged in the sale of a product or service but in no way engaged in the manufacturing of the item, a commission pay basis is appropriate. In some states, the commission-based employee may receive commissions for work even after termination if the sale was completed prior to termination. In many ways, commission-based pay is a contract between the employer and the employee to sell a product. The payment for such a contract may not be reneged upon, even after termination of employment. It should be noted that many states prohibit deductions pertaining to the cost of doing business from an employee's commission. In other words, if a customer received a product that was damaged, lost, or otherwise destroyed, the employee's commission would not be affected.

EXAMPLE:

Sonja works as an outside salesperson with Bayfront Watercraft. Her whole function with Bayfront is to sell the company's products to customers at the customer's facility or other agreed-upon locations, for which she receives a commission of 5% based on the retail price of all sales she makes. During May, she sold $20,000 of products during one week.

Commission = $20,000 × 0.05 = $1,000

© McGraw-Hill Education/David Planchet, photographer

Commission pay can vary by employer, by client, by sales volume, and by employee based on his or her seniority or experience with the company. For instance, sales made by an employee to Client A may have a different commission rate than sales made to Client B, as well as be different for all other clients. Different products may also have varying commission rates, and changes in sales volume can alter commission rates. A sample of a commission-tracking sheet follows.

EXAMPLE: COMMISSION TRACKING SHEET

Salesperson	Client	Product or Service	Total Sales Price	Rate	Commission
Anthony B	Thompson Milbourne	RR-223	$1,245	2%	$ 24.90
Anthony B	Kockran Heights	RS-447	$2,016	5%	$100.80
Anthony B	Hoptop Ranges	RT-11	$ 892	3.5%	$ 31.22

It is important that commissions earned be tracked closely for a variety of reasons:

- Employee pay accuracy.
- Sales employee performance.
- Sales tracking.
- Job order tracking.
- Returns/reductions of commissions paid accuracy.

Commission pay must still meet FLSA minimum wage standards unless the employee is classified as an exempt worker. Similar to salaried nonexempt employees, commission-based employees are subject to the 40-hour workweek as a basis for FLSA minimum wage computations.

EXAMPLE: EFFECTIVE PAY RATE, EXCEED MINIMUM WAGE

In the example concerning Sonja at Bayfront, Sonja's pay was $1,000 for 40 hours of work.

Sonja's effective wage = $1,000/40 hours = $25/hour

EXAMPLE: EFFECTIVE PAY RATE, LOWER THAN MINIMUM WAGE

Anita, another commission-based employee at Bayfront Watercraft, made only $250 in commission for the week during which she worked 40 hours.

Effective hourly rate = $250/40 hours = $6.25/hour.

This amount is below the minimum wage in California. It is the employer's responsibility to compensate the employee at the minimum wage, so Bayfront would have to adjust Anita's compensation to meet FLSA requirements.

Piece-Rate Work

Piece-rate work involves paying employees for each unit they manufacture or each action they perform. This type of pay, based on task completion, is one of the oldest forms of performance-based pay. Dating back to the 16th century, piece-rate pay is thought to have evolved from journeyman artisans whose masters paid them per unit they completed. Prior to computations of hourly wages, piece rate was an accurate measure of how productive an employee was. Frederick Taylor wrote about a piece-rate system in 1896, citing that it placed an emphasis on efficiency and production. A criticism of Taylor's analysis, however, is that the piece-rate system overemphasizes production and may create an adversarial relationship between workers and managers.

> Piece-rate pay rewards workers by connecting individual production to compensation. The challenges arise when individual performance is low and total compensation does not meet minimum wage requirements.

© Ronnie Kaufman/Larry Hirshowitz/
Blend Images LLC, RF

FLSA requirements subjected the piece-rate system to minimum wage requirements. Piece-rate workers must be paid no less than the minimum wage for their location, forcing employers to track their work hours accurately. In many ways, piece-rate pay is more difficult to track and to administer than other types of pay. Not only must the employees be compensated for the work they complete, but they are also subject to FLSA minimum and daily break provisions, including lunch and other breaks.

EXAMPLE: PIECE-RATE PAY, EXCEED MINIMUM WAGE

John is a piece-rate worker in Tennessee who receives $15 per completed piece of work. During a week, he completes 30 pieces and works 40 hours.

John's pay = $15/per piece completed × 30 pieces completed = $450

Hourly rate equivalent = $450/40 hours = $11.25/hour

John's pay exceeds the FLSA minimum wage for his location, so the employer does not have to adjust John's compensation.

EXAMPLE: PIECE-RATE WORKER, BELOW MINIMUM WAGE

Sarah works for the same employer as John and receives the same rate of pay. She completes 15 pieces during the week.

Sarah's pay = $15/piece × 15 = $225.

Hourly rate equivalent = $225/40 = $5.63/hour

Sarah's pay does not meet the minimum wage requirement, so the employer would have to examine Sarah's work and pay rates to ensure that she meets the FLSA minimum wage requirements.

A wide variety of occupations benefit from piece-rate pay systems. Some of these occupations include:

Vineyard workers	Inspectors
Installers	Customer service agents
Machinists/fabricators	Production workers
Sheep shearers	Forest workers

The common thread is that each position has output that is quantifiable and linked to some aspect of a manufacturing or service industry. The important part of piece-rate work is that a quantifiable base must be linked with a specified standard rate per amount of work.

Vineyard workers: Tons of grapes harvested

Inspectors: Number of items inspected

Installers: Number of items installed

Customer service agents: Number of customers assisted

Machinists/ Fabricators: Number of items produced

Sheep shearers: Pounds of wool gathered

Forest workers: Amount of wood cut

At Bayfront Watercraft, the manufacturing department has different types of fabricators, installers, and other production workers in addition to Pat (our hull maker). Let us assume that Joanna works in the upholstery department where she constructs vinyl covers for seats. Rick is in the assembly department and assembles steering mechanisms for the boats.

EXAMPLE: PIECE-RATE COMPUTATION, DIFFERENT EMPLOYEES

Worker	Number of Items	Rate per Item	Gross Pay
Pat	30 hulls	$100	$3,000
Joanna	100 seat covers	$ 25	$2,500
Rick	25 steering mechanisms	$ 40	$1,000

Each worker is compensated based on the work he or she completes. In some companies, workers may work on multiple items for which different rates exist. In cases where one worker completes multiple pieces at different rates, the rates for each different piece must be computed.

EXAMPLE: TOTAL PAY, ONE PIECE-RATE EMPLOYEE

Worker	Item	Number of Items	Pay per Item	Total Pay
John	Motor installation	10 motors	$50 per motor	$500
	Rudder installation	15 rudders	$20 per rudder	$300
			Total pay for John:	$800

A separate record for each employee is important in the case of piece-rate pay, especially when the employee works with multiple production items at different rates. Overtime rates for piece-rate workers are computed differently than for hourly workers. Once the standard number of pieces per hour is determined, the amount per hour per piece can be computed.

EXAMPLE: PIECE RATE WITH OVERTIME PAY

Bayfront determines that 50 ignition assemblies can reasonably be completed in a 40-hour workweek by one worker. Ignition assemblies are paid at a rate of $25 per assembly.

Standard amount paid per 40-hour workweek: $1,250

50 assemblies × $25/assembly = $1,250

Hourly amount = $1,250/40 hours = $31.25/hour

If the employee worked overtime, the rate would be computed as follows:

Overtime rate = regular hourly rate × 1.5 = $46.875.

(continued)

> *(concluded)*
>
> If an employee worked a 45-hour workweek, the pay would be computed as:
>
> Standard amount per week + overtime pay
>
> = $1,250/40-hour week + ($46.875/hour × 5 hours overtime
>
> = $1,484.375, which would be $1,484.38 (rounded)

According to FLSA provisions, piece-rate workers must have a standard number of items that can be reasonably completed each day that allows for breaks and rest periods. To increase compensation, it could be very easy for an employee to engage in overwork so that he or she could complete more items. According to 29 CFR 525.12(h)(2)(ii), piece-rate employees must have a standard number of items per period, and most are subject to minimum wage provisions.

Pay Computations for Different Bases

1. Natasha is a marketing representative who earns a 3% commission based on the revenue earned from the marketing campaigns she completes. During the current pay period, she completed a marketing campaign with $224,800 revenue. How much commission will she receive from this campaign?

2. Jeremy is a specialty artisan for a luxury car maker based in South Carolina. He makes handcrafted dashboards and receives $550.00 per completed assembly. During a semi-monthly pay period, he completes two dashboard assemblies and works 90 hours. How much does he receive for the completion of the assemblies? Does this amount comply with minimum wage requirements? Explain.

3. Lanea is a salaried worker making $57,000 per year for a company using biweekly payroll. Her standard schedule is 40 hours over 5 days per week. She has used all of her vacation time prior to this pay period and fell ill for three days. What effect does this have on the current pay period? Will her gross pay be the same as if she had vacation time available?

LO 3-3 Calculate Pay Based on Hours and Fractions of Hours

Employees, both salaried nonexempt and hourly, are paid based upon the number of hours or fractions thereof. The payroll accountant must learn how to convert a fraction of a 60-minute clock into a fraction of 100. While a few accounting software packages are able to convert minutes into payable units, typically the payroll accountant does this math. Fortunately, the math for this calculation is fairly straightforward.

> **EXAMPLE: CONVERSION OF MINUTES TO DECIMALS AND FRACTIONS**
>
> If an employee works 30 minutes, then the computation for pay purposes is:
>
> 30 minutes ÷ 60 minutes/hour = 0.5 hour or 50/100
>
> If an employee works 33 minutes, the payroll computation is:
>
> 33 minutes ÷ 60 minutes/hour = 0.55 hour, or 55/100*
>
> **Note:** This calculation is necessary when the employer pays using the hundredth-hour method instead of the quarter-hour method. If this had been a quarter-hour computation, the number of minutes would have been rounded to the closest 15-minute increment, which is 0.50 hours.

Calculations of employee wages are broken down by the hour or fraction thereof. Regardless of the classification of employee, a determination of pay per pay period causes the payroll accountant to break down all wages. Salaries are determined based upon a yearly salary and therefore need to be broken down per pay period (monthly, bimonthly, weekly, or biweekly). Companies may pay employees by fractions of an hour (hundredth-hour basis) or by the quarter-hour (rounded to the nearest 15-minute interval), depending upon company policy. The next section will walk you through the calculations of both the hundredth and quarterly processes.

Hourly Calculations

Depending on the company's policy, time payments can be paid either by the individual minute or rounded to the nearest designated interval. Hourly calculations are a combination of minutes and hours. Hours are broken into two categories: regular and overtime. When determining the hourly wage for a salaried individual, the number of average hours required under the salary must be known.

EXAMPLE: HOURLY WAGE COMPUTATION, SALARIED EMPLOYEE

If a manager is expected to work 45 hours per week at $75,000 per year, the effective hourly wage would be:

$75,000/(45 × 52 weeks) = $75,000/2,340 = <u>$32.05 per hour</u>

EXAMPLE: WEEKLY PAY INCLUDING PAID SICK TIME

Jason worked four days during the payroll week. He worked 7.5 hours the first day, 8.75 hours the second day, 7 hours the third day, and 9.5 hours the fourth day. He used 8 hours of his paid sick time on one day during the week. He is paid overtime for any hours worked in excess of 40 per week.

Regular hours: 7.5 + 8.75 + 7 + 9.5 = <u>32.75 hours</u>

He will also receive 8 hours of sick time.

Jason's gross pay = 32.75 regular hours + 8 sick = <u>40.75 hours</u>

Even though Jason has more than 40 hours on his payroll, 8 are not considered "worked" and would therefore not be included in the calculation for the determination of overtime.

EXAMPLE: WEEKLY PAY INCLUDING PAID HOLIDAY TIME

Karen worked four days during the week with a holiday on Monday. Her hours worked were 8.25 hours the first day, 9 hours the second day, 7.75 hours the third day, and 8.5 hours the fourth day. The company pays 8 hours for the holiday. She is paid for any hours worked in excess of 40 hours per week.

Regular hours: 8.25 + 9 + 7.75 + 8.5 = <u>33.5 hours</u>

She will also be paid 8 hours regular pay for the holiday.

Karen's gross pay will contain **41.5** hours of regular pay, which includes **8** hours of holiday pay. Karen has not worked in excess of 40 hours, so she will not receive overtime.

Quarter-Hour System

Some employers compensate employees based upon rounding working hours to the nearest 15 minutes, a system widely known as the *quarter-hour system*. The payroll accountant becomes responsible for rounding the time either up or down consistently across

© Stockbyte/Getty Images, RF

all individuals and pay periods. If an individual worked 8 hours and 6 minutes, he would be paid for 8 hours. However, if that same individual were to work for 8 hours and 10 minutes, he would be paid for 8 hours plus 15 minutes of overtime, if the company pays for overtime on any hours worked over 8 in a day.

EXAMPLE: QUARTER-HOUR SYSTEM COMPUTATION, ROUNDING TO PREVIOUS QUARTER-HOUR

Amanda worked from 8 a.m. until noon. She took one hour for lunch and returned to work at 1 p.m. At the end of the day, Amanda ended up leaving work at 4:20 p.m. Using the quarter-hour system:

> From 8 a.m. to noon: 4 hours
>
> From 1 p.m. to 4:20 p.m.: 3.25 hours
>
> because 4:20 p.m. rounds to 4:15 p.m. under the quarter-hour system.
>
> Total time: 4 + 3.25 = <u>7.25 hours</u>

EXAMPLE: QUARTER-HOUR SYSTEM COMPUTATION, ROUNDING TO NEXT QUARTER-HOUR

Justin worked from 8 a.m. until 12:30 p.m. before taking a half-hour lunch. He returned at 1 p.m. and worked until 4:10 p.m. His employer pays on the quarter-hour system, so Justin would be paid:

> From 8 a.m. to 12:30 p.m.: 4 hours, 30 minutes = 4.5 hours
>
> From 1 p.m. to 4:10 p.m.: 3.25 hours
>
> because 4:10 p.m. rounds to 4:15 p.m. under the quarter-hour system.
>
> Total time for the day: <u>7.75 hours</u>

Hundredth-Hour System

The *hundredth-hour system* is similar to the quarter-hour system in that it calculates partial hours of work performed. Instead of rounding the employee's time to 15-minute intervals, the hundredth-hour system divides the hour into 100 increments. The calculation of partial minutes is simple:

$$\text{Conversion of minutes to hundredth hour} = \frac{\text{Number of minutes in partial hour}}{60 \text{ minutes per hour}}$$

EXAMPLE: CONVERSION FROM MINUTES TO HUNDREDTH-HOUR

If an employee worked 4 hours and 16 minutes:

> 4 hours + 16 minutes/60 minutes per hour = <u>4.27 hours</u>

EXAMPLE: HUNDREDTH-HOUR TIME COMPUTATION

Lesle works an 8-hour shift that had 15 minutes of additional overtime. Her normal hourly rate is $10/hour. Her pay would be computed as follows:

8 hours × $10 per hour = $80 regular pay

15 minutes overtime = 15/60 = 0.25 hours

Overtime = 0.25 hours × $10/hour × 1.5 = $3.75

Total pay for the day = $80 + $3.75 = <u>$83.75</u>

Following is a list of how the time may appear on an individual's time card. Note that an employer should choose only one method of computing partial hours, quarter-hours, or hundredth-hours and apply it to all situations.

EXAMPLE: QUARTER-HOUR COMPUTATION, WEEKLY PAY DETAILS

Amanda Parker: Employee Number 1776M				
Clock In	Clock Out	Clock In	Clock Out	Hours Worked
08:00	11:00	12:00	16:54	7 hours 54 minutes = 8.00 hours
08:00	11:30	12:30	17:05	8 hours 5 minutes = 8.00 hours
07:00	12:09	13:15	17:30	9 hours 24 minutes = 9.5 hours
07:30	12:21	13:24	17:30	9 hours 27 minutes = 9.25 hours
			Total	34.75 hours

Notice in the next example how the same employee with the same time worked would have different hourly computations based on hundredth-hour computations. The difference in the hourly computations leads to a difference in compensation for the period.

EXAMPLE: HUNDREDTH-HOUR COMPUTATION, WEEKLY PAY DETAILS

Amanda Parker: Employee Number 1776M				
Clock In	Clock Out	Clock In	Clock Out	Hours Worked
08:00	11:00	12:00	16:54	7 hours, 54 minutes = 7.9 hours
08:00	11:30	12:30	17:05	8 hours, 5 minutes = 8.08 hours
07:00	12:09	13:15	17:30	9 hours, 24 minutes = 9.4 hours
07:30	12:21	13:24	17:30	8 hours, 27 minutes = 8.45 hours
			Total	33.83 hours

LO 3-4 Create a Payroll Register

A *payroll register* is the payroll accountant's internal tool that helps ensure accuracy of employee compensation. A payroll register can be completed manually, in a spreadsheet program such as Microsoft Excel, in accounting software programs such as QuickBooks, or by payroll outsourcing companies such as ADP or Zen Payroll. Like other worksheets that accountants use, the payroll register is a company confidential document that is not made public.

Quarter-Hour vs. Hundredth-Hour

1. Blue Sky Manufacturing has historically paid its employees according to the quarter-hour system. Software changes have caused them to change to the hundredth-hour system. What is the number of hours worked under the quarter-hour system? What is the time worked under the hundredth-hour system?

Employee	Time In	Time Out	Time In	Time Out	Total
Ann	8:06 a.m.	12:25 p.m.	1:20 p.m.	4:57 p.m.	Quarter-hour: Hundredth:
Nevada	7:58 a.m.	12:02 p.m.	1:02 p.m.	5:05 p.m.	Quarter-hour: Hundredth:
Pat	8:32 a.m.	11:54 a.m.	1:05 p.m.	5:32 p.m.	Quarter-hour: Hundredth:

2. Why do discrepancies exist between the quarter-hour time and the hundredth-hour time totals?

3. Why would it be worthwhile for Blue Sky Manufacturing to switch to the hundredth-hour system?

Payroll Register Data

The payroll register is annotated at the top with the beginning and ending dates of the payroll period. Each employee has a separate row in the register. The register contains columns to reflect each employee's specific pay information, such as:

1. Employee name.
2. Marital status.
3. Number of withholdings.
4. Salary or hourly rate.
5. Number of regular hours worked.
6. Number of overtime hours worked.
7. Regular pay.
8. Overtime pay.
9. Gross pay.
10. Federal income tax withheld.
11. Social Security tax withheld.
12. Medicare tax withheld.
13. State income tax withheld (where applicable).
14. Other state taxes.
15. Local taxes (if applicable).
16. 401(k) or other retirement plan deductions.
17. Insurance deductions.
18. Garnishments or levies.
19. Union dues.
20. Any other deductions.
21. Net pay.
22. Check or payment ID number.

FIGURE 3-2
Sample Payroll Register

Name	M/S	# W/H	Hourly Rate or Period Wage	No. of Regular Hours	No. of Overtime Hours	No. of Holiday Hours	Commissions	Gross Earning	Insurance	Cafeteria Plan

Name	Gross Earning	Taxable Wages for Federal W/H	Taxable Wages for FICA	Federal W/H	Social Security Tax	Medicare W/H	State W/H Tax	Union Dues	Net Pay

It may seem tedious to complete a register each payroll period, but the register offers more information than just the employee compensation. The register also contains information about employer liabilities for taxes and the employees' voluntary deductions that the employer must remit to the appropriate places at a future date. A sample payroll register is shown in Figure 3-2.

Note that other columns may be added to meet the company's needs. Other columns that may appear on a payroll register include commission, piece-rate, stand-by hours, and sleep time. The purpose of the payroll register is to both document the employees' time and hours worked and provide totals of the compensation for each category. Employers use these categorizations as part of labor analysis and planning tasks.

A separate payroll register is maintained for each pay period. To ensure accuracy, the accountant totals, proves, and rules the register.

WHAT DOES TOTAL, PROVE, AND RULE MEAN?

Total: Each column and row are totaled.

Prove: The column totals are added horizontally *and* row totals are totaled vertically. The aggregate column and row totals must be equal.

Rule: Column totals are double underlined to show that the totals have been proven.

Track Employee Compensation Using a Payroll Register

The payroll register is a tool used by payroll accountants to ensure accurate tracking of employee compensation. The following examples will demonstrate different scenarios using a payroll register.

EXAMPLE: WAGE PAYMENTS, NO OVERTIME

Jon Ames is a nonexempt, hourly employee of CM Bakeries. He receives $12.50/hour and receives overtime for any time worked in excess of 40 hours/week. He is single with one withholding allowance. During the week ending April 25, 20XX, he worked 37 hours. The payroll register would appear as follows:

Name	M/S	# W/H	Hourly Rate or Period Wage	No. of Regular Hours	No. of Overtime Hours	No. of Holiday Hours	Commissions	Gross Earning
Jon Ames	S	1	$ 12.50	37				$ 462.50

In example 1, the employee's hourly rate is multiplied by the number of hours worked to obtain the gross pay for the period. The use of the Regular Earnings column is introduced here, although no overtime exists. Example 2 will show how overtime is included in a payroll register.

EXAMPLE: WAGE PAYMENT WITH OVERTIME

Mike Brown is a nonexempt, hourly employee of Strong Coffee Company and earns $18.50/hour. He is married with two withholding allowances. He receives overtime for any hours worked in excess of 40 during a weekly period. During the period ended September 20, 20XX, he worked 45.75 hours. The payroll register would appear as follows:

Name	M/S	# W/H	Hourly Rate or Period Wage	No. of Regular Hours	No. of Overtime Hours	Reg. Earnings	Overtime Earnings	Gross Earning
Mike Brown		2	$ 18.50	40	5.75	$740.00	$ 159.56	$899.56

Overtime earnings = $18.50/hours × 5.75 hours × 1.5 (overtime premium) = $159.56

Notice that the payroll register in example 2 is expanded to include a breakdown of regular earnings and overtime earnings. The purpose of this practice is to facilitate computations, ensure accuracy, and allow for future analysis of overtime worked during a given period.

Example 3 contains a payroll register for a salaried, exempt employee. Notice the difference in the columns used to record the period salary.

EXAMPLE: SALARY PAYMENT

Rae Smith is a manager at Hartshorn Industries. She is a salaried, exempt employee and is married with four withholding allowances. She earns a salary of $2,000 per pay period. For the period ending July 31, 20XX, the payroll register would appear as follows:

Name	M/S	# W/H	Hourly Rate or Period Wage	No. of Regular Hours	No. of Overtime Hours	No. of Holiday Hours	Commissions	Gross Earning
Rae Smith	M	4	$2,000.00					$2,000.00

In a company, it is common to have both salaried and hourly employees, and all employees must be represented on a payroll register. Example 4 contains employees with pay variations that commonly exist in business.

EXAMPLE: PAYROLL REGISTER FOR MULTIPLE EMPLOYEES

PBL Freight pays its employees on a biweekly basis. The standard workweek for hourly employees is 40 hours, and employees receive overtime pay for any hours worked in excess of 40 during a week. The following payroll register is for the period ending March 22, 20XX:

Name	M/S	# W/H	Hourly Rate or Period Wage	No. of Regular Hours	No. of Overtime Hours	Reg. Earnings	Overtime Earnings	Gross Earning
Mary Jahn	S	1	$ 15.25	40		$ 610.00		$ 610.00
John Charles	M	3	$2,750.00			$2,750.00		$2,750.00
Ranea Hu	M	5	$ 21.50	40	6	$ 860.00	$ 193.50	$1,053.50
						$4,220.00	$ 193.50	$4,413.50

Notice how the columns are totaled in example 4. Each earnings column is totaled vertically, and the double underline (i.e., ruling) denotes that the computations are concluded.

The total in the bottom-right corner proves that the sum of the rows in the Gross Earnings column equals the total of the Regular Earnings and Overtime Earnings columns. Once the payroll register is totaled, proved, and ruled, then it is ready for the next step in the payroll process.

The Payroll Register

1. What is the purpose of the payroll register?
2. What are five of the columns that usually appear in a payroll register?
3. Why are computations for regular hours and overtime hours entered in different columns?

LO 3-5 Apply Combination Pay Methods

Employers often offer their employees ***combination pay*** methods. Sometimes the employee performs two different jobs for the same employer, and those two tasks have different compensation bases. Other situations involve payroll-based incentives that link to company productivity. Note how the payroll register reflects these combination pay methods.

Base Salary Plus Commission

A common method includes a base salary plus a commission or piece rate, depending on the nature of the work performed. Another method is a combination of salary plus hourly compensation that reflects a standard set of work hours plus additional hours that are paid only when worked. The purpose of the combination pay method is to meet minimum wage requirements and encourage employees to achieve sales or production goals. The base salary offers both the employer and the employee a level of stability in pay amounts because they will know the minimum amount of compensation for each pay period. Whatever the employees earn above the base salary may vary from pay period to pay period, depending on the employee's capabilities, production needs, and customer needs.

> ### EXAMPLE: BASE SALARY PLUS COMMISSION
>
> Henri Jay is a salaried, exempt employee of Night Lights Security. He is single with two withholding allowances. His compensation package includes commission based on sales of security system packages to customers. During the pay period ending January 15, 20XX, he earned $1,500 in salary and 4% commission on $10,000 of sales.
>
> Commission = $10,000 × 0.04 = $400
>
> | Name | M/S | # W/H | Hourly Rate or Period Wage | No. of Regular Hours | No. of Overtime Hours | No. of Holiday Hours | Commissions | Gross Earning |
> |------|-----|-------|----------------------------|----------------------|-----------------------|----------------------|-------------|---------------|
> | Henri Jay | S | 2 | $1,500.00 | | | | $ 400.00 | $1,900.00 |

Many types of jobs have a combination pay method because it has been found to boost employee productivity and maintain FLSA compliance. Some jobs that use combination pay methods include:

District managers   Account executives

Recruiters   Retail sales workers

Farm workers   College instructors

To compute combination pay methods, knowledge of the employee's base salary plus variable rate is essential.

EXAMPLE: DIFFERENT COMBINATION METHODS, SAME COMPANY

Todd Jones is an account executive for Bayfront Watercraft. He earns a base salary of $36,000 plus a commission of 0.5% on each sale he makes. He is married with six withholding allowances. Suppose that Todd sold $100,000 of boats during a two-week pay period ending June 15, 20XX.

Base salary = $36,000/26 = $1,384.62.

Commission = $100,000 × 0.5% = $500.

The payroll register for Todd's June 15 pay would appear as:

Name	M/S	# W/H	Hourly Rate or Period Wage	No. of Regular Hours	No. of Overtime Hours	Piece Rate Pay	Commissions	Gross Earning
Todd Jones	M	6	$1,384.62				$ 500.00	$1,884.62

Maria Dee installs the seating in the boats for Bayfront Watercraft. She is single with one withholding allowance. In her position, she earns a base salary of $26,000 per year plus a piece rate of $100 for each boat completed during the pay period. During the pay period, Maria installed the seating for eight boats.

Salary = $26,000/26 = $1,000

Piece-rate pay = $100 × 8 = $800

The payroll register including both employees for the June 15, 20XX, pay period would appear as:

Name	M/S	# W/H	Hourly Rate or Period Wage	No. of Regular Hours	No. of Overtime Hours	Piece Rate Pay	Commissions	Gross Earning
Todd Jones	M	6	$ 1,384.62				$ 500.00	$1,884.62
Maria Dee	S	1	$ 1,000.00			$ 800.00		$1,800.00
Totals						$ 800.00	$ 500.00	$3,684.62

Like any other type of pay method, the important element in computing combination pay is accurate maintenance of the base salary, the variable rate, and the number of items or sales for which the variable rate must apply. Use of the payroll register facilitates the computations and ensures the accuracy of the employees' gross pay.

EXAMPLE: HOURLY PIECE RATE WORKER WITH OVERTIME

Amanda Dones, a piece-rate worker for Bayfront Watercraft, worked eight hours on the first two days of the week and nine hours for the remaining three days. She receives $1.50 per gear shift cover she produces. This pay period she produced 150 gear shifts. She is single with no withholdings (done to have the maximum taxes taken out to avoid paying income tax) and earns $7.75 per hour (over minimum wage).

Standard wages: 8 + 8 + 9 + 9 + 9 = 43 hours, 40 regular and 3 overtime.

40 regular hours × $7.75 per hour = $310

3 overtime hours × $7.75 per hour × 1.5 = $34.88

Piece rate: $1.50 × 150 = $225

Name	M/S	# W/H	Hourly Rate or Period Wage	No. of Regular Hours	No. of Overtime Hours	Reg. Earnings	Overtime Earnings	Piece Rate Pay	Gross Earning
Amanda Dones	S	0	$ 7.75	40	3	$ 310.00	$ 34.88	$ 225.00	$ 569.88

Payroll Draw

A special situation in commission-based pay is a situation called a ***draw***. A draw generally involves an employee whose regular compensation is little more than the minimum wage, such as a retail sales position. Employees have sales goals they must meet and receive compensation on a commission basis once they meet or exceed those sales goals. If the sales goal is not met, the employee may draw salary against future commissions. The expectation with a draw is that the employee will eventually generate enough sales to cover any draws during pay periods when sales revenues were lower than expected.

> A draw is generally associated with a commission-only job in which the employer allows new employees to receive money for expected future commissions. With a draw, it is implied that the draw may occur on a regular basis.

EXAMPLE: SALARY PLUS COMMISSION AND DRAW

Karl Lee is an employee in the sales department of Fastball Sports. He is single with one withholding allowance, and his annual base salary is $12,000. He is expected to earn between $1,000 and $3,000 in sales commissions each month and may draw up to $3,000 per month against future earnings

During October, he earned $1,000 in commissions in addition to his salary. He decided to take an additional $1,000 draw against his future earnings. The payroll register would reflect this compensation as follows:

Name	M/S	# W/H	Hourly Rate or Period Wage	No. of Regular Hours	No. of Overtime Hours	Reg. Earnings	Draw	Commissions	Gross Earning
Kari Lee	S	1	$1,000.00			$1,000.00	$ 1,000.00	$ 1,000.00	$3,000.00

In this case, Karl could have withdrawn up to $3,000 against future earnings. If his employment is terminated before he earns enough sales commission to repay the draw, he will have to repay the company for that money. It is important to keep track of employee draws to ensure that the employee repays the draw.

Another example where the company may allow individuals to draw on their payroll exists when the pay period is monthly. In this situation, many employers allow their employees to draw up to 30–40% of their wages at mid-month. Some organizations may not withhold taxes from the draw, and the employee will have the full amount of taxes withdrawn upon the next payroll.

Employers must be careful when allowing employees to draw against future wages. A written and signed authorization must be obtained from the employee that specifies when the draw will be deducted from the employee's future wages to avoid legal issues with deductions, such as wage garnishments, that could be affected by the draw.

EXAMPLE: SALARY PLUS DRAW, EMPLOYEE INELIGIBLE FOR COMMISSION

Scott Fay is a new salesperson with Bayfront Watercraft, hired on September 24, 20XX. He receives a base salary of $19,500 per year, paid biweekly, plus a 5% commission on sales once he achieves his sales quota of $20,000 during a pay period. During the pay period ending September 30, Scott closed $10,000 in sales, making him ineligible for

(continued)

(concluded)

a commission for September. His base pay is $19,500, and he is eligible to draw up to the minimum commission for the pay period. The payroll register would reflect his pay as follows:

Name	M/S	# W/H	Hourly Rate or Period Wage	No. of Regular Hours	No. of Overtime Hours	Reg. Earnings	Draw	Commissions	Gross Earning
Scott Fay	S	1	$ 750.00			$ 750.00	$ 1,000.00		$ 1,750.00

Period salary = $19,500/26 pay periods = $750.00
Commission = $20,000 × 0.05 = $1,000.00.

Incentive Stock Options (ISOs)

Other employee compensation plans, known as *incentive stock options (ISOs)*, allow an employee to report a small base salary for tax purposes and to be issued company stock that must be held for a certain period before being sold. The purpose of ISO stock option plans is a deferral of taxes and salary liabilities for the employer and employee. This type of compensation is often found in executive pay packages.

According to the National Bureau of Economic Research in 2015, chief executive officers (CEOs) in the United States receive more than half of their annual compensation in the form of incentive stock options. In contrast, CEOs received less than 20 percent of their annual compensation as stock options in 1980. The current ISOs are designed as multiyear plans that allow executives to exercise the stock option at a later date, preferably when the market price of the stock is favorable. (Source: National Bureau of Economic Research)

Combination Pay Methods

Stop & Check

1. Shelly, a service administrator, receives a base salary of $42,000 per year paid semimonthly, plus $100 commission for each service contract she sells to her customers. During a pay period, she sells five contracts. What is her gross pay for the period?

2. Adam is a new salesperson with S&D Music. He receives a base salary of $36,000 paid monthly. Company policy allows him to draw 35% of his salary on the 15th of each month. How much will Adam receive at mid-month if he elects to take a draw? How much will he receive at the end of the month if he takes the 35% draw?

3. Joy, an executive for Adarma Chemicals, receives an annual salary of $75,000 plus an additional 3% in an ISO. What amount of stock does she receive annually? What is her total annual compensation?

LO 3-6 Explain Special Pay Situations

Compensation laws have many exceptions. According to the FLSA, every aspect of labor legislation, including minimum wage and overtime provisions, has its less common applications.

© Tetra Images/Alamy, RF

The introduction of new types of knowledge-based employment during the 21st century, as well as the continuance of more traditional agricultural tasks, necessitates an examination of these special pay situations.

Compensatory Time

The FLSA allows public employees to receive ***compensatory time***, often called "comp time," in lieu of overtime. According to section 3(s)(1)(c) of the FLSA, exempt public employees must receive comp time equal to 1.5 times the overtime hours worked. Therefore, if a public employee worked five hours of overtime, the comp time awarded must be 7.5 hours.

Comp time is often misconstrued by the private sector. FLSA provisions for comp time are only for public-sector employees, such as government workers, law enforcement, and seasonally hired laborers. Unless specifically designated by a firm's policies, a private-sector employer is not required to offer comp time. Additionally, many private-sector employers offer comp time on a straight-line basis, meaning that they offer the same number of compensatory hours as the number of overtime hours worked.

When calculating an employee's gross pay, it is prudent to be aware of any effects that a comp time award may have on overtime pay to ensure that the employee's compensation is accurate.

EXAMPLE: PUBLIC EMPLOYEE COMPENSATORY TIME

David works as an exempt employee of the federal government. In the course of his work, he accrues 8 hours of overtime during a pay period when he completes additional work for an absent co-worker. According to FLSA regulations, David must receive 12 hours of comp time because he is not eligible for paid overtime as an exempt government employee.

On-Call Time

Some professions require employees to be available for work outside of normal working hours. This availability is known as ***on-call time***, and two classes of on-call time exist: on-call at the employer's premises and on-call away from the employer's premises.

- If the employee is required to remain at the employer's premises, the employee's freedom is restricted, and he or she must be compensated for the on-call time.
- If the employee is not restricted to the employer's premises for the on-call time, compensation is not required.

In either case, company policy must be specific regarding the conditions of the on-call time. The number of hours specified for on-call compensation must be added to the employee's gross pay.

EXAMPLE: ON-CALL TIME

Kevin Gee works as a service representative for Built Strong, an equipment manufacturer. He earns $19.25/hour and is married with two withholding allowances. Built Strong requires that each service representative rotate on-call duties in one-week increments, during which they remain available for service calls outside of working hours but may otherwise engage in personal activities. During this on-call time, company policy stipulates that on-call service representatives receive two hours of regular pay for each on-call day. Kevin was on-call during the biweekly pay period ending February 25 and would

(continued)

(concluded)

receive 14 hours of additional straight-time pay for his on-call time. The payroll register would reflect the on-call pay as follows:

Name	M/S	# W/H	Hourly Rate or Period Wage	No. of Regular Hours	No. of On-call Hours	Reg. Earnings	On-call Earnings	Gross Earning
Kevin Gee	M	2	$ 19.25	80	14	$1,540.00	$ 269.50	$1,809.50

Travel Time, Wait Time, and Sleeping Time

Employees have traditionally commuted to and from work, although a growing trend toward telecommuting exists in the 21st century. Travel to and from an office is not compensable time; however, many employees do not work at a single location. Additionally, many employees travel for their employer's benefit for training or other business requirements. Similarly, employees may be required to wait by their employer, as in the case of a chauffeur or a bus driver. Other employees such as firefighters or medical personnel may be required to work 24-hour shifts and must be given at least five hours of paid *sleeping time* during that 24-hour period. An agreement between the employer and employee may exist to exclude up to eight hours if the employer provides furnished facilities for uninterrupted sleep.

© Big Cheese Photo/Corbis, RF

According to FLSA, the guideline that assists in the determination of compensable activity in these three situations is if the activity is for the employer's benefit. Travel among customer or business-related sites is compensable as *travel time* because it directly benefits the employer. Requiring a driver to wait as part of the job description also benefits the employer and is compensated as *wait time*. Travel from the employee's home to the office in the morning and returning home in the evening benefits the employee and is not compensable.

EXAMPLE: SLEEP TIME

Dan Morli is a surgical resident at Mercy Hospital and is classified as an exempt employee who earns $124,000 per year, paid semimonthly. The standard workweek is 40 hours. He is single with one withholding allowance. He works two 24-hour shifts per week in the regular course of his employment. His employer provides him a quiet sleeping area, per FLSA requirements. During a single 24-hour shift in the November 15 pay period, he sleeps 7 hours. According to FLSA guidelines, his pay may not be reduced for the first 5 hours that he sleeps. Dan's gross pay will reflect a two-hour reduction for the additional sleep in excess of the five-hour requirement.

The hourly rate needs to be computed to determine the deduction for the excess sleep time: $124,000/(40 × 52) = $59.62

The payroll register would appear as follows:

Name	M/S	# W/H	Hourly Rate or Period Wage	Hourly Rate	Sleep Hours>5	Reg. Earnings	Less Excess Sleep Time	Gross Earning
Dan Morli	S	1	$5,166.67	$ 59.62	2	$5,166.67	$ (119.23)	$5,047.44

Note the inclusion of the sleep hours in excess of five and the deduction. The purpose for tracking this information is to highlight specific issues with employee performance and related costs, which leads to stronger managerial control.

Subminimum Wage Situations

Tipped employees are not the only workers who may legally receive compensation lower than the minimum wage. Other specific classes of employees may receive an hourly wage that is less than the FLSA minimum wage:

- A 1996 amendment to the FLSA allows workers younger than the age of 20 to be paid a minimum wage of $4.25 per hour, but only for the first 90 calendar days of employment.

EXAMPLE: YOUNG EMPLOYEE

Cady Horn is a new employee of The Big Chicken, a fast-food restaurant in Glendale, Arizona, where new employees are paid minimum wage. Cady is 18 years of age and is single with one withholding allowance. During the weekly pay period ending July 18, 20XX, she worked 37 hours. The payroll register would appear as follows:

Name	M/S	# W/H	Hourly Rate or Period Wage	No. of Regular Hours	No. of Overtime Hours	Reg. Earnings	Gross Earning
Cady Horn	S	1	$ 4.25	37		$ 157.25	$ 157.25

- An employer may obtain a certificate to pay a worker with disabilities related to the work performed an amount less than the minimum wage.

EXAMPLE: DISABLED WORKER

Christi Snow is employed as a call-center representative with OEC Dispatch in Bend, Oregon. She is disabled due to a hearing impairment, and OEC Dispatch has obtained a certificate under section 14(c) of the FLSA in order to pay Christi $8.50/hour, which is less than the Oregon minimum wage of $9.25/hour. During the weekly pay period ending March 10, 20XX, Christi worked 44 hours, 4 hours of which were overtime. She is single with three withholding allowances. The payroll register for the period would appear as follows:

Name	M/S	# W/H	Hourly Rate or Period Wage	No. of Regular Hours	No. of Overtime Hours	Reg. Earnings	Overtime Earnings	Gross Earning
Christi Snow	S	3	$ 8.50	40	4	$ 340.00	$ 51.00	$ 391.00

Full-time students in the employ of retail establishments, agriculture, colleges, and universities may receive a wage that is 85% of the federal minimum wage.

EXAMPLE: FULL-TIME STUDENT WAGE

Kay Stone works in the café at Valparaiso University in Valparaiso, Indiana. She is a full-time student of the university and is 20 years old. According to the FLSA, she may receive 85% of the minimum wage.

Indiana minimum wage: $7.25/hour

Full-time student wage = $7.25/hour × 0.85 = $6.16/hour

In her employment at the café, Katie may legally be paid $6.16 per hour while she is a full-time student. During the week of May 4, she worked 35 hours. She is single with two withholding allowances. The payroll register would appear as follows:

Name	M/S	# W/H	Hourly Rate or Period Wage	No. of Regular Hours	No. of Overtime Hours	Reg. Earnings	Overtime Earnings	Gross Earning
Kay Stone	S	2	$ 6.16	35		$ 215.60		

- Student learners in vocational education programs may be paid at a rate of 75% of the federal minimum wage.

EXAMPLE: STUDENT WORKER IN VOCATIONAL EDUCATION PROGRAM

Ben Yoo is enrolled at Middlebury High School in Maine and is taking a shop class as part of his program. Ben is 16 and is single with one withholding allowance. He works for Vining's Cabinets as an apprentice woodworker. After obtaining a certificate from the U.S. Department of Labor's Wage and Hour National Certification Team, Vining's Cabinets pays Ben an hourly wage of $5.44 per worker because of his enrollment in the shop class at his high school. During the weekly pay period ending December 18, 20XX, Ben worked 36 hours. The payroll register would reflect his pay as follows:

Name	M/S	# W/H	Hourly Rate or Period Wage	No. of Regular Hours	No. of Overtime Hours	Reg. Earnings	Overtime Earnings	Gross Earning
Ben Yoo	S	1	$ 5.44	36		$ 195.84		$ 195.84

What is the Correct Pay?

1. Alex is a nonexempt employee of The Silver Club. He works 10 hours of overtime during a pay period and requests that he receive compensatory time instead of overtime pay. The Silver Club's overtime policy states that that compensatory time may be offered at 1.5 times the number of hours worked in excess of 40. His employer grants his request and offers him 10 hours of compensatory time. Alex claims he should receive 15 hours. How much comp time should Alex receive? Explain.

2. Stacy is a student in a vocational program at a cosmetology school. She accepts employment as a shampooer at Cuts & Styles Hair Salon in Alabama. The agreement between the school and the salon is that students receive the student-learner minimum wage. How much should Stacy be paid per hour?

Trends to Watch

EMPLOYEE COMPENSATION

Employee compensation tends to be a hot topic because of the way it affects people on a personal level. Some developments since 2010 in employee compensation include:

*   Increased diligence in overtime tracking and compensation following a lawsuit involving large companies.
*   New types of incentive pay to increase employee engagement, including merchandise rewards, additional company benefits, and other nonmonetary awards.
*   Discussions of the legality of differential pay levels for travel time by nonexempt employees.
*   Discussions about gaps in wages between people with and without a college education.

Some trends to watch in employee compensation include the following:

*   Establishment of an increased salaried minimum wage that may lead to reclassifications of workers as nonexempt employees.
*   Increased scrutiny about equal pay for equal work in the wake of California's passage of SB 358 Fair Pay Act.
*   Pay adjustments and business changes as employers face increased minimum wages.
*   Increased range of performance-based pay to recognize employee efforts.
*   Paid family leave challenges facing state legislators.

Summary of Gross Pay Computation

Gross pay is the employee's compensation before taxes and other withholdings are deducted; net pay is the amount of money an employee receives after taxes and other deductions are subtracted. We discussed the different types of methods for pay computation, including salary, hourly, commission, and piece-rate pay. We looked at the effect of FLSA provisions and applicability of different compensation methods and offered examples of some job classifications that could be compensated using different methods. We discussed the use of a payroll register in computing gross pay. We concluded with a discussion of special compensation situations, especially on-call time, time spent unoccupied for the employer's benefit, and situations in which an employee may receive less than the FLSA minimum wage.

Key Points

- Gross pay is the total amount earned by an employee prior to the deductions for taxes or other withholdings.
- Employees may be subject to the wage and hour provisions of the FLSA (nonexempt) or they may not (exempt), depending on the type of job and employee duties.
- Nonexempt hourly employees are compensated on a basis that recognizes an economic connection between work performed and wages paid.
- Nonexempt salaried employees work a fixed number of working hours per week and receive overtime compensation.
- Exempt employees receive a fixed salary and may work more hours than their nonexempt colleagues.
- Commission-based pay connects employee compensation with sales revenue.
- Piece-rate pay compensates employees based on the manufacturing or completion of goods or services.
- The payroll register is an integral tool to ensure the accuracy of payroll computations, especially in combination pay situations.
- Employees may have the option to draw against future earnings.
- ISOs are a means of offering compensation that is connected to company profitability.
- Compensatory time is legally required for public-sector exempt employees and may be offered to private-sector employees at the employer's discretion.
- Employees may be compensated for time that they are unoccupied if they are required to be available for the employer's benefit.
- In certain circumstances, employees may receive less than the FLSA minimum wage.

Vocabulary

Combination pay	Hundredth-hour	Quarter-hour
Commission	Incentive stock options (ISO)	Salary
Compensatory	Minimum wage	Sleeping time
(comp) time	Net pay	Time card
Draw	Nonexempt	Tipped Employees
Exempt	On-call time	Tipped wages
Gross pay	Overtime	Travel time
Hourly	Payroll register	Wait time

Review Questions

1. How is overtime pay computed for nonexempt salaried workers?

2. When do overtime rates apply?

3. How does minimum wage affect commission employees?

4. How does the tipped minimum wage differ from the FLSA minimum wage?

5. What types of occupations are typically salaried?

6. What is an ISO, and how does it affect employee pay?

7. What is the difference between a salary and a draw?

8. How is overtime computed for piece-rate employees?

9. In what situations could a salaried employee receive overtime pay?

10. What is the primary difference between commission work and piece-rate work?

11. In what situations might an employee draw money against his or her future pay?

12. What is the difference between quarter-hour and hundredth-hour pay?

13. Why are companies moving toward the hundredth-hour system?

14. What is comp time?

15. Under what circumstances may an employee receive compensation for on-call time?

16. When are wait time, travel time, and sleep time compensable?

17. Aside from tipped employees, under what circumstances may an employee receive less than the FLSA minimum wage?

Exercises Set A

E3-1A.

LO 3-1

Rose is a minimum wage worker in Missouri. She is contemplating a move to another state. Which of the following states would be the most favorable in terms of the highest minimum wage?
1. Indiana
2. Arkansas
3. Kansas
4. Tennessee

E3-2A.

LO 3-1

Certain types of businesses are always covered by FLSA provisions. Which of the following businesses are always covered by FLSA? (Select all that apply.)
1. Fruit stands selling only locally obtained goods that conduct no interstate business.
2. A school for children with learning disabilities.
3. A privately run hospital.
4. A Social Security Administration branch office.

E3-3A.

LO 3-1

Ryanne is a tipped employee in Idaho. What is the minimum tipped wage for her state?
1. $2.13/hour
2. $3.95/hour
3. $3.75/hour
4. $3.35/hour

E3-4A.

LO 3-1

Rob, a waiter at a restaurant in Iowa, receives the tipped minimum wage. During a 40-hour workweek, how much must he earn in tips to meet the minimum wage requirement?
1. $31
2. $75
3. $116
4. $195

E3-5A.

LO 3-2

Romeo works for a menswear retail store. His compensation is based on sales of store products to customers. Which type of pay basis represents Romeo's pay?
1. Piece rate
2. Hourly
3. Commission
4. Salary

E3-6A.

LO 3-3

Leah is an account clerk who is paid $11.23 per hour. During a week's pay period, she worked 38 hours and 47 minutes. Based on a hundredth-hour pay method, what is her gross pay for the period? (Round the final answer to two decimal places.)
1. $435.22
2. $435.16
3. $435.54
4. $435.95

E3-7A.

LO 3-4

Of the items in the following list, which ones should appear in a payroll register? (Select all that apply.)
1. Name
2. Marital status
3. Shifts worked
4. Hours worked

E3-8A.

LO 3-4

Alix Phillips is a salaried, exempt employee with HB Inc. She is single with one withholding allowance and earns $52,000 per year. Complete the payroll register for the biweekly pay period ending June 10, 20XX.

Company:							No. of Regular Hours	No. of Overtime Hours	Reg. Earnings	Overtime Earnings	Gross Earning
Name	M/S	# W/H	Hourly Rate or Period Wage	Period Salary	Commissions	Draw					

Period Ended:

E3-9A.

LO 3-5

Mitch Bates is an employee of Wesley Elevators, where his job responsibilities include selling service contracts to customers. Mitch is single with two withholding allowances. He receives an annual salary of $24,000 and receives a 3% commission on all sales. During the semimonthly pay period ending October 12, 20XX, Mitch sold $10,000 of service contracts. Complete the payroll register for the October 12 pay period.

Company:							No. of Regular Hours	No. of Overtime Hours	Reg. Earnings	Overtime Earnings	Gross Earning
Name	M/S	# W/H	Hourly Rate or Period Wage	Period Salary	Commissions	Draw					

Period Ended:

E3-10A.

LO 3-6

Sholem is a full-time student at Yeshiva University in Pittsburgh, Pennsylvania, where he works in the library. What is the minimum hourly wage that he may receive?
1. $7.25
2. $6.50
3. $6.16
4. $5.44

Problems Set A

P3-1A.

LO 3-3

Amanda M. worked the following schedule: Monday, 8 hours; Tuesday, 9 hours; Wednesday, 7 hours 48 minutes; Thursday, 8 hours; Friday, 8 hours. The employer pays overtime for all time worked in excess of 40 hours per week. Complete the following table. Enter Total Time, Regular Time, and Overtime based on whichever method is favorable.

	Total Time	Regular Time	Overtime	Quarter-Hour Time	Hundredth-Hour Time
Amanda M.					

Which pay is more favorable for Amanda, quarter-hour or hundredth-hour?

P3-2A.

LO 3-2

Justin Ullman is a salaried exempt employee at Velvet Chain Company. He is married with five withholding allowances. His contract stipulates a 40-hour workweek at $60,000 per year. During the week ending November 27, there was a company paid holiday for two days. Calculate Justin's weekly pay. Round wages to 5 decimal points.

Name	M/S	# W/H	Hourly Rate or Period Wage	No. of Regular Hours	No. of Overtime Hours	Reg. Earnings	Overtime Earnings	Gross Earning

P3-3A.

LO 3-2

Tessa completed 17 pieces on her 15-piece contract for the company. There is a bonus earned if the individual exceeds 2% of her piece contract. How many pieces must Tessa complete in the remainder of the week to receive the bonus?

P3-4A.

LO 3-4

Aaron works for Pinecone Parasails. He is a shared employee; he works in the manufacturing department and has been trained to work the sales counter in times of need. During other employees' vacations, he was asked to work in the sales department two days for six hours each day. When he works in the manufacturing department, he earns $11.50 per hour. Aaron earns a $2.50 pay differential for working the sales counter. He worked a total of 39.58 hours during the week. Aaron is single with one withholding allowance. Compute Aaron's pay for the week ending May 24. (Use a separate line for each job classification.)

Name	M/S	# W/H	Hourly Rate or Period Wage	No. of Regular Hours	No. of Overtime Hours	Reg. Earnings	Overtime Earnings	Gross Earning

P3-5A.

LO 3-3

Enrique submitted a pay card reflecting the following hours. He earns $13.98 per hour. Compute his pay under both the hundredth-hour and quarter-hour systems. The company pays overtime only on hours worked exceeding 40 per week. Each time the employee clocks in or out, the time is rounded to the nearest quarter-hour. If an individual clocks in at 8:07 a.m., the system records that he clocked in at 8:00. If he clocks in at 8:08 a.m., the system records that he clocked in at 8:15. Calculate hundredth- or quarter-hour on each clock in or out.

In	Out	In	Out	Total Hours with Hundredth-Hour	Total Hours with Quarter-Hour
8:00	11:22	12:17	5:22		
7:29	12:30	1:45	4:10		
9:12	11:45	12:28	3:36		
8:00	11:00	12:02	5:00		

Enrique's total pay in a hundredth-hour system: _____
Enrique's total pay in a quarter-hour system: _____

P3-6A.

LO 3-4

Daniel Wallentine, a single employee with two withholding allowances, is paid $10 per hour and receives commission on net sales. He does not receive commission until his net sales exceed $150,000. Once the minimum sales volume is reached, he receives 2% commission on all of his sales at Carl's Canopies. This week he sold $163,000 of canopies; however, he had $1,500 of returns from last week's sales. Company policy requires he return commissions on sale returns. Compute Daniel's gross pay for the 40 hour weekly pay period.

Name	M/S	# W/H	Hourly Rate or Period Wage	No. of Regular Hours	No. of Overtime Hours	Reg. Earnings	Commissions	Gross Earning

P3-7A.

LO 3-1, 3-2

Cathy, an outside sales representative for a magazine company, receives 10% commission on all new subscriptions she receives in her sales territory. This week she sold $5,000 of new subscriptions and worked 40 hours. What is her gross pay? _____
Is she subject to minimum wage laws? _____
Why or why not?_____

P3-8A.

LO 3-1, 3-2

Telemarketers receive $15 commission on all new customers they sign up for phone service through Birch Phones. Each telemarketer works 40 hours. The company ran a competition this week to see who could sign up the most new people, and the winner would get a bonus of $50. Because these employees are paid solely on commission, the employer must ensure that they earn the federal minimum wage for 40 hours each week. Compute the gross pay for each of the following outbound sales representatives.

Employee	Number of New Customers Signed	Total Commission	Difference Between Commission and Minimum Pay	Total Gross Pay
Kenny	22			
Charles	18			
Laurie	29			
Phyllis	16			

P3-9A.

LO 3-1, 3-2

For each of the piece-rate workers below, determine gross pay. If the employees have a standard 40-hour workweek, what is their affected hourly wage? (Reminder: gross pay divided by 40 hours equals hourly wage.) Based on the FLSA minimum wage, calculate each employee's minimum weekly pay. What is the difference the employer must pay between the calculated gross pay and the calculated FLSA minimum pay?

Worker	Number of Items	Rate per Item	Gross Pay	Gross Pay/40 Hours	Minimum Pay	Difference to Be Paid by the Employer
Mark	25 hulls	$10				
Richie	70 seat covers	$15				
Tony	45 steering mechanisms	$ 4				

P3-10A.

LO 3-1, 3-2

Rick Wallace is a waiter at Palace Eats in Delaware. He is single with one withholding allowance. He receives the standard tipped hourly wage. During the week ending October 20, 20XX, he worked 40 hours and received $160 in tips. Calculate the following:

Name	M/S	# W/H	Hourly Rate or Period Wage	No. of Regular Hours	No. of Overtime Hours	Reg. Earnings	Tips	Gross Earning

How much does Palace Eats need to contribute to Rick's wages to meet FLSA requirements? _____

P3-11A.

LO 3-4

Grace Parker is a salaried, nonexempt administrator for H.E.R. Company and is paid biweekly. Her annual salary is $48,000, and her standard workweek is 35 hours. During the pay period ending January 29, 20XX, she worked 8 hours overtime. She is single with 2 withholding allowances.

Name	M/S	# W/H	Hourly Rate or Period Wage	No. of Regular Hours	No. of Overtime Hours	Reg. Earnings	Overtime Earnings	Gross Earning

P3-12A.

LO 3-5

Nadine is an administrative assistant for her employer. At the end of her shift one day, her employer requires her to deliver a package to a customer before traveling home. Her normal commute is 1 hour. She spends two hours driving to the customer site, and then another hour driving home for a total of 3 hours drive time. How much of Nadine's travel time is compensable?

P3-13A.

LO 3-6

Colin is an 18-year-old worker in the receiving department of a company. On his first paycheck, he notices that he received $170.00 gross pay for 40 hours of work. Did his employer pay him correctly? Explain.

Exercises Set B

E3-1B.

LO 3-1

Brooke is a minimum wage worker in South Dakota. She is contemplating moving to a state with a more favorable minimum wage. Which of the following states should she choose?
1. North Dakota
2. Minnesota
3. Nebraska
4. Montana

E3-2B.

LO 3-1

Which of the following workers is covered by FLSA provisions? (Select all that apply.)
1. Factory manager for an international company.
2. In-home caregiver earning $32,500 annually.
3. Professional chauffeur earning $25,000 annually.
4. Assistant fire chief for a small town.

E3-3B.

LO 3-1

Elmira is a tipped employee in Hawaii. What is the minimum tipped wage for her area?
1. $2.13/hour
2. $4.95/hour
3. $7.75/hour
4. $9.50/hour

E3-4B.

LO 3-1

Kathryn is a waitress at a restaurant in South Carolina. She earns the tipped minimum wage. During a 40-hour workweek, how much must she earn in tips to satisfy the minimum wage requirement?

1. $85.20
2. $204.80
3. $290.00
4. $153.40

E3-5B.

LO 3-2

Peggy is an employee of Yummy Cake Bakery. She is a cake decorator who is paid based on the number and complexity of the cakes she decorates. What pay basis most accurately describes her compensation?

1. Hourly
2. Commission
3. Piece-rate
4. Salary

E3-6B.

LO 3-3

Paul works as a janitor who is paid on an hourly basis and earns $9.50/hour. During a one-week period, he works 38 hours and 40 minutes. How much would his gross pay be under the quarter-hour system? (Round your final answer to two decimal places.)

1. $361.00
2. $365.54
3. $368.13
4. $370.50

E3-7B.

LO 3-4

Of the following items listed, which ones should appear in a payroll register? (Select all that apply.)

1. Gross pay
2. Hourly rate
3. Period ending date
4. Office number

E3-8B.

LO 3-4

Bill Smith works for NMH Industries. He is married with two withholding allowances and earns $18.55 per hour. During a biweekly pay period ending March 5, 20XX, he worked 78.5 hours. Complete the payroll register with the period's information.

Company: _____   Period Ended: _____

Name	M/S	# W/H	Hourly Rate or Period Wage	Period Salary	Commissions	Draw	No. of Regular Hours	No. of Overtime Hours	Reg. Earnings	Overtime Earnings	Commission Earnings	Gross Earning

E3-9B.

LO 3-5

Paula Warren is an employee of Atlas Investments, where she earns a base salary of $57,200 plus a 1% commission on all sales. She is married with four withholding allowances. During the biweekly pay period ended December 5, 20XX, Paula made $500,000 in investment sales. Complete the payroll register for this pay period.

Company: _____   Period Ended: _____

Name	M/S	# W/H	Hourly Rate or Period Wage	Period Salary	Commissions	Draw	No. of Regular Hours	No. of Overtime Hours	Reg. Earnings	Overtime Earnings	Commission Earnings	Gross Earning

E3-10B.

LO 3-6

Jan is 18 years of age and is a new employee of Moral Used Cars in Pullman, Washington. What is the minimum hourly wage that she may receive during the first 90 days of employment?

1. $9.47
2. $8.05
3. $7.10
4. $4.25

Problems Set B

P3-1B.

LO 3-3

Nick B. worked the following schedule: Monday, 8 hours, 24 minutes; Tuesday, 7 hours, 44 minutes; Wednesday, 9 hours, 8 minutes; Thursday, 8 hours, 2 minutes; Friday, 8 hours, 36 minutes. The employer pays overtime for all time worked in excess of 40 hours per week. Complete the following table. Enter Total Time, Regular Time, and Overtime based on whichever method is favorable.

	Total Time	Regular Time	Overtime	Quarter-Hour Time	Hundredth-Hour Time
Nick B.					

Which pay is more favorable for Nick, quarter-hour or hundredth-hour?

P3-2B.

LO 3-2

Shawn Ames is a salaried exempt employee at Rush Elevators with a contract that stipulates 37.5 hours per week at $75,000 per year. He is married with three withholding allowances. This pay period there was a company-paid holiday for three days. Calculate Shawn's biweekly pay based on a standard five-day workweek. Round wages to 5 decimal points. (Hint: determine Shawn's hourly wage to determine holiday pay.)

Name	M/S	# W/H	Hourly Rate or Period Wage	No. of Regular Hours	No. of Overtime Hours	Reg. Earnings	Overtime Earnings	Gross Earning

P3-3B.

LO 3-2

Janet completed 1,200 pieces on her 1,400-piece contract for the company. There is a bonus earned if the individual exceeds 15% of her piece contract. How many pieces must Janet complete in the remainder of the week to receive the bonus?

P3-4B.

LO 3-4

Paris Johnson is a shared employee; she works in the accounting department and has been trained to work at the front desk in times of need. During other employees' vacations, she was asked to work at the front desk four days for five hours each day. When she works in the accounting department, she earns $13.62/hour. Paris earns $12.98/hour for working at the front desk. She worked a total of 38.75 hours during the week. (Use separate lines for each job classification)

Name	M/S	# W/H	Hourly Rate or Period Wage	No. of Regular Hours	No. of Overtime Hours	Reg. Earnings	Overtime Earnings	Gross Earning

P3-5B.

LO 3-3

Jasper submitted a pay card reflecting the following hours. He earns $16.45 per hour. Compute his pay under both the hundredth-hour and quarter-hour systems. Calculate hundredth- and quarter-hour on each clock in or out. Each time the employee clocks in or out, the time is rounded to the nearest quarter hour. If an individual clocks in at 8:07 a.m., the system records that he clocked in at 8:00. If he clocks in at 8:08 a.m., the system records that he clocked in at 8:15.

In	Out	In	Out	Total Hours with Hundredth-Hour	Total Hours with Quarter-Hour
8:08	11:57	12:59	4:57		
9:04	12:17	1:28	5:18		
7:45	11:45	12:43	4:01		
7:57	12:04	1:03	5:06		

Jasper's total pay in the hundredth-hour system _____

Jasper's total pay in a quarter-hour system _____

P3-6B.

LO 3-4

Priscilla Stamper is a commission-based employee who is single with one withholding allowance. She is paid $16.50/hour and receives commission on net sales. She does not receive commissions until her net sales exceed $5,500 during a weekly period at TLA Medicinals. Once the minimum sales volume is reached, she receives 4% commission on all of her sales. For the week ending June 15, 20XX, she worked 40 hours and sold $6,700 of medicinals but had $900 of returns from last week's sales. Company policy requires that she return commissions on sale returns. Compute her gross pay for the week.

Name	M/S	# W/H	Hourly Rate or Period Wage	No. of Regular Hours	No. of Overtime Hours	Reg. Earnings	Commissions	Gross Earning

P3-7B.

LO 3-1, 3-2

Mareka, an outside sales representative for an insurance company, receives 3% commission on all new policies she receives in her sales territory. This week she sold $150,000 of new policies and worked 40 hours.

What is her gross pay? _____

Is she subject to minimum wage laws? _____

Why or why not? _____

P3-8B.

LO 3-1, 3-2

Outbound sales representatives receive a $20 commission on all new customers they sign up for new magazine subscriptions. Each outbound sales representative works 40 hours. During a weekly competition, the outbound sales representative who sold the most subscriptions was awarded a $125 bonus. Because these employees are paid solely on commission, the employer must ensure that they earn the federal minimum wage for 40 hours each week. Compute the gross pay for each of the following outbound sales representatives.

Employee	Number of New Customers Signed	Total Commission	Difference Between Commission and Minimum Pay	Total Gross Pay
Angela	35			
Catherine	22			
Tom	42			
Frank	29			

P3-9B.
LO 3-1, 3-2

For each of the piece-rate workers below, determine gross pay. If the employees have a standard 37.5-hour workweek, what is their effective hourly rate (the gross pay/37.5 hours)? Based on FLSA minimum wages, what is the minimum wage they must receive each week? If they are not receiving the FLSA minimum wage for the pay period, what is the difference that must be paid by the employer? If not, what is the difference between gross pay and minimum that the employer must pay?

Worker	Number of Items	Rate per Item	Gross Pay	Gross Pay/ 37.5 Hours	Minimum Pay	Difference to Be Paid by the Employer
Brenda	25 snowboards	$9				
Mike	30 helmets	$7.75				
Bruce	80 bindings	$4.50				

P3-10B.
LO 3-1, 3-2

Maddie James is a waitress at Quick Lunch in Vermont. She is single with one withholding allowance. She receives the standard tipped hourly wage for the state. During the week ending November 15, 20XX, she worked 40 hours and received $105 in tips. Compute Maddie's pay for the period.

Name	M/S	# W/H	Hourly Rate or Period Wage	No. of Regular Hours	No. of Overtime Hours	Reg. Earnings	Tips	Gross Earning

How much does Quick Lunch need to contribute to Maddie's wages to meet FLSA requirements? _____

P3-11B.
LO 3-4

Eric Matte is a salaried, nonexempt administrative assistant for his company and is paid semimonthly. He is married with 2 withholding allowances. His annual salary is $39,000, and his standard workweek is 37.5 hours. During a pay period, he worked 10 hours overtime. Compute Eric's gross pay for the period ending August 2, 20XX.

Name	M/S	# W/H	Hourly Rate or Period Wage	No. of Regular Hours	No. of Overtime Hours	Reg. Earnings	Overtime Earnings	Gross Earning

P3-12B.
LO 3-5

Marshawn is a sales assistant whose normal commute time is 30 minutes in each direction. At the beginning of his shift one day, his employer requires him to pick up a package from a customer before arriving at work. He spends 1 hour driving to the customer site and then another 30 minutes driving to the office, for a total of 1.5 hours drive time. How much of Marshawn's travel time is compensable?

P3-13B.
LO 3-6

Olivia is a 19-year-old accounting clerk. During the first month of her employment with a firm, she noticed that she received $369.75 for her first semimonthly pay covering 87 regular hours. Did the employer pay her correctly? Explain.

Critical Thinking

3-1. West Virginia State University has a policy of hiring students to work in its bookstores and cafeterias. Assuming that 138 students work for the university at minimum wage rates, what is the amount of pay they will receive for a biweekly pay period, assuming they each work 30 hours per week?

3-2. Daniel owns Veiled Wonders, a firm that makes window treatments. Some merchandise is custom-made to customer specifications, and some is mass-produced in standardized measurements. He has production workers who work primarily on standardized blinds and some employees who additionally work on custom products on an as-needed basis. How should he structure his pay methods for his production workers?

In the Real World: Scenario for Discussion

Motor vehicle service technicians usually must provide their own tools as part of their employment. These tools are the property of the technician, and service technicians generally receive an hourly wage. Some automobile dealerships split service technician wages into classifications such as tool reimbursements and wages. The result of this practice is that the worker's hours are taxed and the tool reimbursements are not because they are classified as a business expense.

Should the tool reimbursement be treated as income on the service technician's W-2? Why or why not? What are some implications of this practice?

Internet Activities

3-1. Using a search engine such as Google, Yahoo, or Bing, search "Commission-based pay." Sites such as the Society for Human Resource Management (www.shrm.com) have a large volume of articles about commission-based pay and workplace cases. Choose a case and find out as much as you can about the company involved. Why do you think that commission-based pay is such a popular topic among human resource professionals?

3-2. Go to www.accountingtools.com/podcasts and look for payroll-related podcasts. Once you have listened to one or more podcasts, what do you feel was the most interesting information you learned?

3-3. Want to learn more about the concepts in this chapter? Check out:

www.dol.gov/whd/minwage/america.htm

www.flsa.com/coverage.html

www.finance.ohiou.edu/financials/100thHourTable.htm

www.fairmark.com/execcomp/iso.htm

Continuing Payroll Project: Prevosti Farms and Sugarhouse

February 12 is the end of the first pay period for Prevosti Farms and Sugarhouse and includes work completed during the week of February 8–12. Compute the employee gross pay using 35 hours as the standard workweek for all employees except Mary Shangraw, who works 20 hours per week and receives overtime for any time worked past that point. The other hourly employees receive overtime pay when they work more than 35 hours in one week. Joel Schwartz has made $5,000 in case sales at a 3% commission rate during this pay period. Remember that the employees are paid biweekly. The first day of work for Prevosti Farms and Sugarhouse for all employees is February 8, 2016. Note that the first pay period comprises only one week of work, but the pay frequency for federal income tax purposes is biweekly.

The hours for the nonexempt employees are as follows:

Name	Hourly Rate	Hours Worked 2/8–2/12	Regular Time Pay	Overtime Pay	Commission Pay	Gross Pay
Towle	$12.00	35 hours				
Long	$12.50	40 hours				
Shangraw	$10.50	21 hours				
Success (You)	$34,000/year	35 hours				

Complete the payroll register for the period's gross pay. Pay will be disbursed on February 15, 2016, starting with check number 6628.

February 26, 2016, is the end of the final pay period for the month. Schwartz has sold $7,500 of product during this pay period at a 3% commission. Complete the payroll register for the period's gross pay. Pay will be disbursed on February 29, 2016, and check numbers will continue from prior payroll.

The hours for the nonexempt employees are as follows:

Name	Hourly Rate	Hours Worked 2/15–2/26	Regular Time Pay	Overtime Pay	Commission Pay	Gross Pay
Towle	$12.00	80 hours				
Long	$12.50	70 hours				
Shangraw	$10.50	42 hours				
Success (You)	$34,000/year	71 hours				

P/R End Date [   ]   Company Name: _____

Check Date [   ]

Name	M/S	# W/H	Hourly Rate or Period Wage	No. of Regular Hours	No. of Overtime Hours	No. of Holiday Hours	Commissions	Gross Earning	401(k)	Sec 125	Taxable Wages for Federal W/H	Taxable Wages for FICA
Totals								–	–	–	–	–

Name	Gross Earning	Taxable Wages for Federal W/H	Taxable Wages for FICA	Federal W/H	Social Security Tax	Medicare W/H	State W/H Tax	Garnish-ment	United Way	Net Pay	Check No
Totals	–	–	–	–	–	–	–	–	–	–	

Answers to Stop & Check Exercises

Pay Your Employees Correctly

1. No. Heather should have received time-and-a-half for the additional 8 hours. Her pay should have been $667.00 ((80 × 7.25) + (8 × 1.5 × 7.25))
2. $345.63 (39.5 × 8.75)

3. $512.00 (32 × 2 × 8.00)
4. $543.75 (7.25 × 75)

Pay Computations for Different Basis

1. $6,744.00 ($224,800 × 3%)
2. $1,100.00. Yes, because $1,100.00 / 90 hours = $12.22 per hour
3. With unpaid time, her current pay will be less; if she had vacation time, there would be no difference.
   Standard salary per biweekly payroll: $57,000 / 26 = $2,192.31
   ($57,000 / (40 × 26)) = $27.40 per hour × (8 × 3) for unpaid leave of $657.60
   Current pay $2,192.31 − 657.60 = $1,543.70

Quarter-Hour vs. Hundredth-Hour

1. Ann:
   Quarter-hour: 8.25 hours
   Hundredth-hour: 7.93 hours

   Nevada:
   Quarter-hour: 8 hours
   Hundredth-hour: 8.12 hours

   Pat:
   Quarter-hour: 8 hours
   Hundredth-hour: 7.82 hours

2. The difference exists because the time worked during a quarter-hour system is rounded to the nearest quarter hour. In a hundredth-hour system, the worker is paid for the exact number of minutes worked.
3. It would be beneficial to adopt a hundredth-hour system to reduce payroll inaccuracies that may affect both employees and company profits.

Payroll Registers

1. To document the employees' time and hours work as well as to provide totals of the compensation by each category.
2. Name, marital status, number of withholdings, hourly rate, number of regular hours, number of overtime hours, commission, piece rate, regular earnings, overtime earnings, gross earnings.
3. To facilitate calculations of regular and overtime, help ensure accuracy, and allow for analysis of overtime worked.

Combination Pay Methods

1. Base pay = $42,000 × 24 = $1,750
   Commission = $100 × 5 = $500
   Gross pay = $2,250
2. $36,000 ÷ 12 = $3,000 per month
   $3,000 × 0.35 = $1,050 mid-month draw
   $3,000 − $1,050 draw = $1,950 received at the end of the month
3. $75,000 × 0.03 = $2,250 received in stock.
   Annual compensation = $75,000 + $2,250 = $77,250

What Is the Correct Pay?

1. 15 hours because comp time must be awarded at 1.5 times regular hours.
2. $5.44 per hour ($7.25 × 75%)

Chapter Four

4

Employee Net Pay and Pay Methods

Death and taxes are the two certainties in life. Taxes are withheld from employees' earnings and remitted to the governing body. Companies operate as the collector and depositor of income taxes, garnishments, and other deductions on behalf of the employee. The tax code permits certain qualifying deductions to be taken out of an employee's pay prior to the income taxes being calculated. These deductions are called pre-tax deductions. Other deductions come out of the employee's pay after income taxes have been calculated; these are called post-tax deductions. Circular E, also known as Publication 15 (and all supplemental materials), from the Internal Revenue Service provides a comprehensive list of employee taxes, employer responsibilities, and guidance for special situations.

The pre-tax deductions reduce the current taxable income of the employee and may be taxed at a later time; for example, contributions to a qualifying retirement program would be a pre-tax deduction. Some pre-tax deductions will not be taxed later. The IRS refers to these pre-tax items as *fringe benefits* and clearly differentiates between taxable and nontaxable fringe benefits.

LEARNING OBJECTIVES

After studying Chapter 4, you should be able to:

LO 4-1   Compute Employee Net Pay

LO 4-2   Identify Pre-Tax Deductions

LO 4-3   Determine Federal Income Tax Withholding Amounts

LO 4-4   Compute Social Security and Medicare Tax Withholding

LO 4-5   Apply State and Local Income Taxes

LO 4-6   Explain Post-Tax Deductions

LO 4-7   Discuss Employee Pay Methods

© Ryan McVay/Getty Images, RF

The Pros and Cons of Paycards

Employers widely use payroll debit cards or "paycards." More than 26 million paycards are issued annually, containing nearly $150 billion in employee compensation. Paycards offer employees instant access to their funds and do not require them to maintain a bank account. They also facilitate secure payments to certain types of workers who earn daily cash wages by offering a secure method of tracking and disbursing pay.

Nearly 30% of all paycards issued do not contain access to an ATM network, forcing the employee to incur fees to access their wages. The bank-related fees for transactions and other restrictions related to paycard use have prompted legislative proposals in many states. Proposed legislation includes a seven-day period during which an employee may elect to have direct deposit to a bank account instead of the paycard, fee disclosure regulations, and prohibitions on employers requiring employees to accept paycards as part of their employment. (Sources: APA, 24/7WallSt)

The convenience and low cost of paycards are balanced by the need for increased vigilance and disclosure about employee fees to access their wages. In Chapter 4, we will explore computations of employee net pay and the methods used to transmit that pay to the employees.

Deductions from Gross Pay

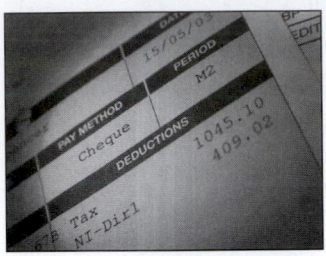

© Powered by Light RF/Alamy

An employer deducts mandatory, voluntary, and mandated deductions from an employee's gross pay. These deductions include federal income tax, Medicare, and Social Security taxes, which are the primary mandatory deductions. Other mandatory deductions that the employee may be subject to include *state income taxes*, city or county income taxes, and regional taxes. For example, Denver has a "head tax" for those employees working within the city and county. Federal Unemployment Tax is the sole employer-only tax. Some states require employees to contribute for the State Unemployment Tax, whereas other states consider it an employer-only tax.

Another class of deductions withheld from employee pay are voluntary deductions. Employees may choose to contribute to retirement programs, additional health or life insurance, or medical insurance through amounts withheld from their pay. Some of these voluntary deductions are pre-tax deductions, and some are post-tax deductions. It is important to classify the deduction correctly so that the proper amount of income taxes may be withheld.

A third class of deductions are mandated deductions, which are required by court order or other legal agreement. Examples of mandated deductions include child support, student loan repayments, and union dues. These items are post-tax deductions and are subject to minimal income requirements typically stipulated within the documentation. Employers are provided documentation by the state regulatory office or other governing body responsible for the redistribution of the withheld amounts to the appropriate parties.

LO 4-1   Compute Employee Net Pay

Now that we have discussed the computation of gross income, it is time to focus on the various taxes and miscellaneous voluntary or court-ordered deductions withheld and to determine the employee's *net pay*. The process of computing gross pay involves several steps, each of which must be completed accurately. We will explore the details of pre-tax deductions, tax computations, and post-tax deductions in the following sections of this chapter.

Pay Computation Steps

This is the process to compute each employee's pay:

1. Start with the employee's gross pay.
2. Subtract the pre-tax deductions to get the total taxable earnings.
3. Compute the taxes to be withheld from the total taxable earnings.
4. Deduct the taxes.
5. Deduct any other voluntary or mandated deductions.
6. The result is the employee's net pay.

EXAMPLE: NET PAY COMPUTATION

Marco Myles receives a salary of $2,000 paid biweekly and has earned $46,000 year-to-date. He is married with two withholding allowances and works for KOR, Inc., in Charleston, West Virginia, where his state income tax is 4.5%. His pre-tax deductions are medical insurance of $50, a cafeteria plan of $75, and a 401(k) of 3% of his gross salary per pay period. He has charitable contributions of $10, union dues of $62, and

(continued)

(concluded)

a court-ordered garnishment for $120. Taxable income computation is the same for both federal and state income tax purposes. Let us compute Marco's net pay step by step:

Gross pay	$2,000.00
less: pre-tax medical insurance deduction	−50.00
less: cafeteria plan	−75.00
less: 401(k) contribution	−60.00
Total taxable earnings	$1,815.00
less: federal income tax (using wage-bracket method)	−140.00
less: Social Security tax*	−116.25
less: Medicare tax**	−27.19
less: West Virginia state income tax	−81.68
less: charitable contribution	−10.00
less: union dues	−62.00
less: garnishment	−120.00
Net pay	$1,257.88

*2000 − 50 − 75 = 1,875 × .062 = 116.25
**2000 − 50 − 75 = 1875 × .0145 = 27.19

The payroll register for Marco Myles's pay would appear as follows:

Name	M/S	# W/H	Hourly Rate or Period Wage	Gross Earning	401(k)	Insurance	Cafeteria Plan	TaxableWages for Federal W/H	TaxableWages for FICA
Marco Myles	M	2	$2,000.00	$2,000.00	$ 60.00	$ 50.00	$ 75.00	$ 1,815.000	$ 1,875.00

Name	Gross Earning	Federal W/H	Social Security Tax	Medicare W/H	State W/H Tax	Charitable Cont.	Union Dues	Garnish-ment	Net Pay
Marco Myles	$ 2,000.00	$ 140.00	$ 116.25	$ 27.19	$ 81.68	$ 10.00	$ 62.00	$ 120.00	$1,257.89

An employer will occasionally want to pay an employee a specific net amount. However, all federal, state, and local taxes must be applied. The amount of the employee's pay must be "grossed up" to satisfy tax liabilities and achieve the net pay desired.

EXAMPLE: "GROSSING UP" AN EMPLOYEE'S PAY

Caitlyn Lanneker is an employee of Pacifica Enterprises, located in the state of Washington. The firm's president wants to award Caitlyn a bonus at the end of the year to reward her. Use the following steps to compute the gross-up amount:

1. Compute the tax rate for federal income tax and FICA. The tax rate on bonuses is 28%. The Social Security (6.2%) and Medicare taxes (1.45%) must be added to this rate. For bonuses, the total tax rate equals 28% + 6.2% + 1.45%, or 35.65%. (For nonbonus gross-up, compute the tax rate using amounts from Appendix C). Add any state or local income tax rates to this computation as necessary.

2. Subtract 100% − tax rate% to get the net tax rate. For this bonus, it is 100% − 35.65%, or 64.35% because no state or local income tax rates apply.

3. Gross-up amount equals the net pay divided by the net tax rate.

For example, for Caitlyn to receive a $150 bonus, the equation is $150/64.35% = $233.10.

Note: Typically voluntary pre-tax or post-tax deductions are not withheld from bonus checks.

Differentiating Between Gross and Net Pay

 **Stop & Check**

1. What is the difference between gross pay and net pay?
2. What are three items that may be deducted from gross pay?
3. What does it mean to "gross up" an amount paid to an employee?

LO 4-2   Identify Pre-Tax Deductions

Two classes of deductions exist: pre-tax and post-tax. Pre-tax deductions are those deductions that are withheld from an employee's *gross pay*, which is the amount of compensation prior to computing tax liability or applying deductions. The effect of pre-tax deductions is that they reduce the taxable income of the employee. Pre-tax deductions are *voluntary deductions* that have been legislated by the federal government as eligible for pre-tax withholding status, including certain types of insurance, retirement plans, and cafeteria plans.

Insurance

Employers may provide subsidized health insurance coverage for their employees. The employees pay a portion of these health insurance expenses out of their paycheck, and the company makes up the difference. How much a company pays is determined by the company and could vary greatly, depending on the costs of health insurance and the policy selected by the employee. For health insurance plans to qualify for pre-tax status, they must meet the guidelines stated in the IRS Code.

According to the IRS, the following guidelines are used to determine if a health insurance plan qualifies for pre-tax status:

- Health plans offered through the state's small or large group market
- A employer's self-insured health plan
- The Department of Defense's Non-appropriated Fund Health Benefits Program
- A governmental plan
- COBRA health coverage
- Retiree health coverage

Source: IRS

EXAMPLE: PRE-TAX MEDICAL PREMIUM

Betty works for Ruthere Phones. Her employer offers medical insurance for which the premiums may be taken on a pre-tax basis. Betty is a salaried employee who earns $48,000 annually and is paid on a semimonthly basis. Her premium for the medical insurance is $125 per pay period. Consider the following difference in taxable income:

	Medical insurance deducted on a pre-tax basis	Medical insurance NOT deduced on a pre-tax basis
Annual salary	$48,000	$48,000
Period salary	$48,000/24 = $2,000	$48,000/24 = $2,000
Medical insurance deduction	$125	$0
Taxable income	$1,875	$2,000

In 2010, the Affordable Care Act was passed, providing small businesses a tax credit when their employees are at low and moderate income levels for providing health insurance coverage. The act extended coverage of children until the age of 26 to be included as an option to employees on a pre-tax basis. This is only for employees covered under a qualifying cafeteria plan.

In response to the Affordable Care Act, the IRS Code 6056 changed the reporting requirements for health insurance programs provided to employees. Employers with more than 50 employees are required to file an information return with the IRS and must provide a detailed summary of health coverage to employees. The value of the insurance coverage contributed by the employer must be reported on the employee's W-2 year-end tax statement within box 12 using code DD and should reflect the amounts contributed by both the employee and the employer. It is important to remember that the amounts reported on the W-2 for the employer's contribution to health insurance do not add to the taxable wages of the employee.

According to the Internal Revenue Service, the Affordable Care Act mandates that individuals have "minimum essential coverage." Examples of minimum essential coverage include:

- Employer-provided health insurance
- Health insurance purchased through an approved health insurance exchange
- Coverage provided under federal auspices such as Medicare and Medicaid
- Privately purchased health insurance

Minimum essential coverage does not include the following limited benefit or limited term coverage plans:

- Vision and dental insurance issued on a stand-alone basis (i.e., not grouped with a medical insurance policy)
- Worker's compensation insurance
- Accidental death and disability plans maintained by the employer

(Source: IRS)

Supplemental Health and Disability Insurance

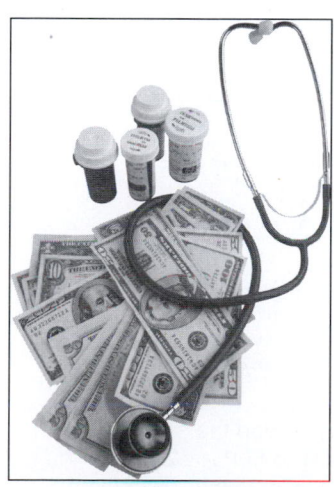

Another option many employers are offering is a flow-through (i.e., the company does not cover any of the costs) of supplemental health and disability insurance. One of the largest providers of this type of insurance is American Family Life Assurance Company of Columbus (AFLAC). There are a variety of policies under AFLAC with separate treatment for taxation purposes (whether pre- or post-tax). The IRS Revision Ruling 2004-55 deals specifically with the tax treatment of short- and long-term disability, and IRS Code Sections 104(a)(3) and 105(a) deal with the exclusion of short- and long-term disability benefits from employees' gross wages. Long-term disability insurance is excluded from taxable income under the ruling. If an employer pays for long-term disability insurance, these amounts may be excluded from or included in gross pay, depending upon the election of the company. When determining the tax treatment for the supplemental health insurance, the IRS guidance provides the following: If the income derived will be estimated to be tax-free, then the cost associated will also be tax-exempt. (Note: Supplemental health and disability plan premiums are not tax-exempt for Social Security and Medicare taxes.)

EXAMPLE: SUPPLEMENTAL HEALTH INSURANCE DEDUCTION

Jim is a salaried exempt employee of LC Holdings. He earns $78,000 annually and is paid biweekly. The employer offers him medical insurance and supplemental health insurance with premiums of $150 and $75, respectively. Jim elects to have both premiums withheld on a pre-tax basis.

Salary per period ($78,000/26)	$ 3,000.00
Less: Medical insurance premium	$ 150.00
Less: Supplemental medical insurance premium	$ 75.00
Taxable income**	$ 2,775.00

**Note: Taxable income computed here pertains to computations of federal income tax. The taxable income for Social Security and Medicare taxes would be $2,850 because supplemental medical insurance premiums are not exempt.

Retirement Plans

Retirement plans were covered under the Employee Retirement Income Security Act (ERISA) of 1974 in conjunction with the Internal Revenue Code. There are two basic types of retirement plans: *defined benefit* and *defined contribution*. In a defined benefit plan, the employer guarantees the employee a specific level of income once retirement has been reached. As an

example, under a defined benefit plan, the employer may guarantee 1% of average salary earned in the final five years of employment.

In a defined contribution plan, the individual places money from his or her payroll, pre-tax, into a retirement plan and the company may or may not match to a percentage. There are several different types of defined contribution plans, such as *401(k)*, *SIMPLE 401(k)*, *403(b)*, *IRA*, *SIMPLE IRA*, *SEP*, *ESOP*, and profit sharing.

Note: Although some qualified 401(k) plans may be considered as cafeteria plans and may be excluded from FICA tax liability, the IRS states in Publication 15b that most 401(k) plans are subject to Social Security and Medicare taxes. For the purposes of this text, we will assume that the 401(k) plans are not included in federal or state tax calculations but are included in Social Security and Medicare tax calculations. See Table 4-1 for an explanation of the different retirement plan types.

© Jim Arbogast/Digital Vision/Getty Images, RF

TABLE 4-1
Retirement Plan Types

Type of Plan	Description
401(k)	A group of investments, typically invested in stock market–based or mutual fund–based plans
403(b)	Similar to a 401(k), but offered by nonprofit employers such as hospitals and schools
Savings Incentive Match Plan for Employees (SIMPLE)	The major limitation is employers may not have more than 100 employees. Funds are specifically set aside for the individual employee in a bank, mutual fund account, or stock market SIMPLE 401(k).
Individual Retirement Account (IRA)	Funds are specifically set aside for the individual employee in a bank or mutual fund account.
Employee Stock Ownership Plan (ESOP)	The company offers employees the ability to earn company stock for the duration of their employment.
Simplified Employee Pension (SEP)	A tax-favorable IRA is set up by or for the employee, and the employer contributes the funds into the account. The SEP is tax-favorable because it reduces the employee's income tax liability.

EXAMPLE: RETIREMENT PLAN EMPLOYEE CONTRIBUTION

Natalie is a salaried, exempt employee of Turner Construction. She is single with one withholding deduction and receives an annual salary of $60,000, paid semimonthly. She elects to contribute 6% of her period pay to the company-sponsored 401(k) plan on a pre-tax basis. Her taxable income would be computed as follows:

Salary per period ($60,000/24)	$2,500.00
Less: 6% contribution to 401(k)	$ 150.00
Taxable income	$2,350.00

Note: The 401(k) deduction is *not* exempt from Social Security and Medicare taxes.

Cafeteria Plans

Cafeteria plans, also known as health plans or Section 125 plans, are offered by the employer and are usually deducted on a pre-tax basis. A cafeteria plan is health insurance coverage that allows employees to make selections from a variety of tax-free, cash, and taxable benefits options. There are many different varieties of health plans. One type of health plan includes a *Health Savings Account (HSA)* that can be used to pay long-term care costs. Another benefit that can be included in the cafeteria plan is a *Flexible Spending Account (FSA)*. FSAs are available to assist in the payment of medical expenses, including copayments and prescriptions, transportation, and certain child-care expenses. Not all HSAs can be considered tax-exempt. Only those included as part of the company's qualifying Section 125 cafeteria plan are deemed exempt from Social Security, Medicare, and federal income taxes.

Although several items are included in the health insurance cafeteria plan, there are also several items that cannot be included in the company's cafeteria plan per IRS regulations. (For a full list, view IRS Publication 15B.)

CAFETERIA PLANS

Section 125 of the IRS code was initially enacted in 1978 and has been revised several times. It permits employers to offer employees a choice between two or more cash and qualified benefits. The employer must explicitly describe the plan benefit, rules governing the benefit, and ways that the employee may both pay for and obtain the benefits. Employee-elected deductions for qualified cafeteria plan benefits are withheld on a *pre-tax* basis.

Examples of qualified benefits include:

- Accident and health benefits
- Long-term care benefits
- Adoption assistance
- Dependent care assistance
- Group term life insurance (including costs not excluded from wages)
- Health Savings Accounts (HSAs)

For plans that have a year starting after December 31, 2015, the maximum annual amount that an employee may contribute to the cafeteria plan is $2,550. Cafeteria plans generally have a "use or lose" provision, meaning that any unused funds at the end of the plan year may not be accessed afterward. However, the IRS permits employers to roll over up to $500 per employee at the employer's discretion.

The following items are specifically *not* included in a Section 125 cafeteria plan. Employee-elected deductions for these benefits must be done on a post-tax basis:

(continued)

(concluded)

- Archer medical savings accounts
- Athletic facilities
- De minimis (i.e., minimal) benefits
- Education assistance
- Employee discounts
- Employer-provided cell phones
- Lodging on the employer's premises
- Meals
- Moving expense reimbursements
- No-additional-cost services
- Transportation benefits (i.e., commuting, rail passes, tollway passes, etc.)
- Tuition reduction
- Working condition benefits

Source: Internal Revenue Service

Fringe Benefits

Fringe benefits are a form of compensation given in return for services performed. The recipient of fringe benefits does not need to be an employee, according to the IRS. Although fringe benefits involve compensation, many are not cash based; however, the value may be subject to taxes. A complete explanation of fringe benefits is included in Publication 15-B. Figure 4-1 details the type of fringe benefit and payroll tax treatment follows.

FIGURE 4-1

Fringe Benefits and Payroll Tax Treatment

Type of Fringe Benefit	Income Tax Exempt	FICA Taxes Exempt	FUTA Tax Exempt
Accident and health benefits*	XX	XX	XX
Achievement awards	XX		
Adoption assistance	XX		
Athletic facilities owned or leased by the employer	XX	XX	XX
De minimis benefits	XX	XX	XX
Dependent care assistance (up to $5,000 annually)	XX	XX	XX
Education (i.e., tuition) assistance (up to $5,250 annually)	XX	XX	XX
Employee discounts (various limits apply)	XX	XX	XX
Employee stock options (depending on the type of option)	XX	XX	XX
Employer-provided cell phone (if not otherwise compensated)	XX	XX	XX
Group term life insurance	XX	XX**	XX
Health savings accounts (HSAs) for qualified individuals	XX	XX	XX
Lodging on the employer premise (for the employer convenience as condition of employment)	XX	XX	XX
Meals (if de minimis or for employer convenience on employer premises)	XX	XX	XX
Moving expense reimbursements	XX	XX	XX
No-additional-cost services	XX	XX	XX
Retirement planning services	XX	XX	XX

FIGURE 4-1 *(continued)*

Fringe Benefits and Payroll Tax Treatment			
Type of Fringe Benefit	Income Tax Exempt	FICA Taxes Exempt	FUTA Tax Exempt
Transportation benefits (commuting and rail passes up to $255, bicycle to $20)	XX	XX	XX
Tuition reduction for undergraduate education	XX	XX	XX
Working condition benefits	XX	XX	XX

*Does not include long-term care benefits if they are included in flexible spending accounts
**Up to cost of $50,000 of coverage

EXAMPLE: FRINGE BENEFIT

Corey is an employee of Cohen Corporation, a company that offers educational assistance as a fringe benefit. According to the IRS, $5,250 per year of Corey's tuition is not subject to payroll taxes. During 2016, Corey received reimbursement from his employer for $7,250 in tuition expenses.

Amount subject to tax = amount in excess of $5,250 = $2,000

The $2,000 in tuition that is beyond the IRS fringe benefit limit for educational assistance would be reported at the end of the year as an addition to Corey's gross pay on Form W-2. For example, if Corey's salary were $54,000, the additional $2,000 in educational assistance would increase his gross salary to $56,000.

The value of non-cash fringe benefits such as the ones listed in the table should be determined by January 31 of the following year and reported on the employee's W-2.

What Counts as Pre-Taxable?

1. What are some examples of pre-tax deductions?
2. Which act offered a small-business tax credit for employees' health insurance premiums?
3. What are examples of different retirement plans that may qualify as pre-tax withdrawals?

LO 4-3 Determine Federal Income Tax Withholding Amounts

Now let us shift our focus to *mandatory deductions* that must be withheld from employee pay. The first class of mandatory deductions is the federal income tax. This is an employee-only tax, meaning that the employer does not contribute a matching amount for the federal income tax withheld from an employee's pay.

Federal Income Taxes

The first tax we will cover is the federal income tax. The federal income tax amounts to be withheld are calculated using the information reported by the employee on Form W-4. The withheld tax is the employee's deposit against income taxes. The employee's federal income tax is determined by four factors:

- Gross pay.
- Pay frequency (weekly, biweekly, semimonthly, etc.).
- Marital status.
- Number of withholding allowances claimed on Form W-4.

The highest taxed federal income tax bracket is single with zero dependents. Employees who work more than one job or have additional income for which no income tax is withheld may request additional amounts as either percentages or dollars to be withheld and submitted to the IRS on their behalf. The employee makes these requests on Form W-4.

The employer acts as a collector and depositor for these funds. When an individual files the income tax return, the amount withheld from his or her pay during the year reduces the amount he or she may have to pay with the return. Federal taxable income is reduced by pre-tax deductions discussed previously.

Federal Income Tax Computation Examples

EXAMPLE: GROSS PAY LESS 401(K) AND INSURANCE

Amanda's gross wages are $950, she has subscribed to the company's cafeteria plan, and she has agreed to a 10% investment of her gross wages to a qualified 401(k) plan. Her portion of the health insurance is $56.90 per pay period. To calculate her taxable pay, we must first determine the 401(k) deduction: $950 × 10% = $95. Therefore, her taxable pay is:

$950.00	gross pay
−95.00	401(k) deduction
−56.90	health insurance
$798.10	taxable income

EXAMPLE: EFFECT OF FIXED AMOUNT VS. PERCENTAGE DEDUCTION FOR 401(K) CONTRIBUTION ON TAXABLE WAGES

Daniel has gross wages of $1,125, participates in the company's 401(k) program at $100 per pay period, and has health insurance and AFLAC (all pre-tax) totaling $113.80. The calculation of Daniel's taxable income is:

$1,125.00	gross pay
−100.00	401(k) deduction
−113.80	health insurance and AFLAC
$ 911.20	taxable income

Had Daniel participated in the company's 401(k) as a percentage instead of a fixed dollar, the percent would be calculated prior to other deductions. For instance, if he elected to invest 3% of his gross pay, his taxable income would be:

$1,125.00	
× 0.03	
33.75	401(k) contribution
$1,125.00	gross pay
−33.75	401(k) contribution
−113.80	health insurance and AFLAC
$ 977.45	taxable income

Note: $1,011.20 would be the taxable amount for Social Security and Medicare.

Regardless of the method used for calculating federal income taxes, the reduction for pre-tax items will remain the same. In manual systems, there are two commonly used methods to calculate the employee's federal income tax: wage bracket and percentage.

Wage-Bracket Method

Using the wage-bracket method, the payroll clerk identifies the individual's marital status, number of exemptions, and taxable income level and then follows the chart located in Publication 15 for the amount to be withheld. If manually calculating the wage-bracket method, it is important to apply the appropriate withholdings prior to calculating the tax amounts. The wage-bracket method may be programmed into an automated payroll system. The wage-bracket method is useful for manual payroll preparation because the process of federal tax withholding is an estimate for the year-end amount of taxes due. Figure 4-2 contains an example of the wage-bracket table that Publication 15 contains.

To determine taxes to withhold using the ***wage-bracket method***, see Figure 4-2, which is for married persons who are paid on a biweekly basis. A married person with three withholding allowances and with $1,639 in biweekly earnings will have $89 of federal income tax withheld. Note that the amount of tax withheld decreases as the number of withholding allowances increases.

FIGURE 4-2
Biweekly Payroll Period—Married Persons, Wage-Bracket Method

Employee A is married and has three withholding allowances. The employee is paid biweekly and earned $1,639. What is the Federal Income Tax for Employee A?

Wage Bracket Method Tables for Income Tax Withholding
MARRIED Persons—BIWEEKLY Payroll Period
(For Wages Paid through December 31, 2016)

At least	But less than	0	1	2	3	4	5	6	7	8	9	10
$1,500	$1,520	$142	$118	$95	$71	$56	$40	$25	$9	$0	$0	$0
1,520	1,540	145	121	98	74	58	42	27	11	0	0	0
1,540	1,560	148	124	101	77	60	44	29	13	0	0	0
1,560	1,580	151	127	104	80	62	46	31	15	0	0	0
1,580	1,600	154	130	107	83	64	48	33	17	2	0	0
1,600	1,620	157	133	110	86	66	50	35	19	4	0	0
1,620	1,640	160	136	113	89	68	52	37	21	6	0	0
1,640	1,660	163	139	116	92	70	54	39	23	8	0	0
1,660	1,680	166	142	119	95	72	56	41	25	10	0	0
1,680	1,700	169	145	122	98	75	58	43	27	12	0	0

And the wages are— / And the number of withholding allowances claimed is— / The amount of income tax to be withheld is—

<u>Important facts:</u>

- The employee is married
- Has 3 withholding allowances
- Pay frequency is biweekly
- Earned $1,639

The page of the table is for married employees with biweekly pay.

Go to the row that contains the bracket containing the employee's pay. In this example, the pay is $1,639, which is in the $1,620–1,640 row.

Go to the column that contains the number of withholding allowances. In this case, the employee has 3 withholding allowances.

*The intersection of the table <u>row and column</u> is the **withholding tax**, which is **$89***.

EXAMPLE: WAGE-BRACKET COMPUTATION OF FEDERAL INCOME TAX, MARRIED, SEMIMONTHLY

Jessa is an employee of Rowan Trees. She earns $48,000 per year and is paid semimonthly. She is married with three withholding allowances. Using the wage-bracket tables in Appendix C, we will determine Jessa's federal income tax in different situations.

1. NO VOLUNTARY PRE-TAX DEDUCTIONS

Period pay ($48,000/24)	$2,000.00
Taxable income	$2,000.00
Federal income tax	$ 133.00

2. PRE-TAX HEALTH INSURANCE DEDUCTION, $150

Period pay ($48,000/24)	$2,000.00
Less: health insurance	$ 150.00
Taxable income	$1,850.00
Federal income tax	$ 109.00

3. PRE-TAX HEALTH INSURANCE DEDUCTION, $150, AND 401(K) CONTRIBUTION, 4%

Period pay ($48,000/24)	$2,000.00
Less: health insurance	$ 150.00
Less: 401(k) contribution	$ 80.00
Taxable income	$1,770.00
Federal income tax	$ 97.00

Note: The taxable income for Social Security and Medicare tax is $1,860

The process of using wage-bracket tables for employees claiming single status is similar. Figure 4-3 is a sample of the wage-bracket table for a single person with semimonthly wages.

Using the table in Figure 4-3, a single person earning a semimonthly wage of $988 with one withholding allowance will have a federal income tax of $90.

EXAMPLE: WAGE-BRACKET COMPUTATION OF FEDERAL INCOME TAX, SINGLE, BIWEEKLY

Alex is an employee at Milliken Metals. He is single with three withholding allowances and earns $45,500 annually, paid biweekly. Using the wage-bracket tables in Appendix C, we will determine Alex's federal income tax in different situations.

1. NO PRE-TAX DEDUCTIONS

Period pay ($45,500/26)	$1,750.00
Taxable income	$1,750.00
Federal income tax	$ 162.00

2. PRE-TAX HEALTH INSURANCE, $75, PRE-TAX SUPPLEMENTAL HEALTH INSURANCE, $55

Period pay ($45,500/26)	$1,750.00
Less: health insurance	$ 75.00
Less: supplemental health insurance	$ 55.00
Taxable income	$1,620.00
Federal income tax	$ 144.00

(continued)

FIGURE 4-3
Semimonthly Payroll Period—Single Persons

Employee B is single and has one withholding allowance. The employee is paid semimonthly and earned $988. What is the Federal Income Tax for Employee B?

Wage Bracket Method Tables for Income Tax Withholding

SINGLE Persons—SEMIMONTHLY Payroll Period
(For Wages Paid through December 31, 2016)

And the wages are—		And the number of withholding allowances claimed is—										
At least	But less than	0	1	2	3	4	5	6	7	8	9	10
						The amount of income tax to be withheld is—						
$800	$820	$88	$63	$38	$21	$4	$0	$0	$0	$0	$0	$0
820	840	91	66	40	23	6	0	0	0	0	0	0
840	860	94	69	43	25	8	0	0	0	0	0	0
860	880	97	72	46	27	10	0	0	0	0	0	0
880	900	100	75	49	29	12	0	0	0	0	0	0
900	920	103	78	52	31	14	0	0	0	0	0	0
920	940	106	81	55	33	16	0	0	0	0	0	0
940	960	109	84	58	35	18	1	0	0	0	0	0
960	980	112	87	61	37	20	3	0	0	0	0	0
980	1,000	115	90	64	39	22	5	0	0	0	0	0

Important facts:

- The employee is single
- Has 1 withholding allowance
- Pay frequency is semimonthly
- Earned $988

The page of the table is for single employees with semimonthly pay

Go to the row that contains the bracket containing the employee's pay. In this example, the pay is $988, which is in the $980–$1,000 row.

Go to the column that contains the number of withholding allowances. In this case, the employee has one withholding allowance.

*The intersection of the table **row and column** is the **withholding tax**, which is **$90***

(concluded)

3. PRE-TAX HEALTH INSURANCE, $75, PRE-TAX SUPPLEMENTAL HEALTH INSURANCE, $55, 401(K) CONTRIBUTION, $100

Period pay ($45,500/26)	$1,750.00
Less: health insurance	$ 75.00
Less: supplemental health insurance	$ 55.00
Less: 401(k) contribution	$ 100.00
Taxable income	$1,520.00
Federal income tax	$ 129.00

*Note: The taxable income for Social Security and Medicare tax is $1,620

FIGURE 4-4
Percentage Method for One Withholding Allowance—2016

Payroll Period	One Withholding Allowance
Weekly	$77.90
Biweekly	155.80
Semimonthly	168.80
Monthly	337.50
Quarterly	1,012.50
Semiannually	2,025.00
Annually	4,050.00
Daily or miscellaneous (each day of the payroll period)	15.40

Percentage Method

There are many tables in Publication 15 from the IRS to assist employers with the correct amount of withholding given the variety of pay period, marital status, and exemption options that can be available. The *percentage method* for calculating employee withholding is tiered, with each layer building upon the previous layer. The table that reflects the amount for one withholding allowance using the percentage method is contained in Figure 4-4. It is important to select the withholding allowance amount that corresponds to the correct pay frequency. Note that if the employee has more than one withholding allowance, the amount in the table should be multiplied by the number of withholding allowances claimed on the employee's Form W-4.

When using the percentage method, the deduction for each withholding allowance is subtracted prior to computing the taxes. Note that the wage-bracket and percentage methods will yield similar results as to income tax withholding; the percentage method shown in Figure 4-5 allows more flexibility for calculations involving high-wage earners or uncommon pay periods.

Using the percentage method tables can be confusing, so let's look at a step-by-step example.

How to calculate federal income tax using the percentage method: Caroline is single and claims two withholding allowances on her Form W-4. She is paid semimonthly and earns $48,000 per year.

Step 1: Total wage payment	$48,000 ÷ 24 = $2,000
Step 2: One withholding allowance for semimonthly pay (Figure 4-4)	$ 168.80
Step 3: Allowances claimed on W-4	2
Step 4: Multiply Step 2 by Step 3	$ 337.60
Step 5: Amount subject to withholding	$2,000 − 337.60 = $1,662.40
Step 6: See Table 3a in Figure 4-5 (Semimonthly wages for single person). Look at the column labeled "of excess over" and choose line 2 "$480.00"	− $ 480.00
Step 7: Subtract Step 6 from Step 5	= $ 1,182.40
Step 8: Multiply Step 7 by 15% (from line 2 in Table 3a)	$1,182.40 × 0.15 = $ 177.36
Step 9: Add Step 8 plus $38.60 (from line 2 in Table 3a) to compute the federal income tax to withhold	$177.36 + 38.60 = $ 215.96

FIGURE 4-5
Percentage Method Tables for Income Tax

Percentage Method Tables for Income Tax Withholding

(For Wages Paid in 2016)

TABLE 1—WEEKLY Payroll Period

(a) SINGLE person (including head of household)—

If the amount of wages (after subtracting withholding allowances) is:
Not over $43 . . . . The amount of income tax to withhold is: $0

Over—	But not over—		of excess over—
$43	—$222 . .	$0.00 plus 10%	—$43
$222	—$767 . .	$17.90 plus 15%	—$222
$767	—$1,796 . .	$99.65 plus 25%	—$767
$1,796	—$3,700 . .	$356.90 plus 28%	—$1,796
$3,700	—$7,992 . .	$890.02 plus 33%	—$3,700
$7,992	—$8,025 . .	$2,306.38 plus 35%	—$7,992
$8,025		$2,317.93 plus 39.6%	—$8,025

(b) MARRIED person—

If the amount of wages (after subtracting withholding allowances) is:
Not over $164 . . . . The amount of income tax to withhold is: $0

Over—	But not over—		of excess over—
$164	—$521 . .	$0.00 plus 10%	—$164
$521	—$1,613 . .	$35.70 plus 15%	—$521
$1,613	—$3,086 . .	$199.50 plus 25%	—$1,613
$3,086	—$4,615 . .	$567.75 plus 28%	—$3,086
$4,615	—$8,113 . .	$995.87 plus 33%	—$4,615
$8,113	—$9,144 . .	$2,150.21 plus 35%	—$8,113
$9,144		$2,511.06 plus 39.6%	—$9,144

TABLE 2—BIWEEKLY Payroll Period

(a) SINGLE person (including head of household)—

If the amount of wages (after subtracting withholding allowances) is:
Not over $87 . . . . The amount of income tax to withhold is: $0

Over—	But not over—		of excess over—
$87	—$443 . .	$0.00 plus 10%	—$87
$443	—$1,535 . .	$35.60 plus 15%	—$443
$1,535	—$3,592 . .	$199.40 plus 25%	—$1,535
$3,592	—$7,400 . .	$713.65 plus 28%	—$3,592
$7,400	—$15,985 . .	$1,779.89 plus 33%	—$7,400
$15,985	—$16,050 . .	$4,612.94 plus 35%	—$15,985
$16,050		$4,635.60 plus 39.6%	—$16,050

(b) MARRIED person—

If the amount of wages (after subtracting withholding allowances) is:
Not over $329 . . . . The amount of income tax to withhold is: $0

Over—	But not over—		of excess over—
$329	—$1,042 . .	$0.00 plus 10%	—$329
$1,042	—$3,225 . .	$71.30 plus 15%	—$1,042
$3,225	—$6,171 . .	$398.75 plus 25%	—$3,225
$6,171	—$9,231 . .	$1,135.25 plus 28%	—$6,171
$9,231	—$16,227 . .	$1,992.05 plus 33%	—$9,231
$16,227	—$18,288 . .	$4,300.73 plus 35%	—$16,227
$18,288		$5,022.08 plus 39.6%	—$18,288

TABLE 3—SEMIMONTHLY Payroll Period

(a) SINGLE person (including head of household)—

If the amount of wages (after subtracting withholding allowances) is:
Not over $94 . . . . The amount of income tax to withhold is: $0

Over—	But not over—		of excess over—
$94	—$480 . .	$0.00 plus 10%	—$94
$480	—$1,663 . .	$38.60 plus 15%	—$480
$1,663	—$3,892 . .	$216.05 plus 25%	—$1,663
$3,892	—$8,017 . .	$773.30 plus 28%	—$3,892
$8,017	—$17,317 . .	$1,928.30 plus 33%	—$8,017
$17,317	—$17,388 . .	$4,997.30 plus 35%	—$17,317
$17,388		$5,022.15 plus 39.6%	—$17,388

(b) MARRIED person—

If the amount of wages (after subtracting withholding allowances) is:
Not over $356 . . . . The amount of income tax to withhold is: $0

Over—	But not over—		of excess over—
$356	—$1,129 . .	$0.00 plus 10%	—$356
$1,129	—$3,494 . .	$77.30 plus 15%	—$1,129
$3,494	—$6,685 . .	$432.05 plus 25%	—$3,494
$6,685	—$10,000 . .	$1,229.80 plus 28%	—$6,685
$10,000	—$17,579 . .	$2,158.00 plus 33%	—$10,000
$17,579	—$19,813 . .	$4,659.07 plus 35%	—$17,579
$19,813		$5,440.97 plus 39.6%	—$19,813

TABLE 4—MONTHLY Payroll Period

(a) SINGLE person (including head of household)—

If the amount of wages (after subtracting withholding allowances) is:
Not over $188 . . . . The amount of income tax to withhold is: $0

Over—	But not over—		of excess over—
$188	—$960 . .	$0.00 plus 10%	—$188
$960	—$3,325 . .	$77.20 plus 15%	—$960
$3,325	—$7,783 . .	$431.95 plus 25%	—$3,325
$7,783	—$16,033 . .	$1,546.45 plus 28%	—$7,783
$16,033	—$34,633 . .	$3,856.45 plus 33%	—$16,033
$34,633	—$34,775 . .	$9,994.45 plus 35%	—$34,633
$34,775		$10,044.15 plus 39.6%	—$34,775

(b) MARRIED person—

If the amount of wages (after subtracting withholding allowances) is:
Not over $713 . . . . The amount of income tax to withhold is: $0

Over—	But not over—		of excess over—
$713	—$2,258 . .	$0.00 plus 10%	—$713
$2,258	—$6,988 . .	$154.50 plus 15%	—$2,258
$6,988	—$13,371 . .	$864.00 plus 25%	—$6,988
$13,371	—$20,000 . .	$2,459.75 plus 28%	—$13,371
$20,000	—$35,158 . .	$4,315.87 plus 33%	—$20,000
$35,158	—$39,625 . .	$9,318.01 plus 35%	—$35,158
$39,625		$10,881.46 plus 39.6%	—$39,625

Percentage Method Tables for Income Tax Withholding (continued)

(For Wages Paid in 2016)

TABLE 5—QUARTERLY Payroll Period

(a) SINGLE person (including head of household)—

If the amount of wages (after subtracting withholding allowances) is: The amount of income tax to withhold is:

Not over $563 . . . . $0

Over—	But not over—		of excess over—
$563	—$2,881 . .	$0.00 plus 10%	—$563
$2,881	—$9,975 . .	$231.80 plus 15%	—$2,881
$9,975	—$23,350 . .	$1,295.90 plus 25%	—$9,975
$23,350	—$48,100 . .	$4,639.65 plus 28%	—$23,350
$48,100	—$103,900 . .	$11,569.65 plus 33%	—$48,100
$103,900	—$104,325 . .	$29,983.65 plus 35%	—$103,900
$104,325	. . . .	$30,132.40 plus 39.6%	—$104,325

(b) MARRIED person—

If the amount of wages (after subtracting withholding allowances) is: The amount of income tax to withhold is:

Not over $2,138 . . . . $0

Over—	But not over—		of excess over—
$2,138	—$6,775 . .	$0.00 plus 10%	—$2,138
$6,775	—$20,963 . .	$463.70 plus 15%	—$6,775
$20,963	—$40,113 . .	$2,591.90 plus 25%	—$20,963
$40,113	—$60,000 . .	$7,379.40 plus 28%	—$40,113
$60,000	—$105,475 . .	$12,947.76 plus 33%	—$60,000
$105,475	—$118,875 . .	$27,954.51 plus 35%	—$105,475
$118,875	. . . .	$32,644.51 plus 39.6%	—$118,875

TABLE 6—SEMIANNUAL Payroll Period

(a) SINGLE person (including head of household)—

If the amount of wages (after subtracting withholding allowances) is: The amount of income tax to withhold is:

Not over $1,125 . . . . $0

Over—	But not over—		of excess over—
$1,125	—$5,763 . .	$0.00 plus 10%	—$1,125
$5,763	—$19,950 . .	$463.80 plus 15%	—$5,763
$19,950	—$46,700 . .	$2,591.85 plus 25%	—$19,950
$46,700	—$96,200 . .	$9,279.35 plus 28%	—$46,700
$96,200	—$207,800 . .	$23,139.35 plus 33%	—$96,200
$207,800	—$208,650 . .	$59,967.35 plus 35%	—$207,800
$208,650	. . . .	$60,264.85 plus 39.6%	—$208,650

(b) MARRIED person—

If the amount of wages (after subtracting withholding allowances) is: The amount of income tax to withhold is:

Not over $4,275 . . . . $0

Over—	But not over—		of excess over—
$4,275	—$13,550 . .	$0.00 plus 10%	—$4,275
$13,550	—$41,925 . .	$927.50 plus 15%	—$13,550
$41,925	—$80,225 . .	$5,183.75 plus 25%	—$41,925
$80,225	—$120,000 . .	$14,758.75 plus 28%	—$80,225
$120,000	—$210,950 . .	$25,895.75 plus 33%	—$120,000
$210,950	—$237,750 . .	$55,909.25 plus 35%	—$210,950
$237,750	. . . .	$65,289.25 plus 39.6%	—$237,750

TABLE 7—ANNUAL Payroll Period

(a) SINGLE person (including head of household)—

If the amount of wages (after subtracting withholding allowances) is: The amount of income tax to withhold is:

Not over $2,250 . . . . $0

Over—	But not over—		of excess over—
$2,250	—$11,525 . .	$0.00 plus 10%	—$2,250
$11,525	—$39,900 . .	$927.50 plus 15%	—$11,525
$39,900	—$93,400 . .	$5,183.75 plus 25%	—$39,900
$93,400	—$192,400 . .	$18,558.75 plus 28%	—$93,400
$192,400	—$415,600 . .	$46,278.75 plus 33%	—$192,400
$415,600	—$417,300 . .	$119,934.75 plus 35%	—$415,600
$417,300	. . . .	$120,529.75 plus 39.6%	—$417,300

(b) MARRIED person—

If the amount of wages (after subtracting withholding allowances) is: The amount of income tax to withhold is:

Not over $8,550 . . . . $0

Over—	But not over—		of excess over—
$8,550	—$27,100 . .	$0.00 plus 10%	—$8,550
$27,100	—$83,850 . .	$1,855.00 plus 15%	—$27,100
$83,850	—$160,450 . .	$10,367.50 plus 25%	—$83,850
$160,450	—$240,000 . .	$29,517.50 plus 28%	—$160,450
$240,000	—$421,900 . .	$51,791.50 plus 33%	—$240,000
$421,900	—$475,500 . .	$111,818.50 plus 35%	—$421,900
$475,500	. . . .	$130,578.50 plus 39.6%	—$475,500

TABLE 8—DAILY or MISCELLANEOUS Payroll Period

(a) SINGLE person (including head of household)—

If the amount of wages (after subtracting withholding allowances) divided by the number of days in the payroll period is: The amount of income tax to withhold per day is:

Not over $8.70 . . . . $0

Over—	But not over—		of excess over—
$8.70	—$44.30 . .	$0.00 plus 10%	—$8.70
$44.30	—$153.50 . .	$3.56 plus 15%	—$44.30
$153.50	—$359.20 . .	$19.94 plus 25%	—$153.50
$359.20	—$740.00 . .	$71.37 plus 28%	—$359.20
$740.00	—$1,598.50 . .	$177.99 plus 33%	—$740.00
$1,598.50	—$1,605.00 . .	$461.30 plus 35%	—$1,598.50
$1,605.00	. . . .	$463.58 plus 39.6%	—$1,605.00

(b) MARRIED person—

If the amount of wages (after subtracting withholding allowances) divided by the number of days in the payroll period is: The amount of income tax to withhold per day is:

Not over $32.90 . . . . $0

Over—	But not over—		of excess over—
$32.90	—$104.20 . .	$0.00 plus 10%	—$32.90
$104.20	—$322.50 . .	$7.13 plus 15%	—$104.20
$322.50	—$617.10 . .	$39.88 plus 25%	—$322.50
$617.10	—$923.10 . .	$113.53 plus 28%	—$617.10
$923.10	—$1,622.70 . .	$199.21 plus 33%	—$923.10
$1,622.70	—$1,828.80 . .	$430.08 plus 35%	—$1,622.70
$1,828.80	. . . .	$502.22 plus 39.6%	—$1,828.80

Source: Internal Revenue Service.

The amount of federal income tax withholding may differ slightly between the wage-bracket and percentage methods. Let's revisit the tax computation for the married employee, this time using the percentage method.

EXAMPLE: MARRIED EMPLOYEE, PERCENTAGE METHOD VS. WAGE-BRACKET TABLE

Employee A earns $1,639 biweekly and is married with three withholding allowances. We will use Table 2b of the percentage method for this computation.

Gross pay	$1,639.00
Less withholding allowances (3 × $155.80)	$ 467.40
Taxable base	$1,171.60
Less: "of excess over $1,042" (line 2)	$1,042.00
Adjusted taxable base	$ 129.60
Multiplied by tax rate (15% or 0.15)	$ 19.44
Plus marginal tax	$ 71.30
Total tax	$ 90.74

Note that the wage-bracket method ended with a result of $89. The reason for the difference is the rounding used in wage-bracket table computations.

Let's now revisit Employee B and compare the percentage method computations to the wage-bracket table.

EXAMPLE: SINGLE EMPLOYEE, PERCENTAGE METHOD VS. WAGE-BRACKET TABLE

Employee B earns $988 semimonthly and is single with one withholding allowance. We will use Table 3a of the percentage method tables for this computation.

Gross pay	$988.00
Less withholding allowance (1 × $168.80)	$168.80
Taxable base	$819.20
Less: "of excess over $480" (line 2)	$480.00
Adjusted taxable base	$339.20
Multiplied by tax rate (15% or 0.15)	$ 50.88
Plus marginal tax	$ 38.60
Total tax	$ 89.48

Note that the wage-bracket method resulted in $90. Again, the reason for the difference is the rounding used in wage-bracket table computations.

LO 4-4 Compute Social Security and Medicare Tax Withholding

The Social Security Act of 1935 mandated the withholding of certain taxes in addition to federal income tax. Two different taxes were part of the Social Security Act legislation: Social Security tax and Medicare tax. Employers collect only federal income taxes on employees without making a corresponding contribution. Social Security and Medicare, collectively known as FICA (Federal Insurance Contributions Act) taxes, contain both the employer's and the employee's portion. When the employer deposits the federal withholding tax, it deposits the Social Security and Medicare amounts at the same time. The deposits are usually done online but may be made by standard mail in certain circumstances. The report provided to

How Much Tax to Withhold?

1. Jennifer earns $52,000 annually. She is married with two allowances and is paid semimonthly.

   Calculate the amount to be withheld using (a) the wage-bracket method and (b) the percentage method.

2. If Jennifer elected to deduct $100 per pay period for her 401(k), how much would that change the tax withheld from her paycheck? (Use the wage-bracket method.)

3. How much would Jennifer's Federal income tax be if her $75 health insurance and $55 AFLAC premiums were deducted each pay period pre-tax? (Use the wage-bracket method, independent of question 2.)

the IRS does not provide a breakdown of tax amounts for individual employees. Specific questions about Social Security or Medicare tax situations should be directed to the Social Security Administration at www.ssa.gov or via telephone at 800-772-1213.

Social Security Tax

Social Security tax, formerly known as OASDI, was designed to cover people for illness, retirement, disability, and old age. As a method of social insurance by which communities will help provide for people who are unable to work, Social Security has evolved into a tax that is levied upon all employees until their annual income reaches a specified level. The maximum income, known as the *wage base*, for the Social Security tax changes annually. In 2016, the wage base is $118,500. The tax rate on employee pay is 6.2% of eligible wages. Remember that eligible wages can be different from gross pay because of pre-tax deductions and the wage base maximum.

Examples of Social Security Tax Computations

Employee	Period Wages	YTD Salary at End of Previous Pay Period	Social Security Tax Computation	Social Security Tax Amount to Be Withheld
1	$ 1,700	$ 55,600	$1,700 × 6.2%	$105.40
2	$ 2,850	$ 90,000	$2,850 × 6.2%	$176.70
3	$ 7,200	$112,600	$5,900 × 6.2%*	$365.80
4	$ 6,200	$118,000	$ 500 × 6.2%**	$31
5	$10,500	$195,000	$0***	$0

*The employee's wage base reaches the maximum during this pay period; thus, only the amount under the $118,500 is taxed for Social Security: $118,500 − $112,600 = $5,900, so only the $5,900 is taxed.
**The employee's wage base reaches the maximum during this pay period; thus, only the amount under the $118,500 is taxed for Social Security: $118,500 − $118,000 = $500, so only the $500 is taxed.
***The employee's wage base maximum was met prior to the current pay period, so no Social Security taxes are withheld.

The employee earnings record is especially important in computing and tracking the Social Security taxes due for each employee. Current records allow payroll accountants to keep track of annual salaries for each employee to avoid exceeding the maximum wage base, preventing excess deductions from employees' pay.

The employer and employee pay the same amount for the Social Security tax. Remember that the Social Security tax has a maximum withholding per year based on the employee's salary. After reaching that maximum, neither the employee nor the employer pay any more Social Security tax.

Medicare Tax

Medicare taxes differ from Social Security taxes in a couple of significant ways. *Medicare taxes* were levied on American employees to help provide basic health coverage for all people older than age 62. The Medicare tax amount for employee wages is 1.45% on all wages earned; there is no maximum wage base for Medicare taxes. The Affordable Care Act of 2010 levied an *additional Medicare tax* of 0.9% on workers with annual wages exceeding $200,000. This made the simple computations and tracking for Medicare taxes a little more challenging for payroll accountants and increased the need for accuracy on the employee earnings report. Note that the additional Medicare tax is levied only on the employees, so there is no employer match.

Examples of Medicare Tax Computations

Employee	Period Wages	YTD Salary at End of Previous Pay Period	Medicare Tax Computation	Total Medicare Tax Liability (Employee and Employer)
1	$ 1,700	$ 55,600	$1,700 × 1.45%	$ 24.65 × 2 = $49.30
2	$ 2,850	$ 90,000	$2,850 × 1.45%	$ 41.33 × 2 = $82.66
3	$ 7,200	$112,600	$7,200 × 1.45%	$104.40 × 2 = $208.80
4	$ 6,200	$118,000	$6,200 × 1.45%	$ 89.90 × 2 = $179.80
5	$10,500	$195,000	Employee: (10,500 × 0.145) + (5,500 × 0.009) = $201.75	Employee: $201.75 + Employer: $152.25 Total = $354.00

Remember that the applicable wages may have pre-tax deductions. Social Security and Medicare taxes apply to the employee's gross pay if an employee elects to have a 401(k) deduction. However, qualified Section 125 (cafeteria) plans are exempt from FICA taxes. When computing employee taxes, understanding the tax effect of the pre-tax deductions is important in computing accurate FICA deductions.

EXAMPLE: COMPUTATION OF SOCIAL SECURITY AND MEDICARE TAXES WITH PRE-TAX DEDUCTIONS

Chris is an employee who earns an annual salary of $58,000, paid biweekly. He is single with one withholding allowance. Chris has pre-tax deductions including $155 for health insurance and a contribution of 5% of his gross pay to a 401(k) plan. Let's compute Chris's net pay using the wage-bracket tables to determine federal income tax.

Gross pay per period	$2,230.77
Less: health insurance	$ 155.00
Less: 401(k)	$ 111.54
Taxable income*	$1,964.23
Federal income tax	$ 269.00
Social Security tax**	$ 128.70
Medicare tax**	$ 30.10
Net pay	$1,536.43

*This taxable income is for federal income tax only
**Social Security and Medicare taxes are computed on taxable income of $2,230.77 − $155.00 = $2,075.77

EXAMPLE: COMPUTATION OF NET PAY, HIGHLY COMPENSATED EMPLOYEE

Morris is the CEO and president of Martens Flooring. His annual salary is $320,000, and he is paid semimonthly. He is married with five withholding allowances and has pre-tax deductions for health insurance of $250 and 401(k) of $1,000.

(continued)

Note that because he is a highly compensated employee, we will need to use the percentage method to compute his federal income tax. He will exceed the Social Security wage base in May 20XX and will incur the additional Medicare tax in September. Let's look at his net pay computations on January 15, May 15, and August 31.

Federal income tax is computed as follows, using Table 3b:

Gross pay	$13,333.33
Less withholding allowance (5 × $168.80)	$ 844.00
Taxable base	$12,489.33
Less: "of excess over $10,000" (line 4)	$10,000.00
Adjusted taxable base	$ 2,489.33
Multiplied by tax rate (33% or 0.33)	$ 821.48
Plus marginal tax	$ 2,158.00
Total federal income tax	$ 2,979.48

JANUARY 15 PAY PERIOD

Gross pay per period	$13,333.33
Less: health insurance	$ 250.00
Less: 401(k)	$ 1,000.00
Taxable income*	$12,083.33
Federal income tax	$ 2,979.48
Social Security tax**	$ 811.17
Medicare tax**	$ 189.71
Net pay	$ 8,102.97

*This taxable income is for federal income tax only
**Social Security and Medicare taxes are computed using a base of $13,083.33

MAY 15 PAY PERIOD

As of April 30, Morris has earned year-to-date gross pay of $106,666.64. This means that he will exceed the Social Security wage base during the next pay period, which ends May 15. Morris's salary is only taxable for Social Security wages up to the wage base of $118,500 (2016 amount), so the amount that may be taxed is $118,500 − 106,666.64 = $11,833.36. After the May 15 pay period, Morris will have no more Social Security tax deducted from his pay. His net pay for May 15 will be as follows:

Gross pay per period	$13,333.33
Less: health insurance	$ 250.00
Less: 401(k)	$ 1,000.00
Taxable income*	$12,083.33
Federal income tax	$ 2,979.48
Social Security tax**	$ 733.67
Medicare tax***	$ 189.71
Net pay	$ 8,180.47

*This taxable income is for federal income tax only
**Social Security tax is computed as $11,833.36 × 0.062 = $733.67
***Medicare tax is computed using a base of $13,083.33

AUGUST 31 PAY PERIOD

As of August 15, Morris has earned year-to-date pay of $200,000.10. His pay is now subject to the Additional Medicare tax of 0.9%, levied only on employees (i.e., no employer match). His net pay for August 31 will be computed as follows:

(continued)

(concluded)

Gross pay per period	$13,333.33
Less: health insurance	$ 250.00
Less: 401(k)	$ 1,000.00
Taxable income*	$12,083.33
Federal income tax	$ 2,979.48
Social Security tax	$ –
Medicare tax**	$ 307.46
Net pay	$ 8,796.39

*This taxable income is for federal income tax only
**Medicare tax is computed using a base of $13,083.33

Maintaining accurate records of taxes withheld through payroll registers and employee earnings records is a critical part of calculating proper FICA tax deductions. Whether a company uses a manual system, an automated system, or outsources the payroll duties, it remains responsible for the accuracy of the deductions and maintenance of associated records.

FICA Taxes

1. Trent is an employee whose annual salary prior to the current pay period is $63,500. His current pay is $5,280. What amount must be withheld for Social Security tax? For Medicare tax?

2. For Trent's FICA taxes, what is the total tax liability including employee and employer share?

3. Sarah is the CEO of a company, making $250,000 per year. Her year-to-date salary for the 19th pay period of the year was $197,916.73. She contributes 5% of her pay to her 401(k) and has a qualified Section 125 deduction of $75 per semimonthly pay period.

    a. For the 20th pay period, what is her Social Security tax liability? Medicare tax liability?

    b. For the 21st pay period, what is her Medicare tax liability?

LO 4-5   Apply State and Local Income Taxes

Many states and localities apply taxes in addition to the federal income tax, Social Security, and Medicare. According to the IRS, all but nine states withhold income taxes. Those states are:

Alaska	Texas
Florida	Tennessee
Nevada	Washington
New Hampshire	Wyoming
South Dakota	

State-Specific Taxes

All other states (except the nine above) withhold income tax from their employees, and many apply other taxes as well. For instance, employees in the state of California have State Disability Insurance (SDI) of 0.9% of gross pay (up to a maximum wage of $106,742 in 2016), in addition to the Personal Income Tax (PIT) that the state levies. Like federal income tax, California's PIT amounts vary by income level, pay frequency, and marital status. California, like many other states, offers both the wage-bracket and the percentage method of determining the PIT amount due. In contrast, Illinois charges a flat rate of 3.75% on all employees for its state withholding tax. (See Appendix D for state income tax information.)

If a firm operates only in one state, deciphering state income tax requirements is reasonably simple but becomes increasingly complex as the firm does business in more locations. State income tax information is readily available through each state's department of revenue as well as through most computerized payroll software programs. (See Appendix E for State Revenue Department List.)

Some states require the collection and remittance of income taxes based upon all wages earned within their state. This could result in the company having several state employer identification numbers, even if the company does not have a physical presence in the state. For example, if a Floridian paper mill worker is stationed at the St. Marys, Georgia, location, the employer could be required to remit the employee's income taxes in Georgia.

EXAMPLE: NET PAY WITH STATE INCOME TAX

Jeremy receives a salary of $850 per week at his job in Joliet, Illinois. He is married with three withholding allowances and is paid weekly. He has pre-tax deductions of $50 for insurance and $50 for 401(k). Using the Illinois state tax rate of 3.75%:

Taxable income	$750.00
State income tax	$ 28.13

His net pay would be computed as follows:

Period pay	$ 850.00
Less: health insurance	$ 50.00
Less: 401(k) contribution	$ 50.00
Taxable income*	$ 750.00
Federal income tax	$ 36.00
State income tax	$ 28.13
Social Security tax**	$ 49.60
Medicare tax**	$ 11.60
Net pay	$ 624.67

*This taxable income is for federal and state income tax only
**Social Security and Medicare taxes are computed on taxable income of $850 − $50 = $800

Local Income Taxes

Another mandatory tax is *local income tax* levied by certain municipalities and counties. Payroll accountants need to be aware of any local taxes that apply to their business. Information about applicable local taxes may be found through city and county governments, often through their Internet sites.

Denver, Colorado, has a local tax called the Occupational Privilege Tax (OPT), also known as the "Head tax." The OPT is $5.75 per month for employees and $4.00 for employers of any business that has any activity in Denver, even if the employee or business does not exist or reside in Denver itself, on wages exceeding $500. The local income tax is applied after any pre-tax deductions. (Source: City and County of Denver, Colorado, Tax Guide)

EXAMPLE: NET PAY WITH LOCAL INCOME TAX

Shalie is an employee at Keiser and Sons in Denver, Colorado. She earns $39,000 annually and is paid biweekly. She is married with two withholding allowances. She has pre-tax deductions including $100 for health insurance and a contribution of 6% of her gross pay to a 401(k) plan. We will use the wage-bracket tables in Appendix C to compute Shalie's federal income tax. Colorado's state income tax is 4.63%. Her net pay would be as follows:

Period pay ($39,000/26)	$1,500.00
Less: health insurance	$ 100.00
Less: 401(k) contribution	$ 90.00
Taxable income*	$1,310.00
Federal income tax	$ 67.00
State income tax	$ 60.65
Denver OPT	$ 5.75
Social Security tax**	$ 86.80
Medicare tax**	$ 20.30
Net pay	$1,069.50

*This taxable income is for federal and state income tax only
**Social Security and Medicare taxes are computed on taxable income of $1,500 − $100 = $1,400

State and Local Income Taxes

Stop & Check

1. April works as a research scientist in Coeur d'Alene, Idaho. She is married with two withholding allowances and earns $62,500 annually, paid biweekly. She has a pre-tax deduction of $150 for her 401(k) and $80 for qualified health insurance. Using the state tax listed in Appendix D, what is her state income tax?

2. Rick works as an accountant in Denver, Colorado. Colorado has a state income tax of a flat 4.63% per employee. Colorado's OPT is $5.75 per month. If Rick is paid monthly and earns $2,850 after pre-tax deductions, what are his state and local taxes?

© Jamie Grill/Getty Images, RF

LO 4-6   Explain Post-Tax Deductions

After the employer withholds the pre-tax and mandatory amounts from an employee's pay, other withholdings may apply. These other withholdings, known as post-tax deductions, comprise both voluntary and *mandated deductions*. An example of a voluntary post-tax deduction is a charitable contribution elected by the employee. Mandated post-tax deductions include *garnishments* and *union dues*. Post-tax deductions are amounts that the IRS has declared cannot reduce the employee's tax liability.

Charitable Contributions

Many companies offer to deduct funds for approved charitable organizations directly from the employee's pay. This *charitable contribution* is typically withheld *after* taxes have been calculated. The individual will report the charitable contribution on his or her itemized tax return, and there are separate requirements for meeting the deductible percentage that are outside the scope of this text.

EXAMPLE: NET PAY WITH CHARITABLE CONTRIBUTION

Shonda is an employee at Mills Printing in Winchester, New Hampshire. She earns $29,000 annually and is paid weekly. She is single with one withholding allowance. She has a pre-tax health insurance of $25 and a charitable contribution to the United Way of $10 per pay period. Her net pay would be as follows:

Period pay	$557.69
Less: health insurance	$ 25.00
Taxable income*	$532.69
Federal income tax	$ 53.00
Social Security tax	$ 33.03
Medicare tax	$ 7.72
United Way contribution	$ 10.00
Net pay	$428.94

*Because there is no 401(k) plan, this taxable income is for all taxes

---

Court-Ordered Garnishments

There are several reasons that a court may order an employer to withhold amounts from an employee's pay and redirect those funds to a regulatory agency. The most common garnishments are for child support, alimony, and student loans. Garnishments apply to ***disposable income***, which is the amount of employee pay after legally required deductions such as income taxes have been withheld. If an employee has one garnishment order for 10% and receives a second for 15%, any further garnishment requests will be deferred until the disposable income is at a level that is available for garnishments.

Consumer credit:
According to Title III of the ***Consumer Credit Protection Act***, garnishments may be not more than: (a) 25% of the employee's disposable earnings OR (b) the amount by which an employee's disposable earnings are greater than 30 times the federal minimum wage, or $217.50.

Child support:
Garnishments for child support or alimony may be up to 50% of disposable income, with an additional 5% for any child support that is more than 12 weeks in arrears.

Nontax debts owed to federal agencies:
Garnishments for nontax amounts to federal agencies may not total more than 15% of disposable income.

EXAMPLE: GARNISHMENTS

In these examples, we will explore the effect of child support and consumer credit garnishments on net pay.

Child Support
Andrew is an employee of Kennesaw Mills. He earns $49,500 annually, paid semi-monthly. He is single with three withholding allowances. He has a pre-tax health

(continued)

(concluded)

insurance deduction of $100 and contributes 3% of his gross pay to his 401(k) per pay period. State income tax rate is 6%. He has a court-ordered garnishment of $300 per pay period. His net pay would appear as follows (amounts rounded to nearest dollar):

Period pay	$2,062.50
Less: health insurance	$ 100.00
Less: 401(k) contribution	$ 61.88
Taxable income*	$1,900.63
Federal income tax	$ 177.00
State income tax	$ 114.04
Social Security tax**	$ 121.68
Medicare tax**	$ 28.46
Garnishment	$ 300.00
Net pay	$1,159.45

*This taxable income is for federal and state income taxes
**Social Security and Medicare taxes are computed on taxable income of $2,062.50 − $100 = $1,962.50

It is important to consider Andrew's disposable income to ensure that the garnishment does not exceed legal maximums. His disposable income is computed as follows:

Gross pay	$2,062.50
Less: federal income tax	$ 177.00
Less: state income tax	$ 114.04
Less: Social Security tax	$ 121.68
Less: Medicare tax	$ 28.46
Total disposable income	$1,621.32
Percent of garnishment to disposable income	18.5%*

*$300/1,621.32 = 0.185 = 18.5%

Consumer Credit

Florence is an employee of Level Two Gallery in Ogden, Utah. She earns $38,500 annually, paid biweekly. She is single with two withholding allowances. She has pre-tax deductions of $50 for health insurance and $30 for her contribution to a 401(k) plan, and she contributes $15 to the United Way. She has a court-ordered consumer credit garnishment of $100 per pay period. Her net pay would appear as follows:

Period pay	$1,480.77
Less: health insurance	$ 50.00
Less: 401(k) contribution	$ 30.00
Taxable income*	$1,400.77
Federal income tax	$ 134.00
State income tax (5%)	$ 70.04
Social Security tax**	$ 88.71
Medicare tax**	$ 20.75
Garnishment	$ 100.00
United Way contribution	$ 10.00
Net pay	$ 977.28

*This taxable income is for federal and state income tax only
**Social Security and Medicare taxes are computed on taxable income of $1,480.77 − $50 = $1,430.77

(continued)

(concluded)

Let's ensure that Florence's consumer credit garnishment is within legal guidelines:

Gross pay	$1,480.77
Less: federal income tax	$ 134.00
Less: State income tax	$ 70.04
Less: Social Security tax	$ 88.71
Less: Medicare tax	$ 20.75
Total disposable income	$1,167.28
Percent of garnishment to disposable income	8.6%*

*$100/$1,167.27 = .086 = 8.6%

© McGraw-Hill Education/Ken
Cavanagh

Union Dues

When employees are part of a union that requires regular dues, the employer must withhold those dues from the employee as a post-tax payroll deduction. The union uses dues to fund its activities, which include representation in employee–employer negotiations and political activism. Some employers may pay the union dues for their employee as part of their noncash compensation.

EXAMPLE: UNION DUES

Forester is an employee of Pacific High School in Washington state, where he is a member of a collective bargaining unit (i.e., union) that negotiates his salary, benefits, and working conditions and has dues of $50 per pay period. He earns $67,500 annually and is paid biweekly. He is married with four withholding allowances. He has pretax deductions of $150 for health insurance and $100 for a qualified Section 125 cafeteria plan. His net pay would appear as follows:

Period pay	$2,596.15
Less: health insurance	$ 150.00
Less: Section 125	$ 100.00
Taxable income	$2,346.15
Federal income tax	$ 174.00
Social Security tax	$ 145.46
Medicare tax	$ 34.02
Union dues	$ 50.00
Net pay	$1,942.67

Additional Withholding

If an employee has more than one job or a spouse who works, an option to avoid having to owe taxes at the end of the year is to withhold additional federal income taxes out of each check. Additional withholdings are requested within the employee's Form W-4. This can be either a straight dollar value or an additional percentage. These amounts are withheld from the employee and submitted with the normal federal payroll tax deposits by the employer. Additional withholdings reduce the employee's tax liability, the same as standard federal income taxes.

Once the payroll clerk determines each employee's gross pay, pre-tax deductions, and taxes withheld, the post-tax deductions are applied to the remaining amount. All deductions, both

FIGURE 4-6

Sample Employee Pay Advice

Payroll End Date	2/21/20XX	Payroll Pay Date	2/25/20XX	Check:	2156
Employee Name	I. M. Smith	Employee number	22692	Rate	$12.00/hour

Description	Earnings	YTD Gross	Description	Deductions	YTD Deductions
Regular	$480.00	$3,275.00	Federal W/H	$21.00	$247.00
Overtime	$36.00	$36.00	Social Security	$35.09	$226.98
			Medicare	$8.21	$53.08
			Section 125	$50.00	$350.00
Net Pay	$306.10	$1,764.73	401(k)	$25.00	$175.00
			Union Dues	$31.00	$217.00
			State W/H	$9.60	$67.20
			Garnishment	$30.00	$210.00
			Total Deductions	$209.90	$1,546.27

voluntary and mandatory, should be listed on an attachment to the paycheck, in both pay-period and year-to-date amounts. An example of a pay advice with deductions is in Figure 4-6.

Post-Tax Deductions

Stop & Check

1. Don has disposable pay of $1,790.00. He receives a court-ordered garnishment for credit card debt of $15,000. What is the maximum amount that may be withheld from Don's pay?

2. Don questions the amount of the garnishment, claiming that he has health insurance of $125 and union dues of $45 that must also be withheld from his pay. How much should be withheld for the garnishment? Explain.

LO 4-7 Discuss Employee Pay Methods

Once the net pay is computed, the next step is to give the employees access to their money. Four common types of payment methods are available: cash, check, direct deposit, and paycard. Each method has its benefits and drawbacks. We will explore each method separately.

Cash

Cash is one of the oldest forms of paying employees but is not widely used as a contemporary payroll practice. The most common use of cash as a payment method involves paying for day laborers, temporary helpers, and odd jobs. Cash is one of the most difficult forms of payroll to manage because it is difficult to track and control. Payments for wages in cash should involve a written receipt signed by the employee. Companies paying by cash must physically have the cash on hand for payroll, which increases the risk of theft from both internal and external sources. Payroll taxes could be withheld, which requires prior preparation so that the appropriate amount of cash is available to pay precisely what is due for each employee. For employees, cash is a very convenient pay method because of its inherent liquidity.

Cash is a convenient way to pay employees but can pose challenges in security of the funds for both the employer and the employee. Cash is difficult to trace and can be transmitted

© Tetra Images/Corbis, RF

from bearer to bearer very rapidly. For the employer, ensuring that the employee receives and acknowledges the appropriate pay amount is the key. When using cash as a payment method for employees, a receipt that contains information about the gross pay, deductions, and net pay (called the *pay advice*) is important. The critical piece is to have the employee sign and date a copy of the pay advice, acknowledging receipt of the correct amount of cash on the specific date. Obtaining the employee's signature and date received can prevent future problems with perceived problems involving timely payments of employee compensation.

Check

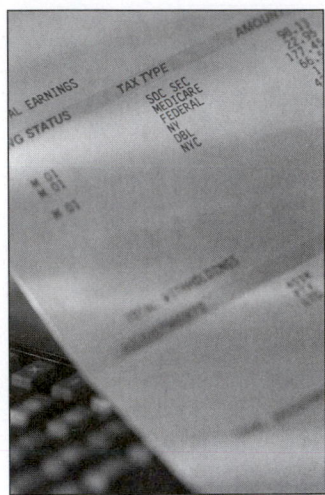

© Comstock Images/Getty Images, RF

Paper checks are a common method of remitting employee compensation. For the employer, a paper check offers traceability and simplicity of accounting records. The use of checks instead of cash means that the employer does not have to maintain large amounts of cash, reducing the vulnerability of keeping currency on hand. Programs such as QuickBooks and Sage50 allow employers to print paychecks directly from the program on specifically designed, preprinted forms. Checks offer a level of security that cash does not because they are issued to a specific employee, the only person who can legally convert the check into cash.

The disadvantage to using paper checks for payroll purposes involves bank account reconciliation. Once issued, the employee may choose not to deposit it into his or her bank account, which can complicate the firm's reconciliation process. Paper checks could be lost or destroyed, requiring voiding of the old check and issuance of a new one. Paper checks may soon be phased out of current practice as other methods of employee pay grow in popularity because of the convenience for both the employer and the employee.

> According to the Pew Internet and American Life Project (2014), more than 53 million consumers in the United States use online banking. The practice of payroll disbursement using paper checks is declining as people shift from traditional banking methods to a culture of electronic money management. (Source: Smart Biz)

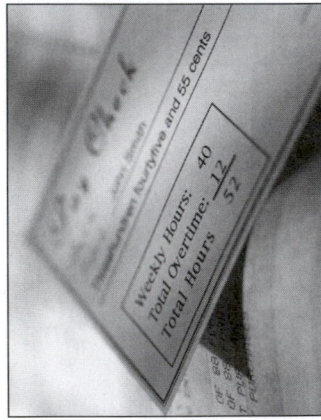

© Steve Cole/Getty Images, RF

For employers who use paper checks as a compensation method, two significant best practices exist: the use of a payroll-only checking account and a procedure for the handling of the payroll checks themselves. A separate payroll-dedicated checking account prevents problems that could occur if the company has difficulties (such as insufficient funds) in the business's main account. For the checks themselves, the payroll accountant needs to maintain a record that notes the use of each and every check, especially for checks that are voided, lost, or never cashed. If a company issues checks, it needs to maintain an unclaimed property account for payroll checks that are never cashed by the employee. The process of leaving a check uncashed, especially if it is a payroll check, is called *escheatment* and is subject to state laws about the handling and distribution of such unclaimed money. Compliance with state escheatment laws is mandatory but not largely enforced—but that does not relieve the employer of the obligation to pay its employee. Use of a record in which the payroll accountant annotates each check's use (i.e., cashed, voided, lost) is imperative.

When a company pays employees by check, the numerical amount of the check must also be represented in specific words for the bank to accept the check for payment to the payee. It is important to note that banks pay the check based on the amount written in words on the check. The highlighted area in the image below shows how the information should appear on the face of the check.

Wings of the North	
121 Nicholas Street	
North Pole, AK 99705	Check No. 23445

Petra Smith   Date   1/3/20XX

One Thousand One Hundred Twenty-four and 13/100   dollars   1,124.13

Payee: Petra Smith
Address: 426 Candy Cane Lane
City/State Zip: North Pole, AK 99705   Signed: *Rudolph Donner*

A relevant concept in using checks for payroll is the potential for fraud by manipulating the information on checks. The check issuer (i.e., the employer) may be liable for the funds until the fraudulent activity is proven. Some red flags that may indicate check fraud include the following:

- Changes in font type between the company's address and the employee's name.
- Low check numbers (e.g., 1001–1500) because payroll fraud often involves new accounts.
- Evidence of typewriter use on the check (most payroll checks are generated via computerized programs).
- Stains or discolorations on the check.
- Notations in the memo line that contain the word "payroll" or "load."
- Handwritten additions to the check, such as the recipient's phone number.
- Absence of the bank's or the recipient's address.
- Check number is either absent or is the same on all checks. (Source: National Check Fraud Center)

Paper checks are more vulnerable to fraud than electronic transfers because of the ease of obtaining preprinted checks. Many employers are transitioning to either direct deposits or paycards to protect company assets.

Direct Deposit

Direct deposit of employee compensation into the individual's bank account offers employers some of the same advantages as checks. Like checks, employee compensation is traceable through both the employer's bank and the optional paper pay advice issued to the employee. Employees often prefer direct deposit because their pay is immediately available in their bank account, eliminating the need to travel to the bank to deposit the paper check. However, for employees to receive their pay through direct deposit, they must have a bank account.

An advantage of direct deposit is that it prevents paper waste, promoting "green" business. In 2009, the National Automated Clearing House Association (NACHA) estimated an average of approximately $175 per employee, amounting to $6.7 billion, was saved per year by using direct deposit. These savings came from lower waste collection, paper usage, and recycling costs. Not only does direct deposit save a

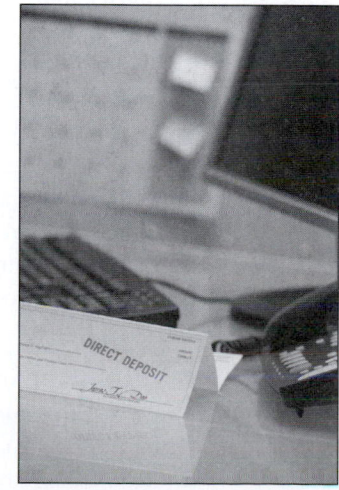

© Comstock/PunchStock, RF

company money, it reduces the time needed for payroll processing, which frees payroll accountants to complete other tasks.

When using direct deposit as an employee compensation method, a suggested best practice is to grant the employees access to a website or online portal by which they can securely view their *pay advice* and pay history, as this may substitute for paper payroll advices. Because direct deposit involves the use of electronic data transmittal, the posting of the pay advice on a secure site could be linked with the human resources data, allowing the employee an element of self-maintenance in payroll records. The potential pitfall in the use of a website for these highly sensitive records is the vulnerability of the information to computer hacking. If an employer chooses to use a website in this manner, he or she must take steps to prevent hacking through data encryption, identity verification, and site security.

> The Federal Communications Commission (FCC) has published guidelines for employer data security procedures, especially as pertains to employee information on websites and the use of paycards. The FCC guidelines include advice about the selection of data to be included on employee-accessible websites, password strength guidelines, update intervals, and data archiving. (Source: FCC)

Paycards

Paycards have been growing in popularity since the beginning of the 21st century. These cards are debit cards onto which an employer electronically transmits the employee's pay. The use of payroll cards started in the 1990s as a convenient way to compensate over-the-road truck drivers who could not be in a predictable place on each payday. Comerica started issuing the paycards that could be used anywhere a conventional MasterCard was accepted, which is nearly everywhere. Unlike the use of paper checks or direct deposit, the paycard does not require an employee to maintain a bank account to access his or her pay. The convenience and ease of use for employees makes the pay card an option that nearly 2 million workers in the United States have opted to use.

What is the disadvantage to paycard use? Unlike the limits to access that a bank has for its account holders, a paycard can be lost or stolen. Some employees may encounter challenges such as withdrawal limits or cash back at point-of-sale (POS) purchases. An issue that haunted the early use of paycards was *Regulation E* of the Federal Deposit Insurance Corporation (FDIC), which protects consumers from loss of the availability of their funds on deposit in the event of bank losses. Until 2006, Regulation E applied to funds on deposit in an FDIC-insured institution. Regulation E was extended to cover payroll funds transferred to paycards, according to 12 CFR Part 205. As a pay method that is growing in popularity among employers and employees, paycards offer more compensation options for employers.

Paycards require different types of security than the other types of employee compensation, but most elements remain the same. In addition to tracking hours and accurately compensating employees based on their marital status and withholdings, the employer must keep the employee's paycard number in a secure file. Software such as QuickBooks offers password encryption abilities for the files of employees who have paycards. Like any other debit card, the funds are electronically coded to the account number. Although the card issuer (not the employer) must remain compliant with Regulation E as far as card loss or theft is concerned, the employer is responsible to ensure this extra step of payroll security.

> In late 2013, Visa, Inc., introduced an improvement to its Visa Advanced Authorization technology, making compensation via paycards more secure and reliable. This new technology improved real-time fraud detection and was projected to prevent nearly $200 million in fraud within a five-year period. (Source: PR Newswire)

TAXES AND PAYMENT METHODS

Mandatory and voluntary deductions from employee pay change each year because of changes in the laws governing these withholdings. Some developments in employee withholdings during the early 2010s include the following:

- Changes to employee net pay because of the Affordable Care Act health insurance requirements for employers.
- Additional Medicare tax deductions that were enacted as part of the Affordable Care Act.
- Changes in the amounts that employees may contribute on a tax-deferred basis to pension plans.
- Increased public awareness of the effect of pay raises, especially for cost of living, on net pay.
- State-level legislation about the percent of disposable earnings that may be subject to garnishments.

Some trends to watch in employee net pay include the following:

- Federally mandated wellness programs to reduce absenteeism and improve financial wellness.
- Changes to rules governing overtime pay that will affect the net pay for salaried employees.
- Changes to the compensation of workers who telecommute or travel regularly for business.
- Questions about paycards being considered as legal money.
- Same-day electronic payments to individuals who have received electronic fund transfers.

Pay Methods

Stop & Check

1. What are the different employee pay methods?
2. What regulation governs paycard loss or theft?
3. For which pay method(s) must an employee have a bank account?

Summary of Employee Net Pay and Pay Methods

Employee pay is subject to a variety of deductions that can be both mandatory and voluntary. Deductions such as federal income tax and Medicare tax are virtually inescapable. Other taxes such as Social Security, state taxes, and local taxes are not applicable in every employee's situation and depend on a variety of factors such as year-to-date pay and state of residence. Of the other deductions, some can be withheld from an employee's pay before taxes are deducted, which benefits an employee by reducing their payroll tax liability. Other deductions must be taken after taxes are withheld. Understanding the difference between gross pay and net pay is vital for payroll accountants because the net pay, not the gross, is the pay that the employee actually receives.

The question of employee pay methods is complex. Which pay method is the best? It is not an easy answer. An employer should consider the needs of the employees, as well as the business, to decide if one method will suit everyone. Sometimes a combination of payment methods is the best solution, although it adds complexity for the payroll accountant. The most appropriate method for the organization will depend on many different factors. Attention to these factors, which include payroll frequency, employee types, and the nature of the business itself, will inform employer decisions about employee pay methods.

Key Points

- Net pay is gross pay less all deductions.
- Pre-tax deductions are used for qualified deductions and to reduce the taxable wage base.
- Federal income tax applies to all workers, and the amount varies based on wages, pay frequency, marital status, and number of withholdings.
- Social Security tax has a maximum wage base that can change each year.
- Medicare tax has no maximum wage base, and an additional Medicare tax is levied on employees who earn more than $200,000.
- Certain pre-tax deductions are subject to FICA taxes.
- Post-tax deductions include garnishments, union dues, and charitable contributions.
- Garnishments are subject to maximum percentages of disposable income, depending on the type of garnishment.
- Employees' pay may be disbursed in cash, by check, by paycard, or via direct deposit.

Vocabulary

401(k)
403(b)
Additional Medicare tax
Cafeteria plans
Charitable contributions
Consumer Credit Protection
  Act
Defined benefit
Defined contribution
Direct deposit
Disposable income
Escheatment
ESOP

Flexible Spending Account
Fringe Benefit
Garnishments
Gross pay
Health Savings account
  (HSA)
IRA
Local income tax
Mandated deductions
Mandatory deductions
Medicare tax
Net pay
Pay advice

Paycard
Percentage method
Regulation E
SEP
SIMPLE
SIMPLE 401(k)
Social Security tax
State income tax
Union dues
Voluntary deductions
Wage base
Wage-bracket method

Review Questions

1. What are the four factors that affect how much federal income tax is withheld from an employee's pay?

2. How is Social Security tax computed? What is the maximum wage base?

3. How is Medicare tax computed? What is the maximum wage base?

4. Name four states that do not have an income tax for employees.

5. What are two examples of voluntary deductions?

6. What are two examples of pre-tax deductions?

7. How is an employee's net income computed?

8. Why is the difference between gross pay and taxable income important?

9. What are garnishments, and how must they be handled?

10. What are the four different pay methods?

11. What are an advantage and disadvantage of paycards?

12. What are an advantage and disadvantage of direct deposit?

13. How does the percentage method work? When should it be used instead of the wage-bracket method?

Exercises Set A

E4-1A.

LO 4-1

Mandella, the payroll accountant, needs to compute net pay for the employees for Hay Industries. Place the following steps in the proper order.

A. Compute income taxes.
B. Subtract pre-tax deductions from gross pay.
C. Compute Social Security and Medicare taxes.
D. Subtract taxes and all other deductions from gross pay.
E. Determine gross pay.
    Order: _____

E4-1A.

LO 4-1

Daryl Simpson is the owner of Padua Products. During the holiday season, he wants to reward his employees for their work during the year, and he has asked you to gross up their bonuses so that they receive the full amount as net pay. What amount(s) should you consider when computing the grossed-up pay? (Select all that apply.)

A. Desired bonus amount.
B. Social Security and Medicare taxes.
C. Mandated deductions.
D. Income tax(es).

E4-3A.

LO 4-2

Larisa is an employee of Yellow Rose Products. She has come to you, the payroll accountant, for advice about her health insurance premiums, specifically if she should have them deducted pre-tax or post-tax. What reason(s) would you give her for having the medical premiums deducted on a pre-tax basis?

A. The premium amounts are reduced by deducting them on a pre-tax basis.
B. The employee's income that is subject to income tax(es) is reduced.
C. The income subject to Social Security and Medicare taxes is reduced.
D. All health insurance premiums must be deducted on a pre-tax basis.

E4-4A.

LO 4-2

Which of the following describes the primary difference between a 401(k) and a 403(b) retirement plan?

A. The 401(k) is a defined benefit only plan.
B. The 403(b) is a defined contribution only plan.
C. The 401(k) is restricted to investments in stocks only.
D. The 403(b) is restricted to use by nonprofit companies.

E4-5A.

LO 4-2

Which of the following is true about fringe benefits?

A. They represent additional cash paid directly to employees.
B. They are only available for employees.
C. They represent additional compensation given for services performed.
D. The amount of the fringe benefit is never subject to income tax.

E4-6A.

LO 4-3

Teddy is a new payroll clerk with B&H Farms. As he prepares to use the wage-bracket tables to determine federal income tax withholdings, what information does he need for each employee? (Select all that apply.)

A. Age
B. Taxable income
C. Pay date
D. Pay frequency

E4-7A.

LO 4-3

Under which circumstances could the percentage method be used to determine federal income tax withholding amounts? (Select all that apply.)

A. When the employee's taxable income exceeds the maximum amount on the appropriate wage-bracket table.
B. When using a computerized accounting system to compute payroll deductions.
C. When using a manual accounting system for a small number of low-pay employees.
D. When computational accuracy is critical.

E4-8A.

LO 4-4

Which of the following is true about Social Security and Medicare taxes as they pertain to earnings limits? (Select all that apply.)
- A. Social Security tax applies to all earnings, regardless of year-to-date amounts.
- B. Employees who earn more than $200,000 annually are subject to additional Medicare tax withholding.
- C. Once an employee's year-to-date earnings exceed the wage base, no additional Social Security tax is withheld.
- D. Employers contribute equally on all Social Security and Medicare taxes.

E4-9A.

LO 4-4

Which of the following are the rates for Social Security and Medicare taxes, respectively?
- A. 4.4%, 6.2%
- B. 4.2%, 1.5%
- C. 6.2%, 1.45%
- D. 1.45%, 6.2%

E4-10A.

LO 4-5

Which of the following statements are true about state and local income taxes? (Select all that apply.)
- A. All states tax employee earnings.
- B. State tax rates on employee earnings vary among states.
- C. Certain states have no personal income tax deduction.
- D. Some localities levy income tax on employees.

E4-11A.

LO 4-6

How is disposable income computed?
- A. Gross pay less pre-tax deductions.
- B. Gross pay less pre-tax deductions and incomes taxes.
- C. Gross pay less mandatory deductions.
- D. Gross pay less Social Security and Medicare taxes.

E4-12A.

LO 4-7

Petra is the accountant for FAB Products, a newly formed company. She is exploring employee pay methods. Which of the following describes a method in which employee earnings is transferred automatically from the employer's bank account to the employee's bank account?
- A. Check
- B. Paycard
- C. Cash
- D. Direct deposit

Problems Set A

P4-1A.

LO 4-1, 4-2

Karen and Katie are looking at the company's health care options and trying to determine how much their net pay will decrease if they sign up for the qualified cafeteria plan offered by the company. Explain the calculations of taxable income when qualified health care deductions are involved. Karen, a married woman with four exemptions, earns $2,000 per biweekly payroll. Katie, a single woman with one exemption, also earns $2,000 per biweekly payroll. The biweekly employee contribution to health care that would be subject to the cafeteria plan is $100.

Karen's taxable income if she declines to participate in the cafeteria plan: _____

Karen's taxable income if she participates in the cafeteria plan: _____

Katie's taxable income if she declines to participate in the cafeteria plan: _____

Katie's taxable income if she participates in the cafeteria plan: _____

P4-2A.

LO 4-1, 4-2, 4-3, 4-6

Using the data in P4-1A, compute the net pay for Karen and Katie. Assume that they are subject to federal income tax (using the wage-bracket method) and FICA taxes and have no other deductions from their pay. When wages fall on the end of a bracket, use the lower end.

Karen's net pay if she declines to participate in the cafeteria plan: _____

Karen's net pay if she participates in the cafeteria plan: _____

Katie's net pay if she declines to participate in the cafeteria plan: _____

Katie's net pay if she participates in the cafeteria plan: _____

P4-3A.

LO 4-1, 4-2, 4-3, 4-5, 4-6

Tooka's Trees in Auburn, Tennessee, has six employees who are paid biweekly. Calculate the net pay from the information provided below for the November 15 pay date. Assume that all wages are subject to Social Security and Medicare taxes. Use the wage-bracket method of determining federal income tax. All 401(k) and Section 125 amounts are pre-tax deductions. The wages are not subject to state taxes.

a. T. Taylor
    Single, four withholdings
    Gross pay: $1,500 per period
    401(k) deduction: $125 per pay period
    Net pay:_____

b. B. Walburn
    Married, six withholdings
    Gross pay: $2,225 per period
    401(k) deduction: $250 per period
    Net pay: _____

c. H. Carpenter
    Single, no withholdings
    Gross pay: $2,100 per period
    Section 125 deduction: $75 per period
    401(k) deduction: $50 per period
    Net pay: _____

d. J. Knight
    Married, three withholdings
    Gross pay: $1,875 per period
    United Way deduction: $50 per period
    Garnishment: $50 per period
    Net pay: _____

e. C. Lunn
    Single, one withholding
    Gross pay: $1,200 per period
    Section 125 withholding: $50 per period
    401(k) deduction: 6% of gross pay
    Net pay: _____

f. E. Smooter
    Married, eight withholdings
    Gross pay: $2,425 per period
    401(k) deduction: $75 per period
    Net pay: _____

P4-4A.

LO 4-1, 4-2, 4-3, 4-4, 4-5, 4-6

The following employees of CIBA Ironworks in Bristol, Illinois, are paid in different frequencies. Some employees have union dues or garnishments deducted from their pay. Calculate their net pay using the wage-bracket method to determine federal income tax, and including Illinois income tax of 3.75% of taxable pay. No employee has exceeded the maximum FICA limits.

Employee	Frequency	Marital Status/ Withholdings	Pay	Union Dues per Period	Garnishment per Period	Net Pay
C. Whaley	Weekly	M, 2	$ 850		$ 50	
F. Paguaga	Semimonthly	M, 6	$2,800	$120		
K. Harvey	Monthly	S, 3	$8,000	$240	$ 75	
L. Bolling	Biweekly	M, 0	$2,500		$100	

P4-5A.

LO 4-1, 4-2, 4-3, 4-4, 4-5, 4-6

Frances Newberry is the payroll accountant for Pack-It Services of Jackson, Arizona. The employees of Pack-It Services are paid semimonthly. An employee, Glen Riley, comes to her on November 10 and requests a pay advance of $750, which he will pay back in equal parts on the November 15 and December 15 paychecks. Glen is married with eight withholding allowances and is paid $50,000 per year. He contributes 3% of his pay to a 401(k) and has $25 per paycheck deducted for a Section 125 plan. Compute his net pay on his November 15 paycheck. The state income tax rate is 4%.

P4-6A.

LO 4-1, 4-2

Milligan's Millworks pays its employees on a weekly basis. Using the wage-bracket tables from Appendix C, compute the federal income tax withholdings for the following employees of Milligan's Millworks:

Employee	Marital Status	No. of Exemptions	Weekly Pay	Federal Tax
D. Balestreri	S	4	$ 845	
Y. Milligan	S	2	$1,233	
H. Curran	M	7	$ 682	
D. Liberti	M	0	$ 755	

P4-7A.

LO 4-2

Wynne and Associates has employees with pay schedules that vary based on job classification. Compute the federal income tax withholding for each employee using the percentage method.

Employee	Marital Status	No. of Exemptions	Pay Frequency	Pay Amount	Federal Income Tax
S. Turner	S	1	Weekly	$ 3,000	
D. McGorray	S	4	Monthly	$ 15,000	
A. Kennedy	M	3	Daily	$ 500	
R. Thomas	M	5	Annually	$120,000	

P4-8A.

LO 4-3

The employees of Agonnacultis, Inc., are paid on a semimonthly basis. Compute the FICA taxes for the employees for the November 15 payroll. All employees have been employed for the entire calendar year.

Employee	Semimonthly Pay	YTD Pay for Oct 31 Pay Date	Social Security Tax for Nov. 15 Pay Date	Medicare Tax for Nov. 15 Pay Date
T. Newberry	$7,500			
S. Smith	$3,500			
D. Plott	$4,225			
I. Ost	$6,895			
D. Bogard	$9,500			
M. Mallamace	$4,100			

P4-9A.

LO 4-4

Fannon's Chocolate Factory operates in North Carolina. Using the state income tax rate of 5.75%, calculate the income tax for each employee.

Employee	Amount per Pay Period	North Carolina Income Tax
K. Jamieson	$ 550	
D. Macranie	$ 4,895	
G. Lockhart	$ 3,225	
K. McIntyre	$ 1,795	

P4-10A.

LO 4-2

Using the percentage method, calculate the federal withholding amounts for the following employees.

Employee	Marital Status	Withholdings	Pay Frequency	Amount per Pay Period	Federal Income Tax
S. Calder	M	6	Quarterly	$20,000	
P. Singh	S	2	Annually	$90,000	
B. Nelson	M	0	Daily	$ 500	

P4-11A.

LO 4-7

Margaret Wilson is the new accountant for a start-up company. The company has cross-country drivers, warehouse personnel, and office staff at the main location. The company is looking at options that allow its employees flexibility with receiving their pay. Margaret has been asked to present the advantages and disadvantages of the various pay methods to senior management. Which would be the best option for each class of workers?

Exercises Set B

E4-1B.

LO 4-1

Chastity is in the process of computing net pay for the employees of the company. Which of the following steps should she do after determining the amount of gross pay? (Select all that apply)
  A. Compute Social Security and Medicare tax withholding.
  B. Compute income tax withholding(s).
  C. Compute pre-tax deductions.
  D. Compute post-tax deductions.

E4-2B.

LO 4-1

Joey Martel is an employee of Overclock Watches. His employer would like to give him a bonus and has asked you to gross it up to ensure that Joey receives the full amount of the desired award. Which of the following should be considered in the denominator to compute the grossed-up amount? (Select all that apply.)
  A. Social Security and Medicare taxes.
  B. 401(k) contribution.
  C. Health insurance premium.
  D. Income tax(es).

E4-3B.

LO 4-2

Cameron Levitt is the payroll accountant for Glowing Yoga. He is preparing a presentation about the Section 125 cafeteria plans. Which of the following items may qualify for inclusion in a cafeteria plan?
  A. Health benefits
  B. Adoption assistance
  C. Childcare expenses
  D. Education assistance

E4-4B.

LO 4-2

Gabrielle Jackson is the payroll accountant of Choice Bakeries. She is researching retirement plan options for her employer. Choice Bakeries has 77 employees and is a for-profit company. Which of the following plans should she consider? (Select all that apply.)
  A. 403(b)
  B. 401(k)
  C. SIMPLE 401(k)
  D. IRA

E4-5B.

LO 4-2

Which of the following is/are examples of fringe benefits? (Select all that apply.)
  A. Education assistance
  B. Shopping club membership
  C. Vacation discounts
  D. Retirement planning services

E4-6B.

LO 4-3

Liam is the payroll accountant for Chop Brothers Coffee. As he prepares to use wage-bracket tables to determine federal income tax withholdings for each employee, which information should he have available? (Select all that apply.)

A. Marital status.
B. Job title.
C. Year-to-date earnings.
D. Number of withholding allowances.

E4-7B.

LO 4-3

Which of the following are steps in computing federal income tax withholding using the percentage method? (Select all that apply.)

A. Compute and deduct withholding allowance.
B. Apply the tax rate to the taxable portion of the earnings.
C. Determine if the employee is exempt or nonexempt.
D. Add the marginal tax.

E4-8B.

LO 4-4

Which of the following are true about Social Security and Medicare tax deductions? (Select all that apply.)

A. They are applied to the gross pay.
B. Contributions to a 401(k) plan are exempt from these taxes.
C. Medicare taxes apply to all earnings.
D. Certain pre-tax deductions are exempt from Social Security and Medicare tax computations.

E4-9B.

LO 4-4

Scout is the Vice President for Marketing at Sun Field Industries. She earns $140,000 annually and is paid on a semimonthly basis. As of October 31, Scout has year-to-date earnings of $116,666.67. The Social Security wage base is $118,500. What is the maximum amount of her taxable earnings that may be subject to Social Security tax for the November 15 pay period?

A. $5,833.33
B. $1,833.33
C. $4,000.33
D. $0

E4-10B.

LO 4-5

Which of the following is true about state and local income tax? (Select all that apply.)

A. Pre-tax deduction rules for federal income tax are generally the same for state and local income taxes.
B. Nine states do not have a personal income tax on earnings.
C. All localities levy income taxes on employees.
D. State income tax computations vary among states.

E4-11B.

LO 4-6

Which of the following are always post-tax deductions? (Select all that apply.)

A. Garnishments
B. Health insurance
C. Charitable contributions
D. Retirement plan contributions

E4-12B.

LO 4-7

Which of the following is true about employee pay methods? (Select all that apply.)

A. Employees must be able to access the full amount of their net pay upon demand.
B. Employers must keep a record of all pay disbursements.
C. Employees do not need to own a bank account to receive their pay via direct deposit.
D. Paycards may be reloaded with an employee's net pay on the pay date.

Problems Set B

P4-1B.

LO 4-1, 4-2

Will and Eric are looking at the company's health care options and trying to determine what their taxable income will be if they sign up for the qualified cafeteria plan offered by the company, which will allow them to deduct the health care contributions pre-tax. Explain the calculations of taxable income when qualified health care deductions are involved. Will, a single man with one deduction, earns $1,600 per semimonthly payroll. Eric, a married man with six deductions, earns $1,875 per semimonthly pay period. The semi-monthly employee contribution to health care that would be subject to the cafeteria plan is $75 for Will, $250 for Eric.

Will's taxable income if he declines to participate in the cafeteria plan: _____

Will's taxable income if he participates in the cafeteria plan: _____

Eric's taxable income if he declines to participate in the cafeteria plan: _____

Eric's taxable income if he participates in the cafeteria plan: _____

P4-2B.

LO 4-1, 4-2, 4-3, 4-6

Using the data in P4-1B, compute the net pay for Will and Eric. Assume that they are subject to federal income tax (using the wage-bracket method in Appendix C) and FICA taxes and have no other deductions from their pay.

Will's net pay if he declines to participate in the cafeteria plan: _____

Will's net pay if he participates in the cafeteria plan: _____

Eric's net pay if he declines to participate in the cafeteria plan: _____

Eric's net pay if he participates in the cafeteria plan: _____

P4-3B.

LO 4-1, 4-2, 4-3, 4-5, 4-6

Hark Enterprises in Taft, Wyoming, has six employees who are paid on a semi-monthly basis. Calculate the net pay from the information provided below for the August 15 pay date. Assume that all wages are subject to Social Security and Medicare taxes. Use the wage-bracket tables in Appendix C to determine the federal income tax withholding.

a. L. Fletcher:
    Married, five withholdings
    Gross pay: $1,320 per period
    401(k) deduction: 2% of gross pay per pay period
    Net pay: _____

b. S. Lince
    Single, no withholdings
    Gross pay: $1,745 per period
    401(k) deduction: $220 per pay period
    Net pay: _____

c. A. Brown
    Single, five withholdings
    Gross pay: $2,120 per period
    Section 125 deduction: $25 per pay period
    401(k) deduction: $150 per pay period
    Net pay: _____

d. R. Kimble
    Married, six withholdings
    Gross pay: $1,570 per period
    United Way deduction: $25 per pay period
    Garnishment: $75 per period
    Net pay: _____

e. F. Monteiro
Married, no withholdings
Gross pay: $2,200 per period
Section 125 deduction: $100 per period
401(k) deduction: 4% of gross pay
Net pay: _____

f. K. Giannini
Single, two withholdings
Gross pay: $1,485 per period
401(k) deduction: $120 per period
Net pay: _____

P4-4B.

LO 4-1,
4-2, 4-3,
4-5, 4-6

The following employees of Memory Bytes of Titusville, Washington, are paid in different frequencies. Some employees have union dues or garnishments deducted from their pay. Calculate their net pay. (Use the wage-bracket tables in Appendix C to determine federal income tax unless otherwise noted.) No employee has exceeded the maximum FICA limits.

Employee	Frequency	Marital Status/ Withholdings	Pay	Union Dues per Period	Garnishment per Period	Net Pay
N. Lawrence	Biweekly	M, 5	$1,680	$102		
D. Gaitan	Weekly	S, 0	$1,300		$70	
N. Ruggieri	Semimonthly	M, 2	$2,525	$110	$90	
P. Oceguera	Monthly	S, 2	$6,600		$45	

P4-5B.

LO 4-1,
4-2, 4-3,
4-4, 4-5,
4-6

Jane Heinlein is the payroll accountant for Sia Lights of Carter, Nebraska. The employees of Sia Lights are paid biweekly. An employee, Melinda Gunnarson, comes to her on September 14 and requests a pay advance of $825, which she will pay back in equal parts on the September 28 and October 12 paychecks. Melinda is single with one withholding allowance and is paid $32,500 per year. She contributes 1% of her pay to a 401(k) plan and has $25 per paycheck deducted for a court-ordered garnishment. Compute her net pay for her September 28th paycheck. The state income tax rate is 5.01%. Use the wage-bracket tables in Appendix C to determine the federal income tax withholding amount.

P4-6B.

LO 4-2

Wolfe Industries pays its employees on a semimonthly basis. Using the wage-bracket tables from Appendix C, compute the federal income tax deductions for the following employees of Wolfe Industries:

Employee	Marital Status	No. of Exemptions	Semimonthly Pay	Federal Income Tax
T. Canter	M	1	$1,050	
M. McCollum	M	5	$1,390	
C. Hammond	S	2	$1,295	
T. Elliott	S	4	$1,165	

P4-7B.

LO 4-2

GL Kennels has employees with pay schedules that vary based on job classification. Compute the federal income tax liability for each employee using the percentage method.

Employee	Marital Status	No. of Exemptions	Pay Frequency	Pay Amount	Percentage Method
C. Wells	M	2	Biweekly	$1,825	
L. Decker	M	0	Weekly	$ 750	
J. Swaby	S	5	Weekly	$ 875	
M. Ohlson	M	3	Semimonthly	$2,025	

P4-8B.

LO 4-3

The employees of Black Cat Designs are paid on a semimonthly basis. Compute the FICA taxes for the employees for the November 30, 2016, payroll. All employees have been employed for the entire calendar year.

Employee	Semimonthly Pay	YTD Pay for 11-15-2016	Social Security Tax for 11-30-2016 Pay	Medicare Tax for 11-30-2016 Pay
P. Gareis	$4,250			
E. Siliwon	$6,275			
G. De La Torre	$5,875			
L. Rosenthal	$2,850			
C. Bertozzi	$5,105			
T. Gennaro	$2,940			

P4-9B.

LO 4-4

Christensen Ranch operates in Pennsylvania. Using the state income tax rate of 3.07%, calculate the state income tax for each employee.

Employee	Amount per Pay Period	Pennsylvania Income Tax
G. Zonis	$1,325	
V. Sizemore	$1,710	
R. Dawson	$ 925	
C. Couture	$2,550	

P4-10B.

LO 4-2

Using the percentage method, calculate the federal withholding amounts for the following employees.

Employee	Marital Status	Withholdings	Pay Frequency	Amount per Pay Period	Federal Income Tax
L. Abbey	S	3	Annually	$63,500	
G. Narleski	M	0	Quarterly	$14,000	
T. Leider	S	1	Monthly	$ 1,200	

P4-11B.

LO 4-7

David Adams has been retained as a consultant for Marionet Industries. The company has had difficulty with its cross-country drivers receiving their pay in a timely fashion because they are often away from their home banks. The company is looking at options that allow its employees flexibility with receiving their pay. Prepare a presentation depicting the advantages and disadvantages of the various pay methods for senior management.

Critical Thinking

For the Critical Thinking problems, use the following steps to compute the gross-up amount:

1. Compute tax rate: The tax rate on bonuses is 28%. The Social Security (6.2%) and Medicare taxes (1.45%) must be added to this rate. For bonuses, the total tax rate equals 28% + 6.2% +1.45%, or 35.65%.
2. Subtract 100% − tax rate% to get the net tax rate. For bonuses, it is 100% − 35.65%, or 64.35%
3. Gross-up amount = net pay / net tax rate. For example, if you want the employee to receive a $150 bonus, the equation is $150/64.35% = $233.10

4-1. Vicky Le, an employee of Sweet Shoppe Industries, receives a bonus of $5,000 for her stellar work. Her boss wants Vicky to receive $5,000 on the check. She contributes 3% of her pay in a pre-tax deduction to her 401(k). Calculate the gross pay amount that would result in $5,000 paid to Vicky.

4-2. Your boss approaches you in mid-December and requests that you pay certain employees their gross pay amount as if there were no deductions as their Christmas bonuses. None of the employees have reached the Social Security wage base for the year. What is the gross-up amount for each of the following employees? (Use the tax rate for bonuses and no state taxes.)

Employee	Regular Gross Pay per Period	Grossed-Up Amount
Yves St. John	$2,500	
Kim Johnson	$3,380	
Michael Hale	$3,178	

In the Real World: Scenario for Discussion

The State of Kansas passed legislation in 2007 that allowed employers to select their employee pay method. The legislation was known as the "paperless payroll law," and many employers opted to give their employees paycards instead of cash, check, or direct deposit. What are some issues with this practice? What are some benefits?

Internet Activities

4-1. Did you know that you can use an online calculator to see how your voluntary deductions will affect your paycheck? Many different payroll calculators exist. Go to one or more of the following sites and use the payroll calculator:

www.paycheckcity.com/

www.surepayroll.com/calculator/payroll-calculators.asp

www.adp.com/tools-and-resources.aspx

4-2. Health insurance is a rapidly changing and evolving field. Employers have many options and concerns to consider. Check out www.npr.org/sections/health-care/ to listen to podcasts about health insurance and employer issues. What issues do employers currently face?

4-3. Want to know more about the concepts in this chapter? Check out these sites:

www.healthcare.gov/law/index.html

www.aflac.com

www.investopedia.com

www.irs.gov/pub/irs-pdf/p15.pdf

www.americanpayroll.org/Visa-Paycard-Portal/

Continuing Payroll Project: Prevosti Farms and Sugarhouse

For the February 12, 2016, pay period, use the gross pay totals from the end of Chapter 3 and compute the net pay for each employee. Once you have computed the net pay (using the wage-bracket tables in Appendix C), state withholding tax for Vermont is computed at 3.55% of taxable wages (i.e., gross pay less pre-tax deductions). Note that the first pay period comprises only one week of work during the February 12 pay period and that the federal income tax should be determined using the biweekly tables in Appendix C.

Voluntary deductions for each employee are as follows:

Name	Deduction
Millen	Insurance: $155/paycheck 401(k): 3% of gross pay
Towle	Insurance: $100/paycheck 401(k): 5% of gross pay
Long	Insurance: $155/paycheck 401(k): 2% of gross pay

Name	Deduction
Shangraw	Insurance: $100/paycheck 401(k): 3% of gross pay
Lewis	Insurance: $155/paycheck 401(k): 4% of gross pay
Schwartz	Insurance: $100/paycheck 401(k): 5% of gross pay
Prevosti	Insurance: $155/paycheck 401(k): 6% of gross pay
You	Insurance: $100/paycheck 401(k): 2% of gross pay

Compute the net pay for the February 12 pay period using the payroll register. All insurance and 401(k) deductions are pre-tax. Update the Employee Earnings Records as of February 12, 2016.

Name	M/S	# W/H	Hourly Rate or Period Wage	No. of Regular Hours	No. of Overtime Hours	No. of Holiday Hours	Commissions	Gross Earning	Insurance	Cafeteria Plan	Taxable Wages for Federal W/H	Taxable Wages for FICA

Name	Gross Earning	Taxable Wages for Federal W/H	Taxable Wages for FICA	Federal W/H	Social Security Tax	Medicare W/H	State W/H Tax	Union Dues	Net Pay	Check No

EMPLOYEE EARNINGS RECORD

NAME	Thomas Millen	Hire Date	01-02-2014
ADDRESS	1022 Forest School Rd	Date of Birth	16-12-1982
CITY/STATE/ZIP	Woodstock/VT/05001	Position	Production Manager
TELEPHONE	802-478-5055	No. of Exemptions	4
SOCIAL SECURITY NUMBER	031-11-3456	Pay Rate	$35,000/year

Period Ended	Hrs. Worked	Reg Pay	OT Pay	Gross Pay	Social Sec. Tax	Medicare	Fed Inc. Tax	State Inc. Tax	SDI	401(k)	Other	Total Deductions	Net pay	YTD

EMPLOYEE EARNINGS RECORD

NAME	Avery Towle	Hire Date	04-02-2014
ADDRESS	4011 Route 100	Date of Birth	14-07-1991
CITY/STATE/ZIP	Plymouth/VT/05102	Position	Production Worker
TELEPHONE	802-967-5873	No. of Exemptions	1
SOCIAL SECURITY NUMBER	089-74-0974	Pay Rate	$12.00/hour

Period Ended	Hrs. Worked	Reg Pay	OT Pay	Gross Pay	Social Sec. Tax	Medicare	Fed Inc. Tax	State Inc. Tax	SDI	401(k)	Other	Total Deductions	Net pay	YTD

EMPLOYEE EARNINGS RECORD

NAME	Charlie Long	Hire Date	07-02-2014
ADDRESS	242 Benedict Rd	Date of Birth	16-03-1987
CITY/STATE/ZIP	S. Woodstock/VT/05002	Position	Production Worker
TELEPHONE	802-429-3846	No. of Exemptions	2
SOCIAL SECURITY NUMBER	056-23-4593	Pay Rate	$12.50/hour

Period Ended	Hrs. Worked	Reg Pay	OT Pay	Gross Pay	Social Sec. Tax	Medicare	Fed Inc. Tax	State Inc. Tax	SDI	401(k)	Other	Total Deductions	Net pay	YTD

EMPLOYEE EARNINGS RECORD

NAME	Mary Shangraw	Hire Date	05-02-2014
ADDRESS	1901 Main St #2	Date of Birth	20-08-1994
CITY/STATE/ZIP	Bridgewater/VT/05520	Position	Administrative Assistant
TELEPHONE	802-575-5423	No. of Exemptions	1
SOCIAL SECURITY NUMBER	075-28-8945	Pay Rate	$10.50/hour

Period Ended	Hrs. Worked	Reg Pay	OT Pay	Gross Pay	Social Sec. Tax	Medicare	Fed Inc. Tax	State Inc. Tax	SDI	401(k)	Other	Total Deductions	Net pay	YTD

EMPLOYEE EARNINGS RECORD

NAME	Kristen Lewis	Hire Date	02-02-2014
ADDRESS	840 Daily Hollow Rd	Date of Birth	06-04-1950
CITY/STATE/ZIP	Bridgewater/VT/05523	Position	Office Manager
TELEPHONE	802-390-5572	No. of Exemptions	3
SOCIAL SECURITY NUMBER	076-39-5673	Pay Rate	$32,000/year

Period Ended	Hrs. Worked	Reg Pay	OT Pay	Gross Pay	Social Sec. Tax	Medicare	Fed Inc. Tax	State Inc. Tax	SDI	401(k)	Other	Total Deductions	Net pay	YTD

EMPLOYEE EARNINGS RECORD

NAME	Joel Schwartz	Hire Date	01-02-2014
ADDRESS	55 Maple Farm Wy	Date of Birth	23-05-1985
CITY/STATE/ZIP	Woodstock/VT/05534	Position	Sales
TELEPHONE	802-463-9985	No. of Exemptions	2
SOCIAL SECURITY NUMBER	021-34-9876	Pay Rate	$24,000/year + commission

Period Ended	Hrs. Worked	Reg Pay	OT Pay	Gross Pay	Social Sec. Tax	Medicare	Fed Inc. Tax	State Inc. Tax	SDI	401(k)	Other	Total Deductions	Net pay	YTD

EMPLOYEE EARNINGS RECORD

NAME	Toni Prevosti	Hire Date	01-02-2014
ADDRESS	10520 Cox Hill Rd	Date of Birth	18-09-1967
CITY/STATE/ZIP	Bridgewater/VT/05521	Position	Owner/President
TELEPHONE	802-673-2636	No. of Exemptions	5
SOCIAL SECURITY NUMBER	055-22-0443	Pay Rate	$45,000/year

Period Ended	Hrs. Worked	Reg Pay	OT Pay	Gross Pay	Social Sec. Tax	Medicare	Fed Inc. Tax	State Inc. Tax	SDI	401(k)	Other	Total Deductions	Net pay	YTD

EMPLOYEE EARNINGS RECORD

NAME ___Student Success___ Hire Date _____

ADDRESS _____ Date of Birth _____

CITY/STATE/ZIP _____ Position _____

TELEPHONE _____ No. of Exemptions _____

SOCIAL SECURITY NUMBER _____ Pay Rate _____

Period Ended	Hrs. Worked	Reg Pay	OT Pay	Gross Pay	Social Sec. Tax	Medicare	Fed Inc. Tax	State Inc. Tax	SDI	401(k)	Other	Total Deductions	Net pay	YTD

Answers to Stop & Check Exercises

Differentiating Between Gross and Net Pay

1. Gross pay consists of wages or commissions earned by the employee before deductions. Net pay consists of an employee's salary or wages less all mandatory and voluntary deductions.
2. Qualifying medical or dental plans, Internal Revenue Code Section 125 plans, 401(k) retirement plans, federal income tax, Medicare tax, Social Security tax, state income tax, garnishments, charitable contributions, union dues.
3. Grossing-up is the process of increasing the gross pay by applicable taxes to ensure net pay achieves the desired amount.

What Counts as Pre-Taxable?

1. Insurance, various retirement plans, cafeteria plans.
2. Affordable Care Act of 2010.
3. 401(k), IRA, SIMPLE, SEP, ESOP.

How Much Tax to Withhold?

1. (a) $183; (b) (($2,166.67 − (2 × 166.70) − 1,127) × 0.15) + $76.90 = $182.84.
2. $168 = $2,166.67 gross pay − $100 for 401(k) deduction per pay period = $2,066.67 taxable pay. This is the amount used in conjunction with the wage-bracket table to calculate the federal income tax withheld. The difference in taxes with the 401(k) deduction is $183 − 168 = $15.
3. $162 = $2,166.67 gross pay − $75 health insurance − $55 AFLAC = $2,036.67 taxable pay.

FICA Taxes

1. $327.36 for Social Security, $76.56 for Medicare.
2. ($327.36 + $76.56) × 2 = $807.84.
3. a. $0 Social Security tax; Medicare taxable would be reduced by the qualified insurance deduction. Year-to-date salary $197,916.73 less the qualified insurance $1,425 ($75 × 19) gives $196,491.67. Medicare base for this payroll, $3,508.33 to reach the $200,000 cap and $6,833.34 ($10,416.67 − 3,508.33 − 75.00) that

will be charged the surcharge. ($3,508.33 × 1.45%) + ($6,833.34 × 2.35%) = $50.87 + $160.58 = $211.45 Medicare tax.

b. ($10,416.67 − 75.00) × 2.35% = $243.03 Medicare tax.

State and Local Income Taxes

1. $34.78 ($62,500 annual salary/26 biweekly = $2,403.85 gross pay − $150 for 401(k) pre-tax deduction − $80 health insurance pre-tax deduction = $2,173.85 taxable pay × 1.6%. From Appendix D, Married.
2. $131.96 ($2,850 × 4.63%) state, $5.75 local.

Post-Tax Deductions

1. $447.50 = $1,790 × 25%.
2. $447.50. The health insurance and union dues deductions are not legal obligations and do not affect disposable income.

Pay Methods

1. Cash, check, direct deposit, and paycard.
2. Regulation E.
3. Direct deposit.

Chapter Five

Employer Payroll Taxes and Labor Planning

All facets of payroll accounting are important because they affect the success of the company and its employees. A particularly important piece of the payroll puzzle is the employer's payroll tax responsibility. The reporting and remittance of payroll taxes is a significant aspect that requires scrupulous attention to detail. Many different tax forms exist that must be filed at regular intervals and with varying governmental bodies. Tax filing requires organizational skills, time management, and continued accuracy. Tax reporting is a huge responsibility of the business and its payroll accountant because of governmental oversight.

Employers must also consider payroll responsibilities as part of labor planning. Besides taxes, other aspects of an employer's payroll responsibilities include maintaining workers' compensation insurance, forwarding amounts withheld through employees' voluntary and mandated deductions, and determining both labor expenses and employee benefits. The Internal Revenue Service and state employment departments have websites that contain important information about filing requirements, due dates, guidelines, and penalties (See Appendix E for state employment department contact information). Insurance responsibilities are a vital consideration when determining labor expenses and employee benefits because they are a significant element in the cost of doing business.

LEARNING OBJECTIVES

After studying Chapter 5, you should be able to:

LO 5-1   List Employer-Paid and Employee-Paid Obligations

LO 5-2   Discuss Reporting Periods and Requirements for Employer Tax Deposits

LO 5-3   Prepare Mid-Year and Year-End Employer Tax Reporting and Deposits

LO 5-4   Describe Payroll Within the Context of Business Expenses

LO 5-5   Relate Labor Expenses to Company Profitability

LO 5-6   Complete Benefit Analysis as a Function of Payroll

© Beathan/Corbis, RF

Benefits Analysis and Employee Economic Security

Employers must weigh different options when considering what benefits they will provide their employees. Employee benefits are now viewed as a way to attract and retain valuable workers. However, offering benefits represents an additional labor expense. Depending on the industry, wages and salaries comprise between 18% and 55% of a firm's operating expenses. In a survey conducted by the SHRM, 35% of employers reported that they increased the amount of sponsored benefits during 2015. To achieve the best return for the investment in their employees, employers surveyed their employees to determine which benefits were the most valuable. The largest increases in benefits spending were reported in employee retirement funds and wellness coverage. (Source: SHRM)

The cost to have employees involves much more than the wage or salary that the employee earns. Employers must match amounts deducted from employee pay for FICA taxes and must contribute the entire amount of FUTA tax. The employer is responsible for the collection, reporting, deposit, and reconciliation of taxes withheld from the employee. When the cost of additional employee benefits, including paid time off, is added to the expense of having employees, it becomes apparent that an employee represents a significant investment by the company.

Labor costs often make up a significant portion of a company's expense. Employee benefits such as company contributions to retirement plans, temporary disability insurance, and educational reimbursements represent additional business expenses. In Chapter 5, we will examine employer payroll tax responsibilities and how payroll is a tool in labor planning.

LO 5-1   List Employer-Paid and Employee-Paid Obligations

Employers must pay some of the same taxes that the employees do. However, a firm has additional liabilities that employees do not, such as certain unemployment taxes and workers' compensation insurance. A comparison of employee-paid and employer-paid taxes is given in Table 5-1.

The taxes that an employer must pay are often known as ***statutory deductions***, meaning that governmental statutes have made the tax a mandatory, legally obligated deduction. An important element of employer tax responsibility is that it continues after writing the paychecks to the employees, often extending well after an employee leaves the firm. Employers must file mandatory reconciliation reports about amounts they have withheld from employee pay, track the employees throughout the company's accounting system, and maintain the personnel files for both current and terminated employees in accordance with the firm's payroll practices and governmental regulations.

Social Security and Medicare Taxes

The ***FICA*** taxes, which include both the Social Security and Medicare taxes, are among the statutory withholdings that employees and employers pay. Employees and employers must each contribute 6.2% (for a total of 12.4%) of the employee's pay up to the maximum withholding amount for Social Security. Additionally, employers must match the employees' payroll deductions for the Medicare tax in the amount of 1.45% (for a total of 2.9%) of the employees' gross pay less applicable deductions. In addition, the Affordable Care Act has mandated an additional 0.9% of Medicare tax for employees whose wages exceed $200,000 annually. The employer does not match this additional Medicare tax.

Let us look at an example of how the employer's share of the FICA tax works.

EXAMPLE: EMPLOYEE AND EMPLOYER SHARE, SOCIAL SECURITY TAX

Courtney works as an hourly worker who earns an annual salary of $36,000 and is paid biweekly. Her gross pay is $1,384.62 per pay period ($36,000 per year/26 pay periods).

Courtney's share of the Social Security tax:	$1,384.62 × 6.2% = $ 85.85
Her employer's share of the Social Security tax:	$1,384.62 × 6.2% = $ 85.85
Total Social Security tax liability for Courtney's pay this period:	$171.70

As shown in the example, the employer and employee contribute the same amounts for the Social Security tax. Remember that the Social Security tax has a maximum withholding per year based on the employee's salary, which is $118,500 for 2016. After reaching that maximum, neither the employee nor the employer contributes any more Social Security tax.

EXAMPLE: EMPLOYEE AND EMPLOYER SHARE SOCIAL SECURITY TAXES, HIGHLY COMPENSATED EMPLOYEE

William is the vice president of Sunny Glassworks. His annual salary is $225,000, which is paid semimonthly. His gross pay per period is $9,375.00 ($225,000/24 pay periods). For the 12th pay period of the year, the Social Security tax withholding is as follows:

William's share of the Social Security tax:	$9,375 × 6.2% = $ 581.25
Sunny Glasswork's share of William's Social Security tax:	$9,375 × 6.2% = $ 581.25
Total Social Security tax liability for William's pay this period:	$1,162.50

(continued)

TABLE 5-1

Employee-Paid and Employer-Paid Taxes

Tax	Employee Pays	Employer Pays
Social Security	XX	XX
Medicare	XX	XX
Federal Income Tax	XX	
Federal Unemployment Tax (FUTA)		XX
State Income Tax (where applicable)	XX	
State Unemployment Tax (SUTA)	Sometimes both are responsible at different percentages; see your local taxation authority for specific details.	XX
Local Income Taxes	XX	
Local Occupational Taxes (where applicable)	XX	XX
Workers' Compensation Premiums		XX
401(k)/Pension (if matching policy exists)	XX	XX
Other Voluntary Deductions	XX	

(concluded)

After the 12th pay period, William's year-to-date pay is $9,375.00 × 12 = $112,500. After the 13th pay period, William's year-to-date pay will be $9,375 × 13 = $121,875, which exceeds the Social Security wage base. The amount subject to Social Security tax for the 13th pay period equals the wage base minus the 12th pay period YTD pay:

$118,500 − $112,500 = $6,000 of William's pay during the 13th pay period is subject to Social Security tax.

William's share of the Social Security tax:	$6,000 × 6.2% = $372.00
Sunny Glasswork's share of William's Social Security tax:	$6,000 × 6.2% = $372.00
Total Social Security tax liability for William's pay this period that must be remitted by Sunny Glassworks:	$744.00

Medicare tax, the other piece of the FICA taxes, has no maximum but does have an additional tax for high-wage employees. Let us look at Courtney's pay again to see how the Medicare tax works.

EXAMPLE: EMPLOYEE AND EMPLOYER SHARE, MEDICARE TAXES

Courtney's share of the Medicare tax:	$1,384.62 × 1.45% = $20.08
Her employer's share of the Medicare tax:	$1,384.62 × 1.45% = $20.08
Total Medicare tax liability for Courtney's pay this period that must be remitted by Sunny Glassworks:	$40.16
Total FICA responsibility from Courtney's pay this period ($171.70 + $40.16):	$211.86

Now let's look at the employee and employer share of Medicare taxes for William, a highly compensated employee.

EXAMPLE: EMPLOYEE AND EMPLOYER SHARE MEDICARE TAXES, HIGHLY COMPENSATED EMPLOYEE

As of the 22nd pay period of the year, William's YTD pay is $206,250. Amount subject to the additional Medicare tax: $6,250.

Medicare tax amounts:	
William's standard Medicare tax liability:	$9,375 × 1.45% = $135.94
Sunny Glasswork's Medicare tax liability:	$9,375 × 1.45% = $135.94
William's additional Medicare tax liability:	$6,250 × 0.9% = 56.25
Total Medicare tax liability:	$328.13
Total FICA responsibility for William's pay this period	$328.13

Remember, no Social Security tax applies because William has exceeded the wage base.

Social Security and Medicare amounts may be listed separately when the company makes its tax deposit. The employer's tax deposit will also include the amount deducted from the employee for federal income tax.

Maintaining accurate records of taxes withheld through payroll registers and employee earnings records is a critical part of calculating proper FICA tax deductions. Whether a company uses a manual system, has an automated system, or outsources the payroll duties, it remains responsible for the accuracy of the deductions and maintenance of associated records.

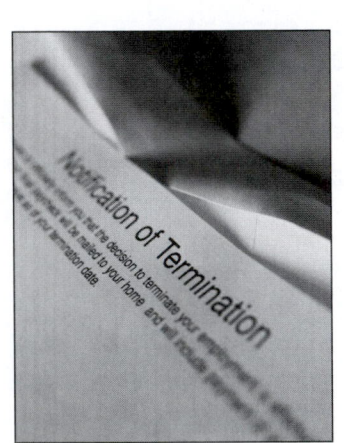

© Janis Christie/Getty Images, RF

Federal and State Unemployment Taxes

Another set of employer-paid payroll taxes includes those mandated by the Federal Unemployment Tax Act (*FUTA*) and State Unemployment Tax Act (*SUTA*). FUTA and SUTA are unemployment compensation funds established to provide for workers who have lost their jobs. Generally, the rate for FUTA tax is lower than that for SUTA tax because the states govern the disbursement of unemployment funds and because unemployment rates vary by region. FUTA taxes pay for the administrative expenses of the unemployment insurance fund. SUTA tax rates provide a localized and individual focus for employer taxes. The unemployment insurance fund pays for half of extended unemployment benefits and provides a fund of additional benefits against which states may borrow as necessary to cover unemployment claims. An interesting note is that FUTA and SUTA are employer-only taxes in all *but* three states: Alaska, New Jersey, and Pennsylvania.

FUTA pertains only to U.S. citizens and workers employed by American companies. According to the IRS, to be classified as an American company, an employer must meet the following criteria:

- An individual who is a resident of the United States,
- A partnership, if two-thirds or more of the partners are residents of the United States,
- A trust, if all of the trustees are residents of the United States, or
- A corporation organized under the laws of the United States, of any state, or the District of Columbia.

American citizens who work for companies outside of the United States who are not classified as American employers are not subject to FUTA provisions. Certain resident aliens and professions are exempt to FUTA provisions, as stipulated by Income Tax Regulation §31.3301-1. The professions from which employee compensation is exempt from FUTA provisions are:

- Compensation paid to agricultural workers.
- Compensation paid to household employees unless the compensation exceeds $1,000 during any calendar quarter of the current year or prior year.
- Compensation paid to employees of religious, charitable, educational, or certain other tax-exempt organizations.
- Compensation paid to employees of the U.S. government or any of its agencies.
- Compensation paid to employees of the government of any state of the United States, or any of its political subdivisions.
- Compensation paid to employees of the government of the District of Columbia, or any of its political subdivisions.

The full 2016 rate for FUTA tax is 6.0% of the first $7,000 of an employee's wages paid during a calendar year. FUTA is paid by the employer. Employees who move to a different company will have the new employer paying additional FUTA taxes. Therefore, if an employer has a high turnover rate among its employees (i.e., a large number of employees remain employed for only a short period before terminating employment), the firm will pay FUTA tax for all employees for the first $7,000 of earnings, including the ones who remained in their employ for only a short time. FUTA is subject to a 5.4% reduction, for which employers may qualify on two conditions:

- Employers make SUTA deposits on time and in full.
- As long as the state is not a credit reduction state.

With the credit, the employer's FUTA rate will be 0.6% on the first $7,000 of every employee's wage. The minimum FUTA tax rate is 0.6%, which means that a minimum of $42 ($7,000 × 0.006) may be paid per employee.

EXAMPLE: FUTA TAX COMPUTATION, ALL EMPLOYEES EARNING IN EXCESS OF $7,000

Snowborn Inc. is a company based in Great Falls, Montana. During 2016, the company had 178 employees, all of whom earned in excess of $7,000 in wages and salaries. At the end of the year, only 145 employees remained with the company. The 2016 FUTA tax liability for Snowborn Inc. would be computed as follows:

Number of employees during 2016	Multiplied by the first $7,000 of wages	Multiplied by .6% tax rate	FUTA tax liability for 2016
178	$7,000	0.006	$7,476

Note that Snowborn Inc. is liable for the FUTA tax on all employees who worked for the company, even if they left employment with the company.

What happens when the employees earn less than $7,000 during the calendar year? The employer is still responsible for the FUTA tax on the employees' earnings, but only the amount earned during the calendar year.

EXAMPLE: FUTA TAX, EMPLOYEES WITH EARNINGS LESS THAN $7,000 DURING THE YEAR

Baja Brothers Wines, based in Tucson, Arizona, has the following employee data for FUTA taxes:

Number of employees during 2016	Multiplied by the first $7,000 of wages	Multiplied by 0.6% tax rate	FUTA tax liability for 2016
59	$7,000	0.006	$2,478.00

(continued)

(concluded)

Employees who earned less than $7,000 during 2016:	Multiplied by the amount of wages earned in 2016	Multiplied by 0.6% tax rate	
Employee A	$5,894.00	0.006	$ 35.36
Employee B	$3,198.00	0.006	$ 19.19
Employee C	$ 975.00	0.006	$ 5.85
		Total FUTA tax	$2,538.40

According to the Federal Unemployment Tax Act, states' wage bases must be a minimum of $7,000. Establishment of the SUTA in each state provided states with local authority to offer unemployment or jobless benefits. Designed as an unemployment insurance program after the Great Depression of the 1930s, the remittance of SUTA payments follows many of the same procedures as other payroll taxes. As a state-run fund, each state can establish its own qualification requirements for both individual claims and business payments. The SUTA wage base and rate fluctuates among states and can be an incentive for businesses to change operations from one state to another. Note that all states' wage bases exceed the minimum required by the law, but the tax rate is variable.

As we noted, the nominal FUTA tax is 6.0%, of which the employer remits 0.6% to the federal government. The remaining 5.4% is a guideline, and many states have rates that vary based on employee retention and other factors. States examine employee turnover during an established period and determine if employers qualify for a credit against the nominal FUTA rate. SUTA is limited on wages collected. Depending upon the state the company is operating in, this limit may be equal to, higher, or lower than the FUTA rate. For example, Alaska's SUTA wage base was $39,700 in 2016. A chart containing the SUTA wage base and rates is shown in Table 5-2.

TABLE 5-2
SUTA Wage Base and Rates 2016

State	Wage Base	Min/Max Rate
Alabama	$ 8,000	0.65%–6.8%
Alaska	$39,700	1.0%–5.4%
Arizona	$ 7,000	0.03%–8.91%
Arkansas	$12,000	0.5%–14.4%
California	$ 7,000	1.5%–6.2%
Colorado	$12,200	0.77%–10.14%
Connecticut	$15,000	1.9%–6.8%
Delaware	$18,500	0.3%–8.2%
D.C.	$ 9,000	1.6%–7.0%
Florida	$ 7,000	0.1%–5.4%
Georgia	$ 9,500	0.04%–8.1%
Hawaii	$42,200	0.0%–5.6%
Idaho	$37,200	0.425%–5.4%
Illinois	$12,960	0.55%–7.75%
Indiana	$ 9,500	0.5%–7.4%
Iowa	$28,300	0.00%–8.0%

State	Wage Base	Min/Max Rate
Kansas	$14,000	0.2%–7.6%
Kentucky	$10,200	1.0%–10.0%
Louisiana	$ 7,700	0.10%–6.2%
Maine	$12,000	0.57%–5.4%
Maryland	$ 8,500	0.3%–7.5%
Massachusetts	$15,000	0.73%–11.13%
Michigan	$ 9,500	0.06%–10.3%
Minnesota	$31,000	0.1%–9.0%
Mississippi	$14,000	0.24%–5.64%
Missouri	$13,000	0.00%–9.75%
Montana	$30,500	0.13%–6.3%
Nebraska	$ 9,000	0.0%–5.4%
Nevada	$28,200	0.3%–5.4%
New Hampshire	$14,000	0.1%–7.5%
New Jersey	$32,600	1.2%–7.0%
New Mexico	$24,100	0.33%–5.4%
New York	$10,700	1.7%–9.5%
North Carolina	$22,300	0.06%–5.76%
North Dakota	$37,200	0.28–10.72%
Ohio	$ 9,000	0.3%–8.7%
Oklahoma	$17,500	0.1%–5.5%
Oregon	$36,900	1.2%–5.4%
Pennsylvania	$ 9,500	2.801%–10.8937%
Puerto Rico	$ 7,000	2.4%–5.4%
Rhode Island	$22,000	1.69%–9.79%
South Carolina	$14,000	0.06%–5.46%
South Dakota	$15,000	0.0%–9.5%
Tennessee	$ 8,000	0.01%–10.0%
Texas	$ 9,000	0.45%–7.47%
Utah	$32,200	0.2%–7.2%
Vermont	$16,800	1.3%–8.4%
Virginia	$ 8,000	0.44%–6.54%
Washington	$44,000	0.13%–7.73%
West Virginia	$12,000	1.5%–8.5%
Wisconsin	$14,000	0.05%–12.0%
Wyoming	$25,500	0.27%–8.77%

Sources: American Payroll Association, ADP.

An employer's SUTA rate is determined by a mix of state unemployment rates and company experience ratings. The SUTA rate for company A may be different from the rate for company B. For example, a construction company may experience higher unemployment claims because of the seasonal nature and higher risk associated with the industry; therefore, the company's rate may be 4.54%, whereas a similar-sized company in a professional services industry may have an unemployment rate of 3.28%. States issue letters on an annual basis to companies with the individually determined SUTA rate for the following year.

The first example is a company that has a SUTA rate of 5.4% and all employees have earned in excess of $7,000 for the year.

EXAMPLE: FUTA AND SUTA LIABILITY, SUTA = 5.4%

JayMac Communications, a California company, has 15 employees, all of whom have met the $7,000 threshold for the FUTA tax. The state portion for which JayMac is liable is 5.4%. The unemployment tax obligations are:

FUTA:	15 employees × $7,000 × 0.006 = $ 630
SUTA:	15 employees × $7,000 × 0.054 = $5,670
Total unemployment tax liability:	$6,300

The next example is a company in Georgia that has a SUTA rate of 2.3% and some employees who have earned less than $7,000 during the year.

EXAMPLE: FUTA AND SUTA LIABILITY, SUTA = 2.3%

Charmer Industries of Georgia has 20 employees: 18 employees have met the FUTA and SUTA thresholds, and 2 employees have not, earning $5,400 and $2,500, respectively. The state obligation for Charmer is 2.3% owing to a favorable employer rating. Charmer's unemployment taxes would be computed as follows:

FUTA:	18 × $7,000 × 0.006 =	$ 756.00
	($5,400 + $2,500) × 0.006 =	$ 47.40
	Total FUTA liability:	$ 803.40
SUTA:	18 × $9,500 × 0.023 =	$3,933.00
	($5,400 + $2,500) × 0.023 =	$ 181.70
	Total SUTA liability:	$4,114.70
Total unemployment tax liability:		$4,918.10

Other State and Local Employer-Only Payroll Taxes

Some states have employer-only taxes unique to the area. Delaware, Colorado, Hawaii, and several other states have additional taxes that are remitted under different names.

- Georgia employers pay an administrative assessment of 0.08% on employee gross wages.
- Maine has an employer-paid Competitive Skills Scholarship Program tax of 0.06%.
- In California, employers pay an Employment Training Tax (ETT) of 0.1% on all wages up to the first $7,000 of wages.

As a payroll accountant, it is very important to be familiar with the tax withholding and employer responsibilities for each state in which the company has employees residing, even if there is not a business office located there.

Individual counties and cities can also impose occupational taxes on the businesses within their jurisdiction. For example, there is the Denver Occupational Privilege "Head" Tax. Individuals are responsible for $5.75 per month, and employers are responsible for $4.00 per employee per month. The reporting periods for the local and city taxes are separate from the filing requirements for federal or state. The payroll accountant must review all tiers of taxes to ensure compliance in collection, submission, and reporting.

Workers' Compensation Insurance

Workers' compensation insurance is another type of employer payroll responsibility. Although it is not considered a tax, states enforce workers' compensation statutes; federal employees are protected by the Federal Employment Compensation Act. Workers' compensation statutes are designed to protect workers who are injured (temporarily or permanently) or killed during the performance of their job-related duties.

Because workers' compensation is an insurance policy maintained by employers, premiums vary based on employees' job classifications and the risk of injury they typically encounter in the normal course of work. Premium amounts are expressed as amounts per $100 of payroll for each job classification. Premium amounts are estimated based on expected payroll amounts for the coming year and then adjusted at the end of the year once the actual payroll amounts are finalized.

EXAMPLE: WORKERS' COMPENSATION PREMIUM COMPUTATION

Jesse Hildreth is the owner of Eastern Freight Lines. She has three categories of employees: drivers, loaders, and administrative staff. The worker's compensation premium rates are as follows:

- Drivers: $1.45/$100 of payroll.
- Loaders: $2.50/$100 of payroll.
- Administrative staff: $0.40/$100 of payroll.

For 20XX, Eastern Freight Lines payroll is expected to be the following:

Job Classification	Premium per $100 of Payroll	Estimated Payroll	Premium Due Jan. 1
Driver	$1.45	$387,500	$ 5,618.75*
Loader	$2.50	$435,200	$ 10,880**
Administrative Staff	$0.40	$320,000	$ 1,280***
Total Premium Due, Jan. 1			$17,778.75

*($387,500/$100) × $1.45 = $5,618.75
**($435,200/$100) × $2.50 = $10,880
***($320,000/$100) × $0.40 = $1,280

The 20XX premium is adjusted based on actual payroll. The difference between the paid estimated premium and the premium based on actual payroll results must either be remitted to the insurance company or refunded to the employer. An analysis of the actual payroll as of December 31, 20XX, revealed the following results:

Job Classifcation	Premium per $100 of Payroll	Actual Payroll	Premium Due Dec. 31
Driver	$1.45	$410,563	$ 5,953.16*
Loader	$2.50	$478,290	$11,957.25**
Administrative staff	$0.40	$338,945	$ 1,355.78***
Total actual premium due December 31			$19,266.19
Less: Premium paid on Jan. 1			$17,778.75
Difference to be remitted to the insurance company			$ 1,487.44

*($410,563/$100) × $1.45 = $5,953.16
**($478,290/$100) × $2.50 = $11,957.25
***($338,945/$100) × $0.40 = $1,355.78

Eastern Freight Lines must remit $1,487.44 to the insurance company due to the difference between the estimated and the actual payroll for 20XX.

Workers' compensation premium rates may also vary based on the employer's safety record. For example, a company with multiple job-related injuries would have a higher premium than another company with few or no injuries. Employer compliance with OSHA guidelines is important to control the cost of workers' compensation insurance.

> The majority of workers' compensation insurance claims occur in five main categories of injuries:
>
> 1. Sprains and strains.
> 2. Puncture or cuts.
> 3. Bruises or other contusions.
> 4. Inflammation.
> 5. Fractured bones.
>
> Most work-related injuries can be avoided through employee safety training, attention to the walking and working conditions of the facility, and employer diligence. (Source: Insurance Journal)

FUTA, SUTA, and Workers' Compensation

1. AMS Enterprises in New Mexico has 30 employees. Of these, 25 have exceeded the FUTA and SUTA wage bases. This is the first quarter of the year, and AMS Enterprises has not yet paid FUTA or SUTA taxes for the year. The other five employees' YTD wages are as follows: Employee A, $15,800; Employee B, $7,800; Employee C, $11,115; Employee D, $22,800; Employee E, $2,575. AMS Enterprises receives the full FUTA tax credit and pays a SUTA rate of 4.2%. How much are AMS Enterprises' FUTA and SUTA liabilities?

2. Noodle Noggins of Maine has 12 employees and is eligible for the full FUTA tax credit; the SUTA rate is 3.26%. Ten of the 12 employees have exceeded the FUTA wage base. Eight employees have exceeded the SUTA wage base. The remaining employees have the following YTD wages: $5,500, $6,800, $11,100, and $9,850. The Competitive Skills Scholarship tax applies to all employees. Noodle's YTD total wages are $279,580. What are the FUTA, SUTA, and Competitive Skills Scholarship tax liabilities for Noodle Noggins?

3. High Flyers Jump School has two classifications of employees: clerical employees and jump instructors. The workers' compensation premium rates are $0.45/$100 for clerical employees, $3.75/$100 for jump instructors. During 20XX, the estimated payroll amounts were $104,550 for clerical employees and $215,690 for jump instructors. How much would the estimated workers' compensation insurance policy cost High Flyers Jump School during 20XX?

LO 5-2 Discuss Reporting Periods and Requirements for Employer Tax Deposits

The frequency of depositing federal income tax and FICA taxes depends on the size of the company's payroll. The IRS stipulates five different schedules for an employer's deposit of payroll taxes:

- Annually
- Quarterly
- Monthly
- Semiweekly
- Next business day

Of these, the most common deposit schedules are monthly and semiweekly. Electronic tax deposits are usually processed through the ***Electronic Federal Tax Payment System (EFTPS)*** website, although the IRS allows employers to transmit payments through certain financial institutions via ***Automated Clearing House (ACH)*** or wire transfer. When using the EFTPS, the employer must register with the IRS to access the site. The EFTPS is used for both Form 941 (Federal income tax, Social Security tax, and Medicare tax) and the quarterly/annual Form 940 FUTA tax deposit. The website for EFTPS is www.eftps.gov.

Lookback Period

The frequency of each company's deposits is determined through a ***lookback period***, which is the amount of payroll taxes an employer has reported in the 12-month period prior to June 30 of the previous year. For example, the lookback period that the IRS would use for 2016 tax deposit frequency would be the July 1, 2014, through June 30, 2015, period. Employers receive notification about their deposit requirements in writing from the IRS in October of each year. Table 5-3 shows the lookback period.

TABLE 5-3
LOOKBACK PERIOD

Lookback Period for 2016 Taxes			
July 1, 2014, through	October 1, 2014, through	January 1, 2015, through	April 1, 2015, through
September 30, 2014	December 31, 2014	March 31, 2015	June 30, 2015

Source: IRS.

Deposit Frequencies

By using the lookback period, the IRS informs businesses in writing if they need to deposit their payroll taxes annually, monthly, or semiweekly. All new companies are monthly schedule depositors unless they have a total payroll liability in excess of $100,000 during any pay period. It is important to note that the tax deposit due date is based on the payroll disbursement date, not the pay period ending date. For example, if a company's pay period ended on June 28, but the payroll was not disbursed until July 1, the payroll tax deposit date would be based on the July 1 disbursement. Table 5-4 outlines the criteria for differences among deposit frequencies.

EXAMPLE: MONTHLY SCHEDULE DEPOSITOR

Generational Coffee is a company based in Wenatchee, Washington. During the lookback period ending June 30, 2015, the company had **$36,549** in total payroll tax liability. Generational Coffee would be a ***monthly*** schedule depositor. Payroll tax deposits would be due on the ***15th*** of the following month (e.g., June 15 for May payroll taxes).

Notice the amount of total payroll tax for Generational Coffee. Because the total amount was less than $50,000, it is classified as a monthly schedule payroll tax depositor, and due dates are the 15th of the following month.

TABLE 5-4

Criteria for Deposit Frequencies

Frequency	Criteria	Due Date
Annually	$2,500 or less in employment taxes to be remitted annually with Form 944.	January 31 of the following year.
Quarterly	For any amounts not deposited during the quarter that may be due to rounding errors or other undeposited amounts.	15th of the month following the end of the quarter.
Monthly	Less than $50,000 in payroll tax liability during the lookback period. The amount of total tax liability is also found on Form 941, line 10. All new businesses are monthly schedule depositors unless they accrue in excess of $100,000 in payroll taxes for any pay period. (See the Next Business Day rule frequency.)	15th of the month following the month during which the company accrued payroll tax deposits. For example, taxes on March payroll would be due on **April 15,** or the next business day if April 15 falls on a weekend or a holiday.
Semiweekly	$50,000 or more in payroll tax liability during the lookback period. The amount of total tax liability is also found on Form 941, line 10. The exception to the semiweekly deposit schedule is the Next Business Day rule.	For payroll paid on a Wednesday, Thursday, or Friday, the payroll tax deposit is due by the following **Wednesday.** For payroll paid on a Saturday, Sunday, Monday, or Tuesday, the payroll tax is due by the following **Friday.**
Next Business Day	$100,000 or more in payroll tax liability for any payroll period.	The payroll tax deposit is due on the **next business day.**

EXAMPLE: SEMIWEEKLY SCHEDULE DEPOSITOR

Pollak Woolens is a company based in Sault Ste Marie, Michigan. During the look-back period ending June 30, 2015, it had **$75,984** in total payroll tax liability. Pollak Woolens would be a *semiweekly* schedule depositor. Depending on the payroll date, tax deposits are due on either the **Wednesday** or the **Friday** following the payroll date.

Notice the total tax liability during the lookback period. For Pollak Woolens, the amount exceeded $50,000 but is less than $100,000; this makes it a semiweekly schedule depositor. Because payroll tax deposits for semiweekly depositors are driven by the day of the week upon which payroll was paid, deposits may be due either on Wednesday or on Friday. For companies with a biweekly payroll frequency, the tax deposit date may remain the same with few exceptions due to holidays. For companies with semimonthly payroll frequencies, the day of the tax deposit will likely vary.

EXAMPLE: NEXT BUSINESS DAY DEPOSITOR

Cornell Companies, based in Ohio, is a semiweekly schedule payroll tax depositor because of the total payroll tax liability of $693,259 during the lookback period ending June 30, 2015. The company had a total payroll tax liability of **$110,290** during the August 26, 2016, payroll period. August 26 is a Friday, so the payroll deposit would be due on **Monday, August 29** because it exceeds $100,000.

In this example, Cornell Companies is already a semiweekly schedule depositor because of its payroll tax liability during the lookback period. Because the company's tax liability exceeds $100,000 for the payroll period, Cornell Companies must deposit those payroll taxes by the next business day.

> ### EXAMPLE: ANNUAL SCHEDULE DEPOSITOR
>
> Wallflower Guitars is based in Ocean Springs, Mississippi. During the lookback period ending June 30, 2015, the company had a total payroll tax liability of $2,154. The payroll tax deposit schedule for Wallflower Guitars would be annual because of the small amount of total tax liability. As long as the total payroll tax liability remains less than $2,500 during 2016, the company may deposit its payroll taxes with its annual payroll tax return.

In this example, Wallflower Guitars has a very small payroll tax liability. It should be noted that ***annual schedule depositors*** are assumed to have very small tax liability. If the company's payroll tax liability grows during the calendar year, the schedule depositors should be mindful of the monthly schedule deposit rules. However, the company will not become a monthly schedule depositor until notified in writing by the IRS.

Reporting Periods

1. Perry Plastics had $46,986 in payroll taxes during the lookback period. How often must the company deposit its payroll taxes?

2. For Perry Plastics, when is the deposit for June payroll taxes due?

3. Charlie's Kitchens has a payroll tax liability of $126,463 on its Friday payroll. When is the payroll tax deposit due?

LO 5-3 Prepare Mid-Year and Year-End Employer Tax Reporting and Deposits

Companies and payroll accountants are responsible for timely filing of the various tax documents required by governmental authorities. Note that the dates for depositing and reporting taxes are not always the same. For example, an employer may be required to file payroll tax deposits through the EFTPS on a semiweekly or monthly basis, depending upon their payroll tax liability during the lookback period. However, that same employer would not be required to file tax forms until after the end of the quarter. Like personal tax reporting, business reporting of statutory tax obligations has specific forms that employers must use. The most common forms used to deposit federal income tax and FICA taxes are Forms 941 (quarterly) and 944 (annual). An additional form used by agricultural businesses is Form 943; it serves the same purpose as Form 941.

Form 941

Monthly payroll tax depositors file ***Form 941*** (see Figure 5-1), which is the employer's quarterly report of taxes deposited and taxes due. The form is used to reconcile the firm's deposits with the tax liability derived through mathematical computations on the form. It is common to encounter minor adjustments during the process of completing the form owing to rounding differences incurred during monthly tax deposits. Form 941 has specific instructions for its completion, as shown in Table 5-5.

FIGURE 5-1
Form 941

Form **941 for 2016:** **Employer's QUARTERLY Federal Tax Return**   950114
(Rev. January 2016)   Department of the Treasury — Internal Revenue Service   OMB No. 1545-0029

Employer identification number (EIN)   9 8 – 7 6 5 4 3 2 1

Name *(not your trade name)*   Patrick Rosenberg

Trade name *(if any)*   Rosenberg Enterprises

Address   1234 Main Street
          Number   Street   Suite or room number

          Mapletown   AR   55394
          City   State   ZIP code

          Foreign country name   Foreign province/county   Foreign postal code

Report for this Quarter of 2016
(Check one.)

☐ **1:** January, February, March

☐ **2:** April, May, June

☐ **3:** July, August, September

☐ **4:** October, November, December

Instructions and prior year forms are available at *www.irs.gov/form941*.

Read the separate instructions before you complete Form 941. Type or print within the boxes.

Part 1:   **Answer these questions for this quarter.**

1   Number of employees who received wages, tips, or other compensation for the pay period including: *Mar. 12* (Quarter 1), *June 12* (Quarter 2), *Sept. 12* (Quarter 3), or *Dec. 12* (Quarter 4)   1   12

2   Wages, tips, and other compensation   2   128,356 . 74

3   Federal income tax withheld from wages, tips, and other compensation   3   18,432 . 50

4   If no wages, tips, and other compensation are subject to social security or Medicare tax   ☐ Check and go to line 6.

		Column 1		Column 2
5a	Taxable social security wages . .	128,356 . 74	× .124 =	15,916 . 24
5b	Taxable social security tips . . .	.	× .124 =	.
5c	Taxable Medicare wages & tips. .	128,356 . 74	× .029 =	3,722 . 35
5d	Taxable wages & tips subject to Additional Medicare Tax withholding	.	× .009 =	.

5e   Add Column 2 from lines 5a, 5b, 5c, and 5d . . . .   5e   19,638 . 59

5f   Section 3121(q) Notice and Demand—Tax due on unreported tips (see instructions) . .   5f   .

6   Total taxes before adjustments. Add lines 3, 5e, and 5f   6   38,070 . 59

7   Current quarter's adjustment for fractions of cents   7   . 01

8   Current quarter's adjustment for sick pay   8

9   Current quarter's adjustments for tips and group-term life insurance   9   .

10   Total taxes after adjustments. Combine lines 6 through 9   10   38,070 . 60

11   Total deposits for this quarter, including overpayment applied from a prior quarter and overpayments applied from Form 941-X, 941-X (PR), 944-X, or 944-X (SP) filed in the current quarter   11   38,070 . 60

12   Balance due. If line 10 is more than line 11, enter the difference and see instructions . . .   12   .

13   Overpayment. If line 11 is more than line 10, enter the difference   .   Check one: ☐ Apply to next return.   ☐ Send a refund.

► **You MUST complete both pages of Form 941 and SIGN it.**   Next ►

For Privacy Act and Paperwork Reduction Act Notice, see the back of the Payment Voucher.   Cat. No. 17001Z   Form **941** (Rev. 1-2016)

950214

Name *(not your trade name)*	Employer identification number (EIN)
Patrick Rosenberg	98-7654321

Part 2:   **Tell us about your deposit schedule and tax liability for this quarter.**

If you are unsure about whether you are a monthly schedule depositor or a semiweekly schedule depositor, see section 11 of Pub. 15.

14   Check one: ☐   Line 10 on this return is less than $2,500 or line 10 on the return for the prior quarter was less than $2,500, and you did not incur a $100,000 next-day deposit obligation during the current quarter. If line 10 for the prior quarter was less than $2,500 but line 10 on this return is $100,000 or more, you must provide a record of your federal tax liability. If you are a monthly schedule depositor, complete the deposit schedule below; if you are a semiweekly schedule depositor, attach Schedule B (Form 941). Go to Part 3.

☐   **You were a monthly schedule depositor for the entire quarter.** Enter your tax liability for each month and total liability for the quarter, then go to Part 3.

Tax liability:	Month 1	12,690 . 20
	Month 2	12,690 . 20
	Month 3	12,690 . 20
Total liability for quarter		38,070 . 60	**Total must equal line 10.**

☐   **You were a semiweekly schedule depositor for any part of this quarter.** Complete Schedule B (Form 941), Report of Tax Liability for Semiweekly Schedule Depositors, and attach it to Form 941.

Part 3:   **Tell us about your business. If a question does NOT apply to your business, leave it blank.**

15   If your business has closed or you stopped paying wages . . . . ☐ Check here, and

enter the final date you paid wages [/ /] .

16   If you are a seasonal employer and you do not have to file a return for every quarter of the year . . ☐ Check here.

Part 4:   **May we speak with your third-party designee?**

Do you want to allow an employee, a paid tax preparer, or another person to discuss this return with the IRS? See the instructions for details.

☐ Yes.   Designee's name and phone number [   ] [   ]

Select a 5-digit Personal Identification Number (PIN) to use when talking to the IRS. ☐ ☐ ☐ ☐ ☐

☐ No.

Part 5:   **Sign here. You MUST complete both pages of Form 941 and SIGN it.**

Under penalties of perjury, I declare that I have examined this return, including accompanying schedules and statements, and to the best of my knowledge and belief, it is true, correct, and complete. Declaration of preparer (other than taxpayer) is based on all information of which preparer has any knowledge.

X   Sign your name here   *Patrick Rosenberg*

Print your name here	Patrick Rosenberg
Print your title here	Owner

Date [/ /]

Best daytime phone   535-555-2340

Paid Preparer Use Only   Check if you are self-employed . . . ☐

Preparer's name		PTIN	
Preparer's signature		Date	/ /
Firm's name (or yours if self-employed)		EIN	
Address		Phone	
City		State		ZIP code	

Page **2**   Form **941** (Rev. 1-2016)

Source: Internal Revenue Service.

TABLE 5-5
Instructions for Completing Form 941

Part 1:

Line 1: The number of employees during the quarter reported, as indicated in the box in the upper right-hand corner.

Line 2: Total wages subject to federal income tax (less pre-tax deductions) for the quarter.

Line 3: Federal income tax withheld from wages paid during the quarter.

Line 4: Check box only if no wages paid during the quarter were subject to taxes. (This is uncommon.)

Lines 5a–5d: Column 1 is for the wages and tips subject to Social Security and Medicare taxes; column 2 is the amount of wages multiplied by the tax percent specified on the form.

Line 5e: Total of column 2, lines 5a–5d.

Line 5f: Tax on unreported tips.

Line 6: Total taxes due before adjustments.

Lines 7–9: Quarterly tax adjustments.

Line 10: Total tax less adjustments: line 6 minus lines 7, 8, and 9.

Line 11: Total taxes deposited during the quarter.

Line 12: Balance due.

Line 13: Overpayment.

Part 2:

Check the first box if the tax liability for the quarter is less than $2,500.

OR

Check the second box if the tax liability is greater than $2,500 and enter the taxes deposited each month during the quarter.

The total deposits must equal the total liability in Part 1.

If the business is a semiweekly depositor, then Schedule B must be completed.

Schedule B

Semiweekly depositors must file Schedule B (Figure 5-2) in addition to Form 941. This form allows firms to enter the details of payroll tax liabilities that occur multiple times during a month. On *Schedule B*, the payroll tax liability is entered on the days of the month on which the payroll occurred. The total tax liability for each month is entered in the right column. The total tax liability for the quarter must equal line 10 of Form 941.

EXAMPLE: PAYROLL TAX LIABILITY

Nicholas Lindeman is the owner of a company that pays its employees on the 15th and the last day of the month. All employees are salaried, exempt workers. Pay dates that fall on the weekend are paid on the preceding Friday. According to the lookback period, the company is required to deposit payroll taxes on a semiweekly basis. Because Lindeman is a semiweekly schedule depositor, he must file Schedule B in addition to Form 941. For the first quarter of 2016, Lindeman's company had the following pay dates and payroll tax liabilities:"

Pay Date	Payroll Tax Liability
January 15	$ 41,486.47
January 31	$ 41,486.47
February 14	$ 41,486.47
February 28	$ 41,486.47
March 15	$ 41,486.47
March 31	$ 41,486.47
Total Tax Liability for the Quarter	$ 248,918.82

Note that the payroll tax liability is (a) listed on the payroll date, and (b) includes the FICA taxes (employee and employer share) and the federal income tax withheld.

FIGURE 5-2
Schedule B for Form 941

Schedule B (Form 941):

960311

Report of Tax Liability for Semiweekly Schedule Depositors

(Rev. January 2014) Department of the Treasury — Internal Revenue Service

OMB No. 1545-0029

Employer identification number (EIN) 1 3 – 2 5 6 9 7 0 4

Name *(not your trade name)*

Calendar year 2 0 1 16 (Also check quarter)

Report for this Quarter...
(Check one.)

- [X] 1: January, February, March
- [ ] 2: April, May, June
- [ ] 3: July, August, September
- [ ] 4: October, November, December

Use this schedule to show your TAX LIABILITY for the quarter; DO NOT use it to show your deposits. When you file this form with Form 941 or Form 941-SS, DO NOT change your tax liability by adjustments reported on any Forms 941-X or 944-X. You must fill out this form and attach it to Form 941 or Form 941-SS if you are a semiweekly schedule depositor or became one because your accumulated tax liability on any day was $100,000 or more. Write your daily tax liability on the numbered space that corresponds to the date wages were paid. See Section 11 in Pub. 15 (Circular E), Employer's Tax Guide, for details.

Month 1

1		9		17		25		**Tax liability for Month 1**
2		10		18		26		82,972 . 94
3		11		19		27		
4		12		20		28		
5		13		21		29		
6		14		22		30		
7		15	41,486 . 47	23		31	41,486 . 47	
8		16		24				

Month 2

1		9		17		25		**Tax liability for Month 2**
2		10		18		26		82,972 . 94
3		11		19		27		
4		12		20		28		
5		13		21		29	41,486 . 47	
6		14		22		30		
7		15	41,486 . 47	23		31		
8		16		24				

Month 3

1		9		17		25		**Tax liability for Month 3**
2		10		18		26		82,972 . 94
3		11		19		27		
4		12		20		28		
5		13		21		29		
6		14		22		30		
7		15	41,486 . 47	23		31	41,486 . 47	
8		16		24				

Fill in your total liability for the quarter (Month 1 + Month 2 + Month 3) ▶
Total must equal line 10 on Form 941 or Form 941-SS.

Total liability for the quarter
248,918 . 42

For Paperwork Reduction Act Notice, see separate instructions. IRS.gov/form941 Cat. No. 11967Q **Schedule B (Form 941)** (Rev. 1-2014)

Source: Internal Revenue Service.

State Tax Remittance

Each state that charges income tax has its own form that it uses for employee income *tax remittance* purposes. State tax forms are similar to federal forms as far as the information included is concerned and generally have similar due dates. An important note is that each state has its own unique taxes. For example, California has an employee-only State Disability Insurance (SDI) tax of 0.9% on earnings up to $106,742 per employee (2016 figure), as well as an employer-only Employment Training Tax (ETT) of 0.1% on the first $7,000 of each employee's earnings. These additional taxes are included on the state's payroll tax return.

Additionally, employers are responsible for reporting any other local or regional taxes. Employers must abide by the filing requirements for each of the taxes or face fines or penalties depending upon state/local tax code. The purpose of these taxes can include the provision of social services and the funding of infrastructure costs. The Denver Head Tax was designed to fulfill both of these purposes in response to the increase of infrastructure and the availability of municipal programs for residents.

Form 944

Firms with a total annual tax liability of less than $2,500 use *Form 944* (see Figure 5-3). Like Form 941, the firm enters the details of wages paid and computes the taxes due. The firm reports the monthly deposits and liabilities in Part 2. However, instead of entering a quarterly liability, the firm enters the annual liability, which is the sum of all the monthly liabilities. The IRS must notify a company in writing of the requirement to file Form 944 prior to its use.

Example:

Madison Poole owns MP Pool Service. MP Pool Service is a sole proprietorship with one part-time employee who works only five months of the year. The IRS has notified Mr. Poole that MP Pool Service is required to report federal payroll tax liabilities using Form 944. The total wages paid to the employee during 2015 were $8,952.20. The federal income tax liability was $800, and total payroll tax liability for the year was $2,169.98. Because the total annual payroll tax liability is less than $2,500, MP Pool Service must file an annual return. The due date for Form 944 is January 31 of the following year.

Unemployment Tax Reporting

Form 940 is the employer's annual report of federal unemployment taxes due, based on employee wages paid during the year. This report is for a calendar year and is due by January 31 of the following year.

According to 26 IRC section 3306, certain fringe benefits are not subject to federal unemployment taxes because they represent noncash compensation that is not intended to be used as disposable income. Specific examples of these fringe benefits are employer contributions to employee retirement plans, such as the 401(k) and 403(b), and payments for benefits excluded under qualified section 125 cafeteria plans.

EXAMPLE: EMPLOYER CONTRIBUTIONS TO RETIREMENT PLANS

Winterguard Products offers its employees a matching 401(k) contribution of 0.5% for each 1% of salary that the employee contributes. During 2015, Susanna Stark, an employee of Winterguard Products, contributed 4% of her $36,500 annual salary to her 401(k) plan.

Susanna's contribution	$36,500 × 0.04 =	$1,460.00
Winterguard's contribution match	Half of employee's contribution =	$ 730.00
Amount exempt from FUTA tax		$ 730.00

The $730 would be listed on line 4 of form 940 as an amount exempt from FUTA taxes.

FIGURE 5-3
Form 944

Form **944 for 2015:** **Employer's ANNUAL Federal Tax Return**

Department of the Treasury — Internal Revenue Service

OMB No. 1545-2007

Employer identification number (EIN) | 2 | 4 | — | 8 | 9 | 7 | 6 | 5 | 0 | 4 |

Name *(not your trade name)*   **Madison K. Poole**

Trade name *(if any)*   **MP Pool Service**

Address   **18196 Arabella Street**
Number   Street   Suite or room number

Fountain Grove   **CA**   **93020**
City   State   ZIP code

Foreign country name   Foreign province/county   Foreign postal code

Who Must File Form 944

You must file annual Form 944 instead of filing quarterly Forms 941 **only if the IRS notified you in writing.**
Instructions and prior-year forms are available at *www.irs.gov/form944.*

Read the separate instructions before you complete Form 944. Type or print within the boxes.

Part 1: **Answer these questions for this year. Employers in American Samoa, Guam, the Commonwealth of the Northern Mariana Islands, the U.S. Virgin Islands, and Puerto Rico can skip lines 1 and 2.**

1	Wages, tips, and other compensation	1	8,952 ▪ 20
2	Federal income tax withheld from wages, tips, and other compensation	2	800 ▪ 00
3	If no wages, tips, and other compensation are subject to social security or Medicare tax	3 ☐	Check and go to line 5.

4   Taxable social security and Medicare wages and tips:

		Column 1		Column 2
4a	Taxable social security wages	8,952 ▪ 20	× .124 =	1,110 ▪ 07
4b	Taxable social security tips	▪	× .124 =	▪
4c	Taxable Medicare wages & tips	8,952 ▪ 20	× .029 =	259 ▪ 61
4d	Taxable wages & tips subject to Additional Medicare Tax withholding	▪	× .009 =	▪

	4e Add Column 2 from lines 4a, 4b, 4c, and 4d	4e	1,369 ▪ 68
5	Total taxes before adjustments. Add lines 2 and 4e	5	2,169 ▪ 68
6	Current year's adjustments (see instructions)	6	▪
7	Total taxes after adjustments. Combine lines 5 and 6	7	2,169 ▪ 68
8	Total deposits for this year, including overpayment applied from a prior year and overpayments applied from Form 944-X, 944-X (PR), 944-X (SP), 941-X, or 941-X (PR)	8	0 ▪ 00
9a	Reserved		
9b	Reserved		
10	Reserved		
11	Balance due. If line 7 is more than line 8, enter the difference and see instructions	11	2,169 ▪ 68
12	Overpayment. If line 8 is more than line 7, enter the difference ▪ Check one: ☐ Apply to next return. ☐ Send a refund.		

▶ **You MUST complete both pages of Form 944 and SIGN it.**   Next ▶

For Privacy Act and Paperwork Reduction Act Notice, see the back of the Payment Voucher.   Cat. No. 39316N   Form **944** (2015)

Name *(not your trade name)*	Employer identification number (EIN)
Madison K. Poole	24-8976504

Part 2:   Tell us about your deposit schedule and tax liability for this year.

13   Check one: [X]   **Line 7 is less than $2,500. Go to Part 3.**

[ ]   Line 7 is $2,500 or more. Enter your tax liability for each month. If you are a semiweekly depositor or you accumulate $100,000 or more of liability on any day during a deposit period, you must complete Form 945-A instead of the boxes below.

	Jan.		Apr.		Jul.		Oct.
13a	.	13d	.	13g	.	13j	.
	Feb.		May		Aug.		Nov.
13b	.	13e	.	13h	.	13k	.
	Mar.		Jun.		Sep.		Dec.
13c	.	13f	.	13i	.	13l	.

Total liability for year. Add lines 13a through 13l. Total must equal line 7.   **13m**   .

Part 3:   Tell us about your business. If question 14 does NOT apply to your business, leave it blank.

14   If your business has closed or you stopped paying wages...

[ ]   Check here and enter the final date you paid wages.

Part 4:   May we speak with your third-party designee?

Do you want to allow an employee, a paid tax preparer, or another person to discuss this return with the IRS? See the instructions for details.

[ ]   Yes. Designee's name and phone number

Select a 5-digit Personal Identification Number (PIN) to use when talking to IRS.   [ ] [ ] [ ] [ ] [ ]

[ ]   No.

Part 5:   Sign Here. You MUST complete both pages of Form 944 and SIGN it.

Under penalties of perjury, I declare that I have examined this return, including accompanying schedules and statements, and to the best of my knowledge and belief, it is true, correct, and complete. Declaration of preparer (other than taxpayer) is based on all information of which preparer has any knowledge.

X   Sign your name here   *Madison K. Poole*

Print your name here   **Madison K. Poole**

Print your title here   **President**

Date

Best daytime phone   **909-555-8760**

Paid Preparer Use Only   Check if you are self-employed   [ ]

Preparer's name		PTIN	
Preparer's signature		Date	
Firm's name (or yours if self-employed)		EIN	
Address		Phone	
City	State	ZIP code	

Form **944** (2015)

Note that a company that files Form 944 has the opportunity to remit payroll taxes using Form 944-V, payment voucher.

Detach Here and Mail With Your Payment and Form 944.

Form **944-V** Department of the Treasury Internal Revenue Service	**Payment Voucher** ▶ Don't staple this voucher or your payment to Form 944.	OMB No. 1545-2007 20**15**

1 Enter your employer identification number (EIN). 24-8976504	**2** Enter the amount of your payment. ▶ Make your check or money order payable to "United States Treasury"	Dollars 2,169	Cents 68

3 Enter your business name (individual name if sole proprietor).

MP Pool Service

Enter your address.

18196 Arabella Street

Enter your city, state, and ZIP code or your city, foreign country name, foreign province/county, and foreign postal code.

Fountain Grove, CA 93020

Source: Internal Revenue Service.

Fringe benefits that may be exempt from FUTA taxes are those excluded from cafeteria plans, such as the ones in the following example:

EXAMPLE: EXCLUDED FRINGE BENEFITS NOT SUBJECT TO FUTA TAXES

Hutcheson Medical Products offers its employees the following fringe benefits:

Benefit	Annual value	Amount paid during the calendar year
Adoption assistance	$5,000 per employee	$15,000.00
Achievement awards	$250 per employee	$10,000.00
Meals	$300 per employee	$15,000.00
Moving expense reimbursements	$500 per employee	$ 2,000.00
Total annual value of excluded fringe benefits		$42,000.00

Hutcheson Medical Products would list $42,000 on Form 940 line 4, "Payments exempt from FUTA tax."

Other fringe benefits specifically exempt from FUTA tax and reported on line 4 include:

- Dependent care (up to $2,500 per employee or $5,000 per married couple).
- Employer contributions to group term life insurance.
- Certain other noncash payments, as outlined in the Instructions for Form 940.

For tax reporting purposes, amounts contributed by employees to these exempt items must be treated in one of two ways on Form 940:

- Deducted from Line 3 "Total payments to all employees."
- Reported on Line 4 "Payments exempt from FUTA taxes."

An example of Form 940 for CJS Creations is found in Figure 5-4.

Example:

Cheryl Sullivan owns CJS Creations, EIN 12-5079864. She filed the Annual FUTA Tax Return (Form 940) to report unemployment tax contributions during 2015. CJS

(continued)

(concluded)

Creations has 12 employees. Lines 9 through 11 are adjustments to the FUTA deposited, which are rare and do not apply in this scenario. (See pages 8–10 of Publication 15 for more details.)

> **Line 1a:** If the company pays unemployment tax in only one state, then the state abbreviation is entered here; otherwise, the company must check the box on line 1b and complete schedule A. CJS Creations has only one location, in Hawaii.
>
> **Line 3:** All wages paid during the calendar year are entered here.
>
> **Line 4:** Wages exempt from FUTA Tax. None of CJS Creations's wages are exempt from FUTA tax.
>
> **Line 5:** Wages for the year that are in excess of $7,000 per employee are entered here. The FUTA wage base is $7,000 per employee. In this example, all employees worked for the entire calendar year, so CJS Creations is responsible for FUTA tax on $7,000 per employee. To compute Line 5:

Total wages	$364,039.32
less FUTA wage base ($7,000 × 12 employees)	(84,000.00)
Wages in excess of $7,000	$280,039.32

> **Line 6:** This is the sum of lines 4 and 5.
>
> **Line 7:** FUTA Taxable wages, which are $84,000 for CJS Creations.
>
> **Line 8:** FUTA Tax ($84,000 × .006) or $504.
>
> **Line 12:** Total FUTA Tax of $504.
>
> **Line 13:** Total FUTA Tax deposited during the year. This total must match Line 17 (side 2). Because all of CJS Creations's employees exceeded their wage base by the end of the second quarter of 2015, all FUTA tax for the year has been deposited prior to completion of the tax return.
>
> **Lines 16a and 16b:** Tax liability during each quarter. These boxes report the employer's FUTA tax liability based on wages paid or accrued during the quarter. In this case, CJS Creations had a FUTA liability of $350 for the first quarter of 2015 and $104 for the second quarter of 2015. The sum of these liabilities (and any other quarterly liability, which does not exist in this example) is recorded on Line 17. The total on Line 17 must match the total on Line 13 (side 1).

Matching Final Annual Pay to Form W-2

One of the more common questions payroll accountants receive following the release of W-2s from the employees at the end of the year is, "why doesn't this match my final paycheck?" In short, it should—if you know how to calculate the income that belongs in each block of the W-2. The W-2 reflects all gross wages received by the employee, less any pre-tax deductions: health insurance, qualified retirement contributions, and other deductions. The total federal income taxes that the employer withheld from the employee and remitted as part of the 941 tax deposits also appears on the W-2 and acts as supporting documentation for the total wages reported on Forms 941 and 940.

Similarly, Form W-2 contains the employee's Social Security and Medicare wages. These wages are not reduced by contributions by the employee to qualified pension accounts (401(k), 403(b), etc.), and therefore may be higher than box 1. The only difference between boxes 3 and 5 will come when employees earn more than the maximum Social Security wage in the given year, or $118,500 for 2016. When this occurs, the Medicare wages reported in box 5 will be greater than the Social Security wages displayed in box 3. Boxes 4 and 6 contain the Social Security and Medicare taxes withheld from the employee and remitted through 941 deposits. Employees who receive tuition reimbursement benefits from their employer may receive up to $5,250 annually, per IRS Publication 970. Any tuition reimbursed to the

FIGURE 5-4
Form 940

Form **940 for 2015:** **Employer's Annual Federal Unemployment (FUTA) Tax Return**   850113

Department of the Treasury — Internal Revenue Service

OMB No. 1545-0028

Employer identification number (EIN)   1 2 – 5 0 7 9 8 6 4

Name (not your trade name)   Cheryl J. Sullivan

Trade name (if any)   CJS Creations

Address   23953 Island Way
Number   Street   Suite or room number

Millilani   HI   99403
City   State   ZIP code

Foreign country name   Foreign province/county   Foreign postal code

Type of Return
(Check all that apply.)

☐ **a.** Amended
☐ **b.** Successor employer
☐ **c.** No payments to employees in 2015
☐ **d.** Final: Business closed or stopped paying wages

Instructions and prior-year forms are available at *www.irs.gov/form940.*

Read the separate instructions before you complete this form. Please type or print within the boxes.

Part 1:   **Tell us about your return. If any line does NOT apply, leave it blank. See instructions before completing Part 1.**

1a If you had to pay state unemployment tax in one state only, enter the state abbreviation .   **1a** H I

1b If you had to pay state unemployment tax in more than one state, you are a multi-state employer . . . . .   **1b** ☐ Check here. Complete Schedule A (Form 940).

2 If you paid wages in a state that is subject to CREDIT REDUCTION . . . .   **2** ☐ Check here. Complete Schedule A (Form 940).

Part 2:   **Determine your FUTA tax before adjustments. If any line does NOT apply, leave it blank.**

3 Total payments to all employees . . . .   **3**   364,039 . 32

4 Payments exempt from FUTA tax . . . .   **4**   .

Check all that apply: **4a** ☐ Fringe benefits   **4c** ☐ Retirement/Pension   **4e** ☐ Other
4b ☐ Group-term life insurance   **4d** ☐ Dependent care

5 Total of payments made to each employee in excess of $7,000 . . . . .   **5**   280,039 . 32

6 Subtotal (line 4 + line 5 = line 6) . . . .   **6**   280,039 . 32

7 Total taxable FUTA wages (line 3 – line 6 = line 7) (see instructions) . . . . .   **7**   84,000 . 00

8 FUTA tax before adjustments (line 7 x .006 = line 8) . . . . . .   **8**   504 . 00

Part 3:   **Determine your adjustments. If any line does NOT apply, leave it blank.**

9 If ALL of the taxable FUTA wages you paid were excluded from state unemployment tax, multiply line 7 by .054 (line 7 × .054 = line 9). Go to line 12 . . . . .   **9**   .

10 If SOME of the taxable FUTA wages you paid were excluded from state unemployment tax, OR you paid ANY state unemployment tax late (after the due date for filing Form 940), complete the worksheet in the instructions. Enter the amount from line 7 of the worksheet . .   **10**   .

11 If credit reduction applies, enter the total from Schedule A (Form 940) . . . . . .   **11**   .

Part 4:   **Determine your FUTA tax and balance due or overpayment. If any line does NOT apply, leave it blank.**

12 Total FUTA tax after adjustments (lines 8 + 9 + 10 + 11 = line 12) . . . . . .   **12**   504 . 00

13 FUTA tax deposited for the year, including any overpayment applied from a prior year   **13**   504 . 00

14 Balance due (If line 12 is more than line 13, enter the excess on line 14.)
• If line 14 is more than $500, you must deposit your tax.
• If line 14 is $500 or less, you may pay with this return. (see instructions) . . . . .   **14**   0 . 00

15 Overpayment (If line 13 is more than line 12, enter the excess on line 15 and check a box below.) . . . .   **15**   .

▶ You **MUST** complete both pages of this form and **SIGN** it.   Check one: ☐ Apply to next return. ☐ Send a refund.

Next ▶

For Privacy Act and Paperwork Reduction Act Notice, see the back of Form 940-V, Payment Voucher.   Cat. No. 11234O   Form **940** (2015)

850212

Name *(not your trade name)*	Employer identification number (EIN)
Cheryl J. Sullivan	12-5079864

Part 5:   Report your FUTA tax liability by quarter only if line 12 is more than $500. If not, go to Part 6.

16 Report the amount of your FUTA tax liability for each quarter; do NOT enter the amount you deposited. If you had no liability for a quarter, leave the line blank.

16a **1st quarter** (January 1 – March 31) . . . . **16a**   350 . 00

16b **2nd quarter** (April 1 – June 30) . . . . **16b**   154 . 00

16c **3rd quarter** (July 1 – September 30) . . . . **16c**   .

16d **4th quarter** (October 1 – December 31) . . . . **16d**   .

17 **Total tax liability for the year** (lines 16a + 16b + 16c + 16d = line 17) **17**   504 . 00   **Total must equal line 12.**

Part 6:   May we speak with your third-party designee?

Do you want to allow an employee, a paid tax preparer, or another person to discuss this return with the IRS? See the instructions for details.

☐ **Yes.**   Designee's name and phone number

Select a 5-digit Personal Identification Number (PIN) to use when talking to IRS   ☐ ☐ ☐ ☐ ☐

☐ **No.**

Part 7:   Sign here. You MUST complete both pages of this form and SIGN it.

Under penalties of perjury, I declare that I have examined this return, including accompanying schedules and statements, and to the best of my knowledge and belief, it is true, correct, and complete, and that no part of any payment made to a state unemployment fund claimed as a credit was, or is to be, deducted from the payments made to employees. Declaration of preparer (other than taxpayer) is based on all information of which preparer has any knowledge.

X Sign your name here   *Cheryl J. Sullivan*

Print your name here   Cheryl J. Sullivan

Print your title here   President

Date   /   /

Best daytime phone   808-555-9876

Paid Preparer Use Only   Check if you are self-employed . ☐

Preparer's name		PTIN	
Preparer's signature		Date	/ /
Firm's name (or yours if self-employed)		EIN	
Address		Phone	
City	State	ZIP code	

Form **940** (2015)

Source: Internal Revenue Service.

employee in excess of $5,250 during a calendar year must be treated as taxable income for the year and included in box 1 wages.

Tipped employees will have amounts represented in boxes 7 and 8 for their reported tips. Box 10 is used to report Dependent Care Benefits. Contributions to nonqualifying retirement plans will be represented in box 11. Employee contributions to qualifying plans are represented in box 12. An alphabetical code is assigned to the specific type of qualified retirement plan the contributions are made to (A through EE). Box 13 denotes specific contributions to deferred compensation plans. Box 14 is used to report other information to employees, such as union dues, health insurance premiums (not pre-tax), educational assistance payments, and other similar items. State and local taxes and wages are represented in boxes 15 through 20.

When completing a *Form W-2*, you will have several copies of the same form. A sample Form W-2 is found in Figure 5-5. According to the order in which they print, the copies of Form W-2 are as follows:

Which Copy?	What Is It For?
Copy A	Social Security Administration
Copy 1	State, City, or Local Tax Department
Copy B	Filing with the Employee's Federal Tax Return
Copy C	Employee's Records
Copy 2	State, City, or Local Tax Department
Copy D	Employer

The following is an example of a Form W-2 for Jill M. Martin.

Example:

Jill Meri Martin worked for LC Enterprises during 2016. The following is on her W-2 for 2016.

Box 1 contains the wages, tips, and other compensation. Jill earned $36,523.34 during 2015.

Box 2 contains the federal income tax withheld: Jill had $3,671.04 withheld based on her W-4 information.

Boxes 3 and 5 contain the Social Security and Medicare wages. Note that these two boxes contain a higher amount than box 1. Jill has a retirement plan into which she contributed $2,000 during 2015.

Boxes 4 and 6 contain the Social Security tax withheld ($2,388.44) and the Medicare tax withheld ($558.59).

Box 12 contains amounts for nontaxable items. Codes for box 12 are contained in *Figure 5-6*.

Boxes 15–17 contain the state tax information. Jill had $1,826.17 withheld for state taxes based on the state withholding certificate that she filed in January 2015.

Form W-3 is the transmittal form that accompanies the submission of Copy A to the Social Security Administration. It contains the aggregate data for all W-2s issued by an employer. Form W-3 and all accompanying W-2s must be filed by February 28 (if filing a paper W-3 form) or March 31 (if filing an electronic W-3). The total annual wages reported on the W-3 must match the annual wages reported on Forms 941 and 940.

The following example from Feola's Cafe depicts the completion of Form W-3 for a company. (See Figure 5-7.)

FIGURE 5-5
Form W-2

22222	Void ☐	**a** Employee's social security number 555-55-5555	**For Official Use Only** ▶ OMB No. 1545-0008	

b Employer identification number (EIN) 34- 1029386	**1** Wages, tips, other compensation 36,523.34	**2** Federal income tax withheld 3,671.04

c Employer's name, address, and ZIP code LC Enterprises 1234 A Street Anytown, IL 66734	**3** Social security wages 38,523.34	**4** Social security tax withheld 2,388.45
	5 Medicare wages and tips 38,523.34	**6** Medicare tax withheld 558.59
	7 Social security tips	**8** Allocated tips

d Control number	**9**	**10** Dependent care benefits

e Employee's first name and initial Last name Suff.	**11** Nonqualified plans	**12a** See instructions for box 12 D 2,000.00

13 Statutory employee ☐ Retirement plan ☒ Third-party sick pay ☐	**12b**

Jill M Martin
573 First Street
Anytown, IL 66734

14 Other	**12c**
	12d

f Employee's address and ZIP code

15 State IL Employer's state ID number 00071053723	**16** State wages, tips, etc. 36,523.24	**17** State income tax 1,826.17	**18** Local wages, tips, etc.	**19** Local income tax	**20** Locality name

Form **W-2** **Wage and Tax Statement**   **2016**   Department of the Treasury—Internal Revenue Service

Source: Internal Revenue Service.

FIGURE 5-6
Box 12 Codes for Form W-2

Form W-2 Reference Guide for Box 12 Codes

A	Uncollected social security or RRTA tax on tips	J	Nontaxable sick pay	S	Employee salary reduction contributions under a section 408(p) SIMPLE
B	Uncollected Medicare tax on tips	K	20% excise tax on excess golden parachute payments	T	Adoption benefits
C	Taxable cost of group-term life insurance over $50,000	L	Substantiated employee business expense reimbursements	V	Income from exercise of nonstatutory stock option(s)
D	Elective deferrals under a section 401(k) cash or deferred arrangement plan (including a SIMPLE 401(k) arrangement)	M	Uncollected social security or RRTA tax on taxable cost of group-term life insurance over $50,000 (for former employees)	W	Employer contributions (including employee contributions through a cafeteria plan) to an employee's health savings account (HSA)
E	Elective deferrals under a section 403(b) salary reduction agreement	N	Uncollected Medicare tax on taxable cost of group-term life insurance over $50,000 (for former employees)	Y	Deferrals under a section 409A nonqualified deferred compensation plan
F	Elective deferrals under a section 408(k)(6) salary reduction SEP	P	Excludable moving expense reimbursements paid directly to employee	Z	Income under section 409A on a nonqualified deferred compensation plan
G	Elective deferrals and employer contributions (including nonelective deferrals) to a section 457(b) deferred compensation plan	Q	Nontaxable combat pay	AA	Designated Roth contributions under a section 401(k) plan
H	Elective deferrals under a section 501(c)(18)(D) tax-exempt organization plan	R	Employer contributions to an Archer MSA	BB	Designated Roth contributions under a section 403(b) plan

Example:

Kevin Feola is the owner of Feola's Cafe, 125 Flat Avenue, Brooklyn, New York, 12002, EIN 49-0030594, phone number 929-555-0904.

Box b: Feola's Cafe will file Form 941 to report quarterly tax liability, so box 941-SS is checked.

Box c: Feola's Cafe had 25 employees who received W-2s.

Box 1: Gross wages and tips for 2016 were $654,087.35.

Box 2: The amount of federal income tax withheld for the 2015 wages was $117,735.

Box 3: Social Security wages were $546,333.35.

Box 4: Social Security tax withheld was $33,872.67.

Box 5: Medicare wages and tips were $570,838.35.

Box 6: Medicare tax withheld was $8,277.16.

Box 7: Social Security tips were $24,505.

Box 12a: Deferred compensation was $83,249.

FIGURE 5-7
Form W-3

DO NOT STAPLE

a Control number	For Official Use Only ▶ OMB No. 1545-0008		
33333			

| b **Kind of Payer** (Check one) | 941 ☑ Military ☐ 943 ☐ 944 ☐ CT-1 ☐ Hshld. emp. ☐ Medicare govt. emp. ☐ | **Kind of Employer** (Check one) | None apply ☑ 501c non-govt. ☐ State/local non-501c ☐ State/local 501c ☐ Federal govt. ☐ | Third-party sick pay (Check if applicable) ☐ |

c Total number of Forms W-2	25	d Establishment number	1 Wages, tips, other compensation	654,087.35	2 Federal income tax withheld	117,735.00
e Employer identification number (EIN)	49-0030594		3 Social security wages	546,333,35	4 Social security tax withheld	33,872.67
f Employer's name	Feola's Cafe		5 Medicare wages and tips	570,838.35	6 Medicare tax withheld	8,277.16
	125 Flat Avenue Brooklyn, NY 12002		7 Social security tips	24,505.00	8 Allocated tips	
			9		10 Dependent care benefits	
g Employer's address and ZIP code			11 Nonqualified plans		12a Deferred compensation	83,249.00
h Other EIN used this year			13 For third-party sick pay use only		12b	
15 State	Employer's state ID number		14 Income tax withheld by payer of third-party sick pay			
16 State wages, tips, etc.	654,087.35	17 State income tax	41,534.55	18 Local wages, tips, etc.		19 Local income tax
Employer's contact person	Kevin Feola		Employer's telephone number	929-555-0904	For Official Use Only	
Employer's fax number			Employer's email address			

Under penalties of perjury, I declare that I have examined this return and accompanying documents and, to the best of my knowledge and belief, they are true, correct, and complete.

Signature ▶   Title ▶   Date ▶

Form **W-3** **Transmittal of Wage and Tax Statements**   **2016**   Department of the Treasury
Internal Revenue Service

Tax Forms

Stop & Check

1. Jacobucci Enterprises is a monthly schedule depositor. According to the information it reported on Form 941, its quarterly tax liability is $8,462.96. During the quarter, it made deposits of $2,980.24 and $3,068.24. How much must it remit with its tax return?

2. Corrado's Corrals paid annual wages totaling $278,452.76 to 15 employees. Assuming that all employees were employed for the entire year, what is the amount of FUTA wages?

3. For Corrado's Corrals in the previous question, what is the FUTA tax liability?

4. Skyrockets, Inc., had the following wage information reported in box 1 of its W-2s:

   Employee A: $25,650
   Employee B: $30,025
   Employee C: $28,550
   Employee D: $31,970
   What amount must it report as total wages on its Form W-3?

LO 5-4   Describe Payroll Within the Context of Business Expenses

© McGraw-Hill Education/John Flournoy, photographer

Understanding employer payroll expenses is important because of the wide range of mandatory activities and lesser-known expenses associated with maintaining employees. Compensation expenses and employer payroll-related liabilities must be accurately maintained in an accounting system. The scope of payroll-related employer responsibilities contributes to the need for knowledgeable payroll accountants.

The amounts withheld from employee pay and the employer liabilities must be deposited in a timely manner with the appropriate authorities. The omission of any of the required filings, activities, or any inaccuracy in the accounting system can lead to problems that could include governmental sanctions and penalties. No statue of limitations exists for unpaid taxes. If a company outsources its payroll processing, it is still liable for any late or unremitted payroll taxes.

The IRS will waive penalties under two conditions:

1. The amount of the shortfall does not exceed the greater of $100 or 2% of the required tax deposit.

2. The amount of the shortfall is deposited either (A) by the due date of the period return (monthly and semiweekly depositors, or (B) the first Wednesday or Friday that falls after the 15th of the month (semiweekly depositors only).

Penalties fall into two classifications: 1) Failure to deposit and 2) Failure to file. The following penalties apply when a ***failure to deposit*** occurs:

2%   - Deposits made 1 to 5 days late.

5%   - Deposits made 6 to 15 days late.

10%   - Deposits made 16 or more days late. Also applies to amounts paid within 10 days of the date of the first notice the IRS sent asking for the tax due.

10%   - Amounts (that should have been deposited) paid directly to the IRS, or paid with your tax return. But see Payment with return, earlier in this section, for an exception.

15%   - Amounts still unpaid more than 10 days after the date of the first notice the IRS sent asking for the tax due or the day on which you received notice and demand for immediate payment, whichever is earlier.

Source: Internal Revenue Service

EXAMPLE: FAILURE TO DEPOSIT PENALTY

Mane Street Hairstylists are monthly schedule payroll tax depositors. The company owed $4,552 in payroll tax liabilities during the month of July. The owner, Billy James, failed to deposit the July payroll taxes until August 27.

The failure to deposit penalty would be calculated as follows:

Tax due	Number of days late	% Penalty	Total Penalty
$ 4,552.00	12	5%	$ 227.60

The ***failure to file*** penalty applies to amounts on Form 941 and is 5% of the unpaid tax due with the return. This penalty accrues for each month or partial month that the tax remains unpaid. Note that failure to file penalties have no maximum that can be charged to the employee.

EXAMPLE: FAILURE TO FILE AND FAILURE TO DEPOSIT PENALTIES

Mary Warren, president of Great Meadows Farms, outsourced the payroll for the company in October 2015. She received a notice on February 15, 2016, that Form 941 for the fourth quarter of 2015 was not filed. After contacting the payroll service, she determined that $32,860 in payroll taxes due with Form 941 were never deposited. The penalties for this oversight would be as follows:

Failure to File penalty

Tax due	Number of months late	% Penalty per month	Penalty
$32,860.00	2*	5%	$3,286.00

Failure to Deposit penalty

Tax due	Number of days late	% Penalty	Penalty
$ 32,860.00	30	10%	$3,286.00
		Total penalties due	$6,572.00

*The number of months is 2 because the Failure to File penalty is based on both months and partial months. Since the notice was issued in February, the penalty would be for 2 months.

Notice how quickly the penalties can accrue for unfiled and undeposited taxes. Keep in mind that these penalties have no maximum and that the failure to file penalty will continue to increase each month. Also keep in mind that the penalties may be subject to interest charges.

A quick summary of general employer payroll expenses and responsibilities follows:

Employee compensation	Tax withholding	Tax matching
Tax remittance	Voluntary deductions from employee pay	Remittance of voluntary deductions
Tax reporting	Tax deposits	Accountability

Employees and Company Framework

Beyond the expenses and responsibilities of the payroll accounting system is the understanding of how the employees fit within the larger framework of the company. Payroll is one part of the cost of employing people. Before the employee ever becomes productive for a company, employers will incur recruiting, hiring, and training costs that vary based on the company's location and minimum job requirements. Other costs include any tools, uniforms, and specific equipment that employees need to perform their jobs. Expenses associated with hiring and retaining well-qualified employees may comprise a significant amount of a company's overhead.

© Brand X Pictures, RF

According to *Entrepreneur* magazine, hiring new employees costs an average of $4,000 each. This figure includes recruiting, hiring, and training costs. Other hidden costs associated with employing people involve workplace integration and worker productivity, which may not peak for several weeks after the initial hire. (Source: *Entrepreneur*)

Tracking employee payroll expenses is an important duty of payroll accountants. The use of payroll reports fosters cost analysis that informs accounting and human resource professionals of specific details needed for budget purposes. Companies need the information generated by payroll records to ensure profitability and competitiveness.

Payroll-Related Business Expenses

Stop & Check

1. What are the two types of penalties associated with payroll taxes?
2. How do payroll expenses relate to other business functions?

LO 5-5   Relate Labor Expenses to Company Profitability

Compensating employees is far more complex than simply paying the hourly wage. The employer's expenses related to taxes, insurance, and benefits are an addition to the employee's annual salary. (See Figure 5-8.) Having employees affects the profitability of a company but is a vital part of doing business. Managers need to associate the proper amount of payroll costs with their department so they can make informed decisions about employee productivity and future budgets.

The Labor Distribution Report

The number of employees in a department is known as the ***labor distribution***. Payroll accounting is a powerful tool in understanding the labor distribution of a company. Accounting records facilitate departmental identification of the number and type of employees, time worked, overtime used, and benefits paid. Integrating the department information into the employee earnings records facilitates labor distribution analysis.

For example, ABD Industries has three departments: administration, sales, and manufacturing. The employees are distributed as follows:

Administration: 15	Sales: 10	Manufacturing: 60

FIGURE 5-8

Percent of Employee Compensation Component to Total Payroll Expense

Compensation component	Civilian workers	Private industry	State and local government
Benefits	31.6%	30.6%	35.9%
Paid leave	7.0%	6.9%	7.3%
Supplemental pay	3.0%	3.5%	0.8%
Insurance	8.8%	8.1%	11.9%
Health benefits	8.4%	7.6%	11.6%
Retirement and savings	5.3%	4.2%	10.1%
Defined benefit	3.3%	2.0%	9.2%
Defined contribution	1.9%	2.2%	0.9%
Legally required	7.6%	8.0%	5.9%
Other fringe benefits	23.1%	26.9%	6.4%

Source: Bureau of Labor Statistics, 2015

Without *departmental classifications*, the payroll costs associated with the 85 employees at ABD would be allocated evenly among the departments. This allocation would result in the administration and sales departments absorbing an amount of the payroll costs that is disproportionate to the number of employees. The departmental classification yields an accurate picture of how the labor is distributed across a company.

EXAMPLE: LABOR DISTRIBUTION, NO DEPARTMENTAL CLASSIFICATION

Total payroll amount for ABD Industries = $500,000

Number of departments = 3

Payroll cost assigned to each department:

$500,000/3 = $166,666.67

Assigning payroll costs without departmental classification works when each department is composed of equal number of employees with reasonably similar skills and job titles.

EXAMPLE: LABOR DISTRIBUTION WITH DEPARTMENTAL CLASSIFICATION

Total payroll for ABD: $500,000 or

Payroll cost per employee: $500,000/85 employees = $5,882.35 per employee (if allocated evenly per employee).

Departmental allocation:

Administration payroll costs = $5,882.35 × 15 = $88,235

Sales payroll costs = $5,882.35 × 10 = $58,823

Manufacturing payroll costs = $5,882.35 × 60 = $352,942

Allocating costs according to the number of employees in each department yields a more accurate amount than equal distribution of the labor costs across the three departments at ABD. However, allocating by number of departmental employees assumes that each employee has equal compensation, which is improbable. A payroll accounting system allows accurate allocation based on the precise amounts paid to each employee per payroll period. Labor distribution reports are among the tools that managers use to determine the productivity and costs specifically associated with their department.

> Labor distribution reports may be used to reveal whatever information is important to a business. Funding sources, payroll accuracy, and budget projections are three common uses of labor distribution reports. Vanderbilt University uses a labor distribution report to ensure that payroll costs are linked to appropriate departments and to specific grant funding. (Source: *Small Business Chronicle*)

Labor Distribution Report

1. Pine Banks Tree Farms has 10 employees on staff: three office staff, five agricultural workers, and two drivers. The annual payroll expense is $300,000.

   a. What would be the labor distribution if Pine Banks Tree Farms uses departmental classification?

   b. What would be the labor distribution if Pine Banks Tree Farms does not use departmental classification?

2. Which method—departmental classification or nondepartmental classification—is most appropriate? Why?

LO 5-6 Complete Benefit Analysis as a Function of Payroll

Companies offer employee benefits both to retain employees after the initial hire and to remain competitive within their industry. The problem with offering benefits is that the cost of the benefits directly affects a company's profitability. The challenge is to find ways to promote employee engagement, reduce employee turnover, and maintain company profitability. Payroll data plays an important role in completing an analysis of benefits offered and their strategic advantage.

Wages and salaries are often a company's largest employee expense. The second largest expense to employers is employee benefits. According to Paychex, employee benefits add an additional 35% to an employee's base pay. Benefits can include paid time off, holiday pay, bonuses, and insurance. Many companies pay a percentage of the employee's insurance benefits, ranging from 70% to 100% in some cases. With the rising costs and mandatory nature of health insurance for certain employers, employee costs have become a major budget concern for many managers.

Payroll-related employee costs need to be compared to the advantages of maintaining the employee, namely, the profitability of the department and the company. To achieve the analysis required, a *benefit analysis* report needs to be compiled. Compiling a benefit analysis report is an important tool in maintaining a balance between employee retention and profitability. The payroll records of the company facilitate the compilation of the benefit analysis report.

The analysis of employee benefits considers all of the variables that comprise their compensation. Many managers are unaware of the full cost of having an employee added to or removed from their department, so the benefit analysis report serves the following purposes:

- Benefit analysis helps employers benchmark their employees' compensation to other companies with similar profiles or in certain geographic locations.
- The report helps employers with labor distribution and budgeting tasks by providing data for decision making.
- The benefit analysis facilitates managerial understanding of departmental impacts prior to hiring or dismissing employees.

Accurate reporting of the benefits costs to employers provides the management with guidance for budget analysis and employee compensation. A sample benefit analysis report is contained in Figure 5-9.

Note the differences between total employee benefit costs and total employer benefit costs. Mandatory and voluntary employee payroll deduction represent a significant monetary investment. When added to the employee's wages and the costs involved with recruitment and hiring, the amount of money dedicated to labor costs becomes a significant portion of a company's expenses.

FIGURE 5-9
Sample Benefit Analysis Report

Statement for: Elizabeth M. Charette

Annual Gross Salary:	$44,137.60
Total Hours Worked Annually:	2,080 Hours

Health & Welfare Benefits:	Annual Employee Cost	Annual Employer Cost
Medical/Dental:	$600	$6,000
Life Insurance:	$0	$1,200
AD&D Coverage:	$0	$980
Dependent Life Insurance:	$300	$600
Disability Insurance:	$600	$3,000
Total Health & Welfare:	$1,500	$11,780
Retirement Plan Benefits:	**Employee Cost**	**Employer Cost**
401(k) Employee Contribution:	$1,324.13	$662.07
Profit Sharing:	$0	$3,000
Total Retirement Plan:	$1,324.13	$3,662.07
PTO & Holiday Pay	**Employee Cost**	**Employer Cost**
Paid Time Off:	$0	$1,697.60
Holiday Pay:	$0	$1,867.36
Total PTO and Holiday Pay:	$0	$3,564.96
Additional Compensation:	**Employee Cost**	**Employer Cost**
Annual Bonus:	$0	$2,500
Bereavement Pay:	$0	$509.28
Production Bonus:	$0	$500
Tuition Reimbursement:	$0	$5,250
Total Additional Comp:	$0	$8,759.28
Government Mandated:	**Employee Cost**	**Employer Cost**
Social Security:	$2,736.53	$2,736.53
Medicare:	$640.00	$640.00
Federal Unemployment:	$0	$253.28
State Unemployment:	$0	$2,279.53
Workers' Compensation:	$0	$353.10
Total Government Mandated:	$3,376.53	$6,262.44
Total Cost of Benefit Provided by WLA Industries	$6,200.66	$34,028.75
Total Cost of Employing E. M. Charette		$78,166.35

Taking the information prepared above, the payroll accountant can determine the cost of each employee to the company. This information can also be used to determine the total cost of offering a particular benefit to the employees. The latter is used when the company is looking at annual renewals of health insurance benefits for comparison.

Annual Total Compensation Report

Some companies provide their employees with an ***annual total compensation report***. The annual total compensation report is similar to the benefit analysis report because it contains detailed analysis of employee costs. The difference between the two reports is the intended audience. The benefit analysis report is an internal report for the company's management, and the annual total compensation report is meant to be distributed to the employee. The work going into the total compensation report can come from either the human resources department or the accounting department, depending on the structure of the company. Either way, the payroll accountant contributes vital information to the report.

> The Credit Union National Association (CUNA) publishes annual total compensation reports that contain the details of CEOs and senior executives at credit unions in the United States. Information from these reports informs each credit union's decisions about base salary, benefits, and retirement packages by providing an industry-wide benchmark. (Source: CUNA)

To prepare the information for the benefit analysis and total compensation reports, the payroll accountant will gather information from many sources: payroll registers, accounts payable invoices, ***payroll tax reports***, and contributions to retirement programs (when employer matching is involved). The payroll accountant will start by printing the annual earnings report for the employee in question. A computerized earnings register can be configured to include taxes and other deductions from the employee's pay. When the total compensation report covers periods greater than one year, it may be necessary for the payroll accountant to obtain Social Security and Medicare tax rates for the years in question. Employer portions of unemployment insurance, workers' compensation, and taxes are added to the benefits provided to the employees in the determination of the total cost.

The payroll accountant will request copies of invoices for health insurance, life insurance, and any other benefits the employer provides, such as on-site meals and gym facilities/memberships, from the accounts payable accountant. Other items that may be added to the cost per employee for benefit analysis could be company-provided awards, meals, clothing, or special facilities (break room, locker room, etc.). Once complete, the annual compensation report is distributed to employees to help them understand the total value of their annual compensation. A sample total compensation report is in Figure 5-10.

Benefit Analysis Report

1. What are the purposes of compiling a benefit analysis report?
2. What is the difference between a benefit analysis report and an annual total compensation report?

FIGURE 5-10
Total Compensation Report

CASH COMPENSATION AND BENEFITS SUMMARY

The amount of your total compensation from ABC Company is much more than what is indicated in your yearly earnings statement. In addition to direct pay, it includes the value of your health care insurance, disability and life insurance, retirement benefits, and government mandated benefits. Below, we break out your total compensation.

CASH COMPENSATION

	Amount
Base Salary	$52,000.00
Total:	**$52,000.00**

BENEFITS	Plan	Coverage	Your Contribution	Company Contribution
Medical Insurance	ABC One		$600.00	$5,400.00
Vision Insurance	ABC Vision		$0.00	$600.00
Dental Insurance	NL Dental		$120.00	$1,080.00
Total:			**$720.00**	**$7,080.00**

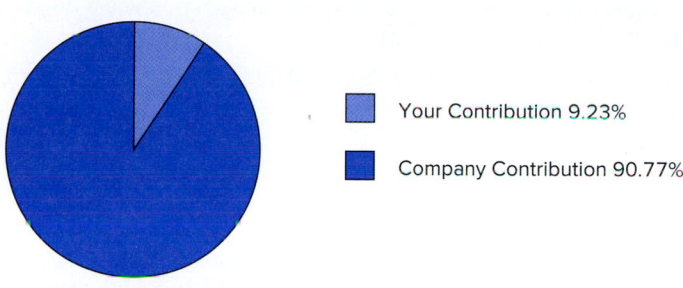

Your Contribution 9.23%

Company Contribution 90.77%

TOTAL COMPENSATION VALUE

The true value of your ABC Company total compensation includes your direct pay, the company's contribution to your benefits, and the consequent tax savings to you.

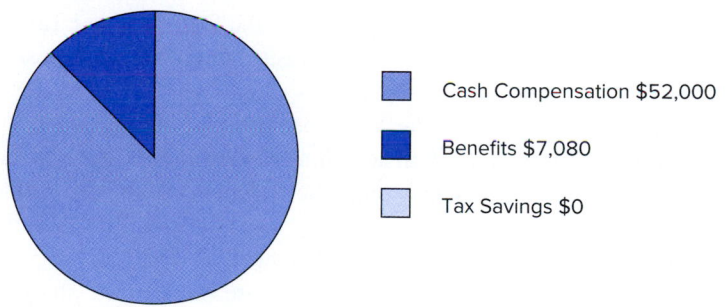

Cash Compensation $52,000

Benefits $7,080

Tax Savings $0

THE TOTAL VALUE OF YOUR COMPENSATION:	**$59,080.00**

OTHER VALUABLE BEBEFITS

ABC Company provides other valuable benefits that are not listed above. Below is a summary of those plans.

Paid Time Off (PTO)	10 Days	$4,520.00
Total:		**$4,520.00**

EMPLOYER TAXES AND BENEFIT ANALYSIS

Tax rates and remittance methods for employers tend to change annually based on directives issued by federal, state, and local governments. Some developments in employer taxes that have changed during the early 2010s include the following:

- The use of the EFTPS as a mandatory tax remittance method for new employers and the preferred method for existing employers.
- Temporary tax deductions for portions of COBRA policies for displaced workers.
- The Work Opportunity Tax Credit that reduces tax liabilities for employers who hired certain groups of workers.
- A reduction in the FUTA tax rate due to the expiration of a 0.2% surtax.

Some trends to watch in employer taxes and benefit analysis include the following:

- A continued increase in wellness programs and employee incentive programs aimed at reducing health care costs.
- Growing concerns among younger employees about the increasing costs of healthcare that may lead to changes in employer labor planning initiatives.
- Active involvement of the employees in their health care that accompanies a decrease in employer-sponsored flexible spending accounts.
- An increase in the number of business offering sign-on incentives and spot bonuses/awards.

Summary of Employer Payroll Taxes and Labor Planning

Taxes are a part of conducting business. Whether taxes are income or employee related, a business must abide by the regulations for the timely submission and reporting of taxes. Employers have responsibilities for collecting federal income tax, Social Security, and Medicare taxes from their employees. In addition, the company is responsible for setting aside federal unemployment taxes per employee based upon taxable wages. Apart from the federal taxes, employers may be liable for the collecting, reporting, and submission of state and local income and unemployment taxes. Privilege taxes, such as the Denver Head Tax, may also be collected in specific districts. Employers who fail to meet the reporting, deposit, or submission requirements may be subject to fines and penalties.

Understanding the connection between the W-2 Form and the final paycheck of the year can save payroll accountants hours of work in searching to find the answers to each employee's query. When the payroll accountant can explain the elements of the W-2 with confidence, fewer employees will come to ask why the difference, especially if the payroll accountant provides a written explanation with the final annual paycheck or W-2.

Although the human resources department could prepare the benefit analysis report, in smaller companies this duty can fall to the payroll accountant. Even in larger organizations, the human resources department will need specific information from the payroll accountant to feed into the benefit analysis report. Managers can examine the benefit analysis to understand how much their employees cost the department. Once receiving a total annual compensation report, the employee has a more complete understanding of their compensation package, thereby feeding wage discussions and building a data-driven understanding of cost changes.

Key Points

- Employers share some of the same tax obligations as their employees. Some examples are the Social Security, Medicare, and (in some states) SUTA taxes.
- FUTA taxes are paid only on the first $7,000 of each employee's annual taxable wage; SUTA tax wage base limits vary by state.

- Workers' compensation is state-mandated insurance that employers carry to protect employees who are injured or killed while performing normal work duties.
- Workers' compensation insurance premium costs vary according to labor classifications.
- Payroll tax deposit frequency is determined by the amount of payroll taxes paid during a "lookback" period.
- All new employers are monthly schedule depositors until the next lookback period.
- Most employers file quarterly payroll tax returns on Form 941.
- Employers who deposit payroll taxes on a semiweekly basis must also file a Schedule B with their Form 941.
- Employers with less than $2,500 of annual tax liability file a Form 944 at the end of the calendar year.
- Employers report FUTA tax liability on an annual basis by using Form 940.
- Employers file an annual Form W-2 for each employee with the Social Security Administration.
- Form W-3 is the transmittal form used to report a company's aggregate annual wages and withholdings.
- Labor distribution has an effect on company profitability, and benefit costs are a significant factor in managerial decisions.
- A total annual compensation report is used to communicate to employees the complete compensation package that they receive.

Vocabulary

Annual schedule depositors
Annual total compensation report
Automated clearing house (ACH)
Benefit analysis
Departmental classification
EFTPS
FICA

Form 940
Form 941
Form 944
Form W-2
Form W-3
FUTA
Labor distribution
Lookback period
Monthly depositors

Next business day depositors
Payroll tax reports
Quarterly depositors
Schedule B
Semiweekly depositors
Statutory deductions
SUTA
Tax remittance

Review Questions

1. What taxes are paid by the employer only?

2. What taxes are the shared responsibility of the employer and employee?

3. What taxes are paid by the employee only?

4. What determines the deposit requirements for employer taxes?

5. How often must a company report Form 941 earnings/withholdings?

6. How often must a company report Form 940 earnings/withholdings?

7. Which of the mandatory withholdings have a maximum wage base?

8. How did the Affordable Care Act change Medicare tax withholding percentages?

9. What is Form 941?

10. Which employers must use Schedule B?

11. How do employers know that they must use Form 944?

12. What is Form 940?

13. What is the difference between Form W-2 and Form W-3?

14. What are the employer's payroll responsibilities?

15. How does payroll relate to a company's costs of doing business?

16. What is meant by the term *labor distribution?*

17. How do payroll records inform managers about labor distribution?

18. What is a benefit analysis report?

19. How can a manager use the benefit analysis report in the decision-making process?

20. How do the payroll reports inform managers about department and company profitability?

Exercises Set A

E5-1A.
LO 5-1

Which of the following are employer-only payroll obligations? (Select all that apply.)
A. Social Security tax
B. SUTA
C. Medicare tax
D. FUTA

E5-2A.
LO 5-1

As of 2016, which of the following accurately represents the full FUTA rate and wage base?
A. 0.6%, $118,500
B. Varies by state
C. 6.0%, $7,000
D. 0.6%, $7,000

E5-3A.
LO 5-1

Davis is the accounting for Heads Up Hat Corporation. As he prepares the payroll for the semimonthly pay period ending December 15, he notices that some of the year-to-date executives' salaries have exceeded $200,000. What payroll tax responsibilities does Heads Up Hat Corporation have, especially regarding FICA taxes? (Select all that apply.)
A. Social security tax must be deducted from the executives' pay and matched by the corporation.
B. An additional 0.9% Medicare tax must be deducted from the employees' pay and matched by the corporation.
C. An additional 0.9% Medicare tax must be deducted from the executives' pay, but no corporate match is required.
D. No Social Security tax should be deducted and matched for the executives because their pay has exceeded the wage base.

E5-4A.
LO 5-2

Annie is a payroll clerk in Wilty Enterprises. She receives a written notice from the IRS that Wilty Enterprises is a monthly schedule depositor. How is the deposit schedule determined?
A. The number of employees in the company.
B. The payroll frequency used by the company.
C. The amount of FUTA taxes paid.
D. The payroll tax liability during the lookback period.

E5-5A.
LO 5-2

Match the amount of payroll tax liabilities from the lookback period with the appropriate tax deposit schedule.

A. $42,300 annual payroll taxes	1. Annual
B. $145,033 annual payroll taxes	2. Monthly
C. $128,450 payroll tax for 1 pay period	3. Semiweekly
D. $1,580 annual payroll taxes	4. Next Business Day

E5-6A.
LO 5-3

Which form(s) should be prepared and filed by companies with employees and payroll tax liabilities exceeding $50,000 as of December 31, 20XX? (Select all that apply.)
A. Form 940
B. Form W-4
C. Form 941
D. Form W-2

E5-7A.
LO 5-4

Wade Pools Company files its second-quarter Form 941 on August 21, after receiving notice from the IRS of the missing form. What is the failure to file penalty?
A. 2%
B. 5%
C. 10%
D. 15%

E5-8A.
LO 5-4, 5-5

Which of the following is true about the cost of employees within a business context? (Select all that apply.)
A. Employees comprise a significant cost of conducting business.
B. Hiring employees involves a significant overhead cost.
C. Costs associated with employees include only salary and limited hiring expenses.
D. The cost of providing employee benefits is minimal and of little importance.

E5-9A.
LO 5-6

Which of the following represent the purpose(s) of the benefit analysis report? (Select all that apply.)
A. Benchmarking with other companies.
B. Understanding of employer and employee benefits costs.
C. Billing employees for benefits costs.
D. Identification of opportunities for increasing profitability.

E5-10A.
LO 5-6

Why is it important to prepare the benefit analysis report or the total compensation report? (Select all that apply.)
A. The reports promote employee education about the total value of their salary and benefits.
B. The reports inform labor planning and employer cost strategies.
C. The reports may be used as employee contracts.
D. The reports may be used to accompany benefits billing.

E5-11A.
LO 5-1, 5-4

Which of the following is a characteristic of workers' compensation? (Select all that apply.)
A. Workers' compensation is an insurance policy.
B. Private employers are federally mandated to provide workers' compensation.
C. The cost of workers' compensation represents a labor expense to the business.
D. Workers' compensation is provided to cover employees who are injured or killed while performing work duties.

Problems Set A

P5-1A.
LO 5-1

Bob works for Seymour Engines, which pays employees on a semimonthly basis. Bob's annual salary is $120,000. Calculate the following:

Pay Date	Prior YTD Earnings	Social Security Taxable Wages	Medicare Taxable Wages	Employer Share Social Security Tax	Employer Share Medicare tax
November 15					
December 31					

P5-2A.
LO 5-1, 5-3

Eyeseeyou Cameras has the following employees:

Employee Name	Annual Taxable Wages
Mia Haskell	$26,000
Viktor Papadopoulos	$35,000
Puja Anderson	$32,000
Cady Billingmeier	$29,000
Carl Johnson	$46,000

Eyeseeyou Cameras' SUTA tax rate is 5.4% and applies to the first $8,000 of employee wages. What is the annual amount due for each employee?

Employee	FUTA Due	SUTA Due
Mia Haskell		
Viktor Papadopoulos		
Puja Anderson		
Cady Billingmeier		
Carl Johnson		

P5-3A.
LO 5-1,
5-2, 5-3

Freedom, Inc., has 16 employees within Denver City and County. All of the employees worked a predominant number of hours within the city. The employees earned $7.25 per hour and worked 160 hours each during the month. The employer must remit $4.00 per month per employee that earns more than $500 per month. Additionally, employees who earn more than $500 per month must have $5.75 withheld from their pay. What is the employee and company Occupational Privilege Tax for these employees?

Employee: _____

Employer: _____

P5-4A.
LO 5-1, 5-3

Joseph earned $68,000 in 2016 for a company in Kentucky. He is single with one dependent and is paid annually. Compute the following employee share of the taxes, using the percentage method in Appendix C.

Federal income tax withholding: _____

Social Security tax: _____

Medicare tax: _____

P5-5A.
LO 5-3

Using the information from P5-4A, compute the employer's share of the taxes. The FUTA rate in Kentucky for 2016 is 0.6% on the first $7,000 of employee wages, and the SUTA rate is 5.4% with a wage base of $10,200.

Federal income tax withholding: _____

Social Security tax: _____

Medicare tax: _____

FUTA tax: _____

SUTA tax: _____

P5-6A.
LO 5-2

Veryclear Glassware is a new business owned by Samantha Peoples, the company president. Her first year of operation commenced on April 1, 2016. What schedule depositor would she be for the first year of operations?

P5-7A.
LO 5-3

Using the information from P5-6A, complete the following Form 941 for second quarter 2016.

EIN: 78-7654398

Address: 23051 Old Redwood Highway, Sebastopol, California 95482, phone 707-555-5555

Number of employees: 7

Form **941 for 2016:** Employer's QUARTERLY Federal Tax Return
(Rev. January 2016)   Department of the Treasury — Internal Revenue Service

950114

OMB No. 1545-0029

Employer identification number (EIN) [ ] [ ] – [ ] [ ] [ ] [ ] [ ] [ ] [ ]

Name (not your trade name)

Trade name (if any)

Address

Number   Street   Suite or room number

City   State   ZIP code

Foreign country name   Foreign province/county   Foreign postal code

Report for this Quarter of 2016
(Check one.)

[ ] **1:** January, February, March

[ ] **2:** April, May, June

[ ] **3:** July, August, September

[ ] **4:** October, November, December

Instructions and prior year forms are available at *www.irs.gov/form941.*

Read the separate instructions before you complete Form 941. Type or print within the boxes.

Part 1:   **Answer these questions for this quarter.**

1	Number of employees who received wages, tips, or other compensation for the pay period including: *Mar. 12* (Quarter 1), *June 12* (Quarter 2), *Sept. 12* (Quarter 3), or *Dec. 12* (Quarter 4)	1 _____
2	Wages, tips, and other compensation	2 _____ . __
3	Federal income tax withheld from wages, tips, and other compensation	3 _____ . __
4	If no wages, tips, and other compensation are subject to social security or Medicare tax	[ ] Check and go to line 6.

		Column 1		Column 2
5a	Taxable social security wages . .	_____ . __	× .124 =	_____ . __
5b	Taxable social security tips . . .	_____ . __	× .124 =	_____ . __
5c	Taxable Medicare wages & tips. .	_____ . __	× .029 =	_____ . __
5d	Taxable wages & tips subject to Additional Medicare Tax withholding	_____ . __	× .009 =	_____ . __

5e	Add Column 2 from lines 5a, 5b, 5c, and 5d	5e _____ . __
5f	Section 3121(q) Notice and Demand—Tax due on unreported tips (see instructions) . .	5f _____ . __
6	Total taxes before adjustments. Add lines 3, 5e, and 5f	6 _____ . __
7	Current quarter's adjustment for fractions of cents	7 _____ . __
8	Current quarter's adjustment for sick pay	8 _____ . __
9	Current quarter's adjustments for tips and group-term life insurance	9 _____ . __
10	Total taxes after adjustments. Combine lines 6 through 9	10 _____ . __
11	Total deposits for this quarter, including overpayment applied from a prior quarter and overpayments applied from Form 941-X, 941-X (PR), 944-X, or 944-X (SP) filed in the current quarter	11 _____ . __
12	Balance due. If line 10 is more than line 11, enter the difference and see instructions . . .	12 _____ . __
13	Overpayment. If line 11 is more than line 10, enter the difference _____ . __ Check one: [ ] Apply to next return. [ ] Send a refund.	

► **You MUST complete both pages of Form 941 and SIGN it.**

Next ►

For Privacy Act and Paperwork Reduction Act Notice, see the back of the Payment Voucher.   Cat. No. 17001Z   Form **941** (Rev. 1-2016)

950214

Name *(not your trade name)*	Employer identification number (EIN)

Part 2:   Tell us about your deposit schedule and tax liability for this quarter.

If you are unsure about whether you are a monthly schedule depositor or a semiweekly schedule depositor, see section 11 of Pub. 15.

14   Check one: ☐   Line 10 on this return is less than $2,500 or line 10 on the return for the prior quarter was less than $2,500, and you did not incur a $100,000 next-day deposit obligation during the current quarter. If line 10 for the prior quarter was less than $2,500 but line 10 on this return is $100,000 or more, you must provide a record of your federal tax liability. If you are a monthly schedule depositor, complete the deposit schedule below; if you are a semiweekly schedule depositor, attach Schedule B (Form 941). Go to Part 3.

☐   **You were a monthly schedule depositor for the entire quarter.** Enter your tax liability for each month and total liability for the quarter, then go to Part 3.

Tax liability: Month 1   [.   ]

Month 2   [.   ]

Month 3   [.   ]

Total liability for quarter   [.   ]   **Total must equal line 10.**

☐   **You were a semiweekly schedule depositor for any part of this quarter.** Complete Schedule B (Form 941), Report of Tax Liability for Semiweekly Schedule Depositors, and attach it to Form 941.

Part 3:   Tell us about your business. If a question does NOT apply to your business, leave it blank.

15   **If your business has closed or you stopped paying wages** . . . .   ☐ Check here, and

enter the final date you paid wages   [/   /   ] .

16   **If you are a seasonal employer and you do not have to file a return for every quarter of the year** . .   ☐ Check here.

Part 4:   May we speak with your third-party designee?

Do you want to allow an employee, a paid tax preparer, or another person to discuss this return with the IRS? See the instructions for details.

☐ **Yes.** Designee's name and phone number   [   ]   [   ]

Select a 5-digit Personal Identification Number (PIN) to use when talking to the IRS.   [ ][ ][ ][ ][ ]

☐ **No.**

Part 5:   Sign here. You MUST complete both pages of Form 941 and SIGN it.

Under penalties of perjury, I declare that I have examined this return, including accompanying schedules and statements, and to the best of my knowledge and belief, it is true, correct, and complete. Declaration of preparer (other than taxpayer) is based on all information of which preparer has any knowledge.

✗   **Sign your name here**   [   ]

Print your name here   [   ]

Print your title here   [   ]

Date   [/   /   ]   Best daytime phone   [   ]

Paid Preparer Use Only   Check if you are self-employed . . .   ☐

Preparer's name	[ ]	PTIN	[ ]
Preparer's signature	[ ]	Date	[/ /]
Firm's name (or yours if self-employed)	[ ]	EIN	[ ]
Address	[ ]	Phone	[ ]
City	[ ] State [ ]	ZIP code	[ ]

Source: Internal Revenue Service.

Wages, tips, and other compensation paid during second quarter 2016: $244,798

Income tax withheld: $48,000

Social Security tax withheld: $15,177.48

Medicare tax withheld: $3,549.57

Monthly tax liability:

April	$28,484.79
May	28,484.79
June	28,484.80

P5-8A.

LO 5-3

Using the information from P5-6A and P5-7A for Veryclear Glassware (California Employer Account Number 999-9999-9), complete the following State of California Form DE-9, Quarterly Contribution and Report of Wages Report. Use 5.4% as the UI rate, 0.1% as the ETT rate, and 0.9% as the SDI rate. All employees have worked a full calendar year with the company, and all wages are subject to UI, ETT, and SDI. The California PIT taxes withheld for the quarter are $22,406. The company has deposited $38,073.07 for the quarter.

P5-9A.

LO 5-3

ZRT, Inc., paid its 25 employees a total of $863,428.49 during 2015. Of these wages, $5,400 is exempt fringe benefits (Section 125 cafeteria plans) and $9,850 is exempt retirement benefits (employer contributions to 401(k) plans). All employees have worked there for the full calendar year and reached the FUTA wage base during the first quarter; taxes were deposited then. ZRT, Inc., is located at 3874 Palm Avenue, Sebring, Florida, 20394. The owner is Hope Daniels, EIN is 99-2039485, phone number is 461-555-9485. Complete Form 940 for ZRT, Inc.

P5-10A.

LO 5-3

Leda, Inc. is located at 433 Augusta Road, Caribou, Maine, 04736, phone number 201-555-1212. The Federal EIN is 54-3910394, and it has a Maine Revenue Services number of 3884019. Owner Amanda Leda has asked you to prepare Form W-2 for each of the following employees of Leda, Inc. as of December 31, 2016.

Sarah C. Niehaus
122 Main Street, #3
Caribou, ME 04736
SSN: 477-30-2234
Dependent Care Benefit: $1,800.00

Total 2016 wages: $34,768.53
401(k) contribution: $1,043.06
Section 125 contribution: $1,500.00
Federal income tax withheld: $4,833.82
Social Security tax withheld: $2,090.98
Medicare tax withheld: $489.02
State income tax withheld $2,561.92

Maxwell S. Law
1503 22nd Street
New Sweden, ME 04762
SSN: 493-55-2049

Total 2016 wages: $36,729.37
401(k) contribution: $1,469.18
Section 125 contribution: $1,675.00
Federal income tax withheld: $4,407.52
Social Security tax withheld: $2,173.37
Medicare tax withheld: $508.29
State income tax withheld $2,670.02

Siobhan E. Manning
1394 West Highway 59
Woodland, ME 04694
SSN: 390-39-1002
Tuition in excess of $5,250: $1,575.00

Total 2017 wages: $30,034.87
401(k) contribution: $712.75
Section 125 contribution: $1,000.00
Federal income tax withheld: $4,833.82
Social Security tax withheld: $1,800.16
Medicare tax withheld: $421.01
State income tax withheld $2,130.38

(continued)

 **Employment Development Department**
State of California

QUARTERLY CONTRIBUTION RETURN AND REPORT OF WAGES

REMINDER: File your DE 9 and DE 9C together.

00090112

PLEASE TYPE THIS FORM—DO NOT ALTER PREPRINTED INFORMATION

		YR	QTR

QUARTER ENDED

DUE

DELINQUENT IF NOT POSTMARKED OR RECEIVED BY

EMPLOYER ACCOUNT NO.

DO NOT ALTER THIS AREA

DEPT. USE ONLY

P1   P2   C   P   U   S   A

T

Mo.	Day	Yr.

EFFECTIVE DATE

FEIN _____

A. NO WAGES PAID THIS QUARTER ☐   **B. OUT OF BUSINESS/NO EMPLOYEES** ☐

ADDITIONAL FEINS _____   _____

B1.   OUT OF BUSINESS DATE

M M D D Y Y Y Y

C. TOTAL SUBJECT WAGES PAID THIS QUARTER ....

D. UNEMPLOYMENT INSURANCE (UI) (Total Employee Wages up to $ _____ per employee per calendar year)

(D1) UI Rate % ____ TIMES

(D2) UI TAXABLE WAGES FOR THE QUARTER ____

=

(D3) UI CONTRIBUTIONS   0:00

E. EMPLOYMENT TRAINING TAX (ETT)

(E1) ETT Rate % ____ TIMES   UI Taxable Wages for the Quarter (D2) ......   =

(E2) ETT CONTRIBUTIONS   0:00

F. STATE DISABILITY INSURANCE (SDI) (Total Employee Wages up to $ _____ per employee per calendar year)

(F1) SDI Rate % ____ TIMES

(F2) SDI TAXABLE WAGES FOR THE QUARTER ____

=

(F3) SDI EMPLOYEE CONTRIBUTIONS WITHHELD   0:00

G. CALIFORNIA PERSONAL INCOME TAX (PIT) WITHHELD ....

H. SUBTOTAL (Add Items D3, E2, F3, and G) 0:00

I. LESS: CONTRIBUTIONS AND WITHHOLDINGS PAID FOR THE QUARTER ....
(**DO NOT** INCLUDE PENALTY AND INTEREST PAYMENTS)

J. TOTAL TAXES DUE OR OVERPAID   (Item H minus Item I) 0:00

If amount due, prepare a *Payroll Tax Deposit* (DE 88), include the correct payment quarter, and mail to: Employment Development Department, P.O. Box 826276, Sacramento, CA 94230-6276. **NOTE:** Do not mail payments along with the DE 9 and *Quarterly Contribution Return and Report of Wages (Continuation)* (DE 9C), as this may delay processing and result in erroneous penalty and interest charges. **Mandatory Electronic Funds Transfer (EFT)** filers must remit all SDI/PIT deposits by EFT to avoid a noncompliance penalty.

K. I declare that the above, to the best of my knowledge and belief, is true and correct. If a refund was claimed, a reasonable effort was made to refund any erroneous deductions to the affected employee(s).

Signature *Required* _____   Title _____   Phone (___) ___   Date ____
                                              (Owner, Accountant, Preparer, etc.)

◉   SIGN AND MAIL TO: State of California / Employment Development Department / P.O. Box 989071 / West Sacramento CA 95798-9071

DE 9 Rev. 2 (7-14) (**INTERNET**)   Page 1 of 2

Fast, Easy, and Convenient!
Visit EDD's Web site at www.edd.ca.gov

Source: Employment Development Department.

Form **940** for **2015:**   **Employer's Annual Federal Unemployment (FUTA) Tax Return**   850113

Department of the Treasury — Internal Revenue Service

OMB No. 1545-0028

Employer identification number (EIN) ☐☐ — ☐☐☐☐☐☐☐

Name (*not your trade name*) _____

Trade name (*if any*) _____

Address _____

Number   Street   Suite or room number

_____

City   State   ZIP code

_____

Foreign country name   Foreign province/county   Foreign postal code

Type of Return
(Check all that apply.)

☐ **a.** Amended

☐ **b.** Successor employer

☐ **c.** No payments to employees in 2015

☐ **d.** Final: Business closed or stopped paying wages

Instructions and prior-year forms are available at *www.irs.gov/form940.*

Read the separate instructions before you complete this form. Please type or print within the boxes.

Part 1:   **Tell us about your return. If any line does NOT apply, leave it blank. See instructions before completing Part 1.**

1a If you had to pay state unemployment tax in one state only, enter the state abbreviation . **1a** ☐☐

1b If you had to pay state unemployment tax in more than one state, you are a multi-state employer . . . . **1b** ☐ Check here. Complete Schedule A (Form 940).

2 If you paid wages in a state that is subject to **CREDIT REDUCTION** . . . . **2** ☐ Check here. Complete Schedule A (Form 940).

Part 2:   **Determine your FUTA tax before adjustments. If any line does NOT apply, leave it blank.**

3 Total payments to all employees . . . . **3** ☐ .

4 Payments exempt from FUTA tax . . . . **4** ☐ .

Check all that apply: **4a** ☐ Fringe benefits   **4c** ☐ Retirement/Pension   **4e** ☐ Other
4b ☐ Group-term life insurance   **4d** ☐ Dependent care

5 Total of payments made to each employee in excess of $7,000 . . . . **5** ☐ .

6 Subtotal (line 4 + line 5 = line 6) . . . . **6** ☐ .

7 Total taxable FUTA wages (line 3 – line 6 = line 7) (see instructions) . . . . . **7** ☐ .

8 FUTA tax before adjustments (line 7 x .006 = line 8) . . . . **8** ☐ .

Part 3:   **Determine your adjustments. If any line does NOT apply, leave it blank.**

9 If ALL of the taxable FUTA wages you paid were excluded from state unemployment tax, multiply line 7 by .054 (line 7 × .054 = line 9). Go to line 12 . . . . . **9** ☐ .

10 If SOME of the taxable FUTA wages you paid were excluded from state unemployment tax, OR you paid ANY state unemployment tax late (after the due date for filing Form 940), complete the worksheet in the instructions. Enter the amount from line 7 of the worksheet . . **10** ☐ .

11 If credit reduction applies, enter the total from Schedule A (Form 940) . . . . . **11** ☐ .

Part 4:   **Determine your FUTA tax and balance due or overpayment. If any line does NOT apply, leave it blank.**

12 Total FUTA tax after adjustments (lines 8 + 9 + 10 + 11 = line 12) . . . . . **12** ☐ .

13 FUTA tax deposited for the year, including any overpayment applied from a prior year . **13** ☐ .

14 Balance due (If line 12 is more than line 13, enter the excess on line 14.)
- If line 14 is more than $500, you must deposit your tax.
- If line 14 is $500 or less, you may pay with this return. (see instructions) . . . . . **14** ☐ .

15 Overpayment (If line 13 is more than line 12, enter the excess on line 15 and check a box below.) . . . . **15** ☐ .

▶ You **MUST** complete both pages of this form and **SIGN** it.

Check one: ☐ Apply to next return.   ☐ Send a refund.

Next ▶

For **Privacy Act and Paperwork Reduction Act Notice, see the back of Form 940-V, Payment Voucher.**   Cat. No. 11234O   Form **940** (2015)

850212

Name *(not your trade name)*	Employer identification number (EIN)

Part 5:   **Report your FUTA tax liability by quarter only if line 12 is more than $500. If not, go to Part 6.**

16   Report the amount of your FUTA tax liability for each quarter; do NOT enter the amount you deposited. If you had no liability for a quarter, leave the line blank.

    16a   **1st quarter** (January 1 – March 31) . . . .   **16a** ☐ .

    16b   **2nd quarter** (April 1 – June 30) . . . .   **16b** ☐ .

    16c   **3rd quarter** (July 1 – September 30) . . . .   **16c** ☐ .

    16d   **4th quarter** (October 1 – December 31) . . . . . .   **16d** ☐ .

17   Total tax liability for the year (lines 16a + 16b + 16c + 16d = line 17)   **17** ☐ .   **Total must equal line 12.**

Part 6:   **May we speak with your third-party designee?**

Do you want to allow an employee, a paid tax preparer, or another person to discuss this return with the IRS? See the instructions for details.

☐ **Yes.**   Designee's name and phone number

             Select a 5-digit Personal Identification Number (PIN) to use when talking to IRS   ☐ ☐ ☐ ☐ ☐

☐ **No.**

Part 7:   **Sign here. You MUST complete both pages of this form and SIGN it.**

Under penalties of perjury, I declare that I have examined this return, including accompanying schedules and statements, and to the best of my knowledge and belief, it is true, correct, and complete, and that no part of any payment made to a state unemployment fund claimed as a credit was, or is to be, deducted from the payments made to employees. Declaration of preparer (other than taxpayer) is based on all information of which preparer has any knowledge.

✗ Sign your name here

Print your name here

Print your title here

Date   /   /

Best daytime phone

Paid Preparer Use Only   Check if you are self-employed   . ☐

Preparer's name		PTIN	
Preparer's signature		Date	/ /
Firm's name (or yours if self-employed)		EIN	
Address		Phone	
City	State	ZIP code	

Source: Internal Revenue Service.

Donald A. Hendrix
1387 Rimbaud Avenue
Caribou, ME 04736
SSN: 288-30-5940

Total 2016 wages: $22,578.89
401(k) contribution: $1,354.73
Section 125 contribution: $2,250.00
Federal income tax withheld: $2,709.47
Social Security tax withheld: $1,260.39
Medicare tax withheld: $294.77
State income tax withheld $1,508.45

Alison K. Sutter
3664 Fairfield Street
Washburn, ME 04786
SSN: 490-55-0293

Total 2016 wages: $45,908.34
401(k) contribution: $2,754.50
Section 125 contribution: $1,750.00
Federal income tax withheld: $5,509.00
Social Security tax withheld: $2,737.82
Medicare tax withheld: $640.30
State income tax withheld $3,291.61

22222	Void ☐	**a** Employee's social security number	For Official Use Only ▶ OMB No. 1545-0008		
b Employer identification number (EIN)				**1** Wages, tips, other compensation	**2** Federal income tax withheld
c Employer's name, address, and ZIP code				**3** Social security wages	**4** Social security tax withheld
				5 Medicare wages and tips	**6** Medicare tax withheld
				7 Social security tips	**8** Allocated tips
d Control number				**9**	**10** Dependent care benefits
e Employee's first name and initial	Last name		Suff.	**11** Nonqualified plans	**12a** See instructions for box 12
				13 Statutory employee ☐ Retirement plan ☐ Third-party sick pay ☐	**12b**
				14 Other	**12c**
					12d
f Employee's address and ZIP code					
15 State Employer's state ID number	**16** State wages, tips, etc.	**17** State income tax	**18** Local wages, tips, etc.	**19** Local income tax	**20** Locality name

Form **W-2** **Wage and Tax Statement**   **2016**   Department of the Treasury—Internal Revenue Service

22222	Void ☐	**a** Employee's social security number	**For Official Use Only** ▶ OMB No. 1545-0008		
b Employer identification number (EIN)				**1** Wages, tips, other compensation	**2** Federal income tax withheld
c Employer's name, address, and ZIP code			**3** Social security wages		**4** Social security tax withheld
			5 Medicare wages and tips		**6** Medicare tax withheld
			7 Social security tips		**8** Allocated tips
d Control number			**9**		**10** Dependent care benefits
e Employee's first name and initial	Last name	Suff.	**11** Nonqualified plans		**12a** See instructions for box 12 Code
			13 Statutory employee ☐ Retirement plan ☐ Third-party sick pay ☐		**12b** Code
			14 Other		**12c** Code
					12d Code
f Employee's address and ZIP code					

15 State Employer's state ID number	**16** State wages, tips, etc.	**17** State income tax	**18** Local wages, tips, etc.	**19** Local income tax	**20** Locality name

Form **W-2** **Wage and Tax Statement**   **2016**   Department of the Treasury—Internal Revenue Service

---

22222	Void ☐	**a** Employee's social security number	**For Official Use Only** ▶ OMB No. 1545-0008		
b Employer identification number (EIN)				**1** Wages, tips, other compensation	**2** Federal income tax withheld
c Employer's name, address, and ZIP code			**3** Social security wages		**4** Social security tax withheld
			5 Medicare wages and tips		**6** Medicare tax withheld
			7 Social security tips		**8** Allocated tips
d Control number			**9**		**10** Dependent care benefits
e Employee's first name and initial	Last name	Suff.	**11** Nonqualified plans		**12a** See instructions for box 12 Code
			13 Statutory employee ☐ Retirement plan ☐ Third-party sick pay ☐		**12b** Code
			14 Other		**12c** Code
					12d Code
f Employee's address and ZIP code					

15 State Employer's state ID number	**16** State wages, tips, etc.	**17** State income tax	**18** Local wages, tips, etc.	**19** Local income tax	**20** Locality name

Form **W-2** **Wage and Tax Statement**   **2016**   Department of the Treasury—Internal Revenue Service

22222	Void ☐	**a** Employee's social security number	**For Official Use Only** ▶ OMB No. 1545-0008		
b Employer identification number (EIN)				**1** Wages, tips, other compensation	**2** Federal income tax withheld
c Employer's name, address, and ZIP code				**3** Social security wages	**4** Social security tax withheld
				5 Medicare wages and tips	**6** Medicare tax withheld
				7 Social security tips	**8** Allocated tips
d Control number				**9**	**10** Dependent care benefits
e Employee's first name and initial	Last name		Suff.	**11** Nonqualified plans	**12a** See instructions for box 12
				13 Statutory employee ☐ Retirement plan ☐ Third-party sick pay ☐	**12b**
				14 Other	**12c**
					12d
f Employee's address and ZIP code					

15 State	Employer's state ID number	16 State wages, tips, etc.	17 State income tax	18 Local wages, tips, etc.	19 Local income tax	20 Locality name

Form **W-2**   **Wage and Tax Statement**   **2016**   Department of the Treasury—Internal Revenue Service

22222	Void ☐	**a** Employee's social security number	**For Official Use Only** ▶ OMB No. 1545-0008		
b Employer identification number (EIN)				**1** Wages, tips, other compensation	**2** Federal income tax withheld
c Employer's name, address, and ZIP code				**3** Social security wages	**4** Social security tax withheld
				5 Medicare wages and tips	**6** Medicare tax withheld
				7 Social security tips	**8** Allocated tips
d Control number				**9**	**10** Dependent care benefits
e Employee's first name and initial	Last name		Suff.	**11** Nonqualified plans	**12a** See instructions for box 12
				13 Statutory employee ☐ Retirement plan ☐ Third-party sick pay ☐	**12b**
				14 Other	**12c**
					12d
f Employee's address and ZIP code					

15 State	Employer's state ID number	16 State wages, tips, etc.	17 State income tax	18 Local wages, tips, etc.	19 Local income tax	20 Locality name

Form **W-2**   **Wage and Tax Statement**   **2016**   Department of the Treasury—Internal Revenue Service

P5-11A.

LO 5-3

Using the information from P5-10A for Leda Inc., complete Form W-3 that must accompany the company's W-2 Forms. Leda Inc. is a 941-SS payer and is a private, for-profit company. Amanda Leda is the owner; phone number is 207-555-8978; no email address to disclose; fax number is 207-555-9898. No third-party sick pay applied for 2016.

DO NOT STAPLE

33333	a Control number	For Official Use Only ▶ OMB No. 1545-0008		

| **b Kind of Payer** (Check one) | 941 ☐ CT-1 ☐ | Military ☐ Hshld. emp. ☐ | 943 ☐ Medicare govt. emp. ☐ | 944 ☐ | **Kind of Employer** (Check one) | None apply ☐ State/local non-501c ☐ | 501c non-govt. ☐ State/local 501c ☐   Federal govt. ☐ | Third-party sick pay (Check if applicable) ☐ |

c Total number of Forms W-2	d Establishment number	1 Wages, tips, other compensation	2 Federal income tax withheld
e Employer identification number (EIN)		3 Social security wages	4 Social security tax withheld
f Employer's name		5 Medicare wages and tips	6 Medicare tax withheld
		7 Social security tips	8 Allocated tips
		9	10 Dependent care benefits
		11 Nonqualified plans	12a Deferred compensation
g Employer's address and ZIP code			
h Other EIN used this year		13 For third-party sick pay use only	12b
15 State Employer's state ID number		14 Income tax withheld by payer of third-party sick pay	
16 State wages, tips, etc.	17 State income tax	18 Local wages, tips, etc.	19 Local income tax
Employer's contact person		Employer's telephone number	For Official Use Only
Employer's fax number		Employer's email address	

Under penalties of perjury, I declare that I have examined this return and accompanying documents and, to the best of my knowledge and belief, they are true, correct, and complete.

Signature ▶   Title ▶   Date ▶

Form **W-3** **Transmittal of Wage and Tax Statements**   **2016**   Department of the Treasury Internal Revenue Service

P5-12A.

LO 5-4, 5-6

Pete's Shelby Shop is a company that restores vintage Ford Mustangs. He has seven employees. Pete wants to perform a benefits analysis report for one of his employees, Kristina Mallhoff, for the year. Kristina's benefits package is as follows:

Salary: $40,000

401(k) contribution: 3% of salary, company match is 50% of employee contribution

Medical insurance deduction: $150 per month

Dental insurance: $25 per month

Complete the following Benefits Analysis Report for Kristina Mallhoff for the year. Do not include FUTA and SUTA taxes.

Yearly Benefit Costs	Company Cost	Kristina's Cost
Medical insurance	$7,200	$
Dental insurance	$1,000	$
Life insurance	$ 200	-0-

(continued)

Yearly Benefit Costs	Company Cost	Kristina's Cost
AD&D	$ 50	-0-
Short-term disability	$ 500	-0-
Long-term disability	$ 250	-0-
401(k)	$	$
Social Security	$	$
Medicare	$	$
Tuition reimbursement	$2,000	-0-
Total yearly benefit costs	$	
Kristina's annual salary	$	
Total yearly benefit costs	$	

P5-13A.

LO 5-4, 5-5

Hoxter Printing has 35 employees distributed among the following departments:

Sales: 10	Factory: 15	Administration: 10

The total annual payroll for Hoxter Printing is $700,000.

Compute the labor distribution based on equal distribution among the departments.

Sales: _____

Factory: _____

Administration: _____

P5-14A.

LO 5-4, 5-5

For Hoxter Printing in P5-13A, compute the labor distribution based on the number of employees per department:

Sales: _____

Factory: _____

Administration: _____

P5-15A.

LO 5-1, 5-4

Wilson's Fine Foods is a specialty grocery store. The employees are classified according to job titles for workers' compensation insurance premium computation purposes.

a. Based on the payroll estimates as of January 1, what is the total estimated workers' compensation premium for 20XX?

Employee Classification	Rate per $100 of payroll	Estimated payroll for 20XX	Workers' Compensation Premium
Grocery Clerk	$0.75	$192,500	
Shelf Stocker	$1.90	$212,160	
Stock Handler	$2.40	$237,120	
		Total Premium =	

b. The actual payroll for 20XX is listed below. What is the workers' compensation premium based on the actual payroll?

Employee Classification	Rate per $100 of payroll	Actual payroll for 20XX	Workers' Compensation Premium
Grocery Clerk	$0.75	$196,588	
Shelf Stocker	$1.90	$215,220	
Stock Handler	$2.40	$242,574	
		Total Premium =	

c. What is the difference between the actual and the estimated premiums? _____

Exercises Set B

E5-1B.

LO 5-1

Of the following taxes, which one(s) is/are examples of statutory deductions that pertain to employers? (Select all that apply.)
A. Social Security tax
B. Employee federal income tax
C. FUTA
D. 401(k) contributions

E5-2B.

LO 5-1

Which of the following is/are true about FUTA obligations? (Select all that apply.)
A. FUTA is an employer-only tax.
B. FUTA is subject to a 5.4% reduction based on employer and state factors.
C. FUTA is subject to a $7,000 wage base per employee.
D. FUTA applies to all companies.

E5-3B.

LO 5-1

Of the IRS-stipulated lookback periods, which one(s) are the most commonly used? (Select all that apply.)
A. Monthly
B. Semiweekly
C. Quarterly
D. Annual

E5-4B.

LO 5-2

The Queen Bee Company has annual payroll taxes of $49,250 during the most recent lookback period. Which payroll deposit frequency will the company have, based on that lookback period?
A. Quarterly
B. Monthly
C. Semiweekly
D. Annual

E5-5B.

LO 5-3

Renny is new payroll accountant with Jupiter Products in Sparks, Nevada. The company had a payroll tax liability of $250,350 during the most recent lookback period. For the quarter ending September 30, 20XX, which federal form(s) should he file? (Select all that apply.)
A. Form 940
B. Form W-2
C. Form SS-8
D. Form 941

E5-6B.

LO 5-3

Which of the following is a form that must accompany all Forms W-2 submitted to the Social Security Administration?
A. Form 941
B. Form 940
C. Form W-3
D. Form W-4

E5-7B.

LO 5-4

What are the penalties associated with the lack of reporting and remitting payroll taxes? (Select all that apply.)
A. Failure to report
B. Failure to file
C. Failure to deposit
D. Failure to remit

E5-8B.

LO 5-4

John Johnson is the accounting supervisor for Block Furnishings, which has chosen to maintain its payroll on an in-house basis for this purpose and has hired new accounting clerks. Which of the following are payroll responsibilities of Block Furnishings? (Select all that apply.)

A. Timely remittance of payroll taxes.

B. Remittance of voluntary deductions.

C. Accountability to employees and governmental agencies.

D. Publication of salary data in company-wide publications.

E5-9B.
LO 5-5

Which of the following represents the difference between the benefit analy-sis report and the annual total compensation report?

A. The benefit analysis report is designed for review by employees.

B. The annual total compensation report's intended audience is company managers.

C. The benefit analysis report reflects actual benefit costs, and the annual total compensation report includes salary data.

D. The reports are maintained as public records.

E5-10B.
LO 5-5

Which of the following represent(s) the purpose(s) of the labor distribution report? (Select all that apply.)

A. Accurate payroll cost allocation among departments.

B. Explanation of individual employee costs.

C. Evaluation of labor planning efforts.

D. Determination of departmental performance.

E5-11B.
LO 5-1, 5-4

Famous Flooring has employees in its manufacturing, sales, and administra-tive departments. Which department will have the highest rate for its work-ers' compensation insurance?

A. Manufacturing.

B. Sales.

C. Administrative.

D. All departments will have the same rate.

Problems Set B

P5-1B.
LO 5-1

Jill works for Mjelde & Fletcher, which pays employees on a semimonthly basis. Jill's annual salary is $210,000. Calculate the following:

Pay Date	Prior YTD Earnings	Social Security Taxable Wages	Medicare Taxable Wages	Employer Share Social Security Tax	Employer Share Medicare Tax
November 30					
December 31					

P5-2B.
LO 5-1, 5-3

Barry's Grill of Andrews, Texas, has the following employees as of December 31:

Employee Name	Annual Taxable Wages
Mark English	$45,750
Shelly Morris	$21,250
TL Radford	$29,850
James Morrow	$36,280
Trella Lyons	$34,900

The company's SUTA tax rate is 6.25% and wage base is $9,000. What is the annual amount of FUTA and SUTA taxes due for each employee?

Employee	FUTA Due	SUTA Due
Mark English		
Shelly Morris		
TL Radford		
James Morrow		
Trella Lyons		

P5-3B.
LO 5-1, 5-2, 5-3

Semolians has 22 employees within Denver City and County. The employees earned $8.50 per hour and worked 160 hours each during the month. The employer must remit $4.00 per month per employee who earns more than $500 per month. Additionally, employees who earn more than $500 per month must have $5.75 withheld from their pay. What is the employee and company Occupational Privilege Tax for these employees?

Employee: _____

Employer: _____

P5-4B.
LO 5-1, 5-2, 5-3

Leslie earned $155,000 in 2016 for a company in Pennsylvania. She is single with four dependents and is paid annually. Leslie contributed $3,550 to her 401(k) plan and $2,000 to her Section 125 plan. Employees in Pennsylvania contribute 0.07% of their gross pay toward SUTA tax, which has a wage base for 2016 of $9,500. Compute Leslie's share of the taxes, using the percentage method tables in Appendix C to determine federal income tax.

Federal income tax: _____

Social Security tax: _____

Medicare tax: _____

SUTA tax: _____

P5-5B.
LO 5-2, 5-3

Using the information from P5-4B, compute the employer's share of the taxes. The FUTA rate within Pennsylvania for 2016 is 0.6% on the first $7,000 of employee wages, and the SUTA rate is 3.456% with a wage base of $9,500.

Federal income tax: _____

Social Security tax: _____

Medicare tax: _____

FUTA tax: _____

SUTA tax: _____

P5-6B.
LO 5-1

Fideaux is a new business owned by Lewis Brooks. His first year of operations commenced on June 1, 2016. What schedule depositor would his company be for the first year of operations?

P5-7B.
LO 5-3

Using the information from P5-6B, complete the following Form 941 for third quarter 2016.

EIN: 98-0050036

Address: 1021 Old Plainfield Road, Salina, California 95670

Phone: 707-555-0303

Number of employees: 8

Wages, tips, and other compensation paid during third quarter 2016: $302,374

Income tax withheld: $51,000

Monthly tax liability:

July	$32,421.08
August	32,421.08
September	32,421.07

P5-8B.
LO 5-3

Using the information from P5-6B and P5-7B for Fideaux, complete the following State of California Form DE-9, Quarterly Contribution Return and Report of Wages. The California employer account number is 989-8877-1. Use 5.4% as the UI rate, 0.1% as the ETT rate, and 0.9% as the SDI rate. All employees have worked since July 1 with the company. The California PIT taxes withheld for the quarter are $40,000. The company has deposited no taxes for the quarter.

Form **941 for 2016:** Employer's QUARTERLY Federal Tax Return

(Rev. January 2016)   Department of the Treasury — Internal Revenue Service

950114

OMB No. 1545-0029

Employer identification number (EIN) ☐☐ – ☐☐☐☐☐☐☐

Name *(not your trade name)* _____

Trade name *(if any)* _____

Address _____
Number   Street   Suite or room number

_____
City   State   ZIP code

_____
Foreign country name   Foreign province/county   Foreign postal code

Report for this Quarter of 2016
(Check one.)

☐ **1:** January, February, March

☐ **2:** April, May, June

☐ **3:** July, August, September

☐ **4:** October, November, December

Instructions and prior year forms are available at *www.irs.gov/form941.*

Read the separate instructions before you complete Form 941. Type or print within the boxes.

Part 1:   Answer these questions for this quarter.

1 Number of employees who received wages, tips, or other compensation for the pay period including: *Mar. 12* (Quarter 1), *June 12* (Quarter 2), *Sept. 12* (Quarter 3), or *Dec. 12* (Quarter 4)   **1** _____

2 Wages, tips, and other compensation   . . . .   **2** _____

3 Federal income tax withheld from wages, tips, and other compensation   . . . . . .   **3** _____

4 If no wages, tips, and other compensation are subject to social security or Medicare tax   ☐ Check and go to line 6.

		Column 1		Column 2
5a	Taxable social security wages . .	_____ .	× .124 =	_____ .
5b	Taxable social security tips . . .	_____ .	× .124 =	_____ .
5c	Taxable Medicare wages & tips. .	_____ .	× .029 =	_____ .
5d	Taxable wages & tips subject to Additional Medicare Tax withholding	_____ .	× .009 =	_____ .

5e Add Column 2 from lines 5a, 5b, 5c, and 5d   . . . .   **5e** _____

5f Section 3121(q) Notice and Demand—Tax due on unreported tips (see instructions)   . .   **5f** _____

6 Total taxes before adjustments. Add lines 3, 5e, and 5f   . . . .   **6** _____

7 Current quarter's adjustment for fractions of cents   . . . .   **7** _____

8 Current quarter's adjustment for sick pay   . . . .   **8** _____

9 Current quarter's adjustments for tips and group-term life insurance   . . . . . .   **9** _____

10 Total taxes after adjustments. Combine lines 6 through 9   . . . . . .   **10** _____

11 Total deposits for this quarter, including overpayment applied from a prior quarter and overpayments applied from Form 941-X, 941-X (PR), 944-X, or 944-X (SP) filed in the current quarter   . . . .   **11** _____

12 Balance due. If line 10 is more than line 11, enter the difference and see instructions   . . .   **12** _____

13 Overpayment. If line 11 is more than line 10, enter the difference   _____ .   Check one: ☐ Apply to next return. ☐ Send a refund.

▶ **You MUST complete both pages of Form 941 and SIGN it.**

Next ▶

For Privacy Act and Paperwork Reduction Act Notice, see the back of the Payment Voucher.   Cat. No. 17001Z   Form **941** (Rev. 1-2016)

950214

Name *(not your trade name)*	Employer identification number (EIN)

Part 2:　**Tell us about your deposit schedule and tax liability for this quarter.**

If you are unsure about whether you are a monthly schedule depositor or a semiweekly schedule depositor, see section 11 of Pub. 15.

14　Check one:　☐　Line 10 on this return is less than $2,500 or line 10 on the return for the prior quarter was less than $2,500, and you did not incur a $100,000 next-day deposit obligation during the current quarter. If line 10 for the prior quarter was less than $2,500 but line 10 on this return is $100,000 or more, you must provide a record of your federal tax liability. If you are a monthly schedule depositor, complete the deposit schedule below; if you are a semiweekly schedule depositor, attach Schedule B (Form 941). Go to Part 3.

☐　**You were a monthly schedule depositor for the entire quarter.** Enter your tax liability for each month and total liability for the quarter, then go to Part 3.

Tax liability:　Month 1　☐ .

Month 2　☐ .

Month 3　☐ .

Total liability for quarter　☐ .　Total must equal line 10.

☐　**You were a semiweekly schedule depositor for any part of this quarter.** Complete Schedule B (Form 941), Report of Tax Liability for Semiweekly Schedule Depositors, and attach it to Form 941.

Part 3:　**Tell us about your business. If a question does NOT apply to your business, leave it blank.**

15　If your business has closed or you stopped paying wages . . . . ☐ Check here, and

enter the final date you paid wages　☐ / / .

16　If you are a seasonal employer and you do not have to file a return for every quarter of the year . . ☐ Check here.

Part 4:　**May we speak with your third-party designee?**

Do you want to allow an employee, a paid tax preparer, or another person to discuss this return with the IRS? See the instructions for details.

☐ Yes.　Designee's name and phone number

Select a 5-digit Personal Identification Number (PIN) to use when talking to the IRS.　☐ ☐ ☐ ☐ ☐

☐ No.

Part 5:　**Sign here. You MUST complete both pages of Form 941 and SIGN it.**

Under penalties of perjury, I declare that I have examined this return, including accompanying schedules and statements, and to the best of my knowledge and belief, it is true, correct, and complete. Declaration of preparer (other than taxpayer) is based on all information of which preparer has any knowledge.

X　**Sign your name here**

Print your name here

Print your title here

Date　/ /

Best daytime phone

Paid Preparer Use Only　　Check if you are self-employed . . . ☐

Preparer's name		PTIN
Preparer's signature		Date / /
Firm's name (or yours if self-employed)		EIN
Address		Phone
City	State	ZIP code

Source: Internal Revenue Service.

 **Employment Development Department**
State of California

QUARTERLY CONTRIBUTION
RETURN AND REPORT OF WAGES
REMINDER: File your DE 9 and DE 9C together.

PLEASE TYPE THIS FORM—DO NOT ALTER PREPRINTED INFORMATION   00090112

QUARTER ENDED   DUE   DELINQUENT IF NOT POSTMARKED OR RECEIVED BY

YR   QTR

EMPLOYER ACCOUNT NO.

DO NOT ALTER THIS AREA

DEPT. USE ONLY

| P1 | P2 | C | P | U | S | A |

T

Mo.   Day   Yr.

EFFECTIVE DATE

FEIN _____   **A.** NO WAGES PAID THIS QUARTER ☐   **B.** OUT OF BUSINESS/NO EMPLOYEES ☐

ADDITIONAL FEINS _____   _____   **B1.** OUT OF BUSINESS DATE
M M D D Y Y Y Y

C. TOTAL SUBJECT WAGES PAID THIS QUARTER ....

D. UNEMPLOYMENT INSURANCE (UI) (Total Employee Wages up to $ _____ per employee per calendar year)

(D1) UI Rate % _____   TIMES   (D2) UI TAXABLE WAGES FOR THE QUARTER _____   =   (D3) UI CONTRIBUTIONS   0:00

E. EMPLOYMENT TRAINING TAX (ETT)

(E1) ETT Rate % _____   TIMES   UI Taxable Wages for the Quarter (D2) ...... =   (E2) ETT CONTRIBUTIONS   0:00

F. STATE DISABILITY INSURANCE (SDI) (Total Employee Wages up to $ _____ per employee per calendar year)

(F1) SDI Rate % _____   TIMES   (F2) SDI TAXABLE WAGES FOR THE QUARTER _____   =   (F3) SDI EMPLOYEE CONTRIBUTIONS WITHHELD   0:00

G. CALIFORNIA PERSONAL INCOME TAX (PIT) WITHHELD ....

H. SUBTOTAL (Add Items D3, E2, F3, and G) 0:00

I. LESS: CONTRIBUTIONS AND WITHHOLDINGS PAID FOR THE QUARTER ....
(**DO NOT** INCLUDE PENALTY AND INTEREST PAYMENTS)

J. TOTAL TAXES DUE OR OVERPAID   (Item H minus Item I) 0:00

If amount due, prepare a *Payroll Tax Deposit* (DE 88), include the correct payment quarter, and mail to: Employment Development Department, P.O. Box 826276, Sacramento, CA 94230-6276. **NOTE:** Do not mail payments along with the DE 9 and *Quarterly Contribution Return and Report of Wages (Continuation) (DE 9C)*, as this may delay processing and result in erroneous penalty and interest charges. **Mandatory Electronic Funds Transfer (EFT)** filers must remit all SDI/PIT deposits by EFT to avoid a noncompliance penalty.

K. I declare that the above, to the best of my knowledge and belief, is true and correct. If a refund was claimed, a reasonable effort was made to refund any erroneous deductions to the affected employee(s).

Signature *Required* _____   Title _____   Phone (___) _____   Date _____
(Owner, Accountant, Preparer, etc.)

SIGN AND MAIL TO: State of California / Employment Development Department / P.O. Box 989071 / West Sacramento CA 95798-9071

DE 9 Rev. 2 (7-14) (**INTERNET**)   Page 1 of 2   Fast, Easy, and Convenient! Visit EDD's Web site at www.edd.ca.gov

Source: Employment Development Department.

P5-9B.

LO 5-3

Blier's Bears paid its nine employees a total of $432,586.40 during 2015. All employees have worked there for the full calendar year and reached the FUTA wage base during the first quarter. Taxes were deposited. The employer contributed $12,470 to Section 125 plans during the year (payments exempt from FUTA). Blier's Bears is located at 783 Morehead Street, Fargo, ND 68383, phone number 701-555-3432. The owner is Noah Jackson, and the EIN is 73-4029848. Complete Form 940 for Blier's Bears.

P5-10B.

LO 5-3

Philip Castor, owner of Castor Corporation, is located at 1310 Garrick Way, Sun Valley, Arizona, 86029, phone number 928-555-8842. The federal EIN is 20-1948348, and the state employer identification number is 9040-2038-1. Prepare Form W-2 for each of the following employees of Castor Corporation as of December 31, 2016. The same deductions are allowed for state income tax as for federal.

Paul M. Parsons 5834 Moon Drive Sun Valley, AZ 86029 SSN: 578-33-3049	Total 2016 wages: $47,203.78 401(k) contribution: $2,832.23 Section 125 contribution: $1,400.00 Federal income tax withheld: $5,664.45 Social Security tax withheld: $2,839.83 Medicare tax withheld: $664.15 State income tax withheld: $1,443.84
Rachel Y. Maddox 32 Second Street Holbrook, AZ 86025 SSN: 734-00-1938 Tuition in excess of $5,250: $750	Total 2016 wages: $37,499.02 401(k) contribution: $1,124.97 Section 125 contribution: $500.00 Federal income tax withheld: $4,409.88 Social Security tax withheld: $2,293.94 Medicare tax withheld: $536.49 State income tax withheld: $1,180.92
Ari J. Featherstone 7784 Painted Desert Road Sun Valley, AZ 86029 SSN: 290-03-4992	Total 2016 wages: $41,904.29 401(k) contribution: $1,885.69 Federal income tax withheld: $5,028.52 Social Security tax withheld: $2,598.07 Medicare tax withheld: $607.61 State income tax withheld: $1,344.63
Connor L. Clearwater 7384 Ridge Road Woodruff, AZ 85942 SSN: 994-20-4837	Total 2016 wages: $29,874.37 401(k) contribution: $597.49 Section 125 contribution: $250.00 Federal income tax withheld: $3,584.92 Social Security tax withheld: $1,836.71 Medicare tax withheld: $429.55 State income tax withheld: $975.30
Tieya L. Millen 229 Second Street #4A Holbrook, AZ 86025 SSN: 477-30-2234	Total 2016 wages: $15,889.04 Federal income tax withheld: $1,906.69 Social Security tax withheld: $985.12 Medicare tax withheld: $230.39 State income tax withheld: $533.87

P5-11B.

LO 5-3

Using the information from P5-10B for Castor Corporation, complete Form W-3 that must accompany the company's Forms W-2. Castor Corporation is a 941-SS payer and is a private, for-profit company. No third-party sick pay was applied for 2016.

P5-12B.

LO 5-5, 5-6

Nanco is a company that makes custom signs and has 12 employees. The owner wants to perform a benefits analysis report for the year for one of its employees, Ben Loomes. Ben's benefits package is as follows:

Salary: $38,950

Form **940 for 2015:** Employer's Annual Federal Unemployment (FUTA) Tax Return

850113

Department of the Treasury — Internal Revenue Service

OMB No. 1545-0028

Employer identification number (EIN)

☐☐ – ☐☐☐☐☐☐☐

Name *(not your trade name)*

Trade name *(if any)*

Address

Number   Street   Suite or room number

City   State   ZIP code

Foreign country name   Foreign province/county   Foreign postal code

Type of Return
(Check all that apply.)

☐ **a.** Amended

☐ **b.** Successor employer

☐ **c.** No payments to employees in 2015

☐ **d.** Final: Business closed or stopped paying wages

Instructions and prior-year forms are available at *www.irs.gov/form940*.

Read the separate instructions before you complete this form. Please type or print within the boxes.

Part 1:   Tell us about your return. If any line does NOT apply, leave it blank. See instructions before completing Part 1.

1a	If you had to pay state unemployment tax in one state only, enter the state abbreviation .	**1a** ☐☐
1b	If you had to pay state unemployment tax in more than one state, you are a multi-state employer	**1b** ☐ Check here. Complete Schedule A (Form 940).
2	If you paid wages in a state that is subject to CREDIT REDUCTION	**2** ☐ Check here. Complete Schedule A (Form 940).

Part 2:   Determine your FUTA tax before adjustments. If any line does NOT apply, leave it blank.

3	Total payments to all employees	**3**
4	Payments exempt from FUTA tax **4**	

Check all that apply: **4a** ☐ Fringe benefits   **4c** ☐ Retirement/Pension   **4e** ☐ Other

4b ☐ Group-term life insurance   **4d** ☐ Dependent care

5	Total of payments made to each employee in excess of $7,000 . . . . **5**	
6	**Subtotal** (line 4 + line 5 = line 6)	**6**
7	Total taxable FUTA wages (line 3 – line 6 = line 7) (see instructions)	**7**
8	FUTA tax before adjustments (line 7 x .006 = line 8)	**8**

Part 3:   Determine your adjustments. If any line does NOT apply, leave it blank.

9	If **ALL** of the taxable FUTA wages you paid were excluded from state unemployment tax, multiply line 7 by .054 (line 7 × .054 = line 9). Go to line 12	**9**
10	If **SOME** of the taxable FUTA wages you paid were excluded from state unemployment tax, **OR you paid ANY state unemployment tax late** (after the due date for filing Form 940), complete the worksheet in the instructions. Enter the amount from line 7 of the worksheet . .	**10**
11	If credit reduction applies, enter the total from Schedule A (Form 940)	**11**

Part 4:   Determine your FUTA tax and balance due or overpayment. If any line does NOT apply, leave it blank.

12	Total FUTA tax after adjustments (lines 8 + 9 + 10 + 11 = line 12)	**12**
13	FUTA tax deposited for the year, including any overpayment applied from a prior year .	**13**
14	Balance due (If line 12 is more than line 13, enter the excess on line 14.)	
	• If line 14 is more than $500, you must deposit your tax.	
	• If line 14 is $500 or less, you may pay with this return. (see instructions)	**14**
15	Overpayment (If line 13 is more than line 12, enter the excess on line 15 and check a box below.)	**15**

▶ You **MUST** complete both pages of this form and **SIGN** it.

Check one: ☐ Apply to next return.   ☐ Send a refund.

Next ▶

For Privacy Act and Paperwork Reduction Act Notice, see the back of Form 940-V, Payment Voucher.   Cat. No. 11234O   Form **940** (2015)

850212

Name *(not your trade name)*	Employer identification number (EIN)

Part 5:   Report your FUTA tax liability by quarter only if line 12 is more than $500. If not, go to Part 6.

16   Report the amount of your FUTA tax liability for each quarter; do NOT enter the amount you deposited. If you had no liability for a quarter, leave the line blank.

16a   **1st quarter** (January 1 – March 31) .   .   .   .   **16a**   [.   ]

16b   **2nd quarter** (April 1 – June 30) .   .   .   .   **16b**   [.   ]

16c   **3rd quarter** (July 1 – September 30) .   .   .   .   .   .   **16c**   [.   ]

16d   **4th quarter** (October 1 – December 31) .   .   .   .   .   **16d**   [.   ]

17   **Total tax liability for the year** (lines 16a + 16b + 16c + 16d = line 17)   **17**   [.   ]   **Total must equal line 12.**

Part 6:   May we speak with your third-party designee?

Do you want to allow an employee, a paid tax preparer, or another person to discuss this return with the IRS? See the instructions for details.

☐ **Yes.**   Designee's name and phone number   [   ]   [   ]

           Select a 5-digit Personal Identification Number (PIN) to use when talking to IRS   [ ] [ ] [ ] [ ] [ ]

☐ **No.**

Part 7:   Sign here. You MUST complete both pages of this form and SIGN it.

Under penalties of perjury, I declare that I have examined this return, including accompanying schedules and statements, and to the best of my knowledge and belief, it is true, correct, and complete, and that no part of any payment made to a state unemployment fund claimed as a credit was, or is to be, deducted from the payments made to employees. Declaration of preparer (other than taxpayer) is based on all information of which preparer has any knowledge.

✗ **Sign your name here**   [   ]   Print your name here [   ]

           Print your title here [   ]

Date   [/   /   ]   Best daytime phone [   ]

Paid Preparer Use Only   Check if you are self-employed . ☐

Preparer's name	[ ]	PTIN	[ ]
Preparer's signature	[ ]	Date	[/ /]
Firm's name (or yours if self-employed)	[ ]	EIN	[ ]
Address	[ ]	Phone	[ ]
City	[ ] State [ ]	ZIP code	[ ]

Page **2**   Form **940** (2015)

Source: Internal Revenue Service.

22222	Void ☐	**a** Employee's social security number	For Official Use Only ▶ OMB No. 1545-0008	

b Employer identification number (EIN)		**1** Wages, tips, other compensation	**2** Federal income tax withheld
c Employer's name, address, and ZIP code		**3** Social security wages	**4** Social security tax withheld
		5 Medicare wages and tips	**6** Medicare tax withheld
		7 Social security tips	**8** Allocated tips
d Control number		**9**	**10** Dependent care benefits
e Employee's first name and initial Last name Suff.		**11** Nonqualified plans	**12a** See instructions for box 12
		13 Statutory employee ☐ Retirement plan ☐ Third-party sick pay ☐	**12b**
		14 Other	**12c**
			12d
f Employee's address and ZIP code			

15 State Employer's state ID number	**16** State wages, tips, etc.	**17** State income tax	**18** Local wages, tips, etc.	**19** Local income tax	**20** Locality name

Form **W-2** Wage and Tax Statement   **2016**   Department of the Treasury—Internal Revenue Service

---

22222	Void ☐	**a** Employee's social security number	For Official Use Only ▶ OMB No. 1545-0008	

b Employer identification number (EIN)		**1** Wages, tips, other compensation	**2** Federal income tax withheld
c Employer's name, address, and ZIP code		**3** Social security wages	**4** Social security tax withheld
		5 Medicare wages and tips	**6** Medicare tax withheld
		7 Social security tips	**8** Allocated tips
d Control number		**9**	**10** Dependent care benefits
e Employee's first name and initial Last name Suff.		**11** Nonqualified plans	**12a** See instructions for box 12
		13 Statutory employee ☐ Retirement plan ☐ Third-party sick pay ☐	**12b**
		14 Other	**12c**
			12d
f Employee's address and ZIP code			

15 State Employer's state ID number	**16** State wages, tips, etc.	**17** State income tax	**18** Local wages, tips, etc.	**19** Local income tax	**20** Locality name

Form **W-2** Wage and Tax Statement   **2016**   Department of the Treasury—Internal Revenue Service

22222	Void ☐	**a** Employee's social security number	For Official Use Only ▶ OMB No. 1545-0008	

b Employer identification number (EIN)		**1** Wages, tips, other compensation	**2** Federal income tax withheld

c Employer's name, address, and ZIP code	**3** Social security wages	**4** Social security tax withheld
	5 Medicare wages and tips	**6** Medicare tax withheld
	7 Social security tips	**8** Allocated tips
d Control number	**9**	**10** Dependent care benefits

e Employee's first name and initial	Last name	Suff.	**11** Nonqualified plans	**12a** See instructions for box 12
			13 Statutory employee ☐ Retirement plan ☐ Third-party sick pay ☐	**12b**
			14 Other	**12c**
				12d

f Employee's address and ZIP code

15 State	Employer's state ID number	**16** State wages, tips, etc.	**17** State income tax	**18** Local wages, tips, etc.	**19** Local income tax	**20** Locality name

Form **W-2** Wage and Tax Statement　　**2016**　　Department of the Treasury—Internal Revenue Service

22222	Void ☐	**a** Employee's social security number	For Official Use Only ▶ OMB No. 1545-0008	

b Employer identification number (EIN)		**1** Wages, tips, other compensation	**2** Federal income tax withheld

c Employer's name, address, and ZIP code	**3** Social security wages	**4** Social security tax withheld
	5 Medicare wages and tips	**6** Medicare tax withheld
	7 Social security tips	**8** Allocated tips
d Control number	**9**	**10** Dependent care benefits

e Employee's first name and initial	Last name	Suff.	**11** Nonqualified plans	**12a** See instructions for box 12
			13 Statutory employee ☐ Retirement plan ☐ Third-party sick pay ☐	**12b**
			14 Other	**12c**
				12d

f Employee's address and ZIP code

15 State	Employer's state ID number	**16** State wages, tips, etc.	**17** State income tax	**18** Local wages, tips, etc.	**19** Local income tax	**20** Locality name

Form **W-2** Wage and Tax Statement　　**2016**　　Department of the Treasury—Internal Revenue Service

22222	Void ☐	**a** Employee's social security number	For Official Use Only ▶ OMB No. 1545-0008	

b Employer identification number (EIN)			**1** Wages, tips, other compensation	**2** Federal income tax withheld
c Employer's name, address, and ZIP code			**3** Social security wages	**4** Social security tax withheld
			5 Medicare wages and tips	**6** Medicare tax withheld
			7 Social security tips	**8** Allocated tips
d Control number			**9**	**10** Dependent care benefits
e Employee's first name and initial	Last name	Suff.	**11** Nonqualified plans	**12a** See instructions for box 12
			13 Statutory employee ☐ Retirement plan ☐ Third-party sick pay ☐	**12b**
			14 Other	**12c**
				12d
f Employee's address and ZIP code				

15 State	Employer's state ID number	**16** State wages, tips, etc.	**17** State income tax	**18** Local wages, tips, etc.	**19** Local income tax	**20** Locality name

Form **W-2**   Wage and Tax Statement   **2016**   Department of the Treasury—Internal Revenue Service

---

DO NOT STAPLE

33333	**a** Control number	For Official Use Only ▶ OMB No. 1545-0008	

b Kind of Payer (Check one)	941 ☐ Military ☐ 943 ☐ 944 ☐ CT-1 ☐ Hshld. emp. ☐ Medicare govt. emp. ☐	**Kind of Employer** (Check one)	None apply ☐ 501c non-govt. ☐ State/local non-501c ☐ State/local 501c ☐ Federal govt. ☐	Third-party sick pay (Check if applicable) ☐

c Total number of Forms W-2	**d** Establishment number	**1** Wages, tips, other compensation	**2** Federal income tax withheld
e Employer identification number (EIN)		**3** Social security wages	**4** Social security tax withheld
f Employer's name		**5** Medicare wages and tips	**6** Medicare tax withheld
		7 Social security tips	**8** Allocated tips
		9	**10** Dependent care benefits
		11 Nonqualified plans	**12a** Deferred compensation
g Employer's address and ZIP code			
h Other EIN used this year		**13** For third-party sick pay use only	**12b**
15 State Employer's state ID number		**14** Income tax withheld by payer of third-party sick pay	
16 State wages, tips, etc.	**17** State income tax	**18** Local wages, tips, etc.	**19** Local income tax
Employer's contact person		Employer's telephone number	For Official Use Only
Employer's fax number		Employer's email address	

Under penalties of perjury, I declare that I have examined this return and accompanying documents and, to the best of my knowledge and belief, they are true, correct, and complete.

Signature ▶   Title ▶   Date ▶

Form **W-3**   Transmittal of Wage and Tax Statements   **2016**   Department of the Treasury Internal Revenue Service

401(k) contribution: 5% of salary, company match is half of employee's contribution up to 6%

Medical insurance deduction: $140 per month

Dental insurance: $36 per month

Complete the following Benefits Analysis Report for Ben Loomes for the year.

Yearly Benefit Costs	Company Cost	Ben's Cost
Medical insurance	$9,600	$
Dental insurance	$ 800	$
Life insurance	$1,200	-0-
AD&D	$ 125	-0-
Short-term disability	$ 500	-0-
Long-term disability	$ 250	-0-
401(k)	$	$
Social Security	$	$
Medicare	$	$
Tuition reimbursement	$5,000	-0-
Total yearly benefit costs	$	
Ben's annual salary	$	
Total yearly benefit costs	$	
Total value of Ben's compensation	$	

P5-13B.

LO 5-4, 5-5

Hammond Enterprises has 52 employees distributed among the following departments:

Sales: 14	Factory: 26	Administration: 12

The total annual payroll for Hammond Enterprises is $1,280,550.

Compute the labor distribution based on equal distribution among the departments.

Sales: _____

Factory: _____

Administration: _____

P5-14B.

LO 5-4, 5-5

For Hammond Enterprises in P5-13B, compute the labor distribution based on the number of employees per department:

Sales: _____

Factory: _____

Administration: _____

P5-15B.

LO 5-1, 5-4

Francesco's Furniture is a retail furniture store. Employees are classified according to job title for workers' compensation insurance premium computation purposes.

a. Based on the following payroll estimates as of January 1, what is the estimated workers' compensation insurance premium for the year 20XX?

Employee Classification	Rate per $100 of Payroll	Estimated Payroll for 20XX	Workers' Compensation Premium
Sales Associate	$0.55	$213,680	
Loader	$2.15	$155,240	
Furniture Builder	$2.95	$102,590	
		Total Premium =	

b. The actual payroll for 20XX is listed below. What is the workers' compensation premium based on the actual payroll?

Employee Classification	Rate per $100 of Payroll	Actual Payroll for 20XX	Workers' Compensation Premium
Sales Associate	$0.55	$228,944	
Loader	$2.15	$163,743	
Furniture Builder	$2.95	$105,389	
		Total Premium =	

c. What is the difference between the actual and the estimated premiums? _____

Critical Thinking

5-1. Maggie's Memories is a semiweekly depositor. Following the success of a special project, Maggie, the owner, pays each of the 250 employees a $20,000 bonus on August 17, 2016. Assuming a 25% income tax rate, when will Maggie need to deposit the payroll taxes?

5-2. Chris is the president of a military regalia antique business, War Arts. His employee, Barry Williams, is due a raise. Barry's current benefit analysis is as follows:

Yearly Benefit Costs	Company Cost (Current)	Employee Cost (Current)
Medical insurance	$ 8,000	$ 1,200
Dental insurance	$ 120	$ 120
Life insurance	$ 300	-0-
AD&D	$ 150	-0-
Short-term disability	$ 60	-0-
Long-term disability	$ 30	-0-
401(k)	$ 750	$ 1,500
Social Security	$ 3,018.16	$3,018.16
Medicare	$ 705.86	$ 705.86
Tuition reimbursement	$ 2,000	-0-
Total yearly benefit costs (employer)	$15,134.02	
Employee's annual salary	$ 50,000	
Total value of employee's compensation	$65,134.02	

Compute the benefit analysis assuming:
- 7% increase in pay.
- 3% contribution to 401(k) will remain the same with a company match of 50%.
- 10% increase in medical and dental insurance premiums.

Yearly Benefit Costs	Company Cost (New)	Employee Cost (New)
Medical insurance	$	$
Dental insurance	$	$
Life insurance	$	-0-
AD&D	$	-0-
Short-term disability	$	-0-
Long-term disability	$	-0-
401(k)	$	$
Social Security	$	$
Medicare	$	$
Tuition reimbursement	$	-0-
Total yearly benefit costs (employer)	$	
Barry's annual salary	$	
Total value of employee's compensation	$	

In the Real World: Scenario for Discussion

In Little Rock, Arkansas, a church pastor was found guilty of payroll tax fraud by withholding employee payroll taxes and failing to remit them from 2006 through 2010. The pastor is serving a sentence of 33 months in prison with 5 years of supervised release and $450,000 in restitution to the IRS. Do you think this was a fair sentence? Why or why not?

Internet Activities

5-1. Try the withholding calculator from the IRS. Go to www.irs.gov/individuals and use the withholding calculator.

5-2. Go to www.bizfilings.com/toolkit/sbg/tax-info/payroll-taxes/unemployment.aspx and check out the unemployment tax laws for your state.

5-3. Want to know more about the concepts in this chapter? Go to one or more of the following sites. What are two or three things you notice about the information on the site?

www.smallbusiness.chron.com/example-employee-compensation-plan-10068.html

http://yourbusiness.azcentral.com/labor-cost-distribution-report-26061.html

www.irs.gov/publications/p80/ar02.html

Continuing Payroll Project: Prevosti Farms and Sugarhouse

The first quarter tax return needs to be filed for Prevosti Farms and Sugarhouse by April 15, 2016. For the purpose of the taxes, assume the February payroll amounts were duplicated for the March 10 and March 24 payroll periods.

Number of employees	8
Quarterly wages	$32,010.17
Federal income tax withheld	$ 988.00
401(k) contributions	$ 1,257.65
Insurance withheld	$ 4,080.00
Month 1	-0-
Month 2	$ 2,133.22
Month 3	$ 3,128.12

Complete Form 941 for Prevosti Farms and Sugarhouse. Prevosti Farms and Sugarhouse was assigned EIN 22-6654454.

Form **941 for 2016:** Employer's QUARTERLY Federal Tax Return

(Rev. January 2016)

Department of the Treasury — Internal Revenue Service

950114

OMB No. 1545-0029

Employer identification number (EIN) [ ][ ] — [ ][ ][ ][ ][ ][ ]

Name *(not your trade name)* [_____]

Trade name *(if any)* [_____]

Address [_____]

Number   Street   Suite or room number

[_____]

City   State   ZIP code

[_____]

Foreign country name   Foreign province/county   Foreign postal code

Report for this Quarter of 2016
(Check one.)

☐ 1: January, February, March

☐ 2: April, May, June

☐ 3: July, August, September

☐ 4: October, November, December

Instructions and prior year forms are available at *www.irs.gov/form941*.

Read the separate instructions before you complete Form 941. Type or print within the boxes.

Part 1: **Answer these questions for this quarter.**

1 Number of employees who received wages, tips, or other compensation for the pay period including: *Mar. 12* (Quarter 1), *June 12* (Quarter 2), *Sept. 12* (Quarter 3), or *Dec. 12* (Quarter 4) **1** [_____]

2 Wages, tips, and other compensation . . . . **2** [_____]

3 Federal income tax withheld from wages, tips, and other compensation . . . . . . **3** [_____]

4 If no wages, tips, and other compensation are subject to social security or Medicare tax ☐ Check and go to line 6.

	Column 1		Column 2
5a Taxable social security wages . .	[_____]	× .124 =	[_____]
5b Taxable social security tips . . .	[_____]	× .124 =	[_____]
5c Taxable Medicare wages & tips. .	[_____]	× .029 =	[_____]
5d Taxable wages & tips subject to Additional Medicare Tax withholding	[_____]	× .009 =	[_____]

5e Add Column 2 from lines 5a, 5b, 5c, and 5d . . . . **5e** [_____]

5f Section 3121(q) Notice and Demand—Tax due on unreported tips (see instructions) . . **5f** [_____]

6 Total taxes before adjustments. Add lines 3, 5e, and 5f . . . . **6** [_____]

7 Current quarter's adjustment for fractions of cents . . . . **7** [_____]

8 Current quarter's adjustment for sick pay . . . . **8** [_____]

9 Current quarter's adjustments for tips and group-term life insurance . . . . **9** [_____]

10 Total taxes after adjustments. Combine lines 6 through 9 . . . . . . **10** [_____]

11 Total deposits for this quarter, including overpayment applied from a prior quarter and overpayments applied from Form 941-X, 941-X (PR), 944-X, or 944-X (SP) filed in the current quarter . . . . **11** [_____]

12 Balance due. If line 10 is more than line 11, enter the difference and see instructions . . . **12** [_____]

13 Overpayment. If line 11 is more than line 10, enter the difference [_____] Check one: ☐ Apply to next return. ☐ Send a refund.

▶ **You MUST complete both pages of Form 941 and SIGN it.**

Next ▶

For Privacy Act and Paperwork Reduction Act Notice, see the back of the Payment Voucher.   Cat. No. 17001Z   Form **941** (Rev. 1-2016)

950214

Name *(not your trade name)*	Employer identification number (EIN)

Part 2: **Tell us about your deposit schedule and tax liability for this quarter.**

If you are unsure about whether you are a monthly schedule depositor or a semiweekly schedule depositor, see section 11 of Pub. 15.

14 Check one: ☐ Line 10 on this return is less than $2,500 or line 10 on the return for the prior quarter was less than $2,500, and you did not incur a $100,000 next-day deposit obligation during the current quarter. If line 10 for the prior quarter was less than $2,500 but line 10 on this return is $100,000 or more, you must provide a record of your federal tax liability. If you are a monthly schedule depositor, complete the deposit schedule below; if you are a semiweekly schedule depositor, attach Schedule B (Form 941). Go to Part 3.

☐ **You were a monthly schedule depositor for the entire quarter.** Enter your tax liability for each month and total liability for the quarter, then go to Part 3.

Tax liability: Month 1 [.]

Month 2 [.]

Month 3 [.]

Total liability for quarter [.]   Total must equal line 10.

☐ **You were a semiweekly schedule depositor for any part of this quarter.** Complete Schedule B (Form 941), Report of Tax Liability for Semiweekly Schedule Depositors, and attach it to Form 941.

Part 3: **Tell us about your business. If a question does NOT apply to your business, leave it blank.**

15 If your business has closed or you stopped paying wages . . . . ☐ Check here, and

enter the final date you paid wages [/   /   ] .

16 If you are a seasonal employer and you do not have to file a return for every quarter of the year . . ☐ Check here.

Part 4: **May we speak with your third-party designee?**

Do you want to allow an employee, a paid tax preparer, or another person to discuss this return with the IRS? See the instructions for details.

☐ Yes. Designee's name and phone number [   ] [   ]

Select a 5-digit Personal Identification Number (PIN) to use when talking to the IRS. ☐ ☐ ☐ ☐ ☐

☐ No.

Part 5: **Sign here. You MUST complete both pages of Form 941 and SIGN it.**

Under penalties of perjury, I declare that I have examined this return, including accompanying schedules and statements, and to the best of my knowledge and belief, it is true, correct, and complete. Declaration of preparer (other than taxpayer) is based on all information of which preparer has any knowledge.

X Sign your name here [   ]

Print your name here [   ]

Print your title here [   ]

Date [/   /   ]

Best daytime phone [   ]

Paid Preparer Use Only   Check if you are self-employed . . . ☐

Preparer's name	[ ]	PTIN [ ]
Preparer's signature	[ ]	Date [/ /]
Firm's name (or yours if self-employed)	[ ]	EIN [ ]
Address	[ ]	Phone [ ]
City	[ ] State [ ]	ZIP code [ ]

Source: Internal Revenue Service.

Answers to Stop & Check Exercises

FUTA and SUTA

1.

$$
\begin{array}{rl}
\text{FUTA: } \$7{,}000 \times 29 \times 0.006 = & \$ \ 1{,}218.00 \\
\$2{,}575 \times 0.006 = & \$ \quad 15.45 \\
\text{FUTA Liability} & \$ \ 1{,}233.45 \\
\text{SUTA: } \$24{,}100 \times 25 \times 0.042 = & \$25{,}305.00 \\
\$60{,}090 \times 0.042 = & \$ \ 2{,}523.78 \\
\text{SUTA Liability} & \$27{,}828.78 \\
\text{Total combined FUTA/SUTA liability} & \$29{,}062.23
\end{array}
$$

2.

$$
\begin{array}{rl}
\text{FUTA: } \$7{,}000 \times 10 \times 0.006 = & \$ \quad 420.00 \\
(\$5{,}500 + 6{,}800) \times 0.006 = & 73.80 \\
\text{Total FUTA liability} & \$ \quad 493.80 \\
\text{SUTA: } \$12{,}000 \times 8 \times 0.0326 = & \$ \ 3{,}129.60 \\
\$33{,}250 \times 0.0326 = & \$ \ 1{,}083.95 \\
\text{Total SUTA liability} & \$ \ 4{,}213.55
\end{array}
$$

Competitive Skills Scholarship tax liability: $\$279{,}580 \times 0.0006 = \$ \quad 167.75$

3.

Job Classification	Premium per $100 of Payroll	Estimated Payroll	Premium Due
Clerical Workers	$0.45	$104,550	$ 470.48
Jump Instructors	$3.75	$215,690	$8,088.38
			$8,528.86

Reporting Periods

1. Monthly.
2. July 15.
3. Monday, the next business day.

Tax Forms

1. $2,414.48.
2. $105,000 (15 employees × $7,000).
3. $630.00 ($105,000 (from problem 2) × 0.006 FUTA rate).
4. $116,195.

Payroll-Related Business Expenses

1. Failure to File and Failure to Deposit penalties.
2. Payroll expenses relate to the company's profitability, worker productivity analyses, employee retention, and business competitiveness.

Labor Distribution Report

1. a. $300,000/10 employees = $30,000 per employee: Office, $90,000; agricultural, $150,000; drivers, $60,000.
   b. Each department would be allocated $100,000 of the payroll.
2. Department classification is the most appropriate because it matches the costs more closely to each department.

Benefit Analysis Report

1. One of the purposes of compiling a benefit analysis report is to represent graphically all of the variables that make up an employee's compensation package. The benefit analysis report provides managers and supervisors a budgetary tool to understand the full cost of hiring or dismissing employees. Additionally, the benefit analysis allows companies to compare benefits and employee costs to geographic or industry standards.
2. The benefit analysis report is an internal report for the company's management, and the annual total compensation report is meant to be distributed to the employee.

CHAPTER SIX

The Payroll Register, Employees' Earning Records, and Accounting System Entries

In this chapter, we will integrate the payroll register with the employees' earnings records and financial statements. In previous chapters, we have examined the effects of payroll on employees, employers, and governmental agencies. This chapter links Generally Accepted Accounting Principles with payroll elements. We will discuss the debits and credits associated with payroll accrual and payment. For this chapter, we will use the accrual basis of accounting, which means that transactions are recognized at the time that they are incurred.

Accounting entries are the transactions that place the payroll amounts into the correct ledger accounts. In automated systems, the software is designed to code each payroll item automatically to the correct General Ledger account. However, for the payroll accountant to record accurate expenses and period end accruals in the correct month, manual entries are necessary. This is the final step of the payroll cycle for each pay period and is the most important piece of the process from an accounting perspective. The final piece of this chapter will include the examination of the ways that payroll costs affect a company's financial reports.

LEARNING OBJECTIVES

After studying Chapter 6, you should be able to:

LO 6-1   Update the Payroll Register to Reflect Net Pay

LO 6-2   Transfer Payroll Data to the Employees' Earnings Records

© Photographer's Choice/Getty Images, RF

LO 6-3   Describe Financial Accounting Concepts

LO 6-4   Complete Payroll-Related General Journal Entries

LO 6-5   Generate Payroll-Related General Ledger Entries

LO 6-6   Describe Payroll Effects on the Accounting System

LO 6-7   Explain Payroll Entries in Accounting Reports

Employee Retention Becomes a C-Level Concern

Companies in the United States have reported growth during recent years. PayScale surveyed 4,700 employers and found that more than half expected to see improved financial performance. These employers reported an intent to hire additional employees to meet growth needs. However, 80% of chief financial officers in the United States expressed concern with employee retention, citing a need to offer existing employees pay raises and promotions to retain their top performers. Payroll data is a critical element that informs decisions regarding employee compensation. The payroll piece of financial reports fosters both analysis of employee pay and benchmarking within appropriate business contexts. (Source: *CGMA Magazine*, PayScale)

Workforce expansion leads to competition for skilled employees. Accurate reporting of payroll costs in the financial statement is a key part of decision making. In Chapter 6, we will examine the accounting system entries for payroll costs, then the effect on the company's financial reports, and finally how those reports influence managerial decisions.

LO 6-1 Update the Payroll Register to Reflect Net Pay

The payroll register is the payroll accountant's primary tool for computing and verifying payroll. Recall that it contains sections to compute all aspects of an employee's gross pay. In this section, we will update the payroll register to reflect the effect of mandatory, voluntary, and mandated deductions on employee net pay.

Complete the Payroll Register

Figure 6-1 contains an example of a payroll register, including columns for net pay and check number. Note that the columns for gross earnings, taxable wages for federal income tax, and taxable wages for FICA (i.e., Social Security and Medicare taxes) are on each block to facilitate computation of the net pay.

Note the addition of an extra set of columns labeled deductions. This is where each employee's tax withholdings, insurance premium, retirement plan contributions, mandated withholdings such as garnishments and union dues, and other post-tax deductions are listed individually. At the far right of the register, note that the net pay and check number are also included on the payroll register. The inclusion of these columns ensures that the net pay computations are accurate, match the disbursement to the employee, alleviate fraud potential, and facilitate proper remittance to third parties.

FIGURE 6-1
Full Payroll Register Sample

Name	M/S	# W/H	Hourly Rate or Period Wage	No. of Regular Hours	No. of Overtime Hours	No. of Holiday Hours	Commissions	Gross Earning	Insurance	Cafeteria Plan	Taxable Wages for Federal W/H	Taxable Wages for FICA
Totals												

Name	Gross Earning	Taxable Wages for Federal W/H	Taxable Wages for FICA	Federal W/H	Social Security Tax	Medicare W/H	State W/H Tax	Union Dues	Net Pay	Check No
Totals											

In May 2016, the owners of Rite-Way Electric were found guilty of failing to remit approximately $275,000 of payroll deductions withheld from employee pay for union fees. These deductions covered union-sponsored health and welfare programs, apprenticeship training, pension, and union dues. The IBEW reported five months of missing remittances and sought involuntary bankruptcy proceedings against Rite-Way Electric, which forced the company to cease operations. The owners were sentenced to five years of probation and full restitution. (Source: Daily Times News)

© Sam Edwards/Getty Images RF

Each company will have different column headings within the deductions section, based on the types of deductions for its employees. Some other columns could be included for state income tax, local income tax, additional Medicare tax (for highly compensated employees), and other tax items. Other deductions columns could include cafeteria plan deductions, charitable contributions, and many other items. Employers may choose to include columns for FUTA and SUTA taxes to facilitate period-based recording.

Recall the explanation of totaling, proving, and ruling the payroll register. This practice is especially important when the deductions and net pay columns are included. The total of the Social Security tax and Medicare tax columns assist with the computation of employer-share taxes. Totals of 401(k), health insurance, and other deductions' columns ensure the accuracy of remittances for these funds to the appropriate agencies.

Connection of the Payroll Register to Other Documents

The payroll register has a related set of documents called the employee earnings records. The employees' earnings records form the link between the accounting and the human resource departments. The information contained within each row of the payroll register is transferred to the employees' earnings records. Additionally, information from the payroll register is used to complete payroll entries in the General Journal.

The following example reflects how a payroll register would reflect the payroll data for an individual employee.

EXAMPLE: FULL PAYROLL REGISTER, INDIVIDUAL EMPLOYEE

Stanley Nobles is an employee of Cornerstone Graniteworks in Boulder, Colorado, which has a 40-hour normal work week. The Colorado income tax rate is 4.63%. Stanley earns $22.00 per hour and is single with one withholding allowance. During the biweekly pay period ending September 30, 20XX, he had the following payroll data:

- 88 hours of work
- $100 pre-tax health insurance premium
- $25 pre-tax cafeteria plan (unqualified)
- $75 union dues

Stanley was paid using check number 10252. The payroll register would appear as follows:

(continued)

(concluded)

Name	M/S	# W/H	Hourly Rate or Period Wage	No. of Regular Hours	No. of Overtime Hours	No. of Holiday Hours	Commissions	Gross Earning	Insurance	Cafeteria Plan	Taxable Wages for Federal W/H	Taxable Wages for FICA
Stanley Nobles	S	1	$ 22.00	80	8			$ 2,024.00	$ 100.00	$ 25.00	$ 1,899.00	$ 1,924.00

Name	Gross Earning	Taxable Wages for Federal W/H	Taxable Wages for FICA	Federal W/H	Social Security Tax	Medicare W/H	State W/H Tax	Union Dues	Net Pay	Check No
Stanley Nobles	$ 2,024.00	$ 1,899.00	$1,924.00	$ 249.00	$ 119.29	$ 27.90	$ 87.92	$ 75.00	$ 1,339.89	10252

Now that we have the example for an individual employee, let's look at the full payroll register that contains more employees within the same firm.

EXAMPLE: FULL PAYROLL REGISTER, MULTIPLE EMPLOYEES

Name	M/S	# W/H	Hourly Rate or Period Wage	No. of Regular Hours	No. of Overtime Hours	No. of Holiday Hours	Commissions	Gross Earning	Insurance	Cafeteria Plan	Taxable Wages for Federal W/H	Taxable Wages for FICA
Stanley Nobles	S	1	$ 22.00	80	8			$ 2,024.00	$ 100.00	$ 25.00	$ 1,899.00	$ 1,924.00
Regina Grey	M	4	$ 1,500.00					$ 1,500.00	$ 175.00	$ 100.00	$ 1,225.00	$ 1,325.00
Chantelle Fry	S	2	$ 15.25	80	3			$ 1,288.63	$ 100.00	$ 20.00	$ 1,168.63	$ 1,188.63
Brianna Watts	S	3	$ 18.50	80				$ 1,480.00	$ 150.00	$ 45.00	$ 1,285.00	$ 1,330.00
Marcus Davis	M	5	$ 1,850.00					$ 1,850.00	$ 175.00	$ 58.00	$ 1,617.00	$ 1,675.00
Totals								$ 8,142.63	$ 700.00	$ 248.00	$ 7,194.63	$ 7,442.63

Name	Gross Earning	Taxable Wages for Federal W/H	Taxable Wages for FICA	Federal W/H	Social Security Tax	Medicare W/H	State W/H Tax	Union Dues	Net Pay	Check No
Stanley Nobles	$ 2,024.00	$ 1,899.00	$1,924.00	$ 249.00	$ 119.29	$ 27.90	$ 87.92	$ 75.00	$ 1,339.89	10252
Regina Grey	$ 1,500.00	$ 1,225.00	$1,325.00	$ 28.00	$ 82.15	$ 19.21	$ 56.72	$ 75.00	$ 963.92	10253
Chantelle Fry	$ 1,288.63	$ 1,168.63	$1,188.63	$ 98.00	$ 73.69	$ 17.24	$ 54.11	$ 75.00	$ 850.59	10254
Brianna Watts	$ 1,480.00	$ 1,285.00	$1,330.00	$ 93.00	$ 82.46	$ 19.29	$ 59.50	$ 75.00	$ 955.76	10255
Marcus Davis	$ 1,850.00	$ 1,617.00	$1,675.00	$ 50.00	$ 103.85	$ 24.29	$ 74.87	$ 75.00	$ 1,289.00	10256
Totals	$ 8,142.63	$ 7,194.63	$7,442.63	$ 518.00	$ 461.44	$ 107.92	$ 333.11	$ 375.00	$ 5,399.15	

Notice that the bottom row of each block contains the column totals and is double underlined. This is how the total, prove, and rule functions work for a full payroll register. Each row will be used to update the employees' earnings records; similarly, columns from the payroll register will be used to form accounting entries in the General Journal.

What Is Contained In The Full Payroll Register?

1. Which columns should exist in all payroll registers?
   a. Gross earnings
   b. Net pay
   c. SUTA tax

    d. Check number

    e. FUTA tax

    f. Local income tax

2. Why is it important to total, prove, and rule the full payroll register?

3. How does the payroll register connect with other company documents?

LO 6-2   Transfer Payroll Data to the Employees' Earnings Records

Employee earnings records form the link between the accounting and the human resource departments and connect closely with the payroll register. The information contained within each row of the payroll register is transferred to the employee's earnings record, an example of which is shown in Figure 6-2.

    The employee earnings record is the master document accountants use to track employees' marital status, deductions (mandatory, voluntary, and mandated), and year-to-date earnings. Remember that Social Security, FUTA, and SUTA taxes have annual earnings limits for each

FIGURE 6-2
Employee Earnings Record

EMPLOYEE EARNING RECORD

NAME		Hire Date	
ADDRESS		Date of Birth	
CITY/STATE/ZIP		Exempt/Nonexempt	
TELEPHONE		Married/Single	
SOCIAL SECURITY NUMBER		No. of Exemptions	
POSITION		Pay Rate	

Period Ended	Hrs. Worked	Reg Pay	OT Pay	Holiday	Comm	Gross Pay	Ins	401(k)	Taxable Pay for Federal	Taxable Pay for FICA

Taxable Pay for Federal	Taxable Pay for FICA	Fed Inc. Tax	Social Sec. Tax	Medicare	State Inc. Tax	Total Deduc	Net Pay	YTD Net Pay	YTD Gross Pay

employee. Accountants update the employees' earnings records during each pay period to track all pay and tax deductions. Any employee changes including pay rate, marital status, and number of withholding allowances should be annotated in the earnings records as soon as possible to ensure the accuracy of the payroll.

EXAMPLE: EMPLOYEE EARNINGS RECORD, INDIVIDUAL EMPLOYEE

Using the example of Stanley Nobles at Cornerstone Graniteworks, we will enter his data into his employee earnings record.

EMPLOYEE EARNING RECORD

NAME	Stanley Nobles	Hire Date	4/22/2013
ADDRESS	2845 Arapahoe Boulevard	Date of Birth	7/15/1988
CITY/STATE/ZIP	Boulder, CO 80305	Exempt/Nonexempt	Nonexempt
TELEPHONE	303-555-1034	Married/Single	Single
SOCIAL SECURITY NUMBER	204-33-5439	No. of Exemptions	1
POSITION	Granite Tech III	Pay Rate	$22.00/hour

Period Ended	Hrs. Worked	Reg Pay	OT Pay	Holiday	Comm	Gross Pay	Ins	Cafeteria	Taxable Pay for Federal	Taxable Pay for FICA
9/30/xx	88	1760	264.00			2,024.00	100.00	25.00	1,899.00	1,924.00

Taxable Pay for Federal	Taxable Pay for FICA	Fed Inc. Tax	Social Sec. Tax	Medicare	State Inc. Tax	Union Dues	Total Deduc	Net Pay	YTD Net Pay	YTD Gross Pay
1,899.00	1,924.00	249.00	119.29	27.90	87.92	75.00	684.11	1,339.89	24,118.03	36,432.00

Note how the following employee information is reflected in the employee earnings record:

- Address.
- Telephone number.
- Social Security number.
- Full-time status.
- Marital status.
- Pay basis (i.e., hourly).
- Hire date.
- Birth date.
- Position.

(continued)

(concluded)

- Pay rate.
- Pay period date.
- Year-to-date net pay.
- Year-to-date gross pay.

These items are common to most employee earnings records because of the connecting between payroll and human resources. The information contained in the employee earnings record is used as the basis for the employee's Form W-2 as well as other company tax and benefits reporting.

The Employees' Earnings Records and Periodic Tax Reports

Period totals are also included on the earnings record. These totals facilitate the preparation of the quarterly and annual reports. Like any payroll record, the earnings records should be retained and destroyed at the same interval as other accounting records. Earning records are typically included as supporting documents for internal copies of quarterly filings of Form 941 as well as state and local tax returns (where applicable). During a payroll audit, the documentation attached to the tax returns provides verification of the information contained in the reports. A secondary use is that, in the event of computer data failure, documents attached to payroll records can be used to re-create files.

Employee Earnings Register

1. How do the employees' earnings records relate to the payroll register?
2. Which of the following fields exist on both the payroll register and the employees' earnings records:
   a. Name
   b. Pay rate
   c. Social Security tax
   d. Net pay
   e. Marital status
3. What reports and forms use information from the employees' earnings records?

LO 6-3   Describe Financial Accounting Concepts

Now that we have explored the principles of computing and reporting payroll data, it is time to connect the information to financial accounting concepts. In financial accounting, the fundamental accounting equation is **Assets = Liabilities + Owners' Equity.**

EXAMPLE: FINANCIAL ACCOUNTING CATEGORIES

Assets: Cash or other items that are used in the operation of the business and amounts owed to the business by customers.
Liabilities: Amounts owed by the business to other people or companies.
Owners' Equity: The net investment that the owner has in the business, including earnings kept in the business.

Financial business transactions, such as the movement of cash used in paying employees and remitting amounts to third parties, are tracked using the accounting system. A fundamental concept in accounting involves the accounting equation, which must remain in balance at all times. As such, transactions will either increase an account (or multiple accounts), decrease an account (or multiple accounts), or a combination thereof. To understand the concept of equation balance, T-accounts are the first step in understanding the classification process that is part of transaction analysis.

EXAMPLE: TRANSACTION ANALYSIS USING T-ACCOUNTS

Barry Larson, the owner of Riptide Sails, invested $4,000 into his business on August 1, 2016. Accountants classify the transaction into two accounts: assets and owners' equity. The cash account would increase because the money was invested in the business. Barry's owner's capital account would increase because he increased his net investment in the business. Using the T-account approach, the transaction would look like this:

Cash	
Dr.	Cr.
4,000	

Larson, Capital	
Dr.	Cr.
	4,000

Debits and Credits

If accountants were to maintain T-accounts for all of a business's transactions, their work would be tedious and vulnerable to a large number of errors. To simplify the addition and subtraction involved, accountants use the terms "debit" (abbreviated Dr.) and "credit" (abbreviated Cr.) to explain the transaction. In accounting parlance, *debit* simply means "the left side of the T-account," and *credit* simply means "the right side of the T-account." No connotation exists about good or bad with the use of these terms in accounting.

EXAMPLE: DEBIT AND CREDIT RULES

Debits Increase:	Credits Increase:
Expenses	Liabilities
Assets	Equity (Capital)
Drawing	Revenue

The General Journal

To simplify the use of T-accounts, accountants use a journal (called the *General Journal*) to record the daily financial transactions. The General Journal is maintained in chronological order. The General Journal is one big T-account and has columns to record the debits and credits involved in each transaction. Complementing the General Journal is the *General Ledger*, in which all journal transactions are recorded in their specific accounts.

In the transaction above, the transaction would appear in the General Journal as follows:

EXAMPLE: TRANSACTION IN THE GENERAL JOURNAL

Trans.	Date	Account Name & Description	Post Ref	Debit	Credit
1	8/1/2016	Cash	101	4,000.00	
		Larson, Capital	301		4,000.00
		Started business			

Note certain accounting conventions present in the journal entry:

- The date of the transaction is noted.
- The debit part of the transaction is on the first line and is flush-left in the column.
- The credit part of the transaction is on the second line and is indented slightly.
- A brief description of the transaction is on line three.
- Account numbers are annotated in the Post Reference (Post Ref) column.
- The post reference in the General Journal is the General Ledger account number.

The General Ledger

Once the transaction has been recorded in the General Journal, the accountant posts the entry to corresponding General Ledger accounts. In the following table, note that (1) the transaction itself is listed, and (2) the balance of each account is adjusted accordingly.

EXAMPLE: GENERAL LEDGER POSTING

			Account: 101 – Cash		
Date	Description	Post Ref.	Debit	Credit	Balance
8/1/2016	Initial Contribution	J1	4,000.00		4,000.00
			Account: 301 – Larson, Capital		
Date	Description	Post Ref.	Debit	Credit	Balance
8/1/2016	Initial Contribution	J1		4,000.00	4,000.00

The General Ledger account balances are used to generate the payroll reports that we have been discussing so far. The elements of the General Ledger and specific posting practices will appear later in this chapter.

Financial Accounting Concepts

Stop & Check

1. What is the fundamental accounting equation?
2. What increases the Wages and Salaries Payable account: a debit or a credit?
3. What increases the Wages and Salaries Expense account: a debit or a credit?

LO 6-4 Complete Payroll-Related General Journal Entries

Recording the specific General Journal entries that correspond to payroll activities is the next step in the process. General Journal entries are the original entry point for events to be recorded within the accounting system. A sample period payroll for NC Bikes follows.

EXAMPLE: NC BIKES PAYROLL DATA

NC Bikes pays its employees biweekly and operates on a calendar fiscal year (i.e., the year-end is December 31). The payroll accountant for NC Bikes has completed the payroll register for the January 28, 2016, payroll. Pay checks will be issued on January 31. Payroll totals are as follows:

Gross pay: $18,050.00

Federal income tax withheld: $1,500.00

Social Security tax withheld: $1,084.38

Medicare tax withheld: $253.61

State income tax withheld: $577.60

401(k) contributions withheld: $750.00

Health insurance premiums withheld: $560.00

United Way contributions withheld: $180.00

Net pay: $13,144.41

The totals row of the payroll register would appear as follows:

Name	Gross Earning	401(k) Contributions	Insurance	Federal W/H	Social Security Tax	Medicare W/H	State W/H Tax	United Way	Net Pay	Check No
Totals	$ 18,050.00	$ 750.00	$ 560.00	$ 1,500.00	$ 1,084.38	$ 253.61	$ 577.60	$ 180.00	$ 13,144.41	

The payroll register is the tool used by payroll accountants to create the pay-related journal entries. Here's how it works:

PAYROLL REGISTER TO GENERAL JOURNAL ENTRIES

Payroll Register Column	General Journal Account	NC Bikes Amount
Gross Earnings	Salaries and Wages Expense	$18,050.00
401(k) Contributions	401(k) Contributions Payable	$ 750.00
Insurance	Health Insurance Premiums Payable	$ 560.00
Federal W/H	FIT Payable	$ 1,500.00
Social Security Tax	Social Security Tax Payable	$ 1,084.38
Medicare W/H	Medicare Tax Payable	$ 253.61
State W/H Tax	State Income Tax Payable	$ 577.60
United Way	United Way Contributions Payable	$ 180.00
Net Pay	Salaries and Wages Payable	$13,144.41

As the payroll data is transferred from the payroll register to the General Journal, notice the following accounting categories:

- Account names ending with the word "expense" are classified as Expense accounts (remember Debit increases).
- Account names ending with the word "payable" are classified as Liability accounts (remember Credit increases).

Employee Pay-Related Journal Entries

The General Journal entry to record the employee's portion of the payroll and the issuance of the checks to employees is in two parts:

EXAMPLE: NC BIKES GENERAL JOURNAL PAYROLL ENTRIES—EMPLOYEE PAYROLL TRANSACTION

Date	Description	Account	Debit	Credit
Jan. 28	Salaries and Wages Expense	511	$18,050.00	
	FIT Payable	221		$1,500.00
	Social Security Tax Payable	222		1,084.38
	Medicare Tax Payable	223		253.61
	State Income Tax Payable	224		577.60
	401(k) Contributions Payable	225		750.00
	Health Insurance Premiums Payable	226		560.00
	United Way Contributions Payable	227		180.00
	Salaries and Wages Payable	231		13,144.41
Jan. 31	Salaries and Wages Payable	231	13,144.41	
	Cash	101		13,144.41

Employer Payroll-Related Journal Entries

The employer's share of the payroll is similarly recorded. NC Bikes's share of the payroll expenses follows:

EXAMPLE: NC BIKES EMPLOYER PAYROLL TAX OBLIGATIONS DATA

Social Security tax: $1,084.38
Medicare tax: $253.61
FUTA tax: $104.94
SUTA tax: $974.70

The General Journal entry for the employer's share of the payroll taxes follows:

EXAMPLE: NC BIKES GENERAL JOURNAL PAYROLL ENTRIES—EMPLOYER PAYROLL TAX TRANSACTION

Date	Description	Account	Debit	Credit
Jan. 28	Payroll Taxes Expense	512	$2,417.63	
	Social Security Tax Payable	222		$1,084.38
	Medicare Tax Payable	223		253.61
	FUTA Tax Payable	228		104.94
	SUTA Tax Payable	229		974.70

Other Payroll-Related Journal Entries

What about the other deductions that NC Bikes withheld from its employees' pay? These other deductions, including federal and state income tax, 401(k) contributions, health insurance premiums, and United Way contributions, are liabilities of the company. These amounts will remain in the liability accounts until NC Bikes *remits* them. Upon remittance, the General Journal entries will appear as a debit to the Liability account and a credit to Cash. An example for the January 28 payroll's voluntary deductions, paid to the appropriate companies on January 31, follows:

EXAMPLE: NC BIKES GENERAL JOURNAL PAYROLL ENTRIES— VOLUNTARY DEDUCTIONS REMITTANCE

Date	Description	Account	Debit	Credit
Jan. 31	401(k) Contributions Payable	225	$750.00	
	Health Insurance Payable	226	560.00	
	United Way Contribution Payable	227	180.00	
	Cash	101		$1,490.00

Remember that the remittance for the governmental taxes has a specific schedule. The General Journal entry for the tax remittances would follow the same pattern as the voluntary deductions: debit the Liability account(s) and credit Cash.

Payroll Accruals and Reversals

A common occurrence is that a payroll may be split between two months, as will be the case for NC Bikes. For example, the majority of the pay for the end of March (i.e., the end of the first quarter) will be paid on the April 1, 2015, payday. For accounting purposes, the accountant needs to record the *accrual* of the payroll for March to represent accurately the *expenses* and liabilities incurred during the period. Some companies choose to record the period's expenses through *adjusting entries* and then reverse the entries after the start of the next period to prevent confusion in the payroll accounting process.

In the case of NC Bikes, the adjusting entry would appear as follows for the end of March:

EXAMPLE: NC BIKES ADJUSTING ENTRY—EMPLOYEE PAYROLL DATA

Gross pay: $16,245.00
Federal income tax withheld: $1,350.00
Social Security tax withheld: $1,007.19
Medicare tax withheld: $235.55
State income tax withheld: $519.84
Net pay: $13,132.42

The adjusting entry for March 31, 2016, would look like this:

EXAMPLE: NC BIKES GENERAL JOURNAL—EMPLOYEE DATA ADJUSTING ENTRIES

Date	Description	Account	Debit	Credit
Mar. 31	Salaries and Wages Expense	511	$16,245.00	
	FIT Payable	221		$1,350.00
	Social Security Tax Payable	222		1,007.19
	Medicare Tax Payable	223		235.55
	State Income Tax Payable	224		519.84
	Salaries and Wages Payable	231		13,132.42

The amount for the employer's share would be:

EXAMPLE: NC BIKES GENERAL JOURNAL—EMPLOYER PAYROLL TAX DATA ADJUSTING ENTRIES

Date	Description	Account	Debit	Credit
Mar. 31	Payroll Taxes Expense	512	$2,217.17	
	Social Security Tax Payable	222		$1,007.19
	Medicare Tax Payable	223		235.55
	FUTA Tax Payable	228		97.47
	SUTA Tax Payable	229		876.96

On April 1, 2016, the accountant could record a reversing entry as follows:

EXAMPLE: NC BIKES GENERAL JOURNAL—EMPLOYEE DATA REVERSING ENTRIES

Date	Description	Account	Debit	Credit
Apr. 1	FIT Payable	221	$1,350.00	
	Social Security Tax Payable	222	1,007.19	
	Medicare Tax Payable	223	235.55	
	State Income Tax Payable	224	519.84	
	Salaries and Wages Payable	231	13,132.42	
	Salaries and Wages Expense	511		$16,245.00

The *reversal* of the General Journal entries, used in accrual-based accounting to represent accrued employer payroll expenditures and liabilities at the end of the prior month, would look like this:

EXAMPLE: NC BIKES GENERAL JOURNAL—EMPLOYER PAYROLL TAX DATA REVERSING ENTRIES

Date	Description	Account	Debit	Credit
Apr. 1	Social Security Tax Payable	222	$1,007.19	
	Medicare Tax Payable	223	235.55	
	FUTA Tax Payable	224	129.96	
	SUTA Tax Payable	229	876.96	
	Payroll Taxes Expense	512		$2,217.17

Note that not all companies and accountants use reversing entries. An advantage of using the reversing entry is that it simplifies the payroll process by avoiding calculating partial payroll periods that occur due to the period end. A disadvantage is that the reversing entry becomes an additional entry that the accountant has to journalize and post. The use of reversing entries is at the company's discretion.

Payroll and the General Journal

1. In the following General Journal entry, which account represents the employees' gross pay?

Description	Debit	Credit
Wages and Salaries Expense	$124,785.00	
Federal Income Tax Payable		$15,280.00
Social Security Tax Payable		$ 7,736.67
Medicare Tax Payable		$ 1,809.38
State Income Tax Payable		$ 4,741.83
Wages and Salaries Payable		$95,217.12

2. Based on the preceding General Journal entry, what would be the entry for the employer's share of the payroll taxes? Omit FUTA/SUTA taxes.

3. In the preceding General Journal entry, assume that $42,795 of the gross pay was accrued for the following period. The accrual amounts are as follows:

Description	Debit	Credit
Wages and Salaries Expense	$42,795.00	
Federal Income Tax Payable		$15,280.00
Social Security Tax Payable		$ 2,653.29
Medicare Tax Payable		$ 620.53
State Income Tax Payable		$ 1,626.21
Wages and Salaries Payable		$22,614.97

What would be the reversing entry?

LO 6-5　Generate Payroll-Related General Ledger Entries

As mentioned before, the process of updating the General Ledger accounts with the transactions that the accountant records in the General Journal is called *posting*. Each account used in the General Journal has a corresponding General Ledger account used to track individual balances of a firm.

For the January 28 payroll and January 31 remittances for NC Bikes that we discussed in the previous section, the postings to the General Ledger would appear as depicted in Figure 6-3. Note that the entries shown reflect only the payroll entries for the end of January and for the end of the first quarter in March.

General Ledger Posting Practices

Note that the columns in the General Ledger are similar to those in the General Journal. Some specific practices in the General Ledger are worth noting:

- Each line has a date. (In the General Journal, only the first line of each transaction is dated.)
- The description is usually left blank, except for adjusting, closing, and reversing entries.

The post reference number is a combination of letters and numbers. The letters denote which journal the entry correlates. In this case, "J" means that the original entry may be found in the General Journal. The number in the Post Ref column reflects the page of the journal on which the entry is recorded.

FIGURE 6-3
NC Bikes General Ledger

						Account: 101 – Cash	
						Balance	
Date		Description	Post Ref	Debit	Credit	Debit	Credit
		Beginning Balance				122,367.43	
Jan	31		J1		13,144.91	109,222.52	
Jan	31		J4		750.00	108,472.52	
Jan	31		J4		560.00	107,912.52	
Jan	31		J4		180.00	107,732.52	

						Account: 221 – FIT Payable	
						Balance	
Date		Description	Post Ref	Debit	Credit	Debit	Credit
Jan	28		J1		1,500.00		1,500.00
Mar	31	Accrue Payroll	J5		1,350.00		2,850.00
Apr	1	Reverse Payroll	J7	1,350.00			1,500.00

						Account: 222 – Social Security Tax Payable	
						Balance	
Date		Description	Post Ref	Debit	Credit	Debit	Credit
Jan	28		J1		1,084.38		1,084.38
Jan	28		J1		1,084.38		2,168.76
Mar	31	Accrue Payroll	J5		974.70		3,143.46
Mar	31	Accrue Payroll – Employer	J6		974.70		4,118.16
Apr	1	Reverse Payroll	J7	974.70			3,143.46
Apr	1	Reverse Payroll – Employer	J7	974.70			2,168.76

						Account: 223 – Medicare Tax Payable	
						Balance	
Date		Description	Post Ref	Debit	Credit	Debit	Credit
Jan	28		J1		253.61		253.61
Jan	28		J1		253.61		507.22
Mar	31	Accrue Payroll	J5		235.55		742.77
Mar	31	Accrue Payroll – Employer	J6		235.55		978.32
Apr	1	Reverse Payroll	J7	235.55			742.77
Apr	1	Reverse Payroll – Employer	J8	235.55			507.22

						Account: 224 – State Income Tax Payable	
						Balance	
Date		Description	Post Ref	Debit	Credit	Debit	Credit
Jan	28		J1		577.60		577.60
Mar	31	Accrue Payroll	J5		519.84		1,097.44
Apr	1	Reverse Payroll	J7	519.84			577.60

						Account: 225 – 401(k) Contributions Payable	
						Balance	
Date		Description	Post Ref	Debit	Credit	Debit	Credit
Jan	28		J1		750.00		750.00
Jan	31		J4	750.00			-

(continued)

Account: 226 – Health Insurance Payable

Date		Description	Post Ref	Debit	Credit	Balance Debit	Balance Credit
Jan	28		J1		560.00		560.00
Jan	31		J4	560.00			-

Account: 227 – United Way Contributions Payable

Date		Description	Post Ref	Debit	Credit	Balance Debit	Balance Credit
Jan	28		J1		180.00		180.00
Jan	31		J4	180.00			-

Account: 228 – FUTA Tax Payable

Date		Description	Post Ref	Debit	Credit	Balance Debit	Balance Credit
Jan	28		J1		144.40		144.40
Mar	31	Accrue Payroll – Employer	J6		129.96		274.36
Apr	1	Reverse Payroll – Employer	J8	129.96			144.40

Account: 229 – SUTA Tax Payable

Date		Description	Post Ref	Debit	Credit	Balance Debit	Balance Credit
Jan	28		J1		974.40		974.40
Mar	31	Accrue Payroll – Employer	J6		876.96		1,851.36
Apr	1	Reverse Payroll – Employer	J8	876.96			974.40

Account: 231 – Salaries and Wages Payable

Date		Description	Post Ref	Debit	Credit	Balance Debit	Balance Credit
Jan	28		J1				13,144.41
Jan	31		J1	13,144.41			-
Mar	31	Accrue Payroll	J5				13,164.91
Apr	1	Reverse Payroll	J7	13,164.91			-

Account: 512 – Payroll Taxes Expense

Date		Description	Post Ref	Debit	Credit	Balance Debit	Balance Credit
Jan	28		J1	2,457.09		2,457.09	
Mar	31	Accrue Payroll	J6	2,217.17		4,674.26	
Apr	1	Reverse Payroll	J7		2,217.17	2,217.17	

Account: 511 – Salaries and Wages Expense

Date		Description	Post Ref	Debit	Credit	Balance Debit	Balance Credit
Jan	28		J1	18,050.00		18,050.00	
Mar	31	Accrue Payroll	J6	16,245.00		34,295.00	
Apr	1	Reverse Payroll	J7		16,245.00	18,050.00	

General Ledger Entries

1. The Medicare Tax Payable account had a credit balance on June 23 of $2,540. As of the June 30 payroll, credits totaling $220 were posted to the Medicare Tax Payable account. What is the balance in the account as of June 30?

2. The post reference for the June 30 journal entry is J34. What does this post reference mean?

The first pair of Debit and Credit columns is used to record the General Journal entry. If the account had a debit in the General Journal transaction, then the amount would appear in the Debit column in the first pair of columns in the General Ledger. The same practice is used for credits.

The second pair of Debit and Credit columns is used to maintain a running balance of the total in the account. These account balances are the foundation for the financial reports generated by the accountant and reviewed by managers, officers, customers, vendors, and governmental agencies.

LO 6-6   Describe Payroll Effects on the Accounting System

Entries in the payroll system are posted into the General Ledger. When a company has an automated payroll system, the journal entries discussed previously are automatically updated to the General Ledger. A payroll accountant needs to understand how the accounts should look after a payroll is completed to ensure the automated system has performed correctly. Glitches within computer programs may cause the payroll entry to be one sided, in which only the debit or credit entry will flow through to the General Ledger. When this occurs, the payroll accountant must discover what has not posted to ensure the entire transaction posts correctly.

© PhotoDisc/Getty Images, RF

Payroll-Related Business Expenses

Payroll represents an expense to the business. As such, it reduces the company's profitability proportional to the wages earned and taxes paid. When the payroll accountant accrues the expenses related to the payroll, the company's expenses will also increase. Companies that operate using a cash basis (i.e., recording activities only when cash is received or spent) will witness the payroll expenses reducing the income when wages and salaries are paid to the employees and when taxes are remitted to governmental agencies.

Employers are increasingly using technology to manage the cost of employee benefits. Employees are requesting transparency in their payroll and benefits statuses, and governmental agencies require accurate and timely remittance of employer payroll obligations. Additionally, the use of payroll technology fosters increased accuracy in employee costs, which allows a company to manage its finances more precisely than ever before. This precision leads to improved data analysis and reliable strategic planning. (Source: *Employee Benefits News*)

Besides administering specific payroll tasks, a responsibility of the payroll accountant is to allocate the employee expenses to specific accounts, departments, or business activities. Regardless of the employee's job description, some amount of time can be allocable to

The Business Effects of Payroll

1. Does the payment of employee wages increase or decrease the profitability of a business?

2. Why is it important to allocate payroll-related expenses properly?

jobs or customers. For example, a fabric manufacturing company will have sewing, accounting, and managerial staff. The bulk of the sewing staff's time will be allocable to specific jobs; however, some time will be considered overhead—cleaning or meetings, for example. The bulk of the accounting department's time will be considered overhead. However, if the accountant is working on the analysis of a specific client's project, that time may be billed to the client. Managerial positions may also have specific times allocated to jobs depending upon the needs of the client and the position.

LO 6-7   Explain Payroll Entries in Accounting Reports

When examining the *income statement*, *balance sheet*, and *trial balance* (Figures 6-4, 6-5, and 6-6), the payroll accountant must know what effect his or her work has on each statement.

Within the expense section of the income statement, you will see several accounts that relate to payroll. Starting with the wages categories, there are salary and hourly divisions. Each of the taxes we have discussed is listed. Note that the expenses related to the taxes are paid by the employer and forwarded to the taxing authority; thus, there is no federal income tax expense. Expenses related to the employer portion of retirement fund matching, health benefits, or other benefits are also located within the income statement.

Moving on to the balance sheet, any unpaid liabilities will be reported in the current liability section. If there are employees who have taken payroll advances, which are amounts to be repaid by the employee, these will show in the current assets section. In accrual accounting, there may also be end-of-period entries to accrue for payroll earned by the employees. Additional liability accounts for accrued salaries, accrued hourly wages, accrued holiday pay, and accrued paid time off could also appear, depending on the timing of the end of the period and the types of employees and benefits with which the company operates.

© Sebastiaan Blockmans/Alamy RF

The trial balance contains all accounts the company uses, spanning all of the financial statements. The accounts listed on the trial balance appear in the order of the chart of accounts. Typically, assets are listed first: short term, and then long term. Following are liabilities: short term, and then long term. Equity accounts are listed next, followed by revenues and expenses. The important thing to remember when examining the trial balance is that it should balance: Debits must equal credits. Should one side not balance with the other, the accountant must determine why and correct the error.

Labor Reports

The payroll accountant may provide specific *labor reports* to management or department heads. These reports may have a variety of names and content depending on the needs of the business.

- The *labor usage* report designates where the labor is used within the company. When a company has several employees who work in different departments, the labor usage report can

FIGURE 6-4
Income Statement Presentation (Partial)

NC Bikes Income Statement For the Quarter Ended March 31, 2OXX		
Expenses:		
Salaries and Wages Expense	$ 34,295.00	
Payroll Taxes Expense	4,674.26	
Utilities Expense	1,725.00	
Telephone Expense	884.00	
Rent Expense	5,175.00	
Total Expenses		46,753.26
Net Income for Quarter		$ 31,550.14

FIGURE 6-5
Balance Sheet Presentation

NC Bikes Balance Sheet March 31, 2OXX		
Assets:		
Cash		$ 78,507.89
Accounts Receivable		39,723.67
Equipment		15,289.00
Inventory		225,960.00
Total Assets		$ 359,480.56
Liabilities		
Accounts Payable		4,085.27
FIT Payable		2,850.00
Social Security Tax Payable		4,118.16
Medicare Tax Payable		978.32
State Income Tax Payable		1,097.44
Health Insurance Payable		560.00
FUTA Tax Payable		274.36
SUTA Tax Payable		1,851.36
Salaries and Wages Payable		13,164.91
Total Liabilities		28,979.82
Owners Equity		
J. Nelson, Capital		195,305.37
A. Nelson, Capital		136,195.37
Total Owners Equity		330,500.74
Total Liabilities and Owners Equity		$ 359,480.56

FIGURE 6-6
Trial Balance Presentation

Account	Debit	Credit
Cash	$ 78,507.89	
Accounts Receivable	39,723.67	
Equipment	15,289.00	
Inventory	225,960.00	
Accounts Payable		$ 4,085.27
FIT Payable		2,850.00
Social Security Tax Payable		4,118.16
Medicare Tax Payable		978.32
State Income Tax Payable		1,097.44
Health Insurance Payable		560.00
FUTA Tax Payable		274.36
SUTA Tax Payable		1,851.36
Salaries and Wages Payable		13,164.91
J. Nelson, Capital		195,305.37
A. Nelson, Capital		136,195.37
	$ 359,480.56	$ 359,480.56

be useful in determining overhead *allocations* by department and the need for increased or decreased staff within a specific department.

- The *billable vs. nonbillable* report tracks the time employees have spent specifically on projects for which customers are paying. This report allows managers to determine if the time allocated to the job in job costing is accurate, the company is operating efficiently, or if the employee is taking too long on a specific job.

- *Overtime* reports allow managers to determine how much overtime has been paid to employees during a specified time period. This report allows managers to monitor labor distribution and scheduling to ensure adherence with budget guidelines.

- Employers can also make use of *trend* reports for payroll staffing needs. Trend reports of income over the period of the year can reveal seasonal increases or decreases in business. An informed business manager will know if the company needs to have seasonal or temporary workers for short-term increases. If the trend reflects a steady increase in business, the manager may determine that hiring a new employee would be beneficial.

> Wells Fargo, N.A., reported the potential for reductions in Information Technology personnel, based on payroll data analysis. The company used payroll data to determine the most efficient use of personnel in accordance with Wells Fargo's mission and objectives. The use of payroll data combined with benefits analysis, total employee compensation reports, and financial statement information led to a critical assessment of personnel needs. (Source: *The Charlotte Observer*)

Analyzing the staffing needs of the company compared to income projections may also lead managers to know if they need to lay off personnel, reduce hours of existing employees, or restructure company operations.

ECONOMIC EFFECTS OF PAYROLL

Although payroll accounting principles remain relatively stable, the role that payroll plays in the broader context of a business is subject to change. Some developments in payroll accounting in the business context that have changed during the early 2010s include the following:

- Issues with employment vulnerability have stemmed from the economic downturn during which employers restructured their operations to remain viable.
- Grassroots movements ("Occupy") brought the issue of wage disparity into the public eye.
- Technology use such as cloud-based payroll services has fostered employee mobility and created challenges to work–life balance.
- Employer-sponsored wellness programs have become a part of strategic human resource management because of the correlation with employee sick time and retention.

Some trends to watch in payroll's economic effects include the following:

- Increases in labor costs for employers resulting from changes to the minimum wage.
- Pressure to expand telecommuting opportunities, challenging accounting policies in regard to labor costs.
- Reclassification of workers as salaried nonexempt employees to avoid exempt minimum wage mandates.

Labor Reports

1. Which of the following reports are affected by the payroll of an organization?
   a. Trial balance
   b. Statement of owners' equity
   c. Interest statement
   d. Income statement
   e. Balance sheet
2. What is a specific type of report that the payroll accountant provides to managerial staff?
3. What are trend reports?

Summary of Payroll Register, Employees' Earnings Records, and Accounting System Entries

The payroll register and employees' earnings records are two tools that payroll accountants need to maintain their work accurately. Both records track employee compensation and contain information about company liabilities to governmental agencies and other organizations. These records also provide information for company decision makers by yielding data about labor distribution and cost allocation. Payroll records provide information about benefits given to employees and how those benefits affect a business's profitability. Information contained in these sources and tools used by payroll accountants provides integral insights for managerial functions.

FIGURE 6-7
Payroll Process Flowchart

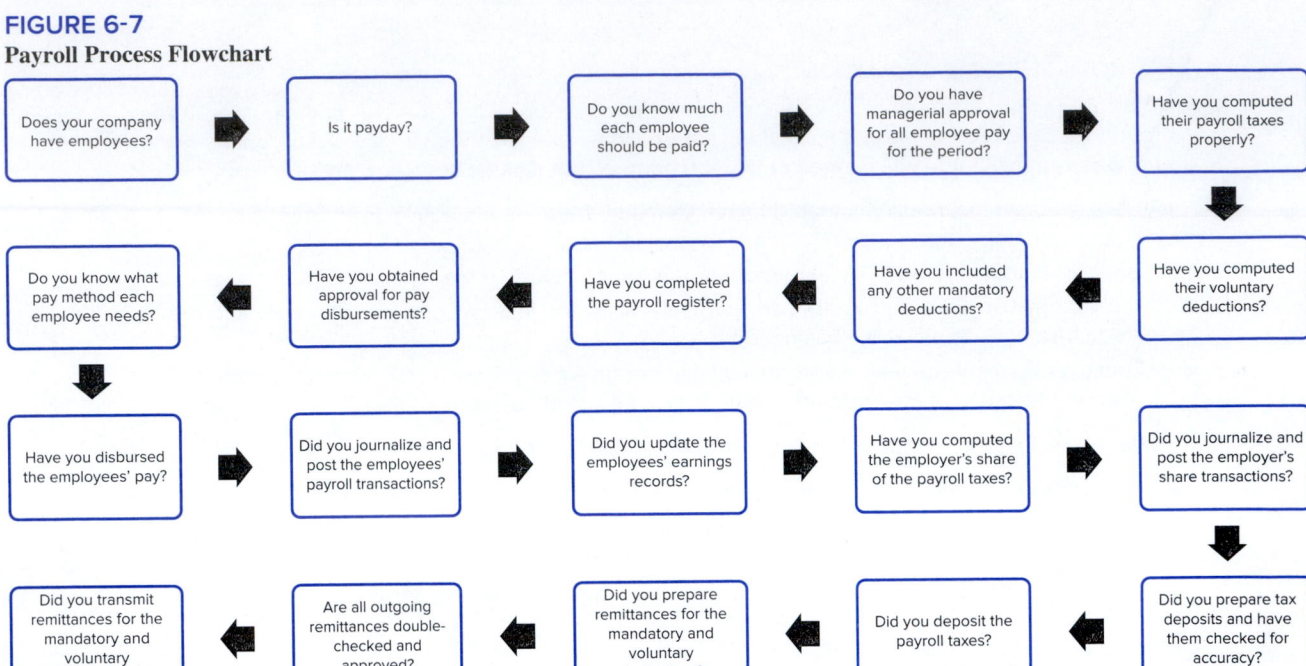

The final piece of the payroll cycle is the creation of accounting system entries. Similar to other business transactions, recording, paying the payroll, remitting money to governmental agencies and other firms requires General Journal and General Ledger entries. Business owners and departmental managers use this accounting information to measure the effectiveness of business plans and to plan both short- and long-term strategies. As an integral part of business operations, payroll-related expenses and liabilities affect the financial reports and company viability as a whole.

With this chapter's explanation of accounting system entries, we have now completed our journey through the payroll process. We have investigated the history of payroll, its many aspects and functions, and the importance of employee compensation within a business context.

We hope that on finishing this book you will have taken away that payroll accounting is complex, involves many different decisions along the way, and deserves your close attention. Figure 6-7 is a depiction of the basic elements of the payroll process that we have discussed.

Key Points

- The payroll register is a tool used by payroll accountants to ensure the accuracy of employee compensation.
- The payroll register yields information about totals for mandatory and voluntary deductions, assisting the accountant with remittances.
- The employees' earnings records are the link between accounting and human resources and contain information from the payroll register.

- Accounting principles assist in the classification of payroll costs and organizational performance.

- Payroll transactions are recorded in the General Journal and posted to General Ledger accounts.

- The balances in the General Ledger accounts form the foundation of financial reports.

- Payroll costs represent an expense of the business.

- Employees are assigned to departments to foster accurate measurements of business segment profitability.

- Trend reports offer business leaders insight about changes in labor costs over a period.

Vocabulary

Accrual	General Journal	Remit
Adjusting entries	General Ledger	Reversal
Allocation	Income statement	Rule
Assets	Labor reports	Total
Balance sheet	Liabilities	Trial balance
Credit	Owners' equity	
Debit	Posting	
Expense	Prove	

Review Questions

1. What types of accounts does a debit increase?

2. What types of accounts does a credit increase?

3. Where are daily accounting entries recorded?

4. Once recorded, to what are the entries posted?

5. What is the purpose of the payroll register?

6. What information is contained in employees' earnings records?

7. How are the payroll register and the employees' earnings records related?

8. For the employee share of the payroll, what type of account is debited for the gross pay?

9. What are three of the accounts that may be credited for the employee payroll?

10. What two accounts are affected upon issuance of paychecks?

11. What accounts are debited and credited for the employer share of the payroll expenses?

12. How do payroll expenses affect the income statement and balance sheet?

13. How can companies use payroll information that is reported in the financial statements to determine labor distribution?

14. How can a company's payroll information contained in financial reports assist in corporate planning?

15. How do the payroll register and employees' earnings records help employers meet their responsibilities to different groups, such as the employees and governmental agencies?

Exercises Set A

E6-1A.
LO 6-1

What is the purpose of the additional columns in the full payroll register? (Select all that apply.)
A. They contain additional information for employees to inspect prior to receiving their net pay.
B. They facilitate accuracy in computing employee net pay.
C. They reflect the effect of deductions on employee gross pay.
D. They reduce the potential for payroll fraud.

E6-2A.
LO 6-1, 6-2

Which column exists in the employees' earnings records but not in the payroll register?
A. Gross pay
B. Net pay
C. YTD pay
D. 401(k) contributions

E6-3A.
LO 6-2

What is the connection between the employees' earnings records and payroll tax reporting? (Select all that apply.)
A. Employees' earnings records do not connect with payroll tax reporting.
B. Employees' earnings records may be used to ensure the accuracy of payroll tax reporting.
C. Employees' earnings records contain details of payroll tax reporting and may be considered as source documents.
D. Employees' earnings records contain year-to-date gross pay, which reflects when employees reach tax bases.

E6-4A.
LO 6-3

A debit increases which of the following types of accounts? (Select all that apply.)
A. Liabilities
B. Expenses
C. Revenue
D. Assets

E6-5A.
LO 6-4

The total of the Gross Earnings column of the payroll register for a given pay period will appear in which account for the payroll-related general journal entry?
A. Salaries and Wages Payable.
B. Cash.
C. Salaries and Wages Expense.
D. Expenses.

E6-6A.
LO 6-5

What is always true about the General Ledger? (Select all that apply.)
A. The process of transferring amounts from the General Journal to the General Ledger is called posting.
B. The General Ledger is a way to represent monthly groupings of entire General Journal entries.
C. The General Ledger contains information about the individual accounts used in General Journal transactions.
D. A debit to an account in a General Journal transaction is a debit to that account in the General Ledger.

E6-7A.
LO 6-5, 6-6, 6-7

How does a payroll accountant use the information in the General Ledger? (Select all that apply.)
A. The account balances form the basis for accounting reports.
B. The payroll accountant uses General Ledger balances to determine the effectiveness of individual employees.
C. General Ledger account balances aggregate data to determine payroll costs.
D. Payroll expenses contained in the General Ledger are not used to make personnel decisions.

E6-8A.

LO 6-7

Which of the following accounts would appear on the income statement? (Select all that apply.)
A. Payroll taxes expense.
B. 401(k) contributions payable.
C. 401(k) employer contributions expense.
D. Social Security tax payable.

E6-9A.

LO 6-7

What is always true about trial balance reports? (Select all that apply.)
A. Only accounts with activity during the period are included on the report.
B. All accounts with balances are included in the report.
C. The total of the debit column must equal the total of the credit column.
D. The report is prepared for a range of dates.

E6-10A.

LO 6-7

The purpose of a labor report is to do what?
A. Report an individual employee's regular time and overtime.
B. Reflect all expenses of a firm.
C. Promote analysis of payroll expenses.
D. Update managers about payroll on a daily basis.

Problems Set A

P6-1A.

LO 6-1

As the accountant for Tooka's Trees, you need to prepare the payroll register for the payroll dated October 14, 2016 (Hint: all dates will be October 14, 2016). Employees are paid biweekly and are subject to a flat 3% state income tax. Use the wage bracket method in the federal tax table in Appendix C. No employee has exceeded the Social Security wage base. The employees are as follows:

a. T. Taylor
Single, four withholdings
Gross pay: $1,500 per period
401(k) deduction: $125 per pay period
b. B. Walburn
Married, six withholdings
Gross pay: $2,225 per period
401(k) deduction: $250 per period
c. H. Carpenter
Single, zero withholdings
Gross pay: $1,500 per period
Section 125 deduction: $75 per period
401(k) deduction: $50 per period
d. J. Knight
Married, three withholdings
Gross pay: $1,875 per period
United Way deduction: $50 per period
Garnishment: $50 per period
e. C. Lunn
Single, one withholding
Gross pay: $2,100 per period
Section 125 withholding: $50 per period
401(k) deduction: 6% of gross pay
f. E. Smooter
Married, eight withholdings
Gross pay: $2,425 per period
401(k) deduction: $75 per period

Complete the payrollngs register for Tooka's Trees for the payroll dated October 14. Check number 14458 is the first available check.

P/R End Date [ ] Company Name _____

Check Date [ ] Check Date _____

Name	M/S	# W/H	Hourly Rate or Monthly Wage	No. of Regular Hours	No. of Overtime Hours	No. of Holiday Hours	Commissions	Gross Earning	401(k)	Sec 125	Taxable Wages for Federal W/H	Taxable Wages for FICA
Totals								-	-	-	-	-

Name	Gross Earning	Taxable Wages for Federal W/H	Taxable Wages for FICA	Federal W/H	Social Security Tax	Medicare W/H	State W/H Tax	Garnishment	United Way	Net Pay	Check No
Totals		-	-	-	-	-	-	-	-	-	

P6-2A.

LO 6-1

Charles Merrill owns a housekeeping service, Charles' Cleaners, in Florida. For the weekly payroll dated July 15, 2016, complete the payroll register. Use the wage bracket method in the federal tax table in Appendix C. No employee has exceeded the Social Security tax wage base. Total, prove, and rule the entries.

P/R End Date 7/15/2016 Company Name Charles' Cleaners _____

Check Date 7/15/2016 Check Date _____

Name	M/S	# W/H	Hourly Rate or Period Wage	No. of Regular Hours	No. of Overtime Hours	No. of Holiday Hours	Commissions	Gross Earning	401(k)	Cafeteria Plan	Taxable Wages for Federal W/H	Taxable Wages for FICA
Clark, M.	M	3	$ 8.50	40	3				$ 50.00			
Toonen, B.	S	1	$ 9.20	35					$ 75.00			
Dahl, P.	S	0	$ 10.10	37.5								
Steverman, S.	S	1	$ 8.04	40								
Bromley, L	M	4	$ 8.90	38					$ 60.00	$ 20.00		
Matte, R.	S	2	$ 10.50	40	5				$ 75.00			
Maddox, F.	S	1	$ 9.95	40						$ 15.00		
Totals												

Name	Gross Earning	Taxable Wages for Federal W/H	Taxable Wages for FICA	Federal W/H	Social Security Tax	Medicare W/H	State W/H Tax	Garnishment	United Way	Net Pay	Check No
Clark, M.											
Toonen, B.									$ 10.00		
Dahl, P.								$ 100.00			
Steverman, S.									$ 25.00		
Bromley, L											
Matte, R.									$ 10.00		
Maddox, F.											
Totals											

P6-3A.
LO 6-2

What follows is the employee earnings record for Sean Steverman of Charles' Cleaners. Record his earnings on the July 15 pay from Exercise 6-2A.

EMPLOYEE EARNING RECORD

NAME	Sean Steverman	Hire Date	May 22, 2011
ADDRESS	2326 Vinings Drive	Date of Birth	November 15, 1991
CITY/STATE/ZIP	Lodi, FL 32039	Exempt/Nonexempt	Nonexempt
TELEPHONE	305-555-5698	Married/Single	Single
SOCIAL SECURITY NUMBER	188-56-7316	No. of Exemptions	1
POSITION	House Cleaner	Pay Rate	8.04/hour

Period Ended	Hrs. Worked	Reg Pay	OT Pay	Holiday	Comm	Gross Pay	Ins	Section 125	Taxable Pay for Federal	Taxable Pay for FICA
7/5/2016	40	$ 321.60				$ 321.60	–	–	$ 321.60	$ 321.60

Taxable Pay for Federal	Taxable Pay for FICA	Fed Inc. Tax	Social Sec. Tax	Medicare	State Inc. Tax	United Way	Net Pay	YTD Net Pay	YTD Gross Pay
$ 321.60	$ 321.60	$ 22.00	$ 19.94	$ 4.66	–	–	$ 275.00	$ 3,500.00	$ 4,502.40

P6-4A.
LO 6-3, 6-4

Using the payroll register from 6-2A for Charles' Cleaners, complete the General Journal entry for the employees' pay for the July 15 pay date. Paychecks will be issued in the future.

	Date	Description	Post Ref.	Debit	Credit	
1						1
2						2
3						3
4						4
5						5
6						6
7						7
8						8
9						9
10						10
11						11
12						12

P6-5A.

LO 6-3, 6-4

Using the payroll register from 6-2A for Charles' Cleaners, complete the General Journal entry for the employer's share of the payroll taxes for the July 15 pay date. Assume 5.4% SUTA and 0.6% FUTA tax rates and that $1,352.40 is subject to FUTA/SUTA taxes

	Date	Description	Post Ref.	Debit	Credit	
1						1
2						2
3						3
4						4
5						5
6						6
7						7
8						8
9						9

P6-6A.

LO 6-3, 6-4

Using the employee payroll entry from 6-4A, post the July 15 employee pay for Charles' Cleaners to the selected General Ledger accounts shown next:

Account: Salaries and Wages Payable

	Date	Description	Post Ref.	Debit	Credit	Balance Debit	Balance Credit	
1								1
2								2
3								3
4								4
5								5
6								6

Account: Employee Federal Income Tax Payable

	Date	Description	Post Ref.	Debit	Credit	Balance Debit	Balance Credit	
1								1
2								2
3								3
4								4
5								5
6								6

Account: Social Security Tax Payable

	Date	Description	Post Ref.	Debit	Credit	Balance Debit	Balance Credit	
1								1
2								2
3								3
4								4
5								5
6								6

Account: Medicare Tax Payable

	Date	Description	Post Ref.	Debit	Credit	Balance Debit	Balance Credit	
1								1
2								2
3								3
4								4
5								5
6								6

Account: Salaries and Wages Expense

	Date	Description	Post Ref.	Debit	Credit	Balance Debit	Balance Credit	
1								1
2								2
3								3
4								4
5								5
6								6
7								7

P6-7A.
LO 6-3, 6-4

Using the employee payroll entry from 6-4A, complete the General Journal entry for the issuance of the pay for the July 15 pay date. The date of the checks is July 18.

	Date	Description	Post Ref.	Debit	Credit	
1						1
2						2
3						3
4						4
5						5

P6-8A.
LO 6-3, 6-4, 6-5

Using the employer payroll entry from 6-5A, post the employer's share of payroll taxes for the July 14 pay at Charles' Cleaners to the appropriate General Ledger accounts. Assume that $1,352.40 is subject to FUTA/SUTA taxes.

Account: Social Security Tax Payable

	Date	Description	Post Ref.	Debit	Credit	Balance Debit	Balance Credit	
1								1
2								2
3								3
4								4
5								5
6								6
7								7

Account: Medicare Tax Payable

	Date	Description	Post Ref.	Debit	Credit	Balance Debit	Balance Credit	
1								1
2								2
3								3
4								4
5								5
6								6
7								7

Account: Federal Unemployment Tax Payable

	Date	Description	Post Ref.	Debit	Credit	Balance Debit	Balance Credit	
1								1
2								2
3								3
4								4
5								5
6								6
7								7

Account: State Unemployment Tax Payable

	Date	Description	Post Ref.	Debit	Credit	Balance Debit	Balance Credit	
1								1
2								2
3								3
4								4
5								5
6								6
7								7

Account: Payroll Taxes Expense

	Date	Description	Post Ref.	Debit	Credit	Balance Debit	Balance Credit	
1								1
2								2
3								3
4								4
5								5
6								6
7								7

6-9A.

LO 6-3, 6-4

KMH Industries is a monthly schedule depositor of payroll taxes. For the month of August 2016, the payroll taxes (employee and employer share) were as follows:

Social Security tax: $3,252.28

Medicare tax: $760.61

Employee Federal income tax: $2,520

Create the General Journal entry for the remittance of the taxes. Use check 2052 in the description.

	Date	Description	Post Ref.	Debit	Credit	
1						1
2						2
3						3
4						4
5						5
6						6
7						7
8						8

P6-10A.
LO 6-3, 6-4

Sophie Sue Breeders has the following voluntary withholdings to remit:

AFLAC payable: $560.00

401(k) payable: $1,280.00

Garnishments payable: $375.00

United Way contributions payable: $200.00

Create the General Journal entry on June 15, 2016, for the remittance of these withheld amounts.

	Date	Description	Post Ref.	Debit	Credit	
1						1
2						2
3						3
4						4
5						5
6						6
7						7

P6-11A.
LO 6-6, 6-7

Sheronda Rowe is the payroll accountant for Great Lake Lamps. The company's management has requested an analysis of the payroll effects on the expenses of the company. Explain which accounting report(s) you would use to construct your analysis. How would you explain the purpose of labor expenses as they affect company productivity?

Exercises Set B

E6-1B.
LO 6-1

What are the differences between the rows and columns in the payroll register? (Select all that apply.)
A. Each row pertains to an individual employee.
B. Each column represents an element in net pay computation.
C. Column totals link to general journal entries.
D. Row totals link to general ledger entries.

E6-2B.
LO 6-1, 6-2

Which of the following information exists in both the employees' earnings records and the payroll register? (Select all that apply.)
A. Marital status.
B. Social Security number.
C. Hourly rate or period wage.
D. Employee home address.

E6-3B.
LO 6-1, 6-2

How do the payroll register and employees' earnings records connect with payroll tax determination and remittance? (Select all that apply.)
A. Payroll register column totals contain information about pay period tax withholdings.
B. Employees' earnings records have pertinent information to determine individual taxable wage base attainment.
C. Employees' earnings records reflect which employees are subject to Medicare tax.
D. Payroll registers contain specific information about each employee's pay period disbursements.

E6-4B.
LO 6-3

Which of the following are categories contained in the fundamental accounting equation? (Select all that apply.)
A. Assets
B. Liabilities
C. Expenses
D. Owners' Equity

E6-5B.
LO 6-3

Which of the following principles are always true about financial accounting? (Select all that apply.)
A. Assets = Owners' Equity.
B. Debits = Credits.
C. Assets = Liabilities + Owners' Equity.
D. Debits + Credits = Owners' Equity.

E6-6B.
LO 6-4

What is true about expenses and liabilities? (Select all that apply.)
A. Expenses usually have the word "expense" in the account title.
B. Expenses represent additional sums earned by the company.
C. Liabilities represent sums of money owed by third parties to the company.
D. Liabilities usually have the word "payable" in the account title.

E6-7B.
LO 6-4, 6-5, 6-6

How do payroll-related expenses affect financial statements? (Select all that apply.)
A. Payroll expenses may be allocable to work performed for a firm's customers.
B. Payroll expense accounts are reported on the Balance Sheet.
C. The period's gross earnings are reported on the Income Statement.
D. Payroll expenses reduce the net income of a company.

E6-8B.
LO 6-7

Which of the following accounts appear on the Balance Sheet? (Select all that apply.)
A. Wages and Salaries Expense.
B. Medicare tax payable.
C. Employee Federal income tax payable.
D. Health insurance premiums payable.

E6-9B.
LO 6-4, 6-7

What is the purpose of payroll-related accrual and reversal entries on financial statements? (Select all that apply.)
A. Accrual entries represent payroll amounts earned but not yet paid.
B. Reversing entries represent disbursement of accrued payroll prior to the end of the payroll period.
C. Accrual entries are used to improve the accuracy of the net income for a period.
D. Reversing entries are omitted from financial statements.

E6-10B.
LO 6-7

Managers use labor reports to do which of the following? (Select all that apply.)
A. Analyze labor trends.

B. Determine staffing needs.
C. Ensure FLSA wage and hour compliance.
D. Formulate strategic plans for the company.

Problems Set B

P6-1B.

LO 6-1

As the accountant for TJ's Tire Company in Illinois, you need to prepare the payroll register for the payroll dated November 18, 2016. Employees are paid semimonthly and are subject to a flat 5% state income tax. Use the wage bracket method in the federal tax table in Appendix C. No employee has met the Social Security wage base. The employees are as follows:

a. P. Hamel
Married, one withholding
Gross pay: $2,357 per period
401(k) deduction: $175 per pay period

b. J. Roberts
Single, one withholding
Gross pay: $1,725 per period
401(k) deduction: $100 per period

c. M. Meyer
Married, four withholdings
Gross pay: $2,625 per period
Garnishment: $125 per period
401(k) deduction: $175 per period

d. C. Moriarty
Married, seven withholdings
Gross pay: $2,430 per period
Section 125 deduction: $80 per period
401(k) deduction: $150 per period

| P/R End Date | | | Company Name | |
| Check Date | | | Check Date | |

Name	M/S	# W/H	Hourly Rate or Period Wage	No. of Regular Hours	No. of Overtime Hours	No. of Holiday Hours	Commissions	Gross Earning	401(k)	Sec 125	Taxable Wages for Federal W/H	Taxable Wages for FICA
Totals									-	-	-	-

Name	Gross Earning	Taxable Wages for Federal W/H	Taxable Wages for FICA	Federal W/H	Social Security Tax	Medicare W/H	State W/H Tax	Garnishment	United Way	Net Pay	Check No
Totals		-	-				-	-	-	-	-

e. T. Brock
Single, three withholdings
Gross pay: $1,590 per period
United Way deduction: $25 per period
401(k) deduction: 3% of gross pay

f. R. Leigh
Married, two withholdings
Gross pay: $2,210 per period
Garnishment: $45 per period
United Way deduction: $10 per period
401(k) deduction: 2% of gross pay

Complete the payroll register for TJ's Tire Company for the payroll dated November 18, 2016. Use the wage bracket table in Appendix C.

P6-2B.

LO 6-1

Tony Stanford owns Cosmic Comics in Greensboro, North Carolina. For the weekly payroll dated September 16, 2016, complete the payroll register. Use the wage bracket method in the federal tax table in Appendix C. Assume 5.8% state income tax. No employee has exceeded the Social Security wage base. Total, prove, and rule the entries.

| P/R End Date | 9/16/2016 | Company Name | Cosmic Cosmics |
| Check Date | 9/16/2016 | Check Date | |

Name	M/S	# W/H	Hourly Rate or Period Wage	No. of Regular Hours	No. of Overtime Hours	No. of Holiday Hours	Commissions	Gross Earning	401(k)	Sec 125	Taxable Wages for Federal W/H	Taxable Wages for FICA
Camacho, N.	M	2	$ 12.20	40	2				$ 50.00			
Rea, A.	S	4	$ 9.45	39						$ 20.00		
Dahl, P.	M	5	$ 11.30	40	5				$ 35.00	$ 10.00		
Hayes, K.	S	1	$ 8.95	37					$ 20.00			
Fortanier, Y.	S	0	$ 10.05	38.5								
Cronan, S.	M	2	$ 13.45	40	6							
Murner, A.	S	2	$ 10.65	37					$ 45.00	$ 10.00		
Zinsli, E.	M	0	$ 9.50	40	1				$ 25.00			
Totals												

Name	Gross Earning	Taxable Wages for Federal W/H	Taxable Wages for FICA	Federal W/H	Social Security Tax	Medicare W/H	State W/H Tax	Garnishment	United Way	Net Pay	Check No
Camacho, N.									$ 10.00		
Rea, A.											
Dahl, P.											
Hayes, K.									$ 60.00		
Fortanier, Y.									$ 50.00		
Cronan, S.											
Murner, A.											
Zinsli, E.											
Totals											

P6-3B.

LO 6-2

What follows is the employee earnings record for Ally Murner of Cosmic Comics. Record her earnings on the September 16, 2016, pay from P6-2B.

EMPLOYEE EARNING RECORD

NAME	Ally Murner		Hire Date	4/2/2009
ADDRESS	522 Shady Lane		Date of Birth	7/1/1989
CITY/STATE/ZIP	Winslow, NC 22203		Exempt/Nonexempt	Nonexempt
TELEPHONE	704-553-5967		Married/Single	Single
SOCIAL SECURITY NUMBER	680-30-2983		No. of Exemptions	2
POSITION	Night Cashier		Pay Rate	$10.65/hour

Period Ended	Hrs. Worked	Reg Pay	OT Pay	Holiday	Comm	Gross Pay	401(k)	Sec 125	Taxable Pay for Federal	Taxable Pay for FICA
9/9/2016	40	$ 426.00				$426.00	$ 45.00	$ 15.00	$ 366.00	$ 411.00

Taxable Pay for Federal	Taxable Pay for FICA	Fed Inc. Tax	Social Sec. Tax	Medicare	State Inc. Tax	Garnish-ment	United Way	Net Pay	YTD Net Pay	YTD Gross Pay
$ 366.00	$411.00	$ 17.00	$ 25.48	$ 5.96	$ 21.23			$ 296.33	$ 5,630.31	$8,256.90

P6-4B.

LO 6-1, 6-3, 6-4

Using the payroll register from P6-2B for Cosmic Comics, complete the General Journal entry for the employees' pay for the September 16, 2016, pay date. Employees' paychecks will be issued on September 19.

	Date	Description	Post Ref.	Debit	Credit
1					
2					
3					
4					
5					
6					
7					
8					
9					

P6-5B.

LO 6-1, 6-3, 6-4

Using the payroll register from P6-2B for Cosmic Comics, complete the General Journal entry for the employer's share of the payroll taxes for the September 16, 2016, pay date. Assume a 5.4% SUTA rate and 0.6% FUTA rate, and assume that $954.05 of the gross pay is subject to SUTA/FUTA taxes.

	Date	Description	Post Ref.	Debit	Credit
1					
2					
3					
4					
5					
6					
7					
8					
9					

P6-6B.

LO 6-4, 6-5

Using the employee payroll entry from P6-4B, post the September 16 employee pay for Cosmic Comics to the selected General Ledger accounts.

Account: Salaries and Wages Payable

	Date	Description	Post Ref.	Debit	Credit	Balance Debit	Balance Credit
1							
2							
3							
4							
5							
6							

Account: Employee Federal Income Tax Payable

	Date	Description	Post Ref.	Debit	Credit	Balance Debit	Balance Credit
1							
2							
3							
4							
5							
6							

Account: Social Security Tax Payable

	Date	Description	Post Ref.	Debit	Credit	Balance Debit	Balance Credit
1							
2							
3							
4							
5							
6							

Account: Medicare Tax Payable

	Date	Description	Post Ref.	Debit	Credit	Balance Debit	Balance Credit
1							
2							
3							
4							
5							
6							

Account: Employee State Income Tax Payable

	Date	Description	Post Ref.	Debit	Credit	Balance Debit	Balance Credit
1							
2							
3							
4							
5							
6							

Account: Salaries and Wages Expense

	Date	Description	Post Ref.	Debit	Credit	Balance Debit	Balance Credit
1							
2							
3							
4							
5							
6							
7							

P6-7B.

LO 6-4, 6-5

Using the employee payroll entry from P6-4B, complete the General Journal entry for the issuance of Cosmic Comics pay on September 19, 2016.

	Date	Description	Post Ref.	Debit	Credit	
1						1
2						2
3						3
4						4
5						5

P6-8B.

LO 6-4, 6-5

Using the employer payroll entry from P6-5B, post the employer's share of payroll taxes for the September 16 pay period at Cosmic Comics to the appropriate General Ledger accounts:

Account: Payroll Taxes Expense

	Date	Description	Post Ref.	Debit	Credit	Balance Debit	Balance Credit	
1								1
2								2
3								3
4								4
5								5
6								6
7								7

Account: Social Security Tax Payable

	Date	Description	Post Ref.	Debit	Credit	Balance Debit	Balance Credit	
1								1
2								2
3								3
4								4
5								5
6								6
7								7

Account: Medicare Tax Payable

	Date	Description	Post Ref.	Debit	Credit	Balance Debit	Balance Credit	
1								1
2								2
3								3
4								4
5								5
6								6
7								7

Account: Federal Unemployment Tax Payable

	Date	Description	Post Ref.	Debit	Credit	Balance Debit	Balance Credit	
1								1
2								2
3								3
4								4
5								5
6								6
7								7

Account: State Unemployment Tax Payable

	Date	Description	Post Ref.	Debit	Credit	Balance Debit	Balance Credit	
1								1
2								2
3								3
4								4
5								5
6								6
7								7

P6-9B.

LO 6-3, 6-4

Legends Leadworks is a monthly schedule depositor of payroll taxes. For the month of April 2016, the payroll taxes (employee and employer share) were as follows:

Social Security tax: $5,386.56

Medicare tax: $1,259.76

Employee federal income tax: $4,978

Create the General Journal entry for the remittance of the taxes on May 13, 2016. Use check 1320 in the description.

	Date	Description	Post Ref.	Debit	Credit	
1						1
2						2
3						3
4						4
5						5
6						6
7						7
8						8

P6-10B.

LO 6-3, 6-4

Candy Farms, Inc., has the following voluntary withholdings to remit as of September 30, 2016:

AFLAC payable: $687.00

Worker's compensation insurance payable: $1,042.00

401(k) payable: $2,104.00

Garnishments payable: $450.00

U.S. savings bonds payable: $200.00

Create the General Journal entry for the remittance of these withheld amounts on October 14, 2016.

	Date	Description	Post Ref.	Debit	Credit	
1						1
2						2
3						3
4						4
5						5
6						6
7						7
8						8

P6-11B.

LO 6-6, 6-7

Pujah Srinivasan is the controller for HHT Industries. She has been asked to explain the payroll accounts on the financial statements for the preceding month. What information will she find about payroll on the income statement? What information will be located on the balance sheet? How could she use the information in the accounting reports to explain the payroll effects on the company?

Critical Thinking

6-1. Your boss asks you for a five-year labor cost trend chart. The labor costs per year are as follows:

2012	$178,967
2013	$185,923
2014	$172,245
2015	$179,905
2016	$182,478

Construct a line chart to depict the data. What conclusions can you derive from the data about labor costs and trends over the past five years? Why?

6-2. Giblin's Goodies pays employees weekly on Fridays. However, the company notices that December 31 is a Saturday. The payroll data for December 26–31 is as follows:

Gross pay: $4,500

Federal income tax: $520

Social Security tax: $279

Medicare tax: $65.25

State income tax: $90

Give the adjusting entry in the General Journal to recognize the employee and employer share of the payroll for the week of December 26. Date the entry December 30. Then give the journal entry to reverse the adjustment on January 1, 2017.

	Date	Description	Post Ref.	Debit	Credit	
1						1
2						2
3						3
4						4
5						5
6						6
7						7
8						8
9						9
10						10
11						11
12						12
13						13
14						14
15						15

In the Real World: Scenario for Discussion

An ongoing discussion among business managers is the return on employee investment (ROEI). Employers want to maximize business profitability, and employees are a significant part of organizational success. An example of this issue faces Uber. The company has a cadre of drivers across the United States who are demanding to be classified as employees. What are some issues Uber faces if it classifies its drivers as employees? How could these issues affect ROEI and company profitability? (Source: *Forbes*)

Internet Activities

6-1. Would you like to know about personal experiences as a payroll accountant? How about videos that detail the completion of payroll-related forms? Go to www.youtube .com and search the term "payroll accounting" to read personal perspectives about payroll practice, outsourcing, and tax form completion. What were three insights you found that were new to you?

6-2. Would you like to build your own favorites list of payroll accounting tools? Go to one or more of the following sites. What are three important items you noticed?

www.accountingtools.com

http://payroll.softwareinsider.com/

www.accountsworld.com

www.americanpayroll.org

6-3. Join a conversation about payroll accounting with industry professionals. Go to www.linkedin.com and establish a profile (if you do not have one). Search groups for payroll accounting and follow the conversations. Which topics did you choose? Why?

6-4. Want to know more about the concepts in this chapter? Check out:

www.americanpayroll.org/payrollmetrics/challenges/

www.moneyinstructor.com/lesson/accountingconcepts.asp

www.cs.thomsonreuters.com/resources/white-papers/15962_Payroll_ Opportunity_WP_.pdf

Continuing Payroll Project: Prevosti Farms and Sugarhouse

Complete the Payroll Register for the 2/12 and 2/26 biweekly pay periods. Use the Wage Bracket Method Tables for Income Tax Withholding in Appendix C. Complete the General Journal entries as follows:

February 12	Journalize the employee pay.
February 12	Journalize the employer payroll tax for the February 12 pay period. Use 5.4% SUTA and 0.6% FUTA. No employees will exceed the FUTA or SUTA wage base.
February 15	Issue the employee pay.
February 26	Journalize the employee pay.
February 26	Journalize the employer payroll tax for the February 26 pay period. Use 5.4% SUTA and 0.6% FUTA. No employee will exceed the FUTA or SUTA wage base.
February 29	Issue the employee pay.

	Date	Description	Post Ref.	Debit	Credit	
1						1
2						2
3						3
4						4
5						5
6						6
7						7
8						8
9						9
10						10
11						11
12						12
13						13
14						14
15						15
16						16
17						17
18						18
19						19
20						20
21						21
22						22
23						23
24						24
25						25
26						26
27						27
28						28
29						29
30						30
31						31
32						32
33						33
34						34
35						35

Post all journal entries to the appropriate General Ledger accounts.

Account: Cash   **101**

	Date	Description	Post Ref.	Debit	Credit	Balance Debit	Balance Credit	
1		Beg. Bal.				15 0 0 0 00		1
2								2
3								3
4								4
5								5
6								6

Account: Employee Federal Income Tax Payable   **203**

	Date	Description	Post Ref.	Debit	Credit	Balance Debit	Balance Credit	
1								1
2								2
3								3
4								4
5								5
6								6

Account: Social Security Tax Payable   **204**

	Date	Description	Post Ref.	Debit	Credit	Balance Debit	Balance Credit	
1								1
2								2
3								3
4								4
5								5
6								6

Account: Medicare Tax Payable   **205**

	Date	Description	Post Ref.	Debit	Credit	Balance Debit	Balance Credit	
1								1
2								2
3								3
4								4
5								5
6								6

Account: Employee State Income Tax Payable   **206**

	Date	Description	Post Ref.	Debit	Credit	Balance Debit	Balance Credit	
1								1
2								2
3								3
4								4
5								5
6								6

Account: 401(k) Contributions Payable   **208**

	Date	Description	Post Ref.	Debit	Credit	Balance Debit	Balance Credit	
1								1
2								2
3								3
4								4
5								5
6								6

Account: Health Insurance Payable   209

	Date	Description	Post Ref.	Debit	Credit	Balance Debit	Balance Credit	
1								1
2								2
3								3
4								4
5								5
6								6

Account: Salaries and Wages Payable   210

	Date	Description	Post Ref.	Debit	Credit	Balance Debit	Balance Credit	
1								1
2								2
3								3
4								4
5								5
6								6

Account: FUTA Tax Payable   211

	Date	Description	Post Ref.	Debit	Credit	Balance Debit	Balance Credit	
1								1
2								2
3								3
4								4
5								5
6								6

Account: SUTA Tax Payable   212

	Date	Description	Post Ref.	Debit	Credit	Balance Debit	Balance Credit	
1								1
2								2
3								3
4								4
5								5
6								6

Account: Payroll Taxes Expense   514

	Date	Description	Post Ref.	Debit	Credit	Balance Debit	Balance Credit	
1								1
2								2
3								3
4								4
5								5
6								6

Account: Salaries and Wages Expense   **515**

	Date	Description	Post Ref.	Debit	Credit	Balance Debit	Balance Credit	
1								1
2								2
3								3
4								4
5								5
6								6

Answers to Stop & Check Exercises

What is contained in the full Payroll Register?
1. a. Gross earnings
   b. Net pay
   d. Check number
   f. Local income tax
2. Total means to compute the total of each row and each column. Prove means to demonstrate that the sum of all rows equals the sum of all columns. Rule means to double-underline each column total. This process ensures accuracy of the calculated payroll and amounts to be remitted to third parties.
3. Employee earnings registers would link payroll to the human resources functions. The payroll register would link to the General Journal to complete payroll entries.

Employees' Earnings Records
1. The payroll register contains the period payroll information for all employees. The employee earnings record lists all payroll data for a single employee.
2. All fields exist on both the employees' earnings records and the payroll register.
3. Quarterly and annual tax reports use the totals from the employees' earnings records.

Financial Accounting Concepts
1. Assets = Liabilities + Owners' Equity
2. Credit
3. Debit

Payroll and the General Journal
1. Wages and Salaries Expense
2.

Account	Debit	Credit
Payroll Taxes Expense	$9,546.05	
Social Security Tax Payable		$7,736.67
Medicare Tax Payable		$1,809.38

3.

	Debit	Credit
Federal Income Tax Payable	$15,280.00	
Social Security Tax Payable	$2,653.29	
Medicare Tax Payable	$620.53	
State Income Tax Payable	$1,626.21	
Wages and Salaries Payable	$22,614.97	
Wages and Salaries Expense		$42,795.00

General Ledger Entries

1. $2,760 Cr.
2. The transaction may be found in the General Journal on page 34.

The Business Effects of Payroll

1. The payment of employee wages decreases profitability because it increases the expenses of a business.
2. Allocation of payroll expenses to specific jobs, clients, and so on allows the company to understand the costs associated with the activity.

Labor Reports

1. a. Trial Balance
   b. Statement of Owners' Equity
   d. Income Summary
   e. Balance Sheet
2. Labor reports
3. Trend reports are used by managers to identify business patterns, needs, and opportunities.

Appendix A

Continuing Payroll Project: Wayland Custom Woodworking

Wayland Custom Woodworking is a firm that manufactures custom cabinets and woodwork for business and residential customers. Students will have the opportunity to establish payroll records and to complete a month of payroll information for Wayland.

Wayland Custom Woodworking is located at 1716 Nichol Street, Logan, Utah, 84321, phone number 435-555-9877. The owner is Mark Wayland. Wayland's EIN is 91-7444533, and the Utah Employer Account Number is 999-9290-1. Wayland has determined it will pay their employees on a semimonthly basis. Federal income tax should be computed using the *percentage* method.

Students will complete the payroll for the final quarter of 2016, and will file fourth quarter and annual tax reports on the appropriate dates. At the instructor's discretion, students may complete a short version, which contains the payroll transactions beginning December 1. Directions for completion of the short version follow the November 30 transactions.

The SUTA (UI) rate for Wayland Custom Woodworking is 2.6% on the first $32,200, and the state withholding rate is 5.0% for all income levels and marital statuses.

Rounding can create a challenge. For these exercises, the rate for the individuals is not rounded. So take their salary and divide by 2,080 (52 weeks at 40 hours per week) for full-time, nonexempt employees.

EXAMPLE: ANNUAL SALARY TO HOURLY RATE, NONEXEMPT EMPLOYEE

Employee Varden's annual salary is $42,000, and he is a nonexempt employee.

Hourly rate = $42,000/ (52 x 40) = $42,000/2,080

Hourly rate = $20.19231 per hour

EXAMPLE: PERIOD GROSS PAY, SALARIED EMPLOYEE

Employee Chinson earns an annual salary of $24,000 and is paid semimonthly.

Period gross pay = $24,000/24 = $1,000 gross pay

For pay periods of greater than 80 hours, use the formula to convert the annual salary to an hourly salary, round the answer to *five* decimal places, and then use that hourly rate to compute the gross pay.

After the gross pay has been calculated, round the result to only two decimal points prior to calculating taxes or other withholdings.

Employees are paid for the following holidays occurring during the final quarter:

- Thanksgiving day and the day after, Thursday and Friday November 24–25.
- Christmas, which is a Sunday. When holidays occur on a weekend, the preceding Friday, December 23, is considered a holiday. Employees receive holiday pay for Monday, December 26.

For the completion of this project the following information can be located in Appendix C. Students will use the Percentage method for federal income tax and the tax tables have been provided for Utah. Both 401(k) and insurance are pretax for federal income tax and Utah income tax. Round calculations to get to final tax amounts and 401(k) contributions after calculating gross pay.

Federal Withholding Allowance (less 401(k), Section 125)	$168.80 per allowance claimed
Federal Unemployment Rate (employer only) (less Section 125)	0.6% on the first $7,000 of wages
Semimonthly Federal Percentage Method Tax Table	Appendix C Page 349 Table #3
State Unemployment Rate (employer only) (less Section 125)	2.6% on the first $32,200 of wages
State Withholding Rate (less 401(k), Section 125)	See Utah Schedule 3, Table 1

TABLE 1

| UTAH SCHEDULE 3 | SEMIMONTHLY Payroll Period (24 pay periods per year) |

SINGLE

1. Utah taxable wages		
2. Multiply line 1 by .05 (5%)		
3. Number of withholding allowances		
4. Multiply line 3 by $ 5		
5. Base allowance	10	
6. Add lines 4 and 5		
7. Line 1 less $500 (not less than 0)		
8. Multiply line 7 by .013 (1.3%)		
9. Line 6 less line 8 (not less than 0)		
10. Withholding tax - line 2 less line 9 (not less than 0)		

MARRIED

1. Utah taxable wages		
2. Multiply line 1 by .05 (5%)		
3. Number of withholding allowances		
4. Multiply line 3 by $ 5		
5. Base allowance	16	
6. Add lines 4 and 5		
7. Line 1 less $750 (not less than 0)		
8. Multiply line 7 by .013 (1.3%)		
9. Line 6 less line 8 (not less than 0)		
10. Withholding tax - line 2 less line 9 (not less than 0)		

October 1

Wayland Custom Woodworking (WCW) pays its employees according to their job classification. The following employees comprise Wayland's staff:

Employee Number	Name and Address	Payroll information
00-Chins	Anthony Chinson 530 Sylvann Avenue Logan, UT 84321 435-555-1212 Job title: Account Executive	Married, 1 withholding allowance Exempt $24,000/year + commission Start Date: 10/1/2016 SSN: 511-22-3333
00-Wayla	Mark Wayland 1570 Lovett Street Logan, UT 84321 435-555-1110 Job title: President/Owner	Married, 5 withholding allowances Exempt $75,000/year Start Date: 10/1/2016 SSN: 505-33-1775
01-Peppi	Sylvia Peppinico 291 Antioch Road Logan, UT 84321 435-555-2244 Job title: Craftsman	Married, 7 withholding allowances Exempt $43,500/year Start Date: 10/1/2016 SSN: 047-55-9951
01-Varde	Stevon Varden 333 Justin Drive Logan, UT 84321 435-555-9981 Job title: Craftsman	Married, 2 withholding allowances Nonexempt $42,000/year Start Date: 10/1/2016 SSN: 022-66-1131
02-Hisso	Leonard Hissop 531 5th Street Logan, UT 84321 435-555-5858 Job title: Purchasing/Shippinkg	Single, 4 withholding allowances Nonexempt $49,500/year Start Date: 10/1/2016 SSN: 311-22-6698

Complete the headers of the Employees' Earnings Register for all company employees. Enter the YTD earnings for each employee. The departments are as follows:

Department 00: Sales and Administration

Department 01: Factory workers

Department 02: Delivery and Customer service

1. You have been hired as of October 1 as the new accounting clerk. Your employee number is 00-SUCCE. Your name is STUDENT SUCCESS. Your address is 1650 South Street, Logan, UT 84321. Your phone number is 435-556-1211, you were born July 16, 1985, your Utah driver's license number is 887743 expiring in 7/2018, and your Social Security number is 555-55-5555. You are nonexempt and paid at a rate of $36,000 per year. Complete the W-4 and, using the given information, complete the I-9 form to start your employee file. Complete it as if you are single with one withholding, you contribute 3% to a 401(k), and health insurance is $50 per pay period.

The balance sheet for WCW as of September 30, 2016, is as follows:

Wayland Custom Woodworking
Balance Sheet
September 30, 2016

Assets		Liabilities & Equity	
Cash	$1,125,000.00	Accounts Payable	$ 112,490.00
Supplies	27,240.00	Salaries and Wages Payable	
Office Equipment	87,250.00	Federal Unemployment Tax Payable	
Inventory	123,000.00	Social Security Tax Payable	
Vehicle	25,000.00	Medicare Tax Payable	
Accumulated Depreciation, Vehicle		State Unemployment Tax Payable	
Building	164,000.00	Employee Federal Income Tax Payable	
Accumulated Depreciation, Building		Employee State Income Tax Payable	
Land	35,750.00	401(k) Contributions Payable	
Total Assets	1,587,240.00	Employee Medical Premiums Payable	
		Notes Payable	224,750.00
		Utilities Payable	
		Total Liabilities	337,240.00
		Owners' Equity	1,250,000.00
		Retained Earnings	-
		Total Equity	1,250,000.00
		Total Liabilities and Equity	1,587,240.00

October 15

October 15 is the end of the first pay period for the month of October. Employee pay will be disbursed on October 20, 2016. Any time worked in excess of 80 hours during this pay period is considered overtime for nonexempt employees. Remember that the employees are paid on a semimonthly basis. The hours for the employees are as follows:

Name	Hourly Rate (round to 5 decimals)	Pay Period Hours 10/1– 10/15	Regular (round to 2 decimal)	Overtime (round to 2 decimal)	Commission
Chinson		80 hours (exempt)			$1,500.00
Wayland		80 hours (exempt)			
Peppinico		80 hours (exempt)			
Varden		88 hours			
Hissop		85.25 hours			
You		82 hours			

Complete the Payroll Register for October 15. Round wages to five decimal points and all other final answers to two decimal points. Update the Employees' Earning Records for the period's pay and update the YTD amount. Insurance qualifies for Section 125 treatment.

Voluntary deductions for each employee are as follows:

Name	Deduction
Chinson	**Insurance: $50/paycheck** **401(k): 3% of gross pay**
Wayland	**Insurance: $75/paycheck** **401(k): 6% of gross pay**
Peppinico	**Insurance: $75/paycheck** **401(k): $50 per paycheck**
Varden	**Insurance: $50/paycheck** **401(k): 4% of gross pay**
Hissop	**Insurance: $75/paycheck** **401(k): 3% of gross pay**
Student	**Insurance: $50/paycheck** **401(k): 3% of gross pay**

Complete the Payroll Register for October 15.

P/R End Date [＿＿＿＿]   Company Name   Wayland Custom Woodworking

Check Date [＿＿＿＿]

Name	M/S	# W/H	Hourly Rate or Period Wage	No. of Regular Hours	No. of Overtime Hours	No. of Holiday Hours	Commissions	Gross Earning	Insurance	Cafeteria Plan	Taxable Wages for Federal W/H	Taxable Wages for FICA
Anthony Chinson												
Mark Wayland												
Sylvia Peppinico												
Stevon Varden												
Leonard Hissop												
Student												
Totals												

Name	Gross Earning	Taxable Wages for Federal W/H	Taxable Wages for FICA	Federal W/H	Social Security Tax	Medicare W/H	State W/H Tax	Union Dues	Net Pay	Check No.
Anthony Chinson										
Mark Wayland										
Sylvia Peppinico										
Stevon Varden										
Leonard Hissop										
Student										
Totals										

EMPLOYEE EARNING RECORD

NAME _____   Hire Date _____
ADDRESS _____   Date of Birth _____
CITY/STATE/ZIP _____   Exempt/Nonexempt _____
TELEPHONE _____   Married/Single _____
SOCIAL SECURITY NUMBER _____   No. of Exemptions _____
POSITION _____   Pay Rate _____

Period Ended	Hrs. Worked	Reg Pay	OT Pay	Holiday	Comm	Gross Pay	Ins	401(k)	Taxable Pay for Federal	Taxable Pay for FICA

Taxable Pay for Federal	Taxable Pay for FICA	Fed Inc. Tax	Social Sec. Tax	Medicare	State Inc. Tax	Total Deduc	Net Pay	YTD Net Pay	YTD Gross Pay	YTD FUTA

EMPLOYEE EARNING RECORD

NAME _____   Hire Date _____
ADDRESS _____   Date of Birth _____
CITY/STATE/ZIP _____   Exempt/Nonexempt _____
TELEPHONE _____   Married/Single _____
SOCIAL SECURITY NUMBER _____   No. of Exemptions _____
POSITION _____   Pay Rate _____

Period Ended	Hrs. Worked	Reg Pay	OT Pay	Holiday	Comm	Gross Pay	Ins	401(k)	Taxable Pay for Federal	Taxable Pay for FICA

Taxable Pay for Federal	Taxable Pay for FICA	Fed Inc. Tax	Social Sec. Tax	Medicare	State Inc. Tax	Total Deduc	Net Pay	YTD Net Pay	YTD Gross Pay	YTD FUTA

EMPLOYEE EARNING RECORD

NAME _____ Hire Date _____

ADDRESS _____ Date of Birth _____

CITY/STATE/ZIP _____ Exempt/Nonexempt _____

TELEPHONE _____ Married/Single _____

SOCIAL SECURITY NUMBER _____ No. of Exemptions _____

POSITION _____ Pay Rate _____

Period Ended	Hrs. Worked	Reg Pay	OT Pay	Holiday	Comm	Gross Pay	Ins	401(k)	Taxable Pay for Federal	Taxable Pay for FICA

Taxable Pay for Federal	Taxable Pay for FICA	Fed Inc. Tax	Social Sec. Tax	Medicare	State Inc. Tax	Total Deduc	Net Pay	YTD Net Pay	YTD Gross Pay	YTD FUTA

EMPLOYEE EARNING RECORD

NAME _____ Hire Date _____

ADDRESS _____ Date of Birth _____

CITY/STATE/ZIP _____ Exempt/Nonexempt _____

TELEPHONE _____ Married/Single _____

SOCIAL SECURITY NUMBER _____ No. of Exemptions _____

POSITION _____ Pay Rate _____

Period Ended	Hrs. Worked	Reg Pay	OT Pay	Holiday	Comm	Gross Pay	Ins	401(k)	Taxable Pay for Federal	Taxable Pay for FICA

Taxable Pay for Federal	Taxable Pay for FICA	Fed Inc. Tax	Social Sec. Tax	Medicare	State Inc. Tax	Total Deduc	Net Pay	YTD Net Pay	YTD Gross Pay	YTD FUTA

EMPLOYEE EARNING RECORD

NAME _____   Hire Date _____

ADDRESS _____   Date of Birth _____

CITY/STATE/ZIP _____   Exempt/Nonexempt _____

TELEPHONE _____   Married/Single _____

SOCIAL SECURITY NUMBER _____   No. of Exemptions _____

POSITION _____   Pay Rate _____

Period Ended	Hrs. Worked	Reg Pay	OT Pay	Holiday	Comm	Gross Pay	Ins	401(k)	Taxable Pay for Federal	Taxable Pay for FICA

Taxable Pay for Federal	Taxable Pay for FICA	Fed Inc. Tax	Social Sec. Tax	Medicare	State Inc. Tax	Total Deduc	Net Pay	YTD Net Pay	YTD Gross Pay	YTD FUTA

EMPLOYEE EARNING RECORD

NAME _____   Hire Date _____

ADDRESS _____   Date of Birth _____

CITY/STATE/ZIP _____   Exempt/Nonexempt _____

TELEPHONE _____   Married/Single _____

SOCIAL SECURITY NUMBER _____   No. of Exemptions _____

POSITION _____   Pay Rate _____

Period Ended	Hrs. Worked	Reg Pay	OT Pay	Holiday	Comm	Gross Pay	Ins	401(k)	Taxable Pay for Federal	Taxable Pay for FICA

Taxable Pay for Federal	Taxable Pay for FICA	Fed Inc. Tax	Social Sec. Tax	Medicare	State Inc. Tax	Total Deduc	Net Pay	YTD Net Pay	YTD Gross Pay	YTD FUTA

General Journal Entries

Complete the General Journal entries as follows:

15-Oct	Journalize employee pay including the issuance of paychecks (use one entry for all checks)
15-Oct	Journalize employer payroll tax for the October 15 pay date
20-Oct	Journalize the payment of payroll

Post all journal entries to the appropriate General Ledger accounts.

Date		Description	Post Ref.	Debit	Credit

October 31

October 31 is the end of the final pay period for the month. Employee pay will be disbursed on November 4, 2016. Any hours exceeding 88 during this pay period are considered overtime for nonexempt employees. Compute the employee pay. Update the Employees' Earning Records for the period's pay and update the YTD amount.

Complete the Payroll Register for October 31. Round wages to five decimal points and all other final answers to two decimal points.

The hours for the employees are as follows:

Name	Hourly rate (round to 5 decimals)	Hours Worked 10/16–10/31	Regular (round to 2 decimal)	Overtime (round to 2 decimal)	Commission
Chinson		88 hours (exempt)			$1,750.00
Wayland		88 hours (exempt)			
Peppinico		88 hours (exempt)			
Varden		92 hours			
Hissop		95 hours			
You		90 hours			

Complete the Payroll Register for October 31.

Run End Date [   ]   Company Name: Wayland Custom Woodworking

P/R Date [   ]

Name	M/S	# W/H	Hourly Rate or Period Wage	No. of Regular Hours	No. of Overtime Hours	No. of Holiday Hours	Commissions	Gross Earning	Insurance	Cafeteria Plan	Taxable Wages for Federal W/H	Taxable Wages for FICA
Anthony Chinson												
Mark Wayland												
Sylvia Peppinico												
Stevon Varden												
Leonard Hissop												
Student												
Totals												

Name	Gross Earning	Taxable Wages for Federal W/H	Taxable Wages for FICA	Federal W/H	Social Security Tax	Medicare W/H	State W/H Tax	Union Dues	Net Pay	Check No.
Anthony Chinson										
Mark Wayland										
Sylvia Peppinico										
Stevon Varden										
Leonard Hissop										
Student										
Totals										

General Journal Entries

Complete the General Journal entries as follows:

31-Oct	Journalize employee pay for the period.
31-Oct	Journalize employer payroll tax for the October 31 pay date.
04-Nov	Journalize the payment of payroll to employees. (Use one entry for all disbursements.)
04-Nov	Journalize remittance of 401(k) and Section 125 health insurance premiums deducted.
04-Nov	Journalize remittance of monthly payroll taxes.

Post all journal entries to the appropriate General Ledger accounts

Date		Description	Post Ref.	Debit	Credit

November 15

Compute the pay for each employee. Update the Employee Earning record for the period's pay and the new YTD amount. Employee pay will be disbursed on November 18, 2016. Any hours exceeding 88 during this pay period are considered overtime for nonexempt employees. Remember that the employees are paid semimonthly.

Complete the Payroll Register for October 31. Round wages to five decimal points and all other final answers to two decimal points.

The hours for the employees are as follows:

Name	Hourly rate (round to 5 decimals)	Pay Period Hours 11/01– 11/15	Regular (round to 2 decimal)	Overtime (round to 2 decimal)	Commission
Chinson		88 hours (exempt)			$1,050.00
Wayland		88 hours (exempt)			
Peppinico		88 hours (exempt)			
Varden		96 hours			
Hissop		91 hours			
You		93 hours			

Complete the Payroll Register for November 15.

Run Date _____ Company Name: Wayland Custom Woodworking

P/R Date _____

Name	M/S	# W/H	Hourly Rate or Period Wage	No. of Regular Hours	No. of Overtime Hours	No. of Holiday Hours	Commissions	Gross Earning	Insurance	Cafeteria Plan	Taxable Wages for Federal W/H	Taxable Wages for FICA
Anthony Chinson												
Mark Wayland												
Sylvia Peppinico												
Stevon Varden												
Leonard Hissop												
Student												
Totals												

Name	Gross Earning	Taxable Wages for Federal W/H	Taxable Wages for FICA	Federal W/H	Social Security Tax	Medicare W/H	State W/H Tax	Union Dues	Net Pay	Check No.
Anthony Chinson										
Mark Wayland										
Sylvia Peppinico										
Stevon Varden										
Leonard Hissop										
Student										
Totals										

General Journal Entries

Complete the General Journal entries as follows:

15-Nov	Journalize employee pay including the issuance of paychecks (use one entry for all checks).
15-Nov	Journalize employer payroll tax for the November 15 pay date
18-Nov	Journalize payment of payroll to employees

Post all journal entries to the appropriate General Ledger accounts.

Date		Description	Post Ref.	Debit	Credit

Date	Description	Post Ref.	Debit	Credit

Post all journal entries to the appropriate General Ledger accounts.

November 30

Compute the Net Pay for each employee. Employee pay will be disbursed on December 5, 2016. Update the Employees' Earning Record with the November 30 pay and the new YTD amount.

The company is closed and pays for the Friday following Thanskgiving. The employees will receive holiday pay for Thanksgiving and the Friday following. All the hours over 88 are eligible for overtime for nonexempt employees as they were worked during the nonholiday week.

The hours for the employees are as follows:

Name	Hourly rate (round to 5 decimal)	Pay Period Hours 11/01– 11/15	Regular (round to 2 decimal)	Overtime (round to 2 decimal)	Holiday (round to 2 decimal)	Commission
Chinson		88 hours (exempt - 16 hours Holiday)				$2,325.00
Wayland		88 hours (exempt - 16 hours Holiday)				
Peppinico		88 hours (exempt - 16 hours Holiday)				
Varden		90 hours (exempt - 16 hours Holiday)				
Hissop		91 hours (exempt - 16 hours Holiday)				
You		89 hours (exempt - 16 hours Holiday)				

Complete the Payroll Register for November 30. Round wages to five decimal points and all other final answers to two decimal points.

Complete the Payroll Register for November 30.

Run Date		Company Name:	Wayland Custom Woodworking
P/R Date			

Name	M/S	# W/H	Hourly Rate or Period Wage	No. of Regular Hours	No. of Overtime Hours	No. of Holiday Hours	Commissions	Gross Earning	Insurance	Cafeteria Plan	Taxable Wages for Federal W/H	Taxable Wages for FICA
Anthony Chinson												
Mark Wayland												
Sylvia Peppinico												
Stevon Varden												
Leonard Hissop												
Student												
Totals												

Name	Gross Earning	Taxable Wages for Federal W/H	Taxable Wages for FICA	Federal W/H	Social Security Tax	Medicare W/H	State W/H Tax	Union Dues	Net Pay	Check No.
Anthony Chinson										
Mark Wayland										
Sylvia Peppinico										
Stevon Varden										
Leonard Hissop										
Student										
Totals										

General Journal entries

Complete the General Journal entries as follows:

30-Nov	Journalize employee pay including the issuance of paychecks (use one entry for all checks)
30-Nov	Journalize employer payroll tax for the November 30 pay date
05-Dec	Journalize payment of payroll to employees
05-Dec	Journalize remittance of 401(k) and health insurance premiums deducted
05-Dec	Journalize remittance of monthly payroll taxes

Post all journal entries to the appropriate General Ledger accounts.

Date		Description	Post Ref.	Debit	Credit

Date		Description	Post Ref.	Debit	Credit

December 15

Compute the net pay and update the Employees' Earning Record with the December 15 pay and the new YTD information. Employee pay will be disbursed on December 19, 2016. Any hours worked in excess of 80 hours during this pay period are considered overtime for non-exempt employees.

The hours for the employees are as follows:

Name	Hourly rate (round to 5 decimals)	Pay Period Hours 12/01–12/15	Regular (round to 2 decimal)	Overtime (round to 2 decimal)	Holiday (round to 2 decimal)	Commission
Chinson		80 hours (exempt)				$1,680.00
Wayland		80 hours (exempt)				
Peppinico		80 hours (exempt)				
Varden		84 hours				
Hissop		80 hours				
Student		83 hours				

Complete the Payroll Register for December 15. Round wages to five decimal points and all other final answers to two decimal points. Employee pay will be disbursed on December 19 , 2016.

Complete the Payroll Register for December 15.

Run Date [   ]   Company Name: Wayland Custom Woodworking

P/R Date [   ]

Name	M/S	# W/H	Hourly Rate or Period Wage	No. of Regular Hours	No. of Overtime Hours	No. of Holiday Hours	Commissions	Gross Earning	Insurance	Cafeteria Plan	Taxable Wages for Federal W/H	Taxable Wages for FICA
Anthony Chinson												
Mark Wayland												
Sylvia Peppinico												
Stevon Varden												
Leonard Hissop												
Student												
Totals												

Name	Gross Earning	Taxable Wages for Federal W/H	Taxable Wages for FICA	Federal W/H	Social Security Tax	Medicare W/H	State W/H Tax	Union Dues	Net Pay	Check No.
Anthony Chinson										
Mark Wayland										
Sylvia Peppinico										
Stevon Varden										
Leonard Hissop										
Student										
Totals										

General Journal entries

Complete the General Journal entries as follows:

15-Dec	Journalize employee pay including the issuance of paychecks (use one entry for all checks)
15-Dec	Journalize employer payroll tax for the December 15 pay date
19-Dec	Journalize payment of payroll to employees

Post all journal entries to the appropriate General Ledger accounts.

Date		Description	Post Ref.	Debit	Credit

Date	Description	Post Ref.	Debit	Credit

December 31

The final pay period of the year will not be paid to employees until January 3, 2017. The company will accrue the wages for the final pay period only. Since the pay period is complete, there will not be a reversing entry for the accrual.

The company pays for the day before and the day of Christmas, and if the holiday is on a weekend, the company pays for the Friday before. Christmas fell on a Sunday, so employees will be paid for both the Friday and Monday as holiday pay.

Employee pay will be disbursed and reflected on the Employees' Earnings Register when paid. Complete all State and Federal tax forms for year end. Generate W-2 and W-3 for employees, recall that these forms only reflect wages actually paid during the year, accrued wages should not be included on Forms W-2 and W-3.

The hours for the employees are as follows:

Name	Hourly rate (round to 5 decimals)	Pay Period Hours 12/16–12/31	Regular (round to 2 decimal)	Overtime (round to 2 decimal)	Holiday (round to 2 decimal)	Commission
Chinson		88 hours (exempt - 16 hours Holiday)				$1,015.00
Wayland		88 hours (exempt - 16 hours Holiday)				
Peppinico		88 hours (exempt - 16 hours Holiday)				
Varden		92 hours (16 Holiday)*				
Hissop		90 hours (16 Holiday)*				
Student		91 hours (16 Holiday)*				

*Employees worked extra hours on Saturday during the week of 12/23–12/29. Reminder, holidays and vacations are not included as hours *worked* for calculation of overtime.

Complete the Payroll Register for December 31.

Run Date [   ]   Company Name: Wayland Custom Woodworking

P/R Date [   ]

Name	M/S	# W/H	Hourly Rate or Period Wage	No. of Regular Hours	No. of Overtime Hours	No. of Holiday Hours	Commissions	Gross Earning	Insurance	Cafeteria Plan	Taxable Wages for Federal W/H	Taxable Wages for FICA
Anthony Chinson												
Mark Wayland												
Sylvia Peppinico												
Stevon Varden												
Leonard Hissop												
Student												
Totals												

Name	Gross Earning	Taxable Wages for Federal W/H	Taxable Wages for FICA	Federal W/H	Social Security Tax	Medicare W/H	State W/H Tax	Union Dues	Net Pay	Check No.
Anthony Chinson										
Mark Wayland										
Sylvia Peppinico										
Stevon Varden										
Leonard Hissop										
Student										
Totals										

General Journal entries

Complete the General Journal entries as follows:

31-Dec   Accrue employee pay including the issuance of paychecks (use one entry for all checks)

31-Dec   Accrue employer payroll tax for the December 31 pay date

Post all journal entries to the appropriate General Ledger accounts.

Date		Description	Post Ref.	Debit	Credit

Date		Description	Post Ref.	Debit	Credit

Employment Eligibility Verification

Department of Homeland Security
U.S. Citizenship and Immigration Services

USCIS
Form I-9

OMB No. 1615-0047
Expires 03/31/2016

▶**START HERE.** Read instructions carefully before completing this form. The instructions must be available during completion of this form.
ANTI-DISCRIMINATION NOTICE: It is illegal to discriminate against work-authorized individuals. Employers **CANNOT** specify which document(s) they will accept from an employee. The refusal to hire an individual because the documentation presented has a future expiration date may also constitute illegal discrimination.

Section 1. Employee Information and Attestation *(Employees must complete and sign Section 1 of Form I-9 no later than the **first day of employment**, but not before accepting a job offer.)*

Last Name *(Family Name)*	First Name *(Given Name)*	Middle Initial	Other Names Used *(if any)*

Address *(Street Number and Name)*	Apt. Number	City or Town	State	Zip Code

Date of Birth *(mm/dd/yyyy)*	U.S. Social Security Number	E-mail Address	Telephone Number
	☐☐☐-☐☐-☐☐☐☐		

I am aware that federal law provides for imprisonment and/or fines for false statements or use of false documents in connection with the completion of this form.

I attest, under penalty of perjury, that I am (check one of the following):

☐ A citizen of the United States

☐ A noncitizen national of the United States *(See instructions)*

☐ A lawful permanent resident (Alien Registration Number/USCIS Number): _____

☐ An alien authorized to work until (expiration date, if applicable, mm/dd/yyyy) _____ . Some aliens may write "N/A" in this field.
(See instructions)

For aliens authorized to work, provide your Alien Registration Number/USCIS Number **OR** Form I-94 Admission Number:

1. Alien Registration Number/USCIS Number: _____

OR

2. Form I-94 Admission Number: _____

If you obtained your admission number from CBP in connection with your arrival in the United States, include the following:

Foreign Passport Number: _____

Country of Issuance: _____

Some aliens may write "N/A" on the Foreign Passport Number and Country of Issuance fields. *(See instructions)*

3-D Barcode
Do Not Write in This Space

Signature of Employee:	Date *(mm/dd/yyyy):*

Preparer and/or Translator Certification *(To be completed and signed if Section 1 is prepared by a person other than the employee.)*

I attest, under penalty of perjury, that I have assisted in the completion of this form and that to the best of my knowledge the information is true and correct.

Signature of Preparer or Translator:	Date *(mm/dd/yyyy):*

Last Name *(Family Name)*	First Name *(Given Name)*

Address *(Street Number and Name)*	City or Town	State	Zip Code

🛑 *Employer Completes Next Page* 🛑

Form W-4 (2016)

Purpose. Complete Form W-4 so that your employer can withhold the correct federal income tax from your pay. Consider completing a new Form W-4 each year and when your personal or financial situation changes.

Exemption from withholding. If you are exempt, complete **only** lines 1, 2, 3, 4, and 7 and sign the form to validate it. Your exemption for 2016 expires February 15, 2017. See Pub. 505, Tax Withholding and Estimated Tax.

Note: If another person can claim you as a dependent on his or her tax return, you cannot claim exemption from withholding if your income exceeds $1,050 and includes more than $350 of unearned income (for example, interest and dividends).

Exceptions. An employee may be able to claim exemption from withholding even if the employee is a dependent, if the employee:

• Is age 65 or older,

• Is blind, or

• Will claim adjustments to income; tax credits; or itemized deductions, on his or her tax return.

The exceptions do not apply to supplemental wages greater than $1,000,000.

Basic instructions. If you are not exempt, complete the **Personal Allowances Worksheet** below. The worksheets on page 2 further adjust your withholding allowances based on itemized deductions, certain credits, adjustments to income, or two-earners/multiple jobs situations.

Complete all worksheets that apply. However, you may claim fewer (or zero) allowances. For regular wages, withholding must be based on allowances you claimed and may not be a flat amount or percentage of wages.

Head of household. Generally, you can claim head of household filing status on your tax return only if you are unmarried and pay more than 50% of the costs of keeping up a home for yourself and your dependent(s) or other qualifying individuals. See Pub. 501, Exemptions, Standard Deduction, and Filing Information, for information.

Tax credits. You can take projected tax credits into account in figuring your allowable number of withholding allowances. Credits for child or dependent care expenses and the child tax credit may be claimed using the **Personal Allowances Worksheet** below. See Pub. 505 for information on converting your other credits into withholding allowances.

Nonwage income. If you have a large amount of nonwage income, such as interest or dividends, consider making estimated tax payments using Form 1040-ES, Estimated Tax for Individuals. Otherwise, you may owe additional tax. If you have pension or annuity income, see Pub. 505 to find out if you should adjust your withholding on Form W-4 or W-4P.

Two earners or multiple jobs. If you have a working spouse or more than one job, figure the total number of allowances you are entitled to claim on all jobs using worksheets from only one Form W-4. Your withholding usually will be most accurate when all allowances are claimed on the Form W-4 for the highest paying job and zero allowances are claimed on the others. See Pub. 505 for details.

Nonresident alien. If you are a nonresident alien, see Notice 1392, Supplemental Form W-4 Instructions for Nonresident Aliens, before completing this form.

Check your withholding. After your Form W-4 takes effect, use Pub. 505 to see how the amount you are having withheld compares to your projected total tax for 2016. See Pub. 505, especially if your earnings exceed $130,000 (Single) or $180,000 (Married).

Future developments. Information about any future developments affecting Form W-4 (such as legislation enacted after we release it) will be posted at *www.irs.gov/w4*.

Personal Allowances Worksheet (Keep for your records.)

A   Enter "1" for **yourself** if no one else can claim you as a dependent . . . . **A** _____

B   Enter "1" if: { • You are single and have only one job; or
• You are married, have only one job, and your spouse does not work; or
• Your wages from a second job or your spouse's wages (or the total of both) are $1,500 or less. }   . . . **B** _____

C   Enter "1" for your **spouse.** But, you may choose to enter "-0-" if you are married and have either a working spouse or more than one job. (Entering "-0-" may help you avoid having too little tax withheld.) . . . . **C** _____

D   Enter number of **dependents** (other than your spouse or yourself) you will claim on your tax return . . . . **D** _____

E   Enter "1" if you will file as **head of household** on your tax return (see conditions under **Head of household** above) . . **E** _____

F   Enter "1" if you have at least $2,000 of **child or dependent care expenses** for which you plan to claim a credit . . . **F** _____
    (**Note:** Do **not** include child support payments. See Pub. 503, Child and Dependent Care Expenses, for details.)

G   **Child Tax Credit** (including additional child tax credit). See Pub. 972, Child Tax Credit, for more information.
    • If your total income will be less than $70,000 ($100,000 if married), enter "2" for each eligible child; then **less** "1" if you have two to four eligible children or **less** "2" if you have five or more eligible children.
    • If your total income will be between $70,000 and $84,000 ($100,000 and $119,000 if married), enter "1" for each eligible child . . **G** _____

H   Add lines A through G and enter total here. (**Note:** This may be different from the number of exemptions you claim on your tax return.) ▶ **H** _____

For accuracy, complete all worksheets that apply.   { • If you plan to **itemize** or **claim adjustments to income** and want to reduce your withholding, see the **Deductions and Adjustments Worksheet** on page 2.
• If you are **single and have more than one job** or are **married and you and your spouse both work** and the combined earnings from all jobs exceed $50,000 ($20,000 if married), see the **Two-Earners/Multiple Jobs Worksheet** on page 2 to avoid having too little tax withheld.
• If **neither** of the above situations applies, **stop here** and enter the number from line H on line 5 of Form W-4 below. }

-------------------------------- **Separate here and give Form W-4 to your employer. Keep the top part for your records.** --------------------------------

W-4

Form **W-4**
Department of the Treasury
Internal Revenue Service

Employee's Withholding Allowance Certificate

▶ Whether you are entitled to claim a certain number of allowances or exemption from withholding is subject to review by the IRS. Your employer may be required to send a copy of this form to the IRS.

OMB No. 1545-0074

2016

1 Your first name and middle initial	Last name		2 **Your social security number**

Home address (number and street or rural route)	3 ☐ Single ☐ Married ☐ Married, but withhold at higher Single rate.
	Note: If married, but legally separated, or spouse is a nonresident alien, check the "Single" box.
City or town, state, and ZIP code	4 If your last name differs from that shown on your social security card, check here. You must call 1-800-772-1213 for a replacement card. ▶ ☐

5	Total number of allowances you are claiming (from line **H** above **or** from the applicable worksheet on page 2)	**5**	
6	Additional amount, if any, you want withheld from each paycheck	**6**	$
7	I claim exemption from withholding for 2016, and I certify that I meet **both** of the following conditions for exemption.		

    • Last year I had a right to a refund of **all** federal income tax withheld because I had **no** tax liability, **and**
    • This year I expect a refund of **all** federal income tax withheld because I expect to have **no** tax liability.
    If you meet both conditions, write "Exempt" here . . . . ▶ **7**

Under penalties of perjury, I declare that I have examined this certificate and, to the best of my knowledge and belief, it is true, correct, and complete.

Employee's signature
(This form is not valid unless you sign it.) ▶ _____   Date ▶ _____

8 Employer's name and address (Employer: Complete lines 8 and 10 only if sending to the IRS.)	9 Office code (optional)	10 Employer identification number (EIN)

For Privacy Act and Paperwork Reduction Act Notice, see page 2.   Cat. No. 10220Q   Form **W-4** (2016)

Account: Cash   101

	Date		Description	Post Ref.	Debit	Credit	Balance Debit	Balance Credit	
Beg Bal									
1									1
2									2
3									3
4									4
5									5
6									6
7									7
8									8
9									9
10									10
11									11
12									12
13									13
14									14
15									15

Account: Employee Federal Income Tax Payable   203

	Date		Description	Post Ref.	Debit	Credit	Balance Debit	Balance Credit	
1									1
2									2
3									3
4									4
5									5
6									6
7									7
8									8
9									9

Account: Social Security Tax Payable   204

	Date		Description	Post Ref.	Debit	Credit	Balance Debit	Balance Credit	
1									1
2									2
3									3
4									4
5									5
6									6
7									7
8									8
9									9
10									10
11									11
12									12
13									13
14									14
15									15

Account: Medicare Tax Payable   205

	Date		Description	Post Ref.	Debit	Credit	Balance Debit	Balance Credit	
1									1
2									2
3									3
4									4
5									5
6									6
7									7
8									8
9									9
10									10
11									11
12									12
13									13
14									14
15									15

Account: Employee State Income Tax Payable   206

	Date		Description	Post Ref.	Debit	Credit	Balance Debit	Balance Credit	
1									1
2									2
3									3
4									4
5									5
6									6
7									7
8									8
9									9
10									10

Account: 401(k) Contributions Payable   208

	Date		Description	Post Ref.	Debit	Credit	Balance Debit	Balance Credit	
1									1
2									2
3									3
4									4
5									5
6									6
7									7
8									8
9									9
10									10

Account: Employee Medical Premiums Payable   209

	Date		Description	Post Ref.	Debit	Credit	Balance Debit	Balance Credit	
1									1
2									2
3									3
4									4
5									5
6									6
7									7
8									8
9									9
10									10

Account: Salaries and Wages Payable   210

	Date		Description	Post Ref.	Debit	Credit	Balance Debit	Balance Credit	
1									1
2									2
3									3
4									4
5									5
6									6
7									7
8									8
9									9
10									10
11									11
12									12

Account: Federal Unemployment Tax Payable   211

	Date		Description	Post Ref.	Debit	Credit	Balance Debit	Balance Credit	
1									1
2									2
3									3
4									4
5									5
6									6
7									7
8									8
9									9
10									10

Account: State Unemployment Tax Payable   212

	Date	Description	Post Ref.	Debit	Credit	Balance Debit	Balance Credit	
1								1
2								2
3								3
4								4
5								5
6								6
7								7
8								8
9								9
10								10

Account: Payroll Taxes Expense   514

	Date	Description	Post Ref.	Debit	Credit	Balance Debit	Balance Credit	
1								1
2								2
3								3
4								4
5								5
6								6
7								7
8								8
9								9
10								10

Account: Salaries and Wages Expense   515

	Date	Description	Post Ref.	Debit	Credit	Balance Debit	Balance Credit	
1								1
2								2
3								3
4								4
5								5
6								6
7								7
8								8
9								9
10								10

Form **941 for 2016:** **Employer's QUARTERLY Federal Tax Return**
(Rev. January 2016)   Department of the Treasury — Internal Revenue Service

950114

OMB No. 1545-0029

Employer identification number (EIN) ☐☐ – ☐☐☐☐☐☐☐

Name *(not your trade name)*

Trade name *(if any)*

Address

| Number | Street | Suite or room number |

| City | State | ZIP code |

| Foreign country name | Foreign province/county | Foreign postal code |

Report for this Quarter of 2016
(Check one.)

☐ **1:** January, February, March

☐ **2:** April, May, June

☐ **3:** July, August, September

☐ **4:** October, November, December

Instructions and prior year forms are available at *www.irs.gov/form941*.

Read the separate instructions before you complete Form 941. Type or print within the boxes.

Part 1:   **Answer these questions for this quarter.**

1   Number of employees who received wages, tips, or other compensation for the pay period including: *Mar. 12* (Quarter 1), *June 12* (Quarter 2), *Sept. 12* (Quarter 3), or *Dec. 12* (Quarter 4) .... **1** ☐

2   Wages, tips, and other compensation .... **2** ☐

3   Federal income tax withheld from wages, tips, and other compensation .... **3** ☐

4   If no wages, tips, and other compensation are subject to social security or Medicare tax ☐ Check and go to line 6.

	Column 1	**Column 2**
5a Taxable social security wages . .	☐ × .124 =	☐
5b Taxable social security tips . . .	☐ × .124 =	☐
5c Taxable Medicare wages & tips. .	☐ × .029 =	☐
5d Taxable wages & tips subject to Additional Medicare Tax withholding	☐ × .009 =	☐

5e   Add Column 2 from lines 5a, 5b, 5c, and 5d .... **5e** ☐

5f   Section 3121(q) Notice and Demand—Tax due on unreported tips (see instructions) . . **5f** ☐

6   Total taxes before adjustments. Add lines 3, 5e, and 5f .... **6** ☐

7   Current quarter's adjustment for fractions of cents .... **7** ☐

8   Current quarter's adjustment for sick pay .... **8** ☐

9   Current quarter's adjustments for tips and group-term life insurance ...... **9** ☐

10   Total taxes after adjustments. Combine lines 6 through 9 .... **10** ☐

11   Total deposits for this quarter, including overpayment applied from a prior quarter and overpayments applied from Form 941-X, 941-X (PR), 944-X, or 944-X (SP) filed in the current quarter .... **11** ☐

12   **Balance due.** If line 10 is more than line 11, enter the difference and see instructions . . **12** ☐

13   **Overpayment.** If line 11 is more than line 10, enter the difference ☐ Check one: ☐ Apply to next return. ☐ Send a refund.

▶ **You MUST complete both pages of Form 941 and SIGN it.**   Next ▶

For Privacy Act and Paperwork Reduction Act Notice, see the back of the Payment Voucher.   Cat. No. 17001Z   Form **941** (Rev. 1-2016)

950214

Name *(not your trade name)*	Employer identification number (EIN)

Part 2:   Tell us about your deposit schedule and tax liability for this quarter.

If you are unsure about whether you are a monthly schedule depositor or a semiweekly schedule depositor, see section 11 of Pub. 15.

14   Check one: ☐ Line 10 on this return is less than $2,500 or line 10 on the return for the prior quarter was less than $2,500, and you did not incur a **$100,000 next-day deposit obligation during the current quarter.** If line 10 for the prior quarter was less than $2,500 but line 10 on this return is $100,000 or more, you must provide a record of your federal tax liability. If you are a monthly schedule depositor, complete the deposit schedule below; if you are a semiweekly schedule depositor, attach Schedule B (Form 941). Go to Part 3.

☐ **You were a monthly schedule depositor for the entire quarter.** Enter your tax liability for each month and total liability for the quarter, then go to Part 3.

Tax liability: Month 1   [.   ]

Month 2   [.   ]

Month 3   [.   ]

Total liability for quarter   [.   ]   **Total must equal line 10.**

☐ **You were a semiweekly schedule depositor for any part of this quarter.** Complete Schedule B (Form 941), Report of Tax Liability for Semiweekly Schedule Depositors, and attach it to Form 941.

Part 3:   Tell us about your business. If a question does NOT apply to your business, leave it blank.

15   If your business has closed or you stopped paying wages . . . . ☐ Check here, and

enter the final date you paid wages   [/   /   ] .

16   If you are a seasonal employer and you do not have to file a return for every quarter of the year . . ☐ Check here.

Part 4:   May we speak with your third-party designee?

Do you want to allow an employee, a paid tax preparer, or another person to discuss this return with the IRS? See the instructions for details.

☐ Yes.   Designee's name and phone number   [   ]   [   ]

Select a 5-digit Personal Identification Number (PIN) to use when talking to the IRS.   ☐ ☐ ☐ ☐ ☐

☐ No.

Part 5:   Sign here. You MUST complete both pages of Form 941 and SIGN it.

Under penalties of perjury, I declare that I have examined this return, including accompanying schedules and statements, and to the best of my knowledge and belief, it is true, correct, and complete. Declaration of preparer (other than taxpayer) is based on all information of which preparer has any knowledge.

X   **Sign your name here**   [   ]   Print your name here   [   ]

Print your title here   [   ]

Date   [/   /   ]   Best daytime phone   [   ]

Paid Preparer Use Only

Check if you are self-employed . . . ☐

Preparer's name		PTIN	
Preparer's signature		Date	/ /
Firm's name (or yours if self-employed)		EIN	
Address		Phone	
City		State	ZIP code

Form **941** (Rev. 1-2016)

Form **940 for 2015:** **Employer's Annual Federal Unemployment (FUTA) Tax Return**   850113

Department of the Treasury — Internal Revenue Service

OMB No. 1545-0028

Employer identification number (EIN) ☐☐ – ☐☐☐☐☐☐☐

Name *(not your trade name)*

Trade name *(if any)*

Address

Number   Street   Suite or room number

City   State   ZIP code

Foreign country name   Foreign province/county   Foreign postal code

Type of Return
(Check all that apply.)

☐ **a.** Amended

☐ **b.** Successor employer

☐ **c.** No payments to employees in 2015

☐ **d.** Final: Business closed or stopped paying wages

Instructions and prior-year forms are available at *www.irs.gov/form940.*

Read the separate instructions before you complete this form. Please type or print within the boxes.

Part 1: **Tell us about your return. If any line does NOT apply, leave it blank. See instructions before completing Part 1.**

1a If you had to pay state unemployment tax in one state only, enter the state abbreviation . **1a** ☐☐

1b If you had to pay state unemployment tax in more than one state, you are a multi-state employer . . . . **1b** ☐ Check here. Complete Schedule A (Form 940).

2 If you paid wages in a state that is subject to **CREDIT REDUCTION** . . . . **2** ☐ Check here. Complete Schedule A (Form 940).

Part 2: **Determine your FUTA tax before adjustments. If any line does NOT apply, leave it blank.**

3 Total payments to all employees . . . . **3** ▯ .

4 Payments exempt from FUTA tax . . . . **4** ▯ .

Check all that apply: **4a** ☐ Fringe benefits   **4c** ☐ Retirement/Pension   **4e** ☐ Other
4b ☐ Group-term life insurance   **4d** ☐ Dependent care

5 Total of payments made to each employee in excess of $7,000 . . . . **5** ▯ .

6 Subtotal (line 4 + line 5 = line 6) . . . . **6** ▯ .

7 Total taxable **FUTA** wages (line 3 – line 6 = line 7) (see instructions) . . . . . **7** ▯ .

8 FUTA tax before adjustments (line 7 x .006 = line 8) . . . . . **8** ▯ .

Part 3: **Determine your adjustments. If any line does NOT apply, leave it blank.**

9 If ALL of the taxable FUTA wages you paid were excluded from state unemployment tax, multiply line 7 by .054 (line 7 × .054 = line 9). Go to line 12 . . . . . **9** ▯ .

10 If SOME of the taxable FUTA wages you paid were excluded from state unemployment tax, OR you paid ANY state unemployment tax late (after the due date for filing Form 940), complete the worksheet in the instructions. Enter the amount from line 7 of the worksheet . . **10** ▯ .

11 If credit reduction applies, enter the total from Schedule A (Form 940) . . . . . . **11** ▯ .

Part 4: **Determine your FUTA tax and balance due or overpayment. If any line does NOT apply, leave it blank.**

12 Total FUTA tax after adjustments (lines 8 + 9 + 10 + 11 = line 12) . . . . . . **12** ▯ .

13 FUTA tax deposited for the year, including any overpayment applied from a prior year . **13** ▯ .

14 Balance due (If line 12 is more than line 13, enter the excess on line 14.)
- If line 14 is more than $500, you must deposit your tax.
- If line 14 is $500 or less, you may pay with this return. (see instructions) . . . . . . **14** ▯ .

15 Overpayment (If line 13 is more than line 12, enter the excess on line 15 and check a box below.) . . . . **15** ▯ .

▶ You **MUST** complete both pages of this form and **SIGN** it.

Check one: ☐ Apply to next return.   ☐ Send a refund.

Next ▶

For Privacy Act and Paperwork Reduction Act Notice, see the back of Form 940-V, Payment Voucher.   Cat. No. 11234O   Form **940** (2015)

850212

Name (not your trade name)	Employer identification number (EIN)

Part 5:   Report your FUTA tax liability by quarter only if line 12 is more than $500. If not, go to Part 6.

16   Report the amount of your FUTA tax liability for each quarter; do NOT enter the amount you deposited. If you had no liability for a quarter, leave the line blank.

16a   **1st quarter** (January 1 – March 31) . . . .   **16a**   ☐   .

16b   **2nd quarter** (April 1 – June 30) . . . .   **16b**   ☐   .

16c   **3rd quarter** (July 1 – September 30) . . . .   **16c**   ☐   .

16d   **4th quarter** (October 1 – December 31) . . . .   **16d**   ☐   .

17   Total tax liability for the year (lines 16a + 16b + 16c + 16d = line 17)   **17**   ☐   .   **Total must equal line 12.**

Part 6:   May we speak with your third-party designee?

Do you want to allow an employee, a paid tax preparer, or another person to discuss this return with the IRS? See the instructions for details.

☐ **Yes.**   Designee's name and phone number   [   ]   [   ]

Select a 5-digit Personal Identification Number (PIN) to use when talking to IRS   ☐ ☐ ☐ ☐ ☐

☐ **No.**

Part 7:   Sign here. You MUST complete both pages of this form and SIGN it.

Under penalties of perjury, I declare that I have examined this return, including accompanying schedules and statements, and to the best of my knowledge and belief, it is true, correct, and complete, and that no part of any payment made to a state unemployment fund claimed as a credit was, or is to be, deducted from the payments made to employees. Declaration of preparer (other than taxpayer) is based on all information of which preparer has any knowledge.

✗ **Sign your name here**   [   ]

Print your name here   [   ]

Print your title here   [   ]

Date   [/   /   ]

Best daytime phone   [   ]

Paid Preparer Use Only   Check if you are self-employed . ☐

Preparer's name		PTIN	
Preparer's signature		Date	/ /
Firm's name (or yours if self-employed)		EIN	
Address		Phone	
City	State	ZIP code	

94181

9998

Name and address

Utah State Tax Commission

Utah Withholding Return

TC-941

Rev. 10/15

☐ Check here to stop receiving paper forms.

☐ Check here to close your account.

Utah Account ID

Federal EIN

Tax Period (mmddyyyy)

From   To

Due Date (mmddyyyy)

☐ Check if AMENDED (replacement, not net difference)

1. Utah wages, compensation and distributions for this period • 1 _____. ____

2. Federal income tax withheld this period for Utah employees • 2 _____. ____

3. Utah tax withheld this period • 3 _____. ____

→ Pay online at **taxexpress.utah.gov**, or use the payment coupon (form TC-941PC), available at **tax.utah.gov/forms**.

Under penalties provided by law, I declare to the best of my knowledge this return is true and correct.

Signature
X _____ Date _____ Phone _____

≡TaxExpress
taxexpress.utah.gov

You can save money!
See the instructions and learn about **taxexpress.utah.gov**.

DWS-UIC
Form 33H
REV 1213

Utah Employer Quarterly Wage List and Contribution Report

Utah Department of Workforce Services, Unemployment Insurance
140 E. 300 S., PO Box 45233, Salt Lake City UT 84145-0233
1-801-526-9235 option 5; 1-800-222-2857 option 5

The preferred method of filing this report is on-line at our website:

http://jobs.utah.gov

Instructions on Back

Registration #: _____
FEIN: _____

■ FEIN change:_____

EMPLOYER NAME & ADDRESS:

A report must be filed even if no wages are paid for the quarter. See Instructions

Yr/Quarter: _____
Qtr End Date: _____
Due Date: _____

Number of Employees this quarter:

1st Month	2nd Month	3rd Month

Type or machine print preferred.

Employee Social Security Number	Employee Name First	Middle Initial	Last	Total Wages Paid to Employee for this Qtr

The Taxable Wage Base for each employee is $ _____

	Grand Total Wages (All Pages)	

■ ☐ Close account, last payroll date: _____

Please Select Reason   ☐ Out of Business
☐ New Owner

Wages in Excess (See Instruction 9)

Subject Wages

Contribution Rate   X _____

■ ☐ Change name, address, or phone: ☐ New Owner
Please Select Reason   ☐ Current Owner

Contribution Due

Interest (1% per month)

Please enter phone number if missing or incorrect.

Name: _____
Address: _____

Late Penalty ($25.00 min)

Total Payment Due

Current Phone
_____

Phone: _____

(Make check payable to Utah Unemployment Compensation Fund)

(   )   -

_____   _____   _____   _____
Name   Title   Date   Contact Phone Number

I certify the information on this report is true and correct to the best of my knowledge.

_____
Signature

22222	Void ☐	**a** Employee's social security number	**For Official Use Only ▶** **OMB No. 1545-0008**	

b Employer identification number (EIN)	**1** Wages, tips, other compensation	**2** Federal income tax withheld
c Employer's name, address, and ZIP code	**3** Social security wages	**4** Social security tax withheld
	5 Medicare wages and tips	**6** Medicare tax withheld
	7 Social security tips	**8** Allocated tips
d Control number	**9**	**10** Dependent care benefits
e Employee's first name and initial Last name Suff.	**11** Nonqualified plans	**12a** See instructions for box 12
	13 Statutory employee ☐ Retirement plan ☐ Third-party sick pay ☐	**12b**
	14 Other	**12c**
		12d
f Employee's address and ZIP code		

15 State Employer's state ID number	**16** State wages, tips, etc.	**17** State income tax	**18** Local wages, tips, etc.	**19** Local income tax	**20** Locality name

Form **W-2** **Wage and Tax Statement**   **2016**   Department of the Treasury—Internal Revenue Service

---

22222	Void ☐	**a** Employee's social security number	**For Official Use Only ▶** **OMB No. 1545-0008**	

b Employer identification number (EIN)	**1** Wages, tips, other compensation	**2** Federal income tax withheld
c Employer's name, address, and ZIP code	**3** Social security wages	**4** Social security tax withheld
	5 Medicare wages and tips	**6** Medicare tax withheld
	7 Social security tips	**8** Allocated tips
d Control number	**9**	**10** Dependent care benefits
e Employee's first name and initial Last name Suff.	**11** Nonqualified plans	**12a** See instructions for box 12
	13 Statutory employee ☐ Retirement plan ☐ Third-party sick pay ☐	**12b**
	14 Other	**12c**
		12d
f Employee's address and ZIP code		

15 State Employer's state ID number	**16** State wages, tips, etc.	**17** State income tax	**18** Local wages, tips, etc.	**19** Local income tax	**20** Locality name

Form **W-2** **Wage and Tax Statement**   **2016**   Department of the Treasury—Internal Revenue Service

22222	Void ☐	**a** Employee's social security number	**For Official Use Only ▶** OMB No. 1545-0008		

b Employer identification number (EIN)		**1** Wages, tips, other compensation	**2** Federal income tax withheld
c Employer's name, address, and ZIP code		**3** Social security wages	**4** Social security tax withheld
		5 Medicare wages and tips	**6** Medicare tax withheld
		7 Social security tips	**8** Allocated tips
d Control number		**9**	**10** Dependent care benefits
e Employee's first name and initial	Last name	Suff.	**11** Nonqualified plans	**12a** See instructions for box 12 Code
			13 Statutory employee ☐ Retirement plan ☐ Third-party sick pay ☐	**12b** Code
			14 Other	**12c** Code
				12d Code
f Employee's address and ZIP code				

15 State	Employer's state ID number	**16** State wages, tips, etc.	**17** State income tax	**18** Local wages, tips, etc.	**19** Local income tax	**20** Locality name

Form **W-2** **Wage and Tax Statement** **2016**

Department of the Treasury—Internal Revenue Service

22222	Void ☐	**a** Employee's social security number	**For Official Use Only ▶** OMB No. 1545-0008		

b Employer identification number (EIN)		**1** Wages, tips, other compensation	**2** Federal income tax withheld
c Employer's name, address, and ZIP code		**3** Social security wages	**4** Social security tax withheld
		5 Medicare wages and tips	**6** Medicare tax withheld
		7 Social security tips	**8** Allocated tips
d Control number		**9**	**10** Dependent care benefits
e Employee's first name and initial	Last name	Suff.	**11** Nonqualified plans	**12a** See instructions for box 12 Code
			13 Statutory employee ☐ Retirement plan ☐ Third-party sick pay ☐	**12b** Code
			14 Other	**12c** Code
				12d Code
f Employee's address and ZIP code				

15 State	Employer's state ID number	**16** State wages, tips, etc.	**17** State income tax	**18** Local wages, tips, etc.	**19** Local income tax	**20** Locality name

Form **W-2** **Wage and Tax Statement** **2016**

Department of the Treasury—Internal Revenue Service

22222	Void ☐	**a** Employee's social security number	**For Official Use Only ▶** OMB No. 1545-0008	

b Employer identification number (EIN)	**1** Wages, tips, other compensation	**2** Federal income tax withheld
c Employer's name, address, and ZIP code	**3** Social security wages	**4** Social security tax withheld
	5 Medicare wages and tips	**6** Medicare tax withheld
	7 Social security tips	**8** Allocated tips
d Control number	**9**	**10** Dependent care benefits

e Employee's first name and initial	Last name	Suff.	**11** Nonqualified plans	**12a** See instructions for box 12
			13 Statutory employee ☐ Retirement plan ☐ Third-party sick pay ☐	**12b**
			14 Other	**12c**
				12d
f Employee's address and ZIP code				

15 State	Employer's state ID number	**16** State wages, tips, etc.	**17** State income tax	**18** Local wages, tips, etc.	**19** Local income tax	**20** Locality name

Form **W-2** Wage and Tax Statement   **2016**   Department of the Treasury—Internal Revenue Service

22222	Void ☐	**a** Employee's social security number	**For Official Use Only ▶** OMB No. 1545-0008	

b Employer identification number (EIN)	**1** Wages, tips, other compensation	**2** Federal income tax withheld
c Employer's name, address, and ZIP code	**3** Social security wages	**4** Social security tax withheld
	5 Medicare wages and tips	**6** Medicare tax withheld
	7 Social security tips	**8** Allocated tips
d Control number	**9**	**10** Dependent care benefits

e Employee's first name and initial	Last name	Suff.	**11** Nonqualified plans	**12a** See instructions for box 12
			13 Statutory employee ☐ Retirement plan ☐ Third-party sick pay ☐	**12b**
			14 Other	**12c**
				12d
f Employee's address and ZIP code				

15 State	Employer's state ID number	**16** State wages, tips, etc.	**17** State income tax	**18** Local wages, tips, etc.	**19** Local income tax	**20** Locality name

Form **W-2** Wage and Tax Statement   **2016**   Department of the Treasury—Internal Revenue Service

DO NOT STAPLE

33333	**a** Control number	**For Official Use Only ▶** OMB No. 1545-0008

| **b**
Kind
of
Payer
(Check one) ▶ | 941 ☐
CT-1 ☐ | Military ☐
Hshld. emp. ☐ | 943 ☐
Medicare govt. emp. ☐ | 944 ☐ | **Kind**
of
Employer
(Check one) ▶ | None apply ☐
State/local non-501c ☐ | 501c non-govt. ☐
State/local 501c ☐ | Federal govt. ☐ | Third-party sick pay
(Check if applicable) ☐ |

c Total number of Forms W-2	**d** Establishment number	**1** Wages, tips, other compensation	**2** Federal income tax withheld
e Employer identification number (EIN)		**3** Social security wages	**4** Social security tax withheld
f Employer's name		**5** Medicare wages and tips	**6** Medicare tax withheld
		7 Social security tips	**8** Allocated tips
		9 	**10** Dependent care benefits
		11 Nonqualified plans	**12a** Deferred compensation
g Employer's address and ZIP code			
h Other EIN used this year		**13** For third-party sick pay use only	**12b**
15 State Employer's state ID number		**14** Income tax withheld by payer of third-party sick pay	
16 State wages, tips, etc.	**17** State income tax	**18** Local wages, tips, etc.	**19** Local income tax
Employer's contact person		Employer's telephone number	For Official Use Only
Employer's fax number		Employer's email address	

Under penalties of perjury, I declare that I have examined this return and accompanying documents and, to the best of my knowledge and belief, they are true, correct, and complete.

Signature ▶ _____   Title ▶ _____   Date ▶ _____

Form **W-3** **Transmittal of Wage and Tax Statements**   **2016**   Department of the Treasury
Internal Revenue Service

Appendix B

Special Classes of Federal Tax Withholding

Special Classes of Employment and Special Types of Payments	Treatment Under Employment Taxes		
	Income Tax Withholding	Social Security and Medicare (Including Additional Medicare Tax when Wages are Paid in Excess of $200,000)	FUTA
Aliens, Nonresident:	See Publication 515, "Withholding of Tax on Nonresident Aliens and Foreign Entities," and Publication 519, "U.S. Tax Guide for Aliens."		
Aliens, Resident:			
1. Service performed in the United States.	Same as U.S. citizen.	Same as U.S. citizen. (Exempt if any part of service as crew member of foreign vessel or aircraft is performed outside United States.)	Same as U.S. citizen.
2. Service performed outside United States.	Withhold	Taxable if (1) working for an American employer or (2) an American employer by agreement covers U.S. citizens and residents employed by its foreign affiliates.	Exempt unless on or in connection with an American vessel or aircraft and performed under contract made in United States, or alien is employed on such vessel or aircraft when it touches U.S. port.
Cafeteria Plan Benefits Under Section 125:	If employee chooses cash, subject to all employment taxes. If employee chooses another benefit, the treatment is the same as if the benefit was provided outside the plan. See Publication 15-B for more information.		
Deceased Worker:			
1. Wages paid to beneficiary or estate in same calendar year as worker's death. See the "Instructions for Forms W-2 and W-3" for details.	Exempt	Taxable	Taxable
2. Wages paid to beneficiary or estate after calendar year of worker's death.	Exempt	Exempt	Exempt

(continued)

Special Classes of Employment and Special Types of Payments	Treatment Under Employment Taxes		
	Income Tax Withholding	Social Security and Medicare (Including Additional Medicare Tax when Wages are Paid in Excess of $200,000)	FUTA
Dependent Care Assistance Programs:	Exempt to the extent it is reasonable to believe amounts are excludable from gross income under section 129.		
Disabled Worker's Wages paid after year in which worker became entitled to disability insurance benefits under the Social Security Act:	Withhold	Exempt, if worker did not perform service for employer during period for which payment is made.	Taxable
Employee Business Expense Reimbursement:			
1. Accountable plan.			
a. Amounts not exceeding specified government rate for per diem or standard mileage.	Exempt	Exempt	Exempt
b. Amounts in excess of specified government rate for per diem or standard mileage.	Withhold	Taxable	Taxable
2. Nonaccountable plan. See section 5 of IRS Publication 15 for details.	Withhold	Taxable	Taxable
Family Employees:			
1. Child employed by parent (or partnership in which each partner is a parent of the child).	Withhold	Exempt until age 18; age 21 for domestic service.	Exempt until age 21.
2. Parent employed by child.	Withhold	Taxable if in course of the son's or daughter's business. For domestic services, see section 3 of IRS Publication 15.	Exempt
3. Spouse employed by spouse. See section 3 of IRS Publication 15 for more information.	Withhold	Taxable if in course of spouse's business.	Exempt
Fishing and Related Activities:	See Publication 334, "Tax Guide for Small Business."		
Foreign Governments and International Organizations:	Exempt	Exempt	Exempt
Foreign Service by U.S. Citizens:			
1. As U.S. government employees.	Withhold	Same as within United States.	Exempt
2. For foreign affiliates of American employers and other private employers.	Exempt if at time of payment (1) it is reasonable to believe employee is entitled to exclusion from income under section 911 or (2) the employer is required by law of the foreign country to withhold income tax on such payment.	Exempt unless (1) an American employer by agreement covers U.S. citizens employed by its foreign affiliates or (2) U.S. citizen works for American employer.	Exempt unless (1) on American vessel or aircraft and work is performed under contract made in United States or worker is employed on vessel when it touches U.S. port or (2) U.S. citizen works for American employer (except in a contiguous country with which the United States has an agreement for unemployment compensation) or in the U.S. Virgin Islands.

Special Classes of Employment and Special Types of Payments	Treatment Under Employment Taxes		
	Income Tax Withholding	Social Security and Medicare (Including Additional Medicare Tax when Wages are Paid in Excess of $200,000)	FUTA
Fringe Benefits:	Taxable on excess of fair market value of the benefit over the sum of an amount paid for it by the employee and any amount excludable by law. However, special valuation rules may apply. Benefits provided under cafeteria plans may qualify for exclusion from wages for Social Security, Medicare, and FUTA taxes. See Publication 15-B for details.		
Government Employment: State/local governments and political subdivisions, employees of:			
1. Salaries and wages (includes payments to most elected and appointed officials).	Withhold	Generally taxable for (1) services performed by employees who are either (a) covered under a section 218 agreement or (b) not covered under a section 218 agreement and not a member of a public retirement system (mandatory Social Security and Medicare coverage), and (2) (Medicare tax only) services performed by employees hired or rehired after 3/31/86 who are not covered under a section 218 agreement or the mandatory Social Security provisions, unless specifically excluded by law. See Publication 963.	Exempt
2. Election workers. Election workers are individuals who are employed to perform services for state or local governments at election booths in connection with national, state, or local elections. **Note.** File Form W-2 for payments of $600 or more even if no Social Security or Medicare taxes were withheld.	Exempt	Taxable if paid $1,700 or more in 2016 (lesser amount if specified by a section 218 Social Security agreement). See Revenue Ruling 2000-6.	Exempt
3. Emergency workers. Emergency workers who were hired on a temporary basis in response to a specific unforeseen emergency and are not intended to become permanent employees.	Withhold	Exempt if serving on a temporary basis in case of fire, storm, snow, earthquake, flood, or similar emergency.	Exempt
U.S. federal government employees.	Withhold	Taxable for Medicare. Taxable for Social Security unless hired before 1984. See section 3121(b)(5).	Exempt
Homeworkers (Industrial, Cottage Industry):			
1. Common law employees.	Withhold	Taxable	Taxable
2. Statutory employees. See section 2 of IRS Publication 15 for details.	Exempt	Taxable if paid $100 or more in cash in a year.	Exempt

(continued)

Special Classes of Employment and Special Types of Payments	Treatment Under Employment Taxes		
	Income Tax Withholding	Social Security and Medicare (Including Additional Medicare Tax when Wages are Paid in Excess of $200,000)	FUTA
Hospital Employees:			
1. Interns.	Withhold	Taxable	Exempt
2. Patients.	Withhold	Taxable (exempt for state or local government hospitals).	Exempt
Household Employees:			
1. Domestic service in private homes. Farmers, see Publication 51 (Circular A).	Exempt (withhold if both employer and employee agree).	Taxable if paid $2,000 or more in cash in 2016. Exempt if performed by an individual younger than age 18 during any portion of the calendar year and is not the principal occupation of the employee.	Taxable if employer paid total cash wages of $1,000 or more in any quarter in the current or preceding calendar year.
2. Domestic service in college clubs, fraternities, and sororities.	Exempt (withhold if both employer and employee agree).	Exempt if paid to regular student; also exempt if employee is paid less than $100 in a year by an income-tax-exempt employer.	Taxable if employer paid total cash wages of $1,000 or more in any quarter in the current or preceding calendar year.
Insurance for Employees:			
1. Accident and health insurance premiums under a plan or system for employees and their dependents generally or for a class or classes of employees and their dependents.	Exempt (except 2% shareholder-employees of S corporations).	Exempt	Exempt
2. Group-term life insurance costs. See Publication 15-B for details.	Exempt	Exempt, except for the cost of group-term life insurance includible in the employee's gross income. Special rules apply for former employees.	Exempt
Insurance Agents or Solicitors:			
1. Full-time life insurance salesperson.	Withhold only if employee under common law. See section 2 of IRS Publication 15.	Taxable	Taxable if (1) employee under common law and (2) not paid solely by commissions.
2. Other salesperson of life, casualty, and so on, insurance.	Withhold only if employee under common law.	Taxable only if employee under common law.	Taxable if (1) employee under common law and (2) not paid solely by commissions.
Interest on Loans with Below-Market Interest Rates (foregone interest and deemed original issue discount):	See Publication 15-A.		
Leave-Sharing Plans: Amounts paid to an employee under a leave-sharing plan.	Withhold	Taxable	Taxable
Newspaper Carriers and Vendors: Newspaper carriers younger than age 18; newspaper and magazine vendors buying at fixed prices and retaining receipts from sales to customers. See Publication 15-A for information on statutory nonemployee status.	Exempt (withhold if both employer and employee voluntarily agree).	Exempt	Exempt

Special Classes of Employment and Special Types of Payments	Treatment Under Employment Taxes		
	Income Tax Withholding	Social Security and Medicare (Including Additional Medicare Tax when Wages are Paid in Excess of $200,000)	FUTA
Noncash Payments:			
1. For household work, agricultural labor, and service not in the course of the employer's trade or business.	Exempt (withhold if both employer and employee voluntarily agree).	Exempt	Exempt
2. To certain retail commission salespersons ordinarily paid solely on a cash commission basis.	Optional with employer, except to the extent employee's supplemental wages during the year exceed $1 million.	Taxable	Taxable
Nonprofit Organizations:	See Publication 15-A.		
Officers or Shareholders of an S Corporation: Distributions and other payments by an S corporation to a corporate officer or shareholder must be treated as wages to the extent the amounts are reasonable compensation for services to the corporation by an employee. See the instructions for Form 1120S.	Withhold	Taxable	Taxable
Partners: Payments to general or limited partners of a partnership. See Publication 541, "Partnerships," for partner reporting rules.	Exempt	Exempt	Exempt
Railroads: Payments subject to the Railroad Retirement Act. See Publication 915, Social Security and Equivalent Railroad Retirement Benefits, for more details.	Withhold	Exempt	Exempt
Religious Exemptions:	See Publication 15-A and Publication 517, "Social Security and Other Information for Members of the Clergy and Religious Workers."		
Retirement and Pension Plans:			
1. Employer contributions to a qualified plan.	Exempt	Exempt	Exempt
2. Elective employee contributions and deferrals to a plan containing a qualified cash or deferred compensation arrangement (for example, 401(k)).	Generally exempt, but see section 402(g) for limitation.	Taxable	Taxable
3. Employer contributions to individual retirement accounts under simplified employee pension plan (SEP).	Generally exempt, but see section 402(g) for salary reduction SEP limitation.	Exempt, except for amounts contributed under a salary reduction SEP agreement.	
4. Employer contributions to section 403(b) annuities.	Generally exempt, but see section 402(g) for limitation.	Taxable if paid through a salary reduction agreement (written or otherwise).	
5. Employee salary reduction contributions to a SIMPLE retirement account.	Exempt	Taxable	Taxable

(continued)

Special Classes of Employment and Special Types of Payments	Treatment Under Employment Taxes		
	Income Tax Withholding	Social Security and Medicare (Including Additional Medicare Tax when Wages are Paid in Excess of $200,000)	FUTA
6. Distributions from qualified retirement and pension plans and section 403(b) annuities. See Publication 15-A for information on pensions, annuities, and employer contributions to nonqualified deferred compensation arrangements.	Withhold, but recipient may elect exemption on Form W-4P in certain cases; mandatory 20% withholding applies to an eligible rollover distribution that is not a direct rollover; exempt for direct rollover. See Publication 15-A.	Exempt	Exempt
7. Employer contributions to a section 457(b) plan.	Generally exempt, but see section 402(g) limitation.	Taxable	Taxable
8. Employee salary reduction contributions to a section 457(b) plan.	Generally exempt, but see section 402(g) salary reduction limitation.	Taxable	Taxable
Salespersons:			
1. Common law employees.	Withhold	Taxable	Taxable
2. Statutory employees.	Exempt	Taxable	Taxable, except for full-time life insurance sales agents.
3. Statutory nonemployees (qualified real estate agents, direct sellers, and certain companion sitters). See Publication 15-A for details.	Exempt	Exempt	Exempt
Scholarships and Fellowship Grants (Includible in Income Under Section 117(c)):	Withhold	Taxability depends on the nature of the employment and the status of the organization. See *Students, scholars, trainees, teachers,* and so on.	
Severance or Dismissal Pay:	Withhold	Taxable	Taxable
Service Not in the Course of the Employer's Trade or Business (Other Than on a Farm Operated for Profit or for Household Employment in Private Homes):	Withhold only if employee earns $50 or more in cash in a quarter and works on 24 or more different days in that quarter or in the preceding quarter.	Taxable if employee receives $100 or more in cash in a calendar year.	Taxable only if employee earns $50 or more in cash in a quarter and works on 24 or more different days in that quarter or in the preceding quarter.
Sick Pay: See Publication 15-A for more information.	Withhold	Exempt after end of 6 calendar months after the calendar month employee last worked for employer.	
Students, Scholars, Trainees, Teachers, etc.:			
1. Student enrolled and regularly attending classes, performing services for:			
a. Private school, college, or university	Withhold	Exempt	Exempt
b. Auxiliary nonprofit organization operated for and controlled by school, college, or university	Withhold	Exempt unless services are covered by a section 218 (Social Security Act) agreement.	Exempt
c. Public school, college, or university	Withhold	Exempt unless services are covered by a section 218 (Social Security Act) agreement.	Exempt

Special Classes of Employment and Special Types of Payments	Treatment Under Employment Taxes		
	Income Tax Withholding	Social Security and Medicare (Including Additional Medicare Tax when Wages are Paid in Excess of $200,000)	FUTA
2. Full-time student performing service for academic credit, combining instruction with work experience as an integral part of the program.	Withhold	Taxable	Exempt unless program was established for or on behalf of an employer or group of employers.
3. Student nurse performing part-time services for nominal earnings at hospital as incidental part of training.	Withhold	Exempt	Exempt
4. Student employed by organized camps.	Withhold	Taxable	Exempt
5. Student, scholar, trainee, teacher, and so on, as nonimmigrant alien under section 101(a)(15)(F), (J), (M), or (Q) of Immigration and Nationality Act (that is, aliens holding F-1, J-1, M-1, or Q-1 visas).	Withhold unless excepted by regulations.	Exempt if service is performed for purpose specified in section 101(a)(15)(F), (J), (M), or (Q) of Immigration and Nationality Act. However, these taxes may apply if the employee becomes a resident alien.	
Supplemental Unemployment Compensation Plan Benefits:	Withhold	Exempt under certain conditions. See Publication 15-A.	
Tips:			
1. If $20 or more in a month.	Withhold	Taxable	Taxable for all tips reported in writing to employer.
2. If less than $20 in a month. See section 6 of IRS Publication 15 for more information.	Exempt	Exempt	Exempt
Workers' Compensation:	Exempt	Exempt	Exempt

Appendix C

Federal Income Tax Tables*

The following is information about federal income tax withholding for 2016. Specific questions about federal income taxes and business situations may be directed to the Internal Revenue Service via the IRS website at https://www.irs.gov/businesses.

Payroll Period	One Withholding Allowance
Weekly	$ 77.90
Biweekly	155.80
Semimonthly	168.80
Monthly	337.50
Quarterly	1,012.50
Semiannually	2,025.00
Annually	4,050.00
Daily or miscellaneous (each day of the payroll period)	15.60

*Note: Appendix C is derived from IRS Publication 15. A comment to refer to pages 42 and 44 exists at the section end for wage-bracket tables when the taxable wages exceed the table. These page references are for Publication 15 itself and not to pages within this text.

Percentage Method Tables for Income Tax Withholding

(For Wages Paid in 2016)
TABLE 1—WEEKLY Payroll Period

(a) SINGLE person (including head of household)—

If the amount of wages (after subtracting withholding allowances) is:
Not over $43 . . . . $0

The amount of income tax to withhold is:

Over—	But not over—		of excess over—
$43	—$222 . .	$0.00 plus 10%	—$43
$222	—$767 . .	$17.90 plus 15%	—$222
$767	—$1,796 . .	$99.65 plus 25%	—$767
$1,796	—$3,700 . .	$356.90 plus 28%	—$1,796
$3,700	—$7,992 . .	$890.02 plus 33%	—$3,700
$7,992	—$8,025 . .	$2,306.38 plus 35%	—$7,992
$8,025	. . . .	$2,317.93 plus 39.6%	—$8,025

(b) MARRIED person—

If the amount of wages (after subtracting withholding allowances) is:
Not over $164 . . . . $0

The amount of income tax to withhold is:

Over	But not over—		of excess over—
$164	—$521 . .	$0.00 plus 10%	—$164
$521	—$1,613 . .	$35.70 plus 15%	—$521
$1,613	—$3,086 . .	$199.50 plus 25%	—$1,613
$3,086	—$4,615 . .	$567.75 plus 28%	—$3,086
$4,615	—$8,113 . .	$995.87 plus 33%	—$4,615
$8,113	—$9,144 . .	$2,150.21 plus 35%	—$8,113
$9,144	. . . .	$2,511.06 plus 39.6%	—$9,144

TABLE 2—BIWEEKLY Payroll Period

(a) SINGLE person (including head of household)—

If the amount of wages (after subtracting withholding allowances) is:
Not over $87 . . . . $0

The amount of income tax to withhold is:

Over—	But not over—		of excess over—
$87	—$443 . .	$0.00 plus 10%	—$87
$443	—$1,535 . .	$35.60 plus 15%	—$443
$1,535	—$3,592 . .	$199.40 plus 25%	—$1,535
$3,592	—$7,400 . .	$713.65 plus 28%	—$3,592
$7,400	—$15,985 . .	$1,779.89 plus 33%	—$7,400
$15,985	—$16,050 . .	$4,612.94 plus 35%	—$15,985
$16,050	. . . .	$4,635.69 plus 39.6%	—$16,050

(b) MARRIED person—

If the amount of wages (after subtracting withholding allowances) is:
Not over $329 . . . . $0

The amount of income tax to withhold is:

Over—	But not over—		of excess over—
$329	—$1,042 . .	$0.00 plus 10%	—$329
$1,042	—$3,225 . .	$71.30 plus 15%	—$1,042
$3,225	—$6,171 . .	$398.75 plus 25%	—$3,225
$6,171	—$9,231 . .	$1,135.25 plus 28%	—$6,171
$9,231	—$16,227 . .	$1,992.05 plus 33%	—$9,231
$16,227	—$18,288 . .	$4,300.73 plus 35%	—$16,227
$18,288	. . . .	$5,022.08 plus 39.6%	—$18,288

TABLE 3—SEMIMONTHLY Payroll Period

(a) SINGLE person (including head of household)—

If the amount of wages (after subtracting withholding allowances) is:
Not over $94 . . . . $0

The amount of income tax to withhold is:

Over—	But not over—		of excess over—
$94	—$480 . .	$0.00 plus 10%	—$94
$480	—$1,663 . .	$38.60 plus 15%	—$480
$1,663	—$3,892 . .	$216.05 plus 25%	—$1,663
$3,892	—$8,017 . .	$773.30 plus 28%	—$3,892
$8,017	—$17,317 . .	$1,928.30 plus 33%	—$8,017
$17,317	—$17,388 . .	$4,997.30 plus 35%	—$17,317
$17,388	. . . .	$5,022.15 plus 39.6%	—$17,388

(b) MARRIED person—

If the amount of wages (after subtracting withholding allowances) is:
Not over $356 . . . . $0

The amount of income tax to withhold is:

Over—	But not over—		of excess over—
$356	—$1,129 . .	$0.00 plus 10%	—$356
$1,129	—$3,494 . .	$77.30 plus 15%	—$1,129
$3,494	—$6,685 . .	$432.05 plus 25%	—$3,494
$6,685	—$10,000 . .	$1,229.80 plus 28%	—$6,685
$10,000	—$17,579 . .	$2,158.00 plus 33%	—$10,000
$17,579	—$19,813 . .	$4,659.07 plus 35%	—$17,579
$19,813	. . . .	$5,440.97 plus 39.6%	—$19,813

TABLE 4—MONTHLY Payroll Period

(a) SINGLE person (including head of household)—

If the amount of wages (after subtracting withholding allowances) is:
Not over $188 . . . . $0

The amount of income tax to withhold is:

Over—	But not over—		of excess over—
$188	—$960 . .	$0.00 plus 10%	—$188
$960	—$3,325 . .	$77.20 plus 15%	—$960
$3,325	—$7,783 . .	$431.95 plus 25%	—$3,325
$7,783	—$16,033 . .	$1,546.45 plus 28%	—$7,783
$16,033	—$34,633 . .	$3,856.45 plus 33%	—$16,033
$34,633	—$34,775 . .	$9,994.45 plus 35%	—$34,633
$34,775	. . . .	$10,044.15 plus 39.6%	—$34,775

(b) MARRIED person—

If the amount of wages (after subtracting withholding allowances) is:
Not over $713 . . . . $0

The amount of income tax to withhold is:

Over—	But not over—		of excess over—
$713	—$2,258 . .	$0.00 plus 10%	—$713
$2,258	—$6,988 . .	$154.50 plus 15%	—$2,258
$6,988	—$13,371 . .	$864.00 plus 25%	—$6,988
$13,371	—$20,000 . .	$2,459.75 plus 28%	—$13,371
$20,000	—$35,158 . .	$4,315.87 plus 33%	—$20,000
$35,158	—$39,625 . .	$9,318.01 plus 35%	—$35,158
$39,625	. . . .	$10,881.46 plus 39.6%	—$39,625

Percentage Method Tables for Income Tax Withholding (continued)

(For Wages Paid in 2016)

TABLE 5—QUARTERLY Payroll Period

(a) SINGLE person (including head of household)—

If the amount of wages (after subtracting withholding allowances) is:
The amount of income tax to withhold is:

Not over $563 . . . . $0

Over—	But not over—		of excess over—
$563	—$2,881 . .	$0.00 plus 10%	—$563
$2,881	—$9,975 . .	$231.80 plus 15%	—$2,881
$9,975	—$23,350 . .	$1,295.90 plus 25%	—$9,975
$23,350	—$48,100 . .	$4,639.65 plus 28%	—$23,350
$48,100	—$103,900 . .	$11,569.65 plus 33%	—$48,100
$103,900	—$104,325 . .	$29,983.65 plus 35%	—$103,900
$104,325	. . . .	$30,132.40 plus 39.6%	—$104,325

(b) MARRIED person—

If the amount of wages (after subtracting withholding allowances) is:
The amount of income tax to withhold is:

Not over $2,138 . . . . $0

Over—	But not over—		of excess over—
$2,138	—$6,775 . .	$0.00 plus 10%	—$2,138
$6,775	—$20,963 . .	$463.70 plus 15%	—$6,775
$20,963	—$40,113 . .	$2,591.90 plus 25%	—$20,963
$40,113	—$60,000 . .	$7,379.40 plus 28%	—$40,113
$60,000	—$105,475 . .	$12,947.76 plus 33%	—$60,000
$105,475	—$118,875 . .	$27,954.51 plus 35%	—$105,475
$118,875	. . . .	$32,644.51 plus 39.6%	—$118,875

TABLE 6—SEMIANNUAL Payroll Period

(a) SINGLE person (including head of household)—

If the amount of wages (after subtracting withholding allowances) is:
The amount of income tax to withhold is:

Not over $1,125 . . . . $0

Over—	But not over—		of excess over—
$1,125	—$5,763 . .	$0.00 plus 10%	—$1,125
$5,763	—$19,950 . .	$463.80 plus 15%	—$5,763
$19,950	—$46,700 . .	$2,591.85 plus 25%	—$19,950
$46,700	—$96,200 . .	$9,279.35 plus 28%	—$46,700
$96,200	—$207,800 . .	$23,139.35 plus 33%	—$96,200
$207,800	—$208,650 . .	$59,967.35 plus 35%	—$207,800
$208,650	. . . .	$60,264.85 plus 39.6%	—$208,650

(b) MARRIED person—

If the amount of wages (after subtracting withholding allowances) is:
The amount of income tax to withhold is:

Not over $4,275 . . . . $0

Over—	But not over—		of excess over—
$4,275	—$13,550 . .	$0.00 plus 10%	—$4,275
$13,550	—$41,925 . .	$927.50 plus 15%	—$13,550
$41,925	—$80,225 . .	$5,183.75 plus 25%	—$41,925
$80,225	—$120,000 . .	$14,758.75 plus 28%	—$80,225
$120,000	—$210,950 . .	$25,895.75 plus 33%	—$120,000
$210,950	—$237,750 . .	$55,909.25 plus 35%	—$210,950
$237,750	. . . .	$65,289.25 plus 39.6%	—$237,750

TABLE 7—ANNUAL Payroll Period

(a) SINGLE person (including head of household)—

If the amount of wages (after subtracting withholding allowances) is:
The amount of income tax to withhold is:

Not over $2,250 . . . . $0

Over—	But not over—		of excess over—
$2,250	—$11,525 . .	$0.00 plus 10%	—$2,250
$11,525	—$39,900 . .	$927.50 plus 15%	—$11,525
$39,900	—$93,400 . .	$5,183.75 plus 25%	—$39,900
$93,400	—$192,400 . .	$18,558.75 plus 28%	—$93,400
$192,400	—$415,600 . .	$46,278.75 plus 33%	—$192,400
$415,600	—$417,300 . .	$119,934.75 plus 35%	—$415,600
$417,300	. . . .	$120,529.75 plus 39.6%	—$417,300

(b) MARRIED person—

If the amount of wages (after subtracting withholding allowances) is:
The amount of income tax to withhold is:

Not over $8,550 . . . . $0

Over—	But not over—		of excess over—
$8,550	—$27,100 . .	$0.00 plus 10%	—$8,550
$27,100	—$83,850 . .	$1,855.00 plus 15%	—$27,100
$83,850	—$160,450 . .	$10,367.50 plus 25%	—$83,850
$160,450	—$240,000 . .	$29,517.50 plus 28%	—$160,450
$240,000	—$421,900 . .	$51,791.50 plus 33%	—$240,000
$421,900	—$475,500 . .	$111,818.50 plus 35%	—$421,900
$475,500	. . . .	$130,578.50 plus 39.6%	—$475,500

TABLE 8—DAILY or MISCELLANEOUS Payroll Period

(a) SINGLE person (including head of household)—

If the amount of wages (after subtracting withholding allowances) divided by the number of days in the payroll period is:
The amount of income tax to withhold per day is:

Not over $8.70 . . . . $0

Over—	But not over—		of excess over—
$8.70	—$44.30 . .	$0.00 plus 10%	—$8.70
$44.30	—$153.50 . .	$3.56 plus 15%	—$44.30
$153.50	—$359.20 . .	$19.94 plus 25%	—$153.50
$359.20	—$740.00 . .	$71.37 plus 28%	—$359.20
$740.00	—$1,598.50 . .	$177.99 plus 33%	—$740.00
$1,598.50	—$1,605.00 . .	$461.30 plus 35%	—$1,598.50
$1,605.00	. . . .	$463.58 plus 39.6%	—$1,605.00

(b) MARRIED person—

If the amount of wages (after subtracting withholding allowances) divided by the number of days in the payroll period is:
The amount of income tax to withhold per day is:

Not over $32.90 . . . . $0

Over—	But not over—		of excess over—
$32.90	—$104.20 . .	$0.00 plus 10%	—$32.90
$104.20	—$322.50 . .	$7.13 plus 15%	—$104.20
$322.50	—$617.10 . .	$39.88 plus 25%	—$322.50
$617.10	—$923.10 . .	$113.53 plus 28%	—$617.10
$923.10	—$1,622.70 . .	$199.21 plus 33%	—$923.10
$1,622.70	—$1,828.80 . .	$430.08 plus 35%	—$1,622.70
$1,828.80	. . . .	$502.22 plus 39.6%	—$1,828.80

Wage Bracket Method Tables for Income Tax Withholding

SINGLE Persons—WEEKLY Payroll Period

(For Wages Paid through December 31, 2016)

And the wages are–		And the number of withholding allowances claimed is—										
At least	But less than	0	1	2	3	4	5	6	7	8	9	10
		The amount of income tax to be withheld is—										
$0	$55	$0	$0	$0	$0	$0	$0	$0	$0	$0	$0	$0
55	60	1	0	0	0	0	0	0	0	0	0	0
60	65	2	0	0	0	0	0	0	0	0	0	0
65	70	2	0	0	0	0	0	0	0	0	0	0
70	75	3	0	0	0	0	0	0	0	0	0	0
75	80	3	0	0	0	0	0	0	0	0	0	0
80	85	4	0	0	0	0	0	0	0	0	0	0
85	90	4	0	0	0	0	0	0	0	0	0	0
90	95	5	0	0	0	0	0	0	0	0	0	0
95	100	5	0	0	0	0	0	0	0	0	0	0
100	105	6	0	0	0	0	0	0	0	0	0	0
105	110	6	0	0	0	0	0	0	0	0	0	0
110	115	7	0	0	0	0	0	0	0	0	0	0
115	120	7	0	0	0	0	0	0	0	0	0	0
120	125	8	0	0	0	0	0	0	0	0	0	0
125	130	8	1	0	0	0	0	0	0	0	0	0
130	135	9	1	0	0	0	0	0	0	0	0	0
135	140	9	2	0	0	0	0	0	0	0	0	0
140	145	10	2	0	0	0	0	0	0	0	0	0
145	150	10	3	0	0	0	0	0	0	0	0	0
150	155	11	3	0	0	0	0	0	0	0	0	0
155	160	11	4	0	0	0	0	0	0	0	0	0
160	165	12	4	0	0	0	0	0	0	0	0	0
165	170	12	5	0	0	0	0	0	0	0	0	0
170	175	13	5	0	0	0	0	0	0	0	0	0
175	180	13	6	0	0	0	0	0	0	0	0	0
180	185	14	6	0	0	0	0	0	0	0	0	0
185	190	14	7	0	0	0	0	0	0	0	0	0
190	195	15	7	0	0	0	0	0	0	0	0	0
195	200	15	8	0	0	0	0	0	0	0	0	0
200	210	16	8	1	0	0	0	0	0	0	0	0
210	220	17	9	2	0	0	0	0	0	0	0	0
220	230	18	10	3	0	0	0	0	0	0	0	0
230	240	20	11	4	0	0	0	0	0	0	0	0
240	250	21	12	5	0	0	0	0	0	0	0	0
250	260	23	13	6	0	0	0	0	0	0	0	0
260	270	24	14	7	0	0	0	0	0	0	0	0
270	280	26	15	8	0	0	0	0	0	0	0	0
280	290	27	16	9	1	0	0	0	0	0	0	0
290	300	29	17	10	2	0	0	0	0	0	0	0
300	310	30	19	11	3	0	0	0	0	0	0	0
310	320	32	20	12	4	0	0	0	0	0	0	0
320	330	33	22	13	5	0	0	0	0	0	0	0
330	340	35	23	14	6	0	0	0	0	0	0	0
340	350	36	25	15	7	0	0	0	0	0	0	0
350	360	38	26	16	8	0	0	0	0	0	0	0
360	370	39	28	17	9	1	0	0	0	0	0	0
370	380	41	29	18	10	2	0	0	0	0	0	0
380	390	42	31	19	11	3	0	0	0	0	0	0
390	400	44	32	20	12	4	0	0	0	0	0	0
400	410	45	34	22	13	5	0	0	0	0	0	0
410	420	47	35	23	14	6	0	0	0	0	0	0
420	430	48	37	25	15	7	0	0	0	0	0	0
430	440	50	38	26	16	8	0	0	0	0	0	0
440	450	51	40	28	17	9	1	0	0	0	0	0
450	460	53	41	29	18	10	2	0	0	0	0	0
460	470	54	43	31	19	11	3	0	0	0	0	0
470	480	56	44	32	21	12	4	0	0	0	0	0
480	490	57	46	34	22	13	5	0	0	0	0	0
490	500	59	47	35	24	14	6	0	0	0	0	0
500	510	60	49	37	25	15	7	0	0	0	0	0
510	520	62	50	38	27	16	8	0	0	0	0	0
520	530	63	52	40	28	17	9	1	0	0	0	0
530	540	65	53	41	30	18	10	2	0	0	0	0
540	550	66	55	43	31	20	11	3	0	0	0	0
550	560	68	56	44	33	21	12	4	0	0	0	0
560	570	69	58	46	34	23	13	5	0	0	0	0
570	580	71	59	47	36	24	14	6	0	0	0	0
580	590	72	61	49	37	26	15	7	0	0	0	0
590	600	74	62	50	39	27	16	8	1	0	0	0

Wage Bracket Method Tables for Income Tax Withholding

SINGLE Persons—WEEKLY Payroll Period

(For Wages Paid through December 31, 2016)

And the wages are–		And the number of withholding allowances claimed is—										
At least	But less than	0	1	2	3	4	5	6	7	8	9	10
		The amount of income tax to be withheld is—										
$600	$610	$75	$64	$52	$40	$29	$17	$9	$2	$0	$0	$0
610	620	77	65	53	42	30	18	10	3	0	0	0
620	630	78	67	55	43	32	20	11	4	0	0	0
630	640	80	68	56	45	33	21	12	5	0	0	0
640	650	81	70	58	46	35	23	13	6	0	0	0
650	660	83	71	59	48	36	24	14	7	0	0	0
660	670	84	73	61	49	38	26	15	8	0	0	0
670	680	86	74	62	51	39	27	16	9	1	0	0
680	690	87	76	64	52	41	29	17	10	2	0	0
690	700	89	77	65	54	42	30	19	11	3	0	0
700	710	90	79	67	55	44	32	20	12	4	0	0
710	720	92	80	68	57	45	33	22	13	5	0	0
720	730	93	82	70	58	47	35	23	14	6	0	0
730	740	95	83	71	60	48	36	25	15	7	0	0
740	750	96	85	73	61	50	38	26	16	8	0	0
750	760	98	86	74	63	51	39	28	17	9	1	0
760	770	99	88	76	64	53	41	29	18	10	2	0
770	780	102	89	77	66	54	42	31	19	11	3	0
780	790	104	91	79	67	56	44	32	21	12	4	0
790	800	107	92	80	69	57	45	34	22	13	5	0
800	810	109	94	82	70	59	47	35	24	14	6	0
810	820	112	95	83	72	60	48	37	25	15	7	0
820	830	114	97	85	73	62	50	38	27	16	8	0
830	840	117	98	86	75	63	51	40	28	17	9	1
840	850	119	100	88	76	65	53	41	30	18	10	2
850	860	122	102	89	78	66	54	43	31	19	11	3
860	870	124	105	91	79	68	56	44	33	21	12	4
870	880	127	107	92	81	69	57	46	34	22	13	5
880	890	129	110	94	82	71	59	47	36	24	14	6
890	900	132	112	95	84	72	60	49	37	25	15	7
900	910	134	115	97	85	74	62	50	39	27	16	8
910	920	137	117	98	87	75	63	52	40	28	17	9
920	930	139	120	100	88	77	65	53	42	30	18	10
930	940	142	122	103	90	78	66	55	43	31	20	11
940	950	144	125	105	91	80	68	56	45	33	21	12
950	960	147	127	108	93	81	69	58	46	34	23	13
960	970	149	130	110	94	83	71	59	48	36	24	14
970	980	152	132	113	96	84	72	61	49	37	26	15
980	990	154	135	115	97	86	74	62	51	39	27	16
990	1,000	157	137	118	99	87	75	64	52	40	29	17
1,000	1,010	159	140	120	101	89	77	65	54	42	30	19
1,010	1,020	162	142	123	103	90	78	67	55	43	32	20
1,020	1,030	164	145	125	106	92	80	68	57	45	33	22
1,030	1,040	167	147	128	108	93	81	70	58	46	35	23
1,040	1,050	169	150	130	111	95	83	71	60	48	36	25
1,050	1,060	172	152	133	113	96	84	73	61	49	38	26
1,060	1,070	174	155	135	116	98	86	74	63	51	39	28
1,070	1,080	177	157	138	118	99	87	76	64	52	41	29
1,080	1,090	179	160	140	121	101	89	77	66	54	42	31
1,090	1,100	182	162	143	123	104	90	79	67	55	44	32
1,100	1,110	184	165	145	126	106	92	80	69	57	45	34
1,110	1,120	187	167	148	128	109	93	82	70	58	47	35
1,120	1,130	189	170	150	131	111	95	83	72	60	48	37
1,130	1,140	192	172	153	133	114	96	85	73	61	50	38
1,140	1,150	194	175	155	136	116	98	86	75	63	51	40
1,150	1,160	197	177	158	138	119	99	88	76	64	53	41
1,160	1,170	199	180	160	141	121	102	89	78	66	54	43
1,170	1,180	202	182	163	143	124	104	91	79	67	56	44
1,180	1,190	204	185	165	146	126	107	92	81	69	57	46
1,190	1,200	207	187	168	148	129	109	94	82	70	59	47
1,200	1,210	209	190	170	151	131	112	95	84	72	60	49
1,210	1,220	212	192	173	153	134	114	97	85	73	62	50
1,220	1,230	214	195	175	156	136	117	98	87	75	63	52
1,230	1,240	217	197	178	158	139	119	100	88	76	65	53
1,240	1,250	219	200	180	161	141	122	102	90	78	66	55

$1,250 and over   Use Table 1(a) for a **SINGLE person** on page 44. Also see the instructions on page 42.

Wage Bracket Method Tables for Income Tax Withholding

MARRIED Persons—**WEEKLY** Payroll Period

(For Wages Paid through December 31, 2016)

And the wages are—		And the number of withholding allowances claimed is—										
At least	But less than	0	1	2	3	4	5	6	7	8	9	10
		The amount of income tax to be withheld is—										
$ 0	$170	$0	$0	$0	$0	$0	$0	$0	$0	$0	$0	$0
170	175	1	0	0	0	0	0	0	0	0	0	0
175	180	1	0	0	0	0	0	0	0	0	0	0
180	185	2	0	0	0	0	0	0	0	0	0	0
185	190	2	0	0	0	0	0	0	0	0	0	0
190	195	3	0	0	0	0	0	0	0	0	0	0
195	200	3	0	0	0	0	0	0	0	0	0	0
200	210	4	0	0	0	0	0	0	0	0	0	0
210	220	5	0	0	0	0	0	0	0	0	0	0
220	230	6	0	0	0	0	0	0	0	0	0	0
230	240	7	0	0	0	0	0	0	0	0	0	0
240	250	8	0	0	0	0	0	0	0	0	0	0
250	260	9	1	0	0	0	0	0	0	0	0	0
260	270	10	2	0	0	0	0	0	0	0	0	0
270	280	11	3	0	0	0	0	0	0	0	0	0
280	290	12	4	0	0	0	0	0	0	0	0	0
290	300	13	5	0	0	0	0	0	0	0	0	0
300	310	14	6	0	0	0	0	0	0	0	0	0
310	320	15	7	0	0	0	0	0	0	0	0	0
320	330	16	8	0	0	0	0	0	0	0	0	0
330	340	17	9	1	0	0	0	0	0	0	0	0
340	350	18	10	2	0	0	0	0	0	0	0	0
350	360	19	11	3	0	0	0	0	0	0	0	0
360	370	20	12	4	0	0	0	0	0	0	0	0
370	380	21	13	5	0	0	0	0	0	0	0	0
380	390	22	14	6	0	0	0	0	0	0	0	0
390	400	23	15	7	0	0	0	0	0	0	0	0
400	410	24	16	8	1	0	0	0	0	0	0	0
410	420	25	17	9	2	0	0	0	0	0	0	0
420	430	26	18	10	3	0	0	0	0	0	0	0
430	440	27	19	11	4	0	0	0	0	0	0	0
440	450	28	20	12	5	0	0	0	0	0	0	0
450	460	29	21	13	6	0	0	0	0	0	0	0
460	470	30	22	14	7	0	0	0	0	0	0	0
470	480	31	23	15	8	0	0	0	0	0	0	0
480	490	32	24	16	9	1	0	0	0	0	0	0
490	500	33	25	17	10	2	0	0	0	0	0	0
500	510	34	26	18	11	3	0	0	0	0	0	0
510	520	35	27	19	12	4	0	0	0	0	0	0
520	530	36	28	20	13	5	0	0	0	0	0	0
530	540	38	29	21	14	6	0	0	0	0	0	0
540	550	39	30	22	15	7	0	0	0	0	0	0
550	560	41	31	23	16	8	0	0	0	0	0	0
560	570	42	32	24	17	9	1	0	0	0	0	0
570	580	44	33	25	18	10	2	0	0	0	0	0
580	590	45	34	26	19	11	3	0	0	0	0	0
590	600	47	35	27	20	12	4	0	0	0	0	0
600	610	48	37	28	21	13	5	0	0	0	0	0
610	620	50	38	29	22	14	6	0	0	0	0	0
620	630	51	40	30	23	15	7	0	0	0	0	0
630	640	53	41	31	24	16	8	0	0	0	0	0
640	650	54	43	32	25	17	9	1	0	0	0	0
650	660	56	44	33	26	18	10	2	0	0	0	0
660	670	57	46	34	27	19	11	3	0	0	0	0
670	680	59	47	35	28	20	12	4	0	0	0	0
680	690	60	49	37	29	21	13	5	0	0	0	0
690	700	62	50	38	30	22	14	6	0	0	0	0
700	710	63	52	40	31	23	15	7	0	0	0	0
710	720	65	53	41	32	24	16	8	1	0	0	0
720	730	66	55	43	33	25	17	9	2	0	0	0
730	740	68	56	44	34	26	18	10	3	0	0	0
740	750	69	58	46	35	27	19	11	4	0	0	0
750	760	71	59	47	36	28	20	12	5	0	0	0
760	770	72	61	49	37	29	21	13	6	0	0	0
770	780	74	62	50	39	30	22	14	7	0	0	0
780	790	75	64	52	40	31	23	15	8	0	0	0
790	800	77	65	53	42	32	24	16	9	1	0	0

Wage Bracket Method Tables for Income Tax Withholding

MARRIED Persons—WEEKLY Payroll Period

(For Wages Paid through December 31, 2016)

And the wages are—		And the number of withholding allowances claimed is—										
At least	But less than	0	1	2	3	4	5	6	7	8	9	10
		The amount of income tax to be withheld is—										
$800	$810	$78	$67	$55	$43	$33	$25	$17	$10	$2	$0	$0
810	820	80	68	56	45	34	26	18	11	3	0	0
820	830	81	70	58	46	35	27	19	12	4	0	0
830	840	83	71	59	48	36	28	20	13	5	0	0
840	850	84	73	61	49	38	29	21	14	6	0	0
850	860	86	74	62	51	39	30	22	15	7	0	0
860	870	87	76	64	52	41	31	23	16	8	0	0
870	880	89	77	65	54	42	32	24	17	9	1	0
880	890	90	79	67	55	44	33	25	18	10	2	0
890	900	92	80	68	57	45	34	26	19	11	3	0
900	910	93	82	70	58	47	35	27	20	12	4	0
910	920	95	83	71	60	48	36	28	21	13	5	0
920	930	96	85	73	61	50	38	29	22	14	6	0
930	940	98	86	74	63	51	39	30	23	15	7	0
940	950	99	88	76	64	53	41	31	24	16	8	0
950	960	101	89	77	66	54	42	32	25	17	9	1
960	970	102	91	79	67	56	44	33	26	18	10	2
970	980	104	92	80	69	57	45	34	27	19	11	3
980	990	105	94	82	70	59	47	35	28	20	12	4
990	1,000	107	95	83	72	60	48	37	29	21	13	5
1,000	1,010	108	97	85	73	62	50	38	30	22	14	6
1,010	1,020	110	98	86	75	63	51	40	31	23	15	7
1,020	1,030	111	100	88	76	65	53	41	32	24	16	8
1,030	1,040	113	101	89	78	66	54	43	33	25	17	9
1,040	1,050	114	103	91	79	68	56	44	34	26	18	10
1,050	1,060	116	104	92	81	69	57	46	35	27	19	11
1,060	1,070	117	106	94	82	71	59	47	36	28	20	12
1,070	1,080	119	107	95	84	72	60	49	37	29	21	13
1,080	1,090	120	109	97	85	74	62	50	38	30	22	14
1,090	1,100	122	110	98	87	75	63	52	40	31	23	15
1,100	1,110	123	112	100	88	77	65	53	41	32	24	16
1,110	1,120	125	113	101	90	78	66	55	43	33	25	17
1,120	1,130	126	115	103	91	80	68	56	44	34	26	18
1,130	1,140	128	116	104	93	81	69	58	46	35	27	19
1,140	1,150	129	118	106	94	83	71	59	47	36	28	20
1,150	1,160	131	119	107	96	84	72	61	49	37	29	21
1,160	1,170	132	121	109	97	86	74	62	50	39	30	22
1,170	1,180	134	122	110	99	87	75	64	52	40	31	23
1,180	1,190	135	124	112	100	89	77	65	53	42	32	24
1,190	1,200	137	125	113	102	90	78	67	55	43	33	25
1,200	1,210	138	127	115	103	92	80	68	56	45	34	26
1,210	1,220	140	128	116	105	93	81	70	58	46	35	27
1,220	1,230	141	130	118	106	95	83	71	59	48	36	28
1,230	1,240	143	131	119	108	96	84	73	61	49	38	29
1,240	1,250	144	133	121	109	98	86	74	62	51	39	30
1,250	1,260	146	134	122	111	99	87	76	64	52	41	31
1,260	1,270	147	136	124	112	101	89	77	65	54	42	32
1,270	1,280	149	137	125	114	102	90	79	67	55	44	33
1,280	1,290	150	139	127	115	104	92	80	68	57	45	34
1,290	1,300	152	140	128	117	105	93	82	70	58	47	35
1,300	1,310	153	142	130	118	107	95	83	71	60	48	36
1,310	1,320	155	143	131	120	108	96	85	73	61	50	38
1,320	1,330	156	145	133	121	110	98	86	74	63	51	39
1,330	1,340	158	146	134	123	111	99	88	76	64	53	41
1,340	1,350	159	148	136	124	113	101	89	77	66	54	42
1,350	1,360	161	149	137	126	114	102	91	79	67	56	44
1,360	1,370	162	151	139	127	116	104	92	80	69	57	45
1,370	1,380	164	152	140	129	117	105	94	82	70	59	47
1,380	1,390	165	154	142	130	119	107	95	83	72	60	48
1,390	1,400	167	155	143	132	120	108	97	85	73	62	50
1,400	1,410	168	157	145	133	122	110	98	86	75	63	51
1,410	1,420	170	158	146	135	123	111	100	88	76	65	53
1,420	1,430	171	160	148	136	125	113	101	89	78	66	54
1,430	1,440	173	161	149	138	126	114	103	91	79	68	56
1,440	1,450	174	163	151	139	128	116	104	92	81	69	57
1,450	1,460	176	164	152	141	129	117	106	94	82	71	59
1,460	1,470	177	166	154	142	131	119	107	95	84	72	60
1,470	1,480	179	167	155	144	132	120	109	97	85	74	62
1,480	1,490	180	169	157	145	134	122	110	98	87	75	63

$1,490 and over	Use Table 1(b) for a **MARRIED person** on page 44. Also see the instructions on page 42.

Wage Bracket Method Tables for Income Tax Withholding

SINGLE Persons—BIWEEKLY Payroll Period

(For Wages Paid through December 31, 2016)

And the wages are—		And the number of withholding allowances claimed is—										
At least	But less than	0	1	2	3	4	5	6	7	8	9	10
		The amount of income tax to be withheld is—										
$ 0	$105	$0	$0	$0	$0	$0	$0	$0	$0	$0	$0	$0
105	110	2	0	0	0	0	0	0	0	0	0	0
110	115	3	0	0	0	0	0	0	0	0	0	0
115	120	3	0	0	0	0	0	0	0	0	0	0
120	125	4	0	0	0	0	0	0	0	0	0	0
125	130	4	0	0	0	0	0	0	0	0	0	0
130	135	5	0	0	0	0	0	0	0	0	0	0
135	140	5	0	0	0	0	0	0	0	0	0	0
140	145	6	0	0	0	0	0	0	0	0	0	0
145	150	6	0	0	0	0	0	0	0	0	0	0
150	155	7	0	0	0	0	0	0	0	0	0	0
155	160	7	0	0	0	0	0	0	0	0	0	0
160	165	8	0	0	0	0	0	0	0	0	0	0
165	170	8	0	0	0	0	0	0	0	0	0	0
170	175	9	0	0	0	0	0	0	0	0	0	0
175	180	9	0	0	0	0	0	0	0	0	0	0
180	185	10	0	0	0	0	0	0	0	0	0	0
185	190	10	0	0	0	0	0	0	0	0	0	0
190	195	11	0	0	0	0	0	0	0	0	0	0
195	200	11	0	0	0	0	0	0	0	0	0	0
200	205	12	0	0	0	0	0	0	0	0	0	0
205	210	12	0	0	0	0	0	0	0	0	0	0
210	215	13	0	0	0	0	0	0	0	0	0	0
215	220	13	0	0	0	0	0	0	0	0	0	0
220	225	14	0	0	0	0	0	0	0	0	0	0
225	230	14	0	0	0	0	0	0	0	0	0	0
230	235	15	0	0	0	0	0	0	0	0	0	0
235	240	15	0	0	0	0	0	0	0	0	0	0
240	245	16	0	0	0	0	0	0	0	0	0	0
245	250	16	1	0	0	0	0	0	0	0	0	0
250	260	17	1	0	0	0	0	0	0	0	0	0
260	270	18	2	0	0	0	0	0	0	0	0	0
270	280	19	3	0	0	0	0	0	0	0	0	0
280	290	20	4	0	0	0	0	0	0	0	0	0
290	300	21	5	0	0	0	0	0	0	0	0	0
300	310	22	6	0	0	0	0	0	0	0	0	0
310	320	23	7	0	0	0	0	0	0	0	0	0
320	330	24	8	0	0	0	0	0	0	0	0	0
330	340	25	9	0	0	0	0	0	0	0	0	0
340	350	26	10	0	0	0	0	0	0	0	0	0
350	360	27	11	0	0	0	0	0	0	0	0	0
360	370	28	12	0	0	0	0	0	0	0	0	0
370	380	29	13	0	0	0	0	0	0	0	0	0
380	390	30	14	0	0	0	0	0	0	0	0	0
390	400	31	15	0	0	0	0	0	0	0	0	0
400	410	32	16	1	0	0	0	0	0	0	0	0
410	420	33	17	2	0	0	0	0	0	0	0	0
420	430	34	18	3	0	0	0	0	0	0	0	0
430	440	35	19	4	0	0	0	0	0	0	0	0
440	450	36	20	5	0	0	0	0	0	0	0	0
450	460	37	21	6	0	0	0	0	0	0	0	0
460	470	39	22	7	0	0	0	0	0	0	0	0
470	480	40	23	8	0	0	0	0	0	0	0	0
480	490	42	24	9	0	0	0	0	0	0	0	0
490	500	43	25	10	0	0	0	0	0	0	0	0
500	520	46	27	11	0	0	0	0	0	0	0	0
520	540	49	29	13	0	0	0	0	0	0	0	0
540	560	52	31	15	0	0	0	0	0	0	0	0
560	580	55	33	17	2	0	0	0	0	0	0	0
580	600	58	35	19	4	0	0	0	0	0	0	0
600	620	61	37	21	6	0	0	0	0	0	0	0
620	640	64	40	23	8	0	0	0	0	0	0	0
640	660	67	43	25	10	0	0	0	0	0	0	0
660	680	70	46	27	12	0	0	0	0	0	0	0
680	700	73	49	29	14	0	0	0	0	0	0	0
700	720	76	52	31	16	0	0	0	0	0	0	0
720	740	79	55	33	18	2	0	0	0	0	0	0
740	760	82	58	35	20	4	0	0	0	0	0	0
760	780	85	61	38	22	6	0	0	0	0	0	0
780	800	88	64	41	24	8	0	0	0	0	0	0

Wage Bracket Method Tables for Income Tax Withholding

SINGLE Persons—BIWEEKLY Payroll Period

(For Wages Paid through December 31, 2016)

And the wages are—		And the number of withholding allowances claimed is—										
At least	But less than	0	1	2	3	4	5	6	7	8	9	10
		The amount of income tax to be withheld is—										
$800	$820	$91	$67	$44	$26	$10	$0	$0	$0	$0	$0	$0
820	840	94	70	47	28	12	0	0	0	0	0	0
840	860	97	73	50	30	14	0	0	0	0	0	0
860	880	100	76	53	32	16	0	0	0	0	0	0
880	900	103	79	56	34	18	2	0	0	0	0	0
900	920	106	82	59	36	20	4	0	0	0	0	0
920	940	109	85	62	39	22	6	0	0	0	0	0
940	960	112	88	65	42	24	8	0	0	0	0	0
960	980	115	91	68	45	26	10	0	0	0	0	0
980	1,000	118	94	71	48	28	12	0	0	0	0	0
1,000	1,020	121	97	74	51	30	14	0	0	0	0	0
1,020	1,040	124	100	77	54	32	16	1	0	0	0	0
1,040	1,060	127	103	80	57	34	18	3	0	0	0	0
1,060	1,080	130	106	83	60	36	20	5	0	0	0	0
1,080	1,100	133	109	86	63	39	22	7	0	0	0	0
1,100	1,120	136	112	89	66	42	24	9	0	0	0	0
1,120	1,140	139	115	92	69	45	26	11	0	0	0	0
1,140	1,160	142	118	95	72	48	28	13	0	0	0	0
1,160	1,180	145	121	98	75	51	30	15	0	0	0	0
1,180	1,200	148	124	101	78	54	32	17	1	0	0	0
1,200	1,220	151	127	104	81	57	34	19	3	0	0	0
1,220	1,240	154	130	107	84	60	37	21	5	0	0	0
1,240	1,260	157	133	110	87	63	40	23	7	0	0	0
1,260	1,280	160	136	113	90	66	43	25	9	0	0	0
1,280	1,300	163	139	116	93	69	46	27	11	0	0	0
1,300	1,320	166	142	119	96	72	49	29	13	0	0	0
1,320	1,340	169	145	122	99	75	52	31	15	0	0	0
1,340	1,360	172	148	125	102	78	55	33	17	2	0	0
1,360	1,380	175	151	128	105	81	58	35	19	4	0	0
1,380	1,400	178	154	131	108	84	61	37	21	6	0	0
1,400	1,420	181	157	134	111	87	64	40	23	8	0	0
1,420	1,440	184	160	137	114	90	67	43	25	10	0	0
1,440	1,460	187	163	140	117	93	70	46	27	12	0	0
1,460	1,480	190	166	143	120	96	73	49	29	14	0	0
1,480	1,500	193	169	146	123	99	76	52	31	16	0	0
1,500	1,520	196	172	149	126	102	79	55	33	18	2	0
1,520	1,540	199	175	152	129	105	82	58	35	20	4	0
1,540	1,560	203	178	155	132	108	85	61	38	22	6	0
1,560	1,580	208	181	158	135	111	88	64	41	24	8	0
1,580	1,600	213	184	161	138	114	91	67	44	26	10	0
1,600	1,620	218	187	164	141	117	94	70	47	28	12	0
1,620	1,640	223	190	167	144	120	97	73	50	30	14	0
1,640	1,660	228	193	170	147	123	100	76	53	32	16	1
1,660	1,680	233	196	173	150	126	103	79	56	34	18	3
1,680	1,700	238	199	176	153	129	106	82	59	36	20	5
1,700	1,720	243	204	179	156	132	109	85	62	39	22	7
1,720	1,740	248	209	182	159	135	112	88	65	42	24	9
1,740	1,760	253	214	185	162	138	115	91	68	45	26	11
1,760	1,780	258	219	188	165	141	118	94	71	48	28	13
1,780	1,800	263	224	191	168	144	121	97	74	51	30	15
1,800	1,820	268	229	194	171	147	124	100	77	54	32	17
1,820	1,840	273	234	197	174	150	127	103	80	57	34	19
1,840	1,860	278	239	200	177	153	130	106	83	60	36	21
1,860	1,880	283	244	205	180	156	133	109	86	63	39	23
1,880	1,900	288	249	210	183	159	136	112	89	66	42	25
1,900	1,920	293	254	215	186	162	139	115	92	69	45	27
1,920	1,940	298	259	220	189	165	142	118	95	72	48	29
1,940	1,960	303	264	225	192	168	145	121	98	75	51	31
1,960	1,980	308	269	230	195	171	148	124	101	78	54	33
1,980	2,000	313	274	235	198	174	151	127	104	81	57	35
2,000	2,020	318	279	240	201	177	154	130	107	84	60	37
2,020	2,040	323	284	245	206	180	157	133	110	87	63	40
2,040	2,060	328	289	250	211	183	160	136	113	90	66	43
2,060	2,080	333	294	255	216	186	163	139	116	93	69	46
2,080	2,100	338	299	260	221	189	166	142	119	96	72	49

$2,100 and over   Use Table 2(a) for a **SINGLE person** on page 44. Also see the instructions on page 42.

Wage Bracket Method Tables for Income Tax Withholding

MARRIED Persons—BIWEEKLY Payroll Period

(For Wages Paid through December 31, 2016)

And the wages are—		And the number of withholding allowances claimed is—										
At least	But less than	0	1	2	3	4	5	6	7	8	9	10
		The amount of income tax to be withheld is—										
$ 0	$340	$0	$0	$0	$0	$0	$0	$0	$0	$0	$0	$0
340	350	2	0	0	0	0	0	0	0	0	0	0
350	360	3	0	0	0	0	0	0	0	0	0	0
360	370	4	0	0	0	0	0	0	0	0	0	0
370	380	5	0	0	0	0	0	0	0	0	0	0
380	390	6	0	0	0	0	0	0	0	0	0	0
390	400	7	0	0	0	0	0	0	0	0	0	0
400	410	8	0	0	0	0	0	0	0	0	0	0
410	420	9	0	0	0	0	0	0	0	0	0	0
420	430	10	0	0	0	0	0	0	0	0	0	0
430	440	11	0	0	0	0	0	0	0	0	0	0
440	450	12	0	0	0	0	0	0	0	0	0	0
450	460	13	0	0	0	0	0	0	0	0	0	0
460	470	14	0	0	0	0	0	0	0	0	0	0
470	480	15	0	0	0	0	0	0	0	0	0	0
480	490	16	0	0	0	0	0	0	0	0	0	0
490	500	17	1	0	0	0	0	0	0	0	0	0
500	520	18	3	0	0	0	0	0	0	0	0	0
520	540	20	5	0	0	0	0	0	0	0	0	0
540	560	22	7	0	0	0	0	0	0	0	0	0
560	580	24	9	0	0	0	0	0	0	0	0	0
580	600	26	11	0	0	0	0	0	0	0	0	0
600	620	28	13	0	0	0	0	0	0	0	0	0
620	640	30	15	0	0	0	0	0	0	0	0	0
640	660	32	17	1	0	0	0	0	0	0	0	0
660	680	34	19	3	0	0	0	0	0	0	0	0
680	700	36	21	5	0	0	0	0	0	0	0	0
700	720	38	23	7	0	0	0	0	0	0	0	0
720	740	40	25	9	0	0	0	0	0	0	0	0
740	760	42	27	11	0	0	0	0	0	0	0	0
760	780	44	29	13	0	0	0	0	0	0	0	0
780	800	46	31	15	0	0	0	0	0	0	0	0
800	820	48	33	17	1	0	0	0	0	0	0	0
820	840	50	35	19	3	0	0	0	0	0	0	0
840	860	52	37	21	5	0	0	0	0	0	0	0
860	880	54	39	23	7	0	0	0	0	0	0	0
880	900	56	41	25	9	0	0	0	0	0	0	0
900	920	58	43	27	11	0	0	0	0	0	0	0
920	940	60	45	29	13	0	0	0	0	0	0	0
940	960	62	47	31	15	0	0	0	0	0	0	0
960	980	64	49	33	17	2	0	0	0	0	0	0
980	1,000	66	51	35	19	4	0	0	0	0	0	0
1,000	1,020	68	53	37	21	6	0	0	0	0	0	0
1,020	1,040	70	55	39	23	8	0	0	0	0	0	0
1,040	1,060	73	57	41	25	10	0	0	0	0	0	0
1,060	1,080	76	59	43	27	12	0	0	0	0	0	0
1,080	1,100	79	61	45	29	14	0	0	0	0	0	0
1,100	1,120	82	63	47	31	16	0	0	0	0	0	0
1,120	1,140	85	65	49	33	18	2	0	0	0	0	0
1,140	1,160	88	67	51	35	20	4	0	0	0	0	0
1,160	1,180	91	69	53	37	22	6	0	0	0	0	0
1,180	1,200	94	71	55	39	24	8	0	0	0	0	0
1,200	1,220	97	73	57	41	26	10	0	0	0	0	0
1,220	1,240	100	76	59	43	28	12	0	0	0	0	0
1,240	1,260	103	79	61	45	30	14	0	0	0	0	0
1,260	1,280	106	82	63	47	32	16	1	0	0	0	0
1,280	1,300	109	85	65	49	34	18	3	0	0	0	0
1,300	1,320	112	88	67	51	36	20	5	0	0	0	0
1,320	1,340	115	91	69	53	38	22	7	0	0	0	0
1,340	1,360	118	94	71	55	40	24	9	0	0	0	0
1,360	1,380	121	97	74	57	42	26	11	0	0	0	0
1,380	1,400	124	100	77	59	44	28	13	0	0	0	0
1,400	1,420	127	103	80	61	46	30	15	0	0	0	0
1,420	1,440	130	106	83	63	48	32	17	1	0	0	0
1,440	1,460	133	109	86	65	50	34	19	3	0	0	0
1,460	1,480	136	112	89	67	52	36	21	5	0	0	0
1,480	1,500	139	115	92	69	54	38	23	7	0	0	0

Wage Bracket Method Tables for Income Tax Withholding

MARRIED Persons—BIWEEKLY Payroll Period

(For Wages Paid through December 31, 2016)

And the wages are—		And the number of withholding allowances claimed is—										
At least	But less than	0	1	2	3	4	5	6	7	8	9	10
		The amount of income tax to be withheld is—										
$1,500	$1,520	$142	$118	$95	$71	$56	$40	$25	$9	$0	$0	$0
1,520	1,540	145	121	98	74	58	42	27	11	0	0	0
1,540	1,560	148	124	101	77	60	44	29	13	0	0	0
1,560	1,580	151	127	104	80	62	46	31	15	0	0	0
1,580	1,600	154	130	107	83	64	48	33	17	2	0	0
1,600	1,620	157	133	110	86	66	50	35	19	4	0	0
1,620	1,640	160	136	113	89	68	52	37	21	6	0	0
1,640	1,660	163	139	116	92	70	54	39	23	8	0	0
1,660	1,680	166	142	119	95	72	56	41	25	10	0	0
1,680	1,700	169	145	122	98	75	58	43	27	12	0	0
1,700	1,720	172	148	125	101	78	60	45	29	14	0	0
1,720	1,740	175	151	128	104	81	62	47	31	16	0	0
1,740	1,760	178	154	131	107	84	64	49	33	18	2	0
1,760	1,780	181	157	134	110	87	66	51	35	20	4	0
1,780	1,800	184	160	137	113	90	68	53	37	22	6	0
1,800	1,820	187	163	140	116	93	70	55	39	24	8	0
1,820	1,840	190	166	143	119	96	73	57	41	26	10	0
1,840	1,860	193	169	146	122	99	76	59	43	28	12	0
1,860	1,880	196	172	149	125	102	79	61	45	30	14	0
1,880	1,900	199	175	152	128	105	82	63	47	32	16	0
1,900	1,920	202	178	155	131	108	85	65	49	34	18	2
1,920	1,940	205	181	158	134	111	88	67	51	36	20	4
1,940	1,960	208	184	161	137	114	91	69	53	38	22	6
1,960	1,980	211	187	164	140	117	94	71	55	40	24	8
1,980	2,000	214	190	167	143	120	97	73	57	42	26	10
2,000	2,020	217	193	170	146	123	100	76	59	44	28	12
2,020	2,040	220	196	173	149	126	103	79	61	46	30	14
2,040	2,060	223	199	176	152	129	106	82	63	48	32	16
2,060	2,080	226	202	179	155	132	109	85	65	50	34	18
2,080	2,100	229	205	182	158	135	112	88	67	52	36	20
2,100	2,120	232	208	185	161	138	115	91	69	54	38	22
2,120	2,140	235	211	188	164	141	118	94	71	56	40	24
2,140	2,160	238	214	191	167	144	121	97	74	58	42	26
2,160	2,180	241	217	194	170	147	124	100	77	60	44	28
2,180	2,200	244	220	197	173	150	127	103	80	62	46	30
2,200	2,220	247	223	200	176	153	130	106	83	64	48	32
2,220	2,240	250	226	203	179	156	133	109	86	66	50	34
2,240	2,260	253	229	206	182	159	136	112	89	68	52	36
2,260	2,280	256	232	209	185	162	139	115	92	70	54	38
2,280	2,300	259	235	212	188	165	142	118	95	72	56	40
2,300	2,320	262	238	215	191	168	145	121	98	75	58	42
2,320	2,340	265	241	218	194	171	148	124	101	78	60	44
2,340	2,360	268	244	221	197	174	151	127	104	81	62	46
2,360	2,380	271	247	224	200	177	154	130	107	84	64	48
2,380	2,400	274	250	227	203	180	157	133	110	87	66	50
2,400	2,420	277	253	230	206	183	160	136	113	90	68	52
2,420	2,440	280	256	233	209	186	163	139	116	93	70	54
2,440	2,460	283	259	236	212	189	166	142	119	96	72	56
2,460	2,480	286	262	239	215	192	169	145	122	99	75	58
2,480	2,500	289	265	242	218	195	172	148	125	102	78	60
2,500	2,520	292	268	245	221	198	175	151	128	105	81	62
2,520	2,540	295	271	248	224	201	178	154	131	108	84	64
2,540	2,560	298	274	251	227	204	181	157	134	111	87	66
2,560	2,580	301	277	254	230	207	184	160	137	114	90	68
2,580	2,600	304	280	257	233	210	187	163	140	117	93	70
2,600	2,620	307	283	260	236	213	190	166	143	120	96	73
2,620	2,640	310	286	263	239	216	193	169	146	123	99	76
2,640	2,660	313	289	266	242	219	196	172	149	126	102	79
2,660	2,680	316	292	269	245	222	199	175	152	129	105	82
2,680	2,700	319	295	272	248	225	202	178	155	132	108	85
2,700	2,720	322	298	275	251	228	205	181	158	135	111	88
2,720	2,740	325	301	278	254	231	208	184	161	138	114	91
2,740	2,760	328	304	281	257	234	211	187	164	141	117	94
2,760	2,780	331	307	284	260	237	214	190	167	144	120	97
2,780	2,800	334	310	287	263	240	217	193	170	147	123	100
2,800	2,820	337	313	290	266	243	220	196	173	150	126	103
2,820	2,840	340	316	293	269	246	223	199	176	153	129	106
2,840	2,860	343	319	296	272	249	226	202	179	156	132	109
2,860	2,880	346	322	299	275	252	229	205	182	159	135	112

| $2,880 and over | Use Table 2(b) for a **MARRIED person** on page 44. Also see the instructions on page 42. |

Wage Bracket Method Tables for Income Tax Withholding

SINGLE Persons—SEMIMONTHLY Payroll Period

(For Wages Paid through December 31, 2016)

And the wages are—		And the number of withholding allowances claimed is—										
At least	But less than	0	1	2	3	4	5	6	7	8	9	10
		The amount of income tax to be withheld is—										
$ 0	$115	$0	$0	$0	$0	$0	$0	$0	$0	$0	$0	$0
115	120	2	0	0	0	0	0	0	0	0	0	0
120	125	3	0	0	0	0	0	0	0	0	0	0
125	130	3	0	0	0	0	0	0	0	0	0	0
130	135	4	0	0	0	0	0	0	0	0	0	0
135	140	4	0	0	0	0	0	0	0	0	0	0
140	145	5	0	0	0	0	0	0	0	0	0	0
145	150	5	0	0	0	0	0	0	0	0	0	0
150	155	6	0	0	0	0	0	0	0	0	0	0
155	160	6	0	0	0	0	0	0	0	0	0	0
160	165	7	0	0	0	0	0	0	0	0	0	0
165	170	7	0	0	0	0	0	0	0	0	0	0
170	175	8	0	0	0	0	0	0	0	0	0	0
175	180	8	0	0	0	0	0	0	0	0	0	0
180	185	9	0	0	0	0	0	0	0	0	0	0
185	190	9	0	0	0	0	0	0	0	0	0	0
190	195	10	0	0	0	0	0	0	0	0	0	0
195	200	10	0	0	0	0	0	0	0	0	0	0
200	205	11	0	0	0	0	0	0	0	0	0	0
205	210	11	0	0	0	0	0	0	0	0	0	0
210	215	12	0	0	0	0	0	0	0	0	0	0
215	220	12	0	0	0	0	0	0	0	0	0	0
220	225	13	0	0	0	0	0	0	0	0	0	0
225	230	13	0	0	0	0	0	0	0	0	0	0
230	235	14	0	0	0	0	0	0	0	0	0	0
235	240	14	0	0	0	0	0	0	0	0	0	0
240	245	15	0	0	0	0	0	0	0	0	0	0
245	250	15	0	0	0	0	0	0	0	0	0	0
250	260	16	0	0	0	0	0	0	0	0	0	0
260	270	17	0	0	0	0	0	0	0	0	0	0
270	280	18	1	0	0	0	0	0	0	0	0	0
280	290	19	2	0	0	0	0	0	0	0	0	0
290	300	20	3	0	0	0	0	0	0	0	0	0
300	310	21	4	0	0	0	0	0	0	0	0	0
310	320	22	5	0	0	0	0	0	0	0	0	0
320	330	23	6	0	0	0	0	0	0	0	0	0
330	340	24	7	0	0	0	0	0	0	0	0	0
340	350	25	8	0	0	0	0	0	0	0	0	0
350	360	26	9	0	0	0	0	0	0	0	0	0
360	370	27	10	0	0	0	0	0	0	0	0	0
370	380	28	11	0	0	0	0	0	0	0	0	0
380	390	29	12	0	0	0	0	0	0	0	0	0
390	400	30	13	0	0	0	0	0	0	0	0	0
400	410	31	14	0	0	0	0	0	0	0	0	0
410	420	32	15	0	0	0	0	0	0	0	0	0
420	430	33	16	0	0	0	0	0	0	0	0	0
430	440	34	17	0	0	0	0	0	0	0	0	0
440	450	35	18	1	0	0	0	0	0	0	0	0
450	460	36	19	2	0	0	0	0	0	0	0	0
460	470	37	20	3	0	0	0	0	0	0	0	0
470	480	38	21	4	0	0	0	0	0	0	0	0
480	490	39	22	5	0	0	0	0	0	0	0	0
490	500	41	23	6	0	0	0	0	0	0	0	0
500	520	43	25	8	0	0	0	0	0	0	0	0
520	540	46	27	10	0	0	0	0	0	0	0	0
540	560	49	29	12	0	0	0	0	0	0	0	0
560	580	52	31	14	0	0	0	0	0	0	0	0
580	600	55	33	16	0	0	0	0	0	0	0	0
600	620	58	35	18	1	0	0	0	0	0	0	0
620	640	61	37	20	3	0	0	0	0	0	0	0
640	660	64	39	22	5	0	0	0	0	0	0	0
660	680	67	42	24	7	0	0	0	0	0	0	0
680	700	70	45	26	9	0	0	0	0	0	0	0
700	720	73	48	28	11	0	0	0	0	0	0	0
720	740	76	51	30	13	0	0	0	0	0	0	0
740	760	79	54	32	15	0	0	0	0	0	0	0
760	780	82	57	34	17	0	0	0	0	0	0	0
780	800	85	60	36	19	2	0	0	0	0	0	0

Wage Bracket Method Tables for Income Tax Withholding

SINGLE Persons—SEMIMONTHLY Payroll Period

(For Wages Paid through December 31, 2016)

And the wages are–		And the number of withholding allowances claimed is—										
At least	But less than	0	1	2	3	4	5	6	7	8	9	10
		The amount of income tax to be withheld is—										
$800	$820	$88	$63	$38	$21	$4	$0	$0	$0	$0	$0	$0
820	840	91	66	40	23	6	0	0	0	0	0	0
840	860	94	69	43	25	8	0	0	0	0	0	0
860	880	97	72	46	27	10	0	0	0	0	0	0
880	900	100	75	49	29	12	0	0	0	0	0	0
900	920	103	78	52	31	14	0	0	0	0	0	0
920	940	106	81	55	33	16	0	0	0	0	0	0
940	960	109	84	58	35	18	1	0	0	0	0	0
960	980	112	87	61	37	20	3	0	0	0	0	0
980	1,000	115	90	64	39	22	5	0	0	0	0	0
1,000	1,020	118	93	67	42	24	7	0	0	0	0	0
1,020	1,040	121	96	70	45	26	9	0	0	0	0	0
1,040	1,060	124	99	73	48	28	11	0	0	0	0	0
1,060	1,080	127	102	76	51	30	13	0	0	0	0	0
1,080	1,100	130	105	79	54	32	15	0	0	0	0	0
1,100	1,120	133	108	82	57	34	17	0	0	0	0	0
1,120	1,140	136	111	85	60	36	19	2	0	0	0	0
1,140	1,160	139	114	88	63	38	21	4	0	0	0	0
1,160	1,180	142	117	91	66	41	23	6	0	0	0	0
1,180	1,200	145	120	94	69	44	25	8	0	0	0	0
1,200	1,220	148	123	97	72	47	27	10	0	0	0	0
1,220	1,240	151	126	100	75	50	29	12	0	0	0	0
1,240	1,260	154	129	103	78	53	31	14	0	0	0	0
1,260	1,280	157	132	106	81	56	33	16	0	0	0	0
1,280	1,300	160	135	109	84	59	35	18	2	0	0	0
1,300	1,320	163	138	112	87	62	37	20	4	0	0	0
1,320	1,340	166	141	115	90	65	40	22	6	0	0	0
1,340	1,360	169	144	118	93	68	43	24	8	0	0	0
1,360	1,380	172	147	121	96	71	46	26	10	0	0	0
1,380	1,400	175	150	124	99	74	49	28	12	0	0	0
1,400	1,420	178	153	127	102	77	52	30	14	0	0	0
1,420	1,440	181	156	130	105	80	55	32	16	0	0	0
1,440	1,460	184	159	133	108	83	58	34	18	1	0	0
1,460	1,480	187	162	136	111	86	61	36	20	3	0	0
1,480	1,500	190	165	139	114	89	64	38	22	5	0	0
1,500	1,520	193	168	142	117	92	67	41	24	7	0	0
1,520	1,540	196	171	145	120	95	70	44	26	9	0	0
1,540	1,560	199	174	148	123	98	73	47	28	11	0	0
1,560	1,580	202	177	151	126	101	76	50	30	13	0	0
1,580	1,600	205	180	154	129	104	79	53	32	15	0	0
1,600	1,620	208	183	157	132	107	82	56	34	17	0	0
1,620	1,640	211	186	160	135	110	85	59	36	19	2	0
1,640	1,660	214	189	163	138	113	88	62	38	21	4	0
1,660	1,680	218	192	166	141	116	91	65	40	23	6	0
1,680	1,700	223	195	169	144	119	94	68	43	25	8	0
1,700	1,720	228	198	172	147	122	97	71	46	27	10	0
1,720	1,740	233	201	175	150	125	100	74	49	29	12	0
1,740	1,760	238	204	178	153	128	103	77	52	31	14	0
1,760	1,780	243	207	181	156	131	106	80	55	33	16	0
1,780	1,800	248	210	184	159	134	109	83	58	35	18	1
1,800	1,820	253	213	187	162	137	112	86	61	37	20	3
1,820	1,840	258	216	190	165	140	115	89	64	39	22	5
1,840	1,860	263	221	193	168	143	118	92	67	42	24	7
1,860	1,880	268	226	196	171	146	121	95	70	45	26	9
1,880	1,900	273	231	199	174	149	124	98	73	48	28	11
1,900	1,920	278	236	202	177	152	127	101	76	51	30	13
1,920	1,940	283	241	205	180	155	130	104	79	54	32	15
1,940	1,960	288	246	208	183	158	133	107	82	57	34	17
1,960	1,980	293	251	211	186	161	136	110	85	60	36	19
1,980	2,000	298	256	214	189	164	139	113	88	63	38	21
2,000	2,020	303	261	218	192	167	142	116	91	66	40	23
2,020	2,040	308	266	223	195	170	145	119	94	69	43	25
2,040	2,060	313	271	228	198	173	148	122	97	72	46	27
2,060	2,080	318	276	233	201	176	151	125	100	75	49	29
2,080	2,100	323	281	238	204	179	154	128	103	78	52	31
2,100	2,120	328	286	243	207	182	157	131	106	81	55	33
2,120	2,140	333	291	248	210	185	160	134	109	84	58	35

| $2,140 and over | Use Table 3(a) for a **SINGLE person** on page 44. Also see the instructions on page 42. |

Wage Bracket Method Tables for Income Tax Withholding

MARRIED Persons—SEMIMONTHLY Payroll Period

(For Wages Paid through December 31, 2016)

And the wages are—		And the number of withholding allowances claimed is—										
At least	But less than	0	1	2	3	4	5	6	7	8	9	10
		The amount of income tax to be withheld is—										
$ 0	$360	$0	$0	$0	$0	$0	$0	$0	$0	$0	$0	$0
360	370	1	0	0	0	0	0	0	0	0	0	0
370	380	2	0	0	0	0	0	0	0	0	0	0
380	390	3	0	0	0	0	0	0	0	0	0	0
390	400	4	0	0	0	0	0	0	0	0	0	0
400	410	5	0	0	0	0	0	0	0	0	0	0
410	420	6	0	0	0	0	0	0	0	0	0	0
420	430	7	0	0	0	0	0	0	0	0	0	0
430	440	8	0	0	0	0	0	0	0	0	0	0
440	450	9	0	0	0	0	0	0	0	0	0	0
450	460	10	0	0	0	0	0	0	0	0	0	0
460	470	11	0	0	0	0	0	0	0	0	0	0
470	480	12	0	0	0	0	0	0	0	0	0	0
480	490	13	0	0	0	0	0	0	0	0	0	0
490	500	14	0	0	0	0	0	0	0	0	0	0
500	520	15	0	0	0	0	0	0	0	0	0	0
520	540	17	1	0	0	0	0	0	0	0	0	0
540	560	19	3	0	0	0	0	0	0	0	0	0
560	580	21	5	0	0	0	0	0	0	0	0	0
580	600	23	7	0	0	0	0	0	0	0	0	0
600	620	25	9	0	0	0	0	0	0	0	0	0
620	640	27	11	0	0	0	0	0	0	0	0	0
640	660	29	13	0	0	0	0	0	0	0	0	0
660	680	31	15	0	0	0	0	0	0	0	0	0
680	700	33	17	0	0	0	0	0	0	0	0	0
700	720	35	19	2	0	0	0	0	0	0	0	0
720	740	37	21	4	0	0	0	0	0	0	0	0
740	760	39	23	6	0	0	0	0	0	0	0	0
760	780	41	25	8	0	0	0	0	0	0	0	0
780	800	43	27	10	0	0	0	0	0	0	0	0
800	820	45	29	12	0	0	0	0	0	0	0	0
820	840	47	31	14	0	0	0	0	0	0	0	0
840	860	49	33	16	0	0	0	0	0	0	0	0
860	880	51	35	18	1	0	0	0	0	0	0	0
880	900	53	37	20	3	0	0	0	0	0	0	0
900	920	55	39	22	5	0	0	0	0	0	0	0
920	940	57	41	24	7	0	0	0	0	0	0	0
940	960	59	43	26	9	0	0	0	0	0	0	0
960	980	61	45	28	11	0	0	0	0	0	0	0
980	1,000	63	47	30	13	0	0	0	0	0	0	0
1,000	1,020	65	49	32	15	0	0	0	0	0	0	0
1,020	1,040	67	51	34	17	0	0	0	0	0	0	0
1,040	1,060	69	53	36	19	2	0	0	0	0	0	0
1,060	1,080	71	55	38	21	4	0	0	0	0	0	0
1,080	1,100	73	57	40	23	6	0	0	0	0	0	0
1,100	1,120	75	59	42	25	8	0	0	0	0	0	0
1,120	1,140	77	61	44	27	10	0	0	0	0	0	0
1,140	1,160	80	63	46	29	12	0	0	0	0	0	0
1,160	1,180	83	65	48	31	14	0	0	0	0	0	0
1,180	1,200	86	67	50	33	16	0	0	0	0	0	0
1,200	1,220	89	69	52	35	18	1	0	0	0	0	0
1,220	1,240	92	71	54	37	20	3	0	0	0	0	0
1,240	1,260	95	73	56	39	22	5	0	0	0	0	0
1,260	1,280	98	75	58	41	24	7	0	0	0	0	0
1,280	1,300	101	77	60	43	26	9	0	0	0	0	0
1,300	1,320	104	79	62	45	28	11	0	0	0	0	0
1,320	1,340	107	82	64	47	30	13	0	0	0	0	0
1,340	1,360	110	85	66	49	32	15	0	0	0	0	0
1,360	1,380	113	88	68	51	34	17	0	0	0	0	0
1,380	1,400	116	91	70	53	36	19	2	0	0	0	0
1,400	1,420	119	94	72	55	38	21	4	0	0	0	0
1,420	1,440	122	97	74	57	40	23	6	0	0	0	0
1,440	1,460	125	100	76	59	42	25	8	0	0	0	0
1,460	1,480	128	103	78	61	44	27	10	0	0	0	0
1,480	1,500	131	106	81	63	46	29	12	0	0	0	0
1,500	1,520	134	109	84	65	48	31	14	0	0	0	0
1,520	1,540	137	112	87	67	50	33	16	0	0	0	0
1,540	1,560	140	115	90	69	52	35	18	1	0	0	0
1,560	1,580	143	118	93	71	54	37	20	3	0	0	0
1,580	1,600	146	121	96	73	56	39	22	5	0	0	0

Wage Bracket Method Tables for Income Tax Withholding

MARRIED Persons—SEMIMONTHLY Payroll Period

(For Wages Paid through December 31, 2016)

And the wages are–		And the number of withholding allowances claimed is—										
At least	But less than	0	1	2	3	4	5	6	7	8	9	10
		The amount of income tax to be withheld is—										
$1,600	$1,620	$149	$124	$99	$75	$58	$41	$24	$7	$0	$0	$0
1,620	1,640	152	127	102	77	60	43	26	9	0	0	0
1,640	1,660	155	130	105	79	62	45	28	11	0	0	0
1,660	1,680	158	133	108	82	64	47	30	13	0	0	0
1,680	1,700	161	136	111	85	66	49	32	15	0	0	0
1,700	1,720	164	139	114	88	68	51	34	17	0	0	0
1,720	1,740	167	142	117	91	70	53	36	19	2	0	0
1,740	1,760	170	145	120	94	72	55	38	21	4	0	0
1,760	1,780	173	148	123	97	74	57	40	23	6	0	0
1,780	1,800	176	151	126	100	76	59	42	25	8	0	0
1,800	1,820	179	154	129	103	78	61	44	27	10	0	0
1,820	1,840	182	157	132	106	81	63	46	29	12	0	0
1,840	1,860	185	160	135	109	84	65	48	31	14	0	0
1,860	1,880	188	163	138	112	87	67	50	33	16	0	0
1,880	1,900	191	166	141	115	90	69	52	35	18	2	0
1,900	1,920	194	169	144	118	93	71	54	37	20	4	0
1,920	1,940	197	172	147	121	96	73	56	39	22	6	0
1,940	1,960	200	175	150	124	99	75	58	41	24	8	0
1,960	1,980	203	178	153	127	102	77	60	43	26	10	0
1,980	2,000	206	181	156	130	105	80	62	45	28	12	0
2,000	2,020	209	184	159	133	108	83	64	47	30	14	0
2,020	2,040	212	187	162	136	111	86	66	49	32	16	0
2,040	2,060	215	190	165	139	114	89	68	51	34	18	1
2,060	2,080	218	193	168	142	117	92	70	53	36	20	3
2,080	2,100	221	196	171	145	120	95	72	55	38	22	5
2,100	2,120	224	199	174	148	123	98	74	57	40	24	7
2,120	2,140	227	202	177	151	126	101	76	59	42	26	9
2,140	2,160	230	205	180	154	129	104	79	61	44	28	11
2,160	2,180	233	208	183	157	132	107	82	63	46	30	13
2,180	2,200	236	211	186	160	135	110	85	65	48	32	15
2,200	2,220	239	214	189	163	138	113	88	67	50	34	17
2,220	2,240	242	217	192	166	141	116	91	69	52	36	19
2,240	2,260	245	220	195	169	144	119	94	71	54	38	21
2,260	2,280	248	223	198	172	147	122	97	73	56	40	23
2,280	2,300	251	226	201	175	150	125	100	75	58	42	25
2,300	2,320	254	229	204	178	153	128	103	77	60	44	27
2,320	2,340	257	232	207	181	156	131	106	80	62	46	29
2,340	2,360	260	235	210	184	159	134	109	83	64	48	31
2,360	2,380	263	238	213	187	162	137	112	86	66	50	33
2,380	2,400	266	241	216	190	165	140	115	89	68	52	35
2,400	2,420	269	244	219	193	168	143	118	92	70	54	37
2,420	2,440	272	247	222	196	171	146	121	95	72	56	39
2,440	2,460	275	250	225	199	174	149	124	98	74	58	41
2,460	2,480	278	253	228	202	177	152	127	101	76	60	43
2,480	2,500	281	256	231	205	180	155	130	104	79	62	45
2,500	2,520	284	259	234	208	183	158	133	107	82	64	47
2,520	2,540	287	262	237	211	186	161	136	110	85	66	49
2,540	2,560	290	265	240	214	189	164	139	113	88	68	51
2,560	2,580	293	268	243	217	192	167	142	116	91	70	53
2,580	2,600	296	271	246	220	195	170	145	119	94	72	55
2,600	2,620	299	274	249	223	198	173	148	122	97	74	57
2,620	2,640	302	277	252	226	201	176	151	125	100	76	59
2,640	2,660	305	280	255	229	204	179	154	128	103	78	61
2,660	2,680	308	283	258	232	207	182	157	131	106	81	63
2,680	2,700	311	286	261	235	210	185	160	134	109	84	65
2,700	2,720	314	289	264	238	213	188	163	137	112	87	67
2,720	2,740	317	292	267	241	216	191	166	140	115	90	69
2,740	2,760	320	295	270	244	219	194	169	143	118	93	71
2,760	2,780	323	298	273	247	222	197	172	146	121	96	73
2,780	2,800	326	301	276	250	225	200	175	149	124	99	75
2,800	2,820	329	304	279	253	228	203	178	152	127	102	77
2,820	2,840	332	307	282	256	231	206	181	155	130	105	79
2,840	2,860	335	310	285	259	234	209	184	158	133	108	82
2,860	2,880	338	313	288	262	237	212	187	161	136	111	85
2,880	2,900	341	316	291	265	240	215	190	164	139	114	88
2,900	2,920	344	319	294	268	243	218	193	167	142	117	91

| $2,920 and over | | Use Table 3(b) for a **MARRIED person** on page 44. Also see the instructions on page 42. |

Wage Bracket Method Tables for Income Tax Withholding

SINGLE Persons—MONTHLY Payroll Period

(For Wages Paid through December 31, 2016)

And the wages are–		And the number of withholding allowances claimed is—										
At least	But less than	0	1	2	3	4	5	6	7	8	9	10
		The amount of income tax to be withheld is—										
$ 0	$220	$0	$0	$0	$0	$0	$0	$0	$0	$0	$0	$0
220	230	4	0	0	0	0	0	0	0	0	0	0
230	240	5	0	0	0	0	0	0	0	0	0	0
240	250	6	0	0	0	0	0	0	0	0	0	0
250	260	7	0	0	0	0	0	0	0	0	0	0
260	270	8	0	0	0	0	0	0	0	0	0	0
270	280	9	0	0	0	0	0	0	0	0	0	0
280	290	10	0	0	0	0	0	0	0	0	0	0
290	300	11	0	0	0	0	0	0	0	0	0	0
300	320	12	0	0	0	0	0	0	0	0	0	0
320	340	14	0	0	0	0	0	0	0	0	0	0
340	360	16	0	0	0	0	0	0	0	0	0	0
360	380	18	0	0	0	0	0	0	0	0	0	0
380	400	20	0	0	0	0	0	0	0	0	0	0
400	420	22	0	0	0	0	0	0	0	0	0	0
420	440	24	0	0	0	0	0	0	0	0	0	0
440	460	26	0	0	0	0	0	0	0	0	0	0
460	480	28	0	0	0	0	0	0	0	0	0	0
480	500	30	0	0	0	0	0	0	0	0	0	0
500	520	32	0	0	0	0	0	0	0	0	0	0
520	540	34	1	0	0	0	0	0	0	0	0	0
540	560	36	3	0	0	0	0	0	0	0	0	0
560	580	38	5	0	0	0	0	0	0	0	0	0
580	600	40	7	0	0	0	0	0	0	0	0	0
600	640	43	10	0	0	0	0	0	0	0	0	0
640	680	47	14	0	0	0	0	0	0	0	0	0
680	720	51	18	0	0	0	0	0	0	0	0	0
720	760	55	22	0	0	0	0	0	0	0	0	0
760	800	59	26	0	0	0	0	0	0	0	0	0
800	840	63	30	0	0	0	0	0	0	0	0	0
840	880	67	34	0	0	0	0	0	0	0	0	0
880	920	71	38	4	0	0	0	0	0	0	0	0
920	960	75	42	8	0	0	0	0	0	0	0	0
960	1,000	80	46	12	0	0	0	0	0	0	0	0
1,000	1,040	86	50	16	0	0	0	0	0	0	0	0
1,040	1,080	92	54	20	0	0	0	0	0	0	0	0
1,080	1,120	98	58	24	0	0	0	0	0	0	0	0
1,120	1,160	104	62	28	0	0	0	0	0	0	0	0
1,160	1,200	110	66	32	0	0	0	0	0	0	0	0
1,200	1,240	116	70	36	2	0	0	0	0	0	0	0
1,240	1,280	122	74	40	6	0	0	0	0	0	0	0
1,280	1,320	128	78	44	10	0	0	0	0	0	0	0
1,320	1,360	134	84	48	14	0	0	0	0	0	0	0
1,360	1,400	140	90	52	18	0	0	0	0	0	0	0
1,400	1,440	146	96	56	22	0	0	0	0	0	0	0
1,440	1,480	152	102	60	26	0	0	0	0	0	0	0
1,480	1,520	158	108	64	30	0	0	0	0	0	0	0
1,520	1,560	164	114	68	34	0	0	0	0	0	0	0
1,560	1,600	170	120	72	38	4	0	0	0	0	0	0
1,600	1,640	176	126	76	42	8	0	0	0	0	0	0
1,640	1,680	182	132	81	46	12	0	0	0	0	0	0
1,680	1,720	188	138	87	50	16	0	0	0	0	0	0
1,720	1,760	194	144	93	54	20	0	0	0	0	0	0
1,760	1,800	200	150	99	58	24	0	0	0	0	0	0
1,800	1,840	206	156	105	62	28	0	0	0	0	0	0
1,840	1,880	212	162	111	66	32	0	0	0	0	0	0
1,880	1,920	218	168	117	70	36	3	0	0	0	0	0
1,920	1,960	224	174	123	74	40	7	0	0	0	0	0
1,960	2,000	230	180	129	78	44	11	0	0	0	0	0
2,000	2,040	236	186	135	84	48	15	0	0	0	0	0
2,040	2,080	242	192	141	90	52	19	0	0	0	0	0
2,080	2,120	248	198	147	96	56	23	0	0	0	0	0
2,120	2,160	254	204	153	102	60	27	0	0	0	0	0
2,160	2,200	260	210	159	108	64	31	0	0	0	0	0
2,200	2,240	266	216	165	114	68	35	1	0	0	0	0
2,240	2,280	272	222	171	120	72	39	5	0	0	0	0
2,280	2,320	278	228	177	126	76	43	9	0	0	0	0
2,320	2,360	284	234	183	132	82	47	13	0	0	0	0
2,360	2,400	290	240	189	138	88	51	17	0	0	0	0

Wage Bracket Method Tables for Income Tax Withholding

SINGLE Persons—MONTHLY Payroll Period

(For Wages Paid through December 31, 2016)

And the wages are—		And the number of withholding allowances claimed is—										
At least	But less than	0	1	2	3	4	5	6	7	8	9	10
		The amount of income tax to be withheld is—										
$2,400	$2,440	$296	$246	$195	$144	$94	$55	$21	$0	$0	$0	$0
2,440	2,480	302	252	201	150	100	59	25	0	0	0	0
2,480	2,520	308	258	207	156	106	63	29	0	0	0	0
2,520	2,560	314	264	213	162	112	67	33	0	0	0	0
2,560	2,600	320	270	219	168	118	71	37	3	0	0	0
2,600	2,640	326	276	225	174	124	75	41	7	0	0	0
2,640	2,680	332	282	231	180	130	79	45	11	0	0	0
2,680	2,720	338	288	237	186	136	85	49	15	0	0	0
2,720	2,760	344	294	243	192	142	91	53	19	0	0	0
2,760	2,800	350	300	249	198	148	97	57	23	0	0	0
2,800	2,840	356	306	255	204	154	103	61	27	0	0	0
2,840	2,880	362	312	261	210	160	109	65	31	0	0	0
2,880	2,920	368	318	267	216	166	115	69	35	1	0	0
2,920	2,960	374	324	273	222	172	121	73	39	5	0	0
2,960	3,000	380	330	279	228	178	127	77	43	9	0	0
3,000	3,040	386	336	285	234	184	133	82	47	13	0	0
3,040	3,080	392	342	291	240	190	139	88	51	17	0	0
3,080	3,120	398	348	297	246	196	145	94	55	21	0	0
3,120	3,160	404	354	303	252	202	151	100	59	25	0	0
3,160	3,200	410	360	309	258	208	157	106	63	29	0	0
3,200	3,240	416	366	315	264	214	163	112	67	33	0	0
3,240	3,280	422	372	321	270	220	169	118	71	37	4	0
3,280	3,320	428	378	327	276	226	175	124	75	41	8	0
3,320	3,360	436	384	333	282	232	181	130	80	45	12	0
3,360	3,400	446	390	339	288	238	187	136	86	49	16	0
3,400	3,440	456	396	345	294	244	193	142	92	53	20	0
3,440	3,480	466	402	351	300	250	199	148	98	57	24	0
3,480	3,520	476	408	357	306	256	205	154	104	61	28	0
3,520	3,560	486	414	363	312	262	211	160	110	65	32	0
3,560	3,600	496	420	369	318	268	217	166	116	69	36	2
3,600	3,640	506	426	375	324	274	223	172	122	73	40	6
3,640	3,680	516	432	381	330	280	229	178	128	77	44	10
3,680	3,720	526	441	387	336	286	235	184	134	83	48	14
3,720	3,760	536	451	393	342	292	241	190	140	89	52	18
3,760	3,800	546	461	399	348	298	247	196	146	95	56	22
3,800	3,840	556	471	405	354	304	253	202	152	101	60	26
3,840	3,880	566	481	411	360	310	259	208	158	107	64	30
3,880	3,920	576	491	417	366	316	265	214	164	113	68	34
3,920	3,960	586	501	423	372	322	271	220	170	119	72	38
3,960	4,000	596	511	429	378	328	277	226	176	125	76	42
4,000	4,040	606	521	437	384	334	283	232	182	131	81	46
4,040	4,080	616	531	447	390	340	289	238	188	137	87	50
4,080	4,120	626	541	457	396	346	295	244	194	143	93	54
4,120	4,160	636	551	467	402	352	301	250	200	149	99	58
4,160	4,200	646	561	477	408	358	307	256	206	155	105	62
4,200	4,240	656	571	487	414	364	313	262	212	161	111	66
4,240	4,280	666	581	497	420	370	319	268	218	167	117	70
4,280	4,320	676	591	507	426	376	325	274	224	173	123	74
4,320	4,360	686	601	517	433	382	331	280	230	179	129	78
4,360	4,400	696	611	527	443	388	337	286	236	185	135	84
4,400	4,440	706	621	537	453	394	343	292	242	191	141	90
4,440	4,480	716	631	547	463	400	349	298	248	197	147	96
4,480	4,520	726	641	557	473	406	355	304	254	203	153	102
4,520	4,560	736	651	567	483	412	361	310	260	209	159	108
4,560	4,600	746	661	577	493	418	367	316	266	215	165	114
4,600	4,640	756	671	587	503	424	373	322	272	221	171	120
4,640	4,680	766	681	597	513	430	379	328	278	227	177	126
4,680	4,720	776	691	607	523	438	385	334	284	233	183	132
4,720	4,760	786	701	617	533	448	391	340	290	239	189	138
4,760	4,800	796	711	627	543	458	397	346	296	245	195	144
4,800	4,840	806	721	637	553	468	403	352	302	251	201	150
4,840	4,880	816	731	647	563	478	409	358	308	257	207	156
4,880	4,920	826	741	657	573	488	415	364	314	263	213	162
4,920	4,960	836	751	667	583	498	421	370	320	269	219	168
4,960	5,000	846	761	677	593	508	427	376	326	275	225	174
5,000	5,040	856	771	687	603	518	434	382	332	281	231	180
5,040	5,080	866	781	697	613	528	444	388	338	287	237	186

$5,080 and over   Use Table 4(a) for a **SINGLE person** on page 44. Also see the instructions on page 42.

Wage Bracket Method Tables for Income Tax Withholding

MARRIED Persons—**MONTHLY** Payroll Period

(For Wages Paid through December 31, 2016)

And the wages are—		And the number of withholding allowances claimed is—										
At least	But less than	0	1	2	3	4	5	6	7	8	9	10
		The amount of income tax to be withheld is—										
$ 0	$720	$0	$0	$0	$0	$0	$0	$0	$0	$0	$0	$0
720	760	3	0	0	0	0	0	0	0	0	0	0
760	800	7	0	0	0	0	0	0	0	0	0	0
800	840	11	0	0	0	0	0	0	0	0	0	0
840	880	15	0	0	0	0	0	0	0	0	0	0
880	920	19	0	0	0	0	0	0	0	0	0	0
920	960	23	0	0	0	0	0	0	0	0	0	0
960	1,000	27	0	0	0	0	0	0	0	0	0	0
1,000	1,040	31	0	0	0	0	0	0	0	0	0	0
1,040	1,080	35	1	0	0	0	0	0	0	0	0	0
1,080	1,120	39	5	0	0	0	0	0	0	0	0	0
1,120	1,160	43	9	0	0	0	0	0	0	0	0	0
1,160	1,200	47	13	0	0	0	0	0	0	0	0	0
1,200	1,240	51	17	0	0	0	0	0	0	0	0	0
1,240	1,280	55	21	0	0	0	0	0	0	0	0	0
1,280	1,320	59	25	0	0	0	0	0	0	0	0	0
1,320	1,360	63	29	0	0	0	0	0	0	0	0	0
1,360	1,400	67	33	0	0	0	0	0	0	0	0	0
1,400	1,440	71	37	3	0	0	0	0	0	0	0	0
1,440	1,480	75	41	7	0	0	0	0	0	0	0	0
1,480	1,520	79	45	11	0	0	0	0	0	0	0	0
1,520	1,560	83	49	15	0	0	0	0	0	0	0	0
1,560	1,600	87	53	19	0	0	0	0	0	0	0	0
1,600	1,640	91	57	23	0	0	0	0	0	0	0	0
1,640	1,680	95	61	27	0	0	0	0	0	0	0	0
1,680	1,720	99	65	31	0	0	0	0	0	0	0	0
1,720	1,760	103	69	35	2	0	0	0	0	0	0	0
1,760	1,800	107	73	39	6	0	0	0	0	0	0	0
1,800	1,840	111	77	43	10	0	0	0	0	0	0	0
1,840	1,880	115	81	47	14	0	0	0	0	0	0	0
1,880	1,920	119	85	51	18	0	0	0	0	0	0	0
1,920	1,960	123	89	55	22	0	0	0	0	0	0	0
1,960	2,000	127	93	59	26	0	0	0	0	0	0	0
2,000	2,040	131	97	63	30	0	0	0	0	0	0	0
2,040	2,080	135	101	67	34	0	0	0	0	0	0	0
2,080	2,120	139	105	71	38	4	0	0	0	0	0	0
2,120	2,160	143	109	75	42	8	0	0	0	0	0	0
2,160	2,200	147	113	79	46	12	0	0	0	0	0	0
2,200	2,240	151	117	83	50	16	0	0	0	0	0	0
2,240	2,280	155	121	87	54	20	0	0	0	0	0	0
2,280	2,320	161	125	91	58	24	0	0	0	0	0	0
2,320	2,360	167	129	95	62	28	0	0	0	0	0	0
2,360	2,400	173	133	99	66	32	0	0	0	0	0	0
2,400	2,440	179	137	103	70	36	2	0	0	0	0	0
2,440	2,480	185	141	107	74	40	6	0	0	0	0	0
2,480	2,520	191	145	111	78	44	10	0	0	0	0	0
2,520	2,560	197	149	115	82	48	14	0	0	0	0	0
2,560	2,600	203	153	119	86	52	18	0	0	0	0	0
2,600	2,640	209	158	123	90	56	22	0	0	0	0	0
2,640	2,680	215	164	127	94	60	26	0	0	0	0	0
2,680	2,720	221	170	131	98	64	30	0	0	0	0	0
2,720	2,760	227	176	135	102	68	34	0	0	0	0	0
2,760	2,800	233	182	139	106	72	38	4	0	0	0	0
2,800	2,840	239	188	143	110	76	42	8	0	0	0	0
2,840	2,880	245	194	147	114	80	46	12	0	0	0	0
2,880	2,920	251	200	151	118	84	50	16	0	0	0	0
2,920	2,960	257	206	156	122	88	54	20	0	0	0	0
2,960	3,000	263	212	162	126	92	58	24	0	0	0	0
3,000	3,040	269	218	168	130	96	62	28	0	0	0	0
3,040	3,080	275	224	174	134	100	66	32	0	0	0	0
3,080	3,120	281	230	180	138	104	70	36	3	0	0	0
3,120	3,160	287	236	186	142	108	74	40	7	0	0	0
3,160	3,200	293	242	192	146	112	78	44	11	0	0	0
3,200	3,240	299	248	198	150	116	82	48	15	0	0	0
3,240	3,280	305	254	204	154	120	86	52	19	0	0	0
3,280	3,320	311	260	210	159	124	90	56	23	0	0	0
3,320	3,360	317	266	216	165	128	94	60	27	0	0	0
3,360	3,400	323	272	222	171	132	98	64	31	0	0	0

Wage Bracket Method Tables for Income Tax Withholding

MARRIED Persons—MONTHLY Payroll Period

(For Wages Paid through December 31, 2016)

And the wages are–		And the number of withholding allowances claimed is—										
At least	But less than	0	1	2	3	4	5	6	7	8	9	10
		The amount of income tax to be withheld is—										
$3,400	$3,440	$329	$278	$228	$177	$136	$102	$68	$35	$1	$0	$0
3,440	3,480	335	284	234	183	140	106	72	39	5	0	0
3,480	3,520	341	290	240	189	144	110	76	43	9	0	0
3,520	3,560	347	296	246	195	148	114	80	47	13	0	0
3,560	3,600	353	302	252	201	152	118	84	51	17	0	0
3,600	3,640	359	308	258	207	156	122	88	55	21	0	0
3,640	3,680	365	314	264	213	162	126	92	59	25	0	0
3,680	3,720	371	320	270	219	168	130	96	63	29	0	0
3,720	3,760	377	326	276	225	174	134	100	67	33	0	0
3,760	3,800	383	332	282	231	180	138	104	71	37	3	0
3,800	3,840	389	338	288	237	186	142	108	75	41	7	0
3,840	3,880	395	344	294	243	192	146	112	79	45	11	0
3,880	3,920	401	350	300	249	198	150	116	83	49	15	0
3,920	3,960	407	356	306	255	204	154	120	87	53	19	0
3,960	4,000	413	362	312	261	210	160	124	91	57	23	0
4,000	4,040	419	368	318	267	216	166	128	95	61	27	0
4,040	4,080	425	374	324	273	222	172	132	99	65	31	0
4,080	4,120	431	380	330	279	228	178	136	103	69	35	1
4,120	4,160	437	386	336	285	234	184	140	107	73	39	5
4,160	4,200	443	392	342	291	240	190	144	111	77	43	9
4,200	4,240	449	398	348	297	246	196	148	115	81	47	13
4,240	4,280	455	404	354	303	252	202	152	119	85	51	17
4,280	4,320	461	410	360	309	258	208	157	123	89	55	21
4,320	4,360	467	416	366	315	264	214	163	127	93	59	25
4,360	4,400	473	422	372	321	270	220	169	131	97	63	29
4,400	4,440	479	428	378	327	276	226	175	135	101	67	33
4,440	4,480	485	434	384	333	282	232	181	139	105	71	37
4,480	4,520	491	440	390	339	288	238	187	143	109	75	41
4,520	4,560	497	446	396	345	294	244	193	147	113	79	45
4,560	4,600	503	452	402	351	300	250	199	151	117	83	49
4,600	4,640	509	458	408	357	306	256	205	155	121	87	53
4,640	4,680	515	464	414	363	312	262	211	160	125	91	57
4,680	4,720	521	470	420	369	318	268	217	166	129	95	61
4,720	4,760	527	476	426	375	324	274	223	172	133	99	65
4,760	4,800	533	482	432	381	330	280	229	178	137	103	69
4,800	4,840	539	488	438	387	336	286	235	184	141	107	73
4,840	4,880	545	494	444	393	342	292	241	190	145	111	77
4,880	4,920	551	500	450	399	348	298	247	196	149	115	81
4,920	4,960	557	506	456	405	354	304	253	202	153	119	85
4,960	5,000	563	512	462	411	360	310	259	208	158	123	89
5,000	5,040	569	518	468	417	366	316	265	214	164	127	93
5,040	5,080	575	524	474	423	372	322	271	220	170	131	97
5,080	5,120	581	530	480	429	378	328	277	226	176	135	101
5,120	5,160	587	536	486	435	384	334	283	232	182	139	105
5,160	5,200	593	542	492	441	390	340	289	238	188	143	109
5,200	5,240	599	548	498	447	396	346	295	244	194	147	113
5,240	5,280	605	554	504	453	402	352	301	250	200	151	117
5,280	5,320	611	560	510	459	408	358	307	256	206	155	121
5,320	5,360	617	566	516	465	414	364	313	262	212	161	125
5,360	5,400	623	572	522	471	420	370	319	268	218	167	129
5,400	5,440	629	578	528	477	426	376	325	274	224	173	133
5,440	5,480	635	584	534	483	432	382	331	280	230	179	137
5,480	5,520	641	590	540	489	438	388	337	286	236	185	141
5,520	5,560	647	596	546	495	444	394	343	292	242	191	145
5,560	5,600	653	602	552	501	450	400	349	298	248	197	149
5,600	5,640	659	608	558	507	456	406	355	304	254	203	153
5,640	5,680	665	614	564	513	462	412	361	310	260	209	159
5,680	5,720	671	620	570	519	468	418	367	316	266	215	165
5,720	5,760	677	626	576	525	474	424	373	322	272	221	171
5,760	5,800	683	632	582	531	480	430	379	328	278	227	177
5,800	5,840	689	638	588	537	486	436	385	334	284	233	183
5,840	5,880	695	644	594	543	492	442	391	340	290	239	189
5,880	5,920	701	650	600	549	498	448	397	346	296	245	195
5,920	5,960	707	656	606	555	504	454	403	352	302	251	201
5,960	6,000	713	662	612	561	510	460	409	358	308	257	207
6,000	6,040	719	668	618	567	516	466	415	364	314	263	213
6,040	6,080	725	674	624	573	522	472	421	370	320	269	219
6,080	6,120	731	680	630	579	528	478	427	376	326	275	225

$6,120 and over	Use Table 4(b) for a **MARRIED person** on page 44. Also see the instructions on page 42.

Wage Bracket Method Tables for Income Tax Withholding

SINGLE Persons—**DAILY** Payroll Period

(For Wages Paid through December 31, 2016)

And the wages are—		And the number of withholding allowances claimed is—										
At least	But less than	0	1	2	3	4	5	6	7	8	9	10
		The amount of income tax to be withheld is—										
$0	$15	$0	$0	$0	$0	$0	$0	$0	$0	$0	$0	$0
15	18	1	0	0	0	0	0	0	0	0	0	0
18	21	1	0	0	0	0	0	0	0	0	0	0
21	24	1	0	0	0	0	0	0	0	0	0	0
24	27	2	0	0	0	0	0	0	0	0	0	0
27	30	2	0	0	0	0	0	0	0	0	0	0
30	33	2	1	0	0	0	0	0	0	0	0	0
33	36	3	1	0	0	0	0	0	0	0	0	0
36	39	3	1	0	0	0	0	0	0	0	0	0
39	42	3	2	0	0	0	0	0	0	0	0	0
42	45	3	2	0	0	0	0	0	0	0	0	0
45	48	4	2	1	0	0	0	0	0	0	0	0
48	51	4	3	1	0	0	0	0	0	0	0	0
51	54	5	3	1	0	0	0	0	0	0	0	0
54	57	5	3	2	0	0	0	0	0	0	0	0
57	60	6	3	2	0	0	0	0	0	0	0	0
60	63	6	4	2	1	0	0	0	0	0	0	0
63	66	7	4	2	1	0	0	0	0	0	0	0
66	69	7	5	3	1	0	0	0	0	0	0	0
69	72	7	5	3	2	0	0	0	0	0	0	0
72	75	8	6	3	2	0	0	0	0	0	0	0
75	78	8	6	4	2	1	0	0	0	0	0	0
78	81	9	7	4	2	1	0	0	0	0	0	0
81	84	9	7	5	3	1	0	0	0	0	0	0
84	87	10	7	5	3	1	0	0	0	0	0	0
87	90	10	8	6	3	2	0	0	0	0	0	0
90	93	11	8	6	4	2	0	0	0	0	0	0
93	96	11	9	6	4	2	1	0	0	0	0	0
96	99	12	9	7	5	3	1	0	0	0	0	0
99	102	12	10	7	5	3	1	0	0	0	0	0
102	105	12	10	8	5	3	2	0	0	0	0	0
105	108	13	11	8	6	4	2	0	0	0	0	0
108	111	13	11	9	6	4	2	1	0	0	0	0
111	114	14	11	9	7	4	3	1	0	0	0	0
114	117	14	12	10	7	5	3	1	0	0	0	0
117	120	15	12	10	8	5	3	2	0	0	0	0
120	123	15	13	10	8	6	3	2	0	0	0	0
123	126	16	13	11	9	6	4	2	1	0	0	0
126	129	16	14	11	9	7	4	3	1	0	0	0
129	132	16	14	12	9	7	5	3	1	0	0	0
132	135	17	15	12	10	8	5	3	2	0	0	0
135	138	17	15	13	10	8	6	3	2	0	0	0
138	141	18	16	13	11	8	6	4	2	1	0	0
141	144	18	16	14	11	9	7	4	2	1	0	0
144	147	19	16	14	12	9	7	5	3	1	0	0
147	150	19	17	15	12	10	8	5	3	2	0	0
150	153	20	17	15	13	10	8	6	3	2	0	0
153	156	20	18	15	13	11	8	6	4	2	1	0
156	159	21	18	16	14	11	9	7	4	2	1	0
159	162	22	19	16	14	12	9	7	5	3	1	0
162	165	22	19	17	14	12	10	7	5	3	1	0
165	168	23	20	17	15	13	10	8	6	3	2	0
168	171	24	20	18	15	13	11	8	6	4	2	1
171	174	25	21	18	16	13	11	9	6	4	2	1
174	177	25	22	19	16	14	12	9	7	5	3	1
177	180	26	22	19	17	14	12	10	7	5	3	1
180	183	27	23	19	17	15	12	10	8	5	3	2
183	186	28	24	20	18	15	13	11	8	6	4	2
186	189	28	25	21	18	16	13	11	9	6	4	2
189	192	29	25	21	18	16	14	11	9	7	4	3
192	195	30	26	22	19	17	14	12	10	7	5	3
195	198	31	27	23	19	17	15	12	10	8	5	3
198	201	31	28	24	20	17	15	13	10	8	6	4
201	204	32	28	24	21	18	16	13	11	9	6	4
204	207	33	29	25	21	18	16	14	11	9	7	4
207	210	34	30	26	22	19	17	14	12	10	7	5
210	213	34	31	27	23	19	17	15	12	10	8	5
213	216	35	31	27	24	20	17	15	13	10	8	6
216	219	36	32	28	24	20	18	16	13	11	9	6
219	222	37	33	29	25	21	18	16	14	11	9	7
222	225	37	34	30	26	22	19	16	14	12	9	7

Wage Bracket Method Tables for Income Tax Withholding

SINGLE Persons—DAILY Payroll Period

(For Wages Paid through December 31, 2016)

And the wages are—		And the number of withholding allowances claimed is—										
At least	But less than	0	1	2	3	4	5	6	7	8	9	10
		The amount of income tax to be withheld is—										
$225	$228	$38	$34	$30	$27	$23	$19	$17	$15	$12	$10	$8
228	231	39	35	31	27	23	20	17	15	13	10	8
231	234	40	36	32	28	24	20	18	15	13	11	8
234	237	40	37	33	29	25	21	18	16	14	11	9
237	240	41	37	33	30	26	22	19	16	14	12	9
240	243	42	38	34	30	26	22	19	17	14	12	10
243	246	43	39	35	31	27	23	20	17	15	13	10
246	249	43	40	36	32	28	24	20	18	15	13	11
249	252	44	40	36	33	29	25	21	18	16	13	11
252	255	45	41	37	33	29	25	22	19	16	14	12
255	258	46	42	38	34	30	26	22	19	17	14	12
258	261	46	43	39	35	31	27	23	19	17	15	12
261	264	47	43	39	36	32	28	24	20	18	15	13
264	267	48	44	40	36	32	28	25	21	18	16	13
267	270	49	45	41	37	33	29	25	21	19	16	14
270	273	49	46	42	38	34	30	26	22	19	17	14
273	276	50	46	42	39	35	31	27	23	19	17	15
276	279	51	47	43	39	35	31	28	24	20	18	15
279	282	52	48	44	40	36	32	28	24	21	18	16
282	285	52	49	45	41	37	33	29	25	21	18	16
285	288	53	49	45	42	38	34	30	26	22	19	17
288	291	54	50	46	42	38	34	31	27	23	19	17
291	294	55	51	47	43	39	35	31	27	24	20	17
294	297	55	52	48	44	40	36	32	28	24	20	18
297	300	56	52	48	45	41	37	33	29	25	21	18
300	303	57	53	49	45	41	37	34	30	26	22	19
303	306	58	54	50	46	42	38	34	30	27	23	19
306	309	58	55	51	47	43	39	35	31	27	23	20
309	312	59	55	51	48	44	40	36	32	28	24	20
312	315	60	56	52	48	44	40	37	33	29	25	21
315	318	61	57	53	49	45	41	37	33	30	26	22
318	321	61	58	54	50	46	42	38	34	30	26	23
321	324	62	58	54	51	47	43	39	35	31	27	23
324	327	63	59	55	51	47	43	40	36	32	28	24
327	330	64	60	56	52	48	44	40	36	33	29	25
330	333	64	61	57	53	49	45	41	37	33	29	26
333	336	65	61	57	54	50	46	42	38	34	30	26
336	339	66	62	58	54	50	46	43	39	35	31	27
339	341	67	63	59	55	51	47	43	39	35	32	28
341	343	67	63	59	55	51	48	44	40	36	32	28
343	345	68	64	60	56	52	48	44	40	36	33	29
345	347	68	64	60	56	52	49	45	41	37	33	29
347	349	69	65	61	57	53	49	45	41	37	34	30
349	351	69	65	61	57	53	50	46	42	38	34	30
351	353	70	66	62	58	54	50	46	42	38	35	31
353	355	70	66	62	58	54	51	47	43	39	35	31
355	357	71	67	63	59	55	51	47	43	39	36	32
357	359	71	67	63	59	55	52	48	44	40	36	32
359	361	72	68	64	60	56	52	48	44	40	37	33
361	363	72	68	64	60	56	53	49	45	41	37	33
363	365	73	69	65	61	57	53	49	45	41	38	34
365	367	73	69	65	61	57	54	50	46	42	38	34
367	369	74	70	66	62	58	54	50	46	42	39	35
369	371	74	70	66	62	58	55	51	47	43	39	35
371	373	75	71	67	63	59	55	51	47	43	40	36
373	375	76	71	67	63	59	56	52	48	44	40	36
375	377	76	72	68	64	60	56	52	48	44	41	37
377	379	77	72	68	64	60	57	53	49	45	41	37
379	381	77	73	69	65	61	57	53	49	45	42	38
381	383	78	73	69	65	61	58	54	50	46	42	38
383	385	78	74	70	66	62	58	54	50	46	43	39
385	387	79	75	70	66	62	59	55	51	47	43	39
387	389	79	75	71	67	63	59	55	51	47	44	40
389	391	80	76	71	67	63	60	56	52	48	44	40
391	393	81	76	72	68	64	60	56	52	48	45	41

$393 and over   Use Table 8(a) for a **SINGLE person** on page 45. Also see the instructions on page 42.

Wage Bracket Method Tables for Income Tax Withholding

MARRIED Persons—DAILY Payroll Period

(For Wages Paid through December 31, 2016)

And the wages are–		And the number of withholding allowances claimed is—										
At least	But less than	0	1	2	3	4	5	6	7	8	9	10
		The amount of income tax to be withheld is—										
$0	$39	$0	$0	$0	$0	$0	$0	$0	$0	$0	$0	$0
39	42	1	0	0	0	0	0	0	0	0	0	0
42	45	1	0	0	0	0	0	0	0	0	0	0
45	48	1	0	0	0	0	0	0	0	0	0	0
48	51	2	0	0	0	0	0	0	0	0	0	0
51	54	2	0	0	0	0	0	0	0	0	0	0
54	57	2	1	0	0	0	0	0	0	0	0	0
57	60	3	1	0	0	0	0	0	0	0	0	0
60	63	3	1	0	0	0	0	0	0	0	0	0
63	66	3	2	0	0	0	0	0	0	0	0	0
66	69	3	2	0	0	0	0	0	0	0	0	0
69	72	4	2	1	0	0	0	0	0	0	0	0
72	75	4	3	1	0	0	0	0	0	0	0	0
75	78	4	3	1	0	0	0	0	0	0	0	0
78	81	5	3	2	0	0	0	0	0	0	0	0
81	84	5	3	2	0	0	0	0	0	0	0	0
84	87	5	4	2	1	0	0	0	0	0	0	0
87	90	6	4	2	1	0	0	0	0	0	0	0
90	93	6	4	3	1	0	0	0	0	0	0	0
93	96	6	5	3	1	0	0	0	0	0	0	0
96	99	6	5	3	2	0	0	0	0	0	0	0
99	102	7	5	4	2	1	0	0	0	0	0	0
102	105	7	6	4	2	1	0	0	0	0	0	0
105	108	7	6	4	3	1	0	0	0	0	0	0
108	111	8	6	5	3	1	0	0	0	0	0	0
111	114	8	6	5	3	2	0	0	0	0	0	0
114	117	9	7	5	4	2	0	0	0	0	0	0
117	120	9	7	5	4	2	1	0	0	0	0	0
120	123	10	7	6	4	3	1	0	0	0	0	0
123	126	10	8	6	4	3	1	0	0	0	0	0
126	129	11	8	6	5	3	2	0	0	0	0	0
129	132	11	9	7	5	4	2	0	0	0	0	0
132	135	12	9	7	5	4	2	1	0	0	0	0
135	138	12	10	7	6	4	3	1	0	0	0	0
138	141	12	10	8	6	4	3	1	0	0	0	0
141	144	13	11	8	6	5	3	2	0	0	0	0
144	147	13	11	9	7	5	3	2	0	0	0	0
147	150	14	11	9	7	5	4	2	1	0	0	0
150	153	14	12	10	7	6	4	3	1	0	0	0
153	156	15	12	10	8	6	4	3	1	0	0	0
156	159	15	13	10	8	6	5	3	2	0	0	0
159	162	16	13	11	9	7	5	3	2	0	0	0
162	165	16	14	11	9	7	5	4	2	1	0	0
165	168	16	14	12	9	7	6	4	2	1	0	0
168	171	17	15	12	10	8	6	4	3	1	0	0
171	174	17	15	13	10	8	6	5	3	2	0	0
174	177	18	15	13	11	8	6	5	3	2	0	0
177	180	18	16	14	11	9	7	5	4	2	1	0
180	183	19	16	14	12	9	7	6	4	2	1	0
183	186	19	17	15	12	10	7	6	4	3	1	0
186	189	20	17	15	13	10	8	6	5	3	1	0
189	192	20	18	15	13	11	8	6	5	3	2	0
192	195	21	18	16	14	11	9	7	5	4	2	0
195	198	21	19	16	14	12	9	7	5	4	2	1
198	201	21	19	17	14	12	10	7	6	4	3	1
201	204	22	20	17	15	13	10	8	6	5	3	1
204	207	22	20	18	15	13	11	8	6	5	3	2
207	210	23	20	18	16	13	11	9	7	5	4	2
210	213	23	21	19	16	14	12	9	7	5	4	2
213	216	24	21	19	17	14	12	10	7	6	4	3
216	219	24	22	19	17	15	12	10	8	6	4	3
219	222	25	22	20	18	15	13	11	8	6	5	3
222	225	25	23	20	18	16	13	11	9	7	5	3
225	228	25	23	21	18	16	14	11	9	7	5	4
228	231	26	24	21	19	17	14	12	10	7	6	4
231	234	26	24	22	19	17	15	12	10	8	6	4
234	237	27	24	22	20	17	15	13	10	8	6	5
237	240	27	25	23	20	18	16	13	11	9	7	5
240	243	28	25	23	21	18	16	14	11	9	7	5
243	246	28	26	24	21	19	16	14	12	9	7	6
246	249	29	26	24	22	19	17	15	12	10	8	6

Wage Bracket Method Tables for Income Tax Withholding

MARRIED Persons—DAILY Payroll Period

(For Wages Paid through December 31, 2016)

And the wages are—		\multicolumn{11}{c}{And the number of withholding allowances claimed is—}										
At least	But less than	0	1	2	3	4	5	6	7	8	9	10
		\multicolumn{11}{c}{The amount of income tax to be withheld is—}										
$249	$252	$29	$27	$24	$22	$20	$17	$15	$13	$10	$8	$6
252	255	30	27	25	23	20	18	16	13	11	8	6
255	258	30	28	25	23	21	18	16	14	11	9	7
258	261	30	28	26	23	21	19	16	14	12	9	7
261	264	31	29	26	24	22	19	17	15	12	10	8
264	267	31	29	27	24	22	20	17	15	13	10	8
267	270	32	29	27	25	22	20	18	15	13	11	8
270	273	32	30	28	25	23	21	18	16	14	11	9
273	276	33	30	28	26	23	21	19	16	14	12	9
276	279	33	31	28	26	24	21	19	17	14	12	10
279	282	34	31	29	27	24	22	20	17	15	13	10
282	285	34	32	29	27	25	22	20	18	15	13	11
285	288	34	32	30	27	25	23	20	18	16	13	11
288	291	35	33	30	28	26	23	21	19	16	14	12
291	294	35	33	31	28	26	24	21	19	17	14	12
294	297	36	33	31	29	26	24	22	19	17	15	12
297	300	36	34	32	29	27	25	22	20	18	15	13
300	303	37	34	32	30	27	25	23	20	18	16	13
303	306	37	35	33	30	28	25	23	21	18	16	14
306	309	38	35	33	31	28	26	24	21	19	17	14
309	312	38	36	33	31	29	26	24	22	19	17	15
312	315	39	36	34	32	29	27	25	22	20	17	15
315	318	39	37	34	32	30	27	25	23	20	18	16
318	321	39	37	35	32	30	28	25	23	21	18	16
321	324	40	38	35	33	31	28	26	24	21	19	17
324	327	41	38	36	33	31	29	26	24	22	19	17
327	330	41	38	36	34	31	29	27	24	22	20	17
330	333	42	39	37	34	32	30	27	25	23	20	18
333	336	43	39	37	35	32	30	28	25	23	21	18
336	339	44	40	37	35	33	30	28	26	23	21	19
339	341	44	40	38	35	33	31	28	26	24	21	19
341	343	45	41	38	36	33	31	29	26	24	22	19
343	345	45	41	38	36	34	31	29	27	24	22	20
345	347	46	42	39	36	34	32	29	27	25	22	20
347	349	46	42	39	37	34	32	30	27	25	23	20
349	351	47	43	39	37	35	32	30	28	25	23	21
351	353	47	43	40	37	35	33	30	28	26	23	21
353	355	48	44	40	38	35	33	31	28	26	24	21
355	357	48	44	40	38	36	33	31	29	26	24	22
357	359	49	45	41	38	36	34	31	29	27	24	22
359	361	49	45	41	38	36	34	31	29	27	24	22
361	363	50	46	42	39	36	34	32	29	27	25	22
363	365	50	46	42	39	37	34	32	30	27	25	23
365	367	51	47	43	39	37	35	32	30	28	25	23
367	369	51	47	43	40	37	35	33	30	28	26	23
369	371	52	48	44	40	38	35	33	31	28	26	24
371	373	52	48	44	41	38	36	33	31	29	26	24
373	375	53	49	45	41	38	36	34	31	29	27	24
375	377	53	49	45	42	39	36	34	32	29	27	25
377	379	54	50	46	42	39	37	34	32	30	27	25
379	381	54	50	46	43	39	37	34	32	30	27	25
381	383	55	51	47	43	39	37	35	32	30	28	25
383	385	55	51	47	44	40	37	35	33	30	28	26
385	387	56	52	48	44	40	38	35	33	31	28	26
387	389	56	52	48	45	41	38	36	33	31	29	26
389	391	57	53	49	45	41	38	36	34	31	29	27
391	393	57	53	49	46	42	39	36	34	32	29	27
393	395	58	54	50	46	42	39	37	34	32	30	27
395	397	58	54	50	47	43	39	37	35	32	30	28
397	399	59	55	51	47	43	40	37	35	33	30	28
399	401	59	55	51	48	44	40	37	35	33	30	28
401	403	60	56	52	48	44	40	38	35	33	31	28
403	405	60	56	52	49	45	41	38	36	33	31	29
405	407	61	57	53	49	45	41	38	36	34	31	29
407	409	61	57	53	50	46	42	39	36	34	32	29

$409 and over	Use Table 8(b) for a **MARRIED person** on page 45. Also see the instructions on page 42.

Appendix D

State Income Tax Information

The employee income tax rates for each state for 2016 are presented below. *Tax Bracket* refers to the year-to-date earnings of the individual. *Marginal Tax Rate* refers to the amount of tax actually collected on each dollar the employee earns and is subject to change as the employee's earnings increase during the year. Note that the tax bracket, although generally pertaining to payroll-related income, also applies to other sources of personal revenue such as interest and dividends. (Source: Tax Foundation)

State	Tax Bracket (Single)	Tax Bracket (Married)	Marginal Tax Rate
Alabama	$0+	$0+	2%
	$500+	$100+	4%
	$3,000+	$6,000+	5%
Alaska	-0-	-0-	0%
Arizona	$0+	$0+	2.59%
	$10,000+	$20,000+	2.88%
	$25,000+	$50,000+	3.36%
	$50,000+	$100,000+	4.24%
	$150,000+	$300,000+	4.54%
Arkansas	$0+	$0+	0.9%
	$4,299+	$4,299+	2.5%
	$8,399+	$8,399+	3.5%
	$12,599+	$12,599+	4.5%
	$20,999+	$20,999+	6.0%
	$35,099+	$35,099+	6.9%
California	$0+	$0+	1%
	$7,850+	$15,700+	2%
	$18,610+	$37,220+	4%
	$29,372+	$58,744+	6%
	$40,773+	$81,546+	8%

(continued)

State	Tax Bracket (Single)	Tax Bracket (Married)	Marginal Tax Rate
	$51,530+	$103,060+	9.3%
	$263,222+	$526,444+	10.3%
	$315,866+	$631,732+	11.3%
	$526,443+	$1,000,000+	12.3%
	$1,000,000+	$1,052,886+	13.3%
Colorado	$0+	$0+	4.63%
Connecticut	$0+	$0+	3.0%
	$10,000+	$20,000+	5.0%
	$50,000+	$100,000+	5.50%
	$100,000+	$200,000+	6.0%
	$200,000+	$400,000+	6.50%
	$250,000+	$500,000+	6.90%
	$500,000+	$1,000,000+	6.99%
Delaware	$2,000+	$2,000+	2.20%
	$5,000+	$5,000+	3.90%
	$10,000+	$10,000+	4.80%
	$20,000+	$20,000+	5.20%
	$25,000+	$25,000+	5.55%
	$60,000+	$60,000+	6.60%
District of Columbia	$0+	$0+	4.0%
	$10,000+	$10,000+	6.0%
	$40,000+	$40,000+	6.50%
	$60,000+	$60,000+	8.50%
	$350,000+	$350,000+	8.75%
	$1,000,000+	$1,000,000+	8.95%
Florida	-0-	-0-	0%
Georgia	$0	$0	1.0%
	$750	$1,000	2.0%
	$2,250	$3,000	3.0%
	$3,750	$5,000	4.0%
	$5,250+	$7,000+	5.0%
	$7,000+	$10,000+	6.0%
Hawaii	$0+	$0+	1.40%
	$2,400+	$4,800+	3.20%
	$4,800+	$9,600+	5.50%
	$9,600+	$19,200+	6.40%
	$14,400+	$28,800+	6.80%
	$19,200+	$38,400+	7.20%
	$24,000+	$48,000+	7.60%
	$36,000+	$48,000+	7.90%
	$48,000+	$96,000+	8.25%

State	Tax Bracket (Single)	Tax Bracket (Married)	Marginal Tax Rate
Idaho	$0+	$0+	1.60%
	$1,452+	$2,904+	3.60%
	$2,940+	$5,808+	4.10%
	$4,356+	$8,712+	5.10%
	$5,808+	$11,616+	6.10%
	$7,260+	$14,520+	7.10%
	$10,890+	$21,780+	7.40%
Illinois	$0+	$0+	3.75%
Indiana	$0+	$0+	3.30%
Iowa	$0+	$0+	0.36%
	$1,554+	$1,554+	0.72%
	$3,108+	$3,108+	2.43%
	$6,216+	$6,216+	4.50%
	$13,896+	$13,896+	6.12%
	$23,310+	$23,310+	6.48%
	$31,080+	$31,080+	6.80%
	$46,620+	$46,620+	7.92%
	$69,930+	$69,930+	8.98%
Kansas	$0+	$0+	2.70%
	$15,000+	$30,000+	4.60%
Kentucky	$0+	$0+	2.0%
	$3,000+	$3,000+	3.0%
	$4,000+	$4,000+	4.0%
	$5,000+	$5,000+	5.0%
	$8,000+	$8,000+	5.8%
	$75,000+	$75,000+	6.0%
Louisiana	$0+	$0+	2.0%
	$12,500+	$12,500+	4.0%
	$50,000+	$100,000+	6.0%
Maine	$0+	$0+	5.80%
	$21,049+	$42,099+	6.75%
	$37,499+	$74,999+	7.15%
Maryland	$0+	$0+	2.0%
	$1,000+	$1,000+	3.0%
	$2,000+	$2,000+	4.0%
	$3,000+	$3,000+	4.75%
	$100,000+	$150,000+	5.0%
	$125,000+	$175,000+	5.25%
	$150,000+	$225,000+	5.50%
	$250,000+	$300,000+	5.75%
Massachusetts	$0+	$0+	5.10%

(continued)

State	Tax Bracket (Single)	Tax Bracket (Married)	Marginal Tax Rate
Michigan	Federal AGI with modification	Federal AGI with modification	4.25%
Minnesota	$0+	$0+	5.35%
	$25,180+	$36,820+	7.05%
	$82,740+	$146,270+	7.85%
	$155,650+	$259,420+	9.85%
Mississippi	$0+	$0+	3.0%
	$5,000+	$5,000+	4.0%
	$10,000+	$10,000+	5.0%
Missouri	$0+	$0+	1.50%
	$1,000+	$1,000+	2.0%
	$2,000+	$2,000+	2.5%
	$3,000+	$3,000+	3.0%
	$4,000+	$4,000+	3.5%
	$5,000+	$5,000+	4.0%
	$6,000+	$6,000+	4.5%
	$7,000+	$7,000+	5.0%
	$8,000+	$8,000+	5.5%
	$9,000+	$9,000+	6.0%
Montana	$0+	$0+	1.0%
	$2,900+	$2,900+	2.0%
	$5,100+	$5,100+	3.0%
	$7,800+	$7,800+	4.0%
	$10,500+	$10,500+	5.0%
	$13,500+	$13,500+	6.0%
	$17,400+	$17,400+	6.9%
Nebraska	$0+	$0+	2.46%
	$3,060+	$6,120+	3.51%
	$18,370+	$36,730+	5.01%
	$29,590+	$59,180+	6.84%
Nevada	-0-	-0-	0%
New Hampshire	-0-	-0-	0%
New Jersey	$0+	$0+	1.40%
	$20,000+	$20,000+	1.75%
	$35,000+	$50,000+	2.45%
	$40,000+	$70,000+	3.50%
	$75,000+	$80,000+	5.53%
	$500,000+	$150,000+	6.37%
		$500,000+	8.97%
New Mexico	$0+	$0+	1.70%
	$5,500+	$8,000+	3.20%
	$11,000+	$16,000+	4.70%
	$16,000+	$24,000+	4.90%

State	Tax Bracket (Single)	Tax Bracket (Married)	Marginal Tax Rate
New York	$0+	$0+	4.00%
	$8,450+	$17,050+	4.50%
	$11,650+	$23,450+	5.25%
	$13,850+	$27,750+	5.90%
	$21,300+	$42,750+	6.45%
	$80,150+	$160,500+	6.65%
	$214,000+	$321,050+	6.85%
	$1,070,350+	$2,140,900+	8.82%
North Carolina	$0+	$0+	5.75%
North Dakota	$0+	$0+	1.10%
	$37,450+	$37,450+	2.04%
	$90,750+	$90,750+	2.27%
	$189,300+	$189,300+	2.64%
	$411,500+	$411,500+	2.90%
Ohio	$0+	$0+	0.50%
	$5,200+	$5,200+	0.99%
	$10,400+	$10,400+	1.98%
	$15,650+	$15,650+	2.48%
	$20,900+	$20,900+	2.97%
	$41,700+	$41,700+	3.47%
	$83,350+	$83,350+	3.96%
	$104,250+	$104,250+	4.60%
	$208,500+	$208,500+	5.00%
Oklahoma	$0+	$0+	0.5%
	$1,000+	$2,000+	1.0%
	$2,500+	$5,000+	2.0%
	$3,750+	$7,500+	3.0%
	$4,900+	$9,800+	4.0%
	$7,200+	$12,200+	5.0%
Oregon	$0+	$0+	5.0%
	$3,350+	$6,500+	7.0%
	$8,400+	$16,300+	9.0%
	$125,000+	$250,000+	9.90%
Pennsylvania	$0+	$0+	3.07%
Rhode Island	$0+	$0+	3.75%
	$60,850+	$60,850+	4.75%
	$138,300+	$138,300+	5.99%
South Carolina	$0+	$0+	0%
	$2,920+	$2,920+	3.0%
	$5,840+	$5,840+	4.0%
	$8,760+	$8,760+	5.0%

(continued)

State	Tax Bracket (Single)	Tax Bracket (Married)	Marginal Tax Rate
	$11,680+	$11,680+	6.0%
	$14,600+	$14,600+	7.0%
South Dakota	-0-	-0-	0%
Tennessee	-0-	-0-	0%
Texas	-0-	-0-	0%
Utah	$0+	$0+	5.0%
Vermont	$0+	$0+	3.55%
	$39,900+	$69,900+	6.80%
	$93,400+	$160,450+	7.80%
	$192,400+	$240,000+	8.80%
	$415,600+	$421,900+	8.95%
Virginia	$0+	$0+	2.0%
	$3,000+	$3,000+	3.0%
	$5,000+	$5,000+	5.0%
	$17,000+	$17,000+	5.75%
Washington	-0-	-0-	0%
West Virginia	$0+	$0+	3.0%
	$10,000+	$10,000+	4.0%
	$25,000+	$25,000+	4.5%
	$40,000+	$40,000+	6.0%
	$60,000+	$60,000+	6.5%
Wisconsin	$0+	$0+	4.0%
	$11,150+	$14,820+	5.84%
	$22,230+	$29,640+	6.27%
	$244,750+	$326,330+	7.65%
Wyoming	-0-	-0-	0%

Appendix E

State Revenue Department Information

Alabama

Alabama Department of Revenue
50 North Ripley Street
Montgomery, AL 36104
334-242-1300
www.revenue.alabama.gov

Alaska

Juneau Commissioner's Office
P.O. Box 110400
Juneau, AK 99811-0400
907-465-2300
www.revenue.state.ak.us

Arizona

Arizona Department of Revenue
P.O. Box 29086
Phoenix, AZ 85038-9086
602-255-2060
www.azdor.gov

Arkansas

Department of Finance and Administration
1509 West 7th Street
Little Rock, AR 72201
501-682-7290
www.dfa.arkansas.gov

California

Employment Development Department
P.O. Box 826880
Sacramento, CA 94280-0001
888-745-3886
www.edd.ca.gov

Colorado

Colorado Department of Revenue
1375 Sherman Street
Denver, CO 80261
(303) 238-7378
www.colorado.gov/revenue

Connecticut

Department of Revenue Services
25 Sigourney Street, Suite 2
Hartford, CT 06106-5032
860-297-5962
www.ct.gov/drs

Delaware

Delaware Department of Revenue
Carvel State Office Building
820 North French Street
Wilmington, DE 19801
302-577-8200
www.revenue.delaware.gov

Florida

Florida Department of Revenue
5050 West Tennessee Street
Tallahassee, FL 32399
800-352-3671
dor.myflorida.com/dor

Georgia

Georgia Department of Revenue
1800 Century Blvd. NE, Suite 12000
Atlanta, GA 30345-3205
877-423-6711, option #1
dor.ga.gov/withholding-0

Hawaii

Department of Taxation (Oahu District)
Princess Ruth Keelikolani Building
830 Punchbowl Street
Honolulu, HI 96813-5094
808-587-4242
www.tax.hawaii.gov

Idaho

Idaho State Tax Commission
800 E. Park Blvd., Plaza IV
Boise, ID 83712-7742
(208) 334-7660
www.tax.idaho.gov

Illinois

Illinois Department of Revenue
James R. Thompson Center—Concourse Level
100 West Randolph Street

Chicago, IL 60601-3274
800-732-8866
www.revenue.state.il.us

Indiana

Indiana Department of Revenue
Indianapolis Taxpayer Services
100 N. Senate IGCN Rm N105
Indianapolis, IN 46206
317-233-4016
www.in.gov/dor

Iowa

Iowa Department of Revenue
Hoover State Office Building, 4th Floor
1305 E. Walnut
Des Moines, IA 50319
800-367-3388
www.iowa.gov/tax

Kansas

Kansas Department of Revenue
915 SW Harrison St.
Topeka, KS 66612-1588
785-368-8222
www.ksrevenue.org

Kentucky

Kentucky Department of Revenue
501 High Street
Frankfort, KY 40601-2103
502-564-4581
www.revenue.ky.gov/wht

Louisiana

Louisiana Department of Revenue
617 North Third Street
Baton Rouge, LA 70802
855-307-3893
www.rev.state.la.us

Maine

Maine Revenue Services
51 Commerce Drive
Augusta, ME 04330
207-626-8475
www.maine.gov/revenue

Maryland

Comptroller of Maryland
80 Calvert Street
P.O. Box 466
Annapolis, MD 21404-0466
800-638-2937
www.taxes.marylandtaxes.com

Massachusetts

Massachusetts Department of Revenue
P.O. Box 7010
Boston, MA 02204
800-392-6089
www.mass.gov/dor

Michigan

Michigan Department of Treasury
Lansing, MI 48922
517-373-3200
www.michigan.gov/treasury

Minnesota

Minnesota Department of Revenue
600 North Robert St.
St. Paul, MN 55101
651-556-3000
www.revenue.state.mn.us

Mississippi

Mississippi Department of Revenue
500 Clinton Center Drive
Clinton, MS 39056
601-923-7700
www.dor.ms.gov

Missouri

Missouri Department of Revenue
Harry S. Truman State Office Building
301 West High Street
Jefferson City, MO 65101
573-751-3505
www.dor.mo.gov

Montana

Montana Department of Revenue
Sam W. Mitchell Building
125 N. Roberts, 3rd Floor
Helena, MT 59601-4558
406-444-6900
www.revenue.mt.gov

Nebraska

Nebraska Department of Revenue
Nebraska State Office Building
301 Centennial Mall South
Lincoln, NE 68508
402-471-5729
www.revenue.nebraska.gov

Nevada

Nevada Department of Taxation
1550 College Parkway, Suite 115

Carson City, NV 89706
775-684-2000
www.tax.nv.gov

New Hampshire

New Hampshire Department of Revenue Administration
Governor Hugh Gallen State Office Park
109 Pleasant Street (Medical & Surgical Building)
Concord, NH 03301
603-230-5000
www.revenue.nh.gov

New Jersey

New Jersey Division of Taxation
Taxation Building
50 Barrack Street, 1st Floor Lobby
Trenton, NJ 08695
609-292-6400
www.nj.gov/treasury/taxation

New Mexico

Taxation & Revenue New Mexico
1100 South St. Francis Drive
Santa Fe, NM 87504
505-827-0700
www.tax.newmexico.gov

New York

New York State Department of Taxation and Finance
Building 9
W. A. Harriman Campus
Albany, NY 12227
518-485-6654
www.tax.ny.gov

North Carolina

North Carolina Department of Revenue
501 N. Wilmington St
Raleigh, NC 27604
877-252-3052
www.dornc.com

North Dakota

Office of State Tax Commissioner
600 E Boulevard Ave., Dept. 127
Bismarck, ND 58505-0599
701-328-1248
www.nd.gov/tax

Ohio

Ohio Department of Taxation
4485 Northland Ridge Blvd.
Columbus, OH 43229
888-405-4039
www.tax.ohio.gov

Oklahoma

Oklahoma Tax Commission
Connors Building, Capitol Complex
2501 North Lincoln Boulevard
Oklahoma City, OK 73194
405-521-3160
www.tax.ok.gov

Oregon

Oregon Department of Revenue
955 Center St. NE
Salem, OR 97301-2555
503-378-4988
www.oregon.gov/dor

Pennsylvania

Pennsylvania Department of Revenue
Strawberry Square Lobby, First Floor
Fourth and Walnut Streets
Harrisburg, PA 17128
717-783-1405
www.revenue.state.pa.us

Rhode Island

Rhode Island Division of Taxation
One Capitol Hill
Providence, RI 02908
401-574-8941
www.tax.ri.gov

South Carolina

South Carolina Department of Revenue
300A Outlet Pointe Blvd
Columbia, SC 29210
803-896-1450
www.sctax.org

South Dakota

South Dakota Department of Revenue
445 E Capitol Avenue
Pierre, SD 57501-3185
800-829-9188
dor.sd.gov

Tennessee

Tennessee Department of Revenue
Andrew Jackson Building
500 Deaderick Street
Nashville, TN 37242
615-253-0600
www.tn.gov/revenue

Texas

Texas Comptroller of Public Accounts
Lyndon B. Johnson State Office Building

111 East 17th Street
Austin, TX 78774
800-252-5555
http://www.comptroller.texas.gov/

Utah

Utah State Tax Commission
210 North 1950 West
Salt Lake City, UT 84134
801-297-2200
www.tax.utah.gov

Vermont

Vermont Department of Taxes
133 State Street
Montpelier, VT 05633
802-828-2505
http://tax.vermont.gov/

Virginia

Virginia Department of Taxation
1957 Westmoreland Street
Richmond, VA 23230
804-367-8037
www.tax.virginia.gov

Washington

Washington State Department of Revenue
Executive Office
P.O. Box 47450
Olympia, WA 98504-7450
800-647-7706
www.dor.wa.gov

West Virginia

West Virginia Department of Revenue
Taxpayer Services
1206 Quarrier Street
Charleston, WV 25301
800-982-8297
http://www.Tax.WV.Gov/

Wisconsin

Wisconsin Department of Revenue
2135 Rimrock Road
Madison, WI 53713
608-266-2772
www.revenue.wi.gov

Wyoming

Wyoming Department of Revenue
122 West 25th Street, 2nd Floor West
Cheyenne, WY 82002-0110
307-777-5200
http://revenue.wyo.gov

Appendix F

Payroll Certification Information

Payroll certification examinations are available to document mastery of payroll accounting topics. The National Association of Certified Professional Bookkeepers (NACPB), the American Institute of Professional Bookkeepers (AIPB), and the American Payroll Association (APA) each offer certification exams. Contact details for each exam are at the end of this appendix.

Correlation of Certification Exam Topics and Specific Learning Objectives

The following table contains information about the topics covered by each payroll certification and the location of that information in this text.

Payroll Certification Exam Topics	Learning Objective
401(k) plans	4-2
Account classification	6-3
Accounting terminology	6-3
Additional Medicare tax—highly compensated employees	1-2, 4-4
Affordable Care Act Form 1095	1-2
Benefits costs and benchmarking	5-6, 6-7
Bonuses and commissions	3-5
Cafeteria (section 125) plans	4-2
Calculation of FICA taxes (Social Security and Medicare): Employee	4-4
Calculation of FICA taxes (Social Security and Medicare): Employer	4-4, 5-1
Calculation of involuntary (mandated) deductions	4-6
Communication with IRS and SSA	2-2, 4-4
Data privacy	1-4
Data retention	2-4
De minimis fringe benefits	4-2
Deferred compensation	3-5
Docking exempt employee pay	3-2
Employee benefits	4-2, 4-5, 5-6
Employee classification	1-6

Payroll Certification Exam Topics	Learning Objective
Employee vs. independent contractor	1-2, 1-6, 2-2
Employer-provided benefits: Cafeteria plan, awards, personal use of company vehicle, Group-term life insurance	4-2
Employment forms	2-2
Enterprise test	3-1
Exempt vs. nonexempt	1-6
Expatriate taxation	2-6
Fair Labor Standards Act	1-2
Federal forms	1-4, 5-3
Federal income tax calculation: Taxable wages, tax computation	4-3
FLSA provisions	1-2
Form W-4: Additional withholding, employee changes	2-2
Fringe benefits	4-1, 4-2, 4-6
General Journal entries	6-4
Gross pay calculation	3-2, 3-3, 3-4, 3-5, 3-6
Gross-up of compensation	4-1
Identifying payroll job requirements	3-2, 3-4, 3-5
Internal controls	2-4
IRS regulations	4-3
Legislations affecting payroll, Contract acts	1-1, 1-2
Multiple worksite reporting	1-4, 1-5, 2-2
Net pay calculations	4-1, 4-6
New hire documentation	2-2
Nonproductive time	3-6
Nonqualified plans	4-2
Nontaxable benefits	4-2
On-premises benefits: Athletic facilities, child care, etc.	4-2
Overtime premium calculation: FLSA, weighted average, commission, salary, piece-rate	3-2, 3-3, 3-4
Pay calculation: Regular, tipped, time worked, other pay situations	3-2, 3-3, 3-5, 3-6
Payment methods: Cash, check, direct deposit, paycard	4-7
Payroll in the United States: Employee documentation	2-2
Payroll practices, confidentiality	1-4, 1-5, 2-3
Payroll systems	1-4, 1-5
Payroll: Process and challenges	1-4, 1-5, 6-6, 6-7
Penalties	5-4
Pension payments and withholding	4-2
Planning and organizing payroll operations	1-4, 1-5, 2-1
Qualified employee discounts	4-2
Qualified moving expenses	4-2
Reconciling wages and taxes	5-3
Recording accruals and reversals	6-4, 6-5
Recordkeeping requirements	2-3, 2-4, 2-5
Repaying employer loans	4-6
Retirement plans: qualified	4-2
State wage and hour laws	4-5
Stock compensation	3-5, 3-6

(continued)

Payroll Certification Exam Topics	Learning Objective
Tax deposits: requirements, lookback period, deposits	5-2, 5-3
Time management	1-4, 1-5
Trends and technology	1-4, 1-5
Unemployment and disability taxes	5-1, 5-2, 5-3
Voluntary deductions/other deductions calculations computation	4-2, 4-6
Withholding taxes, FICA taxes	4-4

Contact Information for Payroll Certifications

National Association of Certified Professional Bookkeepers

877-444-9385
http://certifiedpublicbookkeeper.org/certification.cfm

Requirement

- Successful completion of the NACPB Payroll Certification Exam.

American Institute of Professional Bookkeepers

800-622-0121
https://www.aipb.org/certification_program.htm

Requirements

- A minimum of 2 years' professional full-time (or part-time equivalent) experience, which may be obtained either before or after the exam.
- Successful completion of a two-part exam.
- Signed acknowledgement of the AIPB's Code of Ethics.

American Payroll Association

210-226-4600
http://www.americanpayroll.org/certification

Two levels of payroll certification are available from the American Payroll Association: Certified Payroll Professional (CPP) and Fundamental Payroll Certification (FPC). The following are the criteria for eligibility for each certification available from the APA.

Certified Payroll Professional

The Certification Board of the American Payroll Association (APA) requires that payroll professionals fulfill **ONE** of the following criteria before they take the Certified Payroll Professional Examination.

Criteria 1

The payroll professional has been practicing a total of three (3) years out of the five (5) years preceding the date of the examination. The practice of payroll is defined as direct or related involvement in at least one of the following:

- Payroll production, payroll reporting, payroll accounting.
- Payroll systems and payroll taxation.
- Payroll administration.
- Payroll education/consulting.

Criteria 2

Before a candidate takes the examination, the payroll professional has been employed in the practice of payroll as defined in Criteria 1 for at least the past 24 months *and* has completed within the last 24 months ALL of the following courses within **ONE** of the following three options offered by the APA:

Option 1

- Payroll Practice Essentials (three-day course: live or virtual) and
- Intermediate Payroll Concepts (two-day course: live or virtual) and
- Advanced Payroll Concepts (two-day course: live or virtual) and
- Strategic Payroll Practices (two-day course: live or virtual)

Option 2

- Payroll 101: Foundations of Payroll Certificate Program and
- Payroll 201: The Payroll Administration Certificate Program

Option 3

- Certified Payroll Professional Boot Camp

Criteria 3

Before a candidate takes the examination, the payroll professional has been employed in the practice of payroll as defined in Criteria 1 for at least the past 18 months, has **obtained** the **Fundamental Payroll Certification (FPC),** *and* has completed within the past 18 months ALL of the following courses within **ONE** of the following two options offered by the APA:

Option 1

- Intermediate Payroll Concepts (two-day course: live or virtual) and
- Advanced Payroll Concepts (two-day course: live or virtual) and
- Strategic Payroll Practices (two-day course: live or virtual)

Option 2

- Payroll 201: The Payroll Administration Certificate Program

Fundamental Payroll Certification (FPC)

The Fundamental Payroll Certification (FPC) is open to all those who wish to demonstrate a baseline of payroll competency. The FPC is designed for all of the following:

- Entry-level payroll professionals.
- Sales professionals/consultants serving the payroll industry.
- Systems analysts/engineers writing payroll programs.
- Payroll Service Bureau client representatives.

  APA membership is not required to take the FPC examination.

Glossary

401(k):   A defined contribution plan in which employees may contribute either a specific amount or a percentage of their gross pay on a pre-tax or post-tax basis through payroll deductions.

403(b):   A retirement plan designed for employees of certain nonprofit organizations.

A

Accrual: An accounting method in which revenues and expenses are recorded when they occur, not necessarily when any cash is exchanged.

ADA: The Americans with Disabilities Act of 1990.

Additional Medicare tax: An additional 0.9% Medicare tax levied upon employees who earn in excess of $200,000 per year, as mandated by the Affordable Care Act.

Adjusting entries: Journal entries created at the end of an accounting period to allocate income and expenses to the proper accounts.

Affordable Care Act of 2010:   Mandated health care coverage for all Americans regardless of employment status.

Allocation: The storing of costs in one account and then dividing the costs based on a quantifiable activity.

Annual Schedule depositors   Employers who have an annual payroll tax liability of less than $1,000 during the lookback period and are notified in writing by the IRS that they submit Form 944 and remit taxes on an annual basis.

Annual Total Compensation Report: A list of all compensation that an employee earns per year, including (but not limited to) salary, commissions, bonuses, and all fringe benefits; examples include health insurance, employer contributions to the employee's retirement plan, life insurance, and tuition reimbursement.

ARRA: The American Recovery and Reinvestment Act of 2009.

Asset: An item of value that a business uses in the course of its operations and from which it expects future economic benefit.

ATRA: The American Taxpayer Relief Act of 2012.

Automated Clearing House (ACH):   The electronic network of financial institutions in the United States through which monetary transactions are transmitted in batches.

B

Balance sheet: A financial statement that lists the totals in the assets, liabilities, and owners' equity accounts of a firm for a specific date.

Benefit analysis: A calculation of the costs and benefits of a company, department, project, or employee.

Biweekly payroll: A pay frequency in which employees are paid 26 times per year.

C

Cafeteria plan: A benefit plan pursuant to Section 125 of the Internal Revenue Code that allows employees to designate specific amounts to be deducted from their payroll to pay for health and child care expenses on a pre-tax basis.

Certified payroll: A report mandated for certain federal government contracts that verifies the accuracy of labor expenses incurred during completion of contract-related activities.

Charitable contributions: A payroll deduction in which an employee designates a specific amount of gross pay to be paid to community, religious, educational, or another IRS-designated charitable organization.

COBRA: The Consolidated Omnibus Budget Reconciliation Act of 1985.

Combination pay: Employee compensation that reflects two or more discrete pay bases during the same pay period.

Commission: Employee compensation paid upon completion of a task, often pertaining to sales-based activities.

Compensatory (comp) time: Paid time off granted to employees instead of paid overtime.

Consumer Credit Protection Act: Federal law that pertains to the percentage of wage garnishment that may be withheld from employee pay to satisfy legal obligations.

Copeland Anti-Kickback Act: Federal legislation enacted in 1934 that prohibits a federal contractor or subcontractor from inducing an employee to forego a portion of the wages guaranteed by the contract.

Credit: The right side of the T-account.

Current Tax Payment Act of 1943:   Federal law enacted in 1943 that required employers to submit a timely remittance to the government of any taxes withheld from the employee pay.

D

Daily payroll: A pay frequency in which employees are paid each business day.

Davis-Bacon Act of 1931:   Federal legislation enacted in 1931 that requires federal contractors to pay employees an amount commensurate with the prevailing local wage.

Debit: The left side of the T-account.

Defined benefit: A company-sponsored pension plan that uses the employee's salary and length of service to compute the amount of the benefit.

Defined contribution: A retirement plan to which the employee, and sometimes the employer, makes a regular contribution.

Departmental classification: The division of payroll-related costs by employee function or organizational department.

Direct deposit: The electronic transmission of employee wages from the employer to the employee's account at a financial institution.

Disposable income: The amount of employee wages remaining after withholding federal, state, and local taxes.

Document destruction: The act of destroying documents that contain sensitive payroll and employee information.

DOMA: The Defense of Marriage Act of 1996, which was repealed in 2013.

Draw: A loan against future earnings that employees will repay from commissions.

Due care: The caution that a reasonable person would exercise to avoid being charged with negligence.

E

EEOC: The Equal Employment Opportunity Commission.

EFTPS: The Electronic Federal Tax Payment System.

ERISA: The Employee Retirement Income Security Act of 1974.

Escheatment: The transfer of personal property to the employee's state of residence when no legal owner claims the property.

ESOP: Employee Stock Ownership Plan.

Ethics: An individual's definition of right and wrong.

Exempt: An employee who is not subject to the overtime provisions of the Fair Labor Standards Act.

Expense: The cost of doing business, which may contain both cash and noncash amounts.

F

FICA: The Federal Insurance Contributions Act of 1935.

File maintenance: The application of all transactions, including any necessary modifications, to an employee's file.

File security: The protection of sensitive payroll information by restricting access and securely storing files.

Firing: Involuntary termination of employment.

Flexible Spending Account: A tax-advantaged employee spending account as designated by the Internal Revenue Code.

FLSA: The Fair Labor Standards Act of 1935.

FMLA: The Family Medical Leave Act.

Foreign Account Tax Compliance Act (FATCA): Federal law that regulates the income tax withholdings of foreign employees.

Form 940: The Employer's Annual Federal Unemployment Tax Return.

Form 941: The Employer's Quarterly Federal Tax Return.

Form 944: The Employer's Annual Federal Tax Return.

Form W-2: Wage and Tax Statement.

Form W-3: Transmittal of Wage and Tax Statements.

Fringe benefit: A company-sponsored benefit that supplements an employee's salary, usually on a noncash basis.

FUTA: Federal Unemployment Tax Act of 1939.

FWH: Federal Withholding.

G

Garnishments: A legal procedure for the collection of money owed to a plaintiff through payroll deductions.

General Journal: A chronological record of a firm's financial transactions.

General Ledger: A record of a firm's financial transactions, grouped by account.

Gross pay: The amount of wages paid to an employee based on work performed, prior to any deductions for mandatory or voluntary deductions.

H

Health savings account (HSA): A savings account that provides tax advantages for individuals with health plans that have high deductions via pre-tax payroll deductions.

HIPAA: The Health Insurance Portability and Accountability Act of 1996.

Hiring packet: A package of forms that a firm issues to new employees; examples are Form W-4, Form I-9, and health insurance enrollment.

Hourly: Wage determination based on the number of complete and partial hours during which an employee performs work-related tasks.

Hundredth-hour: The division of an hour into 100 increments used to compute employee wages as accurately as possible.

I

I-9: The Employment Eligibility Verification.

Incentive stock options (ISOs): A type of employee compensation in which the employee receives a firm's stock on a tax-advantaged basis.

Income statement: A financial report used to determine a firm's net income by computing the difference between revenues and expenses for a period; also known as the Profit and Loss statement.

Independent contractor: An individual who contracts to do work for a firm using his or her own tools and processes without being subject to direction by a firm's management.

Integrity: Possessing honesty and high moral principles.

Internal control: A firm's process of maintaining efficiency and effectiveness, work quality, accurate and reliable financial reports, and legal compliance.

IRA: Individual Retirement Account.

IRCA: Immigration Reform and Control Act of 1986.

ISO: Incentive Stock Options.

L

Labor distribution: The classification of a firm's labor by internally designated classifications.

Labor reports: A report that contains details about the number of hours worked and the wages paid to employees.

Liability: A financial obligation of the firm arising from revenues received in advance of services or sales or expenses incurred but not paid.

Local income taxes: Payroll taxes levied by a city or county government.

Local taxes: Payroll taxes levied by a city or county government.

Lookback period: The time frame used by the IRS to determine the payroll tax deposit schedule for a firm.

M

Mandated deductions: Post-tax payroll deductions ordered by a court of law or otherwise nonvoluntary in nature.

Mandatory deductions: Payroll deductions over which the employee has no control; examples include taxes, garnishments, and certain retirement contributions.

Medicare tax: A payroll tax mandated to be paid by all employees of a firm to fund the Medicare program.

Minimum wage: The minimum hourly amount that employers may legally pay to employees.

Monthly depositor: A firm that must deposit its Federal Income Tax and FICA payroll withholdings and contributions on a monthly basis, based on the lookback period.

Monthly payroll: A pay frequency in which employees are paid 12 times per year.

N

Net pay: An employee's wages or salary less all mandatory and voluntary deductions.

New hire reporting: A process by which a firm notifies governmental authorities of any new hires shortly after the hire date.

Next business day depositor: A semiweekly schedule depositor whose payroll tax liabilities exceed $100,000 for any pay period.

Nonexempt: An employee who is subject to all overtime provisions of the Fair Labor Standards Act; generally, an hourly employee.

O

Objectivity: Making decisions that are free from bias or subjectivity.

On-call time: The nonwork time that an employee is expected to be available for workplace-related emergencies.

OSHA: The Occupational Safety and Health Act of 1970.

Outsourced vendor: A party external to a firm that provides goods or services.

Overtime: Time that an employee works beyond his or her normal working hours.

Owner's equity: The financial investment and any accumulated profits or losses of the owner of a firm.

P

Pay advice: A document detailing employee pay and deductions that either accompanies the paycheck or notifies the employee of the direct deposit of net pay.

Pay period: The recurring period during which a firm collects employee labor data and pays employees in accordance with wage or salary agreements.

Paycard: A debit card, issued to employees, that contains electronically transmitted wages.

Payroll allocation: The total of all compensation that a firm pays its employees, divided into functional units or other internal designations.

Payroll audit: An examination of a firm's payroll records to determine legal compliance.

Payroll deposits: The firm's remittance of payroll taxes through the EFTPS or via check.

Payroll Register: A payroll register is the payroll accountant's internal tool that helps ensure accuracy of employee compensation.

Payroll review: Verification of payroll accuracy for a period.

Payroll tax reports: Reports offering details of the period's tax liability that an employer must file with governmental authorities.

Percentage method: A method used to compute an employee's income tax liability that involves computations based on the employee's wages, marital status, pay frequency, and number of withholdings claimed on Form W-4.

Period-end adjustments: General Journal entries used in accrual-based accounting to recognize appropriate costs and revenues during a period.

Piece-rate: Employee compensation based on production of unit or completion of an action during a specified time period.

Posting: Transferring the details of Journal entries to the General Ledger accounts.

Privacy Act of 1974:   Protecting employees by removing personal identifiers from payroll records and restricting access to personnel records.

Prove: Ensuring that the sum of the rows of the payroll register equals the sum of the columns.

PRWOR: Personal Responsibility and Work Opportunity Reconciliation Act of 1996.

Public interest: A process reflecting the transparency and public accountability of accounting records.

Publication 15:   The Employer's Tax Guide published by the Internal Revenue Service.

Q

Quarter-hour: The division of an hour into 15-minute increments as a means of computing hourly work.

Quarterly depositors   Monthly schedule depositors who have a payroll tax liability of less than $2,500 during the preceding or current quarter may remit the payroll tax liability when filing Form 941.

Quarterly depositors   Monthly schedule depositors who have a payroll tax liability of less than $2,500 during the preceding or current quarter may remit the payroll tax liability when filing Form 941.

R

Regulation E: Federal legislation protecting consumers who use electronic funds transfer to access their net pay.

Remit: To send money in payment of an obligation.

Resignation: Voluntary termination of employment.

Revenue: Money earned by a firm in the course of conducting its principal business operations.

Reversal A general journal entry recorded at the start of the following month to undo the accruals recorded in the prior month.

Review process: Examination and analysis of accounting records to ensure accuracy and completeness.

Rule: The accounting practice in which the final totals of financial reports are double-underlined.

S

Salary: A fixed amount paid to an employee on a regular basis, often expressed in annual terms.

Sarbanes-Oxley Act of 2002: Public law 107-204, concerning publicly owned companies and auditing firms to ensure appropriate internal controls and the integrity of financial statements.

Schedule B: The report of tax liability for semiweekly depositors.

Semimonthly payroll: The payroll frequency in which employees are paid 24 times per year.

Semiweekly depositor: A firm that must deposit its federal income tax and FICA payroll withholdings and contributions within three days of the pay date, based on the lookback period.

SEP: A Simplified Employee Pension individual retirement account.

Separation of duties: An internal control method in which payroll duties are spread among two or more employees.

SIMPLE 401(k): A retirement plan for employees of companies that employ 100 or fewer workers. An annual investment limit of $11,500 exists for this type of retirement plan.

SIMPLE: The Savings Incentive Match Plan for Employees.

Sixteenth Amendment to the U.S. Constitution Allowed the United States government to levy and collect income taxes on individuals.

Sleep time: Time spent sleeping at an employee's premises as a part of an employee's work schedule.

Sleeping time: Employees who are required to be on duty for 24 hours or more may be allowed up to 5 hours of sleep without a reduction in pay.

Social Security Act An Act that was passed to promote social welfare for old-age workers and surviving families of workers who had been disabled or deceased in the course of their employment.

Social Security tax: A tax paid by both employers and employees that is used to fund the Social Security program.

SOX: The Sarbanes-Oxley Act of 2002.

State income taxes: Income taxes levied by a state government on employee payroll.

State taxes: Income taxes levied by a state government on employee payroll.

Statute of limitations: The time limit attached to certain legal actions.

Statutory deductions: Payroll deductions mandated by law.

Statutory employee: A special class of employees who run their own business but must be treated as employees for tax reasons.

Supporting documents: Paperwork that supports the payroll calculations; for example, time sheets and the payroll register.

SUTA: The State Unemployment Tax Act of 1939.

T

Tax matching: The process in FICA taxes where the employer and employee pay the same amount of tax for the wages earned during a pay period.

Tax rate: The percentage to be used when computing certain types of taxes.

Tax remittance: The payment of a firm's payroll tax liability.

Tax table: A set of precalculated tables issued by federal and state governments to facilitate income tax computations for employee payroll.

Termination: Ceasing employment with a firm.

Time card: A record of the time worked during a period for an individual employee.

Tipped employee: An employee who engages in an occupation in which he or she customarily and regularly receives more than $30 per month in tips.

Tipped wage: The base wage paid to employees who earn the majority of their income through customer tips.

Total: Computing the sum of each row and each column of the payroll register.

Travel time: Time that an employee spends traveling for the employer's benefit.

Trial balance: An internal accounting statement in which the accountant determines that the debits equal the credits for the amounts in the General Ledger.

U

Union dues: Amounts paid on a regular basis by employees who are required to be part of a union as a condition of their employment.

USERRA: The Uniformed Services Employment and Reemployment Rights Act of 1994.

V

Voluntary deductions: Amounts that an employee elects to have deducted from his or her paycheck and remitted to a third party; examples include charitable contributions, savings bond purchases, and health club fees.

VPN: Virtual Private Network.

W

W-4:   The Employee Withholding Allowance Certificate.

Wage base: The maximum annual salary that is subject to tax liability, commonly used for Social Security, FUTA, and SUTA taxes.

Wage-bracket method: The use of tax tables located in federal and state publications that facilitate the determination of employee income tax deductions for payroll.

Wait time: The time that an employee is paid to wait on the employer's premises for the benefit of the employer.

Walsh-Healey Public Contracts Act: Legislation enacted in 1936 that required employers working on federal contracts in excess of $10,000 to pay employees the federal minimum wage and follow the overtime provisions of the Fair Labor Standards Act.

Weekly payroll: The payroll frequency in which employees are paid 52 times per year.

Worker's compensation: A mandatory insurance policy paid by employers that provides wage replacement and medical benefits to employees who are injured in the course of their employment.

Index

A

Accountants. *See also* Payroll accountants
   certification for, 384–387
   code of ethics for, 13
   integrity of, 14
   objectivity and independence
      of, 14, 15
   responsibility of, 14
   salaries for, 4
   sources of information for, 15
Accounting. *See also* Payroll accounting
   ethical guidelines for, 12–15
   payroll effects on, 275–278
   trends in, 279
Accounting reports, 276–278
Accruals, 270–271
ADP, 113
Affordable Care Act of 2010
   explanation of, 12, 143
   Medicare tax and, 157, 190
   reporting requirements for, 143
   trends in, 169
Age Discrimination in Employment
      Act of 1967 (ADEA), 5
American Family Life Assurance Company of
      Columbus (AFLAC), 143
American Institute of Certified Public
      Accountants (AICPA), Code of
      Ethics, 13, 15
American Institute of Professional
      Bookkeepers, 386
American Payroll Association (APA), 23,
      386–387
American Payroll Association (APA)
      Certification Board, 384
American Recovery and Reinvestment
      Act of 2009 (ARRA), 8
Americans with Disabilities Act of 1990
      (ADA), 6

Annual total compensation report
   example of, 223
   explanation of, 222
Apple, 21
Arthur Andersen, 41
Assets, 265
Audits, 18, 62, 63
Automated Clearing House (ACH), 199

B

Balance Sheet
   explanation of, 276, 277
Banking
   direct deposit, 167–168
   online, 166
Banking Secrecy Act, 52
Bank of America, 8
Bartels v. Birmingham, 44
Base salary plus commission method, 117–118
Bayfront Watercraft, 109
Ben and Jerry's, 18
Benefit analysis
   explanation of, 189
   as function of payroll, 220–222
   trends in, 224
Benefit analysis report, 220, 221
Billable vs. nonbillable report, 278
Biweekly payroll, 43
Brinker Restaurant Group, 35
Business expenses
   payroll as, 216–218
   payroll-related, 275–276

C

Cafeteria plans, 145–146
California
   Employment Training Tax in, 196
   Personal Income Tax in, 160